1 $28

MANAGEMENT INFORMATION SYSTEMS

MANAGEMENT INFORMATION SYSTEMS

Second Edition

RAYMOND McLEOD, Jr.

Texas A&M University

SCIENCE RESEARCH ASSOCIATES, INC.
Chicago, Palo Alto, Toronto, Henley-on-Thames, Sydney

A Subsidiary of IBM

To Francis Cox, band director, 1935–1968

C. H. Yoe High School, Cameron, Texas

Acquisition Editor	Terry Baransy
Project Editor	Judith Fillmore
Copy Editor	Amy Klatzkin
Compositor	Graphic Typesetting Service
Illustrator	Patrick Long
Cover and Text Designer	Carol Harris
Cover Photographer	Erich Hartmann/Magnum

ACKNOWLEDGMENTS

Figures 1-1, 1-8, 5-3, 5-18, 5-19, 6-9, 7-19, 9-18, 9-19, 10-2, 10-10, 10-11, 10-14, 17-13, 19-17: *International Business Machines Corporation;* Figure 2-7: *from* Management and Performance *by Andrew D. Szilagyi, Jr., copyright © 1981 Scott, Foresman and Company, reprinted by permission;* Figure 2-11: *Lawrence D. White Associates;* Figure 3-1: *General Motors Corporation;* Figures 5-2, 5-7, 5-8, 6-16, 6-22, 9-20: *The Burroughs Corporation;* Figures 5-4, 5-5, 10-5, 10-6: *Texas Instruments;* Figure 5-17: *Cray Research, Inc.;* Figure 6-6: *Maxell Corporation of America;* Figure 6-7: *BASF Systems;* Figure 6-8: *Mohawk Data Sciences Corp.;* Figures 6-10, 9-10: *Southwestern Bell Telephone Company;* Figure 6-11: *TAB Products Co., Palo Alto, CA;* Figures 6-12, 6-14, 6-23: *Dataproducts Corporation;* Figures 6-15, 6-17, 6-18, 6-19, 15-5: *Recognition Equipment Incorporated;* Figures 6-20, 14-10: *NCR Corporation;* Figure 6-21: *Interstate Electronics Corporation;* Figure 6-24: *Xerox Corporation;* Figures 6-24, 6-26: *California Computer Products, Inc. (CalComp), Anaheim, CA;* Figure 6-27: *Computer Pictures Corp.;* Figure 6-28: *produced using DISSPLA and/or TELL-A-Graf, proprietary software products of ISSCO, San Diego, CA;* Figures 6-29, 6-30: *Eastman Kodak Company;* Figures 7-2, 7-14: *Storage Technology Corp.;* Figures 7-13, 7-18: *from* Introduction to IBM Direct Access Storage Devices *by Marilyn Bohl, copyright © Science Research Associates, Inc. 1981, reprinted by permission;* Figure 7-20: *Intel;* Figures 8-18, 8-19, 8-20, 8-21: *copyright, Software AG Systems Group, Inc. COM-PLETE and NATURAL are trademarks of Software AG Systems Group, Inc.;* Figure 9-14: *Universal Data Systems;* Figure 10-4: *Apple Computer Inc.;* Figure 10-7: *Data General Corporation;* Figures 10-12, 10-13: *VisiCorp;* Figures 10-15, 10-16: *Datapoint Corporation;* Figures 11-7, 11-13, 11-14, 11-15: *reproduced from Infodata User Language Tutorial with permission of the author, Infodata Systems Inc.;* Figures 11-8, 15-4: *Aluminum Company of America;* Figure 11-6: *informatics inc;* Figure 13-2: *Burke Marketing Services, Inc.;* Figure 13-6: *Yamaha Motors;* Figure 13-8: *Procter & Gamble;* Figure 15-3: *Smithsonian Institution;* Figure 15-8: *SAS Institute Inc.;* Figures 15-17, 15-18: *Execucom;* Figures 16-13, 16-14: *Systonetics, Inc., Fullerton, California;* Figures 18-10, 18-11: *TOTAL® and MANTIS are trademarks of Cincom Systems, Inc., all rights reserved;* Figures 18-13, 18-14: *Clyde Campbell Menswear, Inc.;* Figure 18-15: *Electronic Data Systems.*

Library of Congress Cataloging in Publication Data

McLeod, Raymond.
  Management information systems.

  Includes index.
  1. Management information systems.   I. Title.
T58.6.M424   1983   658.4'0388   82-19174
ISBN 0-574-21410-0

10 9 8 7 6 5 4 3 2 1

Preface

Although the subject of management information systems (MIS) is usually offered in schools of business, it is difficult to conceive of a career path that will not eventually involve use of the computer as a management tool. All people who have managerial responsibilities—including those in organizations such as churches, military branches, museums, and hospitals as well as business firms—need more than a computer literacy. They need an MIS literacy. These people are the users of the MIS.

In addition to managers are information specialists—systems analysts, programmers, data base administrators, and EDP auditors—who support them. Such specialists help managers recognize problems that can be solved with the aid of the MIS, formulate computer-based solutions, and implement workable information systems. These specialists also need to understand the managerial role and the importance of information to that role.

Future managers and future information specialists travel different routes during their collegiate programs. But at some point the two bodies of material—the managerial and the technical—must merge. That point is the MIS course. Both groups of students study the same material in the same setting of managerial problem solving. This is a good approach, because the two groups eventually will work together in designing and implementing information systems. It is important that cooperation and understanding develop as soon as possible, and the MIS course is the perfect place. This textbook is written especially for such a course.

Realizing that little course standardization exists from campus to campus, every effort has been made to provide instructional flexibility. Material has been included to observe curricula suggestions provided by the Association for Computing Machinery in their course IS3 and by the Data Processing Management Association in their course CIS-10.

Further flexibility is provided by an updated case book and a software package. These items permit the student to become personally involved in solving MIS-related problems and using the computer as a decision support system. In addition, an instructor's guide includes a range of items designed to support the various activities of the instructor in presenting the course material.

Like the first edition, this book has a management orientation. Emphasis is on the problem to be solved and the information needed. It is both possible and preferable for the manager to obtain information without getting wrapped up in the technical details of the computer, so those details are omitted here. A set of schematic models, many new as well as many carried over from the first edition, provide the framework that holds all of the pieces together. Each chapter now concludes with a short case to further illustrate and apply chapter concepts in realistic settings.

The narrative of the text fills out and explains the framework of the models. All terms are explained and all processes described—each part and each step. The intent is to provide a solid foundation of the MIS material on which instructors in this and following courses can build in explaining the subject and describing its specific application to particular career areas.

Although the first edition was well accepted and widely adopted, it needed to reflect the rapidly changing computer field. A survey of faculty users suggested added topics, expanded coverage, different approaches, and other improvements. These suggestions have been incorporated into this second edition, along with valuable feedback from my students at Texas Christian University and Texas A&M University. Final improvements came from reviewers who read all or part of the manuscript and recommended changes. Users of the first edition will find three new chapters, covering data base, mini/micro systems, and the future of MIS. Such additional concepts as decision support systems, informal information systems, contingency management theory, word processing, and computer security have been added, along with many more examples of how firms are actually using MIS.

Organization

This edition has the same basic organization as the first. Part One consists of a single chapter introducing the entire topic. It is an overview that describes what an MIS is and why you should be studying it.

Part Two is devoted to theory and its application to problem solving. A process that can be followed in solving problems is explained, using the computer as a decision support system. A mastery of this process, called the systems approach, is a valuable skill for every person entering an organization.

Part Three deals with the computer. Chapter 5 provides an overview, and separate chapters focus on input/output devices, storage devices, the data base, data communications, mini/micro systems, and the computer as a decision support system. Each chapter is related to the theory presented earlier.

Part Four answers the question "What does an MIS do?" Chapter 12 is an overview of functional information systems. A functional system is one tailored to fit the needs of a functional area of business—marketing, manufacturing, and finance. Each area is described in a separate chapter that provides a wide range of examples of MIS use. These examples are presented both to explain the material and to whet the appetites of future managers and information specialists for what can be accomplished with MIS. The examples are realistic in that firms are performing the tasks every day, but they are also creative, insightful uses of the computer, representing effective targets at which the designers of future information systems might aim.

Finally, Part Five describes the life cycle of an MIS, detailing the step-by-step process that the manager and the information specialist follow in developing an MIS. As with the discussion of hardware and software, this explanation of the MIS life cycle is presented in the context of the computer as a decision support system. The role of the manager is emphasized because manager involvement is the key to successful computer installations. The involvement of the user is more important today than ever. We are in the midst of an evolution from an era of user dependency on the information specialist to one of user self-sufficiency. New user-friendly natural languages and design tools are making it easier for managers to build and use their own systems.

Acknowledgments

I have had much help in writing this book. I recognize the contributions of the many people with whom I worked while with IBM, Recognition Equipment Incorporated, and the consulting firm Lifson, Wilson, Ferguson, and Winick. I recognize the influence of my professors, students, and colleagues while at the University of Colorado, Metropolitan State College in Denver, Texas Christian University, and Texas A&M University. I appreciate the inputs provided by the professors who responded to the survey: Wynn A. Abranovic of the University of Massachusetts, Michael Ball of the University of Maryland, David R. Cooke of Campbell University, Roy Kerby of Arizona Western College, L. I. Pete Morgan of the University of Wisconsin at Stevens Point, Paul A. O'Hop of Marywood College, and Jerry Wegenast of Moorhead State University. I am especially indebted to the reviewers who read the complete manuscript and made many constructive suggestions: Marilyn Bohl of IBM, Deane M. Carter of Colorado State University, Donald W. Kroeber of James Madison University, Gene T. Sherron of the University of Maryland, and Robert Stokes of the University of Wisconsin at Parkside. Three members of the Texas A&M faculty deserve recognition for their assistance on selected chapters: Robert Albanese (management and organization theory), Donald L. Davis (data base), and Marietta J. Tretter (mini/micro systems). Thanks should also go to the companies that provided information and photographs. I thank my contacts at SRA—Terry Baransy, senior editor; Judith Fillmore, project editor; and Amy Klatzkin, copy editor—professionals all. I willingly acknowledge the contribution of all these sources, but I take full responsibility for the final product.

And, finally, I want to recognize the support of my wife, Martha, and my daughter, Sharlotte, who often heard me say: "I have to go work on the book."

Raymond McLeod, Jr.

Contents

PART FOUR   FUNCTIONAL INFORMATION SYSTEMS   381

Part One

INFORMATION MANAGEMENT

Managers have always used information to perform their tasks, so the subject of management information is nothing new. What *is* new is the recent availability of better information. The innovation that makes this possible is the electronic computer.

The computer is a relatively new tool, since it became popular only about twenty-five years ago. It was first applied to business tasks mainly as an accounting tool. More recently, the value of the computer as a producer of management information has been recognized. The term *management information system (MIS)* is by now quite popular, and almost all firms have some type of MIS.

The information systems of some firms are better than those of others. And some systems are computer-based, whereas others use keydriven machines, punched card machines, or manual methods. These two differences do not necessarily relate to each other; the better systems are not always the computer-based ones. The quality of the MIS is determined by the people who design it—the managers and computer professionals—not by the type of equipment.

The control over information that MIS designers have is called *information management*. The manager can use information as another resource. A body of knowledge has been assembled that describes how information can, and should, be managed. The objective of Part One is to introduce the topic of information management.

Chapter 1

Introduction to Information Management

Learning Objectives

After studying this chapter, you should:

- Understand why there is so much interest in the use of computers for management support
- Know what is meant by a physical system, supersystem, and subsystem, and how they relate to a business organization
- Appreciate the importance of a conceptual information system as it relates to the physical system
- Know the difference between data and information, and the basic processes for transforming data into information
- Understand one definition of the MIS, and know the necessary components and how they are integrated
- Be familiar with how the MIS concept has evolved and how MIS relates to the DSS (decision support system) concept
- Appreciate the difficulty of economically justifying the MIS
- Understand how the MIS evolves through a series of phases, and recognize the primary roles played by the manager and the information specialist

Overview

This book regards information as one of the basic resources available to the manager—just as valuable as human, material, or financial resources. Information is especially valuable because it *represents* the other, tangible, resources. This representation becomes more important as the scale of business increases.

The manager of a small newsstand in the lobby of a hotel can manage by observing the tangible ingredients—himself or herself, the merchandise, the cash register, the room, and the customer flow. As the scale increases to a firm with several hundred or several thousand employees, with operations scattered over a wide area, the manager relies less on observation of the physical operation and more on information representing that operation. He or she uses many reports or information displays to reflect the firm's condition. It is easy to imagine the almost complete reliance that the chairman of the board of General Motors or IBM or Sears must place on information. These executives probably regard information as their most valuable resource.

If information is recognized as a resource, then it follows that information, like other resources, can be managed. The other resources (personnel, money, material, and machines) are acquired and assembled to be available for use when needed. Very often the assembly process entails converting an essentially raw material into a refined form, such as training an employee or constructing a piece of special machinery. Once these resources are assembled, the manager is responsible for using them in the most efficient way. The manager attempts to minimize the amount of time during which resources are idle and to keep them functioning at their highest efficiency. Finally, the manager must replace these resources at a critical time—before inefficiency or obsolescence affects the entire organization.

The management of information as a resource follows the same pattern. The manager is responsible for gathering raw data and processing it into usable information. He or she must assure that appropriate individuals within the organization receive the information in the proper form at the proper time so that it can assist in the management process. And finally, the manager must discard out-of-date, incomplete, or erroneous information and replace it with information that is usable.

Importance of Information Management

Interest in information management has increased during recent years—both in the college classroom and in the world of business. Two main reasons account for this: the increasing complexity of the management task and improved decision-making tools.

Increasing complexity of the management task

Management has always been a difficult task, but it is more so today than ever before. One reason is the sheer *size of organizations.* In addition to an increase in the number of organizations (especially the very small ones) in the past decade, the large ones have grown larger. For example, the number of employees in the nation's 500 largest industrial firms increased from 11.3 million in 1965 to 16.2 million in 1979, and assets increased from $252 to $1,035 billion.[1]

---

[1] *Statistical Abstract of the United States 1980* (Washington, D.C.: U.S. Department of Commerce, Bureau of the Census, 1980), p. 570.

Another factor is the *increasing complexity of technology* employed within the organization. The effort to keep pace with technology must be continuous. And the computer is not the only example of increasing complexity. Increasing mechanization is occurring in almost every part of the firm; examples include factory robots, automated merchandise storage and movement, electronic inspection and quality control, and even automated vending machines in the lunchroom.

In addition to this increase in the scale and complexity of operations, the manager's *time frame* for action is shrinking. Managers must act quickly in response to pressures from customers, competition, and stockholders. The entire span of business operations is moving more rapidly today than ever before; sales representatives cover their territories by jet, sales orders arrive at headquarters by telephone or satellite transmission, and filled orders are shipped the same day.

Not all environmental pressures favor production; some, ironically, favor *non*production. This is true in the case of products and services that society, or some part of it, finds undesirable. Thus, *social pressure* adds another dimension to the task of business decision making. Decisions must be based on economic factors, but social costs and payoffs must be considered as well. Plant expansion, new products, new sales outlets, and similar actions affecting the local and national community must all be weighed in terms of their short- and long-term impact.

Each of these factors—the scale and complexity of operation, the demands of time, and social pressure—influences the management task at all levels.

Availability of decision-making tools

Even as the manager's task has become more complex, there has been a movement under way to develop means to improve the effectivenes of decision making. Some means involve quantitative techniques; others involve the application of electronic devices such as computers. During the 1950s, efforts to solve business problems with advanced mathematics were called *operations research* (OR). These efforts were usually designed to prevent or solve manufacturing problems. During the 1960s, the term *management science* became popular, as quantitative methods were applied on a broader scale—in finance and marketing, for example. The increasing popularity of the computer in the late sixties and seventies led to attempts to harness the power of this electronic giant for mathematical computations. Terms such as *management information system* (MIS) and *decision support system* (DSS) represent currently popular means of assisting the manager with computer-produced information. MIS refers to the overall application of the computer in a firm, with the emphasis on supporting management's information needs. DSS refers to a subset of the MIS, intended to provide information relating to specific problems.

Increasing computer literacy

Of course, in order to use operations research, management science, MIS, or DSS, a manager must understand them. More harm than good can come from uninformed use. Asking someone to learn to manage information by trial and error is like giving a high-performance racing car to someone just learning to drive.

Today most college graduates who enter management training programs have had courses in both quantitative techniques and computers. These management trainees know the basics and can communicate with the firm's OR and systems staffs. Thus managers and specialists can jointly develop computer-based systems to help solve business problems.

Many of the senior managers in today's organizations, however, studied neither quantitative solutions to business problems nor computers in college. Some never went to college, and those who did took courses that were generally nonquantitative. Senior managers who have seen the need to augment their education have enrolled in programs conducted by business societies such as the American Management Association or pursued Master of Business Administration (MBA) degrees through special evening or weekend programs. Very often, computer companies offer executive classes in particular techniques and systems.

During the early years of the computer, few people in any organization understood the new technology, and their level of understanding was often low. This problem is gradually disappearing as more and more computer-trained managers enter organizations and work their way to the top. Not all companies have management staffs who are generally knowledgeable about computers, but many do. Surprisingly, company size is not the key factor. Some small firms with progressive leadership are making very effective use of computers.

To be computer literate, managers need not know a lot of technical details. It is more important that they appreciate the positive influence that the computer can have on our society and our business system. Nor is it necessary for managers to know all the technical jargon. The computer-literate manager will overcome the jargon barrier through study and communication to focus on how the computer can be used to solve problems.

Improving technology

By today's standards the early computers were primitive. Computers have become smaller, faster, and less expensive while offering greater capacity and convenience. Today you can buy a pocket calculator more powerful than one of the first room-sized computers—and a great deal less expensive. Fifteen years ago, only large firms could afford to purchase or lease computers. A small system could be leased for about $10,000 a month. Today a firm or even an individual can buy a much more powerful computer for the same price.

All of this means that computer technology is more readily available. The lack of a computer with sufficient power and capacity is no longer a deterrent to solving a problem. More likely, the deterrent will be the difficulty of formulating a solution in terms of logical expressions that the computer can act on. Today managers throughout many companies can access a central computer through typewriterlike terminals in their offices, as in Figure 1-1. In some companies, managers have small computers by their desks. Very often, these small computers are linked to a central computer to form an integrated problem-solving network.

Figure 1-1 Many managers have a computer terminal in their office.

The Modern Manager

In early business organizations the manager was a generalist, knowledgeable about all the firm's activities. As the size and scope of the firm increased, general knowledge gave way to specialization. During the 1950s and 1960s, large organizations became essentially accumulations of specialists, each knowing more about a particular field than any generalist; but these specialists did not always work together.

This situation often resulted in not only a lack of communication and cooperation within the firm but also a performance that was less than efficient. Figure 1-2 shows the wall-building aspect of specialization.

Computers have played an important role in keeping the walls of specialization from growing and in some cases have broken them down altogether. The essence of the MIS concept is a computing resource supporting the entire orga-

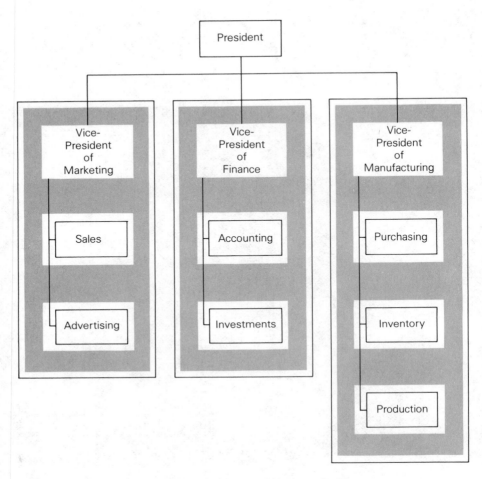

Figure 1-2 Extreme specialization builds walls in an organization.

nization. The various data and information systems of the firm are integrated, and data and information flow from one area to another. Managers not only know what is happening throughout the organization but also appreciate how the success of their area depends on working effectively with other areas.

Good managers use business judgment, assess situations, take risks, weigh subjective factors, and think creatively. In addition, the modern manager must be able to see the firm as an integrated system of resources working toward a primary goal.

According to George Kanawaty, chief of the International Labor Office's management development branch, the manager of the 1980s

must be sensitive to the changing environment, able not only to understand it, but to predict it. This requires an ability to handle and analyze information, as well as an adaptability and flexibility of style and approach. He must be able to comprehend the forces that will shape his social policy and balance it with the economic goals of his enterprise. He must be able to coordinate activities in a more flexible organization and to share his views with others seeking a wider participation in goalsetting and policy implementation.[2]

Computer literacy is not explicitly included in the preceding description, but computer use can contribute to an understanding of a firm's environment and an ability to predict that environment, which is crucial to success. The availability of information also enables a manager to coordinate activities within the organization and to communicate ideas and knowledge throughout the firm.

The Manager and Systems

A manager who thinks of a firm as an integration of functional areas working toward a common goal is actually regarding the firm as a system. The areas are integrated by flows of resources, such as material and information, and each area depends on the others for survival. The firm is then a physical system just as a machine (such as an automobile or a computer) is a system.

To complete this systems orientation, the manager must recognize the importance of the firm's environment. The firm not only depends on its environment for life-giving resources but also makes a contribution to that environment. Regarding business operations as systems embedded within larger systems is an abstract way of thinking. But this abstraction prevents the manager from getting lost in the details of the job and emphasizes the importance of ensuring that the major parts work together harmoniously. A systems orientation is a key ingredient of something called the *systems approach*—the topic of Chapter 4.

What is a system?

When the word *system* is used in relation to business operations, it identifies a group of elements or parts that are integrated through the common purpose of achieving some objective. Let's take the key terms in the definition and expand on them.

1. *A group of elements:* A system must have more than one elemental part. A rock, for example, is not a system. But it can be part of a system, such as a wall.

2. *Integrated elements:* Not all parts of a system must necessarily work together, but they must have some logical relationship. Parts that do not fit the relationship cannot be regarded as part of the system.

    Mechanical systems have this logical relationship. For example, watches, cars, bicycles, and tape decks have been designed to do specific jobs and all the parts contribute to performing those jobs.

---

[2] George Kanawaty, "Managers of the 1980s," *ILO Information* 7 (December 1979): 8.

Many people assume that the elemental parts of a system must work together in a synchronized manner. Although this is desirable, it is not necessary. A wristwatch that does not keep time is still a system; it is just a poor system.

3. *Common purpose to achieve an objective:* A system is designed to achieve one or more objectives. All elements work toward the achievement of the system goal rather than toward separate goals for each element.

Purely mechanical systems are designed to achieve a coordinated operation. Purely human systems, such as workers in an office, lack this built-in coordination, and it is difficult to attain. The manager or leader of such human systems must motivate participants to coordinate so that system objectives can be reached.

Elements of a system

The elements of a system are integrated, as illustrated in Figure 1-3. In this view, the system transforms input into output. A control mechanism monitors the system and regulates its operation so that the transformation process is executed properly.

When this diagram, or model, is used to explain a heating system in a building, the input represents the fuel—electricity, natural gas, coal, and so on. The heating process transforms this fuel into heat—the output. The control mechanism is the thermostat, which can be set at a desired level of performance.

When the model illustrates a business firm, the input consists of basic resources—machinery, materials, money, personnel, and information. The transformation process converts these resources into the output of the firm—products or services. The control is performed by the management. As in the example of the heater, the performance of the firm can be established to achieve a certain level. It is the manager's job to assure this level of performance.

What is a subsystem?

Systems often comprise smaller systems, or subsystems. A *subsystem* is simply a system contained within a larger one. Therefore a subsystem is also a system. This means that systems exist on several levels, and sometimes small ones are part of larger ones.

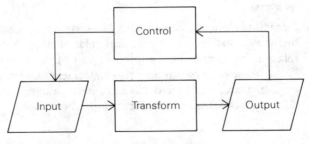

Figure 1-3 Component parts of a system.

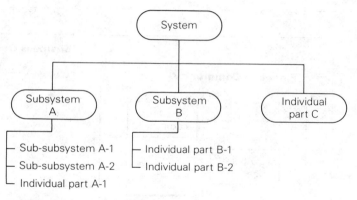

Figure 1-4 System composition.

An automobile can be regarded as a system. But it is made up of several subsidiary, or lower-level, systems—the engine system, the body system, and the frame system. Each in turn may be composed of lower-level systems; for example, the engine system is a combination of a carburetor system, a generator system, a fuel system, and so on. And these systems may be subdivided further into subsystems or elemental parts. The parts of a system therefore may be either systems (groups of parts) or individual parts. Figure 1-4 illustrates this relationship.

In a business firm, the subsystems—such as marketing, finance, and manufacturing—are the basic functional units. Each of these in turn consists of sub-subsystems and parts. The marketing department, for example, is made up of advertising, sales, and marketing research sub-subsystems.

When a system is a part of a larger system, that larger system is often called a *supersystem,* or *suprasystem*. For example, the U.S. Postal Service is itself a system, and it is also part of a larger system—the federal government. Here the federal government is a supersystem, or suprasystem.

The business system

What the manager manages is the system of the firm or the organization. The organization may have *profit* objectives; or it may be *nonprofit*. Also, it may be *private,* as in the case of a corporation or proprietorship, or it may be *governmental*. In the discussion that follows, the term *firm* is not restricted to profit-seeking business organizations. The term applies to any type of organization. The fundamentals of information management described in this book apply to any type of organization.

The manager's major responsibility is to assure that the firm meets the established goals or objectives. Effort is required to make the various parts of the firm work together as they should. The manager is the control element in the system, keeping it on course as it moves forward to achieve its goals.

Of course, the system of the firm fits into one or more larger systems or suprasystems. If the firm is a bank, for example, it is part of the financial com-

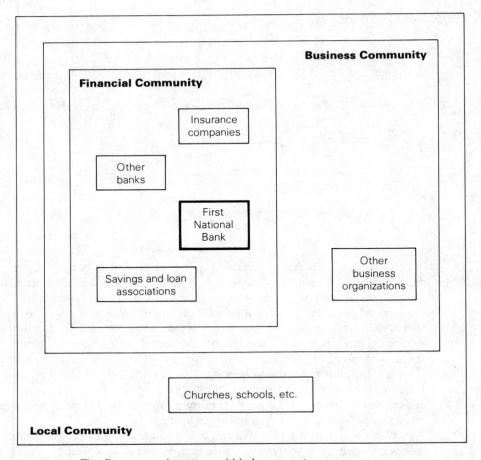

Figure 1-5 The firm as a subsystem within larger systems.

munity. Also, it is part of both the local community and the business community. See Figure 1-5.

The system of the firm also comprises smaller systems, or subsystems. The subsystems of the bank may be the departments for savings accounts, demand deposits (checking accounts), installment loans, and so on. Although each of these subsystems has its own objectives and goals, these subsidiary objectives support and contribute to the overall objectives of the firm (the bank).

Physical systems and conceptual systems

The business firm is a *physical system*—that is, it exists physically. The system is tangible; it can be seen, touched, or kicked. The business firm exists physically; the buildings, trucks, employees, machines, and materials are all physical entities. The manager, in this case, is concerned with managing this physical system.

What, then, is a conceptual system? A *conceptual system* is a system that *represents* a physical one. The conceptual system commonly exists as an idea in someone's mind, as figures or lines on a sheet of paper, or as magnetized areas of a computer storage medium. The forms themselves are unimportant. What matters is what the system represents. The physical system is important for what it is; the conceptual system is important for its representation of the physical system. For example, the data in a computer storage unit is a conceptual system representing the physical system of the firm.

Perhaps some more examples will help. The knowledge and experience of the newsstand proprietor can be viewed as a conceptual system. The proprietor understands his or her physical system and knows its operational details. The proprietor can talk about it, write about it, or even draw pictures of it. All of this knowledge and information represents the physical system—the newsstand with its shelves, magazines, cash register, and so on.

Similarly, the board chairman of General Motors receives periodic reports of his operation. These reports are conceptual descriptions of the physical system. One of the reports, dealing with the manufacturing process, represents the physical manufacturing system. Another report, dealing with the performance of the dealer network, represents that physical dealer network. The board chairman uses these conceptual representations to monitor the corresponding physical systems. Just as a physician can monitor the condition of a patient by examining charts and graphs showing key indicators, so a manager can monitor the condition of a firm by consulting computer-generated indicators. The indicators are the conceptual system representing the physical system.

Data versus Information

Many people use the terms *data* and *information* interchangeably. This is acceptable in informal conversation, but to computer people there is a difference. According to the dictionary, *data* is the plural of datum, defined as something used as a basis for discussion, decision making, calculating, or measuring. Therefore, *a datum is* a single item or element of fact, such as the number of hours an employee worked last week, and *data are* several of these facts, such as the figures for hours worked for all employees in the company. When these data are processed, they can be converted into information. For example, when the hours worked by each employee are multiplied by his or her hourly rate, the product is the gross earnings. And, when the figures for gross earnings are added, the sum is the total payroll amount for the entire firm. This payroll amount would be information to the owner of the firm. *Information* is processed data, or meaningful data. Information tells someone something that he or she did not previously know.

Before we go on, we should clarify one point. Most people do not use the word "datum." Instead, they use data as both a singular and a plural noun. This usage has become so commonplace that it is reflected in more and more of the literature. In this book, we will use data to mean one or more facts, and we will say "data is" rather than "data are."

Now let us say something more about information. You might have heard the expression "One person's junk is another person's treasure." In discussing data and information, we could say, "One person's data is another person's information." Let's get back to our example of the gross earnings figures for a firm's employees. These separate figures are information to each employee—each figure tells an employee how much money he or she earned last week. But to the company's owner, these figures are data. The owner wants to know the total payroll for the firm, and the individual figures (the data) must be processed to produce this amount.

Data and information processing

The system that processes the data is called either a *data processing system* or an *information processing system*. Both terms are common, and are usually used interchangeably. Figure 1-6 illustrates a data or an information processing system.

Data or information processing can be performed manually, with the help of a keydriven device such as a pocket calculator or typewriter, with punched card machines, or with a computer. The processing consists of one or more of the following operations:

1. *Recording* transaction data to create a file of transaction records
2. *Sorting,* sequencing, or arranging the records of a single file
3. *Merging* the ordered contents of two or more files
4. *Calculating* amounts by performing one or more mathematical operations
5. *Accumulating* amounts to develop summary totals
6. *Storing* data or information for future use
7. *Retrieving* stored data or information when it is needed
8. *Reproducing* or duplicating data or information for multiple uses
9. *Displaying* or printing the output of the processing (the information) for the intended users

During the early years of computer use, the emphasis was on the processing of data. The computer was used mainly for traditional accounting functions, and little output was generated for the firm's managers. Today information output is receiving most of the attention as firms design management information systems and decision support systems.

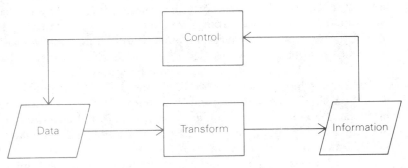

Figure 1-6 A data or information processing system.

The Management Information System (MIS)

Although the term *MIS* has been around since the mid-sixties, there is still no universal agreement as to its meaning. In this book, we are going to use MIS to include *all* data processing within an organization. This comprehensive definition means that the MIS does more than just produce information for managers, even though this will be our focus. We will not pay particular attention to information generated for the firm's employees or environment. We will, however, pay attention to the processing that is necessary to produce the information. And we will assume that the MIS is computer-based, although that is not a requirement.

Definition of MIS

One of the first widely publicized definitions of MIS was offered by Walter J. Kennevan, who called it

> an organized method of providing past, present, and projection information relating to internal operations and external intelligence. It supports the planning, control, and operational functions of an organization by furnishing uniform information in the proper time frame to assist the decision-making process.[3]

The depth of Mr. Kennevan's description can be appreciated when each of the component parts is considered:

1. *Organized method:* The MIS is organized. Since the MIS is a system, the parts should work together in an organized manner to achieve efficient performance.

2. *Past, present, and projection information:* Information is provided to the manager to make it possible to appraise where the firm has been, where it is now, and where it is going. Before computers were available most systems used by managers were designed to provide only past information. Those systems, using punched card machines, keydriven machines, or manual processes, generated historical reports for the manager. The manager used these reports as a basis for deciding what should be done in the future. The systems were so slow that the manager seldom had a good idea of what was happening presently. By the time present performance was reported, it was past history.

   An important characteristic, then, of the modern MIS is the ability to report information about the present and the future—information that was generally unavailable before the computer era.

---

[3] Walter J. Kennevan, "MIS Universe," *Data Management,* September 1970, p. 63. This definition was cited by John Dearden in his criticism of early MIS efforts in "MIS Is a Mirage," *Harvard Business Review* 50 (January–February 1972): 90–99. It is not clear whether Dearden disliked the definition or Kennevan, who had criticized Dearden in the "MIS Universe" article. For other reactions to the Dearden article, see Letters to the Editor, *Harvard Business Review* 50 (May–June 1972): 22 ff.

3. *Internal and external information:* Information is provided about what is happening both inside and outside the firm. Compared to previous systems that provided mainly internal information, the MIS places great value on external, or environmental, information. This environmental information is especially important to top-level managers. The president of Ford Motor Company, for example, pays more attention to the effect of Japanese-automobile imports than to the many internal matters left to competent administrators.

4. *Planning, control, and operational functions:* The MIS should help the manager plan what to do, execute plans, and control the firm's activity to assure that the plans are carried out. No part of the manager's activity should be left unsupported by the MIS. The MIS is a broad, comprehensive system, then, in its support of the manager.

5. *Uniform information:* The MIS should be ongoing, providing information on a continuing basis. This factor separates MIS from other business information-gathering activities, such as marketing research or financial research, that are directed at solving a particular problem. Once the problem is solved, the data-gathering activity is terminated. An example of uniform information is a monthly report prepared for the sales manager showing the return on investment (ROI) for each of the sales offices.

6. *Proper time frame:* The information provided by the MIS must be quickly available. This requirement of responsiveness is especially critical for information describing the current operation. Often the conceptual information system must respond immediately to the needs of the physical system—perhaps within seconds. The term *realtime* describes systems with such fast response ability. As the size of the firm increases, the need for responsiveness demands a computer—and often a larger and more expensive computer as the need for a fast response intensifies.

7. *Assists in decision making:* The MIS is designed to help the manager make decisions. The intent is not for the computer to make decisions for the manager, but for the computer to provide information support to the manager while he or she is making decisions to solve problems. This is the decision support system concept. Although managers do not spend all of their time making decisions and solving problems, these activities are the focus of the MIS and the DSS.

MIS components

If a firm wants to develop an MIS, it must acquire the necessary resources. Perhaps the easiest to acquire is the computer. The variety and selection of computer equipment, called *hardware,* are mind-boggling—and the prices keep coming down. The price of an adequate computer system is within the reach of almost all firms.

But developing an MIS is more involved than just plugging in a computer. The computer needs the instructions, the programs or *software,* that direct the accomplishment of processing tasks. There are basically two types of software. The first is *applications software,* which processes the firm's data. Payroll programs, inventory programs, and forecasting programs are good examples. The second type of software is *systems software,* which causes the computer to perform certain operations such as compiling programs (converting them from a programming language such as BASIC or Pascal to a machine language that the computer can understand), sorting data, or retrieving data from storage. Applications software can be prepared by the firm's programming staff or acquired from a software vendor. Systems software is almost always acquired from a vendor.

If a firm elects to prepare applications software, then it must have a staff of computer specialists. It must have programmers, systems analysts, data entry operators and other operational-area personnel, and managers. These human resources are organized into an *information services staff.* As more companies pursue computer implementation projects, qualified personnel become increasingly scarce.

If the hardware and software are to convert data into information, a firm must first acquire a data resource. The term *data base* has been coined to describe the data resource. A data base usually includes data describing all of the important transactions and details of the firm's operations, which is stored in one or more computer storage devices in some logical, organized manner. The gathering and editing of this data can be time-consuming and expensive.

With all of the resources identified so far—the hardware, the software, the information services staff, and the data base—a firm can now produce information. To close the loop, the firm needs an *information-oriented management staff* to identify what information they need, to use that information, and to work to refine and improve both the information and the MIS over time. These managers are the users of the information product, and they are perhaps the most difficult to acquire. The ideal management staff comprises a large number of people in various areas of the firm, on different levels, who understand and appreciate the importance of the MIS. In short, the managers are computer literate.

Last but not least, the firm must possess *progressive executive leadership* in the form of a president, board of directors, or executive committee to serve as a motivating force. Even when all the other resources are present, if top management isn't enthusiastic about the MIS and doesn't provide the necessary support, developing a good information system will be difficult.

An MIS model

The resources of a good information system are illustrated in Figure 1-7. At the bottom is the *physical system of the firm*—the workers and all of the facilities and equipment used to produce the firm's products and services. *Internal data* is gathered throughout the physical system and directed to the *information processing resources.* These resources include the computer and the information services staff. The *software library* (or collection of programs) and the *data base* are used to convert *data* into *information* that is directed to the *executive leadership and management staff*—the users. These users make *decisions* directed at the physical system of the firm and at the information processing resources. These decisions produce changes designed to improve operations.

The model illustrates a loop—data is gathered from the firm, transformed into information, and used to make decisions that are transmitted back to the

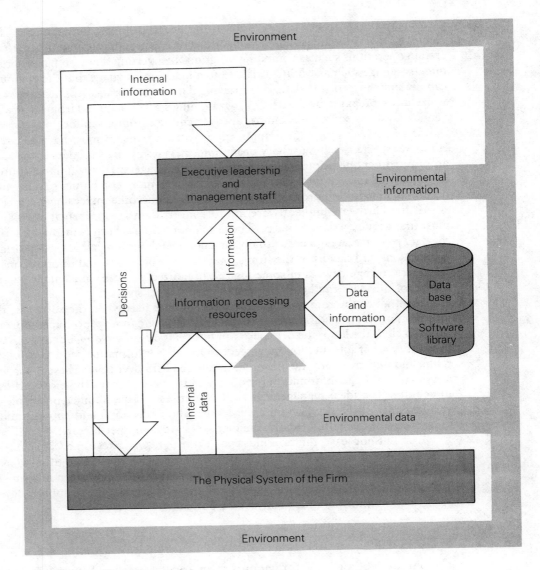

Figure 1-7 An MIS model.

data origin. The ongoing looping process keeps the firm in equilibrium with its environment.

The *environment* is important to the firm and to the MIS. As the model shows, *environmental data* is also used to produce information. And some *environmental information* is transmitted directly to the users from the environment without passing through the computer system. Although this noncomputerized information flow is less formal than computer-generated information, it is no less important. Managers acquire a great deal of environmental information by reading business publications such as the *Wall Street Journal,* by developing good relationships with customers and suppliers, and by engaging in community and industry activities. In fact, environmental information can flow as easily at social functions and on the golf course as it does in the board room.

You will also notice another arrow labeled *internal information* that bypasses the computer. This is information passed along by word of mouth, observation, conversation, interoffice memos, and the like, describing activities within the firm. Internal information ranges from highly organized reporting activities to informal communications among employees around the water cooler.

In sum, the model illustrates not only the resources of the MIS, but also the important looping activity, the interrelationships between the firm and its environment, and the noncomputerized information flows. The MIS is a network of data and information flows similar to the nervous system of the body, reporting on both internal and external conditions and facilitating appropriate responses to those conditions. Computers speed this information flow and make it possible to process certain types of data that would otherwise be impractical or impossible to convert into information.

The evolution of the MIS concept

During the precomputer era, firms generally ignored the possibility of generating information for managers. Computers changed all this—but not overnight. Not until the mid-fifties did manufacturers such as IBM, Univac, Burroughs, and National Cash Register begin marketing computer products on a widespread basis. Acceptance of these products was gradual, with application limited to the same areas handled by the keydriven and punched card machines (i.e., accounting applications).

Before long, however, users and vendors recognized the inherent power of the computer—its ability to do jobs never before possible. Managers in the manufacturing area realized that the computer could be used for superior production scheduling and more sophisticated inventory control. Engineers saw the potential for design work. News of the power of computers spread throughout the firm.

During this period, which lasted until the mid-sixties, the use of computers was called *electronic data processing,* or *EDP.* The term is hardly used at all anymore; today *EDP* is used almost exclusively to identify a person specially trained to audit the effectiveness of a computer system—an *EDP auditor.* Otherwise, the term has a somewhat negative connotation—the limited use of computers for processing accounting data rather than producing management information.

During the EDP era, however, a few farsighted individuals recognized that the computer could do more than just process data. Among them were H. P. Luhn and Stephen E. Furth of IBM, who developed a use of computers (and also of punched card machines) known as *information retrieval.* This development occurred during the late fifties and early sixties. Information retrieval is the most likely predecessor of the MIS. It involves the storage of particular data files for the subsequent purpose of retrieving selected portions. An example is the storage of abstracts of scientific journals so that scientists can selectively retrieve those that relate to their projects.

Although information retrieval and MIS are similar, there are two major distinctions. First, information retrieval is less ambitious, since it seeks only to store selected data, such as titles and abstracts of printed publications or the contents of court records. Many colleges and universities offer computer-based information-retrieval services in their libraries. Similar services are offered by many private firms and governmental agencies.

The second distinction between information retrieval and MIS deals with the degree of processing performed. Information retrieval does not calculate or accumulate; it is primarily concerned with storing, retrieving, and displaying. Information retrieval is an important subset of the MIS.[4]

In 1964 a new generation of computer hardware was introduced that exerted a strong influence on the manner in which computers were employed. Hardware improvements are classified by generation. In the first generation, computers were constructed of vacuum tubes; in the second, they were constructed of transistors. The third generation, introduced in 1964, consisted of the first use of semiconductor chip circuitry. This generation offered much greater processing speed and data storage capacity per user's dollar. A firm could use a computer with large-capacity storage units and data communication equipment for a relatively small increase in overall cost. The concept of the MIS was promoted by computer vendors to justify this additional equipment. The concept was accepted readily by many computer users, since a real need existed for better management information. The time was ripe for the development of a new use for the computer.

The road these pioneering firms traveled during the last decade was not easy. As with many new ideas, actual accomplishments seldom matched those initially envisioned. There are several reasons why many of the first MIS efforts failed— a general lack of computer literacy among users, an ignorance of the management role among system designers, expensive and limited hardware and software, and so on. But one error in particular characterized the early systems—they were too ambitious. Firms believed they could build a giant information system to support all managers. System designs snowballed, and the task became overwhelming. Some firms stuck it out, invested more resources, and eventually developed workable systems, although more modest in size than originally projected. Other firms decided to scrap the entire MIS idea and retreated to EDP.

While many watched from the sidelines as firms grappled with their giant system designs, some information scientists at the Massachusetts Institute of Technology (MIT) formulated a different approach to information for managers. These scientists were Michael S. Scott Morton, G. Anthony Gorry, and Peter G. W. Keen, and their approach was named *decision support systems,* or *DSS.* A DSS is

---

[4] For more information on information retrieval, see Gerard Salton and M. J. McGill, *Introduction to Modern Information Retrieval* (New York: McGraw-Hill, 1983).

an information-producing system aimed at a particular decision a manager must make. The problems the DSS can best attack are semistructured ones—those with some aspects that can be described quantitatively and others that must be handled subjectively. Instead of attempting to install one giant MIS, DSS proponents recommend focusing on separate problems and designing a computer-based management support system for each.[5]

Some people feel that DSS replaces MIS, and they criticize the MIS concept—often unfairly. These critics claim that the MIS is an effort to replace managers. In fact, this was never the intent; MIS from its beginning was meant to support the manager. The error was to envision this support initially on too grand a scale.

Another view holds that DSS is a new part of the MIS concept, in which MIS is the overall structure, encompassing both DSS and data processing. This view provides the underlying organization of our text and will be developed in the following chapters.

Before we leave the discussion of the evolution of MIS, we should note a new area of activity that is becoming an important part of the computing industry. The new area is *office automation*—an activity involving people, procedures, and electronic equipment to increase the productivity of office workers. Office automation started in 1964 when IBM announced its Magnetic Tape/Selectric Typewriter (MT/ST)—a typewriter that could type automatically from words recorded on magnetic tape. The automatic typing operation was soon transferred to small-scale computers, and these small systems were called *word processors*. IBM, a leading seller of word processing equipment, has been joined in this booming market by firms such as Wang, Hewlett-Packard, Xerox, Lanier, and Philips. A typical system is the IBM Displaywriter, pictured in Figure 1-8, which includes a typewriterlike keyboard with a televisionlike screen, a logic unit, a printer, and a device that records and reads data on a small magnetic disk or diskette. The system can store document data, rearrange or reformat the data, and even transmit the data across the country over a telephone line. In addition, the print quality is very good, making the system ideal for business communications.

Word processing can be performed on a terminal attached to a large computer as well as on small stand-alone systems. Software packages such as the University of Waterloo's SCRIPT enable the terminal to be used to perform the same functions as a stand-alone system. In addition, the terminal has access to the firm's data base housed in the computer's storage units.

Initially, word processing was regarded separately from data processing. During the past few years, however, many firms have integrated their word processing

---

[5] For additional information on decision support systems, see G. Anthony Gorry and Michael S. Scott Morton, "A Framework for Management Information Systems," *Sloan Management Review* 13 (Fall 1971): 55–70; Steven Alter, "A Taxonomy of Decision Support Systems," *Sloan Management Review* 19 (Fall 1977): 39–56; Peter G. W. Keen, "Decision Support Systems: Translating Analytic Techniques into Useful Tools," *Sloan Management Review* 21 (Spring 1980): 33–44; and Ralph H. Sprague, Jr., "A Framework for Development of Decision Support Systems," *MIS Quarterly* 4 (December 1980): 1–26.

Figure 1·8 The IBM Displaywriter.

with data processing. Some firms have recognized the information value of word processing and are integrating it with their MIS.[6]

The popularity of word processing is only part of a larger application of electronics to office work. Office automation also includes electronic mail, tele-conferencing, document retrieval, and other means of increasing the productivity

---

[6]For information on integrating word processing and data processing, see Donald H. Bender, "A Convergence of Data Processing and Word Processing," *Best's Review* 81 (March 1981): 38 ff; Paul H. Cheney, "You Can Merge DP and WP," *Computer Decisions* 12 (October 1980): 110–112; Edith Meyers, "The Link Between WP and DP," *Datamation* 27 (February 1981): 50–52; and Edith Meyers, "Weaving WP and DP Together," *Datamation* 27 (August 1980): 61–63. For an explanation of how the MIS can be affected by word processing, see John A. Murphy, "Merging Word and Data Processing: A First Step Toward Total Information Integration," *Computerworld*, 29 December 1980, pp. 49–50.

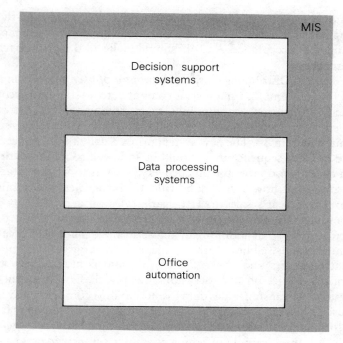

Figure 1-9 MIS provides the overall structure for
decision support systems, data processing,
and office automation.

of the office worker. There is a real need for improvement here. During the 1960s, factory productivity increased by 83%, whereas office productivity increased by only 4%.[7] Where the movement toward office automation will lead is anybody's guess; in any case, it will be widespread.

The view taken in this book—that the MIS provides the overall structure for data processing, decision support systems, and office automation—is illustrated in Figure 1-9.

Some MIS examples

Managers receive information from the MIS in three basic ways. They can receive *periodic reports,* they can *inquire* into the data base and receive answers on the display screen to specific questions (such as "How much did Fred Winfield sell last month?") or they can use sophisticated programs called *mathematical models* to project the likely consequences of decisions. The periodic reports are the tra-

---

[7]Elio R. Rotolo, "Entering the '80s with a Challenge," *IE* 12 (July 1980): 32. Other sources of information on office automation are Michael D. Zisman, "Office Automation: Revolution or Evolution?" *Sloan Management Review* 19 (Spring 1978): 1–16; "Voice Mail Arrives in the Office," *Business Week,* 9 June 1980, pp. 80–84; "Office Productivity," *Business Week,* 2 March 1981, pp. 50 ff; and Louis H. Mertes, "Doing Your Office Over—Electronically," *Harvard Business Review* 59 (March–April 1981): 127–135.

ditional way to provide the manager with information, and they are still the most popular approach. The inquiry and modeling abilities are more modern and are gaining in acceptance. An MIS should make all three approaches available to the manager.

Sound Distributing Corp., a *distributor of beer products* in New York, installed an IBM System/32, a small-scale computer, to do standard accounting applications such as preparing customer bills, maintaining accounts receivable, and analyzing sales. The system worked well, and the System/32 was later replaced with a larger unit, a System/34. The new system prints a daily report for each driver suggesting the delivery sequence that should be followed to minimize driving time. Also, if an order is too large for one delivery, such as to Yankee Stadium, the computer recommends how best to subdivide it. Management gets a sales report that compares this year's sales to last year's sales on a product-by-product basis. The computer can perform an ethnic analysis to identify product preferences of particular groups. In addition, an analysis can be made on a location basis, showing which brands sell best, for example, at a golf course. Customers are also rated so that managers know who the best customers are and can assure that they get priority service on rush occasions, such as the Fourth of July. Once a week the System/34 transmits sales data to another IBM computer, a System/1, at Anheuser-Busch's headquarters in St. Louis. In this way, the computers facilitate an interfirm information network so that both organizations can serve their customers better.[8]

Another example of how a computer can provide management information is a farmer's use of a small computer to determine which crops should be planted. Jack Scarth and his son Pat farm a 2000-acre *grain and livestock operation* near the Texas–New Mexico border. They were considering planting sunflowers on a 260-acre portion but decided to use their $7000 microcomputer for analysis first. The computer identified soybeans as a better crop, the Scarths acted accordingly, and the result was an additional $20,000 in revenue. The Scarth's computer, linked to an agricultural computer network, includes a keyboard terminal with a televisionlike screen, a printer, and a central processing unit. Farmers like the Scarths are becoming increasingly involved in computer processing in order to maintain their standard of living in the face of constantly increasing costs. In addition to recordkeeping, computers enable farmers to play "what-if" games to simulate the consequences of decisions. For example, farmers can consider the effects of a price change, flood, or drought as they plan for the coming season.[9]

On a much larger scale, Lever Brothers, a leading *soap manufacturer,* developed a sophisticated computer program to forecast, based on consumer-attitude data, the market share for a particular brand of soap. This program, called FAM (Franchise Analysis Model), is a mathematical model that projects the likely percent of market sales using consumer ratings of a Lever Brothers brand and two or three others on thirty-six attributes. Consumers complete a form by marking the box that most closely describes an attitude (such as "not important") about an attribute (such as "fragrance"). Once the data is entered into the computer,

---

[8] "On-line Distributor," *Viewpoint,* July–August 1981, pp. 18–19.

[9] "Computers Benefit Farming," *The Battalion,* 8 October 1981, p. 12.

the program computes a market share for each of the brands. The model was validated using attitudinal data for two new brands—Tone and Coast. The model predicted a 5% market share for Tone and an 8.3% share for Coast. Actual sales figures for both of the brands were very close to these predictions. Using a model such as FAM can be very helpful in speeding the flow of products to meet consumer needs.[10]

Another example of a sophisticated program is the mathematical model called Simu-School, which permits the simulation of events affecting a *school district*. Developed by the Dallas Independent School District under a U.S. Office of Education grant, Simu-School consists of three programs written in the COBOL and FORTRAN languages for a Burroughs 5500 computer. The set of programs was used in Terrell, Texas, when an unexpectedly high enrollment of 3300 students shocked the town into passing a school bond issue. The school board was uncertain how to use the money. Simu-School came to the rescue. The model was fed historical data, current information, and some assumptions about trends. The model digested this data and forecast school-building needs for the next ten years. Using the model output, the school board directed the construction of one new junior high school and the addition of several portable classrooms at other locations. Computer use in schools may become so common that each superintendent will soon have an Apple on his or her desk.[11] (The Apple is one of the most popular small-scale, personal computers.)

Justifying the MIS

MIS resources should be economically justified in the same manner as any other sizable expenditure. During the EDP era, firms usually justified the cost of a computer and its associated expenses by comparing the costs with those of the displaced manual, keydriven, or punched card systems. Even though the computer costs exceeded the costs of the keydriven and punched card equipment, fewer people were required for the computer system. The computer was then justified on the basis of displaced clerical costs. Few of these clerical workers actually lost their jobs, however, since they were usually transferred elsewhere in the company.

Another way of justifying EDP was the added efficiency or reduced investment it made possible. This approach was common in the manufacturing and marketing areas. One of the first computer applications was inventory control, and firms often reduced their inventory investment with EDP. If EDP could reduce a $10 million inventory by 3%, then $300,000 was available to invest elsewhere.

With the advent of MIS, computer justification became more difficult. An MIS can produce a valuable report, such as the analysis of beer sales by ethnic group used by Sound Distributing Corp. management. But how valuable is the report? Under normal circumstances a report's monetary value is difficult to assess. A firm could implement the report and then, using the report, compare total profit

---

[10] "Lever Brothers Uses Micromodel to Project Market Share," *Marketing News,* 27 November 1981, sec. 2, p. 2.

[11] William Pohl, "Clearing Away Academic Debris," *Datamation* 25 (November 1979): 121.

for the period with the profit during a prior period. For this comparison to be valid, the report would have to be the only change in the firm's operations—hardly a feasible possibility in a dynamic business setting. There are usually many actions or combinations of actions that could contribute to increased profit, and singling out one is almost impossible.

So the modern manager faces a problem. How does he or she justify something when its worth can't be exactly measured? Quite simply, the manager has to have faith that the MIS contributes more to revenues than to costs. This is not an unusual approach. Millions of dollars are spent on advertising each year, even though the revenue value of advertising is impossible to measure. Of course, some firms spend money on advertising because their competitors do. The same logic could apply to computer use. A firm with a good MIS will do a better job of managing its resources and will probably be more competitive than a firm with a poor MIS.

Because of the difficulty of justifying an MIS, firms approach the decision very seriously. Much manager and staff time is spent evaluating the impact the MIS will have on the organization. Although the process is largely subjective, justifying the MIS is a key step in the achievement of this valuable resource.[12]

Not true. It can be measured. That's what market research is for.

Achieving the MIS

All firms have an MIS. It might not be computer-based, and it might be lacking in many respects, but there is one. What we are talking about is a computer-based MIS designed to support particular management decisions. This goal is achieved by assembling the MIS resources identified earlier. Some firms are farther along in this assembly process than others, and probably no firm feels that it has assembled all of the resources it needs. The process of developing an MIS is never-ending, as firms strive to take advantage of new technology and methodology. Although much has been accomplished in MIS design in recent years, much more remains to be accomplished. Firms will be involved in MIS implementation projects for years to come.

The MIS life cycle

The evolutionary process that is followed in achieving an MIS is called the *MIS life cycle*. In some respects, the MIS is like a living organism—it is born, it grows and matures, it functions, and sooner or later it dies. A given MIS will eventually be replaced by a newer or better one as the firm's needs change.

---

[12] More information on justifying the MIS can be found in Willis R. Greer, Jr., "Value Added Criterion for Decision Support System Development," *Journal of Systems Management* 31 (May 1980): 15–19; Charles A. Gallagher, "Perceptions of the Value of a Management Information System," *Academy of Management Journal* 17 (March 1974): 46–55; and C. W. Axelrod, *Computer Effectiveness* (Arlington, Va.: Information Resources Press, 1979).

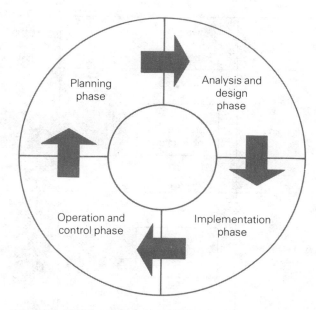

Figure 1-10 The continuous MIS life cycle.

As the MIS develops, it passes through several phases. In Part Five of this book, the MIS life cycle phases are identified as:

- Planning
- Analysis and design
- Implementation
- Operation and control

Figure 1-10 illustrates how these phases fit in a circular pattern. When an MIS becomes obsolete and must be replaced, the firm begins a new life cycle by initiating the planning phase.

Management responsibility for the MIS

The manager is ultimately responsible for the MIS. She or he is responsible both for developing it and for using it. The information specialist, the systems analyst or programmer, serves as a valuable technical assistant. As the MIS evolves, the manager must plan the life cycle and then control the various specialists as they set out to achieve the new system. After the MIS has been implemented, the manager must control the resources to keep system performance within tolerances. The manager's overall responsibility and phase-by-phase support of the information specialists is illustrated in Figure 1-11.

The information specialists play a vital role in the development of an MIS. They often trigger the manager's interest in a new system by informing the man-

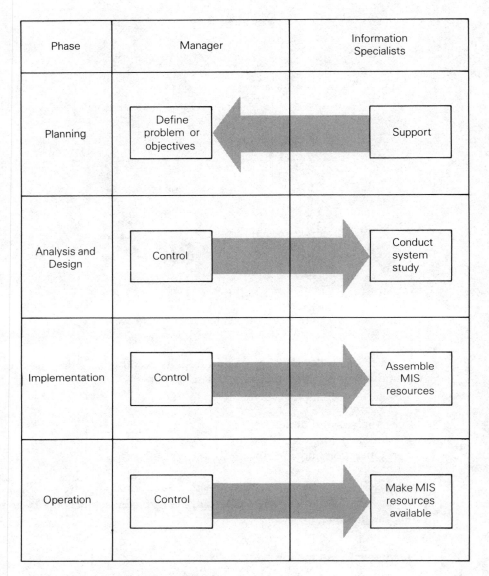

Figure 1-11 The cooperative development process.

ager of a new technology or method. The specialist is trained to solve systems problems and knows the correct procedure to follow to convert an ill-defined problem or symptom into a specific description of how the MIS can help solve the problem. Both the manager and the specialist follow this procedure to identify, evaluate, and select alternate solutions and to identify appropriate hardware and software. The specialist recommends a particular system design, but it is the manager's responsibility to approve implementation. Once the manager makes the decision, it is the information specialist's responsibility to implement the system.

Summary

This first chapter placed considerable emphasis on the subject of systems. This emphasis will continue throughout the book because of the importance of the subject to the modern manager. A system is an integration of parts, all contributing to the achievement of an overall goal. This structural system consists of a transformation process that converts input resources to output and that is controlled in some manner. The manager can see his or her firm as a system. With a systems orientation, managers can fully appreciate the importance of the environment to the system, and they can conceptualize the subdivision of the system into subsystems. A subsystem is simply a small system contained within a larger one.

The manager must manage this physical system. But this task becomes more difficult as the size of the firm increases. The manager of a large firm must monitor the physical system by using another system, a conceptual system that represents the physical one. This conceptual system is an information system—a management information system (MIS).

The MIS provides information to the manager for decision making. The information describes both the internal operation of the firm and its environment. Also, the information describes what has happened in the past, what is happening now, and what is likely to happen in the future.

There is a difference between information and data. Data includes items and elements of fact that are transformed into information—processed or meaningful data. This transformation is called data or information processing.

The MIS is composed of resources—hardware, software, an information services staff, a data base, an information-oriented management staff, and progressive executive leadership. Before the MIS, computers were used for electronic data processing (EDP) and for information retrieval. Recently, the emphasis has shifted to decision support systems (DSS), word processing, and office automation.

It is rather easy to identify the costs of an MIS. More difficult, however, is a measurement of the value of the information produced. Yet decisions to implement an MIS are usually made in a sound, businesslike manner. Managers are confident that the value of the MIS exceeds its cost, even though the value cannot be measured exactly.

It is the manager's responsibility to see that an information system is designed and implemented. This responsibility cannot be delegated. Information specialists and managers must work together, but the manager must both initiate and control the effort.

Key Terms

information management

operations research (OR)

management science

system, subsystem, supersystem, suprasystem

physical system, conceptual system

data, information

data processing system, information processing system

MIS

realtime system

hardware, software, software library

applications software, systems
  software

data base

internal data, information

environmental data, information

electronic data processing (EDP)

EDP auditor

information retrieval

decision support system (DSS)

office automation

word processor, word processing

MIS life cycle

Key Concepts

The synergistic effect of the
  computer and quantitative
  techniques

Why the manager should think in
  systems terms

The firm as a physical system

The MIS as a conceptual system

Data and information processing

Components of an MIS and how
  they interrelate

The evolution of EDP, MIS, and DSS

The MIS life cycle

Questions

1. How can information be managed? Explain.
2. Is information more valuable to the manager of a large firm than of a small one? Explain.
3. Is a manager of a large firm more likely to have a computer-based MIS than a manager of a small firm? Explain your answer, and describe how the situation has changed over the past ten years.
4. How does a manager become computer literate?
5. Is the trend in management toward specialization or generalization? What effect has the computer had on this trend?
6. Why should a manager think of the organization as a system? Is it a physical system or a conceptual system?
7. A recent ad for a razor with a replaceable double blade referred to it as a "shaving system." Is the razor really a system? What are its elements? What is the objective?
8. What is the control mechanism in a firm?
9. Can a subsystem also be a system? Explain.
10. Each day, a large metropolitan telephone company will print thousands of bills. Are the bills data or information? Explain.
11. What are the nine data processing operations?

12. When you go into a McDonald's restaurant and the sales clerk keys your order into the cash register–like device, what data processing operations are being performed?

13. Distinguish between the two types of software.

14. Must a firm have a computer to have a data base?

15. Give an example of (1) environmental information, (2) environmental data, (3) internal information, and (4) internal data. Which of these would you probably find in the *Wall Street Journal*?

16. Distinguish between EDP, information retrieval, MIS, and DSS.

17. What type of hardware is used to perform word processing? Is software also needed?

18. What are some of the costs associated with an MIS? Does an MIS increase the firm's revenue? Explain.

19. While playing handball, a president learns that the firm's leading competitor has just ordered a computer. The president immediately places an order for an identical model. Is this sound business strategy? Explain.

20. Why do firms continually repeat the phases of the MIS life cycle?

CASE PROBLEM: Automobile Software, Inc.

You are a sales representative for Automobile Software, Inc., a national firm that markets a software package for car dealers. One day while you are talking with James Kahler, the sales manager for Freeway Ford, you learn that his firm has a problem with its inventory. The manual records they maintain do not accurately reflect the inventory status—the numbers and types of automobiles and trucks on the lot. Whenever a new shipment arrives from Detroit, it takes several days to update the inventory cards. A salesperson might have a buyer who wants a particular car, and the car may be on the lot, but the salesperson will never know it. A sale is lost because of poor information. Another problem arises when two salespersons sell the same car to two buyers. This happens because the inventory records are not updated immediately after a sale.

You know that your software package, called SMART (Sales Management Analysis in Real Time), will solve the problem. Once a dealer gets SMART, the computer records are updated from a typewriterlike terminal as soon as a new-car shipment arrives or a sale is made. The computer records always reflect exactly what is on the lot. Versions of SMART are available for most popular small computers—the Apple, TRS-80, PET, and IBM Personal Computer. The cost of both the software and hardware is well within the reach of most metropolitan new-car dealerships.

Your next step is to approach the new president of Freeway Ford, Chip Sprague, and give your sales pitch. As you begin to tell Sprague of your product's merits, he stops you and says: "Listen, I'm new on the job. I'm a recent graduate of a top Ivy League school, with a degree in systems theory. If you could just explain how your product will help us, in systems terms, I think I can understand. Now, go ahead."

Question

Describe, in systems terms, how SMART can benefit Freeway Ford.

Part Two

FUNDAMENTAL PRINCIPLES

Management information systems are very real. They consist of managers, information specialists, data, information, communication channels, and often computers for storage and processing. The business student can expect soon to be a part of such a system, either as a provider of information or as a user.

There is a great deal to learn about management information systems. Actually, the subject is a composite of two complete fields—management and computer science. Much of the MIS material has developed during the past few years as firms created their computer-based systems. Other material, however, has evolved over the past century as the subject of business management has become more refined. To the person first encountering this new subject matter, the volume of material can appear overpowering. It cannot be learned overnight, but it can be learned. The process of learning can be expedited and facilitated by an orderly, systematic approach.

The purpose of Part Two is to provide a theoretical foundation—a basic structure—upon which to build an understanding of information systems. This is a general framework, applying to a wide variety of situations. The framework should prove useful in preparing for any type of business career.

This part addresses three basic topics. The first is *theory*. Theories of both management and organization are presented in systems terms. The second is a *general model* of a firm as a physical system with a conceptual information system. The third is an approach to business problem solving, the *systems approach*.

Each topic relates to the idea of a system. This relatively new way to view business is used in this book to help you understand an important part of a business organization—its management information system.

Chapter 2

Theory of Management and Organization

Learning Objectives

After studying this chapter, you should:

- Understand and appreciate how theory facilitates both the study and the practice of business
- Recognize that management theory concerns all managerial activity, and that organization theory is a subset concerning the allocation of all resources—not just personnel
- Be able to identify the different schools of management and organization theory, and understand their different concepts
- Appreciate the contributions of the different schools to MIS design and use
- Understand what is meant by a systems theory of management and by a systems theory of organization

Overview

This chapter lays the theoretical foundation for the material to follow. It describes theories of both management and organization, the two large and important bodies of theory in the study of business management. We will not attempt a full description of management and organization theories. That task is best accomplished in a general management textbook. Our task is to focus on one area of management—information management. Thus the sole purpose of discussing theory in this text is to lay the groundwork for studying information management. Consequently, we will be selective in our coverage of theory, keeping this objective in sight.

Theory

Many people don't get excited about theory. In fact, some dislike it. To these people, theory is unrealistic. They say, "That's just a theory," when they feel something is not true.

Actually, these people are not altogether wrong. Theory does not mean truth; nor does it mean untruth. When something always holds true it is no longer a theory, but a *law*. Probably the most widely understood law is the law of gravity, which relates to the behavior of physical objects. It has been proven and everyone accepts it. A number of such laws provide the basis for the physical sciences, such as physics and chemistry.

What is theory?

Nearly everyone has heard the term *theory* and has a conception of its meaning. Because the term has several different meanings, *theory* probably means one thing to one person and another to somebody else. Any dictionary will show six or eight different definitions.

The definition or meaning of theory that is of interest to the study of management deals with a set of propositions. Theory is a *coherent group* of *general propositions* that are used as *principles* to *explain* some class of *phenomena*. The italicized terms are elaborated below.

Coherent group   Just as an efficient system comprises multiple parts that work together, a theory comprises a coherent group of parts that fit together in a logical way. A theory then, is a type of system. The system consists of propositions designed to explain certain phenomena. The interest here, however, is not in theory *as a system* but in a theory *of* systems.

The general propositions   A proposition is something offered for acceptance. A general proposition is one offered in a variety of situations or used to apply to a variety of situations.

Principles   Principles are generally accepted rules of behavior or action. These are the component parts of a theory. A theory, then, contains multiple principles that fit together in a logical, coherent manner.

Explanation   The purpose of theories in business is to help explain the various business phenomena.

Class of phenomena   A class of phenomena relates to some particular part of business. The phenomena of interest here are those generally accepted rules used to explain management. More specifically, this chapter seeks to address those theories that can be offered as explanations of management and organizations in terms of systems. When the firm is viewed as a system and the manager as the control mechanism of that system, the importance of information becomes clear.

Theory in business

Business is not a physical science. In fact, some doubt it is a science of any kind. At best, it is a social science—one dealing with people. And in general it is much harder to predict what people will do than what a nonliving object will do. For this reason the social sciences have fewer laws than the physical sciences. In business there are more theories than laws. These theories represent what people believe to be true but have not proven true in all cases. The manager applies judgment to the use of theories. The manager realizes that the theory does not tell the entire story, but that it does provide an idea of what to expect under general conditions. The manager must then determine whether the theory applies to the situation at hand.

Since business is so complex and covers so many areas, there is no single theory *of* business. There are theories *in* business, however, and these can be expected to increase in importance and in number.[1] They will increase in importance as the need arises to learn more about particular business areas. They will increase in number as this higher level of understanding is achieved.

Why study theory?

A theory in isolation is worth very little. The real value of theory is in its application to a real situation in order to explain that situation accurately. Theories of business do not seek to answer the question *What exists?* Usually *what exists* is very apparent to the observer, in this case the manager. The manager knows what is happening if an adequate information system is available. What the manager usually does not know, however, is *why it exists*. Theories seek to provide the needed explanation.

As an example, assume a manager knows that certain employees are motivated better by nonmonetary than by monetary rewards. The manager knows this situation exists but does not know why. If the manager knows why nonmonetary rewards work better for certain employees, then that type of reward can be applied intelligently in appropriate situations. Thus the manager can make better decisions because he or she understands why a certain behavior occurs.

Essentially, theory provides the manager with a better understanding of the complex system of business. This understanding helps the manager do a better job.

Information and theory

Many managers use theories learned in school. Others develop their own from experience. Most theories begin as crude approximations, then undergo

---

[1] One area of business that has inspired many theories is the study of consumer behavior. Efforts have mainly focused on applying theories developed in psychology and sociology to business situations. For examples of this work, see any textbook on consumer behavior, and also see issues of the *Journal of Marketing Research* and the *Journal of Consumer Research*.

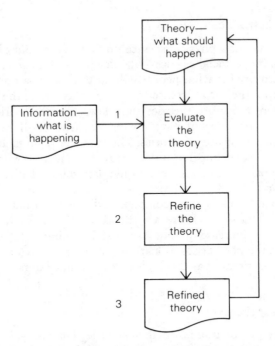

Figure 2-1 Information is used to refine theories.

refinement as more is learned about the phenomena involved (Figure 2-1). In effect, the manager's information system helps the manager develop theories.

The theory tells the manager what to expect. The information system tells what is happening. If real activity differs from what was expected, the theory is refined. Over a period of time, the manager can develop theories that accurately predict the behavior of the business system.

A Very Short Course in Flowcharting

Up to this point, our diagrams have all been schematics showing how parts fit together. Figure 2-1 is a flowchart that shows a series of steps. Systems analysts and programmers draw flowcharts to illustrate the steps of computerized business procedures.

The symbols used in flowcharts represent types of processes and forms of input and output. (For a full explanation of flowchart symbols, see the Appendix.) Of the symbols used in Figure 2-1, the rectangle represents a processing step, and the curved shape represents a document. In this figure, the processes are steps performed by the manager, and the documents represent descriptions of theories and information describing what is happening in the firm. The arrows represent the flow of activity relating to the documents.

Management Theory

We will direct most of our attention in this chapter to the development of theories of management. We can paraphrase our earlier definition of theory to define *management theory* as a coherent group of general propositions used as principles to explain the practice of management. This general body of knowledge describes the roles managers play, the functions they perform, and the skills they need to do both jobs well.

For the most part, these theories have been developed by managers who have learned through trial and error and who have gradually identified propositions that serve as useful guidelines. The managers and other people who study the art of management have assembled these propositions into the theories that now form an integral part of the literature of business.

Management theory includes everything relating to the managerial task—including organization. In fact, organization theory is so important to the MIS that we will treat it separately later in the chapter.

Schools of management theory

There have been many theories of business management. Those that share a number of basic principles are grouped into *schools*. The first school was the *classical* school, followed by the *behavioral,* the *quantitative,* and most recently, the *contingency* schools.[2] As we discuss each of these schools, we will highlight their relevance to the MIS; then we will describe a *systems* theory of management.

The classical school[3]

Frederick W. Taylor (1856–1915) is known as the *father of scientific management.* Taylor was the first industrial engineer (IE), or systems analyst. He studied the activities of American steelworkers. Using time-and-motion studies, Taylor sought to identify the best way to perform menial tasks such as shoveling coal. By experimenting with shovels of different sizes for different materials, he was able to increase worker productivity from 16 to 59 tons per day. Taylor believed that maximizing productivity was the key to maximizing the profits of the firm and the earnings of the employees. Management was quick to embrace scientific management, but organized labor resisted it, claiming that it was dehumanizing.

Taylor's attention was aimed at the worker level in the organization; he didn't contribute much to improve upper-level management. His main contribution, in terms of a systems theory of management, was his attention to *performance standards.* Taylor believed that standards should be established to regulate the meth-

---

[2] Although the classifications used here are common, there is no universal agreement on the number of schools or their names.

[3] Based on Andrew D. Szilagyi, Jr., *Management and Performance* (Santa Monica: Goodyear Publishing Co., 1981), pp. 57–84.

ods used and time taken for each task. Taylor's idea of standards is equally applicable to upper levels of management.

Standards represent acceptable levels of performance that individuals are expected to meet as they perform their tasks. These standards are similar to a thermostat setting that establishes an acceptable temperature range for a heater or an air conditioner. If the workers and the managers meet their standards, then the firm will accomplish its objectives. The objectives represent an accomplishment to be achieved in the future. For the heater or air conditioner, the objective is human comfort.

The difference between standards and objectives is very important, for we will be using both terms throughout the remainder of the book. *Objectives* are what the organization attempts to accomplish. *Standards* are measures of performance that, when met, should accomplish the stated objectives. Objectives are usually defined for the firm and for its important units. They tend to be broad, general statements. Standards can apply to the firm, its units, and even individual employees. They must be stated in specific, quantifiable terms so that the degree of accomplishment can be measured. Table 2-1 presents a list of several objectives that a firm might adopt, along with some standards of performance.

Each manager is the control mechanism of her or his system. The manager keeps the system performance on target with respect to its objectives by comparing the performance to standards.

The idea of comparing performance to standards can be carried one step farther. The information processor of the MIS can be programmed to perform this comparison automatically and to inform the manager only when the limits are exceeded. This is an example of *management by exception*—the manager only becomes involved in cases of exceptional (very good or very bad) performance. Management by exception conserves the manager's time by directing attention to problems and opportunities, and this is facilitated by the MIS.

A second important contributor to classical theory was a Frenchman, Henri Fayol (1841–1925), who was the first to develop a theory of administrative management. Fayol recognized a difference between operating and managerial activities and sought to improve management, whereas Taylor concentrated on operations. Fayol is most famous for his definitions of *management functions*—the activities that managers perform.

According to Fayol, all managers plan, organize, staff, direct, and control. Listed in a logical order, the first task is to *plan* what is to be done. Then the proper *organization* structure must be established to permit implementation of the plan. The manager then must *staff* for the planned activity by acquiring the necessary resources. While the term *staff* suggests personnel resources, all types of resources should be included. Once these resources have been assembled, the next task is to *direct* their use in the performance of the planned activities.Finally, the manager must *control* the activities in order to meet the designated objectives.

Fayol believed that all managers perform these functions, regardless of their level in the organization. This theory has been called the *universality of management functions*—it applies universally to all managers on all levels.

While the universal applicability is most certainly true, managers on the top level have different responsibilities and needs from those on the bottom. Names

Table 2-1 Examples of objectives and corresponding standards of performance

Objectives	Standards of Performance
Satisfy customer needs	Achieve an annual sales volume of at least $25 million
	Maintain a 20% share of the market
	Maintain an annual growth rate of 15%
Produce a return on investment for the owners	Pay dividends to stockholders each quarter
	Maintain the price of the firm's common stock above $85 per share
Operate efficiently	Realize an after-tax profit of 15% of sales
	Maintain a record of accident-free days
	Keep employee turnover below 10%
Invest in the future	Invest a minimum of 15% of sales in research and development
Develop sources of supply	Achieve stockouts on no more than 2% of the items in inventory during the year
	Keep the number of backorders to less than 5% of all orders processed
	Have no plant shutdowns due to unavailable raw materials
Operate ethically	Successfully defend the firm against legal actions filed by customers, suppliers, and the government
Take advantage of modern methods	Invest no less than 10% of sales revenue in automation, computerization, and mechanization

have been given to three management levels in the firm: *strategic* (top), *tactical* (middle), and *operational* (lower). Figure 2-2 shows the hierarchy of managerial positions in a manufacturing organization, subdivided within each level.

All levels *plan*, but managers on the top levels plan farther into the future than those on the bottom. Strategic-level managers plan the firm's activities five or more years into the future. These managers do not actively engage in solving the day-to-day problems of the firm, or even those of the near future. Those problems are left to lower-level managers. Tactical-level managers are involved with what the firm will be doing from one to five years into the future. The managers who solve current problems are on the operational level.

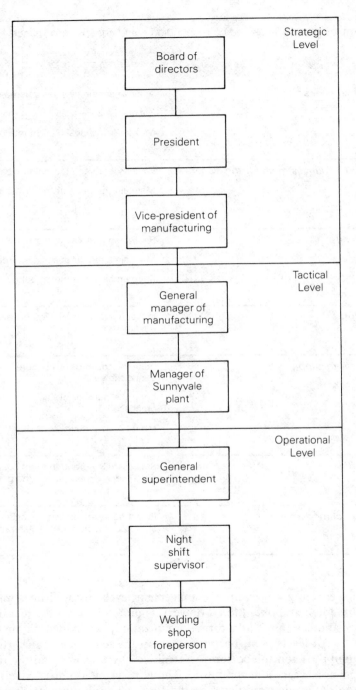

Figure 2-2   Hierarchy of manager positions, by level.

Figure 2-3 Influence of management level on management function.

Although all levels *organize,* they organize different parts of the firm. Strategic-level managers determine the overall, general organization of the firm. The details of how each part is organized are left to lower-level managers.

The *staff* function also is performed on all levels, but in a different manner. Strategic management is concerned with the acquisition of those resources used by top management. For example, the president will personally select the vice-presidents, but leave the selection of lower-level employees to lower-level managers.

All managers *direct* resources to attain objectives. But the strategic level is most interested in accomplishing long-range, general objectives. Lower levels are more interested in immediate, specific objectives.

As the managers direct their resources, they exercise *control* over them. Top levels aim for long-range control, whereas lower levels have more short-term concerns.

Figure 2-3 shows that managers on different levels divide their time differently among the various functions. As a general rule, the higher you are in the organization, the more time you spend planning. The lower you are, the more time you spend staffing, directing, and controlling. These time allocations are only approximations, and they vary with the managerial situation. In a particular company, a tactical-level manager can spend considerable amounts of time controlling, for example.

The management levels have a significant effect on two basic aspects of MIS design. First, they influence the source of data or information; and second, they influence how the information is presented. These design aspects are shown in Figure 2-4.

The different levels demand information from different sources. Top-level managers have a greater need for environmental information than for internal. The opposite is true for the lower levels. According to the figure, a manager on the strategic level mostly needs information describing what is happening in the environment, with some information on what is happening within the firm. Tactical-level managers need both environmental and internal information.

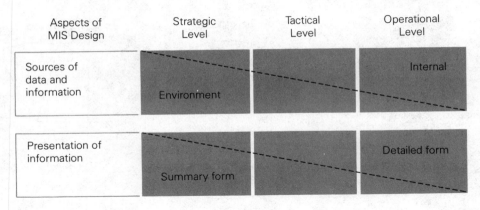

Figure 2-4 Influence of management level on MIS design.

The management level also influences how the information should be presented to the manager. Operational-level managers need detailed descriptions: exactly how many overtime hours were worked last week, the average hourly cost of operating a forklift truck, how many units were produced on machine A, and so on. Top-level managers are exposed to so much information that it must be summarized into only the most important facts. Tactical-level managers work with both detailed and summary information.

These are general rules about the information needs of the three management levels. You should understand that individual preference is also a factor. Some top-level managers like detailed information. One executive, commenting on his newly found ability to use the computer, said, "I've always felt that the answers were in the detail. Now, at last, I can pore through some of that detail. That's my style."[4]

Early MIS efforts were criticized for helping only lower-level managers. There were two reasons for this. First, the systems analysts were able to grasp the information needs of lower-level managers more quickly. The work of the upper-level managers was less routine and repetitive, and thus more difficult to analyze. Second, the first information systems were used mainly for control. The computer reports compared actual performance with standards, pointing out areas needing attention. As Figure 2-3 shows, most of this control occurs on the lower level.

More recently, the MIS has been applied to planning. Statistical techniques such as forecasting methods, and also mathematical models facilitating "what-if" simulations, enable managers to look into the future. Since planning is more of an upper-level function (see Figure 2-3), recent MIS efforts have supported mainly strategic- and tactical-level managers.

There is evidence that chief executive officers (CEOs) are beginning to use

---

[4]John F. Rockart and Michael E. Treacy, "The CEO Goes On-line," *Harvard Business Review* 60 (January–February 1982): 86.

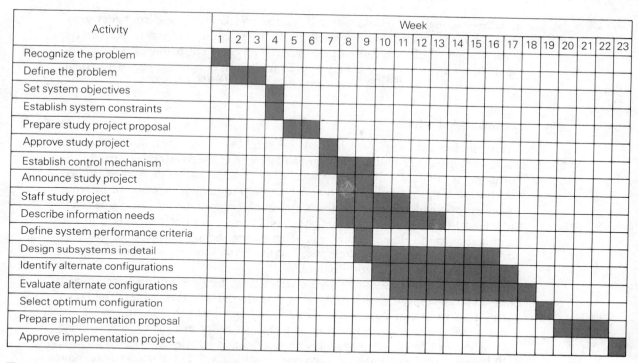

Activity	Week
	1 | 2 | 3 | 4 | 5 | 6 | 7 | 8 | 9 | 10 | 11 | 12 | 13 | 14 | 15 | 16 | 17 | 18 | 19 | 20 | 21 | 22 | 23
Recognize the problem	
Define the problem	
Set system objectives	
Establish system constraints	
Prepare study project proposal	
Approve study project	
Establish control mechanism	
Announce study project	
Staff study project	
Describe information needs	
Define system performance criteria	
Design subsystems in detail	
Identify alternate configurations	
Evaluate alternate configurations	
Select optimum configuration	
Prepare implementation proposal	
Approve implementation project	

Figure 2-5 A Gantt chart of an MIS life cycle (planning phase and analysis and design phase).

computers personally. Some CEOs have terminals in their offices, some write their own programs, and others use prewritten programs for graphical analyses.[5]

These examples of different uses of the MIS, based on management level, are easy to observe. Fayol's theory of management functions helps us understand why these differences exist. This understanding is very important to the people designing the MIS.

An associate of Frederic W. Taylor's, Harry L. Gantt (1861–1919) was also a member of the classical school and is best known for his charting technique—the Gantt chart. The *Gantt chart* illustrated in Figure 2-5 is a bar chart showing how the major activities needed to implement an MIS (the bars) are scheduled over time. This type of chart is a simple way to plan and control a project. When the project becomes complex, however, the Gantt chart is less effective than other methods. We will take a closer look at the alternatives in Chapter 16, when we discuss planning for the MIS.

The husband-and-wife team of Frank B. Gilbreth (1869–1924) and Lillian M. Gilbreth (1878–1972) carried on the Taylor tradition by studying the detailed motions of workers to identify the most efficient combinations. The Gilbreths

[5] Ibid., pp. 82–88.

classified the motions, calling them "therbligs" (Gilbreth spelled backward). Although labor resisted Taylor's scientific management, it was generally receptive to the Gilbreths' ideas because of the reduced physical effort their studies advocated. In addition, many workers appreciated management's concern for their physical well-being.

The behavioral school

A team of Harvard researchers, headed by Elton Mayo and Fritz J. Roethlisberger, studied the effects of illumination on productivity at the Western Electric Hawthorne plant at Cicero, Illinois, between 1927 and 1932. The more they studied the relationship, the more confusing it became. Productivity seemed to increase regardless of whether the lighting was increased, reduced, or kept the same. As it turned out, experimental groups of employees were not responding to the lighting, but to the attention that was being shown them. This response to attention was named the *Hawthorne effect,* and the Hawthorne experiments heralded the beginning of the behavioral school.

The behavioral school has been characterized by two groups, both placing more emphasis on the *people* in the jobs than on the jobs themselves. The Hawthorne researchers, as part of the *human relations movement,* were among the first to gain a better understanding of people at work in organizations. These researchers were later joined by highly trained behavioral scientists (psychologists, sociologists, social psychologists, and anthropologists).[6] These scientists became known as the *social systems* group. More sophisticated research techniques were applied by this group, whose efforts produced the body of material describing *organizational behavior.* The social systems group has greatly influenced the study of management in modern business schools, as evidenced by the many textbooks and courses titled *Organizational Behavior.*

It is more difficult to relate the MIS to the behavioral school than to the classical school. The classical school, with its emphasis on efficiency and productivity, is highly compatible with the design of many computerized management systems. This is unfortunate. The designers of early systems paid little attention to the people involved. The systems looked good on paper, but they were unacceptable to the employees who were expected to provide the input data, and to the managers who were expected to use the output information.

Had the designers of early information systems paid more attention to behavioral theory, both the number and the severity of MIS failures would most certainly have been reduced. Employees felt threatened by the computer; they feared they would lose their jobs. Management made little effort to communicate the objectives of the computer project to the employees. When the computer was installed, employees in effect sabotaged it by doing their computer-related jobs poorly or not at all. The support from the managers was frequently no better. Although intended primarily to help the managers, systems were often designed without

---

[6]Psychology is the study of individual behavior. Sociology is concerned with group behavior, and social psychology with the influence of groups on individual behavior. Anthropology is the study of human origins and the development of culture.

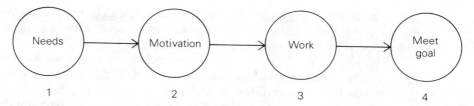

Figure 2-6 Goals are met by satisfying needs.

managers' participation. Many managers rejected the MIS, feeling it was forced on them without their consent or involvement.

The designers of the early systems often rationalized the failure of their systems by claiming that people resist change. On the contrary, people in our society generally thrive on change. Most wouldn't think of wearing the same clothes two days in a row, and many who have owned a car for only a few years start looking around for a new one. People generally resist change only when it is forced on them or when they perceive it as a threat.

The research that came out of the human relations group can be applied toward the success of an MIS. These findings recognized that employees have various types of needs, and that there are ways these needs can be satisfied. The chain reaction from needs to goals is pictured in Figure 2-6. The first step is to recognize the needs of the employees. In step 2 the manager develops motivators to inspire the employees to work toward the goals of the firm. The work is performed in step 3, and the firm meets its goals in step 4.

The social systems group worked along the same lines as this model. They also recognized the importance of the individual if the group, or firm, is to meet its goals. They believed that the goals of both the individual and the group must be compatible. Therefore when the manager sets a goal for a system, it must be one the employees will regard as compatible with their personal goals.

The behavioral school has made some solid contributions to a systems theory. The school concentrates on the importance of goals and how they can be achieved. It would be foolish for a manager of a business system to ignore these suggestions. The business system is not simply a mechanical structure. Its performance level is determined by the people working in it. The behavioral school suggests how these people can be motivated to work together as a system.[7]

The quantitative school

During World War II, new quantitative techniques were developed for military purposes in order to use limited resources more efficiently and to improve decision making. After the war, the techniques were applied in business situations to

---

[7] For examples of some of the current research on the behavioral effect of computerized systems, see Frank Collins and Robert E. Seiler, "Causes of Erroneous Data Input," *Journal of Systems Management* 30 (July 1979): 18–21; Henry C. Lucas, Jr., "MIS Affects Balance of Power," *Management Accounting* 61 (October 1979): 8 ff; and Charles A. O'Reilly III, "Individuals and Information Overload in Organizations: Is More Necessarily Better?" *Academy of Management Journal* 23 (1980): 684–696.

accomplish the same results. At the same time, the electronic computer arrived on the scene, and together the two innovations—quantitative techniques and the computer—formed an exciting problem-solving tool.

The name given to these quantitative techniques is *operations research,* or *OR.* The term *management science* is also used. Larger organizations and the government formed operations research staffs composed of persons with the necessary quantitative expertise. The OR people used quantitative methods such as linear programming, the Monte Carlo method, and multiple regression. *Linear programming* is used either to minimize costs or to maximize returns, within constraints. For example, the travel costs of a salesperson incurred in covering her or his territory can be minimized by determining the shortest route through the territory. The constraints are the distances that separate the customers. *Monte Carlo* involves the use of randomly generated numbers to represent the random fluctuations of business activity. For example, a manager wishing to study an inventory system can use Monte Carlo to simulate the random activity of daily sales volume. *Multiple regression* is used to forecast future activity, such as sales, based on several influencing factors, such as the national economy, an advertising budget, and so on. We will learn more about these quantitative techniques later in the book when we turn our attention to MIS applications.

The OR researchers and managers who believed in quantitative solutions to business problems formed the quantitative school of management theory. Quantitative theory concentrates on decision making and provides tools for improving this aspect of managerial work. Central to the quantitative approach is the *mathematical model*—an equation or a set of equations that represents a business situation. The process of using a model in decision making consists of the following steps:

1. Study the problem well enough to understand the elements involved and their interactions. For example, if the problem concerns how much of a product to order from a supplier, the elements can be identified as:

   A: acquisition (or purchase) cost
   S: annual sales
   R: retention (or carrying) cost

2. Build a model consisting of the elements and their relationships. The economic order quantity (EOQ) model appears as

$$EOQ = \sqrt{\frac{2AS}{R}}$$

3. Test the model by providing test data and analyzing the results. Verify that the model does in fact achieve its objective—in this case, minimum cost.

4. Use the model in day-to-day business activities.

5. Continually evaluate and update the model to guard against obsolescence. For example, change the value for the variable S when the sales rate changes.

The quantitative school has greatly influenced MIS design and use. Quantitative techniques demand the use of a computer, and the problems attacked are some of the most difficult a manager can face. There are managers, however, who have not embraced the quantitative school. These managers are more concerned with applying human skills to the interpersonal problems of organization, motivation, staffing, and leadership. Additionally, the following significant problems occur with the quantitative approach.

1. *Development time:* The time to create and test the model may be excessive for a problem that demands a quick decision.
2. *Lack of good input data:* The models require good input data, which is not always available. The model can be no better than its input.
3. *Requirement for quantitative skills:* Many managers do not have the necessary quantitative skills and cannot communicate effectively with people who do. Managers often hesitate to turn over decision-making authority to an OR specialist.
4. *Difficulty of modeling business problems:* Some business situations are so complex that it is difficult to see all of the variables and their effects. Attempts to solve these problems with overly simple models lead to poor decisions.

As we go about the task of describing the modern MIS, you will recognize the influence of the quantitative school. Always remember that its techniques are not ends in themselves, but only contributions to improved management, supplementing the contributions of other schools of management theory.[8]

The contingency school

Efforts to apply the principles of the classical, behavioral, and quantitative schools have not always been successful. None of the principles works in all situations. It became apparent that the situation influenced the chance of success for any of the theories. One group of theorists believed that no theory worked all the time, and that success was contingent on the situation. This group became known as the contingency, or situational, school. The school has a large following because it encourages a flexibility in the solution of complex problems that the other schools, with their specialized focus, cannot offer.

According to this school of thought, the situation affecting management practice is the environment of the organizational unit. This environment consists of the *external environment* (the *economic, political,* and *social* influences on the firm) and the *internal environment* (the constraints imposed by a firm's limited

---

[8] Examples of the application of OR to business problems are found in William C. Hellriegel, "OR/MS Modeling in Long Range Bank Planning," *Omega* 9 no. 1 (1981): 33–36; Cornelis A. de Kluyver and Graeme M. McNally, "Corporate Planning Using Simulation," *Interfaces* 10 (June 1980): 1–7; Helen Deresky, "Analytical Tools for Increased Productivity," *Journal of Systems Management* 32 (July 1981): 28–30; and Lawrence F. Young, "The Birth, Maturation, and Death of Management Science in an Advertising Agency," *Interfaces* 10 (August 1980): 62–67.

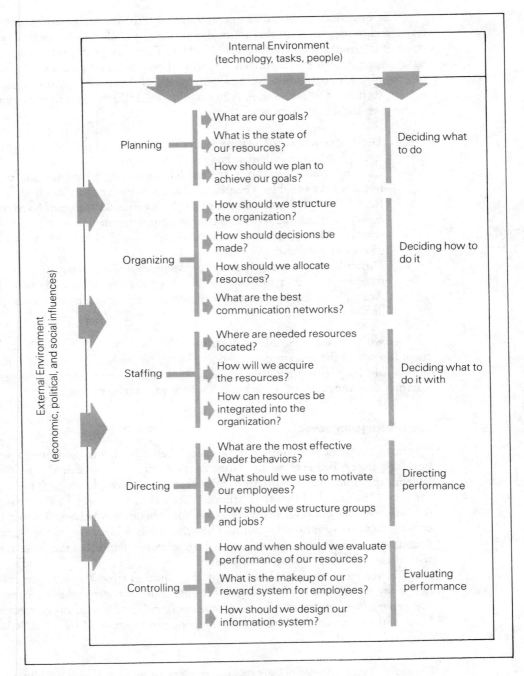

Figure 2-7 A summary of contingency management.

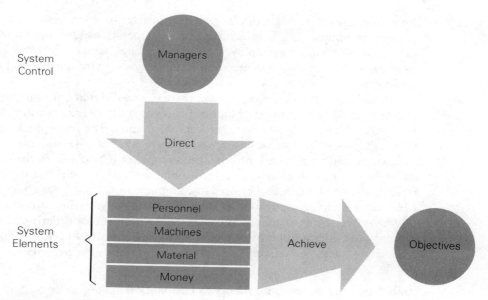

Figure 2-8 The firm as a physical system.

resources).[9] The internal constraints consist of the *technology* used in the production process, the *tasks* performed by the employees, and the *people* themselves. To cite an example, the internal environment of a foreperson of a welding shop, where a majority of the workers have little or no college education, is different from that of a project leader of a group of R&D (research and development) engineers.

The influence of both environments on the manager's performance is shown in Figure 2-7, along with questions that must be answered. Since answers to the questions vary from one situation to the next, the manager must be constantly aware of changes in both environments and capable of obtaining the information necessary to revise the answers accordingly. In this view of management the MIS can play an important role by providing good information and facilitating good decisions.

A systems theory of management

To date, a bona fide *systems school* of management theory has not emerged. There are managers, however, who apply a *systems theory* in conjunction with principles from one or more of the schools. A systems theory draws on the existing schools of management theory and uses certain principles in a systems context.

Central to systems theory is the idea of a system composed of inputs, transformation processes, outputs, and a control mechanism. This is the *physical system of the firm,* with the manager serving as the control mechanism. Figure 2-8

---

[9]Based on Szilagyi, pp. 79–82.

illustrates how the manager directs resources to achieve objectives. Classical management techniques can help achieve efficient operations, and behavioral techniques can help motivate employees to work toward system objectives. Management decisions and direction are contingent on both environmental and internal constraints.

In addition to the physical system, there is a *conceptual information system*. This system—also composed of inputs, processes, outputs, and a control mechanism—transforms data into management information. The conceptual system, or MIS, is illustrated by the shaded arrows in Figure 2-9. The MIS gathers the internal and external environmental information and makes it available to the managers on all levels. Including system objectives in the MIS permits management by exception. The MIS can also be used to communicate actions (plans, instructions, directives, policies, and so on) to the physical system to keep the system on course.

A systems theory of management provides a basis for the orderly examination of a complex organization by attending to the major parts and their influence on goal achievement. We will build on this concept in the next two chapters.

Importance of management theory to information management

The firm's information system is intended to help the manager manage. In order to do so, the people designing the MIS must understand management. This is why

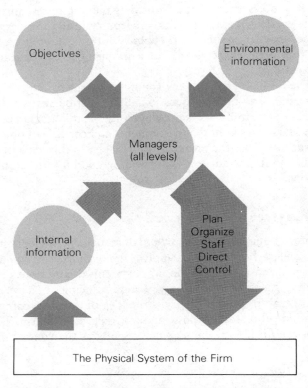

Figure 2-9 Using information to manage the physical system.

the manager must be directly involved in the design of the MIS. He or she is more likely to have this understanding than is an information specialist.

The manager should understand theories of management. The MIS can then be designed to help the manager apply these theories to the management of available resources. The understanding of management must come first, however. It is a prerequisite for a good MIS.

Before a firm can consider an MIS, an adequate management resource must be available. An MIS will help improve this resource. But a poor management resource probably could never develop a good MIS. Therefore an MIS should not be regarded as a cure for poor management. The basic management skill must be present for an effective MIS to be realized.

The manager's recognition of the psychological impact of an MIS on a firm and its employees is another reason why management theory is important. Since much of management theory is concerned with the psychology of management, this understanding can help win acceptance of the MIS.

Organization Theory[10]

Organization theory concerns the arrangement or assembly of a firm's resources. It deals with structure. Usually, the structure is thought of as relating only to people, as with an organization chart. But this arrangement of people also entails an arrangement of other resources—money, machines, and material. For example, the people in the marketing department have available operating funds, any machines required (such as company cars), and any needed material (such as sales manuals and free samples). When people are classified by organizational unit, these other resources go along with them.

Organization theory is a subset of management theory. Management theory applies to everything relating to the task of management. Organization theory concerns only that part dealing with the arrangement of resources.

Schools of organization theory

Like management theory, organization theory has evolved through a series of schools: first the *classical* school, followed by the *behavioral* school, and then the *contingency* school. We will discuss each of these schools and then present a *systems* theory of organization.

The classical school

Frederick Taylor and his scientific management group viewed employees in a strictly economic sense—more or less as appendages of their machines, working to achieve higher productivity. They ignored the firm's environment, and their emphasis was strictly on making internal operations as efficient, rational, and predictable as possible. High productivity was considered a direct result of the

---

[10]Based on Szilagyi, pp. 291–317; and Robert Albanese, *Managing: Toward Accountability for Performance,* 3rd ed. (Homewood, Ill.: Richard D. Irwin, 1981), pp. 492–501, 579–602.

best work methods. The scientific management group believed that the best organizational structure for implementing these methods was one with clear lines of authority and responsibility, management control, and economic (monetary) rewards for good work.

Henri Fayol had a wider view of management, as we have seen, and he contributed more toward the organization of workers into groups. Fayol identified a set of *principles* related to organization. We have singled out and explained in systems terms some of Fayol's principles that apply to the firm as a system.

- *Division of labor:* Resources are grouped into specialized units, or subsystems. Such specialization can improve efficiency and productivity.
- *Unity of command:* There is one control point in the system.
- *Unity of direction:* Subsystems should work together toward the system's goals.
- *Subordination of individual interest to the common goal:* All subsystems should contribute to the achievement of the system's goals.
- *Order:* The resources of the system—materials, machines, and personnel—should be in the right place at the right time.

Although these principles were almost fifty years old when the systems concept became popular, they still serve as guidelines for good system performance.

Another principle deserves mention, since it affects MIS design. The principle of *span of control* deals with the number of subordinates a manager can manage. The span, along with the number of bottom-level employees, determines the number of layers of managers. Figure 2-10 compares two structures, one with a span of control of 4 and another of 2. These layers are important to the MIS designer,

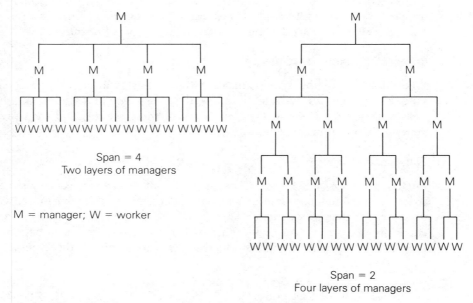

Span = 4
Two layers of managers

M = manager; W = worker

Span = 2
Four layers of managers

Figure 2-10 Span of control influences management layers.

since information and decisions must be communicated vertically through the organization. The span of control influences how many layers are involved. As a rule, a system with few layers is more responsive than a system with many layers—information and decisions can be communicated more quickly.

Another principle important to MIS designers is that of *functional organization.* Fayol used the term *departmentation,* meaning that the firm's resources should be segregated in departments based on purposes, processes, customers, geographic area, and so on. Today the functional form of organization is most prevalent, with resources distributed among the functional areas of manufacturing, marketing, and finance. Figure 2-11 is the organization chart of an architec-

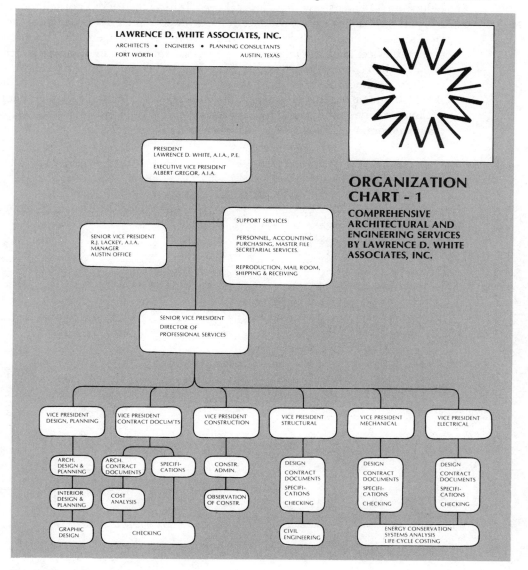

Figure 2-11 An organization chart is a graphic model.

tural firm, showing the groupings of people according to the type of work they perform. All the resources of the firm are grouped in this manner.

In summary, classical organization theory is very formal and rigid. The resources must be arranged along functional lines in an exact manner. The structure should be reflected in an organization chart, and all members of the organization should have specific, well-defined duties.

The behavioral school

Behavioral scientists saw that classical organization theory did not tell the whole story. It was too inflexible. Managers and workers alike grew tired of the formal, rigid structure and established their own "unofficial" arrangement. This informal structure exists in all organizations. It does not appear on an organization chart, but it is there. It is also known as "the grapevine," and its main purpose is to facilitate communications.

The informal network enables one employee to communicate with another without following the lines of the organizational chart. Horizontal, vertical, and diagonal communication coexist, as illustrated in Figure 2-12.

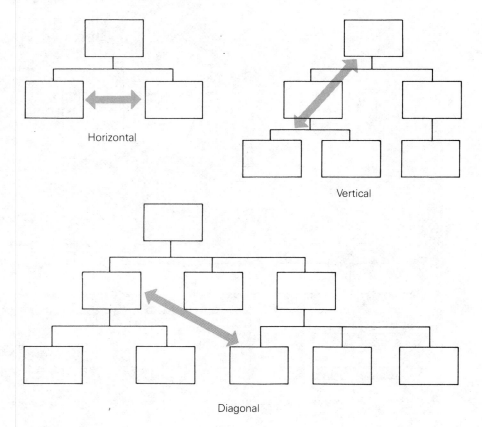

Figure 2-12 Informal communication flows.

The informal organization is of special interest because the MIS is responsible for an important part of the communication within a firm—the information and decision flow. Up until now, however, the MIS has been unsuccessful in capturing the information of the informal network. Henry Mintzberg, a modern-day management theorist, states that "most work just cannot get done without some informal communication."[11] According to Mintzberg, the formal MIS is too slow, unreliable, and limited. He refers to the information of the informal network as *soft information,* as opposed to the *hard* information of the MIS. Mintzberg has conducted studies indicating that managers spend 65–80% of their time communicating verbally, and about 45% of their time communicating outside of their formal organizational structure.

It is likely that the incorporation of word processing technology into the MIS will make some of this informal information flow more formal. Word processing can handle intrafirm communications—such as interoffice memos, letters, procedures, and so forth—much better than conventional computing equipment. But it would be foolish to assume that the MIS could ever embrace all informal communications.

In addition to informal communication flows, there are informal flows of influence or power that fail to show up on the charts. Some people accumulate power over and above that of their formal positions. As the MIS designer becomes involved in an MIS project, he or she should attempt to identify all the individuals who will have an effect on the success of the project. The designer must gain insight into the informal power structure in order to identify the influences that do not appear on the chart. All of the people influencing the success of the MIS should be involved in its design—regardless of their formal position in the organization.

The contingency school

In practice, none of the theories of organization discussed up to now is effective in all situations. Functional organization is the most widespread, but it becomes cumbersome as the firm grows larger. Firms that outgrow the functional structure often superimpose another structure on top of it. Figure 2-13 shows a departmentation by product superimposed on a traditional functional structure.

This two-dimensional approach to organization can be visualized as a matrix. In fact, when an organization is structured as in Figure 2-14, it is called a *matrix organization.* The rows of the matrix represent one organizational subdivision, and the columns represent another. In the figure, the rows represent the products, and the columns represent the areas of activity. The matrix structure is popular in firms with large government contracts, such as aerospace. Someone is designated *project manager,* and he or she assembles a staff that cuts horizontally across functional lines. In food companies such as Procter & Gamble and General Mills, a *product manager,* or *brand manager,* is responsible for all activities relating to

---

[11] Henry Mintzberg, *The Structuring of Organizations* (Englewood Cliffs, N.J.: Prentice-Hall, 1979), p. 49.

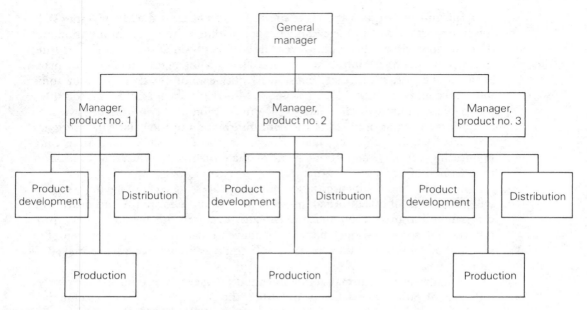

Figure 2-13   A simplified product organization structure.

a particular brand. These efforts are intended to overcome the problems inherent in a large functional organization.

A contingency theory of organization is based on the notion that there is no single best way to organize. Different approaches are possible, and the appropriate one should be used in each situation. Matrix organization, for example, might be right for aerospace but wrong for a bank. The contingency theory recognizes the influence of the environment on organization and sees different structures as ways of coping with environmental demands and changes. Finally, this theory recognizes that several different structures usually exist within a firm at the same time.

Centralized versus decentralized organization

In addition to matrix structure, another tactic for coping with large organization size is *decentralization*. This involves the decentralization of authority and power, not the dispersion of a firm's operations over a geographic area. When power is concentrated in a few individuals, a firm is *centralized;* when the power is dispersed, it is *decentralized*.

General Electric has always been decentralized, with its various divisions operating like separate companies; Du Pont decentralized in 1921. But the real shift to decentralization came much later. In 1950 only 20% of the *Fortune 500* firms were decentralized; by 1970 the number had reached 80%.[12]

---

[12] Robert H. Waterman, Jr., Thomas J. Peters, and Julien R. Phillips, "Structure Is Not Organization," *Business Horizons* 23 (June 1980): 19.

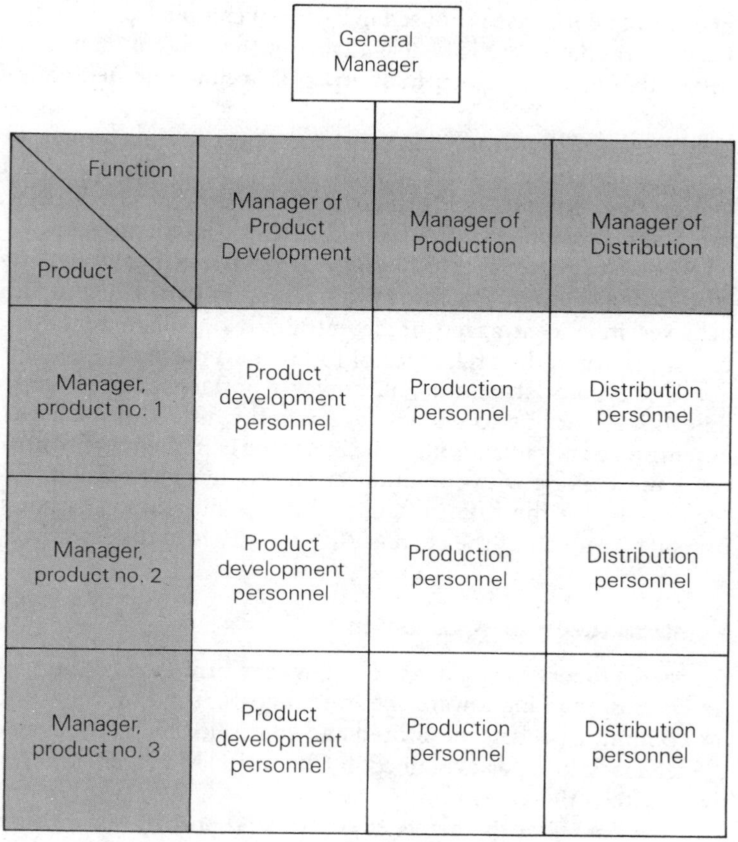

Figure 2-14 A matrix organization structure.

Centralization offers top management the tightest control possible. This control is delegated only when the task becomes too great for those people with the power. Ideally the control should be delegated as far down the hierarchy as possible—to the lowest competent level. This frees upper-level managers for other tasks.

The swing to decentralization has been facilitated in part by improvements in computer and data communication technology. Today companies routinely use networks of computers, terminals, and data communications facilities to transmit information between headquarters and field offices. Multiple computers, very often minicomputers, can be dispersed throughout the firm and can communicate with each other. This is *distributed data processing* (DDP), a hot computer application during the past seven or eight years. This type of intrafirm communication was impossible as little as ten years ago. Today a manager in an Atlanta office can have a minicomputer and a data base of the office's data and information. This system can be used to solve Atlanta problems without going through headquarters in Chicago. And the Atlanta manager can link that system to others in the firm, such as the one in Albuquerque, to solve special problems. Quite possibly, a corporate data base is housed in a central computer, called the *host,* in Chicago. This central data base is also available to the Atlanta manager, and it is updated with Atlanta transactions. In short, MIS technology definitely facilitates decentralization.

On the other hand, this same computer equipment can be used to further centralized management. Top management in an organization can gather information describing the performance of a geographically dispersed operation, and can make decisions that are relayed to lower-level managers.

Therefore computer technology does not specifically encourage centralization or decentralization. On the contrary, a firm can use computing equipment to achieve either centralized or decentralized organizational structure. The determining factor is the preference of top management.

The type of structure can, however, influence the process of implementing the MIS. According to one study, it is more difficult to achieve a good MIS in a decentralized organization.[13] The increased complexity of control in decentralized companies, along with communication problems between different divisions, are the reasons for the MIS difficulty. But this situation does not seem to hold any firms back; much of the current MIS activity is in decentralized organizations.

A systems theory of organization

A systems theory of organization views the firm as a system with all elements, or subsystems, working toward the overall goals. The firm transforms input resources into output, a process monitored and controlled by management. Management is the feedback loop, as explained in Chapter 1. Management uses the firm's objectives to keep the system on course.

The resources the manager controls do not remain within the firm but flow through it. The firm can be regarded as a system of flow networks representing physical resources and information, as shown in Figure 2-15. These networks originate outside the firm, flow through the firm, and finally return to the environment.

Four of the flow networks carry physical resources—personnel, material, machines, and money. The fifth flow is that of information—the conceptual representation of the physical system. Managers use information to manage the other, physical, resources when direct contact with those resources becomes difficult. While information is valuable to all managers, it is an absolute necessity for managers in large firms and for managers on upper levels.

Most of the flow of physical resources occurs at the lower, or operational, level. The flows of machines and material are at this level as they move through the manufacturing process. Money also flows at the operational level—between the firm and its customers, vendors, and financial institutions. Management is very interested in these flows, but does not participate in them directly.

---

[13] Phillip Ein-Dor and Eli Segev studied the effect of organization on the MIS and reported their findings, in terms of twenty-two propositions, in "Organizational Context and the Success of Management Information Systems," *Management Science* 24 (June 1978): 1064–1077.

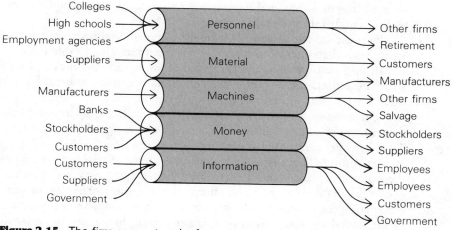

Figure 2-15 The firm as a network of resource flows.

Managers monitor the physical flows by using the information flow. The only physical flow at upper levels is personnel; management is actively involved in personnel through organizing, staffing, directing, and motivating other employees on those same levels.

Even though the firm may be considered in flow network terms, it is seldom organized along those lines. Instead, firms are normally organized by functional group. Some firms have approached the flow network structure while maintaining an essentially functional organization. This is usually done by separating the material flow and assigning it to a new function—logistics. This new functional area is responsible for all material flows from the environment, through the firm, and back to the environment. Other firms have separated out particular parts of the material flow and assigned them to product or brand managers.

If firms have organized or subdivided other than by flow network, what is the value of thinking in flow network terms? The main advantage is that it recognizes the firm as a single system, not a conglomeration of several systems. It is possible to trace a single flow from the environment, through the firm, and back to the environment without getting caught up in the functional complexities that vary from one type of organization to another.[14] Even when an organization is organized functionally, the manager and the systems analyst can think in flow network terms to isolate and understand problems. Flow network organization

---

[14]There have been a number of good efforts to describe the organization as a system of flow networks. See, for example, Jay W. Forrester, "Industrial Dynamics: A Major Breakthrough for Decision Makers," *Harvard Business Review* 36 (July–August 1958): 37–66; idem., "Advertising: A Problem in Industrial Dynamics," ibid. 37 (March–April 1959): 100–110; Richard J. Hopeman, *Systems Analysis and Operations Management* (Columbus: Charles E. Merrill, 1969), pp. 125–151; Otis Dudley Duncan, "Social Organization and the Ecosystem," in Robert E. L. Faris, ed., *Handbook of Modern Sociology* (Chicago: Rand McNally, 1964), pp. 36–44; and Mintzberg, *The Structuring of Organizations,* pp. 35–64.

is an abstraction that enables managers to focus on important elements without getting tangled up in details.

Because functionalism is so widely accepted, and because it can be followed along with the systems approach, it has been included in this book. A structure for an information system is presented along functional lines in Part Four. This structure reflects the direction that functionally organized firms have followed in the design of management information systems.

Once the flow network idea is understood, it is easy to regard the manager as a controller of these flows. This concept of management is illustrated in Figure 2-16. The owners of the firm entrust certain resources to the manager and expect certain results. There is a limit to the resources available to a manager. When these resources are committed to an assigned task, they are removed from the pool of available resources and allocated to the transformation process. They are returned to the pool when the transformation is complete. Resources that cannot be employed for one reason or another remain in the pool—either they cannot perform the required tasks or there are no tasks to perform.

When management is viewed in this manner, the efficiency of the management task can be measured to a certain extent by the size of the resource pool. Resources in the pool are essentially wasted; they are costing the firm and are returning nothing. It might appear that the manager's ultimate objective is to eliminate the pool completely. While desirable, this is not realistic. If profit is to be maximized, resources must be directed to the most profitable tasks, not to those resulting in the lowest cost by reducing the resource pool. Over the long term the manager seeks to acquire resources that can be used in the most profitable activities; but in the short term the day-to-day changes in business prevent a perfect match between resources and tasks.

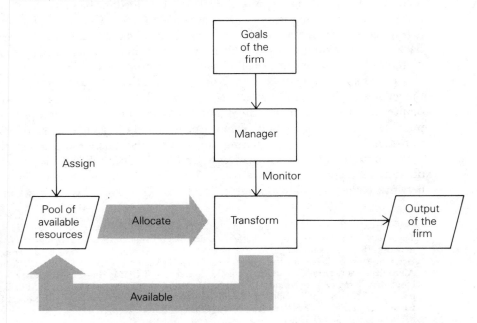

Figure 2-16 The manager strives for optimum use of the firm's resources.

Importance of organization theory to information management

The MIS provides an opportunity for improved communication and decision flow in organizations of all forms. In designing the MIS, attention must be given to the levels of management and the organizational groupings (by functional area, product, and so on) and to the effect these structures have on information needs.

Attention must also be directed to the informal organization structure. Management should try to identify information needs that are not being fulfilled by the formal system and to incorporate as many of these flows into the formal MIS as possible. Certainly those informal power centers of the organization that can influence the success of the MIS should be identified and included in the design effort.

Finally, the MIS can keep management informed of environmental needs and changes that influence the organizational structure. The structure can then be changed to respond to environmental demands.

In addition to the influence of the MIS on the organization, the organization influences the MIS. A good MIS cannot be expected in a firm where the parts—the divisions and departments—do not work together. And as we have seen, a decentralized organization probably makes the MIS task more difficult.

The organizational implications of the MIS go beyond setting up a new department. An understanding of the basics of organizational theory is a must for MIS designers.

Summary

Our purpose in this chapter has been to lay a foundation for the study of the MIS. Although the MIS is relatively new, theoretical work that went on long before is still applicable. A knowledge of management and organization theory is important in the design of an MIS. The theory enables the manager and the information specialist to understand *why* certain behavior occurs. With this understanding, the MIS and its development project can be designed to meet the needs of the participants, thereby assuring their cooperation.

Management theory is the overall body of knowledge related to every aspect of the management process. The classical theorists, including Frederick W. Taylor, Henri Fayol, Harry L. Gantt, and Frank B. and Lillian M. Gilbreth, were concerned with increasing productivity. Taylor's work with standards of performance and management by exception contribute significantly to modern MIS design and use. Fayol's management functions provide the information specialist with an understanding of the activities needing information support.

The behavioral theorists were more concerned with the people performing the work than with the work itself. The human relations group grew out of the Hawthorne studies and was later joined by behavioral scientists, forming a social systems group. The importance of behavioral theory is easily overlooked—which is exactly what happened in early MIS designs. Early system failures were due in part to the insufficient attention given to the human aspects. Present-day system designers are more aware of the importance of behavioral theory than were designers of early systems.

The quantitative management theory has assumed a key role in the MIS.

Systems are designed to use mathematical models to support the manager's decision making. But you must be careful not to lose sight of the fact that decision modeling presents several problems and that it does not address all of the areas of managerial responsibility.

The unique limitations of each of the schools of management theory led to the establishment of a new school that recognizes the relative effectiveness of different techniques in different situations. This is the contingency school, which uses the manager's environment (external and internal) as the starting point. The environment influences how problems are solved.

A systems theory of management is not as widely recognized as the other schools. Yet systems theory is especially useful in studying the MIS, as it positions the MIS in the feedback loop. The MIS enables the manager to control the physical system of the firm by gathering and presenting information describing the firm's operations. The MIS enables the manager to adapt the firm to changing needs and influences.

Organization theory is the subset of management theory that concerns the arrangement of the firm's resources. The classical school, led by Fayol, stressed formal, functional relationships. Several classical principles (such as unity of command, unity of direction, and order) relate to the firm as a system.

The behavioral school emphasized informal relationships and power centers in the organization. These topics are important to the MIS designer, who must capture more of the informal information flows and achieve cooperation during the MIS implementation project.

The contingency school recognizes the influence of the situation on organization. Matrix structure as well as product and brand management concepts are modern ways of coping with organizational problems. Another way is decentralization of decision-making authority. The computer can facilitate either decentralization or centralization, depending on management's preference.

A systems theory of organization integrates flows of both physical and conceptual resources through the firm. Management's task is to maintain the flows at the proper rate. The conceptual information flow—the MIS—facilitates the physical flow.

In this chapter we introduced systems theories of management and organization. These theories will be expanded in the next two chapters.

Key Terms

theory	strategic, tactical, and operational management levels
proposition	
management theory	Gantt chart
classical school	behavioral school
scientific management	Hawthorne effect
performance standards	human relations movement
management by exception	social systems group
management functions	organizational behavior

quantitative school

mathematical model

contingency school

systems theory

organization theory

organization principles

division of labor

unity of command

unity of direction

order

span of control

functional organization

soft information, hard information

matrix organization

project manager, product manager, brand manager

decentralization, centralization

distributed data processing (DDP)

Key Concepts

The role of theory in explaining and understanding phenomena

How information is used to develop theory

The grouping of theorists into schools

The contributions of the schools to MIS design and use

The universality of management functions

Levels of management

The importance of human behavior to a successful MIS

The specialized nature and limited scope of the quantitative school of management theory

The importance of the environment to the contingency school

A systems theory of management and organization

Functional organization structure

Informal organizational relationships

Hard and soft information

How the computer facilitates both centralized and decentralized organization

Questions

1. Does a theory have to be true all the time? If not, what is its value?
2. What is theory?
3. What is the question that theory enables the user to answer?
4. How is information used to develop theories?
5. What are the different schools of management theory? Which have corresponding schools of organization theory?
6. Name four classical management theorists.
7. Who is the father of scientific management? Is scientific management the same as systems analysis? Explain.
8. Are the performance standards that Taylor envisioned the same as company goals and objectives? Explain your answer.
9. What is the concept of management by exception? Explain.

10. Are management functions the same as functional areas? Explain.

11. What are the three management levels? What distinguishes them from each other? What significance does the concept of levels have to the information specialist?

12. How can a manager achieve improved employee performance by using the Hawthorne effect?

13. Which management theory did designers of early information systems overlook?

14. What is the primary tool of the quantitative school of management theory? What are the steps in developing this tool? What are some problems with its use?

15. Which theorist contributed the most to classical organization theory? Have his ideas become obsolete because of the computer? Explain.

16. What is the difference between hard and soft information? Give an example of each.

17. How can a manager use the computer to achieve a centralized organization structure? Explain.

18. Does distributed data processing encourage a centralized or decentralized organization?

19. Can a manager be evaluated based on the size of resources in the resource pool? Why or why not?

20. On which management level is the personnel flow the greatest in terms of volume? What about the machine flow? The material flow? The data flow? The information flow? In your opinion, what resource is most valuable to the operational-level manager? To the tactical-level manager? To the strategic-level manager?

CASE PROBLEM: Palm Springs Publications, Inc.

Palm Springs Publications, Inc. (PSPI), is a chain of West Coast newspapers with headquarters in San Diego. A large, centralized computer installation is used to set the type for each of the eighteen member newspapers. Story copy is transmitted to headquarters, where the computer aligns the copy into columns with proper hyphenation. The copy is sent back to the newspaper, where a punched paper tape is automatically created to operate the typesetting equipment.

The computer configuration includes an optical character reader—a unit that reads characters typed on paper. This reading process permits someone with a typewriter to create computer input, eliminating the need for keypunch machines or terminals. PSPI uses the reader to input copy written by the reporters at headquarters.

All of the decisions concerning PSPI's MIS operation are made by an MIS committee composed of Frank Ruiz (the board chairman), Roberta Guenther (the president), and Cecil McGregor (the vice-president of MIS). These decisions concern hardware and software selection, project planning, and project management.

The optical reader was ordered by the MIS committee over the objections of Jack Stone, the manager of computer operations. Stone claimed that neither the technology nor the reliability of the manufacturer had been proven, and that terminals should be used for input.

The reader has been installed for eighteen months and has never worked properly. The error rate is high, and the unit frequently suffers electronic and mechanical failure. Even with an on-site repairperson, the unit is inoperative for long periods.

You are the new sales representative for Cyclops Systems, the manufacturer of the reader, and you are concerned that PSPI might cancel their lease because of the poor performance. You call on Ruiz, and he assures you that all is well. He understands the problems with new technology and is confident that the bugs will be worked out. Subsequent calls on Guenther and McGregor inspire less enthusiasm, but they assure you that no plan is underway to cancel the lease.

Before you call it a day, you decide to meet Stone. You find him extremely bitter about the reader. He claims that the excessive downtime causes him problems since he must use backup keypunch machines, which are slow and also subject to mechanical failure. Stone says, "I've been with PSPI for four years, and I have been denied promotions and salary increases because of the poor operations record caused by this reader. If something isn't done to remedy the situation, I'm going to quit. I'm going to have to cut our talk short, since Frank and I have a golf date at four. I've got to run."

When you get back to your office, your boss, Roger Potuzak, tells you, "I'm glad you got to meet the people at PSPI. I don't want to lose that account. I'll consider anything that will retain their confidence—and business. There's a lot of potential out there. Now, tell me what strategy you think is best."

Questions

1. What is the problem at PSPI?
2. Who makes the decisions relating to the MIS operation?
3. Which school of organization theory provides assistance in solving this problem? Explain how.
4. How can the work of the human relations group be applied in this situation?
5. Provide your boss, Mr. Potuzak, with the recommended strategy that he has requested.

Chapter 3

The General Systems Model of the Firm

Learning Objectives

After studying this chapter, you should:

- Know what a model is, what types exist, and how they are used
- Appreciate the special capability of the mathematical model when used in decision support
- Appreciate the value of a general model
- Know the elemental parts of the general systems model, their relationships, and their roles
- Understand the concept of management by exception
- Be able to visualize how the general systems model can be used as the basis for evaluating any type of organization
- Be able to use the general systems model in a real business setting, with practice

Models

The model has become a popular device in business. It is used to facilitate understanding and to aid in decision making. An analysis of business literature during the past fifteen years shows an almost geometric increase in the discussion of models in textbooks, professional business journals, and periodicals. If the scope of the analysis were pushed back thirty or forty years, it would appear that modeling is a recent innovation that, like the computer and management science techniques, came into its own only recently. This conclusion is not completely true. Modeling has probably always been an important decision-making tool, but only recently has it attracted the attention of business writers.

What is a model?

A model is an abstraction of something; it is something that represents something else.

The word *model* usually brings to mind the people pictured in fashion ads. This type of model is an abstraction of something, as the person viewing the ad puts himself or herself in the model's place. Fashion models—female and male alike—are employed by advertisers to show viewers how they could look wearing a particular dress or suit. The model represents the hundreds or thousands of potential purchasers who view the ad.

The idea of a conceptual system was presented in Chapter 1. A conceptual system also has the function of representing something—in this case, a physical system. Therefore, both a model and a conceptual system are used to represent something else. In fact, the two terms can be used interchangeably.

Types of models

Since models of all kinds have become popular in recent years, a number of efforts have been made to classify the various kinds. The classification scheme discussed below consists of four types:

1. Physical models
2. Narrative models
3. Graphical models
4. Mathematical models

The fashion model is a *physical model,* as are childhood toys such as dolls and toy airplanes. Most physical models are three-dimensional representations and in many cases they are smaller than the object represented. For instance, dolls and toy airplanes are smaller than what they represent, and fashion models are usually slimmer than the prospective purchasers of the garments. But reduced size is not a requirement and some models are the same size as their counterparts. Life-size dolls and the styling models used by automakers are examples.

Regardless of size, these physical models represent something else—consumers, babies, and automobiles. For one reason or another, the model serves a purpose that cannot be fulfilled practically by the real thing; real babies cannot stand the physical wear suffered by dolls, and automakers can hardly stand the financial wear of using automobiles as styling prototypes.

The physical model pictured in Figure 3-1 is a Hybrid II anthropomorphic dummy developed by General Motors for use in automobile crash testing. The model serves its purpose by providing some characteristic not evident in the object being modeled. In some cases this characteristic is *economy;* in others it is *availability*—the model is more readily available than the real object. Availability is the reason for the GM crash dummy. There wasn't a long line of human volunteers for the work.

Of the four types, the physical model probably has the least value for the

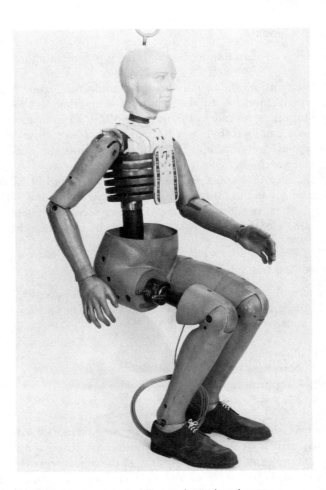

Figure 3-1 An automobile crash-testing dummy—
a physical model.

business manager. Managers usually do not need to see something in three-dimensional form in order to understand it or to make decisions.

One type of model managers use daily is seldom recognized as a model; this is the *narrative model*. Since the narrative can be either written or spoken, the narrative model is used by everyone who speaks or writes, which makes it the most popular type.

The narrative represents a subject or topic, and the representation is accomplished with words. The listener or reader can understand the subject from the narrative. At least, that is the intent. All written and oral communications in business are narrative models. Therefore both the hard information of the MIS and the soft information of the informal communication system are examples of narrative models.

Another type of model in constant use is the *graphical model*. This is an

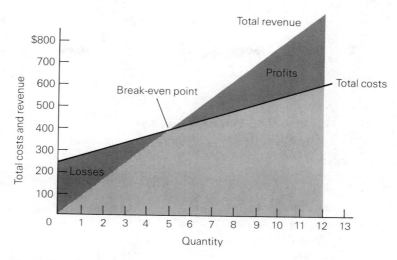

Break-Even Chart with Selling Price of $80 per Unit

Figure 3-2 A graphical model.

abstraction of lines, symbols, or shapes, often with a narrative explanation. The graphical model in Figure 3-2 is called a break-even chart. It depicts the point at which revenues and costs are equal. Beyond that point, the firm begins to show a profit. The most popular graphical model in the computer field is the flowchart. The symbols represent processes to be performed or input and output files. The systems analyst and the programmer use the flowchart both to help understand the system and to communicate with each other and with system users. Examples of other graphical models used for the same purposes are decision logic tables (DLTs), decision trees, and HIPO diagrams. These will be discussed in more detail in Chapter 17.

The fourth type of model, the *mathematical model,* has stimulated most of the recent interest in models for decision making. Any mathematical formula or equation is a model, and most of you have had years of experience with mathematics dating back to elementary school. The mathematical model, then, is no stranger.

Many of the mathematical models business managers use are similar to those used in mathematics courses. For example, the break-even formula used to calculate the break-even point in Figure 3-2 is no more complex than models studied in high school. The formula, or mathematical model, is simply

$$BEP = \frac{TFC}{P - C} \quad \text{where:} \quad \begin{aligned} BEP &= \text{break-even point} \\ TFC &= \text{total fixed costs} \\ P &= \text{sales price} \\ C &= \text{unit variable cost} \end{aligned}$$

```
10    PRINT "ENTER TOTAL FIXED COSTS";
20    INPUT F
30    PRINT "ENTER UNIT VARIABLE COST";
40    INPUT C
50    PRINT "ENTER SALES PRICE";
60    INPUT P
70    LET B = F / (P - C)
80    PRINT
90    PRINT "BREAKEVEN POINT IS"; B
100   PRINT
110   PRINT "DO YOU WANT TO TRY ANOTHER PRICE? ENTER Y-YES/N-NO";
120   INPUT R$
130   IF R$ = "Y" THEN 60
140   IF R$ = "N" THEN 999
150   PRINT "YOU SHOULD ENTER Y OR N, TRY AGAIN"
160   GO TO 120
999   END
```

Figure 3-3   A BASIC program to compute the break-even point.

Figure 3-3 shows a computer program, written in the BASIC language, to compute the break-even point. A manager can use this model to simulate the effect of different prices on the break-even point. The BASIC program is a mathematical model, representing the calculations in a program language. Assuming total fixed costs of $250 and unit variable costs of $30, a price of $80 produces a break-even point of 5 units, and a price of $100 produces a break-even point of 3.6 units. The manager can sit at a terminal and play the "what-if" game, trying out different prices until a preferred one is identified. Figure 3-4 shows the output—the dialog between the manager and the computer.

Because the language of mathematics is universal, mathematical models know no cultural, political, or geographic boundaries. Anyone who understands the language and knows the meaning of the symbols can understand the model regardless of its origin; this is one of the main advantages of a mathematical model.

Another advantage is precision in describing the interrelationships among the parts of an object. Mathematics can handle relationships expressed in more than the two dimensions of the graphical model or the three of the physical model. To the mathematician, and to the business manager who recognizes the complexity

```
ENTER TOTAL FIXED COSTS? 2000
ENTER UNIT VARIABLE COST? 75
ENTER SALES PRICE? 125
BREAKEVEN POINT IS 40
DO YOU WANT TO TRY ANOTHER PRICE? ENTER Y-YES/N-NO? N
```

Figure 3-4   Output from the break-even-point model.

of the many factors affecting the outcome of business decisions, the multidimensional ability of the mathematical model is of great value.

The break-even model uses only one equation. Many of the more complex mathematical models used in business use numerous equations—often hundreds of them. A financial planning model developed by the Sun Oil Company during the early years of MIS used approximately 2000 equations.[1] But large models tend to be cumbersome and difficult to use. The trend today is toward smaller models serving as decision support systems.

Use of models

We noted earlier that the value of the model lies in its ability to depict some characteristic not evident in the object being modeled. Economy and availability are important reasons to use a model rather than the real thing. Another reason is simplicity. It is common to use a model more simple in construction than the real object. While this leads to benefits in economy—a desirable goal—the primary reason for using simplified models is *understanding*. When the system being modeled is complex, it is easier to understand its interrelationships and workings if these are presented in a simplified way. For example, a map only shows the cities, towns, highways, lakes, and so forth. If more detail were included, the map would be too cluttered to be useful.

Each type of model discussed above can vary in detail. But as a rule, less detail is included when the objective of the model is to facilitate understanding. A physical model can represent only features of interest; a narrative can be boiled down to a summary; a diagram can show only the main relationships; and a mathematical equation can contain only primary ingredients. In each, an effort is made to present the model in a simplified form, frequently the first step to understanding. Once these simple models are understood, they can be made more complex, but they still represent the system being modeled and *never* match it exactly.

A model is an abstraction of reality, and models exist in various degrees of abstraction. Mathematical models are perhaps the most abstract; in fact, it is difficult for many to understand how a physical system, such as a business firm, can be represented by a series of mathematical equations. If you can accept that the equations represent different parts of the system in an extremely precise way, you can appreciate the value of the mathematical model to the manager.

The recent interest in modeling has been due less to the value of models as aids to understanding, however, than to a second important feature—their ability *to predict*. Because the manager is concerned with the impact of decisions on the firm, the ability to look into the future before deciding is of great value. Only the mathematical model offers this predictive power. If the manager is able to predict with the other types of models, it is because of the greater understanding that the model provides. The manager must use this understanding to project what might happen in the future. The mathematical model, on the other hand, does the pro-

[1] George W. Gershefski, "Building a Corporate Financial Model," *Harvard Business Review* 47 (July–August 1969): 39.

jecting for the manager. For example, the break-even model provides the manager with a projection of when total revenue will equal total cost. Although the manager should understand the basis of the computation when developing the model, it is not necessary for the manager to understand the greater complexities when using the model.

You should not get the idea that mathematical models enable the manager to predict the future perfectly. *No* model is ever that good. Because the model is only a simplification or approximation of the real system, the result is a device that can be expected to behave similarly but not identically to the real system. Despite this lack of perfect accuracy, the model is such an improvement over anything previously available that the manager accepts its shortcomings and takes advantage of its strong points. As long as the manager is aware of the shortcomings, and considers their possible influence on the behavior of the model, this situation is acceptable.

The mathematical model adds a dimension to decision support that was not present twenty years ago. There are many types of mathematical models—each designed to address a particular type of business problem.[2] The models permit the analysis of multiple influences, which interact in various ways to effect some aspect of the firm's operations. The models provide the manager with a look into the future and enable the manager to see the possible outcomes of a particular decision strategy. Using models therefore helps managers better understand the complexity of the systems they manage. And mathematical models in particular help them project the operation of the system into the future. We will return to the subject of mathematical modeling in Chapter 11.

General versus Specific Models

Because all models only aproximate the system being modeled, they are all somewhat general in nature. As Table 3-1 illustrates, however, some models are more general than others. Efforts can be made to construct a model so that it is very specific. Models can fit on a continuum ranging from the very general to the very specific. The type of model (graphical, mathematical, or other) has no bearing on the degree of generality. All types can be at any point on the continuum.

The examples of very general models in Table 3-1 have the primary advantage of wide applicability. The baby doll can represent any baby, and the break-even formula can be used by any type of firm. This wide applicability is also a limitation. While describing many objects in a rough way, the general model fails to describe any object specifically.

If you want to describe a relationship or condition unique to a particular situation, a specific, rather than a general, model must be used. Using organiza-

---

[2] For more information on the use of mathematical models in business, see Hugh J. Watson, *Computer Simulation in Business* (New York: John Wiley & Sons, 1981). A good discussion of how modeling can be used to manage a firm's resources can be found in Paul S. Bender, William D. Northup, and Jeremy F. Shapiro, "Practical Modeling for Resource Management," *Harvard Business Review* 59 (March–April 1981): 163–173.

Table 3-1 Degrees of generality in models

Model	Very General	Very Specific
Physical	An ordinary baby doll	A likeness of John F. Kennedy in a wax museum
Narrative	An article on "Ethics in Business"	The Continental Oil Company policy manual
Graphical	The break-even chart (Figure 3-2)	The Lawrence D. White Associates, Inc., organization chart (Figure 2-11)
Mathematical	The break-even formula	The Sun Oil Company financial planning model

tional relationships as an example, an organization chart can show the exact relationships within the particular firm. The advantage is accuracy, gained at the expense of another advantage—general applicability. One firm's chart probably cannot describe the organizational structure of any other firm.

Each type of model has its purpose, and the type selected depends entirely on the needs to be fulfilled. If a manager wants to understand a particular situation, the specific model is helpful. If the purpose is to understand a wide variety of situations, the general model is more applicable.

General systems theory

We have led up to our discussion of the general systems model by discussing models—what they are, what types exist, and how they are used. We could have followed another approach by describing the theoretical basis of the model. In effect, we have laid the theoretical groundwork by addressing management and organization theory in the previous chapter. The general systems model is an expression of some of that theory. But another body of theory is also relevant— the general systems theory.

The *general systems theory* suggests that the various academic disciplines can be represented in systems terms. The concept of the system therefore provides a common denominator between physics, history, chemistry, psychology, and so on. The initial contribution to the theory was made by German biologist Ludwig von Bertalanffy in 1937 when he pointed out the similarities among various scientific disciplines.[3] More recently, economist Kenneth E. Boulding explained general systems theory in terms of a hierarchical ranking of system types—from the most simple to the most complex.[4] Boulding's hierarchy is:

---

[3] Ludwig von Bertalanffy, "General System Theory: A Critical Review," *General Systems* 7 (1962): 1–20.

[4] Kenneth E. Boulding, "General Systems Theory—The Skeleton of Science," *Management Science* 2 (April 1956): 197–208. For an extensive bibliography of general systems theory, see Gerald M. Weinberg, *An Introduction to General Systems Thinking* (New York: John Wiley & Sons, 1975).

1. Framework
2. Clockwork
3. Cybernetic
4. Open, self-maintaining
5. Genetic-societal
6. Animal
7. Human
8. Social organization
9. Unknown

The simplest type is the *framework* that integrates several nonmoving parts, such as a straight chair or a hammer. Next is the *clockwork* system that includes parts with predetermined motions, such as a hair dryer or an electric drill. *Cybernetic* systems are more complex in that they are self-controlled, such as heaters with thermostats. These are all nonliving systems. The next level of complexity is represented by the simplest type of living system—the cell. This system type is called an *open, self-maintaining* system. The cells can be integrated to form the next higher system—*genetic-societal* systems, such as a plant. *Animal* systems are followed by *human* systems and then groups of humans forming *social organizations*. Boulding believes that the most complex type of system is the one not yet discovered—the *unknown* system.

The general systems model of the firm is an expression of this general systems theory. Instead of being limited to scientific disciplines, the general model is concerned with organizations of all types. The idea is that all of these organizations can be represented by the same model.

The value of a general model

Business education at the college level is general in approach. Students take courses that will help them in the wide variety of employment situations they may encounter later. Few business courses are aimed at a particular type of organization or profession.

This book is also general in approach. The principles and fundamentals found here can be applied to any type of information system in any type of organization. This chapter will present a general model of a business firm. The model is intended for use in a wide variety of situations. It should provide an effective way to view any type of firm and its information system.

The simplicity of the general model of the firm facilitates a basic understanding of the firm. This basic understanding will be augmented by additional material later in the book and in later business courses. When you begin your business career with a particular company, you need only add the unique characteristics of that company to the model.

The transition from the classroom to the firm is often an awkward period in the business student's career. The first few days on a new job can be confusing. The environment is new and different—new faces, facilities, and terminology. When something familiar appears, it can serve as a reference point and help generate a feeling of stability. The general model of a firm can provide such a reference point. You can learn the basic activities performed in any organization and their fundamental interrelationships. You will therefore be prepared to encounter these activities and to use the model as a useful framework.

Besides providing a framework for orientation, the general model can be a yardstick for evaluating the new firm. You expect certain elements and relationships. Using the general model as a checklist of what should be encountered can help you identify the parts of the firm that offer opportunities for improvement. You need not always accept the new firm as it is; you will eventually be asked to suggest improvements. The general model can indicate the need for improvement and pinpoint where this improvement is needed.

The General Systems Model

The systems theory of management and organization recognizes the firm as a physical system. In addition, management uses a conceptual system, the MIS, to manage the physical system. In this chapter, both of these systems are integrated to form a *general systems model of the firm.* First we will describe the physical elements, and then we will add the conceptual elements.

The physical system

The system model presented in the first chapter provides the basis for studying the physical system of the firm. As seen in Figure 3-5, input resources are transformed into output resources. Input resources come from the environment, and output resources are returned to the same environment. The physical system of the firm is therefore an *open system,* interacting with its environment by means of physical resource flows.

Most systems are open. An example of a *closed system*—one that is not dependent on its environment—would be a carefully controlled scientific experiment or a battery-powered, shockproof, waterproof wristwatch (except when new batteries are added). Human beings, puppies, flowers, and business firms are all open systems that depend on an outside environment.

Figure 3-5 represents a manufacturing operation where raw materials are transformed into finished goods. This is essentially a flow of materials without reference to any of the other flows of physical resources, such as personnel, machines, and money, that enter into the transformation process. There is no doubt that these other flows are involved—personnel and machines transform the raw materials into finished goods and money pays for the material, personnel, and machines. These latter resources also flow through the firm much like the material flow.

Figure 3-5 The physical system of the firm.

This is the flow network concept presented in Chapter 2, which is part of a systems theory of organization. Each of the physical flows is described below.

Material flow Input materials are received from vendors or suppliers of raw materials, parts, and assembled components. These materials are held in a storage area (raw-materials inventory) until required for the transformation process; then they are released to the manufacturing activity (work-in-process inventory). At the conclusion of the transformation, the materials, now in some finished form, are placed in a storage area (finished-goods inventory) until they are shipped to customers.

Personnel flow Personnel input originates from several points in the environment. Some workers come through organized labor unions, some do not. Some are recruited by the firm and some by private employment agencies. Some are found in the local community and some result from a nationwide search. Some come from college campuses and others do not. A firm obtains personnel from many sources to meet a wide range of requirements.

This personnel input is usually processed by the personnel department of the firm and assigned to separate work areas. While in those areas, the employees are used in the transformation process, either directly or indirectly. They might be available to the firm briefly or for a long period. Some may leave the firm shortly after joining it. Others remain for fifty years or more to receive their gold watches. Whether the duration is short or long, the personnel resource flows through the firm, and at some point each employee exits. The personnel department processes the termination and the resource is returned to its environment—the local community, a competitor, organized labor, or some other environmental element.

Machine flow Machines are obtained from specialized vendors and suppliers who manufacture and distribute them. Unlike the other physical resources, machines invariably remain in the firm for an extended period. Rarely is a machine acquired one day and released the next. Ultimately, however, all the machines must return to the environment. In many cases machines wear out or become obsolete and are scrapped. Some machines can be traded in on newer models or sold to other organizations that have a use for them.

While in the firm, machines are seldom stored. Rather, they are almost continually available, either as delivery trucks in the marketing department, desktop calculators in the accounting department, or machine tools in the manufacturing department. Because of special supply sources, the lack of in-firm storage, and special disposal outlets, the machine flow is the simplest flow of physical resources.

Money flow Money is obtained from many sources, though primarily from the stockholders or owners, who provide investment capital, and the firm's customers, who provide sales revenue. Other sources include loans from financial institutions, government loans or grants, and interest income from investments.

While many sources provide money, the responsibility for the money flow lies with the accounting department. The accounts receivable section collects money owed the firm by its customers, and the accounts payable section pays debts owed by the firm.

The flow of money through the firm is unusual in one respect. Physical money seldom flows through the firm. Rather, there is a flow of something representing money—checks, credit card slips, and so forth. Only on the retail level does cash change hands, and even here cash is giving way to credit transactions and electronic funds transfers.

The money flow therefore connects the firm to its financial institutions, customers, vendors, stockholders, and employees. In some cases the firm holds specific funds for a long time, such as certificates of deposit representing an interest-bearing investment with a bank. In other cases there is a quick turnover of money, as when sales revenue is quickly converted into checks payable to vendors and employees.

The conceptual system

As illustrated in Figure 3-5, the physical system is an open system in terms of its environmental links. It has no feedback loop or control mechanism. Such a system is called an *open-loop system*. There is no feedback from system output to effect changes in system input.

Examples of open-loop systems are not hard to find. A good example is a small electric space heater. When the heater is turned on, it gives off heat. It may give off too much or too little. It has no self-regulating mechanism to maintain a certain temperature.

There are probably a few business firms of the open-loop type. They set off on a particular course and never change direction. If they get out of control nothing is done to restore equilibrium. The result is system destruction, or bankruptcy.

The feedback loop   Most business firms have a closed feedback loop. The control mechanism built into this loop is the management. A business firm, therefore, can be regarded as a type of *closed-loop system*—one where a control mechanism monitors system output and makes necessary changes to system input.

Figure 3-5 could have included feedback and control elements. Those additions are reflected in Figure 3-6.

The reason management and the feedback loop were not included in the discussion of the physical system is that they are both integral parts of the con-

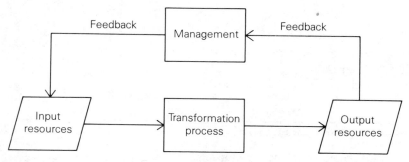

Figure 3-6   The physical system of the firm as a controlled system.

ceptual information system. It is true that both managers and devices contributing to the flow of information (such as computers, telephone networks, and the like) are physical resources; but they are also elements of the conceptual information system. Because we are primarily interested in studying how resources work together to form a conceptual system, we have included the physical feedback elements in our discussion of the conceptual, rather than the physical, system.

With the addition of the feedback loop to the physical system, management can control the system by becoming an integral part of the loop. The control process involves receiving information about the system, evaluating it, and transmitting information back to the system when some type of change must be made. The feedback loop therefore provides a communication channel for the fifth basic resource—information.

Management control   As shown in Figure 3-6, management receives information about the system's output. Many management reports fall into this category— sales analyses by customer, product, and salesperson, distribution costs, inventory statistics, and so on. Since the main purpose of the firm as a system is to produce some type of output, a measure of the output is an integral part of system control.

Figure 3-7 is an example of a report of systems output—a sales report of fast-moving products. The detailed sales data during the month is retained on a computer storage medium such as magnetic tape, which is used to print the report at the end of the month. A computer program arranges all of the detailed data by product number, accumulates the sales amounts for each product, sorts these amounts into descending order, selects the products at the top of the list (such as

ITEM NUMBER	ITEM DESCRIPTION	YEAR-TO-DATE SALES VOLUME	PERCENT OF TOTAL YEAR-TO-DATE SALES*
400293	BRAKE PIPE	$ 1,702.93	.068
319421	DOOR HANDLE GASKET	1,624.00	.065
786402	CLUTCH DRIVEN PLATE	1,403.97	.056
190796	CARPET SNAP	1,102.00	.044
001007	SPARK PLUG	1,010.79	.040
739792	HOST CLIP	949.20	.038
722210	RUBBER PLUG	946.73	.038
410615	UPPER DOOR HINGE	938.40	.038
963214	REAR TUBE SHOCK	922.19	.037
000123	NEEDLE VALVE	919.26	.037
	TOTALS	$11,519.47	.461

BASED ON YEAR-TO-DATE SALES OF $24,988.00

Figure 3-7   A sales report of fast-moving products.

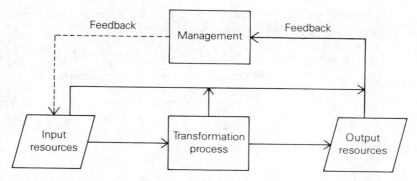

Figure 3-8 Multiple information sources monitor the physical system.

the top 10%), and prints the report. The report calls the manager's attention to the products that are selling best. The manager then tries to determine why these products sell well and possibly uses the findings to increase the sales of other products.

Figure 3-6 is a simplified model of the conceptual information system (added to the physical system). However, certain additions and refinements can be made to describe the conceptual system better. First, the manager gathers information other than that relating to the firm's output. The manager also must know the status of the firm in terms of internal processes and inputs. For example, the manager wants information describing how well vendors are meeting the firm's needs for input material. In addition, the manager wants information describing the production efficiency of the manufacturing operation. Figure 3-8 reflects the addition of information-gathering activities to the input and processing parts of the physical system.

In Figure 3-9 we can see a report describing one aspect of the system's input. This vendor analysis compares all the vendors used to procure a certain raw material in the past. The comparison includes price, delivery time, and product quality. A purchasing director could request such a report before deciding on the supplier of the next order of the raw material.

ITEM NUMBER   410615
ITEM DESCRIPTION   UPPER DOOR HINGE

VENDOR NUMBER	VENDOR NAME	—LAST TRANSACTION—			UNIT PRICE	DAYS TO RECEIPT	PERCENT REJECTS
		DATE	PURCH ORD NO	QTY			
3062	CARTER AND SONS	7/12	1048-10	360	$8.75	12	.00
4189	PACIFIC MACHINING	4/13	962-10	350	9.10	8	.02
0140	A. B. MERRILL & CO.	1/04	550-10	350	8.12	3	.00
2111	BAY AREA METALS	8/19	1196-10	360	11.60	19	.04

Figure 3-9 A vendor analysis report.

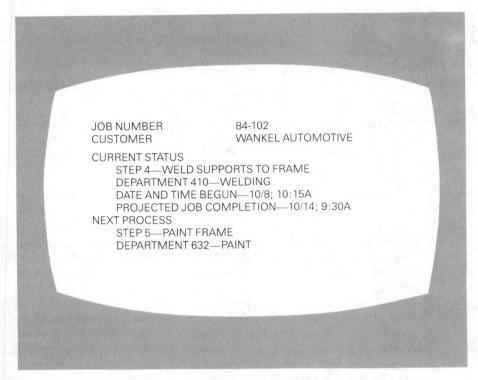

JOB NUMBER   84-102
CUSTOMER   WANKEL AUTOMOTIVE

CURRENT STATUS
    STEP 4—WELD SUPPORTS TO FRAME
    DEPARTMENT 410—WELDING
    DATE AND TIME BEGUN—10/8; 10:15A
    PROJECTED JOB COMPLETION—10/14; 9:30A
NEXT PROCESS
    STEP 5—PAINT FRAME
    DEPARTMENT 632—PAINT

Figure 3-10 A job status report displayed on a televisionlike terminal.

Figure 3-10 illustrates an aspect of internal processing that can be reported to management. In this example, a production manager wants to know the status of a certain job. The job number is keyed into a terminal, and the terminal displays the information, as shown in the figure. The manager knows that the job has reached step 4 in department 410, that the step was begun at 10:15 A.M. on October 8, and that the job should be completed by 9:30 A.M. on October 14.

Getting back to our discussion of the general model, we should realize that information does not always travel directly from the physical system to the manager. The manager is usually removed from the physical system and must get information through some type of communication network. Sometimes the information is not immediately made available to the manager but is held in temporary storage until it is needed. An example is the storage of detailed data during the month for use in preparing a monthly summary report.

The information processor Figure 3-11 includes the addition of an element called the *information processor*. In this discussion we assume that the information processor is a computer. You may recall from Chapter 1 that there are other ways to process data—manually, with keydriven machines, and with punched card machines. The general systems model is just as applicable to those noncomputer systems. The important point is that data is processed to produce information.

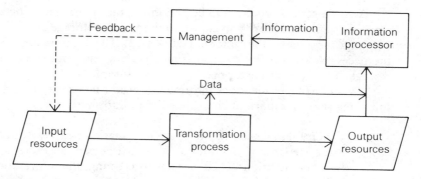

Figure 3-11 Adding the information processor to the conceptual information system.

Part Three of this book will provide a description of the computing equipment that constitutes the information processor. For the time being, this element can be recognized to contain two basic parts: a place to store data, and the computer routines that convert this data into information. Figure 3-12 identifies the important parts of a computer-based information processor.

The distinction between data and information (recognized in Chapter 1) is very important. The concept of a data base is also very important. A *data base* is a storage area containing data gathered from throughout the firm and from the environment. If the information system is computerized, the data base is housed in some type of computer storage. The data records are arranged logically, so that selected data items can be assembled from various parts of the data base.

The computer uses programs in the software library to perform the processing. The *software library* is the collection of all applications and systems programs, which enable the computer to process the firm's data in the desired manner. One of the systems programs is the data base management system (DBMS), which is used to manage the data in the data base.

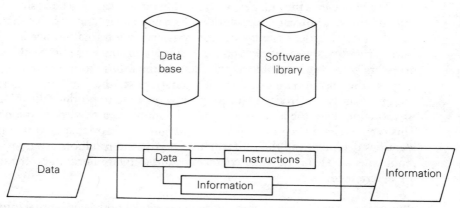

Figure 3-12 An information processor.

When a certain process is to be performed, the appropriate program is selected from the software library and copied in the primary storage area of the computer (the large rectangle in the center of Figure 3-12). The program is executed, causing the necessary data to be selected from the data base and copied into primary storage. The data is transformed into output information.

As the manager identifies information needs, he or she should consider the following several important characteristics of information.

1. *Quality:* How accurate must the information be? Very often, as in monetary accounting, the information must be very accurate—to the penny. In other situations, such as sales forecasting, the information need only approximate what actually exists or can be expected to happen.

2. *Quantity:* How much information is needed? The computer can produce information faster than the manager can digest it. The manager should receive only the amount of detail necessary to understand the situation and make a decision. The MIS can be designed to produce information initially in summary form, and to produce increasing levels of detail on demand.

3. *Timing:* How quickly must an action in the physical system be reported to the manager? All managers would like an instantaneous signal, but that may not be necessary. Perhaps the manager cannot take immediate action even if the information is made available without delay.

4. *Cost versus return:* As the manager considers requirements in terms of quality, quantity, and timing, the cost also must be recognized. Most firms simply cannot afford a perfect system and must settle for something less. The cost of information should never exceed its value.

5. *Presentation mode:* How will the information be presented—in the form of numbers, narrative, or graphics? Will the information be printed or displayed on a television-type terminal, or will it be presented in an audible form?

The manager is the best person to identify the information he or she needs. The systems analyst, however, can work with the manager, and provide the stimulus and the logical, systematic format for considering information needs. Together, manager and analyst identify and understand a problem, delineate the decisions necessary to solve the problem, and identify the information the manager needs to make the appropriate decisions. The analyst uses these information specifications to identify the processes (or programs) required to produce the information. At the same time, the analyst identifies the input data needed by the programs. This type of chain reaction, illustrated in Figure 3-13, originates with a problem, identifies decisions and their information needs, and produces program and data requirements. This is how the contents of the software library and the data base are determined.

Standards   Another element in the evolving model of the conceptual information system addresses the manager's need for standards to measure the firm's actual performance. The importance of standards was recognized by Frederick W. Taylor

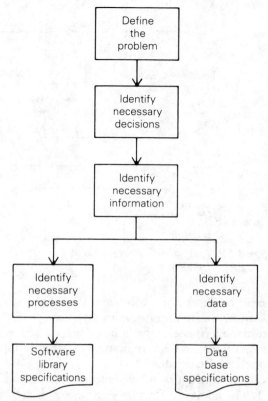

Figure 3-13 Software library and data base
specifications begin with
definitions of problems.

(see Chapter 2), who saw the need to set standards for production workers. Here we are talking about one or more *standards* for the firm and for each of its subsystems.

If the manager receives a report indicating that yesterday's sales were $25,000, is that good or bad? Without some standard of performance, it would be impossible to tell. If the firm never before had reached that sales level, the performance would be good; if sales normally averaged $30,000, the performance would be bad. The need for performance standards can also be seen in a thermostatically controlled heating system. If the thermostat is to maintain a certain temperature, it must first be set to the appropriate level. Similarly, if a business firm is to perform at a certain level or rate, some standard of performance must be established. In many cases the managers set the performance level; but in others the level is established by an element in the environment such as the government or the local community.

The manager controls the system by comparing (1) actual performance, as reflected by information provided by the information processor, to (2) the standards of performance. Figure 3-14 illustrates the addition of standards.

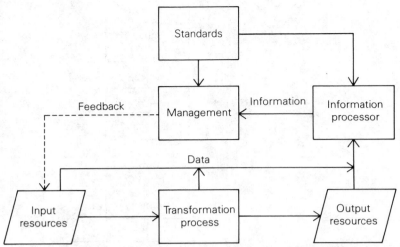

Figure 3-14 Adding performance standards to the conceptual information
system.

Management by exception Most managers have so many responsibilities that
they find it practically impossible to give each the attention it deserves. This is
why most managers work long hours. Theirs is not a nine-to-five job. Managers
learn to direct their attention to matters of greatest importance. Situations of low
priority often go unattended.

This is the concept of management by exception, which was introduced in
Chapter 1. The manager deals only with exceptional situations. The exceptional
situations can be either extremely bad or extremely good performance. Students
of management often fail to appreciate why exceptionally good performance should
be called to the attention of the manager. But clearly if something good happens,
the manager should know why so that she or he can get the same thing to happen
more often.

Management by exception requires that both high and low standards of
performance be clearly established. As long as performance remains within these
bounds, there is no need for management attention. You will notice in Figure
3-14 that the standards are made available to both the manager and the information processor. By making the standards a part of the data base, the information
processor can compare actual performance to the standards and notify the manager when the boundaries have been crossed. For example, if daily shoe sales
should range from 125 to 200 pairs, the manager is signaled only when the sales
fall below 125 or rise above 200.

Management by exception offers three basic *advantages:*

1. The skills of the manager are used to the fullest.
2. Since fewer decisions are made, each can receive more thorough attention.
3. It is a positive approach since opportunities as well as problems are identified.

These advantages enable the firm to achieve a more efficient use of scarce
management resources.

There are some *limitations,* however, that must be recognized:

1. It is not always easy to measure certain types of business performance quantitatively. An example is behavioral measures, such as customer attitudes.

2. An effective information system that accurately monitors various types of performance is essential.

3. Attention must continually be directed to the standards. Are they at the correct level? Have they become obsolete?

4. The manager must not grow passive and simply wait for standards to be exceeded. The manager must supplement the automatic monitoring by the information system with an aggressive search for new opportunities and new problem areas.

Management by exception is an integral part of the MIS. The manager's time is effectively used as the MIS assumes some of the responsibilities for monitoring the physical system.

Decision flow Another addition to the general model is necessary to reflect the manner in which management decisions can change the physical system. Just as the manager must gather data from all three elements of the physical system—input, processing, and output—it is important that the manager also be able to effect changes in the performance of all three elements. In the model drawn in Figure 3-14, the manager can only communicate feedback instructions or decisions to the input element. This limitation would prohibit the manager from responding quickly to changes throughout the entire system. If information from the data base indicates that activity in either the transformation processing or the output area requires adjustment, the manager must be able to effect such change directly, without having to work through the input area. This modification is made in Figure 3-15; the feedback from the manager to the physical system is relabeled

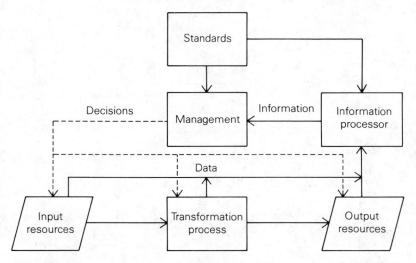

Figure 3-15 Changes made in the physical system through the decision flow.

"decisions" to reflect the manner in which the manager changes the system's performance.

The basic feedback loop as drawn initially in Figure 3-6 still represents signals from the physical system used for control; but the signals are in three different forms—data, information, and decisions. The data is transformed into information by the information processor, and the information is transformed into decisions by the manager. The information processor and the manager are the two key elements in the feedback loop—they work together to transform data into needed decisions. This is the decision support system (DSS) concept.

The environment   In Chapter 2, the discussion of the contingency school of management theory used the terms *external environment* and *internal environment*. These are the environments of the *manager,* and they include elements both outside and inside the firm. Here, and for the remainder of the text, we are concerned with the environment of the *firm*. We will use the term *environment* to describe all of the influences outside the firm.

As the discussion in the next chapter will indicate, the influence of the environment on the firm can be very complex. An attempt to show this effect in the general model would complicate it unnecessarily. Therefore, the final form of the general model recognizes only that resources flow into the firm from the environment and from the firm back to the environment. That addition is made in Figure 3-16.

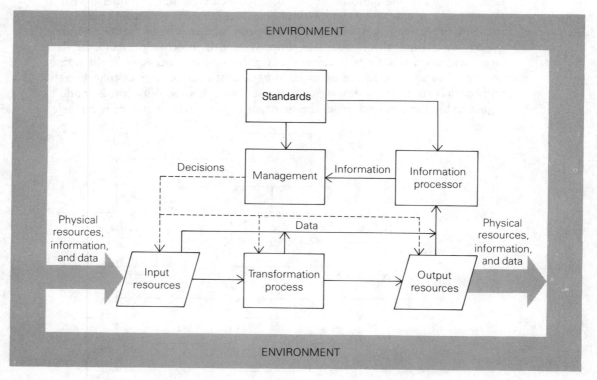

Figure 3-16   The general systems model of the firm.

All five types of resources—personnel, machines, material, money, *and information*—enter the firm from the environment. The physical resources flow through the physical system at the bottom of the model. The conceptual resource—information—first enters the input area of the physical system and then enters the information processor, where it is stored or made available to the manager. Data gathered from the environment follows the same path.

Use of the General Model

It is rather easy to relate our general model to a manufacturing firm. The flow of materials through the physical system and the control exercised by the manager in assuring that production goals are met by the firm are both very apparent. It is not quite so easy to relate the model to other types of organizations, especially those providing services rather than products, and those of a nonprofit nature. In the sections below, three types of organizations are explained in terms of the model. Our objective is to show that the model is general in the true sense and can provide a basic structure for the analysis of any type of organization.

A football team

The management control of a football team is exercised by the coaching staff. The coaches must use their resources in the most efficient way. Most teams have standards that they wish to meet during a season (such as winning at least eight games) or during a single game (such as limiting the opposition to no more than 10 first downs). The team's standards are mostly quantitative and there is little question of whether they have been reached. Fans and sportswriters can make this determination very easily.

The most important resource available to the coaches is personnel. Some material is involved (such as uniforms, footballs, adhesive tape, and the like), but it is of much less value to the coaches than the players. Very little machinery is involved. Movie projectors, whirlpool baths, and weight machines are about the extent of it. Money may or may not be an important resource, depending on the type of team; certainly, no professional team could exist without it. For a team that is more modest in its performance level, money plays a lesser role.

Clearly the management of the organization—the coaching staff—has a mixture of resources with which to work, and these resources have different relative values. Naturally, much of the success of a football team is due to the skill of the coaching staff, but much is determined by the resources available. The coach must do the best he can with what he has.

These resources flow through the organization. In a college team, the players are available for only four years, equipment is used for only a single season, and supplies often last only days. The team begins the season with a budgeted amount of funds, which are probably spent by the time the last game rolls around. While the resources are available, the coaches must integrate them into a smoothly functioning team.

All coaches have a conceptual information system of some sort. Those on the sandlot level rely entirely on observation from the sidelines. This basic approach to monitoring the performance of the system can be augmented by assistant coaches in the pressbox, by game films, and even by computer systems. Many professional teams use computers to recruit players and to decipher the strategy of opponents. As a general rule, data does not reside in the data base for a long period of time. During a game, the coaching staff can usually determine by half-time the causes of their team's problems so that they can take corrective action. As this information becomes available to the coaches, they make decisions that alter the team's performance. The purpose of such changes is to help the team meet its objectives.

The football team is a service organization. It produces only entertainment for its followers. It uses resources gathered from its environment and returns an output to the environment in the form of entertainment. Although the organization is quite different in many respects from a business firm, there are also many similarities to the general model. The model provides a useful framework with which to evaluate the team. A new head coach will most certainly take stock of his resources, evaluate the nature of the goals, and pass judgment on the information system in preparing for the upcoming season. The model serves as a normative, or ideal, model of how the organization should be structured.

A law firm

There are several obvious differences between a law firm and a football team. The law firm usually comprises a small number of people who perform their tasks through mental, rather than physical, activity. The objective of the law firm usually is profit, while that of a football team usually is to provide a service.

Even with these differences, a law firm can be described by the same general model used for the football team. Each law firm has some management function that controls the organization. In a large firm this control is exercised by the partners; in a small firm of only a single lawyer, this control is performed on a part-time basis by that person.

The main responsibility of the person or persons managing the law firm is to assure that it meets its objectives. It is doubtful that the goals of the law firm are as specific as those of the football team. A law firm probably does not strive to win a certain percentage of court cases or to handle some minimum number of divorce settlements. We can assume a profit objective, however, since management realizes that profit is the key to continued operation and service.

The transformation process in the law firm is one of converting the raw materials (clients with legal problems) into finished products (clients whose legal problems have been solved). This transformation is accomplished by the lawyers, who probably represent the most important resource available to the firm. But we could also argue that information is the most important resource. That ingredient is absolutely necessary in legal practice. Everyone has seen pictures of attorneys' offices with bookshelves filled with law books; the books are evidence of the importance of information in the transformation process.

Some law firms use computers to provide information in a fraction of the time required to obtain it through library research. A special information retrieval system called WESTLAW is offered by the West Publishing Company on a subscription basis. For about $2600 per month, you get a terminal connected by telephone communications to a legal data base in St. Paul, Minnesota. The legal data base contains results of court cases dating back as far as 1932 (for Supreme Court cases).

Systems such as WESTLAW underscore the importance of information to the lawyer. However, if information were the most important resource, people with legal problems would seek out those lawyers with the largest libraries or the fastest computer systems. This is not done. The lawyers most in demand are those who can apply professional skills to the solution of a problem. The ability to identify information requirements and sources is only one of those skills.

The performance of a law firm therefore lends itself to the general model. Management of the firm monitors the process by which legal problems are transformed into solutions. Information facilitating this control is provided from the physical system and derived from a data base. When standards are not being met, decisions are made to alter the physical system. If too few legal problems are being converted into solutions (the firm is losing too many cases), the partners can hire additional lawyers, replace existing lawyers, reassign lawyers to different types of cases, hire legal secretaries, etc.

The general model provides a structure for the basic elements of a legal firm. A new partner can expect to find these elements regardless of whether he or she has ever before served in that particular firm or has any previous knowledge of its structure. The new partner expects to find standards (for the firm and perhaps for individual lawyers), an information system, and a personnel resource capable of performing the transformation process in a manner acceptable to the managing partners.

A newspaper publisher

A newspaper publisher is usually a profit-seeking organization. A management team is formed to assemble the resources necessary to achieve and maintain profitable operations. These resources include personnel such as reporters, press operators, and carriers, who play roles in creating and delivering the printed product. Machines such as computer-controlled typesetting equipment, printing presses, and delivery vehicles are all necessary to the production process. The primary materials are newsprint and ink, and all of these resources are acquired with money.

The transformation of the raw material into the finished product is very rapid. You can go to bed before a Monday night football game is over and read the final score in your morning paper, printed a hundred miles away. It is management's responsibility to achieve this responsive system. The management uses an MIS to monitor both the environment and the physical system of the firm. The cry "Stop the presses!" captures the urgency of newspaper management. This expression was famous long before the computer. Today it could easily be "Stop the computer!" since most big-city papers and many smaller ones have computerized typesetting operations. Televisionlike terminals have replaced typewriters for many reporters and data entry personnel.

For a modern newspaper publisher, the computer plays two roles. As a piece of production equipment, it is part of the physical system of the firm, transforming the input copy into a printed newspaper. It is also part of the conceptual system, keeping management informed of the status of the overall physical system.

The newspaper organization needs standards specifying market coverage, readership rates, level of advertising revenues, daily deadlines, profit margins, and so on. The MIS helps management channel resources toward the achievement of specified goals.

Managers of the newspaper organization can use the general model to pinpoint the source and nature of problems in the physical system. If the newspaper doesn't get out on time, or if it contains too many errors, management knows the cause of the problem is a resource flow that doesn't measure up to the standards. Perhaps there are not enough resources, such as reporters or carriers, or perhaps the resources are not being used efficiently. But the real cause of the poor resource flow might not be with the physical system. The poor performance of the physical system might be due to the conceptual system. Perhaps the physical system is poorly managed. The general model shows three elements integrated into the feedback control loop—management, the information processor, and standards. If any of these elements are missing or are deficient in any way, the physical system will not be in control.

Systems analysts working for the newspaper can use the general model just as they would for any firm trying to improve its MIS. Neither the managers nor the systems analysts would necessarily recognize that the general model was being used during the analysis process. But they would have developed a good understanding of business operation in general, and of the newspaper business in particular. They know that their firm—any firm—must contain the basic ingredients of the model, arranged in the specified manner.

For a new employee of the newspaper, however, a conscious use of the general model can provide a useful technique for evaluating how well the newspaper measures up to the normative model. The new employee can study the quantity and quality of the resources, and the efficiency with which they are used. She or he can check to determine how data and information are gathered from the physical system and from the environment. The information processor and its data base and software library can be studied, as well as the information flow to management. The employee can verify that standards exist, and that they are being used by management for decision making. When the newspaper—or any other firm—is given this type of scrutiny, the areas needing improvement are easily identified. The general systems model of the firm is therefore an effective systems analysis tool.

Summary

The main objective of this chapter was to present a general systems model of the firm that can be used to understand the structure of both the physical system of the firm and the conceptual information system and how they interrelate.

The term *model* was introduced,, and four types were identified—physical, narrative, graphical, and mathematical. All provide some feature not evident in the object being modeled. These features, economy and availability, permit the user to better understand the object being modeled and often (for mathematical models) to predict the future with a limited degree of accuracy.

All four types of models can range from the general to the specific. A general model has wide applicability, but does not specifically address any particular situation. The general systems model of the firm can be used to analyze any type of organization, but it does not describe any type specifically. The general systems model is, in effect, two models—a graphical model and a narrative model. The narrative explains the graphical relationships in greater detail.

We introduced the general systems model element by element, with attention to both the resource flow through the physical system and the feedback flow through the conceptual system. The feedback flow originates as data, is transformed into information by the information processor, and is then used by the manager to make decisions.

The general model depicts the firm as an open system (it interacts with its environment) and as a closed-loop system (it has a feedback loop). No firm can be a closed system, shut off from its environment. But a poorly managed firm can resemble an open-loop system—one with no feedback mechanism.

Management follows a practice of management by exception by using the information processor to monitor the physical system. By entering standards into the data base, the manager prepares the information processor to determine whether system performance is within established upper and lower limits.

This chapter serves only to introduce the general systems model. Each part of the model will be analyzed in more detail in the following chapters. As you will see, the beauty of the general systems model is its simplicity: it is useful to anybody in any situation. It is also a basic tool of the systems approach to business analysis, which is the subject of the next chapter.

Key Terms

model

physical, narrative, graphical, mathematical model

break-even point

general model, specific model

general systems theory

framework system

clockwork system

cybernetic system

genetic-societal system

animal system

human system

social organization system

general systems model of the firm

open system, closed system

open-loop system, closed-loop system

information processor

software library

management by exception

Key Concepts

A model as an abstraction of some phenomenon

Different types of models

The two basic uses of models

How the general systems model is an expression of general systems theory, on an organizational level

Boulding's hierarchy of systems

The value of a general model as a systems analysis tool

How the general systems model represents any type of organization

Closed and open system types versus closed-loop and open-loop system types

The three different forms of the feedback loop—data, information, and decisions

Basic components of an information processor

Characteristics of information

Management by exception

Questions

1. Why is the term *model* used to describe someone who poses for clothing ads?

2. Name the four basic types of models. Which is used the least in management decision making? Which has a predictive ability?

3. What are the two characteristics offered by models?

4. Why do managers use models?

5. What is the name of the theory that encourages the use of the systems concept as a means of studying various disciplines? Who is credited with originating this theory?

6. What are the three types of nonliving systems, according to Boulding? What distinguishes each type?

7. Does the systems analyst work at the human or social-organization level of systems? Explain.

8. What is the difference between an open and a closed system? An open-loop and a closed-loop system? Which of these types describe a business firm?

9. The physical system of the firm is composed of four resource flows. What are they? Should the manager try to speed up or slow down these flows? Explain.

10. Are managers and the information processor a part of the physical or the conceptual system? Explain.

11. Is the sales report of fast-moving products pictured in Figure 3-7 an example of a management-by-exception report? What about the vendor analysis report in Figure 3-9, and the production status report in Figure 3-10? Explain your reasoning.

12. What part of the information processor contains stored data? Stored programs?

13. Name five characteristics of information that the manager should consider.

14. Comment on the following statements:

    a. Information produced by the MIS should contain no errors.

    b. An MIS should provide the manager with as much information as possible.

    c. A good MIS must produce information no later than five seconds after it is requested.

15. Arrange the following items in sequence, based on the order in which they are specified by the systems analyst: data, information, problem, processes, decisions.

16. How does the work of Frederick W. Taylor relate to the general systems model?

17. In what form(s) does the feedback loop exist in a firm?

18. Which resources enter the firm from the environment? Which exit to the environment?

19. By what route does information gathered from the environment travel to the manager?

20. What machines might flow through a law firm? What materials? What information?

Problems

1. Draw the general systems model of the firm. Label all symbols, including the arrows. Briefly explain each part.

2. Use the general systems model to describe a hospital.

3. Use the general systems model to describe a supermarket.

4. Assume that you are a purchasing agent (buyer) analyzing the vendor analysis report in Figure 3-9. Which vendor would you select for your next purchase? Why?

CASE PROBLEM: Conway Container Corp.

Conway Container Corp. is a manufacturer of metal and plastic containers, such as motor oil cans, milk cartons, and frozen-juice cans. Ralph McCann, Jr., assumed the presidency of Conway upon graduation from college. One of McCann's first actions was to install an Apple computer—one of the hottest-selling small systems. The Apple is used to compute payroll, maintain inventory records, prepare purchase orders, and handle the firm's accounts payable.

In the inventory system, the Apple maintains a master record for each inventory item, describing its balance on hand, reorder point, order quantity, and so on. Each time an inventory transaction is processed, the new balance is compared to the reorder point. When the balance drops below the reorder point, the computer prints a purchase order. The purchase orders are sent to McCann so that he can check them for accuracy, verify the need to make the purchase, and initial them. After Ralph's approval, (which might take as long as two days, because of his busy schedule), the multiple-part purchase order forms are separated. The original copy is sent to the supplier, the second copy is placed in an unfilled-purchase-order file, and the third copy is sent to the receiving department.

Quite often the ordered materials do not arrive soon enough, and production must be delayed. This results in missed deliveries and lost business. McCann is dismayed over the poor system performance, especially after having made it one of his top-priority computer applications. If the situation doesn't improve, McCann is going to revert back to a manual system and take the Apple home to his children so that they can play some electronic games.

Questions

1. Is McCann using his Apple as an information processor or as a data processor?
2. Is the Apple properly positioned in the feedback loop of Conway's inventory system?
3. Is McCann properly positioned in the feedback loop of the inventory system?
4. What is the problem?
5. How can it be solved? Briefly outline a strategy that you would recommend to McCann.

Chapter 4

The Systems Approach

Learning Objectives

After studying this chapter, you should:

- Understand how the MIS is involved in the decision-making process
- Know the difference between structured and unstructured problems, and how they relate to the DSS concept
- Be familiar with all the elements of the systems approach and how they fit together to form a powerful problem-solving tool
- Know the difference between objectives and standards and their respective roles in relation to the MIS
- Be able to use the systems approach to solve business problems
- Appreciate individual differences in problem-solving styles and how they affect MIS design
- Understand how the manager's environment affects decision making

The Importance of Decision Making

The purpose of the information system is to help the manager make decisions. Certainly managers do other things. In fact, decision making might account for only a small portion of a particular manager's time. However, the importance of decision making is not based on the amount of time a manager spends doing it, but rather on the consequences. A decision might require only a few hours, but could affect the firm's profits to the tune of thousands or even millions of dollars.

The history of a firm, therefore, becomes a series of key decisions that have definite influences on the firm's ability to meet its objectives and to survive. Successful firms can point to a series of correct decisions. Unsuccessful firms can point to a series of incorrect decisions, or perhaps even a single fatal one.

Decisions are made to solve problems. A particular problem—say, low sales for a product such as ski boots—may require multiple decisions to solve. The manager will have to choose among several alternate solutions such as (1) develop a new product, (2) modify the existing one, (3) change the price, or (4) implement a new advertising program. For each alternative, the manager will have to decide whether or not to accept it as the best solution.

Elements of a Problem-Solving Process

Several elements are critical if a manager is to begin a successful problem-solving process. Naturally, there must be a *problem* and a *problem solver* (the manager). The other elements are less obvious; but if any are absent, the end results are likely to be poor. All of these elements are pictured in Figure 4-1.

The solution to the problem must best enable the system to meet its performance standards. Therefore the *standards* must be specified clearly. These standards describe the "desired state" the system should achieve. In addition, the manager must have available *information* that describes the "current state" of the system. If the current state and the desired state are the same, there is no problem and the manager takes no action. If the two states are different, some problem is the cause and must be solved. In some cases, there is more than one problem to solve.

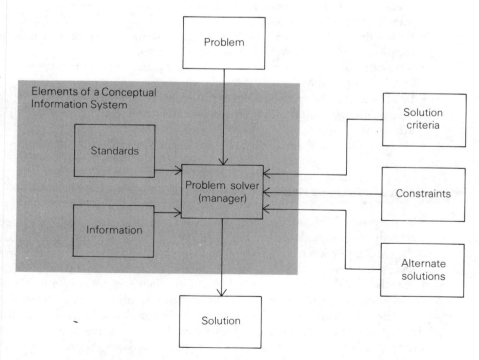

Figure 4-1 Elements of a problem-solving process.

The figure indicates that the problem-solving elements—managers, standards, and information—are also the elements of the conceptual information system from the general model. In fact, these are the elements that achieve the solution. The information system is therefore a problem-solving system.

Information enables the manager to understand the problem in the physical system. Perhaps the information system itself is the problem. However, for the sake of simplicity, let's assume that the problem lies elsewhere. The difference between the current state of the system and the desired state represents the *solution criterion,* or what it will take to bring the current state to the desired state. For example, if the standard is to sell a minimum of 125 pairs of ski boots a day, and sales are averaging 75 pairs, the solution to the problem must be one that can increase sales by at least 50 pairs. This is the solution criterion.

We have recognized that an important part of problem solving is the consideration of *alternate solutions.* It is the manager's responsibility to identify these alternatives and to evaluate each one. Perhaps the information system can identify alternatives, or perhaps the manager uses creativity, ingenuity, and experience. Most certainly, once the alternatives have been identified, the information system can be used to evaluate them individually.

As the alternate solutions are considered, the manager must be aware of any possible constraints. These can be internal or environmental. *Internal constraints* are in the form of limited resources—personnel, money, material, machines, or information. Perhaps additional resources can be obtained to solve the problem, but there are limits, and the manager must work within them. Some alternate solutions can be eliminated because they demand resources that are unavailable.

Environmental constraints can be just as real. Government laws may prohibit certain solutions. A whole host of laws, mostly on the federal level, establish constraints on practically every facet of business operation. Also, constraints applied by the other elements of the external environment, such as competition, vendors, and so on, can prohibit certain alternatives.

Once all these elements exist and the manager understands them, a *solution* to the problem is possible. All problems have solutions. Some solutions may be difficult to recognize, some may not be easy to achieve, and some may not be optimal, but they do exist.

Problems versus Symptoms

It is important to recognize the distinction between problems and symptoms. Very often the manager sees symptoms rather than the problems themselves. The symptoms, in this respect, are like the tip of the iceberg. The manager must look beneath the symptoms to locate the real cause of the difficulty.

This process of sorting through symptoms to find problems is the task facing a medical doctor when a patient complains of some ailment, such as constant headaches. Something is causing the headaches, and the doctor must determine whether it is nervous tension, poor vision, poor diet, or something else. The manager faces the same task when he or she is confronted with a symptom such as low profits. Something is causing the low profits. The problem is the *cause* of the trouble. A symptom is only the manner in which the problem appears to the observer; the symptom is *caused by* the problem.

Types of Problems

The various kinds of problems encountered in the day-to-day operation of a business firm can be classified into broad types. The most popular classification scheme in use today in the MIS area was originated by G. Anthony Gorry and Michael S. Scott Morton in their original description of the decision support system (DSS) concept.[1] Gorry and Scott Morton showed that problems fall on a continuum, with one end representing structured problems and the other end representing unstructured problems. *Structured problems* are those of a routine nature for which a prescribed solution procedure exists. *Unstructured problems* are novel, nonrepetitive challenges that must be solved with creativity, initiative, and originality. An example of a structured problem is the economic order quantity (EOQ) decision. The key variables have been identified and assembled in the EOQ formula. The break-even formula is another example. These formulas can be used by nonmanagers and even by computers to solve structured problems. An example of a truly unstructured problem is hard to find. Almost all problems have some structure. Nevertheless, we could argue that the problem of how to determine the social value of a corporation is essentially unstructured. The solution would involve some measure of the firm's contribution to the good of society, which would differ from the traditional economic value measured by profit. No suitable measure has yet been found to solve this difficult unstructured problem.

Computers can solve structured problems without the manager's involvement, once appropriate procedures have been established. But the manager has to do most of the work to solve unstructured problems. In between the two extremes lies a vast area of *semistructured problems* that can be solved by the manager with help from the computer. This is the area of the decision-support system (DSS).

Problem Solving and the Systems Approach

Central to the DSS concept is the identification and isolation of a single problem, followed by a systematic solution process. The idea is to subdivide the complexity of business into manageable units—separate problems—which you handle one at a time.

The task of solving a problem is usually described as a series of steps. These steps have been named the *systems approach*.

---

[1]G. Anthony Gorry and Michael S. Scott Morton, "A Framework for Management Information Systems," *Sloan Management Review* 13 (Fall 1971): 55–70.

1. Define the problem.
2. Gather data describing the problem.
3. Identify alternate solutions.
4. Evaluate the alternatives.
5. Select the best alternative.
6. Implement the solution and follow up to assure that the solution is effective.

The systems approach has received much attention in business literature during the past ten years or so.[2] The approach is an effort to lend a certain amount of procedure to a task that has been more of an art than a science. The basis of the systems approach is the *scientific method,* used in the physical sciences (such as chemistry and physics) and in the behavioral sciences (such as psychology and sociology).[3] The steps of the scientific method are:

1. Observing
2. Formulating a hypothesis
3. Predicting what will happen in the future
4. Testing the hypothesis

The systems approach is a modern term used to describe the time-honored process of using common sense. John Dearden, a Harvard professor, referred to the systems approach as nothing more than "good management."[4] But the fact that it is nothing new or different does not diminish its value. The systems approach is today the most popular problem-solving technique.

The systems approach and decision making

So far our discussion has centered on problem solving. What about decision making? Several decisions are necessary to solve a single problem. In fact, each step of the systems approach requires at least one decision. The relationship between the systems approach and decision making is illustrated in Table 4-1.

---

[2] For some examples of the application of the systems approach, see Buddy Robert Stephen Silverman, "Systems Approach to Baseball Players' Compensation," *Journal of Systems Management* (September 1981): 7–13; Samir Chakraborty, "Strategic Planning for Telecommunications—A Systems Approach," *Long Range Planning* 14 (October 1981): 46–55; and H. Peter Holzer and John S. Chandler, "Systems Approach to Accounting in Developing Countries," *Management International Review* 21, no. 4 (1981): 23–32.

[3] For example, assume that psychologists have *observed* that rats physically handled by researchers learn faster than those left alone. Their *hypothesis* states "Physical handling facilitates learning." The psychologists *predict* that rats handled physically will learn faster than those that aren't handled. The hypothesis is *tested* by designing an experiment in which some rats are handled and others are not. The results are then evaluated.

[4] John Dearden, "MIS Is a Mirage," *Harvard Business Review* 50 (January–February 1972): 90–99.

Table 4-1 The systems approach requires decision making at each step

Step	Decisions
1. *Define the problem.*	Where is the problem? What is causing the problem? Is this the true cause?
2. *Gather data describing the problem.*	Does new data need to be gathered, or does data already exist? Who will gather the data? How will the data be gathered?
3. *Identify alternate solutions.*	How many alternatives should be identified? Are there other alternatives? Are these alternatives feasible?
4. *Evaluate the alternatives.*	Which criteria should be used? How does each alternative measure up to each criterion? Do all criteria have equal weight?
5. *Select the best alternative.*	Do I have enough information to make a selection? Which alternative measures up best to the criteria? Has the selection process been fair and unbiased?
6. *Implement the solution and follow up to assure that the solution is effective.*	When should this solution be implemented? How should the solution be implemented? Who should perform the evaluation? How well is the solution meeting the objectives?

The systems approach and the MIS

The MIS should be used as a support system for each decision made in applying the systems approach. A DSS can be designed to support each decision, as illustrated in Figure 4-2. The systems approach serves as a bridge between the problem and the DSS, providing a framework for the various decisions.

This figure indicates that one DSS is used to solve a single problem. Some might prefer to think of one DSS for each decision. The size of the problem would be the determining factor. If the problem is too large and complex for a single DSS, then you must design multiple support systems.

Characteristics of the Systems Approach

In recent years much has been written about the systems approach. In many instances there has been no attempt to explain what it is. It has been assumed that the term is self-explanatory. In those instances where definitions have been offered, they have not always agreed. All of this can be very confusing to the manager or student of business looking for a usable technique.

Most definitions of the systems approach refer to the series of steps that have just been described. Sometimes they are presented in a different form, but the main ideas are the same. Other definitions present the systems approach in terms of analyzing a system. The manager is described as a systems analyst, first address-

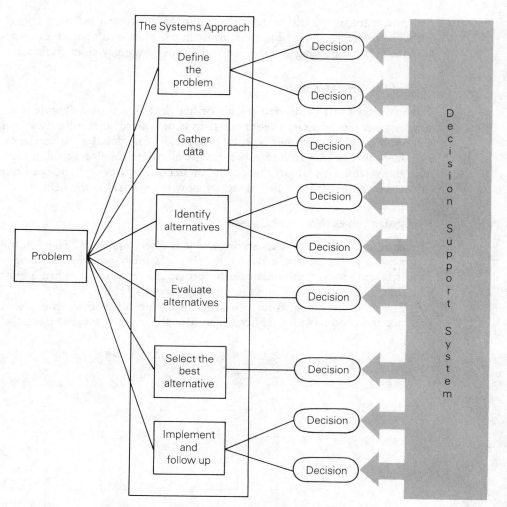

Figure 4-2 A decision support system helps the manager solve a problem.

ing the total system and then dividing it into subsystems. This process of dividing a problem or a system into its elemental parts is called *analysis*. Then, when the subsystems have been understood and redesigned, they are reassembled by a process known as *synthesis*.

These constitute the most frequent explanations of the systems approach. But although they are important, they do not convey the whole story. The other dimensions of the systems approach should be recognized in order to appreciate the full power of this problem-solving technique.

If the manager is to use the systems approach, he or she must *regard the firm as a system,* as we have done in the previous two chapters. Second, the manager must recognize the *environmental system* that embraces the firm. Third, the system of the firm must be seen to comprise several *subsystems.* Fourth, in analyzing the firm the manager should proceed from the *system to the subsystem* level. And fifth, the manager should follow a particular *sequence* to analyze the parts of a system. In the following sections we will discuss these key characteristics.

Regard the firm as a system

The manager must be able to see his or her firm as a system (Figure 4-3). This requirement must be met even if the firm is organized some other way, such as geographically, by customer type, by product, by functional area, and so on. The manager must be able to integrate mentally all of the resources so that they form a single system. This is how the general model of the firm described in Chapter 3 fits in. The manager must be able to see how the model fits the firm.

Recognize the environmental system

The firm's relationship to its environment is also important. The environment represents a larger system, of which the firm is a subsystem. By requiring certain products and services, this environment provides a reason for the firm's existence. The firm's objectives are geared to meeting certain of these needs.

    The environment also furnishes the firm with all of the resources used to produce the products and services. The firm therefore is created from the envi-

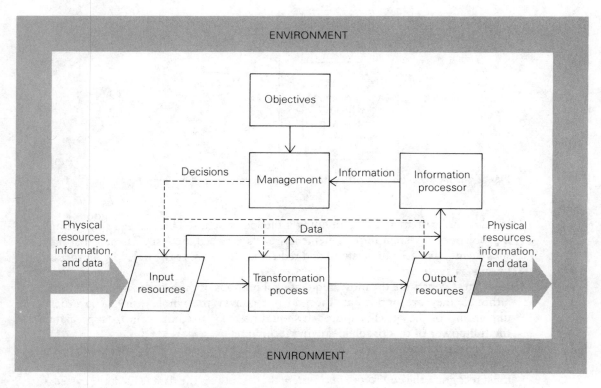

Figure 4-3 The manager sees the firm as a system.

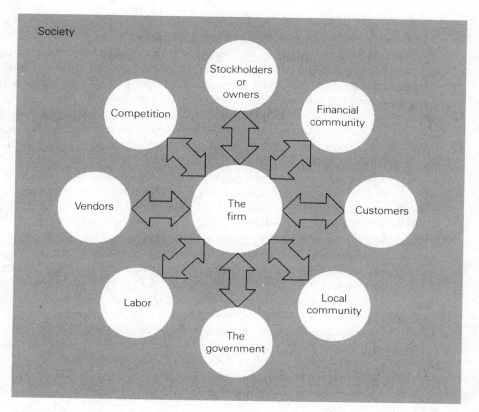

Figure 4-4 Elements in the environment of the firm.

ronment. The management of the firm, performing an entrepreneural function, recognizes environmental needs, acquires the resources to meet those needs, and then manages the resources.

There are many ways to look at the environment. One is to identify eight separate members or elements, as shown in Figure 4-4.[5] Each element is actually a subsystem within a larger system called *society*.

The *vendors* supply the materials used by the firm to produce goods and services for the *customers*. *Labor* provides the personnel resources, and the *financial community* provides the money resources, as do the *stockholders* or *owners*. *Competition* provides a constraint on what the firm does and often serves as a motivating force to better meet the needs of the environment. The *government*, on the federal, state, and local levels, also provides constraints; in addition, it can assist the firm by buying products and services, providing information, and providing research and development funds. In recent years the *local community* has assumed a bigger role in this environmental system. The firm demonstrates its

---

[5]Based on Richard J. Hopemen, *Systems Analysis and Operations Management* (Columbus: Charles E. Merrill, 1969).

responsibility to this community, for example, by using antipollution and safety measures and by supporting charitable and civic programs.

Resource flows connect the firm with the other environmental elements. All types of resources flow back and forth between the firm and these elements. Some flows are more frequent than others. Material flow to customers, money flow to stockholders, machine flow from vendors, and personnel flow from labor are all primary. Other flows such as money flow from the government (for research, for example), material flow to vendors (for returned merchandise), and personnel flow to the competition (for employees "pirated" by other firms)—all exist, but on a secondary level.

Not all resources flow between the firm and all environmental elements. For example, machines normally do not flow from the firm to the stockholders, money should not flow to competitors, and material should not flow to labor. The only resource that connects the firm with all of the elements is information. In most cases the manager strives to expedite the information flow connecting the firm with the environmental elements. The manager attempts to build an interfirm information network, exclusive of the competition; at the same time, the manager strives to suppress the flow of information from the firm to its competitors.

Resource flows are further complicated by the influence one environmental element can have on another. An element can have an indirect influence on the firm, often as effective as the direct. An example is a strike by organized labor against a firm we order materials from, resulting in a lack of needed materials. The supplying firm might have to shut down its manufacturing process. The result is as serious as if our firm's own factory workers went on strike. Similar indirect influences involve the competition, the government, the financial community, and the local community.

Identify subsystems in the firm

Once the firm is seen as a single system in a larger environmental system, it is next necessary to identify the major parts of the system. These parts are the subsystems of the firm, and they can take several forms. Perhaps the easiest for the manager to see are the *functional areas* of finance, manufacturing, and marketing. Each can be regarded as a separate subsystem. Each subsystem exists on the same level within the firm; one is not superior to the others. This arrangement is shown in Figure 4-5.

The president of the firm must integrate these subsystems into a single system. To do so the president must think in systems terms. So should the vice-presidents in charge of the functional areas.

How are these subsystems integrated or connected? They are connected by the resources that flow through the firm. This is where a systems theory of organization is useful. When the manager can see how resources should flow from one functional area to another, he or she can appreciate the need for an integrated system.

Figure 4-5 is redrawn in Figure 4-6 to show some of the more important resource flows that connect the subsystems. The numbered paths in the figure are explained as follows:

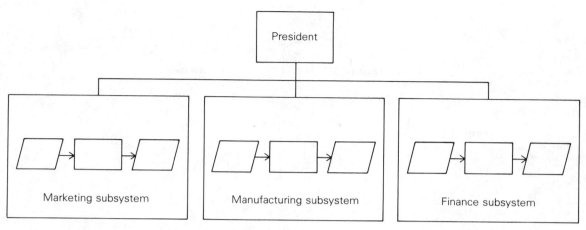

Figure 4-5 Functional subsystems in the firm.

1. The marketing subsystem gets information from the environment describing needs for products and services.
2. This information is transmitted to the other functional subsystems so that they can determine what the firm must produce if the needs are to be met.
3. The finance subsystem obtains money from the environment and makes it available to the manufacturing and marketing subsystems so that they can perform their functions.
4. The manufacturing subsystem transforms raw material resources into finished goods.
5. These goods are then distributed to customers by the marketing subsystem.

An organizational structure based on functional subdivisions is an example of decentralization. You will recall from the discussion of organization theory in Chapter 2 that decentralization is very common, especially in large firms. There are many ways to decentralize. One approach is to establish separate divisions to handle different groups of customers—such as large firms and small firms, or government organizations and industrial organizations. Other approaches to subdividing the firm are based on the product line, geography, and services offered. All of these subdivisions are subsystems within the larger system.

The manager also can regard the *level of management* as subsystems. This concept is pictured in Figure 4-7. Here the subsystems have a superior-subordinate relationship and are connected by information flows. The top management, on the strategic level, makes decisions that filter down through the organization. These decisions enable the organization to meet its objectives. Information flows up through the organization from the operational level, where the firm creates the products and services for the environment. When the manager sees the firm arranged in this manner, the importance of information flows is clear. Without these flows, upper-level management is cut off from the physical system of the firm.

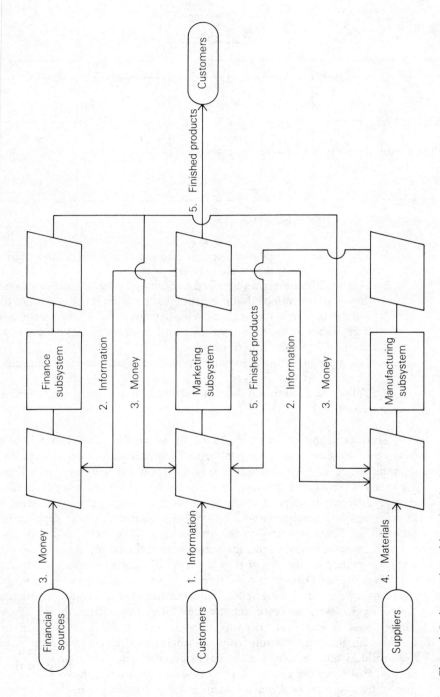

Figure 4-6 Interaction of functional subsystems in the firm.

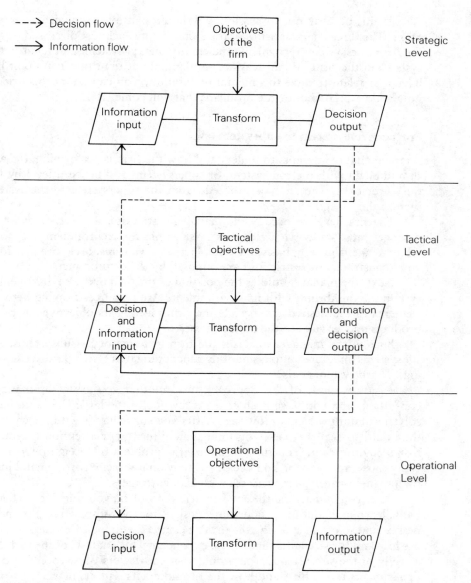

Figure 4-7 Management levels as subsystems.

While this book does not describe information systems by management level, the practice is not uncommon. The literature of business frequently refers to strategic-level information systems, tactical-level information systems, and so on.

Figure 4-7 in its simplified form fails to illustrate two key points about information flow. First, it is not necessary that the information flow up through the tactical level to get to the strategic level. The strategic level can get information directly from the operational level. Second, only internal information is shown. Management on all three levels must make use of environmental information as well. The environmental information can enter the firm on any level.

At this point in our discussion, we should pause to recognize an important point. The three characteristics of the systems approach just discussed (regarding the firm as a system, recognizing the environmental system, and identifying subsystems in the firm) are all ways of thinking about the firm. You don't have to have a problem to have this mental orientation. You can adopt this orientation now and be prepared for the problems that will come later.

Proceed from system to subsystem level

As the manager attempts to understand how the firm is performing, the analysis should begin with the top system, or supersystem, and proceed level by level to the lower ones. The analysis proceeds from the supersystem to the system and then to the subsystem.

The first level to occupy the manager's attention is the *environment*. The manager must know what elements exist within the environment and how they relate to the firm. Emphasis must be placed on what resources are provided and what constraints or restrictions are imposed by the environment.

Next, the manager studies the position of the firm in the environment. Is the system in equilibrium with its environment? Are resources flowing between the elements in the desired manner? Is the firm meeting its objectives of providing products and services to the environment?

Finally, the manager analyzes the firm in terms of its subsystems. Are the subsystems integrated into a smoothly functioning unit? Are all subsystems working toward system goals?

As an example of this approach, assume that you are a top-management consultant, and you have been called in by one of the large U.S. automakers to solve its major problem of low sales. After you shake hands with the chairman of the board to seal the pact, you immediately turn your attention to your client firm's environment. You fully recognize the problem of foreign imports—especially those from Japan. You decide to study an indirect environmental impact—the Japanese automakers' success with U.S. customers.

After you understand the environmental problem, you study your client company, learning about the product line, designs for the future, strengths and weaknesses, and so on. In studying the firm's resources, you look for reasons why sales are low and for strengths that can be expanded. This analysis of the firm leads to a study of the subsystems. You would visit car dealers' showrooms and service departments to see firsthand how the firm interacts with its market.

Once you have completed this top-to-bottom study, you assemble your facts and report back to the top with your recommendations. You describe the problem and specify the levels in the system where the problem exists. To complete your report, you recommend changes in different subsystems that you believe will correct the problem. The same approach can be followed for any size firm, by managers and systems analysts as well as consultants, and for any system level, such as a division or a department.

This vertical sweep through the organization aims at recognizing problems, locating their source, and understanding them. This is the phase of *problem identification*, the *analysis* portion of the systems approach.

Analyze system parts in a certain sequence

After studying the environment, the manager focuses attention on the firm. Is the firm meeting its responsibilities to the environment? If not, what part is defective? To answer this question, the manager must examine each part of the system. This process can be expedited when the parts are examined in a logical sequence, as shown in Figure 4-8. The steps correspond to the numbered blocks in the figure.

1. *Evaluate standards:* The performance standards for a firm are usually stated in the form of annual plans, budgets, and quotas. The annual performance is subdivided into the desired performance level by month. As the firm meets these standards, it moves toward the short- and long-term objectives that have been established.

   The standards must have certain characteristics. They must be *valid*. That is, they must be a good measure of system performance. For example, a certain high sales volume may not be a valid standard if the goal of the firm is to achieve a certain level of profitability. Perhaps high profits can be achieved at low sales volumes. The standards also must be *realistic*. A 20% increase in sales is not very realistic if it has never before been achieved and there is nothing to warrant such optimism. Standards must be *understandable* to those who are expected to meet them. And they should be *measurable*. If the standard is maximum profits, the manager never knows whether the standard has been achieved. "Realize a profit of 10% of sales" is the type of standard that leaves no doubt about its degree of attainment.

2. *Compare output with standards:* Once the manager is satisfied with the standards, he or she next evaluates the performance of the firm. First, the output of the firm is compared with the standards.

   If the firm is meeting its standards, there is no need to continue with the systems approach to problem solving. There is no problem to solve.

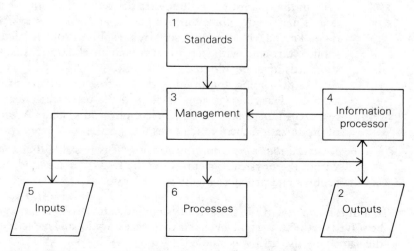

Figure 4-8 Each part of the system is analyzed in sequence.

The manager can reevaluate the standards in the light of good current performance. Perhaps this performance level can be increased in the future.

If the firm is not meeting its standards—in all or in part—the manager must identify the cause or causes. A problem exists that must be solved. The remaining system elements are possible locations of the problem or problems.

3. *Evaluate management:* A critical appraisal is made of the firm's management. Are there adequate numbers of managers in the different areas and on the different levels? The signals that indicate this is a problem include managers working excessively long hours and projects that never get completed.

    The quality of the management team also must pass inspection. Do the managers have the skills and experience needed to perform their duties? Errors in judgment, excessive costs, and high employee turnover are signals that management quality might not be satisfactory. A good knowledge of management theory is valuable in this part of the analysis.

4. *Evaluate the information processor:* It is possible that a good management team is present, but the team is simply not getting the information it needs. If this is the case, the needs must be identified and an adequate information system must be designed and implemented.

5. *Evaluate the firm's resources:* The management resource has already been evaluated. When this level of the system analysis is reached, the adequacy of the management resource is no longer a question. But what about the rest of the employees? Does the firm have the right number of employees, and do they have the right skills? And what about the machine and material resources? Are they adequate? What about money? Is there enough available for the firm to obtain the physical resources it needs to meet its objectives?

    Some compromise may be necessary here. Some resources may not exist in the quantities and qualities desired. Even if this is true, the limitations may be overcome through good management of available resources. If good management cannot solve the resource problem, then the manager should start over with step 1 and reevaluate the standards. Some realistic standards must be adopted.

    At this point, the organizational structure of the firm can also be assessed. Has management assembled the resources effectively? Are the resources functioning as an efficient physical system? A good knowledge of organization theory facilitates this portion of the analysis.

6. *Evaluate the transformation process:* It is possible that the problem lies within the physical system—how the resources are used. Inefficient procedures and practices might be the cause.

If the analysis of the firm as a system indicates problems, they will probably be solved on the subsystem level. It is then necessary to analyze selected subsystems the same way the firm was studied.

Take, for example, a firm that is having problems with a new product. The information system reports that too many products are being returned because of defective parts. An evaluation of the firm's resources indicates a shortage of quality control inspectors. The manager then shifts attention to the manufacturing subsystem of the firm. Each of the elements of the manufacturing subsystem is examined in the same sequence as the overall firm. The sequence in Figure 4-8 is followed on successively lower levels until the cause of the problem is found.

Because a business system is so complex, it is doubtful that any manager will conduct all the analyses alone. He or she will probably lack both the specialized skills and the time required for detailed study. For these reasons specialists are frequently employed to assist the manager. General management consultants can be used at any point in the analysis but are especially effective in evaluating standards, management, organization, and resources. Information specialists and EDP auditors help evaluate the MIS; industrial engineers study the efficiency of the transformation processes.

Let's pause again and review our progress. After adopting a systems way of thinking, we become alerted to the possibility of a problem. Perhaps we sought out the problem, or it was called to our attention. We examined the firm in its environment by starting at the top system level and working down. This is a *vertical analysis*. On each level, we studied the elements of that system in a certain sequence. This is a *horizontal analysis*. We are therefore searching vertically and horizontally at the same time.

Figure 4-9 shows this vertical and horizontal analysis process. The analysis starts with the top system level—that of the firm—and proceeds from one system element to another. As soon as the problem element is identified, the analysis

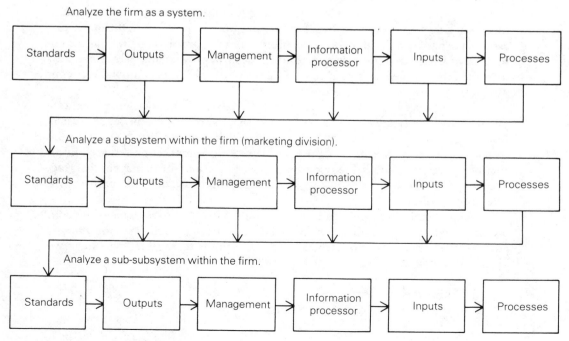

Figure 4-9 Vertical and horizontal analysis process.

drops to the next lower system level. That level is analyzed, element by element, and the problem element on that level is identified. If necessary, the analysis drops to still lower system levels.

In the case shown in Figure 4-9, it is unnecessary to analyze all six elements on each level. As soon as the problem element is identified, attention is focused on that element by studying it on a lower system level. For example, assume that a firm's top management is alerted to the fact that the firm is not meeting its annual sales standards. Each month, the firm is below quota. Hence the output of the firm is not up to standard. The next system element, management, is studied and determined to be deficient. There is no need at this point to continue with the analysis on the firm level, as the subsequent elements are of a lower priority. We follow the priority sequence on each level, studying the most important elements first.

The problem element (in this case, management) must be understood once it is identified. The nature of the management deficiency must be explored. Perhaps you learn that a high turnover of managers in the marketing division has kept the firm from meeting its standards. The analysis turns to the marketing division to learn more about the problem.

In analyzing the marketing system, you learn that managers have been leaving the firm because they felt the annual sales quotas were unreasonable. The problem lies within the standards established for marketing management. Continued study of the problem on the marketing level discovers that the primary reason for the unrealistic quotas is a poorly functioning marketing research department. The department is not doing a good job of measuring the market potential that the managers should be expected to achieve.

Analysis next drops to the lower system level—the marketing research department—and its elements are analyzed. You learn that the problem in the marketing research department is an inadequate information processor. The firm has a computer, but the marketing research routines need improvements. You have now identified the problem and defined it in sufficient detail. You can now direct your attention toward solving the problem.

The route we have followed to trace the problem to the marketing research department is illustrated in Figure 4-10. The signals received at the higher system levels—low sales, deficient management, high management turnover, and poor quotas—were only symptoms of the problem: a poor marketing research information processor. Usually the symptoms appear first, and the manager must trace the symptoms to the problem. The systems approach provides the path for the manager to follow.

The procedure we followed in this example is one of *problem identification*. We first tried to pinpoint the problem and its location. This activity is the *analysis* portion of the systems approach, and it corresponds to the first two steps we identified initially:

1. Define the problem.
2. Gather data describing the problem.

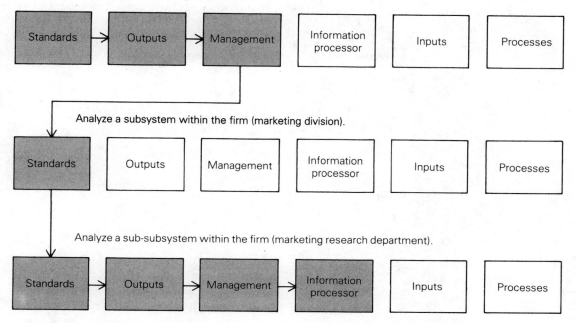

Figure 4-10 The systems approach provides the path to problem identification.

We are now ready to embark on a phase of *problem solution*. This is the *synthesis* portion of the systems approach.

At this point, we revert back to our original list of steps and conduct the final four:

3. Identify alternate solutions.
4. Evaluate the alternatives.
5. Select the best alternative.
6. Implement the solution and follow up to assure that the solution is effective.

Review of the Systems Approach

We have identified several elements, or characteristics, of the systems approach. Although it is not difficult to understand each one separately, fitting them together effectively requires some effort. Managers develop this integrative skill through experience.

A good starting point is the orientation the manager should adopt before problem solving begins. The manager should see the firm as a system residing within a larger environmental system and consisting of several subsystems. This

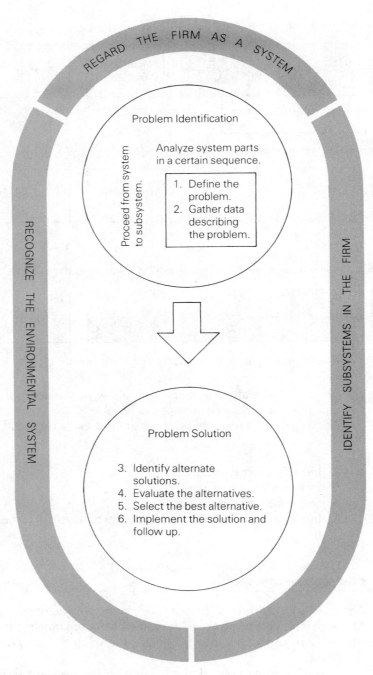

Figure 4-11 Integrative model of the systems approach.

orientation represents the outer ring in Figure 4-11. Now the manager is ready to look for a problem, or to understand one if it presents itself.

The manager searches for problems by proceeding from system to subsystem and by analyzing system parts in a certain sequence for each level. By doing this, the manager accomplishes the first two steps of the systems approach: (1) define the problem, and (2) gather data describing the problem. Together these activities constitute *problem identification,* in the upper circle in Figure 4-11.

Once the problem has been identified, it can be solved by following the remaining four steps of the systems approach, as illustrated in the lower circle of the figure.

What we have done is separated the six steps of the systems approach into two groups—problem identification and problem solution. In addition, we have placed these activities within a larger network—a systems orientation for the manager. Also, we have recommended a sequence for the analysis of system levels and parts.

Now we have a basic framework to follow when solving problems. In Chapter 11 we will learn how the MIS supports the manager in problem identification and solution.

Examples of the Systems Approach

Let's look again at the three types of organizations described in the previous chapter—a football team, a law firm, and a newspaper publisher. We will describe how each organization's management can use the systems approach to understand and solve a problem that is having a negative effect on the firm.

A football team

Assume that a four-year college has just hired a new head football coach. He must decide if he has any problems. If he thinks in systems terms, he views his squad as a system, composed of subsystems, existing in a larger environment. The subsystems are offensive players, defensive players, and specialty players (kickers, returners, and so on). The offensive and defensive systems are divided into line and backfield subsystems. The environment consists of the team's athletic conference.

First, the coach must search for a problem. He starts with the team's *output* and reviews the past won-lost record. Last year it was 2-9. The year before that it was 0-11. Now he's beginning to understand why the school changed coaches. The previous teams were not meeting their standards. He remembers the last words of the chancellor as he signed his one-year contract: "Win the championship next year, or else." He knows what his *standards* are. He must somehow raise the quality of the output to championship caliber in one year.

The team's *management* is the next focus. The new coach was able to select his own staff of assistants, and he got the people he wanted. He is confident that he has the right leadership. He is also satisfied with the quality of his *information processor.* He has hired assistant coaches who have proven abilities for preparing team scouting reports and serving as observers in the press box. Further, two experienced student statisticians are available.

What about *input resources?* Looking at the files on the team members, he notices very few highly recruited high-school players. His team is composed mainly of players that nobody else wanted. Here is a problem. The team has inadequate input resources. The coach drops down to the subsystem level to learn more about this personnel shortage. He reviews last season's game films and sees that most of the losses were caused primarily by a poor kicking game. The team needs a better kicker. This completes the problem identification phase. Now, the coach must start solving the problem.

The coach *identifies the alternatives.* He can develop the kicking ability of a player already on the squad. He can recruit a graduating high-school kicker. Or he can recruit a graduating junior-college kicker. He *evaluates the alternatives,* looking at the advantages and disadvantages of each. He remembers what the chancellor said about next year and decides to *select the alternative* of recruiting the junior-college kicker, since that alternative offers the best chance for a quick solution. He *implements the solution* by taking the next plane to California and signing an All-American junior-college kicker. He has to wait a while to *follow up on the solution*—until the end of the coming season. If his team meets its standards, he will know that he made the right decisions. If he must look for another job, he will know to try something else the next time a kicking problem arises.

A law firm

Our firm consists of three partners, two secretaries, a part-time bookkeeper, and a part-time researcher (a law school student). The founder of the firm (one of the partners) has become increasingly concerned about the firm's financial condition. The loss of a highly publicized case last year seems to have affected the firm's image. The client load is down; several clients have switched to other firms.

The founder reviews the past year's trial record and sees too many lost cases. This *output* is unacceptable, even though no specific *standards* exist for the percentage of cases that should be won. The founder is satisfied, however, with the firm's standards. He and the other partners have agreed on the importance of the image of being winners.

Since the partners also serve as lawyers, they represent the *management* and an important *input resource.* The founder believes that the partners are good managers, but as lawyers they often have difficulty with certain types of cases. For example, one lawyer took on a trademark infringement case even though he had little background in business law. He lost the case, and the client company was critical of the counsel they had received.

The problem does not seem to involve an inadequate *information processor.* The part-time researcher has done an excellent job, and one of the secretaries has performed some good research. There is no evidence that better information would have made a difference in the firm's past performance.

The problem appears to be a legal staff inadequate to their task. The firm is spread too thin—cases are taken on without reference to the lawyers' abilities to handle them. The standards are too ambitious for the resources. The problem of unreasonable standards is reflected in the symptoms: a poor financial condition, a tarnished image, a low client load, lost clients, lost cases, and difficulty with certain kinds of cases.

The partners discuss the founder's conclusions and agree that the firm should have a more central focus. They decide that the firm should select some type of law and specialize in it. There are not enough resources to be all things to all clients. While the *standards* appeared satisfactory the first time through the analysis of the system elements, a comparison with the resources indicates the need to rethink what the firm is attempting to accomplish.

The firm selects criminal law as its specialty, since the partners all have that experience. The standards are revised so that expectations focus on the area of specialization.

In this example, the firm is so small that the analysis can be performed without studying subsystems. The systems approach is applied to fit the unique characteristics of the system under study.

A newspaper publisher

The *Rapid City Herald* has been gradually losing its market leadership to its crosstown rival, the *Rapid City Bugle*. After reviewing the *Herald's* annual financial report, the board of directors hired a marketing research firm to survey area readers and find out how each of the two papers is perceived.

The survey of the *environment* revealed a conservative and mature, yet old-fashioned and boring, image of the *Herald*. The *Herald* appeals to an older market, while the *Bugle* is seen as youthful, fresh, and exciting. *Herald* readers most enjoyed the column on needlepoint and the series on Lawrence Welk.

The problem is that management has been out of touch with market needs. The image of the *Herald* must change, but more importantly, steps must be taken to ensure that management doesn't again lose contact. The MIS can help keep the managers informed.

When the board meets to decide on the solution, one member recommends a column on vacation spots for swingers, but it is voted down as too piecemeal an approach. The chairman of the board, just back from an American Management Association conference on decision making, suggests that they follow the systems approach. The other members agree to try it.

The board forms a project team, consisting of the president and the four vice-presidents, to apply the approach. The team examines each element in the system of the firm in sequence. The *standards* are restated by subdividing the market into submarkets based on age, income, and ethnic origin. Specific standards are established for each group. The *management* team is evaluated as strong and competent. The *information system,* however, is almost nonexistent. The computer has been used almost solely for typesetting and generates no worthwhile management reports. The team decides to reorganize the data processing organization—moving it from a department within the controller's division to separate divisional status. The director of data processing is told that if she can develop an effective MIS during the next two years, she will be promoted to vice-president.

The MIS is to be used to keep management informed about internal and external environmental events. Special attention will be given to uniform environmental information. Annual readership surveys will be conducted, and economic and demographic (age, income, education, and so on) statistics will be maintained in the data base. Management intends to use the MIS to do a better job of keeping in touch with its market. A new set of standards, a revised organizational structure, and new plans for using the computer as part of an MIS are expected to solve the problem.

In this example, the analysis began at the appropriate level, the environment. The marketing researchers gathered data for a better understanding of environmental relationships. They could identify the problem on this level without studying the firm as a system. They directed their attention to the problem's solution and evaluated the elements of the firm as a system. For each element they asked, "How can this element contribute to a better understanding of environmental needs?"

The application of the systems approach to each of the three examples above has been quite different. The systems approach is only an organized problem-solving format. It does not guarantee success. *How* it is used is the key. The manager must use the technique with skill, ingenuity, and imagination.

Personal Factors Influencing Decision Making

Throughout this book, we paint a picture of an MIS that the manager can use aggressively to seek out problems to solve. Intuitively, that seems to be the way things should work. In actual practice, all managers do not adopt such an aggressive posture for at least two reasons. First, it may not be their nature; second, they may not have time.

Each manager has a unique decision-making style. This is one reason why MIS design is so challenging. Three dimensions appear to provide an opportunity for individual differences among managers. These dimensions are their problem-sensing styles, their information-gathering styles, and their information-using styles.[6]

Managers fall into three basic categories in terms of their *problem-sensing styles:*

- *Problem avoider*—The manager who takes a positive attitude and assumes that everything is fine. An effort is made to block out the possibility of problems by ignoring information or avoiding thorough planning.
- *Problem solver*—The manager who neither looks for problems nor blocks them out. If a problem arises, it gets solved.
- *Problem seeker*—Here is our aggressive manager.

In addition to the differences in how managers sense problems, there are differences in how they develop and evaluate alternatives. Managers can exhibit

---

[6]Based on Andrew D. Szilagyi, Jr., *Management and Performance* (Santa Monica: Goodyear Publishing Co., 1981), pp. 220–225.

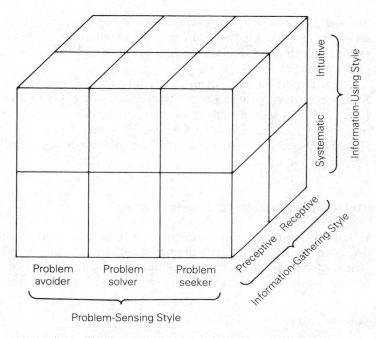

Figure 4-12 The three dimensions of decision-making style.

one of two *information-gathering styles*—the way they organize the various sources of information received daily:

- *Preceptive style*—The manager adheres to management by exception and screens out everything not meeting certain criteria, such as relevance to his or her area of responsibility.

- *Receptive style*—The manager wants to look at everything and then determine its meaning. This style is illustrated by the CEO who said, "Your staff really can't help you think. The problem with giving a question to the staff is that they provide you with the answer. You learn the nature of the real question you should have asked when you muck around in the data."[7]

Managers also tend to favor one of two different *information-using styles*—the way they go about using information to solve a problem:

- *Systematic style*—The manager pays particular attention to following a prescribed method of problem solving, such as the systems approach.
- *Intuitive style*—The manager does not favor any certain method, but rather uses the approach that seems suited to the situation.

Figure 4-12 illustrates these three dimensions of decision-making style. There are twelve (3 × 2 × 2) unique combinations of these styles. For example, a

---

[7]John F. Rockart and Michael E. Treacy, "The CEO Goes On-Line," *Harvard Business Review* 60 (January–February 1982): 86.

manager can be a problem solver, have a preceptive information-gathering style, and favor a systematic procedure for problem solution. These are basic categories that the information specialist can use to better understand the information needs of the manager.

It is important to recognize these individual differences. All too often, the MIS is described with statements that supposedly apply to all cases. Statements such as "Upper-level managers use summarized information" probably hold true *most* of the time but not all of the time. The most important element in the MIS is the manager, and he or she is only human. No two are exactly alike, and they use the MIS in different ways.

Environmental Factors Influencing Decision Making

In addition to unique personal factors, the manager's environment influences how decisions are made. The environmental situation is influenced by culture, the degree of centralization in the organization, the availability of information, the degree of control over the decision process, and the importance of the decision.

Culture[8]

The Japanese follow a more collective (or group) approach to decision making than U.S. managers. In Japan, managers on all levels of the hierarchy circulate memos discussing elements of an upcoming decision and examining the consequences. Fellow managers initial the memos in a manner indicating their degree of concurrence. Initials written sideways on the memo indicate reservations; upside-down initials indicate that a dissenting memo is forthcoming. Supporters claim three advantages to this group approach:

- Decision making receives more thorough treatment.
- Broader participation is a good way to obtain broader commitment.
- Decisions tend to be bolder and more radical.

Degree of centralization in the organization

In a highly centralized organization, power rests at the top. Top-level managers make most of the decisions—the important ones, anyway. Lower-level managers have relatively few decision-making responsibilities.

As the organization grows, the top-level managers suffer from *information overload*—the more information the brain tries to absorb, the less actually gets through.[9] When this happens, responsibility for decisions gets funneled to lower and lower levels.

---

[8] Based on Szilagyi, pp. 219–220.

[9] Henry Mintzberg, *The Structuring of Organizations* (Englewood Cliffs, N.J.: Prentice-Hall, 1979), p. 183.

When decision making is decentralized, managers who are in direct touch with the problem activities make the decisions. This way the organization can respond more quickly to problems than if the decision has to be sent up the organizational hierarchy.

Information availability

For the past several years, the trend in computer use has been toward *distributed processing*—spreading information processors throughout the organization. This trend has made possible more decentralized decision making, since lower-level managers now have access to the information they need.

There is a potential problem here. It is easier now to make information available to levels that are not competent to make a given decision. Poor decision making under such conditions can damage the credibility of the MIS and, more importantly, the performance of the firm.

Degree of control over the decision process

According to Henry Mintzberg, "What matters . . . is not control over decisions but over actions: what the organization actually does. . . ."[10] Mintzberg describes a *decision process* consisting of the following steps:

1. Collect *information*.
2. Process the information to present *advice* to the decision maker.
3. Make the *choice*.
4. *Authorize* activity to solve the problem.
5. *Execute* the activity.

A decision maker has the most power when he or she personally controls all of these steps. Power is lost when it is delegated to lower levels (*vertical decentralization*) or to support-staff personnel (*horizontal decentralization*). For example, when a manager relies on the information services department to provide information, control over the first two steps is lost and the manager has less power. The computer-based information processor collects the information, processes it, and in some instances recommends certain decisions to the manager.

Some top-level managers rely on staff assistants not only to screen and interpret output from the MIS, but also to determine what requests are made for information. The power of such an *MIS gatekeeper* (the staff assistant) and the effect that such power can have on the organization is very great.

The importance of the decision

The more important the decision, the higher the level of the decision maker. A decision is important if it is significant to the success of the organization, such as

---

[10]Ibid., p. 187.

the decision whether to develop a new product. A decision that has long-range effects is also considered important. We have seen that strategic-level managers make decisions affecting the firm five or more years into the future, and that tactical-level managers' decisions have a time range of from one to five years. All of these personal and environmental factors influence the decision-making process.

Summary

The conceptual information system is a problem-solving system consisting of the manager, information, and standards. Other elements enter into the problem-solving process—solution criteria, constraints, and alternate solutions.

A popular way to classify problems is to place them on a continuum ranging from structured to unstructured. The computer can solve structured problems, the manager must solve the unstructured problems, and the manager and computer working together can solve the semistructured problems. The semistructured area is the target of the DSS concept.

Modeled after the scientific method, the systems approach is used in business to solve problems. Most definitions of the systems approach include a series of steps from problem definition to evaluation of alternatives to implementation and follow-up. Often the systems approach is explained in terms of analysis and synthesis.

The systems approach requires decision making at each step. And the MIS can support the manager by providing information for each decision. The steps of the systems approach provide a bridge between a single problem and the multiple decisions needed to solve it. A single DSS can support the manager in solving a manageable problem; larger problems require more than one DSS.

In addition to the steps, the systems approach requires that the manager regard the firm as a system, recognize the environmental system, and identify subsystems in the firm. These are all orientations that the manager should adopt before a problem arises. While looking for the source of a problem and understanding it, the manager proceeds from system to subsystem and analyzes the parts in a certain sequence.

The systems approach is a general method, applicable to any type of organization. We used the systems approach to identify a problem of inadequate input resources for a football team, unreasonable standards for a law firm, and a nonexistent information processor for a newspaper publisher. The systems approach is not an inflexible procedure, but rather a guideline adaptable to specific decision-making situations.

Descriptions of decision making and decision makers frequently overlook exceptions to the rule. Personal factors create three basic problem-sensing styles—problem avoiders, solvers, and seekers. Managers also differ in how they gather information (preceptive and receptive), and how they use the information to solve problems (systematic and intuitive). Additionally, environmental factors such as culture, the degree of centralization in the organization, the availability of information, the degree of control over the decision process, and the importance of the decision affect how decisions are made.

We have now completed the theory part of our study of the MIS. This theory should provide a solid foundation as we proceed to study the computing equipment that can be used in an MIS, the various types of MIS software, functional information systems, and the MIS life cycle. Theory serves to put these remaining topics into perspective.

Key Terms

desired state, current state

constraint

symptom

structured problem, unstructured problem, semistructured problem

systems approach

scientific method

analysis

synthesis

environmental element

vertical analysis, horizontal analysis

problem avoider, problem solver, problem seeker

preceptive style, receptive style

systematic style, intuitive style

information overload

vertical decentralization, horizontal decentralization

MIS gatekeeper

Key Concepts

The elements that must be present to solve a problem

The varying degrees of problem structure and how they relate to the DSS concept

The logical nature of the systems approach as a problem-solving tool

The multiple decisions needed to solve a single problem

The relationship between the problem, the systems approach, and the DSS

How the elements of the environment form a supersystem

The flow of resources between environmental elements, and between subsystems of the firm

The separation of the problem-solving process into problem identification and problem solution activities

The difference between symptoms and causes

Individual differences in decision-making styles

The influence of the manager's environment on decision making

The decision-making power represented by information gathering, processing, and presenting

---

Questions

1. What are the elements of the problem-solving process? Which of these elements also appear in the general systems model of the firm?

2. What type of problem, if any, is the DSS intended to solve?

3. List the six traditional steps of the systems approach.

4. In what way does the systems approach relate to the scientific method?

5. Explain the difference between decision making and problem solving.

6. How many decision support systems are needed to solve one problem? Explain.

7. Which of the six steps listed in question 3 represent analysis? Which represent synthesis?

8. Explain how the interaction of a firm's customers and competition can exert an indirect influence on the firm's operations. Also provide an explanation of the influence caused by an interaction of the financial community and the government.

9. Identify one example of useful information that could flow to the firm from each of the eight environmental elements.

10. What can the manager do to adopt a systems orientation in preparation for problem solution?

11. What steps does the manager follow during problem identification?

12. What steps does the manager follow during problem solution?

13. Could a good MIS conceivably change a problem solver into a problem seeker? Explain your reasoning.

14. In what ways could an MIS support a manager who has a receptive style of information gathering?

15. Can you see any relationship between information-using style (systematic versus intuitive) and degree of managerial experience? Explain.

16. How can the information specialist guard against designing a system that produces information overload?

17. Can decision making become too decentralized? Explain.

18. What are Mintzberg's problem-solving steps?

19. Compare Mintzberg's problem-solving steps to the systems approach. Are they similar or different?

20. At what level in the managerial hierarchy would you be most likely to find an MIS gatekeeper? What skills should this person possess?

CASE PROBLEM: Micro-Scan Corp.

By age 35, Herb Thompson had amassed a fortune through shrewd deals in the commodities market. A finance major in college, he developed a "system" for knowing when to buy and sell. His college roommate, Bill Stanton, an electronics engineering major, wrote a program to perform the logical analysis Herb had devised. The program, which was run on a local bank's computer, provided Herb with the feel for the market that he needed.

Everything worked so well that life for Herb was no longer a challenge. He grew bored. He had surpassed his investment goals and was looking for other worlds to conquer. One day, while having a cup of coffee at the corner Walgreen's, who should walk in but Bill Stanton. It had been years since they last saw each other, and each brought the other up to date on his career. Bill explained that he had developed an electronic device that could read data into a computer from microfilm. Microfilm output devices for computers had been in use for years, but the secret of microfilm reading had never been broken. The more Bill described his invention, which he had patented, the more interested Herb became. Before they left Walgreen's, they had agreed to form a company to manufacture the reader. Herb would put up the money, and Bill would provide the product. Within two months, Micro-Scan was a reality, operating out of a rented store with an employee force of eighteen.

The first three years of operations exceeded the owners' highest expectations, although they had set no specific goals. A key order came in from a large oil company, and the dominoes began to fall. By the end of the fifth year, virtually every major oil company in the United States was a user. The reader seemed perfectly tailored to the credit card processing most oil companies performed.

At this point, in January of 1982, Bill suggested that the firm get its own computer. He sought to convince Herb that Micro-Scan had outgrown its manual system. With 1500 employees and sales hovering at the $75 million mark, Bill saw the need to computerize. Herb was not the conservative sort, especially when it came to computers, but he had seen too many organizations get a computer before they were ready. He was a firm believer in the service bureau approach—letting someone else do the processing for a monthly fee. "That way, they have all of the problems," he said. Herb convinced Bill that the service bureau route was the way to go, and they decided to start with some basic accounting applications—inventory, payroll, billing, and accounts receivable.

Shortly after the service bureau arrangement had begun, company sales began to slip. The oil company market had been saturated, and nobody else was buying. They attempted to get into the banking industry, but bankers had no interest in microfilm reading. Similar attempts to enter the retailing, insurance, and government markets also ended in failure. Within a year, a third of the work force was laid off, and Herb and Bill were forced to sell much of their stock at a very low price in order to avoid bankruptcy. The stock was bought by Pacific Investors, which became the majority stockholder with 32% of the shares.

The first thing Pacific did was to replace Herb as president with one of their own executives, Lisa Tanaka. Herb was named executive vice-president, and Bill kept his title of chief scientist.

On Lisa's first day, she called Herb and Bill into her office and reassured them that their continued contribution to the firm was needed. She explained that she wanted to make a complete reappraisal of the firm, its products, its market, and its future. A new start was needed, and Pacific was looking to her to get Micro-Scan moving again. After listening intently, Bill took advantage of a lull in the conversation to ask, "And just how do you plan to solve our problems?" To which Lisa replied, "With the systems approach, of course."

Questions

1. Did Herb Thompson and Bill Stanton follow the systems approach in forming their company? Explain.
2. Where did Herb and Bill go wrong?
3. Did Herb's reluctance to get a computer lead to Micro-Scan's downfall? Why or why not?
4. How do you think that Lisa is going to apply the systems approach to get Micro-Scan back on its feet?

Part Three

THE COMPUTER

We recognized earlier that a firm need not have a computer to have an information system. Most of the material presented in the first four chapters applies to any kind of information system, whether it be manual, keydriven machine, punched card, or computer. This book deals mainly with computer-based management information systems, and the computer plays an important role in the remainder of the chapters. But the computer does not play the most important role—that role must be played by the manager. The manager not only uses the information output, but also participates in the design and implementation of the system.

To perform these duties effectively, the manager must have a good understanding of the role played by the computer in the information system. The purpose of this part is to enhance that understanding.

The information specialists assisting the manager must have an even greater understanding. These computer professionals must provide the expertise in design and use of computer-based information systems that the manager cannot be expected to possess.

Chapter 5 provides an overview describing how computers have evolved, what goes on inside the central processing unit, sizes of systems, and basic approaches to processing data. Chapters 6 through 10 provide more details on special input, output, secondary storage, and mini/micro equipment. The focus in the Chapter 8 discussion of data bases is not so much on hardware as on software—the data base management system (DBMS). Chapter 11 also emphasizes software by describing the basic ways a manager can use a computer system to solve problems.

Chapter 5

Introduction to the Computer

Learning Objectives

After studying this chapter, you should:

- Know the basic types of information processors and what conditions encourage their use
- Understand the evolutionary development process of the computer in terms of hardware, software, and use
- Appreciate the impact the small-computer boom is having on the computer industry and on the MIS concept
- Know the basic parts of a computer system
- Know the five uses of primary storage
- Know how characters are represented in storage
- Be familiar with the basic functions of the operating system
- Know the different size categories of computers and their distinguishing characteristics
- Understand how computer configurations are dependent on user needs
- Know the difference between batch processing, online processing, timesharing, realtime processing, and distributed processing
- Know the difference between a star and a ring network

Computer Popularity

Most of the interest in using the computer originated in the mid-fifties, so the computer era is only a few decades old. As recently as thirty years ago, the sharpest minds in the largest business equipment firms forecast only a handful of sales—less than a hundred. Today you need a computer to keep up with computer deliveries. By the end of 1979, there were approximately 370,000 *desktop* computers installed in the U.S., and this number is expected to reach approximately 849,000 by 1984.[1] You and many of your classmates may even own your own computers.

Business organizations have become increasingly dependent on computers. Without computers, for example, airlines could not make reservations and the telephone company could not offer low-cost, long-distance service. In addition to processing data, the computer plays an important role in the MIS.

The Information Processor in the General Systems Model

Chapter 3 presented the general systems model of the firm as a basic structure showing the important resource flows in any type of organization. The conceptual system gathers data from the physical system and transforms that data into information for the manager. This chapter introduces the information processor and provides a description of some of the different forms the processor can take.

Figure 5-1 illustrates the parts of the general systems model discussed in this chapter. Most of the discussion will center on the information processor itself, but attention will also be directed to data gathering, data communications, storage, and software.

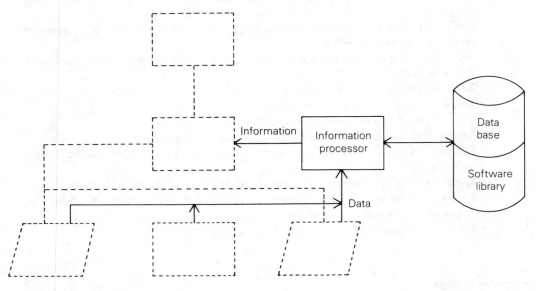

Figure 5-1 Information processor components.

[1] "All About Personal Computers," in *Datapro 70: The EDP Buyer's Bible* (Delran, N.J.: Datapro Research Corp., 1981), p. SC10-100-102.

Noncomputerized Systems

The most sophisticated computer is not the electronic variety; it is the human brain. The brain monitors and controls the most complex of all physical systems—the human body. In monitoring the conditions of the body, the brain functions as an *analog computer*. An analog is something that is similar to something else; it is a conceptual representation of some physical thing. The brain monitors the body by using physical inputs to represent the state of the body. Heart beat, pulse rate, body temperature, and other signals convey the condition of the body to the brain so that changes to the physical system can be made. When the need for change is recognized by the brain, other physical signals are sent out that result in faster breathing, perspiration, rest, sleep, and so on.

Electronic computers also serve as analog control devices. They monitor the condition of electrical power plants, paper mills, and oil refineries. But the precision of these computer applications does not match the precision with which the brain monitors and controls the human body.

The brain also functions in another capacity. It solves problems by processing data stored in the brain or captured by the sensory perceptors. When the brain performs in this manner, it functions as a type of *digital computer*. Scientists still do not know how data is stored in the brain, but such data is used to solve problems of a digital, or numeric, nature. The human brain can solve problems involving anything from algebra, to household budgets, to selecting TV channels, to baking cakes.

Electronic computers are best known as digital devices. But the electronic computer has solved only a very narrow range of digital problems compared to the human brain. This fact is evidenced by the interest in using computers to assist the manager in making decisions, rather than to make decisions for the manager. The primary processor used in making especially difficult decisions is still the human brain. Essentially, the decision support system uses the electronic brain to supplement the processing done by the human brain.

But before information can be used in problem solving, it must be created from data. There are four basic approaches to information processing—manual, keydriven machine, punched card machine, and computer.

Manual systems

A system in which people process information with only pencil and paper is a *manual system*. There are no labor-saving devices of a mechanical nature. The person does all the work. In all probability, more data is processed manually than in any other way. This is because every person is a functioning manual processor.

If you visit a company with a large computer operation, you will also find manual systems. Not all jobs lend themselves to computer processing. Usually, the low-volume, one-of-a-kind jobs are better handled manually.

In the days before small-scale computers—before the 1970s—small organizations had little choice in how their data was processed. Some of the important data processing tasks—payroll, billing, and accounts receivable—were performed manually. Today fewer and fewer firms cling to manual methods for these important data processing tasks. Manual systems are gradually giving way to computerized systems, but there will always be some data processed manually.

Keydriven systems

The first devices applied to reduce the manual-processing workload were mechanical and keydriven. The most familiar of these systems is the *typewriter*. First developed in the late 1800s as a manual device, it has been continually improved with electric power and computer-age components. Its low cost, flexibility, and high-quality output make the typewriter the most popular printing device in business today.

Other keydriven systems have been developed to solve digital problems; *adding machines* add and subtract, while *calculators* also multiply and divide. Modern forms of these machines, such as the *pocket calculator,* use computer-age circuitry and display output electronically. The calculator is a good example of how the economies of computer technology have been applied in a wide range of products, including keydriven machines.

As the scale of business increased, a need arose for an electromechanical system that would combine the printing ability of the typewriter with the arithmetic ability of the calculator. These machines, called *billing, posting,* and *accounting machines* (see Figure 5-2), were very popular for a few decades before about 1960. They are in use today with modern components, usually handling specialized jobs in small organizations.

Punched card systems

A third basic approach to data processing was developed shortly before the turn of the century by Dr. Herman Hollerith, a Buffalo, New York, statistician. Dr. Hollerith invented a group of machines that could process data punched into cards. These machines were used first by the Bureau of the Census in 1890.

In 1912 the rights to Dr. Hollerith's machines were acquired by a company that would later become International Business Machines. The IBM organization, under the leadership of its founder, Thomas J. Watson, Sr., became a worldwide giant in manufacturing and marketing punched card systems. These systems enjoyed their heyday from the mid-twenties to the mid-fifties and represented the best way to process large volumes of data.

While practically all of the punched card systems have been replaced by computers, the cards are still being used in some applications for computer input. In utility billing, customers return punched cards with their payments, and the cards are read by a card-reading unit. In production control, factory workers insert punched cards into card-reading terminals to transmit production data to the computer.

As we conclude our discussion of these noncomputerized approaches, one point should be made clear. The three noncomputerized systems (manual, key-

Figure 5-2 A keydriven billing machine.

driven, and punched card) have been used more as *data processing systems* than as information systems. It is possible to produce information with noncomputerized systems, but their real value has been in processing large volumes of (primarily) accounting data.

Computerized Systems

When computers were first introduced, they simply provided another way to do jobs previously done by other means. More recently, users have recognized the value of the computer as an information processing system. When the output of the computer is used in decision making, the computer is functioning as an *information processing system*. Otherwise, it is functioning as a *data processing system*. This is a refinement of the discussion in Chapter 1 that used the terms data processing system and information processing system interchangeably. We will continue to use this distinguishing characteristic in the remainder of the book.

Computer evolution[2]

The roots of computer technology can be found in the work of Blaise Pascal and Gottfried Wilhelm von Leibniz in the seventeenth century. Pascal built a mechanical device that could add and subtract, and von Leibniz built a machine that could multiply and divide. In addition to Herman Hollerith's punched card machines, the nineteenth century witnessed contributions from Joseph Marie Jacquard and Charles Babbage. Jacquard fashioned a weaving loom controlled by holes punched in paper rolls. Babbage conceived of a device containing the basic architecture of the computer; but the device, called the *analytical engine,* was never built.

The first generation   There has been no agreement on who invented the electronic computer. A court decision awarded the honor to Dr. John Atanasoff, a professor at Iowa State University, who built a device using vacuum tubes to solve equations. IBM uses the work of Harvard professor Howard H. Aiken on his Mark I (a project funded by IBM) as an indication of its role in computer evolution. But most observers consider that the real founders were J. Presper Eckert and Dr. John W. Mauchly of the University of Pennsylvania, who produced a device called ENIAC (Electronic Numerical Integrator And Calculator) in 1946. Eckert and Mauchly formed their own company, which was acquired in 1949 by Remington Rand.

Remington Rand used the ENIAC technology as the basis for developing the first commercially available computer—the UNIVAC (Universal Automatic Computer). In 1951, the U.S. Census Bureau became the first computer user, accepting delivery of a UNIVAC-I. The first business firm to obtain a computer was General Electric, which installed a UNIVAC-I at its Louisville, Kentucky, plant in 1954.

The UNIVAC captured the interest of both the government and large U.S. firms. For a few years, the term UNIVAC was synonymous with computer. IBM was slow to respond to the need for large-scale computing ability until 1952, when it announced its 701 scientific computer. IBM forecast only eleven 701 sales, but sold seventeen. Then in 1953 IBM announced the 650 commercial computer. Fifty units were forecast, but over four hundred sold. IBM subsequently added a large-scale 705 commercial computer and introduced the 704—an improved version of the 701. All of these systems used punched card input, vacuum tube circuitry, storage constructed of tiny doughnut-shaped magnetic cores, magnetic tape units, and slow (about 150 lines per minute) printed output. This stage of technology, characterized by vacuum tube circuitry, is called the *first generation.*

A significant innovation appeared toward the end of the first generation. IBM announced the 305 RAMAC (Random Access Method of Accounting and Con-

---

[2]Three excellent descriptions of computer history have been prepared during the past few years. They are N. Metropolis, J. Howlett, and Gian-Carlo Rota, eds., *A History of Computing in the Twentieth Century* (New York: Academic Press, 1980); Nancy Stern, *From ENIAC to UNIVAC: An Appraisal of the Eckert-Mauchly Computers* (Bedford, Mass.: Digital Press, 1981); and the twenty-fifth anniversary issue of the *IBM Journal of Research and Development* 25 (September 1981): 353–846. Also see Nancy Stern, "In the Beginning, There Was Mauchly," *Datamation* 26 (March 1980): 55ff; and Marguerite Zientara, *History of Computing* (Framingham, Mass.: Computerworld Communications, 1982).

Figure 5-3 The IBM 305 RAMAC.

trol)—the first computer to offer magnetic disk storage.[3] A photograph of the RAMAC appears as Figure 5-3. The stack of magnetic disks provided for *direct access storage*—a reading and writing mechanism could go directly to an area in storage without the searching process required when magnetic tape was used. The term *direct access storage device (DASD)* describes the class of devices, including disks, that offers the direct access capability.

The second generation In 1958 the first transistorized computer appeared—the UNIVAC Solid State 80 and 90 systems. The first transistors, though much larger than today's, were only 1/200 the size of a vacuum tube. They permitted faster operations, were more reliable, and generated less heat than the tubes. Computers produced between 1958 and 1964 used transistors; they were designated the *second generation*.

IBM followed UNIVAC later in 1958 by announcing the 7070, a large-scale transistorized system designed to replace the 705. Then in 1959 the 1401 was announced, destined to be even more successful than the 650, with over 8000 units sold. The number of computer manufacturers gradually increased, with Control Data Corporation and Honeywell joining the industry pioneers—Sperry Rand (previously Remington Rand), IBM, Burroughs, and National Cash Register.

---

[3] For a description of the impact of the RAMAC on the computing industry, see Mitchell E. Morris, "Professor RAMAC's Tenure," *Datamation* 27 (April 1981): 195 ff.

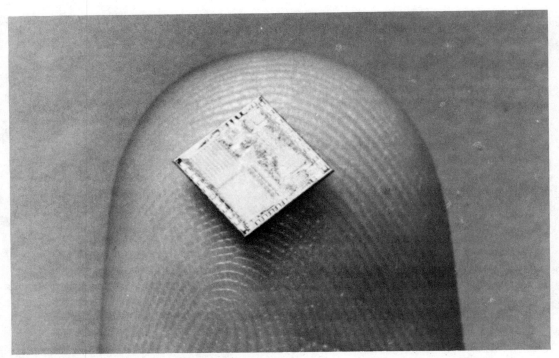

Figure 5-4   The semiconductor chip is extremely small.

*More
memory;
w. operating
system*

The third generation   The third generation was ushered in during 1964 when IBM announced its System/360 line, boasting integrated circuits consisting of tiny transistors (28/1000 inch square) mounted on half-inch ceramic modules. These integrated circuits were referred to as *SLT*—solid logic technology. Somewhat less than 1000 circuits were integrated on a single semiconductor chip. Other systems of this generation using chip circuitry were the RCA Spectra 70 and the NCR Century. All of these systems continued to use magnetic cores for primary storage.

*Cheap
Memory;
Virtual
machines.
remote
terminals*

The fourth generation   Cores were finally obsoleted in 1970 with the announcement of the IBM System/370, using chips for primary storage. During the next few years, other manufacturers also replaced the slower, bulkier, and more expensive cores with chips. The use of semiconductor chip storage in these systems can be regarded as the primary hardware characteristic of the fourth generation.

During recent years, the size of the chip has become smaller and its storage capacity has increased. A chip the size of the one pictured in Figure 5-4 can store from 64,000 to 256,000 characters.

The small-computer boom

There isn't much interest today in counting computer generations. There have been so many advances in both hardware and software that it is difficult to isolate unique families of technology. The innovations that have done the most to add a new dimension of difficulty to computer chronology are the minicomputer and, more recently, the microcomputer.

The *minicomputer era* got its start in 1963, when Digital Equipment Corporation (DEC) announced its PDP-5, selling for $27,000. The PDP-5 was followed in 1965 by the more powerful PDP-8, selling for only $18,000. These first two minicomputers set the trend toward smaller size, more powerful performance, and lower cost.

At first, minicomputers were not applied to business data processing tasks, but to scientific and production problems. In manufacturing, minis were used to monitor and control production machines, to test products, and to control heating, power, and water systems.[4] Perhaps one reason why business applications were not attempted on the early minis is that the established computer manufacturers, such as IBM, Burroughs, and so on, did not offer minicomputer systems. They did not want to replace their larger, more expensive units with minis. Also early minis, offered by firms with little commercial experience (such as DEC, Data General, Hewlett-Packard, and Wang), did not have the systems or applications software the commercial users demanded.

But the momentum of the minicomputer was unstoppable. In 1976 IBM announced its first mini, the Series/1. Other old-line manufacturers, such as Burroughs, Honeywell, UNIVAC, and NCR, followed suit with their small systems. These systems, marketed for business applications, are often called *small business computers*.

The early minis were easily distinguished from their larger counterparts. These small systems were limited in terms of internal operations, software support, and input/output equipment. Purchase prices ranged from $3000 to $50,000, and primary storage seldom exceeded 32KB. The letters *KB* mean *kilobyte*—a thousand (actually 1024) bytes, or characters. Larger system memories are measured in *megabytes* (MB), millions of bytes, and *gigabytes* (GB), billions of bytes.

The distinctive features of the minis soon blurred. Minis often had more storage, processed data faster, and generally outperformed larger systems. The name "mini" no longer seemed appropriate.

Then in the early seventies an even smaller computer came onto the scene, heralding the *microcomputer era*. The microcomputer is often called a "computer on a chip" since all of the logic and arithmetic circuitry are housed on a single *metal-oxide-semiconductor* (MOS) chip as shown in Figure 5-5. The pioneer in MOS technology was the Intel Corporation, which developed the Intel 4004 *microprocessor* in 1971. The 4004 consisted of 2250 transistors on a silicon chip measuring 0.117 by 0.159 inch. Within four years of the 4004 introduction, approximately twenty different microprocessors were placed on the market by firms such as Rockwell International and National Semiconductor. Microproces-

---

[4] See Frank L. Staudulis, "Computers in Production—How to Get Started," *Automation* 20 (October 1973): 70–76; "Minicomputers That Run the Factory," *Business Week,* 8 December 1973, pp. 68–78; and Gene Bylinsky, "Here Comes the Second Computer Revolution," *Fortune* 92 (November 1975): 134 ff.

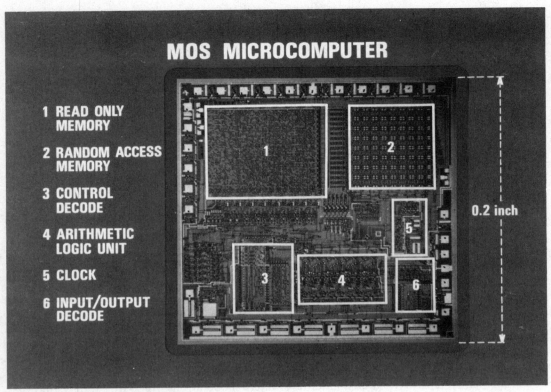

MOS MICROCOMPUTER

1 READ ONLY MEMORY

2 RANDOM ACCESS MEMORY

3 CONTROL DECODE

4 ARITHMETIC LOGIC UNIT

5 CLOCK

6 INPUT/OUTPUT DECODE

0.2 inch

Figure 5-5 A computer on a chip.

sors are now used in automobiles, microwave ovens, pocket calculators, and electronic games.

A microprocessor is not a computer. It only provides part of the circuitry needed in a central processing unit. In order for the microprocessor to have a special value in business information processing, it must be integrated with storage and input/output units. This integration produces the *microcomputer*. Today a wide range of microcomputers are available to serve as information processors for small firms and as components in distributed computing networks in large firms.

In addition to these commercially popular systems is a newer group of systems marketed successfully to individuals—the *personal computers*. The first personal computer was the Altair 8800, produced by MITS, Inc., in kit form during 1975. It sold for about $400. A year later Steve Wozniak and Steve Jobs began building a computer called the Apple in their garage. In 1977 the Commodore PET (*Per-*

---

[5] A survey of personal computers appears in Stan Miastkowski, "Choosing Your Popular Computer," *Popular Computing* 1 (November 1981): 16 ff.

sonal *Electronic Transactor*) and the Radio Shack TRS-80 were placed on the market. The market exploded in 1979–80, and today there are dozens of models available.[5] In addition, there are over 500 separate sources of software and add-on devices.

Summary of computer history

Our discussion of computer history has centered on hardware improvements. The circuitry, primary storage, input/output, and secondary storage technologies provide handy ways to isolate the generations, as illustrated in Table 5-1. The input/output and secondary storage devices will be explained in Chapters 6 and 7. Future technology is the subject of Chapter 20.

Table 5-1 Computer hardware characteristics

Genera-tion	Dates	Circuitry	Primary Storage	Secondary Storage	Input/Output
First	To 1958	Vacuum tubes	Magnetic cores	Magnetic tape Magnetic drum	Punched cards Line printers
Second	1958–1964	Transistors	Magnetic cores	Magnetic tape Magnetic disk	Punched cards Magnetic ink character recognition (MICR) Optical character recognition (OCR) Line printers
Third	1964–1970	Integrated circuits, small-scale integration (SSI)	Magnetic cores	Magnetic tape Magnetic disk Magnetic tape cartridge	Punched cards Terminals Character printers Optical character recognition (OCR) Line printers
Fourth	1970s	Large-scale integration (LSI)	Metal-oxide-semiconductor	Magnetic tape Magnetic disk Magnetic tape cartridge Floppy disk	Terminals Page printers Color graphics
Present and future	1980s	Very large-scale integration (VLSI)	Metal-oxide-semiconductor	Optical disk	Document image Audio input

Table 5-2 Computer software innovations

Generation	Systems Software	Applications Software
First and second	Assemblers Compilers (COBOL, FORTRAN, RPG) Sort/merge routines Input/output control systems	Accounting applications Scientific computations
Third	Operating systems Compilers and interpreters, (PL/I, APL, and BASIC)	Information-oriented report writers Operations research
Fourth	Virtual storage Data base management systems Compilers (Pascal) Query languages	Data retrieval routines Decision support models
Present and future	More "user-friendly" languages Data communications software	More sophisticated data retrieval and decision support modeling capability

The generations can also be explained in terms of software improvements. Table 5-2 summarizes some of the most important software characteristics of each generation. All of these software topics receive additional explanation in subsequent chapters.

During the first and second generations, the popular programming languages were Assembler, FORTRAN, COBOL, and RPG. In addition to the programs offered by the manufacturers to convert user programs written in these languages to machine language, systems software included sort/merge routines and input/output control systems (IOCS). Applications software invariably processed accounting and scientific data.

The big software innovation in the third generation was the operating system, which took over many of the tasks previously performed by human operators. The role of the operating system has grown, and today it is impossible to use a computer without one. The interest in MIS grew with the third generation, and for the first time, applications programs emphasized information output.

Significant software improvements continued in the fourth generation. A new operating system with a virtual storage capability enables a computer to execute programs that exceed the size of the available primary storage. Also, a software system to manage the data base, a DBMS (data base management system), has been widely adopted.

As we conclude this brief history of computing, we should put it into perspective in terms of our topic—the MIS. The main trend has been toward equipment with vastly improved reliability and performance capabilities, at continually reduced prices. Earlier we recognized that computer hardware and software are two of the MIS resources. These resources are available to more and more firms each year. It is hard to conceive of any business that could not afford a computerized information processor. Not every organization *needs* one, but the technology is certainly available.

The computer as a physical system

We made a distinction in Chapter 1 between a physical system and a conceptual system. The computer is a physical system; it is a group of integrated elements with the common purpose of achieving some objective. The elements are the various electronic units connected with wires and cables. The objective is the satisfactory execution of the instructions contained in the storage.

The technology of computer systems has changed dramatically, as we have seen. But the basic architecture has remained the same as that envisioned by Charles Babbage in the nineteenth century. The diagram in Figure 5-6, showing the basic architecture, is called a *computer schematic*. In all probability a similar diagram was drawn on the chalkboard by the teacher of the first computer class.

The computer has one or more input devices for entering data into the transformation and control part of the system—called the *central processing unit,* or the *CPU*. The CPU contains a storage unit where data and programs are stored. Any calculations or logical decisions are made in the arithmetic and logic unit, and the entire computer system is controlled by the control unit. Processed data and information are transmitted from the storage unit to one or more output devices.

In addition to the primary storage unit, constructed of integrated circuits and containing thousands of locations where characters are stored, there is a secondary

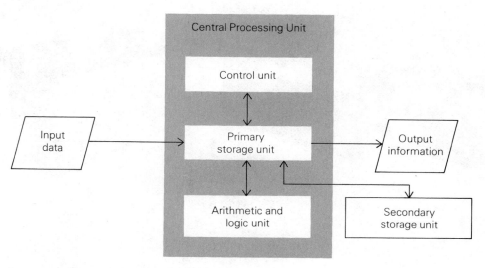

Figure 5-6 The computer schematic.

Figure 5-7 A small computer system.

Figure 5-8 A large computer system.

storage unit. The secondary storage unit maintains data on a medium such as magnetic disk or magnetic tape, and contains millions or billions of locations.

In a small computer (Figure 5-7), several devices and units can be packaged in a single cabinet. As a general rule, however, a separate cabinet is used for each unit. In a large system (Figure 5-8), twenty or thirty or more separate cabinets can be interconnected. Even though the above computer systems are quite different in appearance and performance, they can be represented by the general model of a computer system shown in Figure 5-6.

Computer storage

The storage portion of the CPU has five different uses. These may be described as the *five conceptual areas* of storage. The areas are not physical, in that the storage is not permanently partitioned in this manner. In fact, nothing physically distinguishes the five areas; the distinction is only in how the areas are used. The conceptual areas are illustrated in Figure 5-9.

As data enters the storage from an input device, such as a terminal, it is placed in the *input area*. The program in the *applications program area* is the list of instructions that guides the computer to the solution of a problem or the completion of a task. The applications program performs the necessary calculations, logical decisions, movements, and so on, and places data and information in the *output area*. The data and information are transmitted from this output area to an output device, such as a printer. Most programs require a separate storage area to contain intermediate totals, constants, descriptive characters, and the like. This separate area is the *working area*. The execution of the applications program is controlled by programs, primarily the operating system, in the *systems program area*.

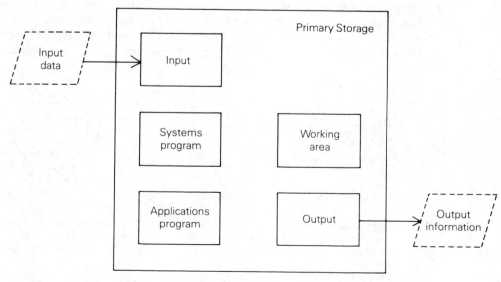

Figure 5-9 The five conceptual areas of primary storage.

Figure 5-9 does not attempt to show the relative sizes of the areas—they vary from one situation to another. The area required by the operating system can be quite large. For example, the UNIX V32 operating system used with the DEC VAX 11/780 computer occupies up to 55,000 positions. A DBMS also requires a great deal of storage area. The TOTAL system requires a minimum of 28,000 positions.

Although the conceptual areas do not represent physical boundaries, such boundaries are frequently established. Computers of all sizes often feature primary storage subdivided into *partitions,* with a separate applications program, or part of a program, residing in each partition. For example, a 128KB micro might feature three applications program partitions of, say, 20KB each.

The speed of the CPU has increased with each computer generation. During the first generation, internal CPU speeds were measured in *milliseconds* (thousandths of a second). Second and third generations were measured in *microseconds* (millionths) and *nanoseconds* (billionths) respectively. We are presently in the low-nanosecond range. Future speeds will be measured in *picoseconds* (trillionths of a second).

Representation of material in storage

All of the material (data and instructions) contained in storage is represented in a coded form. The code permits the computer to operate at maximum speeds for minimum costs.

Since the computer is an electronic device, it can represent numbers, letters, and special characters with groups of tiny electronic elements. Each element is called a *bit*—a contraction of *binary digit.* The bit can either be *on* or *off*—its binary states.

The most popular form of electronic storage element in earlier systems was the magnetic core. A core, illustrated in Figure 5-10, can be magnetized in one of two directions by passing an electrical current through the center.

In integrated-circuit, semiconductor storage, a single chip is capable of storing 64,000 elements, or bits of data. There is a tiny memory cell on the chip for each

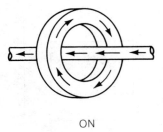

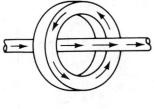

ON   OFF

Electrical current sets the
magnetic field of the core in
one direction—the "on" state.

Reversal of the current sets the
magnetic field in the opposite
direction—the "off" state.

Figure 5-10 Magnetic core storage.

of the bits. Each cell consists of a capacitor and a transistor, as illustrated in Figure 5-11. The capacitor can hold an electrical charge. When the capacitor is charged, it represents an *on* condition; when it is not charged, it represents an *off* condition. The transistor serves as a gate that can be used to test the condition of the capacitor. A pathway through the transistor exists only when the capacitor is on.

Characters are coded for computer storage with different combinations of on and off bits. Early computers (the first two generations) coded characters with six bits. A six-bit code offers sixty-four different combinations—enough for all twenty-six letters and ten digits, and for quite a few special characters, such as the dollar sign and dash. This six-bit code was called the *BCD* (*Binary Coded Decimal*) code.

Some computer users needed larger character sets to represent, for example, both upper- and lowercase letters. In response, the third generation offered both seven- and eight-bit codes. IBM incorporated an eight-bit code, called *EBCDIC*

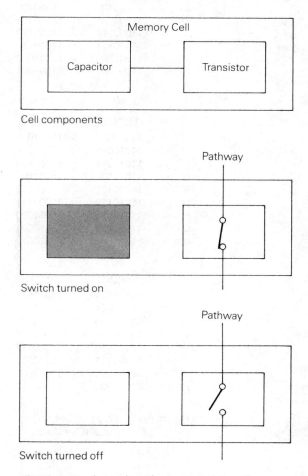

Figure 5-11 A semiconductor memory cell.

	EBCDIC	ASCII-8
0	11110000	10110000
1	11110001	10110001
2	11110010	10110010
3	11110011	10110011
4	11110100	10110100
5	11110101	10110101
6	11110110	10110110
7	11110111	10110111
8	11111000	10111000
9	11111001	10111001

	EBCDIC	ASCII-8
A	11000001	11000001
B	11000010	11000010
C	11000011	11000011
D	11000100	11000100
E	11000101	11000101
F	11000110	11000110
G	11000111	11000111
H	11001000	11001000
I	11001001	11001001

	EBCDIC	ASCII-8
J	11010001	11001010
K	11010010	11001011
L	11010011	11001100
M	11010100	11001101
N	11010101	11001110
O	11010110	11001111
P	11010111	11010000
Q	11011000	11010001
R	11011001	11010010

	EBCDIC	ASCII-8
S	11100010	11010011
T	11100011	11010100
U	11100100	11010101
V	11100101	11010110
W	11100110	11010111
X	11100111	11011000
Y	11101000	11011001
Z	11101001	11011010

Figure 5-12 Two popular computer codes—
EBCDIC and ASCII-8.

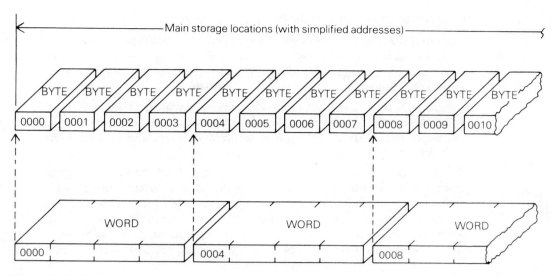

Figure 5-13 Bytes and words.

(*Extended Binary Coded Decimal Interchange Code*) into its System/360. The EBCDIC code, pictured in Figure 5-12, is the most widely used code for conventional computer systems.

Another eight-bit code is named *ASCII-8* (*American Standard Code for Information Interchange*). ASCII-8, also illustrated in Figure 5-12, is popular with mini and micro systems. An eight-bit code provides for 256 different characters. There is also a seven-bit code called ASCII-7, which is used primarily for data communication rather than internal storage.

A group of bits representing a character is called a *byte*. With EBCDIC or ASCII-8, a byte consists of eight bits. Several bytes are often processed as a unit, called a *word*. For larger systems, the most common word size is four bytes, or thirty-two bits (four bytes times eight bits per byte). Figure 5-13 shows the relationship between bytes and words. You will notice that the bytes and words have four-digit addresses that are used to locate data and instructions in storage. Many small computers can only handle one byte at a time. Large systems can handle one or two words at a time.

The operating system

Before the third generation, computer operators were in complete control of the computer. Operators decided *which* programs the computer would run—and *when*. They readied input and output devices, set console switches, and executed a program. Then they repeated the process for the next program. It became apparent that the computer was being used inefficiently. Precious minutes were lost between programs, and very often only a part of the system was used by the program being executed. The solution was to let the computer control itself, using software—the operating system.

An operating system includes three types of programs.

- The *control program,* often called the *supervisor* or *executive,* controls the computer as it executes programs. This portion of the operating system is *main memory resident*—it is always located in the primary storage (or main memory).

- *Language processors* convert programs written in languages such as COBOL and BASIC to the only language that the computer can understand—*machine language.* These processors reside in secondary storage and are called into primary storage by the control program as needed.

- *Service programs* include special programs such as the librarian, sort/merge, and utilities. The *librarian* (software, not the human variety) obtains applications programs from the software library when they are needed. The *sort/merge* performs those two data-processing tasks. The *utilities* convert data from one medium to another. As an example, a tape-to-print utility prints the contents of a magnetic tape file. A disk-to-tape utility copies records from a disk file onto a magnetic tape file.

Figure 5-14 illustrates the arrangement of the different parts of the operating system in the primary and secondary storage units. When the parts in secondary

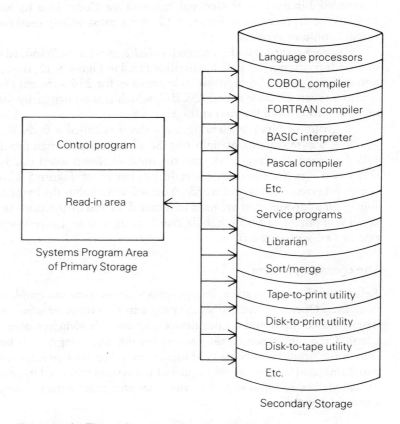

Figure 5-14 The major parts of an operating system.

storage are needed, they are called into primary storage by the control program. Program instructions can only be executed in primary storage, not in secondary storage. When one program enters the read-in area, it is *overlaid* on the previous program, erasing it.

The *control program* enables the operating system to perform three basic tasks:

- *Job management:* The operating system stores jobs to be run in an *input queue,* as shown in Figure 5-15. This queue resides on a secondary storage device such as magnetic disk. A *scheduling algorithm* is used to select the jobs. The algorithm considers things such as user priority, amount of primary storage needed, data needed, how long the job has been in the queue, and so on. The operating system calls the job into primary storage, executes it, and records the output in an *output queue*. When the appropriate output devices are free, the output is transferred from the queue to the device.

- *Task management:* The operating system allocates its resources to the various jobs. The operating system permits *multiprogramming*—the concurrent processing of several programs. Before operating systems were available, computers could work only on one program at a time; the ability to handle several was an important improvement. Several programs can reside

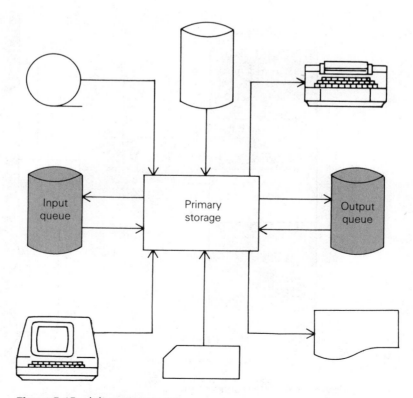

Figure 5-15 Job management.

in primary storage at the same time, along with the control program. The operating system, in conjunction with the control unit of the CPU, makes the arithmetic and logic unit (ALU) available to one program. Then, after a short period of time, execution of that program is stopped and a second program is allowed to use the ALU. Perhaps additional programs are also given their turn. At some point, the operating system returns to the first program, giving it more processing time. In this manner, several programs can be processed concurrently.

- *Data management:* The programs in primary storage interface with the input/output devices referenced by the program. As an example, assume that the computer is executing an inventory program that requests a data record from a disk file. Figure 5-16 illustrates the steps involved. (1) Control passes from the applications program to the data management portion of the operating system. (2) Data management then issues a signal to a *channel* that provides a pathway between the CPU and the input/output devices. The channel is actually a small computer that provides all the necessary instructions to the attached devices. (3) The data record is retrieved from disk storage, and (4) the data is transferred by the channel to an input data area in primary storage. The channel signals the operating system that the data has been retrieved. While the channel is retrieving the data, the oper-

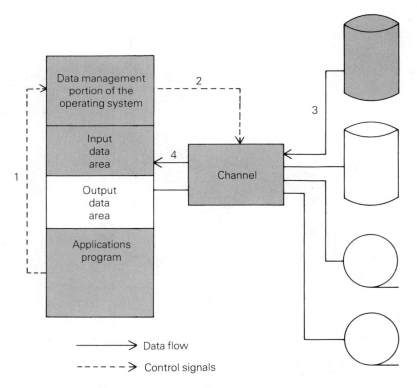

Figure 5-16 Data management.

ating system can shift to processing another program. When the data is available, the operating system can resume processing the interrupted program. Writing data from the output area of primary storage follows roughly the same pattern. The data management program signals the channel to take data in the output area and write it on a particular output device. While the channel is doing this, the operating system can resume executing the same, or another, program.

Small computers have only one channel. Large systems may have as many as three different types, capable of handling input/output devices of various speeds. The IBM 3033 has up to sixteen channels. Each channel can handle multiple input/output devices.

Larger computers offer a choice of operating systems. With the IBM 3033, for example, you can select from OS/VS2 (also called MVS), OS/VS1, and VM/370. Each offers different combinations of special features, such as multiprogramming, virtual storage (discussed in Chapter 7), and timesharing (discussed later in this chapter).

The Computer Program

The computer is a general-purpose device. It can handle a wide range of data and information processing tasks. It can print payroll checks and then screen customers' credit requests. The program causes the computer to do specialized jobs. A program is written for each job. A small program may contain only eight or ten instructions. A large one may contain several thousand. (Chapter 18 discusses the way these programs are written.)

A single instruction is required to cause the computer to take a specific action, such as read a card, multiply one number by another, write a line on the printer, and so on.

The programmer writes the instructions in a programming language. There are a large number of these languages, the more popular being FORTRAN (*Formula Translator*), BASIC (*Beginner's All-purpose Symbolic Instruction Code*), and COBOL (*COmmon Business Oriented Language*). A programming language consists of a set of different types of instructions—perhaps a hundred. The programmer selects those types needed and arranges them in the correct sequence.

All of the units of a computer system are interconnected electronically. The program determines when each device or unit is needed and what it will do.

Computer Sizes

As we have noted, computers come in different sizes. The smallest are the *microcomputers,* followed by the slightly larger *minicomputers*. These are the small-scale systems. On a higher level are the *medium-scale* and *large-scale* systems. At the top of the ranking are the *supercomputers*.

Microcomputers

Microcomputers cost about $400 to $30,000. These small systems can serve as information processors for small firms or as intelligent terminals in a distributed processing network. An *intelligent terminal* can perform some limited processing, such as editing data, in addition to serving as an input/output device. Primary storage for most micros ranges up to about 64KB. The system consists of a file-drawer-size CPU, a keyboard terminal (usually with a televisionlike display), a floppy disk unit that can hold one or two disks, and a printer. The most popular language is BASIC. Systems software includes an operating system and perhaps a DBMS. Packaged, off-the-shelf applications software is just now beginning to appear.

Minicomputers

Minicomputers cost about $4,000 to $150,000. These systems can serve as information processors in small- to medium-size firms or as distributed processors in large firms. Primary storage capacity starts at about 32KB and can go as high as 512KB. A system typically consists of a CPU, several hard disk drives, a high-speed printer, perhaps a few magnetic tape units, and a number of terminals. Programming languages include BASIC, Pascal, and FORTRAN. Systems software includes an operating system, DBMS, and data communications monitor. Most packaged, off-the-shelf applications software is prepared for minis.

Medium- and Large-Scale Systems

Medium- and large-scale systems are the direct descendants of the hardware and software developed over the four computer generations. Prices start at about $80,000 and can go as high as $10 million. Any type of hardware configuration can be assembled, using a wide variety of input/output and secondary storage devices. Although the full range of programming languages is offered, FORTRAN, COBOL, PL-1, and APL are the most popular. Systems in this range offer the most varied and advanced systems software on the market. Considerable packaged applications software is available, but users tend to develop their own. These systems serve as information processors or as central (host) systems for larger business organizations.

Supercomputers

There have been only three systems in the supercomputer category—the Burroughs ILLIAC IV, the Cray-1, and the CYBER 205. Only one ILLIAC was built, and it was installed at NASA's Ames Research Center in California. The ILLIAC has been replaced by a Cray-1, manufactured by Cray Research, Inc., pictured in Figure 5-17. The Cray and the CYBER 205, manufactured by Control Data Corporation, are designed to handle very complex computations such as those used in meteorology, atomic physics, and aerodynamics.

To qualify for this category, a computer must be able to perform at least 20 million arithmetic operations per second and solve problems involving a data base

Figure 5-17 The Cray-1 supercomputer.

of a million or more words.[6] As of January 1982, some 34 Crays and a half dozen or so CYBERs had been shipped or placed on order worldwide. The total market is estimated at between 100 and 200 systems by 1987.

Realistically, these systems are not designed to handle business data processing, even for the largest firms. The value of the supercomputers to the MIS is their influence on future, lower-priced, smaller-scale computer design.

Computer Configurations

Most computers have a single CPU, but the systems differ in the number and types of devices attached. Two general classes of devices, called *peripherals,* are attached to the CPU—input/output and secondary storage. Some examples of these peripherals are listed on the next page.

---

[6] Ronald D. Levine, "Supercomputers," *Scientific American* 246 (January 1982): 118 ff.

Figure 5-18   Industry-oriented peripheral equipment.

Input/output units	*Secondary storage units*
Card readers	Magnetic tape units
Card punch units	Magnetic disk units
Printers	Floppy disk units
Graph plotters	Magnetic tape cassette units
Optical character readers	Magnetic tape cartridge units
Magnetic ink character readers	
Terminals	

Most input/output units perform only one function—either input or output. Card readers are used only for input and printers only for output. Some of the units, however, can do both. Most terminals can transmit data to the CPU and receive information from it.

In the period before the mini/micro revolution, computer configurations differed greatly depending on the size of the system. The smallest computers were *card-oriented*—a card reader served as the input device, and a card punch and a printer served as output devices. A step up in performance produced a *tape-oriented* system—the addition of several magnetic tape units and larger primary

Figure 5-19 General-purpose peripheral equipment.

storage. Also possible was a *disk-oriented* system—secondary storage provided by magnetic disks. Some configurations were *tape and disk* systems.

Low-cost hardware has changed the way configurations are determined. Today it is possible to buy a microcomputer that has all the hardware and software options previously restricted to large systems. The feature that distinguishes the computer configurations is not the devices attached to the CPU but the performance capabilities of the devices. A microcomputer can use terminal input, secondary storage on floppy disks, and printed output from a slow-speed character printer. A large-scale system can include many terminals for input, several hard disk units for secondary storage, and one or more high-speed line printers. Both systems are disk-oriented, but the large system can greatly outperform the micro.

Card input and output units are rapidly becoming obsolete and are being replaced with various models of terminals. Some of the terminals, such as the IBM 4700 Finance Communication System shown in Figure 5-18, are designed to meet the particular needs of certain industries. Other terminals, such as the IBM 3270 display terminal in Figure 5-19, are general-purpose in nature and can be used in a variety of situations. Some of the other peripherals have also been designed for special industry use. Magnetic ink character recognition (MICR) units are used primarily in banking, and optical character recognition (OCR) devices have proven extremely popular in retailing and credit card industries.

A computer configuration is assembled to meet the unique data and information processing requirements of an organization. Low-cost hardware has made it possible for small as well as large organizations to match systems to their needs.

Basic Approaches to Computer Processing

There are two basic ways that a computer can process business data. It can do it now, or it can do it later. If a transaction is to be processed *now,* the data must be entered into the computer while the transaction occurs or immediately afterward. The computer then performs all of the necessary processes and produces the needed outputs. Then it can handle another transaction. This approach is called *transaction* or *online processing.* We will use the term online. *Online* means that a device, such as a terminal, is connected to a computer. A device that is not connected to a computer, such as a keypunch machine, is said to be *offline*.

If a transaction is to be processed *later,* it can be held until a number of such transactions can be processed as a group. This assembly-line approach to data processing offers the advantage of low cost and is the most popular way to handle large data volumes. The approach that has been followed since punched card days is called *batch processing*. The main disadvantage to batch processing is the lack of current files as the transactions build up. The files are only current immediately after they are updated, which might be only once a day. For example, if a firm batches its sales transactions and processes them against the inventory master file in the evening, the file only reflects the real inventory situation until the beginning of the next work day. As the next day's sales transactions build up, the file gradually becomes less valuable as a conceptual representation of the physical system.

Batch processing

Figure 5-20 illustrates how batched transaction data passes through a series of sort and update steps to update three master files. The flowchart symbol for the files indicates that they are recorded on magnetic tapes. Before a master file can be updated, the transactions must be sorted into the sequence of the master file. Batch processing is also called *sequential processing* because all records must be in a certain sequence.

The various data files can be stored in punched card, magnetic tape, or disk form. Regardless of the medium, a completely new file is created with each update—changes are not made directly to the old file. This way the old files can be retained for backup.

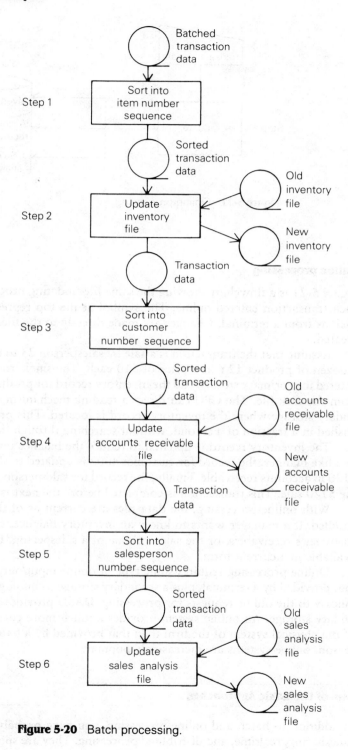

Figure 5-20 Batch processing.

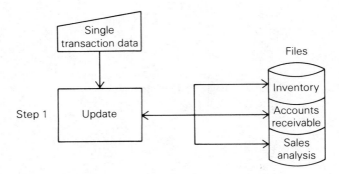

Figure 5-21 Online processing.

Online processing

Figure 5-21 is a flowchart showing the same file-updating process, this time with each transaction entered online. The symbol at the top represents keyed input, such as from a terminal. Changes are made directly to the file—a new file is not created.

Assume that the transaction is a sale by salesperson 23 to customer 4002 for a dozen of product 12Y at a price of $10 each. The single transaction record is entered into primary storage and the inventory record for product 12Y is obtained from the disk file. The CPU can direct a reading mechanism to the area in secondary storage where the inventory record is located. This procedure is accomplished in a fraction of a second, without searching through the file.

The inventory record is updated to reduce the balance on hand by a dozen. In a like manner, the record for customer 4002 is updated to show an increase of $120 in accounts receivable. Finally, the record for salesperson 23 is updated with the $120 sale. This transaction is completed before the next is entered.

With online processing, the data files are current as of the last transaction handled. If a manager wants to know an inventory balance, or the amount of a customer's receivables, or the sales volume of a salesperson, that information is available in a current form.

Online processing requires some type of online input/output ability, such as that provided by a terminal, plus a secondary storage technology that can respond quickly to the online requests for processing. DASD provides the responsive secondary storage. An online system provides a much more current representation of the physical system of the firm than that provided by a batch system. For this reason, online systems are increasingly popular.

Adaptations of the Basic Approaches

In addition to batch and online processing, you have probably heard the terms timesharing, realtime, and distributed processing. They are special adaptations of the two basic approaches.

Timesharing

Modern computers operate at such fast speeds that users must work hard to keep up with them. It takes a lot of jobs to keep the computer busy. Indeed, the more users, the merrier. One approach developed to permit this multiple use is known as *timesharing*. All that is needed is a central computer with a multiprogramming capability and data communication terminals.

Many terminals can be attached to a central computer, online. The terminal users can thus *share* the *time* of the computer. As far as each user is concerned, his or her terminal is the computer itself. Data can be entered through a keyboard and transmitted to the central computer. The operating system allocates the CPU time to the various users. The processing required by each terminal user is performed, perhaps using central data files, and the output is transmitted back to the appropriate terminal, where it is printed or displayed.

An individual or firm can purchase timesharing services from a computer service center. The user furnishes the data, programs, and terminal, and pays for the communication and computer time used. This can be an attractive alternative for a new computer user, especially a small firm. More computing power can often be obtained for less money than if the firm acquired its own system.

Realtime processing

There is a fine line between realtime processing and online processing, if one exists at all. The distinguishing feature is the response of the conceptual information system to the physical system. In *realtime*, the conceptual information system must be able to respond quickly enough to effect a change in the physical system if one is needed. An example is a point-of-sale transaction in a department store. The salesclerk keying transaction data into the terminal includes the customer's driver's license number. The computer uses this number to verify the customer's credit rating and advises the clerk accordingly. If the credit is bad, the clerk can void the sale. This is realtime—the conceptual information system is actually controlling the physical system.

In online processing, the data need only be entered into the conceptual information system as the transaction occurs. There is no requirement for a quick response. An online system only reflects the status of the physical system. A realtime system controls the physical system.

Distributed processing

During the mid-seventies firms began to spread their computing power throughout the organization. They distributed computers, often minis, to regional, area, and branch offices and plants. This approach is called *distributed processing*, or *distributed data processing (DDP)*.[7] Distributed processing requires that more than

---

[7]For more information on distributed processing, see Jack R. Buchanan and Richard G. Linowes, "Understanding Distributed Data Processing," *Harvard Business Review* 58 (July–August 1980): 143–153; idem., "Making Distributed Data Processing Work," ibid. 58 (September–October 1980): 143–161; Jon C. French, "Selecting a Distributed System," *Datamation* 27 (February 1981): 67–69; and Harold Lorin, "DDP: How to Fail," *Datamation* 27 (February 1981): 60 ff.

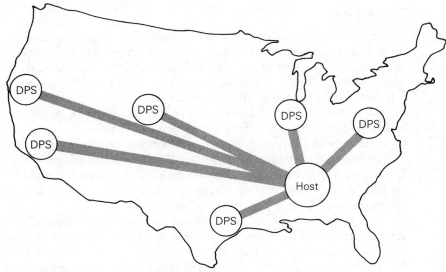

DPS = distributed processing system

Figure 5-22   A star network.

one information processor be available within the organization and that they be in different locations. The processors can be used in a batch or online manner.

According to some observers, a firm can have a distributed processing system even if the processors are not interconnected in any way. To most, however, the processors must be able to transmit data back and forth, using some type of communication link.

Two network arrangements are in current use. One, called the *star network,* includes a *host* computer (usually larger than the others) and any number of satellite systems. The star network concept is illustrated in Figure 5-22. The satellite systems are called *distributed processing systems (DPS).*

In the other arrangement, called a *ring network,* there is no host. All systems are comparable in importance. Figure 5-23 illustrates this approach.

The availability of the necessary hardware and software makes distributed processing an attractive alternative for large, geographically disbursed operations.

Selecting an Information Processor

Many different information processors are available. A firm can select from among manual, keydriven, and computerized systems. Punched card systems, however, are effectively obsolete. A firm typically starts with a manual system and uses it until the volume of activity makes it impractical. Then the firm can add keydriven devices and/or acquire a computer processing capability. If computer processing is believed necessary, still more alternatives exist. The firm can acquire its own system, subscribe to a timesharing service, or have a computer service bureau do the work.

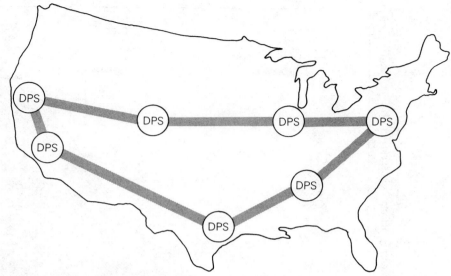

DPS = distributed processing system

Figure 5-23   A ring network.

The selection of an alternative is based on the firm's data and information processing requirements and on its resources. Computer processing is usually indicated if the firm uses large volumes of data, performs complex and/or lengthy calculations, and needs rapid response, high accuracy, or management information. One or more of these needs must exist to justify the expense of the computer and its related resources. If a firm with such needs has or can acquire a competent staff of information specialists, it will probably use its own computer. Timesharing is a good option when the firm needs a limited amount of computer processing and has some in-house expertise among its users and/or information specialists. The service bureau is attractive for firms that need computer processing but do not have the in-house expertise.

The selection of an information processor should be a deliberate, well-planned process beginning with a definition of the firm's needs. This process is part of the MIS life cycle described in Part Five.

Figure 5-24 is a conceptual model showing how a firm can evolve through the various information processor stages. The model is greatly simplified, using the size of information needs as the only determining factor. Many firms leapfrog certain stages. For example, a new firm can acquire its own computer right from the start. Or it can begin with manual methods and then subscribe to a timesharing service. The reverse sequence is also possible. A computer user can use a time-sharing service for applications that cannot be handled on the firm's system, such as long-range forecasting. The figure does, however, reflect a general progression of alternatives facing the firm.

Figure 5-24 conveys another key point—a firm usually retains old information processors even when it implements a new one. All firms have manual systems

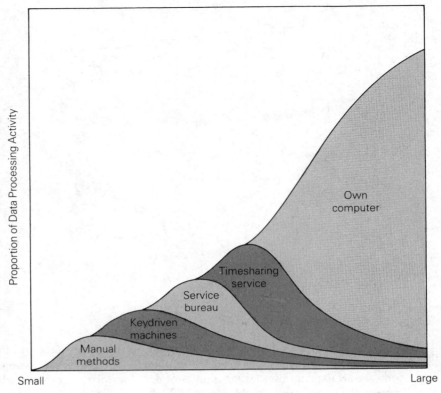

Figure 5-24 Information processor alternatives.

of some kind and use some keydriven machines, such as typewriters. A firm with large information needs can use all five approaches simultaneously.

Summary

This chapter focuses primarily on the computer-based MIS, but three other types of information processors could serve as a basis—manual, keydriven machine, and punched card machine. Both manual and keydriven systems are found in all organizations, used especially for small jobs. Punched card systems, however, are virtually obsolete.

The computer has evolved through at least four generations in terms of its hardware and software. Although no single person is credited with inventing the computer, Eckert and Mauchly are generally presumed to have contributed the most to early system design. Atanasoff and Aiken also played important roles. Sperry Rand offered the first mass-produced computer, the UNIVAC-I, and the first transistorized computer, the UNIVAC Solid State 80 and 90 systems. IBM finally gained a position of leadership in the market with the System/360 and System/370 models, which introduced the third and fourth generations respectively.

The small-computer boom has made it difficult to classify computer technologies and system sizes. Although the minicomputer started small, it has reached higher levels of performance than many conventional, medium-size computers. And the microcomputer has had a surprisingly large impact on the bottom end of the market. Minis and micros, including small business systems and personal computers, account for most of the activity in the computing field. It is a case of the tail wagging the dog—the small-system boom is now a major part of computer evolution.

Even though computers come in different sizes, the basic architecture of all systems can be illustrated with the computer schematic. As we look more closely at the CPU, we see primary storage divided into five conceptual areas, based on how the storage is used.

CPU speeds are measured in nanoseconds, and storage capacities are measured in kilobytes, megabytes, and gigabytes. A byte is storage space for a character, represented in most cases by seven or eight bits, or binary elements. The EBCDIC and ASCII-8 codes represent characters with eight bits, and ASCII-7 uses seven bits. Bytes are usually assembled to form words. Primary storage is constructed of metal-oxide-semiconductor (MOS) chips. The density of the memory cells and circuits on each chip has increased with each new product announcement.

The operating system is a software system that manages the computer. The control program resides in memory and performs job, task, and data management. Language processors convert programs written in languages such as COBOL and BASIC to machine language. Service programs perform functions such as software library management, sorting and merging, and converting data from one medium to another.

The two basic approaches to computer processing are batch and online. Time-sharing is a form of online processing, as is realtime. Distributed processing simply means that more than one processor is used. Processing can be either batch or online. Distributed processing uses one of two network arrangements—star or ring.

This concludes our overview of the computer. In the next six chapters we will expand on this material to increase our knowledge of an important part of the MIS—the information processor.

Key Terms

analog computer, digital computer	computer generation
manual system	direct access storage, direct access storage device (DASD)
keydriven system	
punched card system	solid logic technology (SLT)
analytical engine	minicomputer

small business computer

kilobyte (KB), megabyte (MB),
    gigabyte (GB)

metal-oxide-semiconductor (MOS)

microprocessor

microcomputer

personal computer

computer schematic

central processing unit (CPU)

conceptual storage area

partition

millisecond, microsecond,
    nanosecond, picosecond

bit, byte, word

BCD (Binary Coded Decimal)

EBCDIC (Extended Binary Coded
    Decimal Interchange Code)

ASCII-8 (American Standard Code
    for Information Interchange)

operating system

control program, supervisor,
    executive

main memory resident

language processor

machine language

service program

librarian

sort/merge program

utility program

overlay

job management

input queue, output queue

scheduling algorithm

task management

multiprogramming

data management

channel (data)

medium-scale system

large-scale system

supercomputer

intelligent terminal

peripheral

card-oriented, tape-oriented,
    disk-oriented, tape and disk-
    oriented systems

batch processing, sequential
    processing

online, offline

online processing, transaction
    processing

timesharing

realtime processing

distributed processing, distributed
    data processing (DDP)

star network, ring network

host

distributed processing system (DPS)

Key Concepts

The difference between manual,
    keydriven, and computer systems,
    and the conditions that encourage
    the use of each

The special ability of the computer
    (as compared with other alterna-
    tives) to produce management
    information

The contributions of many people
    and organizations to computer
    evolution

The evolution in computer
    hardware, software, and use
    through a series of generations

The basic parts of a computer system

The different uses of primary storage

How characters are represented in storage

How the operating system controls the computer system and facilitates certain operations

Grouping of computers in categories based on size

The manner in which computer configurations are determined based on user needs

The different approaches to computer processing

The general conditions influencing the selection of an information processor

Questions

1. Distinguish between an analog and a digital computer. Which type is the subject of this chapter?

2. What data processing applications might be performed manually in a doctor's office? When would keydriven methods be used?

3. Name the keydriven machines that might be found in a lawyer's office, department store, a restaurant, an accountant's office, and a president's office.

4. Who invented the computer?

5. Which company introduced the first computer generation? the second? the third? the fourth? the minicomputer era? the microprocessor? the personal computer?

6. What significant feature did the RAMAC offer?

7. Why were minicomputers not initially applied to business problems?

8. Distinguish between minicomputer, microcomputer, and microprocessor.

9. Could the same piece of equipment be a microcomputer, a small business computer, and a personal computer at the same time? Explain.

10. Why has the computer schematic not changed over the years, even though there have been many changes in computer technology?

11. What are the five conceptual areas of storage? Why is the term, "conceptual" used?

12. How would you represent one millisecond in decimal form? One microsecond? One nanosecond?

13. How many memory cells (capacitor plus transistor) would be needed to represent a character using EBCDIC?

14. Distinguish between bit, byte, and word.

15. What are the three types of programs included in an operating system?

16. What are the three basic tasks of the control program?

17. Why is the term *sequential* used to describe batch processing? Why is the term *transaction* used to describe online processing?

18. Which is better suited to an MIS—batch or online processing? Explain.

19. How many computer systems are used in a timesharing network? How many in a distributed processing network?

20. Must a firm first use manual, keydriven, service bureau, and timesharing systems before purchasing its own computer? Explain.

Problems

1. Draw the computer schematic.
2. Code the following characters, using EBCDIC and ASCII-8. Refer to Figure 5-12 for the codes. Example: an EBCDIC "Z" is 11101001.

Character	EBCDIC	ASCII-8

B																
L																
A																
C																
K																
S																
M																
I																
T																
H																

3. Draw a flowchart (similar to Figure 5-20) of a tape-oriented batch processing system that performs the following functions:
   a. Sorts sales transactions into customer number sequence
   b. Updates the accounts receivable file
   c. Resorts the transactions by sales region number
   d. Updates the sales region activity file.

CASE PROBLEM: Elcon Construction Company

Elcon was founded in 1946 by Edward Lampkin, who bought a used steamroller and began installing asphalt driveways. Ed did all the work himself until business prospered and he hired employees. The company continued to expand, eventually offering a full range of capabilities in highway, bridge, and airfield construction. Ed retired in 1968, and his son Ralph assumed the presidency.

The economic slump of the 1970s put a damper on growth. It was all Ralph could do to maintain the employee force at 635 and keep revenues above the $40 million mark. Beginning in 1980, things grew even worse as the tight money situation slowed all types of construction. At the end of 1980, Ralph was forced to lay off eighty workers, and plans to purchase additional earth-moving equipment were put on hold.

Elcon had always used manual and keydriven systems for payroll, inventory, and general accounting. About ten years ago it experimented with a computer model that would estimate project costs. The model, offered by a local service bureau, failed miserably. Although the service bureau salesperson maintained that the problem was faulty input data, Ralph and the other top managers were "burned" on computer processing.

Then in late 1982, Ralph's college alma mater sponsored an executive seminar titled "The Use of the Computer in the Construction Industry." The seminar sounded interesting to Ralph, since he had great respect for the capabilities of his school's engineering faculty. He felt that they had something worthwhile to say and decided to give them the chance. He attended the seminar and was well pleased with the results. He especially liked the part describing how the computer can be used to plan and control projects using a method called Critical Path Method (CPM). He had heard of CPM and knew how it worked, but he was not aware of the potentially valuable outputs that were possible. The computer could prepare charts and graphs that would be especially valuable to him and his managers.

Upon his return to the office, Ralph called in his executive committee, consisting of Manny Rosen, the controller, and Zeke Villaneuva, the vice-president of operations. Together they discussed the ramifications of computer processing. Manny was quick to point out that nobody within the organization had any real computer experience. He further reminded Ralph and Zeke of the highly efficient manual system they had refined over the years. "I'm as progressive as the next person," Manny protested, "but it would be foolish to scrap this system and go through the trials and tribulations of installing a computer."

Neither Ralph nor Zeke objected, because they knew he was right. Manny ran a tight ship, and there was no real reason to discard something that was working so well. However, something kept gnawing at Ralph. He wanted to use information outputs like those prepared by CPM. Manny admitted that his system couldn't now provide that kind of information, and it would be prohibitively expensive to add the number of people and keydriven machines that would be necessary. All three executives realized that they had reached another impasse as far as the computer issue was concerned. But since all three had other things to attend to, they decided to table the discussion.

That evening, as Ralph drove home, he thought about the CPM application. The application seemed so simple. There are a number of canned CPM programs on the market, fitting practically any kind of computer. You don't even have to be a programmer to use one. Oh well, he thought, its probably like anything else—it seems simple until you try it.

Questions

1. Should Manny scrap his manual system and replace it with a computer? Explain your reasoning.

2. Does Elcon have a good information processing operation?

3. How might Ralph go about obtaining the benefits offered by CPM?

4. Will that solve the problem?

Chapter 6

Computer Input and Output

Learning Objectives

After studying this chapter, you should:

- Know the different input and output alternatives
- Understand the roles played by channels and control units
- Appreciate the constraint that the input bottleneck has on computer performance and the methods that have been aimed at relieving it
- Appreciate the value of punched cards for certain applications
- Know the different types of keyboard terminals
- Recognize characteristics of applications that lend themselves to MICR (magnetic ink character recognition) and OCR (optical character recognition)
- Be able to project how audio response and voice recognition will be integrated into future MIS designs
- Evaluate the relative advantages and disadvantages of the different types of printers
- Appreciate the manager's need for both special hardware and special software to provide graphical output
- Understand how computer output microfilm (COM) is used in conjunction with a data base
- Be able to determine the combination of input and output units needed to satisfy the requirements of certain applications

The preceding chapter discussed the general performance of the computer. This chapter will describe the different methods of entering data into the computer and receiving information and data from it. These *input/output* (I/O) devices are important to the MIS for two basic reasons. First, they provide the hardware interface between the manager and the central processing unit. The manager often enters data, such as specifications required by a mathematical model, into the computer using an input device. The manager receives information from the MIS by means of output devices. Second, the I/O devices are used by employees in processing the daily transaction data of the firm. This data is entered in the data base, where it represents a valuable resource for the manager.

Input/Output Devices in the General Systems Model

Figure 6-1 illustrates the position of I/O devices in the general systems model. The input devices enter data from three sources: (1) data gathered from the physical system of the firm, (2) data gathered from the environment, and (3) data provided by the manager. The output devices (4) make information available to the manager.

Some of the gathered data is first recorded on some type of medium, such as punched cards, magnetic tape, or magnetic disk. *Offline keydriven machines,* operated by data entry operators, convert source data to a computer-readable medium. Then another group of machines—*input devices* attached to the CPU by means of a data channel—enter the media-recorded data into the CPU.

Other data is originally recorded in a form that is acceptable to the computer. Little or no keying is required. Examples are magnetic ink character recognition (MICR) and optical character recognition (OCR). This approach is called *source data automation*—the source data medium is automated so that its data can enter the computer directly, a process also called *direct entry*. The OCR units in supermarkets that read the bar code on packaged items are a good example, as are the MICR units in banks that read data from checks. In the latter case, the only data that must be keyed onto the check is the amount.

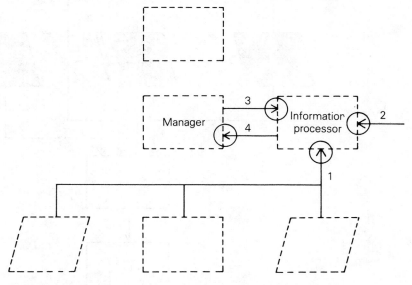

Figure 6-1 Input/output devices in the general systems model.

A third basic way to enter data into the computer is to key it into an *online keydriven device,* such as a keyboard terminal. With this option, no computer-readable medium is required.

A fourth option permits data input in audible form, using a *voice recognition unit.* These relatively new units recognize specific vocabularies spoken by designated users.

The various approaches to data entry are pictured in Figure 6-2. The input hardware units are shaded. The flowchart symbol for keydriven machines indicates a keying operation using an offline device, such as a keypunch machine. The

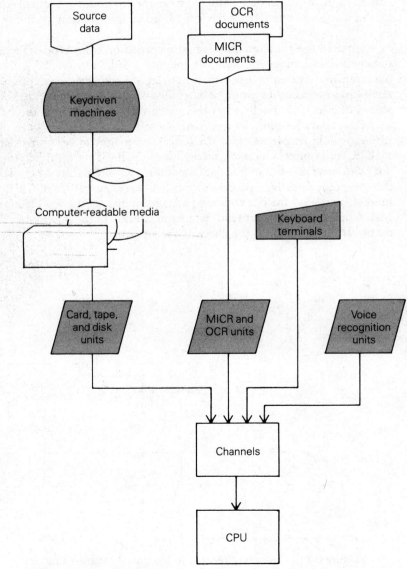

Figure 6-2 Input options.

flowchart symbol for a keyboard terminal indicates a keying operation using an online device, such as a terminal. The parallelogram is the flowchart symbol representing input and output.

Output offers similar options. Information or data can be recorded on a permanent medium, such as paper, microfilm, or punched cards, or the information can be displayed on a televisionlike screen or presented audibly. (Although we have described these screens as "televisionlike," the popular name is *CRT—cathode ray tube*.) In addition, data or information recorded on microfilm can be converted to printed form or displayed on a viewer. These output options are the subject of Figure 6-3. The symbol for a terminal display indicates output produced when processing occurs, such as that displayed on or printed by an online terminal.

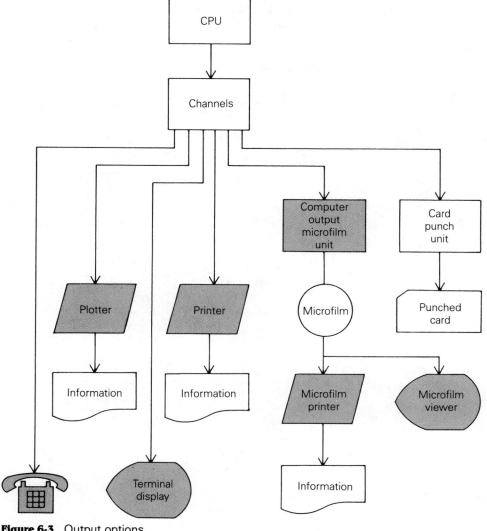

Figure 6-3 Output options.

Computer Channels and Control Units

A large number and variety of devices can be linked to a CPU. If these devices (the peripherals) were attached directly to the CPU, the CPU could not function efficiently because it would have to halt processing whenever one of the units was operating. Since I/O units perform at very slow speeds compared to the CPU, much CPU time would be wasted. For this reason, it is necessary to place intermediate units between the CPU and the I/O devices. These intermediate units are the channels and the I/O device control units. They provide a pathway between the CPU and the I/O devices. In fact, they provide several pathways that can be used for multiple transmissions at the same time. The role played by the channels and the control units is illustrated in Figure 6-4.

The *control unit* contains the logic circuitry and storage needed for the control of multiple I/O devices. The *channel* contains the logic circuitry and storage needed to monitor several I/O device control units and provide pathways to and from the CPU.

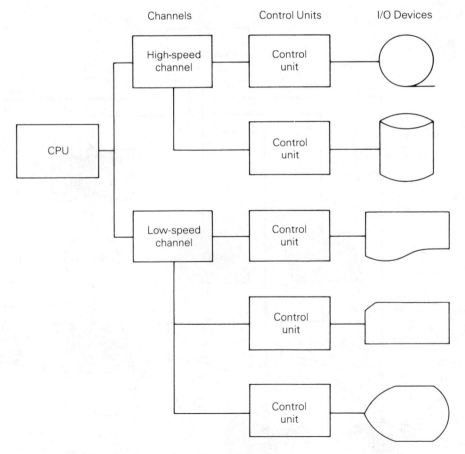

Figure 6-4 The role of channels and control units.

The transfer of data between the I/O unit, the control unit, and the channel is *serial,* or one byte at a time. For example, as a magnetic tape unit reads data recorded on tape, the data is transmitted to the control unit and then to the channel one byte at a time. While this operation is performed, the CPU can process other data in primary storage. When the channel's buffer storage is filled, the channel signals the CPU that the data is ready to enter primary storage. The CPU halts processing just long enough to enter the data from the channel. The interruption of the program in process is very brief because all of the bytes from the channel are transmitted to primary storage at once—in *parallel.* For faster channels, such as those of the IBM 3033, the transfer speed is as high as 3MB per second.

The transfer of data from primary storage to an I/O unit works in the reverse sequence. Data is transmitted from the CPU to the channel in parallel, and the CPU resumes processing. Data is then transmitted one byte at a time first to the control unit and then to the I/O unit.

Smaller computers have only one channel; larger systems have many. The large-scale IBM 3033 can have as many as twenty-four. When there are multiple channels, it is common for one to be dedicated to slow-speed devices such as printers, card readers and punches, and terminals. Other channels are dedicated to the faster magnetic tape and direct access storage devices. The computer configuration in Figure 6-4 features one low-speed and one high-speed channel.

The importance of the channels is easy to overlook, but without them CPU performance would be drastically reduced. The channel hardware and the operating system permit the multiprogramming that maximizes computer productivity. Without the channels, there could be no timesharing or distributed processing, and batch processing would be extremely slow and costly.

Keydriven Input Devices

CPU speeds are measured in millionths and billionths of a second, yet most input data is originated at human speeds by an operator using a keyboard device. This is why people in the computer industry speak of an *input bottleneck.* Although there have been many attempts to reduce this bottleneck, keyed input remains the primary means of data entry.

Offline keydriven devices

The most common input device during the first three computer generations was the keypunch machine. In the mid-sixties, computer manufacturers sought improvements in keyed input. They offered key-to-tape and key-to-disk machines that recorded on magnetic media rather than punched cards. Figure 6-5 illustrates the options for creating computer-readable media offline. The first key-to-tape and key-to-disk units used conventional magnetic tape reels and hard disks. Later, magnetic tape cassettes and cartridges as well as floppy disks (also called diskettes) were added as input media options. The five parallelograms in the figure represent computer input units.

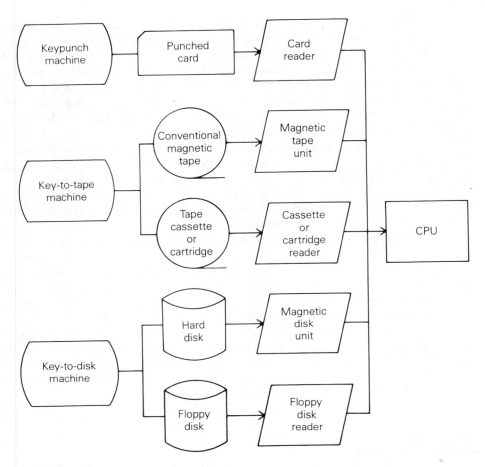

Figure 6-5   Offline keydriven machines.

Figure 6-6   Magnetic tape cassettes.

Figure 6-7 Floppy disks.

Figure 6-6 shows two tape cassettes. Each cassette contains 285 feet of polyester on which data can be recorded at a density of 800 bytes per inch. The capacity of a cassette is equivalent to approximately 2000 punched cards.

Floppies come in two sizes—5¼ inches and 8 inches in diameter (see Figure 6-7). Disk capacity is the equivalent of 2000 to 8000 punched cards, depending on disk size, number of recording tracks (similar in concept to grooves on a phonograph record), recording density (such as 3200 or 6800 bytes per inch), and whether recording is on one or both sides of the disk.

Key-to-tape and key-to-disk machines are faster and easier to operate than keypunch machines. And computer input units can read tape and disk data much faster than data from punched cards. Figure 6-8 pictures a multistation keyboard

Figure 6-8 A multistation key-to-disk system.

entry system consisting of several keyboards linked to a single disk unit by a small processor. Systems such as this have become popular replacements for keypunch machines. Nevertheless, the future of all offline keydriven devices is dim, since the trend is away from batch and toward online processing.

Keyed Media Input Units

After the input media have been created, they (the cards, tapes, and disks) must be processed by an input unit that reads the data and transmits it to the CPU through the control unit and channel. Figure 6-5 showed five of these input units—card reader, magnetic tape unit, cassette or cartridge reader, magnetic (hard) disk unit, and floppy disk reader. We will not discuss the magnetic tape and disk units here, including them instead in our discussion of secondary storage in Chapter 7.

Card-reading and -punching units

Many medium- and large-scale computer systems include a card-reading unit and a card-punching (or card punch) unit. A card punch unit is illustrated in Figure 6-9. Cards can be read much faster than they can be punched. Card-reading speeds

Figure 6-9 A card punch unit.

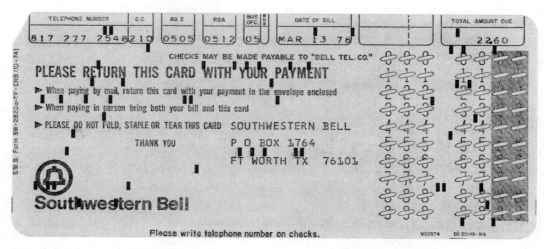

Figure 6-10 A turnaround document.

of 2000 per minute are not uncommon, but punching speeds are in the range of 100 to 250 per minute.

Some readers incorporate checking circuitry to assure that the data is read correctly. One approach is to have two reading stations and to compare the impulses read at both stations. The impulses must match exactly before the data is allowed to enter the computer.

Punched cards are used as *turnaround documents*. A turnaround document is pictured in Figure 6-10. Cards such as these are prepared by the card punch unit and mailed to customers along with printed invoices. The customers return the cards with their payments. Since the cards are already punched with the necessary data (customer number and amount), there is no need for the keypunching operation. This is an example of an approach designed to relieve the input bottleneck.

Punched cards are also used to track materials as they flow through a plant or a distribution network. In a factory, workers insert punched cards in special terminals to "clock on" and "clock off" their assigned jobs. The cards accompany the materials from one work station to another. A similar application involves the attachment of a packet of cards to an item, such as a sofa or television set, so that wholesalers and retailers can report the location of the item to the manufacturer. Perhaps you have seen such cards attached to items you have purchased.

Floppy disk, cassette, and cartridge readers

When floppy disks, magnetic tape cassettes, and magnetic tape cartridges are created offline, they require an online reading unit. Because of this, the offline approach is much less attractive than an online approach using a terminal.

Cassette and cartridge tapes have not enjoyed the same popularity as floppies. In some instances, cassette and cartridge tapes are produced as a by-product of another operation. For example, data can be recorded offline on cassette tape by point-of-sale terminals in a retail store or by data collection terminals in a factory.

Figure 6-11   A CRT (cathode ray tube) terminal.

Online keydriven devices

There are two basic types of keyboard terminal—one displays output on a CRT, the other prints output on a continuous paper form. Both types use typewriterlike keyboards for data entry. Unlike offline keydriven devices, online terminals provide convenient and effective means of *output* as well as input.

A *CRT terminal,* also called an *alphanumeric display terminal* and a *video display terminal,* is all-electronic, noiseless, and economical. CRTs can display information very rapidly, filling the screen with characters much faster than the characters can be printed on paper. This speed makes the CRT ideal for displaying information in response to a manager's inquiries (or queries). For example, a complete stock status report for an inventory item can be displayed within a few seconds after the query is made. A photograph of a CRT terminal appears as Figure 6-11.

CRT terminals offer a variety of special features:

- *Color:* Multiple colors can be displayed on certain models.
- *Reverse video:* Characters can be green on a white background or white on a green background.
- *Blinking:* Single characters or data items can be made to blink so that they stand out.

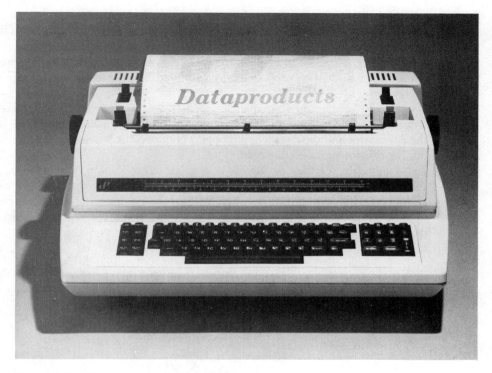

Figure 6-12 A hardcopy terminal.

- *Cursor:* A special character such as an underline mark can move about on the screen to identify, for example, the position where the next character should be entered. Cursors can be controlled by the host computer (for some terminals) or by the operator.
- *Scrolling:* Lines move up or down by one line as a new line is added.
- *Paging:* Some terminals have enough storage capacity to store two or more "pages" of data and can display a page upon request.
- *Protected format:* Some characters on the screen can be protected from inadvertent erasure. In this procedure a "form" is displayed on the screen for the operator to complete.

A terminal with paper output is called a *hardcopy terminal,* since the term *hardcopy* describes anything in printed form. Another name is *teleprinter terminal.* The hardcopy terminal uses a mechanical printing device. Therefore it is noisier, somewhat slower, and more subject to failure than a CRT. In addition, the hardcopy terminal is usually more expensive. In the light of this comparison, perhaps you are wondering why anyone would select the hardcopy terminal over the CRT. The reason is the hardcopy. If you want or need a printed record of terminal input and/or output, you use a hardcopy terminal. A photograph of a hardcopy terminal appears in Figure 6-12.

Hardcopy terminals provide several different printing alternatives. The mechanisms fall into two basic categories—impact and nonimpact. An *impact* printer causes a print "hammer" to strike the paper to form the character (as in a typewriter). A *nonimpact* printer causes characters to be printed by means of some chemical or heat process, or by spraying the characters on the paper from an ink jet.

Impact printers are capable of speeds from 10 to over 600 characters per second (cps), depending on the technology. Popular impact technologies include the dot matrix and the daisywheel. Popular nonimpact technologies include thermal, ink jet, and xerographic processes.

One model of the *dot matrix* printer moves a column of seven pins across the paper and selectively actuates the pins at five successive intervals to form the character. This mechanism is called a "5 by 7" dot matrix—the characters are formed by a matrix of five columns across and seven rows down. Figure 6-13 illustrates this approach. Other matrix dimensions are available.

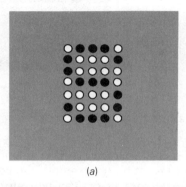

(a)

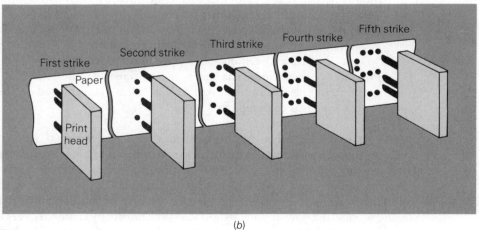

(b)

Figure 6-13   The dot matrix printing approach: (a) the matrix arrangement for printing the letter S; (b) the printing process (an ink ribbon between the print head and the paper is not shown).

Figure 6-14   The daisywheel technology.

The *daisywheel* printer uses a flat plastic disk with petallike projections, each containing an embossed character, as on a typewriter print bar. A daisywheel is pictured in Figure 6-14.

Nonimpact printers are capable of speeds better than 2000 cps. The most common technology is the *thermal* printer, which uses a heat process. *Ink-jet* printers spray droplets of ink on the paper. Xerox uses the *xerographic* principle (naturally) to achieve speeds of 4000 lines per minute. Because of their high cost and inability to print more than a single copy, nonimpact terminals are still quite rare.

Both types of terminals (CRT and hardcopy) are good I/O devices in an MIS. The units can be located in the manager's office, and information can be produced in a report or a graphic format. The CRT is especially good for graphs, which can be displayed in two or more colors. Not all terminals have a graphics capability, however.

We will describe only keyboard terminals in this chapter. Several other types of terminals will be covered in Chapter 9, where the topic is data communications.

Source Data Automation

Source data automation (SDA) requires that data documents be in a special form so that the data can be read by a reading unit. Two such technologies have developed—magnetic ink character recognition (MICR) and optical character recognition (OCR).

Magnetic ink character recognition

The American banking industry was among the first to establish a standard approach to computer use. In the mid-fifties, the American Banking Association devised a standard *type font* (or style) to be used in processing checks. The font, named *E-13-B,* consists of the ten digits plus four special symbols, as shown in Figure 6-15. Also shown is the CMC-7 font, popular in Europe and South America. The E-13-B font is also used in Europe.

When you receive blank checks from the bank, they are preprinted with numbers identifying both the customer (you) and the bank. These numbers appear at the bottom on the left side. When you write a check, the amount is encoded in the E-13-B font by the first bank to process it. The amount is entered by a key-driven machine called an *encoder*. This keying operation does not actually represent an extra step. Banks like to accumulate batches of checks and tabulate a total amount for all of the checks in the batch. The tabulation is accomplished on a keydriven device. The encoder can accumulate these totals while encoding. All of the characters on the check are printed in a special ink that can be magnetized just prior to reading. The equipment can only read characters printed in this special ink.

After the amount is encoded, the check can be processed on a *reader sorter,* as in Figure 6-16. The reader sorter performs two main activities. First, it reads the MICR encoded data and records it on a storage medium such as tape or disk. Second, it sorts all of the checks for each bank into separate stacks. Checks on other banks are forwarded to the clearinghouse, and checks written by the bank's own customers are then sorted into customer batches. At the end of the month, the computer prints a statement for each customer using tape or disk data created by the reader sorter. The statement and the checks are mailed to the customer.

ABA E-13-B

CMC-7

Figure 6-15 MICR (magnetic ink character recognition) type fonts.

Figure 6-16 A magnetic ink reader sorter.

The reader sorter can be either a standalone unit or an online unit. A *standalone unit* operates independently of the CPU. A keypunch is a good example of a standalone unit. When operating online, the reader sorter inputs data to the CPU.

Had it not been for MICR, the banking system could not have handled the large volume of checks during the past twenty-five years. But MICR is not a permanent cure. Bankers fear that the future volume of checks will be too great, even for MICR. Thirty-two billion checks were written in 1979, and the number increases by about 7% each year. One alternative being implemented on a gradual basis to reduce the number of checks is called *electronic funds transfer* (EFT).

In electronic funds transfer, money is transferred from one account to another electronically. Employers deposit employees' earnings directly into the employees' checking accounts. Withdrawals from the accounts are authorized by customers as purchases are made at retail stores, for example. The paper documents (the checks) are eliminated; all transfers are electronic. The automated teller machines currently in use by many banks are also part of the EFT system.

Optical character recognition

In addition to checks, there are other types of paper documents that present processing problems because of their large volumes. Examples are credit card invoices, airline tickets, insurance claims, vehicle registrations, and court records.

Optical character recognition (OCR) equipment has been designed to read the data from these and other forms at high speeds. The data is printed in ordinary ink, but the forms usually must be specially designed to facilitate the reading process.

A standard OCR type font, called OCR-A, has been adopted for use in the U.S. In Europe, the standard font is OCR-B. Manufacturers of OCR equipment produce machines specially designed to read these or other fonts. Some examples appear in Figure 6-17. A machine designed to read only one font is called a *single-font* reader. A machine designed to read several specific fonts is called a *multiple-font* reader. A machine that can read nearly all fonts intermixed, without being restricted to a predetermined set, is called a *multifont* reader.

In addition to reading *machine-printed* characters, OCR units can read *marks* made with any type of writing instrument, not just a soft-lead pencil. As long as the mark is dark, it can be read. Many colleges use OCR reading units for scoring true-false and multiple-choice tests. Readers designed to read only marks are much

IBM

IBM 1403 #022

ABCDEFGHIJKLMNOPQRSTUVWXYZ
1234567890   +-/◻*ə#$%¢&( )=≠

IBM 1428 OCR 009

ABCDEFGHIJKLMNOPQRSTUVWXYZ
1234567890   +-/*≢

OCR-A (The American Standard)

OCR-A

ABCDEFGHIJKLMNOPQRSTUVWXYZ
1234567890 +-/ ΥΗ♪$%&*?

OCR-B (The European Standard)

OCR-B

ABCDEFGHIJKLMNOPQRSTUVWXYZ
1234567890   +-/*ə£$&( )#¤≤≥<>%↑

Figure 6-17 Several OCR (optical character recognition) type fonts.

Figure 6-18 The Input 80 optical character recognition system.

less expensive than those designed to read characters. The units need only determine the presence of a mark—not its shape.

The use of OCR that seems to have the most potential is reading hand-printed data. Several manufacturers, including Cognitronics, IBM, National Computer Systems, Recognition Equipment, and Scan-Data, produce equipment that can read *hand-printed numbers.* The numbers must be printed in boxes, and must match a predefined pattern or style, such as:

$$0\ |\ 2\ 3\ 4\ 5\ 6\ 7\ 8\ 9$$

In addition to numeric data, some of these readers can read selected alphabetic letters (three or four) and special characters. At present, no unit on the market can read *hand-printed alphanumeric* data, which would include all letters, all numbers, and a set of special characters. There has been even less success in reading *hand-written* data. The irregularities of handwriting continue to be a problem to the designers of OCR equipment.

OCR units also differ in the sizes of paper documents they handle. Some, called *page readers,* read full-size 8½-by-11-inch pages; others, called *document readers,* read small, coupon-size slips. Some, such as the Recognition Equipment Input 80, can read intermixed documents varying in size from 2.9 by 2.75 inches to 12 by 14 inches. Paper weight can vary from 18-pound to card stock. The Input 80 is pictured in Figure 6-18.

Figure 6-19 A retail terminal with an OCR wand.

Point-of-sale recording The use of MICR by the banking industry never varied from its original course, but OCR use has been more dynamic. We are presently in the midst of an OCR boom in retailing. Many department stores use *point-of-sale (POS)* terminals with *OCR wands*. In Figure 6-19, a retail clerk optically reads product identification data from a price tag. The large chains such as J. C. Penney, Sears, and Wards have adopted this technology in an effort to speed up service and reduce errors. Many local stores use OCR-equipped POS terminals as well. Manufacturers of this equipment claim error-free data entry and transaction times reduced by as much as 20–30%.

Data from a POS terminal can be transmitted to the store's central computer, perhaps miles away, where the appropriate records are updated immediately. For example, inventory records can be updated to reflect the sale. This is an example of online processing. In some instances, the sales clerk will key in the customer's driver's license number, and the computer will perform a credit check. When the computer responds to the physical system with signals that affect the performance of the system, the computer is operating in realtime.

Another retail application of OCR is in the supermarket industry. The bar code printed on food labels is called the *universal product code (UPC)*. This code was adopted in the early seventies by a trade association of food marketing firms. Part of the bar code identifies the manufacturer, and part identifies the specific item. The price is not included in the code, nor is it printed on the item. While eliminating the expense of price marking, this practice of omitting the price from the item has caused some consumer resistance. The price is attached to the shelf

Figure 6-20 A universal product code reader in a supermarket.

for the consumer's benefit and stored in an onsite mini or micro for calculating the bill. But consumers want the price on the item as well, so they know at the checkout stand whether the price in the computer is consistent with the price on the shelf. Such consumer resistance has led several state legislatures to pass laws requiring all merchandise to be price-marked.

Each checkout register in a POS system contains an OCR unit that reads the bar code, as in Figure 6-20. If an item has no code printed on it, the clerk must enter the code on a keyboard. As each item is handled, the store computer retrieves the price from storage. When all item data has been entered, the computer calculates the tax and totals the bill.

The store computer can record transaction data on cassette tape or floppy disk, or it can communicate with a large central computer. The store manager can use a terminal to obtain information describing the store's performance.

OCR has been used primarily to reduce the cost of large-volume jobs. One state government saves more than $250,000 a year in the area of driver and vehicle licensing alone. Another state saves $1.2 million annually in processing medical claims and has reduced payment turnaround time from two months to two weeks. Table 6-1 lists some application areas where OCR has proven effective.

Table 6-1 OCR Application Areas

Business or Agency	Application	OCR Requirements
Government Agencies		
Department of Motor Vehicles	• Driver's license processing • Bonded insurance inquiries • Vehicle renewal registrations • Court records • Vehicle inspection reports	• Multifont reading • Carbon-copy reading • Handprint recognition, mark-sense capability • High-volume throughput • Wide variety of form sizes
Human Resources Development Agency	• Wage and salary reports • Applications for disability and unemployment insurance • Testing & evaluation forms	• Multifont reading • High-volume throughput • Handprint recognition, mark-sense capability
Social Service Organizations, Mental Health and Mental Rehabilitation Agencies	• Social service applications • MEDICAID claims • Timekeeping/functional accounting & recording • Inspection & licensing of various public functions including eating establishments, etc.	• High-volume throughput, multifont reading • Handprint recognition, mark-sense capability • Handprint recognition, mark-sense capability
State Controllers' Offices	• Payroll • Claims	• Wide variety of form sizes, high-volume throughput
Banking	• Customer services such as loan applications • Interbank transfers • Bank card processing • Lock box processing	• High-volume throughput • Handprint recognition, multifont and multiple font reading
Insurance Industry		
Service Bureaus	• Claims processing services for independent insurance agencies	• Multifont reading • Carbon-copy reading • High-volume throughput
Fire, Life, Casualty Insurance	• Daily reports • Claims processing • Premium billings • Account status changes	• Multifont reading • Carbon-copy reading • High-volume throughput • Handprint recognition • Wide variety of form sizes • Intermixed document sizes
Health Insurance	• Subscribers' providers' claims processing for MEDICARE and MEDICAID programs • Private business • Payment processing	• Multifont carbon-copy reading • Reading of carbon imprint from subscribers' plastic cards, imprinters' date wheels, or providers' plastic cards • Reading of both carbon and other impressions on same line • Processing of documents with labels attached

Table 6-1 (Continued)

Business or Agency	Application	OCR Requirements
Education	• Student recordkeeping • Enrollment • Test grading	• Mark-sense capability • High-volume throughput • Carbon-copy reading • Handprint recognition
Retail	• Inventory • Payment processing • Order entry	• Handprint recognition • High-volume throughput • Wide variety of form sizes

SOURCE: Recognition Equipment Incorporated.

Audio Response and Voice Recognition

Audio output, or *audio response,* has not been difficult for computer equipment manufacturers to achieve. Words are recorded on a magnetic drum in much the same manner as sound is recorded by a tape recorder. The stored computer program can select words from the drum to form a sentence, which is usually transmitted over a communication line or circuit.

In use since the third generation, audio response units can store a vocabulary of from 30 to as many as 1500 words. The user can choose between a male and a female voice. With an audio response unit as part of the computer system, any push-button telephone becomes a terminal. For example, assume that a manager wants to know the stock status of a particular inventory item. The manager dials the computer number and, when a connection is made, keys in a code identifying a "request for a stock status" along with the item number. The keying is done on the telephone's push-buttons. The computer retrieves the inventory record from the data base and selects vocabulary words to form a response. The computer might respond, for example, "Item one-four-three-six balance on hand four-six-two-nine, quantity on order eight-four-six." Audio response provides another mode for the presentation of information to the manager—information limited in volume, such as brief query responses.

Audio input has been a more difficult task for computer manufacturers. In 1970 Threshold Technology began to manufacture commercial voice recognition systems. Today the firm has systems installed to perform applications such as warehousing, numerical control of production machines, quality control, and banking and commodity exchange procedures. Centigram Corporation, another manufacturer, produces a low-cost system called MIKE that can learn to recognize up to sixteen words. This unit has become popular with hobbyists who like to build their own equipment.

In 1978 Interstate Electronics Corporation introduced the first voice-operated intelligent terminal. The user tailors the system to recognize her or his voice

Figure 6-21 A voice recognition unit.

by repeating a word from three to ten times. This is an example of a *speaker-dependent* system. (See Figure 6-21.) The Interstate Electronics system has been used in oil exploration, aircraft maintenance, geophysics, and quality control. The unit works well when a person (such as a quality-control inspector in a factory) would otherwise have to stop working to record data.

Verbex, Inc., a member of the Exxon Information Group, has developed a system that does not have to be conditioned to a specific user's voice. This type of system is *speaker-independent*. There are still problems, however, with accents, dialects, and frequency (for instance, females have higher voices than males). Industry experts believe we are still five to fifteen years away from natural-speech recognition.

Voice recognition can play an important role in the MIS. Handicapped programmers, for example, can use a voice recognition unit to code programs by speaking the instructions: "Compute gross equals rate times hours." Rick Pilgrim, a quadriplegic programmer for the National Institute of Health, uses an Interstate unit to code programs in the COBOL language. The unit, located in his home, is conditioned to recognize Rick speaking the special COBOL words. The system operates 95–100% accurately and automatically compensates for the slight change in voice when Rick catches a cold.

Voice recognition is also expected to make it easier to use word processing systems. It will be possible to speak certain key phrases and control words rather than use a keyboard. In addition, voice recognition will make it easier for managers to use certain software packages. A manager can enter decisions and data into a mathematical model, for example, by means of a voice recognition unit.

Printers

Beginning with the first computer, the most common way to obtain human-readable output has been the printer. Currently there are three types of printers in use. The first printers were called *line printers* since they print a line at a time. Next came slower-speed, less expensive *serial printers* that print one character at a time like a typewriter. Most recently there have been efforts to produce very high speed printers, called *page printers*. Both line and serial printers are online devices. Some page printers can be operated offline.

Line printers

All line printers are impact printers that can print multiple characters on a line simultaneously. The first line printers used a mechanism of 120 *print wheels*— one wheel per printing position. Each wheel had the characters embossed around the perimeter. Next came the *print drum,* a metal cylinder with embossed characters around the surface. Drums, still in use, have a set of characters for each printing position. Most line printers today print a 132-character line. Another popular technology is the *print chain,* which looks like a bicycle chain with two embossed characters on each link. There are five sets of characters on the chain. The chain rotates in a horizontal plane, and hammers fire at the appropriate time to cause the characters to print. A recent improvement in the print chain has been the *print train*—the same basic principle, but the links are not connected. The links move in a track to achieve greater speed. The most recent development is the *print band,* a steel ribbon with embossed characters that moves in the same horizontal plane as the chain.

Drum and chain printers operate in the range of 600 to 1000 lines per minute (lpm). Train printers are capable of 2500 lpm. Band printers operate from relatively slow speeds of 300 lpm up to 1800 lpm. The Burroughs B9246-6 band printer in Figure 6-22 prints at 450, 600, or 650 lpm, depending on the number of characters in the character set.

Throughout the computer era, line printers have been the workhorse output device, capable of high volumes. They are found on most medium- and large-scale systems. Some systems include multiple printers operating under the control of a single control unit.

Figure 6-22   A line printer.

Serial printers

Serial printers are often called *character printers* because they print one character at a time. Their development has coincided with the expansion of the small-system market. Serial printers provide the printed output for practically all micro systems and for a large number of minis.

Figure 6-23 shows a photograph of a Dataproducts M-100 matrix printer attached to a Digital PDP-11/34 mini. The M-100 uses a 9 by 9 dot matrix that makes possible the high-density printing required for graphics. Printing is bidirectional at a speed of 140 characters per second (cps).

Serial printers use the same technology and are capable of the same speeds as hardcopy terminals. In some cases, the mechanisms are identical. In other cases, such as the M-100 in Figure 6-23, the keyboard has been removed. The print quality of serial printers is superior to that of line printers. In fact, some serial printers are capable of "letter quality" printing. This high quality, plus the ability of some models to prepare graphical output, makes the serial printer an effective output unit for preparing management information.

Figure 6-23 A serial printer as part of a mini.

Page printers

Page printers are used by organizations with tremendous volumes of printed output, such as the federal government, insurance companies, and banks. The printers produce mostly data documents, such as claim checks and bank statements, rather than management reports.

Three manufacturers have introduced page printers:

Manufacturer	Model	Speeds (lpm)
Honeywell	Page Processing System	2000–18,000
IBM	3800 Printing Subsystem	13,360
Xerox	Model 9700	8000–18,000

The Xerox and Honeywell systems are offline, standalone units controlled by a mini and a micro respectively. The IBM is used online with a System/370. All three printers use laser technology for nonimpact printing. The Xerox unit is pictured in Figure 6-24.

Because page printers are nonimpact, they produce only single copies. If you want six copies, you print the same document six times. In addition to the high speed, page printers permit printing at greater densities than line printers. (Some serial printers also have this feature.) This means that reports normally printed

Figure 6-24 A page printer.

on oversize paper can be reduced to a convenient 8½ by 11 inches. In addition, the 3800 offers eighteen different character sets and a forms overlay feature, which produces documents on blank paper that look as if they have been printed on custom forms. For example, the form of an insurance premium notice can be printed first and then data can be printed in the boxes. The paper cost is much lower than if preprinted forms were used.

The line printer has been the primary means of producing human-readable output. Its days seem numbered, however. The trend toward distributed processing will see more reports and documents printed on the serial printers of distributed systems, and fewer on the line printers of centralized systems. Page printers will continue to be used by organizations with massive volumes of printed output.

Today printed output represents an important way for the manager to receive information from the computer. But interest in online devices and graphics is increasing. This interest, combined with the high cost of printed output, indicates that the printer will probably become less significant in future MIS designs.[1]

---

[1] For several years a number of people in the computer industry have predicted the demise of printed output. For a good analysis of the problem, see Tim Tyler, "Don't Bet on Paper Output," *Datamation* 24 (September 1978): 266 ff.

Figure 6-25 An electrostatic plotter.

Plotters

Special output devices called *plotters* are used to display information graphically on paper. There are two types—the pen plotter and the electrostatic plotter.

The *pen plotter* uses from one to eight pens with different colored ink to draw lines. The pens can be pressurized ball point, liquid ink, nylon tip, or liquid ball. The pen plotter moves the pen quite rapidly, at speeds approximating 30 inches per second. But since only one pen can be used at a time, a rather complex graph can require several minutes to complete.

Pen plotters come in two styles. In the *flatbed* plotter, the paper remains stationary on a large table. The pens move in two directions across the width and length of the paper, tracing the path of both the X and Y axes. In the *drum* plotter, the paper is wrapped around two rollers, with the pen mechanism in between. The rollers move the paper back and forth, and this action, combined with the movement of the pens, draws lines at the proper angles on the paper.

The nonimpact technology developed with printers has been applied to plotters. Nonimpact plotters use an electrostatic process (as does a copying machine) and are called *electrostatic plotters*. These plotters are capable of speeds of up to 3.25 inches per second. Output is in black and white. Electrostatic plotters come in only one style—with plotting accomplished on a continuous roll of paper as it moves through the unit at a fixed rate.

A photograph of the CalComp 5500 electrostatic plotter appears in Figure 6-25. The 5500 plots on 36-inch-wide paper at a speed of 1.62 inches per second.

Figure 6-26 A controller, used for offline plotting.

It can be used online with minicomputers, or it can be used offline with the CalComp 953 Controller, pictured in Figure 6-26. The Controller includes a microcomputer that translates plot data from prerecorded magnetic tape and outputs the data to an electrostatic plotter (such as the 5500) or to a pen plotter.

To prepare graphical output on a computer, you need a computer (naturally), a plotter, data, and software to guide the plotter.[2] During recent years, big advancements have been made in the software. With a software system such as Trend-Spotter '82, marketed by Computer Pictures Corporation, a manager can use very simple language to obtain the sales graphs in Figure 6-27. Some of the graphics packages can present the information in a three-dimensional form, as shown in Figure 6-28. This three-dimensional graph showing the top hundred U.S. computer markets was prepared using the DISSPLA package marketed by

---

[2]Two excellent manuals on the design of computer graphics have been prepared by ISSCO Graphics: Alan Paller, Kathryn Szoka, and Nan Nelson, *Choosing the Right Chart;* and Anders Vinberg, *Designing a Good Graph.*

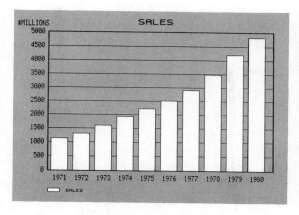

To get a bar graph of sales,
we simply type
BAR SALES.

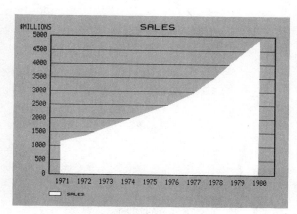

To get an area chart,
we would type
AREA SALES.

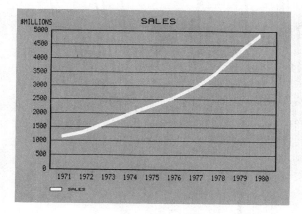

To get a line graph,
we would type
LINE SALES.

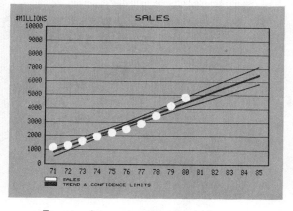

To get a dot graph, plus a 4-year forecast
with confidence limits, type
HORIZONTAL + 4 DOT SALES LIMITS.

Figure 6-27 With a graphics software package such as Trend-Spotter '82, the manager uses very simple language.

ISSCO Graphics. Graphics such as these—and the relative ease with which they can be obtained—provide the modern manager with an information form not possible twenty years ago.[3]

[3] For more information on computer graphics, see Alan T. Paller, "Improving Management Productivity with Computer Graphics," *IEEE Computer Graphics and Applications* 1 (October 1981): 9–16; Robrt L. Janson, "Graphic Indicators of Operations," *Harvard Business Review* 57 (November–December 1980): 164–170: and Anders Vinberg and James E. George, "Computer Graphics and the Business Executive—The New Management Team," *IEEE Computer Graphics and Applications* 1 (January 1981): 57–71.

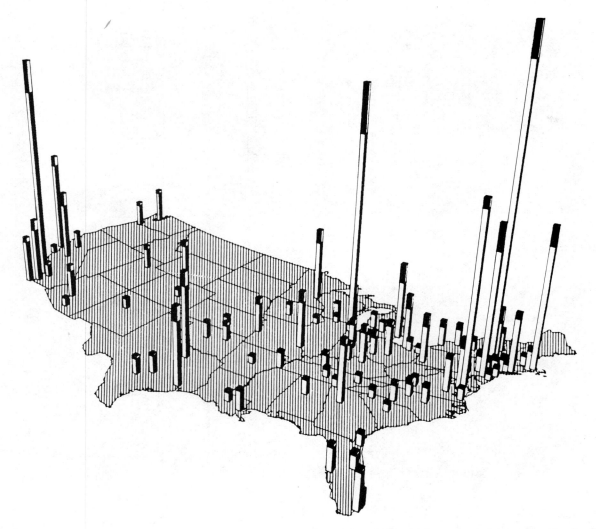

Figure 6-28 This three-dimensional graph showing the top hundred U.S. computer markets was prepared using the DISSPLA graphics system from ISSCO Graphics.

Computer Output Microfilm

Organizations have long been plagued by large volumes of paper. And high-speed computer printers have only intensified the problem. Computer users must continually work to maintain paper volumes within reasonable limits and to control the use and storage of necessary documents.

Microfilm has been an effective way to cope with these paper volumes. Paper documents can be microfilmed and stored in about 2% of the space required for paper documents. Additional devices are used to retrieve, view, and print selected microfilm images.

Figure 6-29 An online computer output microfilm (COM) unit.

This microfilming, storage, and retrieval process has been computerized. It is possible to attach an output unit to a computer channel that will prepare *computer output microfilm* (COM) images online. The Kodak Komstar 200 pictured in Figure 6-29 is a COM unit. The Kobstar 200 includes (1) a controller for attaching the unit to the channel, (2) a minicomputer that controls the microfilming process, and (3) the laser printer, film transport, and dryer.

Microfilm refers to rolled film in 16-, 35-, or 105-mm widths. Microfilm is one type of *microform,* which is the general term identifying all types of miniaturized records. In addition to microfilm, another type of microform is *microfiche,* a 4-by-6-inch card that contains up to 690 page images. The Komstar 200 prepares both 16-mm microfilm and microfiche at speeds four to eight times faster than an impact printer.

Figure 6-30 A microimage terminal.

After the microform is created, it is stored in an access file, such as the one at the operator's left in Figure 6-30. The unit at the right is a Kodak IMT-150 microimage terminal that retrieves a microfilm image from a reel and displays it on the screen. The terminal also prepares a dry printed copy in 12 seconds. The terminal includes a microprocessor that can search for as many as forty images at a time—each identified by reference number. The film is searched at speeds of up to 15 feet per second.

The microimage terminal and a conventional keyboard terminal (the unit in the center) can be used together for information retrieval. An insurance company, for example, may need to know the current status of a certain policy. The operator enters the policy number into the computer terminal, and the CPU retrieves the policy data from the data base and displays it on the CRT screen. In addition to policy data, a microfilm retrieval code is also displayed. The operator selects the microfilm magazine from the access file and inserts the magazine in the microimage terminal. The appropriate frame is automatically displayed on the screen.

This example of *image processing* is an integral part of office automation. A clerical employee can retrieve data from the data base and document images from a microform access file.

It is also possible to make image processing available to a manager, although little work has been done in this area. The manager's terminal of the future will undoubtedly combine both information and image retrieval capabilities. For example, an image of a graph can be retrieved in seconds, along with pages from competitors' annual reports, pages of economic data, and so on.

Putting the I/O Devices in Perspective

We have identified many of the available I/O devices. Obviously not all firms need all of the devices. And not all of the devices have the same level of importance to an MIS.

The manager works with some of the devices or with their output. These devices make a *direct* contribution to the MIS. This group includes hardcopy and CRT terminals that a manager can use to interact with the computer, printers of all types that produce printed information, plotters that produce graphics, microimage terminals that provide images of documents, and both audio response and voice recognition units that permit audible interaction with the computer.

Other devices make an *indirect* contribution to the MIS. These devices convert large volumes of data to computer-readable form for entry into the data base. Although these devices do not produce information, they do provide the data resource from which information is produced. These data input devices include both offline and online keydriven devices, keyed media input units, MICR, OCR, and voice recognition units.

Figure 6-31 illustrates the role of these units in (1) providing a path for the data flow from the physical system of the firm to the data base, (2) providing a two-way communication path between the manager and the computer, and (3) providing a communication path from the manager to the physical system.

Of these three paths, the third is the least developed. If the manager is to communicate to the physical system through the MIS, the link will primarily involve word processing and, more generally, office automation developments such as electronic mail and teleconferencing. The I/O hardware and software on the market today address primarily the first two paths in Figure 6-31.

The figure illustrates vividly how the I/O devices, as part of the formal MIS, provide a link between the manager and the firm. In conjunction with the other MIS resources, these devices provide a "window" through which the manager can view the operation of the firm.

Summary

In terms of input/output equipment, early computers were relatively uncomplicated—card input and line printer output. Things are different now, with a wide variety of devices available, and card input and line printer output playing increasingly minor roles.

I/O devices are attached to the CPU by control units and channels. The channels facilitate multiprogramming by providing intermediate buffer storage

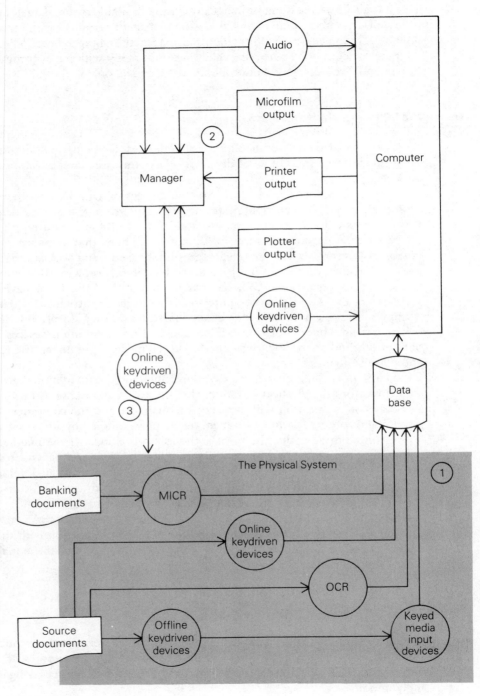

Figure 6-31 I/O devices in the MIS.

for data being read and written while the CPU is executing instructions. A single control unit can control several I/O devices, and a computer can have one or more channels.

Keydriven input devices create an input bottleneck. Efforts to replace the keypunch machine have included other offline media-recording devices such as key-to-tape and key-to-disk units. When offline media (cards, tapes, and disks) are created, a special input unit enters the data into the CPU. Punched cards, though rapidly decreasing in use, serve as turnaround documents and as records to track materials through one or more organizations.

The input device accounting for most of the interest today is the keyboard terminal. This online approach eliminates the need for both media and input units to read the media. Keyboard terminals come in two basic styles—CRT and hardcopy. CRT terminals can offer an excellent graphics capability, in color on certain models. It is also possible to produce graphs on some hardcopy terminals. Hardcopy terminals use two basic methods for printing—impact and nonimpact. A number of impact technologies are used, including dot matrix and daisywheel. Most hardcopy terminals use impact technology. Nonimpact terminals are more expensive and can produce only one copy at a time.

Source data automation (SDA) is a way to ease the input bottleneck. Documents are designed so that their data is computer-readable. Magnetic ink character recognition (MICR) and optical character recognition (OCR) are examples of SDA. MICR is still limited to banking applications, but OCR applies to a number of industries. Currently retailing is embracing the OCR approach with the increasing use of OCR wands in department stores and universal product code readers in supermarkets. MICR is gradually being replaced by electronic funds transfer (EFT). The point-of-sale retailing terminals are rapidly becoming a part of EFT.

Computer manufacturers and users have long been intrigued by the idea of audio input and output. Audio response provides the manager with the opportunity to use an ordinary push-button telephone as a terminal. Improvements in MIS performance made possible by voice recognition should be realized during the next few years.

Printers have always produced most of the human-readable computer output. Line printers are giving up much of this volume to serial printers attached to minis, micros, and distributed systems. Page printers are restricted to use by organizations with extra-large printing volumes. Most of the output produced by all of these printers is data rather than information. Line and serial printers come in impact and nonimpact styles; all page printers are nonimpact.

Plotters were initially used for design and engineering jobs, but more recently they have been integrated into MIS configurations. The plotters, combined with CRT terminals, give the manager an excellent tool for distilling large quantities of data into the essential elements.

Another means of combatting large data quantities is computer output microfilm (COM). With COM it is possible to prepare printed output in a form that requires only a fraction of the space required by paper, often at speeds faster than those of impact printers. The COM units, like the plotters, can be operated either online or offline.

Some of the I/O devices, such as keyboard terminals, printers, and plotters, provide the manager with a direct link to the MIS. Other devices, such as OCR readers and COM recorders, play important roles in creating and maintaining the data base. Today there are a wide variety of I/O devices available to meet the unique needs of a manager, a firm, or an industry.

Key Terms

cathode ray tube (CRT)

control unit

channel

serial transfer, parallel transfer

input bottleneck

turnaround document

alphanumeric display terminal, video display terminal

cursor

hardcopy terminal, teleprinter terminal

impact printer, nonimpact printer

dot matrix printer

daisywheel printer

ink jet printer

thermal printer

source data automation (SDA)

magnetic ink character recognition (MICR)

E-13-B type font

encoder

reader sorter

standalone unit

electronic funds transfer (EFT)

optical character recognition (OCR)

single-font, multiple-font, multifont reader

page reader, document reader

point of sale (POS)

OCR wand

universal product code (UPC)

audio response

speaker-dependent, speaker-independent voice recognition

line printer

serial printer, character printer

page printer

pen plotter

flatbed plotter, drum plotter

electrostatic plotter

computer output microfilm (COM)

microfilm, microform, microfiche

image processing

Key Concepts

The trend to medialess input

The manner in which the CPU, channel, control unit, and I/O unit work as a system in input and output operations

Steps taken to relieve the input bottleneck

The use of the punched card as a turnaround document

The advantages of a keyboard terminal as a link between the manager and the MIS

How source data automation relieves the input bottleneck

The potential role of audible input and output in an MIS

The changing role of printed output in an MIS

The requirement for both special hardware and special software to obtain graphical output

How image processing operates in conjunction with data and information processing

The direct and indirect contributions of I/O devices to the MIS

Questions

1. Name the four basic ways to enter data into a computer.

2. Name the three permanent forms of output media. Name two nonpermanent forms.

3. Why do computer systems include channels?

4. What is the input bottleneck? Name three devices that have been developed to relieve the bottleneck.

5. In your opinion, why are keyboard terminals more popular than key-to-disk and key-to-tape units?

6. Describe two application areas where punched cards are still used.

7. Why would a manager prefer a CRT terminal over a hardcopy terminal? When would a hardcopy terminal be preferred?

8. What hardware do banks need to read magnetically encoded characters and route checks to their destination?

9. Why are UPC readers used in supermarkets? Which group has resisted the use of the readers? What is their complaint?

10. Which has been easiest to achieve, audio input or output? Why?

11. Can a voice recognition unit handle the differences in speech patterns between users? Explain your answer.

12. What is the difference, if any, between a serial printer and a hardcopy terminal?

13. Rank the three basic types of printers in terms of their importance in a *data* processing system (such as accounting applications). Do the same for an *information* processing system (such as a DSS).

14. What are the two types of plotters? Name one advantage of each.

15. What elements are needed in order to produce graphical output on a computer?

16. What are the characteristics of firms that use COM?

17. What are the two types of microform?

18. What is image processing?

19. List the I/O devices that make a direct contribution to the MIS. List those that make an indirect contribution.

20. Which I/O devices provide both an input and an output capability?

Problems

1. Fill in the following diagram to show the various types of printers.

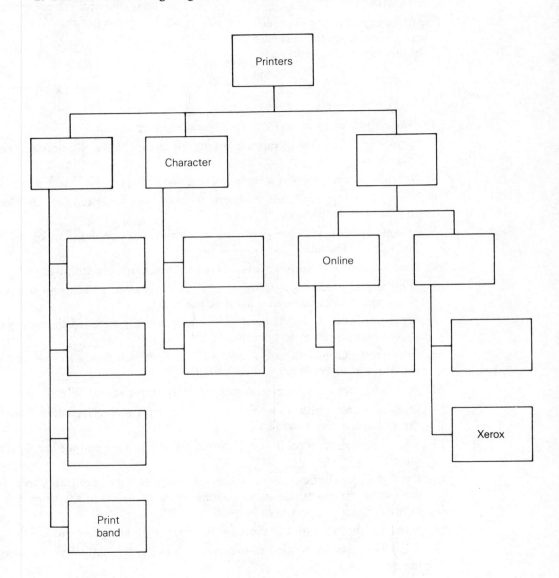

2. Fill in the following diagram to show the various types of keyboard terminals.

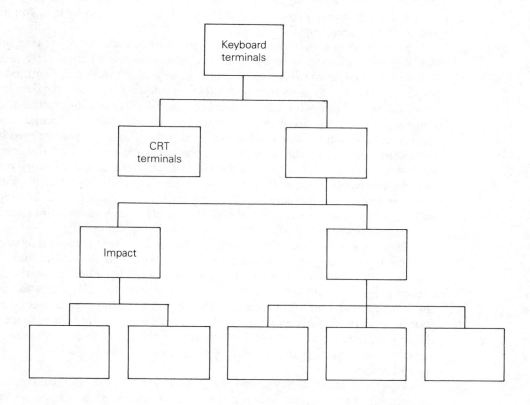

CASE PROBLEM: Wellborn's Department Stores

Wellborn's is a Midwest chain of seventeen department stores, with headquarters in Chicago. The IBM 4331-1 at headquarters is used for inventory, sales analysis, and charge account collections. The 4331 is a medium-scale computer with sufficient speed and capacity to handle the Wellborn's volume with room to spare. Any type of input/output device can be attached to the 4331.

You are a senior business systems major and you sign up for an interview with Wellborn's. At the appointed time, you meet Joe Biggs, the vice-president of information systems. You and Joe chat for a while, and then he tells you about the Wellborn operation.

Sales clerks in each of the seventeen stores write up sales on paper sales forms. All of the information is recorded on the forms—customer name and address, items purchased, quantities, and prices. Charge account sales are identified with a special code. The forms are mailed daily to headquarters, where the data is keypunched on one of twelve keypunch machines. The data is then entered into the computer, where the inventory and sales records are updated. Charge account data is recorded on a collection file that is used monthly to prepare printed statements. In addition to the statement, a punched card turnaround document is enclosed. When the customer pays the bill, the card data is read by a card reader, and the receivable amount is removed from the collection file. Printed management reports are also prepared on the line printer on a monthly basis. The reports include a list of inventory items showing monthly sales and quantities on hand and a list of all past-due collections (those over thirty days old).

Biggs explains to you that the store managers have been complaining because they don't have enough information on inventory status and collections. They claim that their information is outdated when they receive it because of the delays caused by mailing and keypunching. As a rule, it takes four days after the end of the month to enter all of the month's sales data in the computer. It takes three or four more days for the reports to reach managers by mail. And the managers get the reports only once a month. The reports are practically useless, the managers complain, because they do not represent the actual status of the stores' inventories and collections.

Biggs looks you in the eye and says, "You have had the opportunity to study modern input and output devices during your academic program. I want you to think about our situation and to recommend the new equipment that you think we need. Cost is no problem. Just tell me which units we need and how they will be used."

Questions

1. What is the problem?
2. Can the problem be solved with I/O hardware? Explain.
3. Can the same I/O equipment affect both the inventory and the collections applications? Explain.

Chapter 7

Secondary Storage Media and Devices

Learning Objectives

After studying this chapter, you should:

- Know the data hierarchy within a data base
- Know the two basic types of secondary storage and the media representing each type
- Know how data is recorded on magnetic tape
- Know the uses of magnetic tape
- Appreciate early direct access storage device (DASD) technology, as represented by the IBM 305 RAMAC
- Understand some of the basics of current DASD technology
- Know how data is recorded in a magnetic disk unit
- Have a general understanding of the characteristics of several IBM DASDs
- Recognize three types of DASD in addition to magnetic disks—two successful and the third unsuccessful
- Know the basic DASD file organization methods
- Know the uses of DASD
- Understand what the term virtual storage means and generally how it works

When we introduced computer storage in Chapter 5, we presented the *computer schematic,* recognizing the two basic types of storage—the *primary storage* of the CPU and the *secondary storage* that augments it. Most of our discussion centered on primary storage. We saw how it is used in five basic ways—the five conceptual areas. We also took note of the physical construction in terms of its organization (bits, bytes, and words) and its technology (magnetic core and metal-oxide-semiconductor). Finally, we identified three coding systems (BCD, EBCDIC, and ASCII) that have been used to represent data in storage. Our discussion of primary storage in Chapter 5 is adequate for our study of the MIS. But we have not devoted much attention to secondary storage. In Chapter 5 we recognized that magnetic tapes and magnetic disks are used for secondary storage. In this chapter we will provide more information on these two media. In addition, we will describe a third type—magnetic tape cartridge. These are three common forms of secondary storage. We will discuss two others in later chapters. Floppy disks are used as secondary storage on mini/micro systems, and we will include them in Chapter 10. Optical disks are a possible medium of the future, and they will be described in Chapter 20.

Secondary Storage in the General Systems Model

The first computers used secondary storage to augment the limited capacity of primary storage—usually 32KB or less. Primary storage capacities have continually expanded since those early days, but so have total storage needs. Consequently, the current demand for secondary storage is greater than ever before. A study of users of large-scale IBM systems revealed an increase in secondary storage capacity at a compounded growth rate of 45% since 1971.[1] Another estimate puts the growth as high as 70% a year.[2]

Figure 7-1 positions secondary storage within the general systems model. As the figure indicates, the storage has two basic uses, housing two important elements of the MIS—the data base and the software library. Both of these elements have increased in importance during recent years, and this has produced an accompanying increase in storage demands.

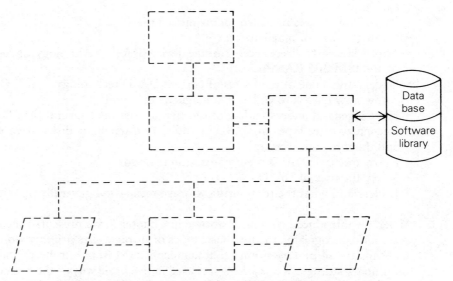

Figure 7-1 Secondary storage in the general systems model.

[1] Marilyn Bohl, *Introduction to IBM Direct Access Storage Devices* (Palo Alto: Science Research Associates, 1981), p. 116.

[2] John W. Verity, "Storage for the Masses," *Datamation* 27 (October 1981): 56.

The data base contains the logically integrated records of many of the firm's activities. The software library contains both systems and applications software. Efficient use of the data base and software requires secondary storage that offers large capacity, rapid access, and low cost.

Data Hierarchy

Data exists in a hierarchy, with names identifying each level. At the lowest level is the *data item,* such as an employee number. All of the data items that describe an object or subject are assembled to form a *record.* For example, all of the payroll data about an employee form a payroll record. All of the records of a type are accumulated in a *file.* A firm has one or more payroll files—perhaps a salaried payroll file, an hourly payroll file, and so forth. (Another name used to describe a computer-based file is *data set,* but we will not use that term here.) When several files are integrated logically, they are called a *data base.* The data base is covered in the next chapter.

Types of Secondary Storage

There are two basic types of secondary storage—sequential and direct. In *sequential storage* the data records are arranged in sequence based on a code called the key. The *key* is simply a data item that identifies a record. For example, the key for a payroll file would most likely be the employee's number. The key field in each record identifies that particular record. If the payroll file is arranged sequentially, the records are ordered with the lowest numbered record first and the highest numbered record last. This is an ascending sequence; it is also possible to arrange records in a descending sequence. This arranging is accomplished by the sort/merge program, which is part of the operating system. The most common medium for sequential storage is magnetic tape.

Sequential storage offers both economy and efficiency. Very little storage space and time are wasted in creating and updating the files. However, the main restriction is that records must be processed sequentially; i.e., the first record on the tape must be processed first, the second must be processed second, and so on. Sequential processing is required because there is no practical way to directly access individual records in the file without a sequential search.[3] Since it is impractical to search a sequential file to process each transaction separately, the transactions are usually accumulated in batches. Sequential files require batch processing.

Direct storage was invented to overcome the sequential processing requirement of sequential storage. With direct storage an access mechanism can move a

---

[3] One approach to retrieving a record from a sequential file is to use a technique called *binary search.* The key of the desired record is compared to the key of the record in the middle of the file to determine which half contains the desired record. Then the key is compared to that of the record in the middle of the selected half. This comparison continues until only a small area remains, which is then searched sequentially. For more details, see Bohl, p. 123.

read/write head directly to the desired record. The device making this possible is called a *direct access storage device (DASD).*

Magnetic disk storage has been, is now, and probably will be in the near future the most common type of DASD. There are two basic types of disks in use at the present time—the hard disks of the larger systems, and the floppies of the mini/micro systems.

In addition to disks, other types of DASD are magnetic tape cartridges, magnetic cards, magnetic drums, and metal-oxide-semiconductor (MOS) chips. Of these four types, only the tape cartridges and MOS chips are in current use. The cartridges provide exceptionally large capacities at modest speeds. The MOS devices provide the opposite support—modest capacities at high speeds. Disks represent an attractive compromise for the vast area between the two.

Direct storage is designed for direct access, facilitating online processing. But it is also possible to use a DASD as a sequential medium and to process the data in batches. When we discussed batch and online processing in Chapter 5, we drew the distinction between "now" and "later." If you handle a transaction now (online processing), you need DASD. If you handle a transaction later (batch processing), you can use magnetic tape or a DASD. DASD can be used for *both* online and batch processing, but magnetic tape can be used only for batch.

The remainder of the chapter will address magnetic tape, DASD, and a relatively new concept in storage use—virtual storage.

Magnetic Tape Storage

Magnetic tape has consistently provided an attractive storage alternative. It is fast—data can be read or written at speeds from 20KB to 1250KB per second. It is compact—a 2400-foot reel of half-inch-wide tape can contain more than 141.5 million bytes of data.[4] It is economical—a reel of tape costs in the neighborhood of $30.

Computer tape is used in basically the same manner as sound recording tape. But instead of recording sound magnetically in frequencies, computer tape records data magnetically in combinations of bits. The eight data bits of a byte are written across the width of the tape, along with a check bit. The check bit is used to signal an error caused by adding or losing bits accidentally. A large number of bytes can be recorded on an inch of tape. The standard *recording densities* are 200, 556, 800, 1600, and 6250 bytes per inch (bpi).

To record data, you place a reel of tape on a *magnetic tape unit,* often called a *tape drive,* shown in Figure 7-2. The leading portion of the tape is automatically threaded through a read/write mechanism and wrapped around the hub of a takeup reel. As data is written onto the tape or read from it by the read/write

---

[4]This capacity is calculated by subtracting a 25-foot header and a 16-foot trailer leader from the 2400-foot length, multiplying the available area (2359 feet) by 12 to obtain the number of recording inches (28,308), multiplying this figure by 0.8 for the 80% of the area that will be used for data recording (22,646.4), and finally multiplying by the recording density of 6250 bpi. The 80% figure is an estimate.

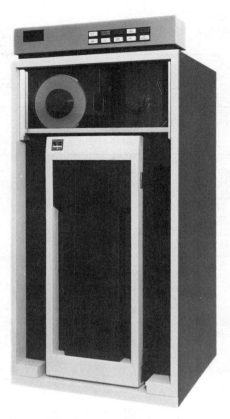

Figure 7-2 A magnetic tape unit.

mechanism, the tape winds onto the takeup reel. When all the data has been read from the file or written onto it, the reels rewind and you remove the source reel.

There is considerable variation in the performance characteristics of the many tape units on the market. The Burroughs unit in Figure 7-2 handles 1600-bpi tape at a data transfer rate of 40KB per second. When the last record is written on the reel, the tape rewinds at 100 inches per second, taking a little over two minutes for a 2400-foot reel. The fastest IBM unit, the 3420 model 8, handles 6250-bpi tape at a transfer rate of 1250KB per second. Rewind time is 45 seconds.

How data is recorded on tape

The capacity of a tape reel in bytes depends on how the data is recorded on the tape. Figure 7-3 shows how the parts of a tape are used for different purposes. Part of the tape is used to attach the tape to the two reels. These parts are called *leaders*. Data is not recorded on these areas.

In many systems the first and last records on the tape are used for control purposes. These records are known as *labels*. The one at the beginning of the tape is the *header label*. The one at the end is the *trailer label*. The header identifies

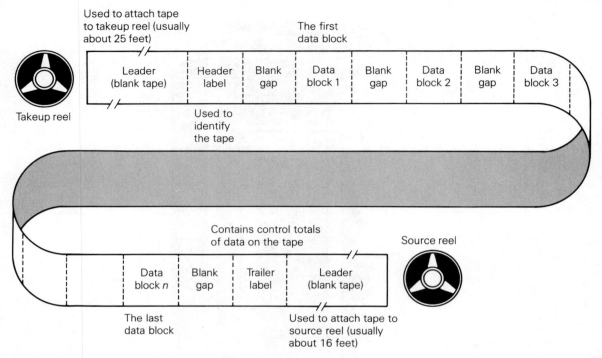

Figure 7-3 A computer tape.

the reel to assure that the operator mounts the reel required by the program. The trailer label includes totals accumulated from records on the reel; the totals are used for control purposes.

Most of the tape is used for recording data. This data is written as *blocks* in the area between the labels. The tape unit writes the blocks and later reads them separately, one at a time. A block can contain a single record, as in Figure 7-4, or multiple records.

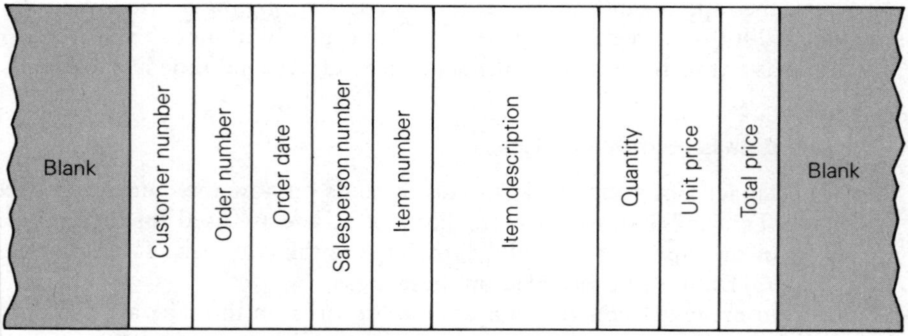

Figure 7-4 A single record written on tape.

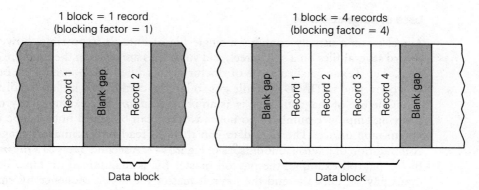

Figure 7-5 Blocks of data on magnetic tape.

Figure 7-5 illustrates how single or multiple records can be written in blocks. The number of records in a block is called the *blocking factor*. One block is read or written at a time, as shown in Figure 7-6. Each time the CPU directs the tape unit to write a block, the tape starts to move past the read/write mechanism. As the tape gets up to speed, some of it passes over the read/write mechanism before the first byte is written. Then, after the last byte is written, more tape passes over before coming to a stop. These blank areas are the gaps separating the blocks. They are called *interblock gaps* and usually occupy 0.6 inch.

There are two basic reasons for blocking records. First, blocking uses more tape for data and less for the blank gaps separating the blocks. If a tape unit records data at a density of 1600 bpi and the length of the interblock gap is 0.6 inches, the area occupied by the gap represents 960 bytes of wasted space. Second, the frequent starts and stops required by unblocked records waste valuable tape unit time. The time required to accelerate the tape unit to its rated speed so that a block can be read or written is measured in milliseconds. The unit could be reading thousands of bytes in the time it takes to stop and start.

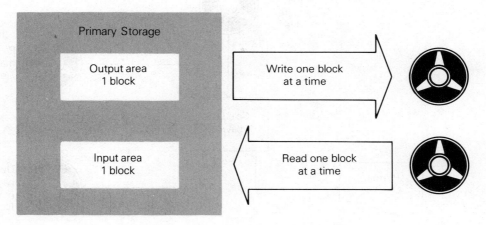

Figure 7-6 Tape data is written and read one block at a time.

Uses of magnetic tape

A reel of tape usually contains a single file of data. It is possible, however, to record several files on a single reel, and some files are so large they require several reels. The Texas Medicare file of doctor claims filled forty-seven reels before it was converted to DASD. The file got so large it couldn't be updated daily.

One use of magnetic tape is as an *input medium*. For example, payroll data showing employee number and hours worked can be keyed onto a tape using a key-to-tape device. The tape data can then be read into primary storage for a computation of payroll amounts, as in Figure 7-7. A second use is as a *file medium*. In the payroll example, the payroll master file is maintained on tape. Both the input payroll data file and the payroll master file are in sequence by employee number. This is an example of batch processing.

In Figure 7-7, an input payroll data record is read into primary storage along with the payroll master record. With both records for an employee in primary storage, the computer can multiply hourly rate (from the master record) by hours worked (from the payroll data record) to obtain gross pay. Then deductions are made, using data from the master record, to calculate net pay. While all of this data is in primary storage, a payroll check is printed on the line printer.

When a master record is involved in a transaction, it is said to be *active*. A high-activity file is one in which a large percentage of the records are active. Magnetic tape becomes more suitable as the storage medium as the activity increases, since read and write operations are not wasted on inactive records.

Before the next employee's records are read, an updated payroll master record is written. This updated record contains data such as gross pay to date, income tax to date, social security tax to date, and so on. These amounts reflect the results of the calculations just completed.

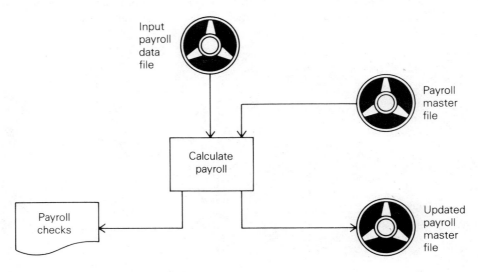

Figure 7-7 Updating the payroll master file.

The updated file is never written back onto the input reel. It is always written onto another reel. This is the third use of magnetic tape—as an *output medium*. The new file will provide the master data next time payroll computations are made; it now contains the curent data.

Magnetic tape also can be used as a *historical storage medium*. Since a reel of tape is so inexpensive and contains so much data in a small area, tape is ideal for historical storage. Accounting procedures require that historical data be retained for a period of time. This data provides the detailed description of what the firm has done. The firm may need to review this data for some reason, but the probability or frequency is too low to keep it in a more expensive form.

A final use of magnetic tape is as a *communication medium*. A reel can provide the communication from one computer program to another, such as from the payroll computation described above to a program that prints a payroll report for management. In addition, tape reels can be mailed or delivered to other computer sites.

During early generations, more computer systems were tape-oriented than disk-oriented. Today the opposite is true. DASD has replaced magnetic tape in many installations. Tape is still popular for both file and historical storage media. But as an input medium, tape plays a minor role compared to floppies and online terminal input. And with the trend away from batch processing, there is no great need to create an output tape to communicate with another program. Overall, magnetic tape remains valuable for its high performance and economical use. It should still be an important secondary storage medium for selected uses in the years to come.

Direct Access Storage Devices

In Chapter 5 we recognized the RAMAC as the first system to offer magnetic disk storage. By today's standards, RAMAC technology is extremely primitive.[5] There are two reasons, however, why a brief study of that early system is worthwhile. First, it provides a benchmark for measuring the advancement of technology over the past twenty-five years. Second, the simple design of the RAMAC makes it an excellent learning tool. From it we can learn some fundamentals that apply to modern units.

The RAMAC's input/output units were extremely slow, as were its CPU speeds. What made it special was a stack of fifty rotating metal disks—a *disk stack*. The stack was permanently housed in its cabinet and could contain 5 million characters. Data was organized in 100-character records, and any of the records could be retrieved in a maximum of 8/10 of a second. There was no need to scan records sequentially. The access mechanism could be directed to any record in the

---

[5]The following excellent reviews of the history of IBM magnetic storage media (tape and disk) can be found in the *IBM Journal of Research and Development* 25 (September 1981): L. D. Stevens, "The Evolution of Magnetic Storage," pp. 663–675; J. M. Harker et al., "A Quarter Century of Disk File Innovation," pp. 677–689; and J. P. Harris et al., "Innovations in the Design of Magnetic Tape Subsystems," pp. 691–699.

file. This meant transactions could be processed as they occurred; there was no need to batch them. This development marked the beginning of online processing.[6]

Record Addressing

Just as each location of primary storage has an address, so each recording location in a DASD has one also. The computer program using DASD data must provide this address to the access mechanism. In effect, the program says, "Get me the record at location 12345." The access mechanism moves to that part of the disk file and reads the record into primary storage. There the data is processed, and

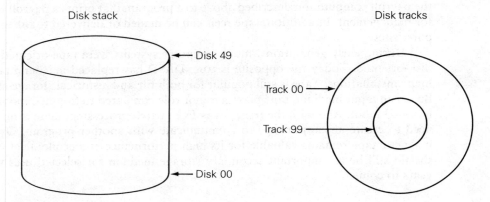

Figure 7-8 Data disks and tracks.

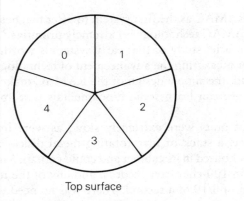
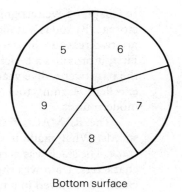

Figure 7-9 Recording sectors.

---

[6] At the time, IBM used the term *inline* instead of *online*. Inline meant that a transaction was completely handled before the next one was entered through the card reader. The term inline is no longer used.

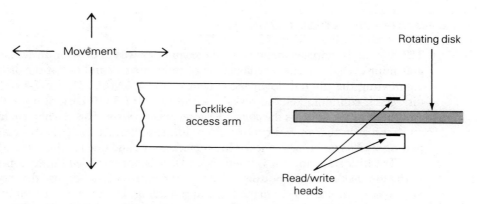

Figure 7-10   A single forklike access arm serves all 50 disks.

the updated record is written in the *same area* of the disk stack where it was recorded originally.

This constitutes a basic difference between disk and tape updating. Updated tape records are never written back on the same area from which they were read. Disk records usually are.

In the RAMAC, each of the fifty disks had a number—from 00 to 49—as in Figure 7-8. Data was recorded on both the top and bottom of each disk in *tracks*. There were 100 tracks on each side, numbered from 00 to 99.

Each disk was also divided into ten *sectors* like slices of a pie, as in Figure 7-9. The top surface of a disk included sectors 0 to 4, and sectors 5 to 9 were on the bottom. Each track in each sector had a capacity of 100 characters. (The recording density was greater for the inner tracks.)

The RAMAC had a single forklike access arm, shown in Figure 7-10. The fork could move from one disk to another, and in and out of the disk stack. The fork straddled each disk but did not touch the disk surface. Two small read/write heads were attached to the end of the arm, one for the top surface and one for the bottom.

Assume that the program calls for RAMAC record 12345. The positions of the address had special meanings, as shown in Figure 7-11. The access arm moved to *disk 12;* then it moved to *track 34.* As the disk rotated past the arm, the read/write head read the 100-character record from *sector 5.* When the updated record was written back to the file, the read/write head waited until sector 5 was reached before writing the data.

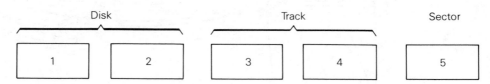

Figure 7-11   A DASD address.

Some Basics of Current DASD Technology

The first major improvement in DASD technology was to provide an access mechanism for each disk. The mechanism need only move in and out of the disk stack, eliminating the up-and-down movement of the RAMAC. Figure 7-12 shows a disk stack containing eleven disks, used in the IBM 3330 Disk Storage Facility. At the left of the figure is the *comblike access mechanism*. The mechanism includes an *access arm* that moves between two disk surfaces. At the end of the arm is a pair of *read/write heads*—one for the surface above and one for the surface below.

The disk stack includes eleven disks. Data is not recorded on the top surface of the top disk or on the bottom surface of the bottom disk because these surfaces are exposed to possible damage from mishandling. Data is recorded only on the inner surfaces. Of the twenty disk surfaces used for recording, only nineteen contain data. The other is used by one of the read/write heads to synchronize the movement of the access arm.

The disk stack in Figure 7-12 provides 404 tracks per surface. Each track has a capacity of 13,030 bytes. When the access mechanism is positioned to read one

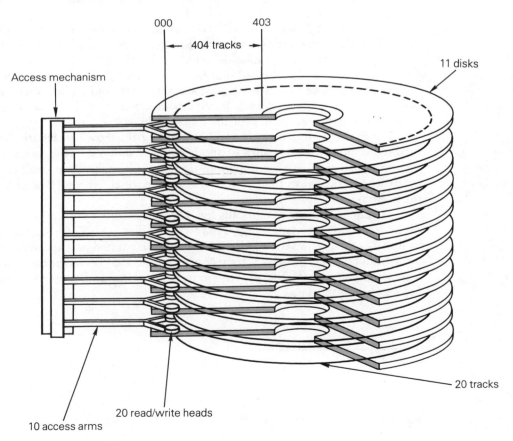

Figure 7-12 A comblike access mechanism.

of the 404 tracks of a disk, there are actually 19 tracks arranged in a vertical stack, or *cylinder*. Figure 7-13 illustrates the cylinder concept.

The cylinder of data is created by all read/write heads moving in unison. If one head is positioned on, say, track 103, then all the heads must be positioned on their tracks 103. The cylinder concept is important because it recognizes how data should be stored in a disk stack to minimize access time. The *access time* is the interval from the time the control unit transmits a command (such as seek, read, or write) to a DASD, until the read/write head begins to read data from or write data on the record location. The access time consists of three time-consuming activities:

- *Access motion time*—the time required to move the access mechanism to the cylinder containing the record to be processed
- *Head selection time*—the activation of the proper read/write head that is to read or write data on a particular track in the cylinder
- *Rotational delay time*—the time required for the disk to rotate so that the record to be read or written is positioned under the read/write head.

Because the head selection is electronic, the time required is negligible. The access motion and rotational delay times are largely the result of mechanical activity and are very time-consuming. The cylinder concept is intended to reduce the need for mechanical movements of the access mechanism.

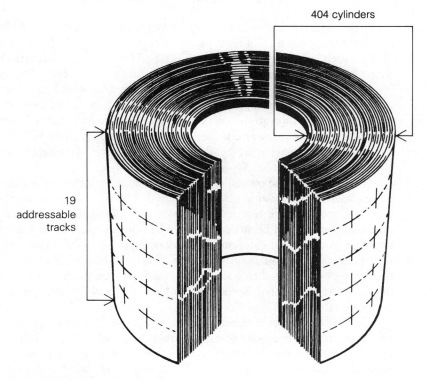

Figure 7-13 The cylinder concept.

Figure 7-14   The Storage Technology STC 8650 disk drive.

The capacity of a cylinder is quite large. For example, the IBM 3380 Direct Access Storage has a cylinder capacity of slightly over 712KB. Capacities of other IBM models range from 100.4 to 572KB. These cylinder capacities are greater than the primary storage capacity of most minis and micros. This means that a great amount of data is retrievable with a single movement of the access mechanism. The cylinder concept encourages the storage in one cylinder of all the data needed to process a transaction. The access mechanism is moved to that cylinder, and then multiple reads and writes can be performed with no access motion time. The only delay comes from head selection (negligible) and rotational delay (unavoidable).

In addition to the comblike access mechanism, another advancement in DASD design was the *removable disk pack*. The RAMAC disk stack was built into the unit and could not be removed. This was a disadvantage compared to magnetic tape reels, which can be stored offline when not in use. The disk pack solved this problem. An operator can remove a disk pack, put it in the library, obtain another disk pack, and mount it on the same *disk unit*, or *disk drive*. The disk unit is therefore not restricted to a single disk stack—it can process data from any stack or pack that is mounted. Some DASDs feature removable disk packs; others have nonremovable stacks.

Actually, the recent trend has been away from removable packs. As the storage capacities of the units increased over the years, it became less necessary to exchange packs. The exchange requires operator time, which is eliminated with nonremovable packs. The Storage Technology STC 8650 disk drive pictured in Figure 7-14 contains two disk stacks, each with a capacity of 635MB.

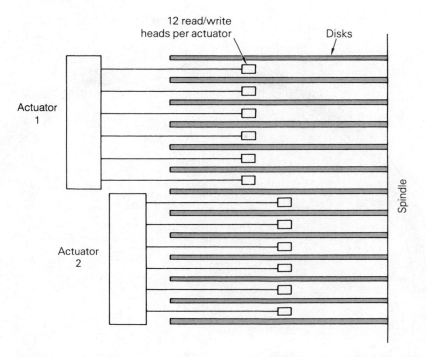

Figure 7-15 Some disk stacks have more than one access mechanism (actuator).

Some of the more recently introduced disk units feature two access mechanisms per stack. The IBM 3370 Direct Access Storage Facility consists of a single nonremovable stack with two access mechanisms, called *actuators*. Figure 7-15 shows how one actuator can seek a record on one cylinder while the other actuator seeks, reads, or writes a record on another cylinder. When one realizes that the access time of the 3370 is twenty times as fast as that of the RAMAC, and the capacity is 457 times as great, it is not difficult to see why disks remain the most popular DASD medium.

How data is recorded on a disk

As on magnetic tape, the characters are recorded on a disk in the form of magnetized bits using the same coding structure of eight data bits per byte. But on disks the bytes are recorded *serially* (one bit after the other) along the track, rather than in the *parallel* form of the tape (across the width). Also, the records in a DASD are separated by gaps.

But the gaps are not caused by starting and stopping, since the disk rotates continuously. Rather, the gaps provide time for certain functions (such as data transfer) to take place.

Figure 7-16 shows a track with three data records. The records can be blocked or unblocked. There is a gap before and after each record. In addition, each record is preceded by its address, separated by gaps. These addresses enable the computer to identify a particular record on the track.

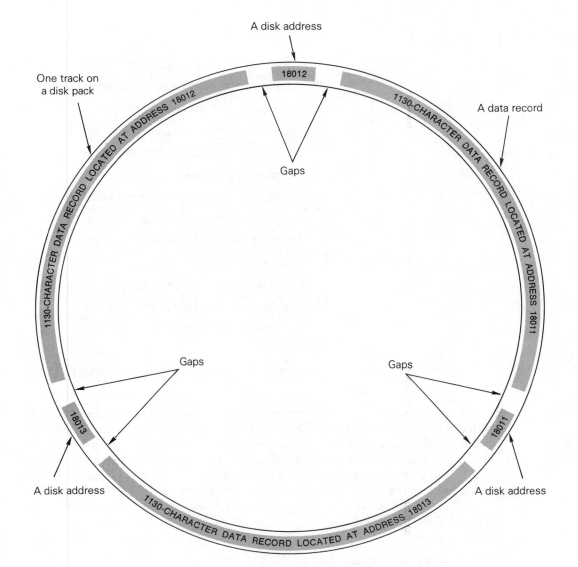

Figure 7-16 Gaps separate data records and addresses on the disk track.

Unlike tape, the check bit associated with the byte is not recorded on the DASD. During a DASD write operation, the control unit removes the check bits from the data transmitted from the CPU. The control unit replaces the check bits with a special *error correction code* (ECC) that is added to the data record. When the record is read from the DASD, the ECC is removed and the parity bits added as the data is transmitted to the CPU. The ECC enables the control unit not only to detect certain errors, but to correct some of them as well. The check bit only detects errors.

How DASD records are addressed

We have seen that the RAMAC used a five-position address identifying the disk, the track, and the sector. Modern units use addresses constructed in a similar manner. The form of the address appears in Figure 7-17. The first three digits identify the cylinder. The access mechanism is positioned so that all of the read/write heads are over the cylinder's tracks—in this example, cylinder 104. The next two digits identify which read/write head is to be activated. That head, number 12 in the example, is switched on. The last two digits identify the location on the track where the record is located. The sample record is the fifteenth record on the track. The size of the address (number of digits) will vary from one DASD to another. This particular address format (cylinder, head, and record), however, is used in most systems.

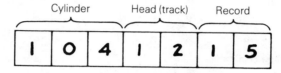

Figure 7-17   A DASD address identifying cylinder, head and record locations.

IBM's DASDs

IBM pioneered DASD technology, and its line still offers the widest variety of any on the market.[7] Other vendors build similar units that are *plug-compatible* with the IBM CPUs. For these reasons, we will use the IBM units as examples of what is available today.

IBM offers nine different DASD models for use with its 370, 303X, 3081, and 43XX systems.[8] These DASD models are summarized in Table 7-1. The models are listed in the order of their introduction to the market. The 3330 was introduced in the early seventies, and the 3380 was introduced in 1980.

The 2305 is a completely different technology from the others. The disk stack consists of six disks, and each disk has four permanently mounted access mechanisms, as shown in Figure 7-18. This arrangement eliminates the access motion time, as shown in Table 7-1. The average access time of each model can be calculated by adding the two rightmost columns.

Table 7-1 also shows the trend away from removable packs that was mentioned earlier. You can see that all disks are 14 inches in diameter except those of the 3310, which are 8 inches. Most units have only a single actuator except for the fixed-head 2305 and the three most recently announced models. The dual

---

[7] For a more detailed description of the IBM units, see Bohl, pp. 15–43.

[8] The Xes stand for the various model numbers in the series, such as 3031, 3032, 3033, 4331, and 4341.

Table 7-1 IBM DASD Models

DASD Model	Used with			Removable?	Disk Size	Pack or Module Capacity (in megabytes)	Number of Actuators	Average Access Motion Time (in milliseconds)	Average Rotational Delay (in milliseconds)
	370	303X, 43XX	3081						
3330 Disk Storage	X	X	X	Yes	14″	200	1	30	8.4
2305 Fixed-Head Storage	X	X	X	No	14″	11.3	4	0	5.0
3340 Direct Access Storage Facility	X	X	X	Yes	14″	70	1	25	10.1
3344 Direct Access Storage Facility	X	X	X	No	14″	279.5	1	25	10.1
3350 Direct Access Storage Facility	X	X		No	14″	317.5	1	25	8.4
3310 Direct Access Storage Facility			X	No	8″	64.5	1	27	9.6
3370 Direct Access Storage Facility			X	No	14″	571.4	2	20	10.1
3375 Direct Access Storage Facility		X	X	No	14″	819.7	2	19	10.1
3380 Direct Access Storage Facility	X	X	X	No	14″	1260.5	2	16	8.3

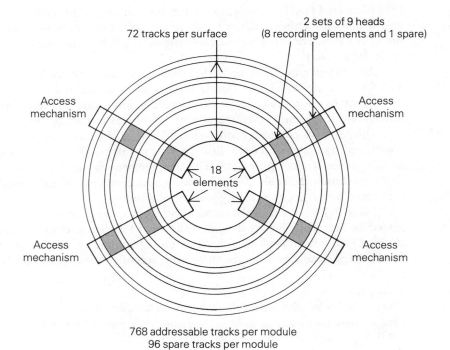

72 tracks per surface

2 sets of 9 heads
(8 recording elements and 1 spare)

Access mechanism

Access mechanism

18 elements

Access mechanism

Access mechanism

768 addressable tracks per module
96 spare tracks per module

Figure 7-18 A fixed-head access mechanism.

Figure 7-19 The IBM 3850 Mass Storage Facility.

actuator approach taken by the 3370, 3375, and 3380 models permits low access times of 10.1 milliseconds or less.

The trend is clearly toward greater capacity and reduced access time. These improvements in performance have been achieved without comparable increases in cost. The most recent units offer significantly lower costs per megabyte.

Some other DASD technologies

Shortly after disk storage became available to computer users, electronics engineers began to look for other technologies. One alternative is magnetic tape, packaged in such a way that it can provide direct access. In 1974 IBM introduced its *3850 Mass Storage System (MSS)*, which provides extremely large capacity in the form of data cartridges. The photograph in Figure 7-19 shows these cartridges stored in honeycomb-shaped chambers. Each cartridge is about 4 inches long and contains a roll of magnetic tape about 3 inches wide and 770 inches long. The mechanism at the left can perform the following operations:

1. Retrieve a cartridge from its storage location
2. Remove the tape from the cartridge
3. Wrap the tape around a drum so that data can be written on or read from the tape

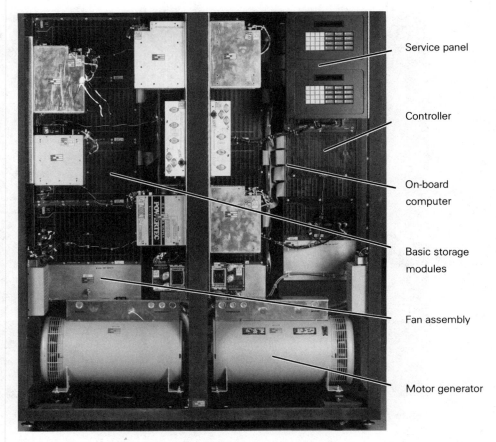

Service panel

Controller

On-board
computer

Basic storage
modules

Fan assembly

Motor generator

Figure 7-20   Inside the Intel FAST 3805 semiconductor secondary
storage.

4. Read and write data
5. Transfer the data read to a 3330 disk storage drive or write on the cartridge tape from a 3330
6. Reinsert the tape into the cartridge
7. Return the cartridge to its storage location

The process of making the data available to the 3330 (steps 1–5 above) is called *staging*. The process of returning the cartridge is called *destaging*.

As you might have guessed, access speed is not the 3850's strong point. Rather, the main reason for using it is the huge capacity—up to 472 *billion* bytes (gigabytes). The 3850 offers a way to mechanize a tape library so that tapes can be retrieved without operator intervention.

Another technology that once appeared promising but has apparently fizzled is *bubble memory*. In 1977 Texas Instruments (TI) announced a memory device 1 inch square that contained 92,000 bits. Bits were stored in the form of magnetic bubbles that could be moved around in thin films of magnetic material. A bubble represents a binary *1;* no bubble is a *0*.

Bubble memory looked promising as a type of DASD in the 20MB range. Quite possibly things would have worked out had not new breakthroughs in disk technology made the bubble memory too expensive. Most of the big manufacturers of bubble devices—TI, National Semiconductor, and Rockwell—have dropped out. Only Intel and Motorola are left. At present, it looks as if the bubble has burst.[9]

Still another approach is to use *semiconductor memory* for secondary storage. Intel has such a unit—the FAST 3805, announced in 1979—which is aimed at applications requiring very fast access times with modest capacity needs. The FAST 3805 has a maximum capacity of 72MB, but average access time is only 400 microseconds, making it over twelve times faster than the fastest IBM unit in Table 7-1. Since there is no rotating disk, there is no access movement or rotational delay time. Figure 7-20 gives an idea of what is housed inside a DASD, in this case the Intel 3805. The unit includes a microcomputer that performs error detection and correction.

The FAST 3805 is not intended for large data bases, but rather for program storage. Portions of programs can be maintained on the 3805 and brought into primary storage when needed. This type of memory is called *paging memory*. We will say more about this use later in the chapter.

How records are arranged in a DASD file

As seen earlier, magnetic tape records can be blocked and are arranged sequentially. In a payroll file, for example, the record with the lowest employee number is first. The record with the highest number is last.

Records can be recorded on a DASD in the same way, as shown in Figure 7-21. This *sequential* organization permits the DASD to be used like a magnetic

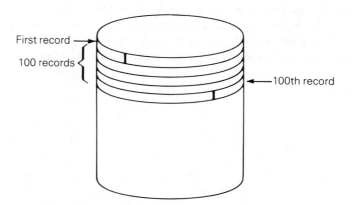

Figure 7-21 Sequential organization of a DASD file.

---

[9] For a clear, concise explanation of bubble memory, see Leslie Solomon, "A New Approach to Data Storage: Bubble Memories," *Popular Electronics* 15 (February 1979): 74–76. A description of the once-optimistic market projections can be found in "The Bubble Memory Finally Arrives," *Business Week,* 28 March 1977, pp. 72, 74.

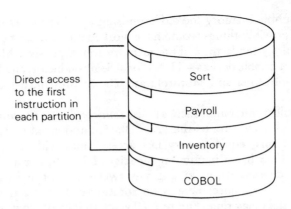

Figure 7-22 Partitioned organization of a DASD file.

tape. This is especially useful for applications where the economies of batch processing can be realized and direct access is not required.

There are other ways to organize records in a DASD file. A DASD unit can be *partitioned* into separate areas for each program or subprogram, as shown in Figure 7-22. The access mechanism can be directed to the location of the first instruction in a partition by means of a *directory*. The directory contains the name and beginning address of each *member* (program) in the file. The entire program or subprogram can then be called into primary storage sequentially, one instruction at a time.

Another type of file organization is *indexed sequential,* shown in Figure 7-23. As the name implies, the records are arranged sequentially, as in sequential storage. But there is something extra—an index. The *index* serves as a directory of the records in the file. Although Figure 7-23 shows the index separate from the file, it is usually recorded on the first few tracks.

The index contains a key for each record in the file. The keys are listed in the index sequentially, and with each key is the DASD address of the record. The index is used in much the same manner as a telephone directory, with the key

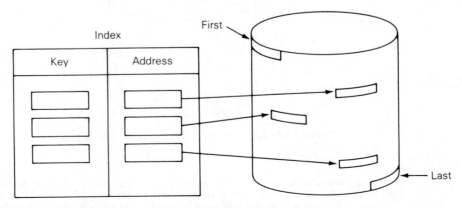

Figure 7-23 Indexed sequential organization of a DASD file.

identifying the needed record and the address identifying where that record can be found. The key is provided by the computer program needing the record. The index is read into primary storage from the DASD, and the key is compared with each entry in the index until a match is found. The corresponding address is then used to send the access mechanism to the location where the record is stored. The advantage of this approach is direct access. The disadvantage is the time-consuming routine that must be followed in order to access the record. First, the index must be accessed and read into primary storage. Then, the data record must be accessed. Two movements of the access mechanism are required (unless the data record is located in the same cylinder as the index). This disadvantage can be overcome by using the direct type of file organization, as illustrated in Figure 7-24.[10]

With *direct organization,* the data address can be generated by the program needing the record. The address is used to send the access mechanism to the correct location. The easiest approach is to use the key as the address. For example, part number 34125 could identify cylinder 34, read/write head 12, and the fifth record on the track. Unfortunately, few coding schemes exactly match the addressing scheme of the DASD. For example, part numbers contain too many positions, include letters as well as numbers, and do not run in continuous sequences.

Some type of arithmetic can be used to convert the key into an acceptable address. This use of arithmetic is called a *hashing scheme.* In Figure 7-24, part number 149107432 is divided by 1,000,000, and the remainder, 107432, is used as the address. This is only one approach. Often the divisor is the prime number (a number evenly divisible only by itself and 1) closest to but less than the number of tracks allotted to the file. For example, if 500 tracks are allotted to the file, the divisor would be 499. In addition to the division/remainder method, there are other address conversion methods such as digit analysis, folding, and radix transformation that are not described here.[11]

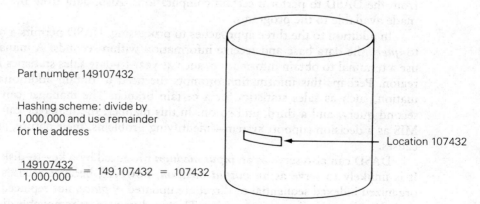

Part number 149107432

Hashing scheme: divide by
1,000,000 and use remainder
for the address

Location 107432

$$\frac{149107432}{1,000,000} = 149.107432 = 107432$$

Figure 7-24 Direct organization of a DASD file.

---

[10] The term *random* is often used to describe the direct method, but it will not be used here.

[11] For information on each of these address conversion methods, see Bohl, pp. 151–155.

A potential advantage of direct addressing is that it may require only a single movement of the access mechanism to access a particular record. Since access movements are time-consuming (compared with reading, processing, and writing DASD data), more efficient computer use is possible with direct organization than with the other file organizations. A potential disadvantage is that records may well get distributed unequally in the DASD device. It is possible for the hashing scheme to produce the same address for more than one key. These duplicates are called *synonyms*. In this case, all but the first record assigned to a given location must be placed in an overflow area. The access mechanism is sent to the first location, finds that the record is elsewhere, and looks in the overflow area. One or more additional movements of the access mechanism might be required. This time-consuming activity should not occur very often. If it does, a new hashing scheme should be devised—one producing fewer synonyms. A rule of thumb is a maximum of 20% synonyms.[12] When more than one out of five calculated storage addresses produces a synonym, it is time to find a new hashing scheme.

Uses of DASD

DASD makes its greatest contribution to the MIS as a *file medium*. DASD units are used for both data and programs that are active enough to warrant the expense. It costs more to maintain data on DASD than on magnetic tape. A file should not be kept on DASD unless the cost is justified.

In Chapter 5 we identified two basic processing approaches—batch and online. We also identified three variations—realtime, timesharing, and distributed processing. Of these five approaches, three (online, realtime, and timesharing) require DASD. In each of these situations, it is impossible to anticipate which program, file, or record will be required next by a user. For this reason, all must be kept in a "ready" state—recorded on a DASD unit available to the CPU. This procedure is shown in Figure 7-25. In all three approaches, programs are called from the DASD to perform certain computations. Also, data from the DASD is made available to the programs.

In addition to the three approaches to processing, DASD permits a manager to *query* the data base and receive information within seconds. A manager can use a terminal to obtain information, such as year-to-date sales statistics for each region. Perhaps this information prompts the need to obtain additional information, such as sales statistics for a certain branch. The manager can enter a second query, and a third, and so on. In this manner, the manager can use the MIS as a decision support system—identifying problems, their nature, and their causes.

DASD can also serve as an *input medium* produced by a key-to-disk system. It is unlikely to serve as an *output medium*, however, because records of files organized indexed sequential or direct are updated *in place*, not replaced by new records as in magnetic tape processing. The trend away from removable disk packs also reduces the effectiveness of DASD as a *communication medium* from one computer installation to another. But the fast reading and writing speeds make

---

[12]Bohl, p. 151.

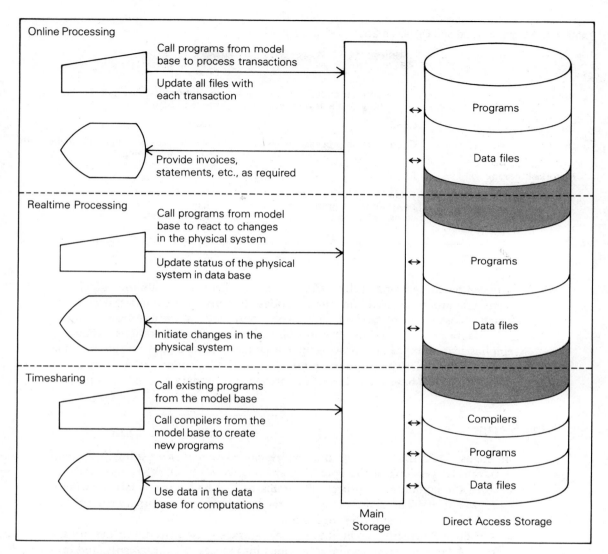

Figure 7-25 DASD makes data and programs immediately available.

DASD very attractive for communicating data from one program to another at a single site. And finally, the cost of the DASD storage space, while continuing to decrease, is too great to consider for use as a *historical storage medium*.

A Comparison of Magnetic Tape and DASD

Table 7-2 compares magnetic tape and DASD for the five major uses. Both types of secondary storage are best suited for file media. Tape is good with high-activity files and in situations where there is no need to query the file for status information

Table 7-2 Magnetic Tape and DASD as Secondary Storage Media

Use	Magnetic Tape	DASD
Input	Both secondary storage media play minor roles as input media—the trend is toward online data entry and SDA.	
File	Good	Excellent
Output	Good in batch processing	Not a large volume of activity with online processing
Historical Storage	Excellent	Poor
Communication	Good for both site-to-site and program-to-program communication	Poor for site-to-site communication. Excellent for program-to-program communication

between batch updating cycles. DASD offers excellent file capabilities—facilitating online processing and immediate response to a manager's queries. Because of its lower cost, magnetic tape is the most commonly used historical storage medium.

Magnetic tape was effective during early computer generations, when the emphasis was on the batch processing of accounting data. The evolution to online processing and decision support systems, coupled with continued refinements in disk technology, have made DASD the preferred secondary storage medium.

Virtual Storage

In August 1972 IBM announced a feature named *virtual storage* for its System/370. Special versions of the operating system (DOS/VS, OS/VS1, and OS/VS2) enabled the computer to process programs as if it had a much larger primary storage capacity. This is desirable, since the lack of adequate primary storage has always been a constraint on programming.

There is "virtually" no limit to primary storage space with the virtual storage feature. A large program can be subdivided into pieces called *segments,* and into even smaller pieces called *pages*. The program is stored in pages in secondary storage, as shown in Figure 7-26, and the pages are brought into primary storage as they are needed. The process is called *paging,* and the areas in primary storage where the pages are stored are called *page frames*. After a page has been executed, another page can be brought in from secondary storage and *overlaid* on the same area as the previous page, erasing the previous page contents. There can be multiple pages from one program in primary storage as long as there is enough space.

Virtual storage is important to the manager. It means that a computer can execute a program that would otherwise be too large for primary storage. Primary storage capacity doesn't represent a constraint on the type or size of problem the computer can handle.

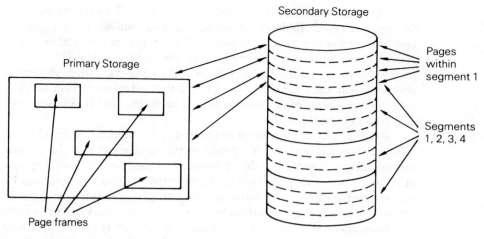

Figure 7-26 The paging process involving virtual storage.

Summary

Secondary storage performs two vital functions in the MIS—it houses both the data base and the software library. In the data base, data exists in a hierarchy ranging from data items, at the lowest level, to files, at the highest level.

There are two basic types of secondary storage—sequential and direct. Magnetic tape is used for sequential storage. Magnetic disks are the most popular medium for direct storage.

Data is recorded on 2400-foot reels of ½-inch tape at densities as high as 6250 bpi. Records are usually blocked to conserve space and reduce start/stop time. The primary use of tape is as a file medium. The file must be arranged and processed sequentially. Magnetic tape is very efficient and economical when the records in a file are highly active; it permits a mass-production approach to data processing. The main limitation is the need for sequential processing. Another limitation that is significant to the MIS is the inability to facilitate an immediate response to a manager's queries. Magnetic tape is useful, however, as a means of historical storage.

Disk storage, a type of DASD, was developed to overcome the sequential limitation of magnetic tape. Direct access is achieved with a mechanism that can access, read, and write data on the surfaces of rotating metal disks. Each record in the DASD has an address that identifies the cylinder, read/write head, and record number on the track. The cylinder concept is important in that it reduces the time required to retrieve records by arranging related records in the same cylinder. There are as many cylinders in a disk stack as there are tracks on the surface of a disk.

Data is recorded along the tracks in bytes, with gaps separating the records. Each record has an address, and the records can be blocked or unblocked. An error correction code is used to detect and correct some errors.

IBM offers nine different disk models, as well as the 3850 Mass Storage System. Each model is designed to offer some combination of capacity, speed, and cost that meets the particular needs of an organization. Other manufacturers provide units with similar performance/cost ratios. Other DASD technologies, such as magnetic bubble memory, have seldom measured up to expectations. Intel and Motorola may yet develop a bubble that offers an attractive alternative to disk. Intel presently offers another DASD medium—an MOS-based unit designed as a paging memory.

Records can be organized sequentially, partitioned, indexed sequential, or direct. Sequential organization produces the same effect as if the records were on magnetic tape. There is no direct access, and the records must be processed one after the other. This approach is characteristic of batch processing. Partitioned organization is effective for retrieving programs from the software library. Indexed sequential may require two movements of the access mechanism—one to retrieve the index and one to retrieve the record. Direct may require only a single movement and uses an address-producing algorithm called a hashing scheme.

Batch processing, using magnetic tape or sequentially organized DASD, is the most economical way to process large volumes of data. Many data processing applications such as payroll, accounts receivable, and billing are performed in a batch fashion, with files arranged sequentially. For information processing applications—those providing decision support for managers—online processing is best. When files are organized indexed sequential or direct, the records can be updated as transactions occur and managers can query the file contents for up-to-date status information. It would be possible to design a highly effective MIS using magnetic tape and batch processing. But the support provided by DASD and the file organizations facilitating direct access are so excellent that they are often automatically assumed to be part of the MIS.

Virtual storage is a technique for subdividing a program into pages and transferring them between secondary and primary storage when they are needed. A computer can handle a larger program with virtual storage.

Our objective in this chapter has been to provide a solid foundation in secondary storage technology and methodology. We have not elaborated on how this storage is used in an MIS. That explanation will begin in the next chapter as we discuss the software that manages the data base—the data base management system. Then, in Chapters 11 through 15, we will discuss a number of MIS applications and examples. The importance of secondary storage will become more apparent as we learn more about the MIS.

Key Terms

data item, record, file, data set	recording density
sequential storage	magnetic tape unit, tape drive
key	header label, trailer label
direct storage	block
direct access storage device (DASD)	blocking factor

interblock gap

disk stack

track

sector

access mechanism, access arm

cylinder

access time

access motion time

head selection time

rotational delay time

disk pack

disk unit, disk drive

actuator

error correction code (ECC)

staging, destaging

bubble memory

paging memory

sequential organization

partitioned organization

directory

member

indexed sequential

index

direct organization

hashing scheme

synonym

query

virtual storage

segment

page, paging, page frame

Key Concepts

How data is organized in a hierarchy

The two basic types of secondary storage and how they influence data and information processing

How data is recorded on magnetic tape

How magnetic tape is used

How data is stored in disk storage

How DASD records are addressed

DASD file organization methods

How DASD is used

Virtual storage

Questions

1. What are the two basic types of computer storage?

2. What is the data hierarchy?

3. What would the key probably be in an inventory master file? a customer master file? a vendor master file? a salesperson commission file?

4. Why do interblock gaps appear on magnetic tape?

5. Give two reasons why magnetic tape records are blocked.

6. List five uses of magnetic tape. For which use does magnetic tape seem best suited? Explain.

7. When magnetic tape is used as a communication medium, what is it communicating with?

8. If a RAMAC record had an address of 49999, exactly where would it be located?

9. Did the cylinder concept apply to the RAMAC? Explain your answer.

10. Which of the three components of access time does the cylinder concept attempt to minimize?

11. Why is the trend away from removable disk packs?

12. Do data bytes on a DASD contain a parity bit? Explain.

13. Which of the three components of access time does the IBM 2305 eliminate?

14. Is the IBM 3850 Mass Storage System an example of a sequential or direct storage?

15. Why is bubble memory no longer considered the secondary storage of the future?

16. How is the Intel FAST 3805 intended to be used?

17. Which DASD file organization method uses a directory? an index? Which generates synonyms?

18. What happens to a record when its key is converted to an address already assigned to another record? What happens when there are too many synonyms?

19. Does virtual storage expand the capacity of primary storage?

20. How does virtual storage benefit the manager?

Problems

1. Assume you have a 2400-foot reel of magnetic tape with a 25-foot header and a 16-foot trailer leader. With an interblock gap of 0.6 inch, how many unblocked 100-byte records can be recorded on the tape at 6250 bpi? If you used a blocking factor of 10, how many records could be written on the tape?

2. Calculate the average access time of each IBM DASD model listed in Table 7-1.

3. Historically, the largest DASD units have had the slowest access times, and the smallest have had the fastest. Draw a graph that compares the access time (y axis) with the pack or module capacity (x axis), using data from Table 7-1. Does the historical relationship exist?

CASE PROBLEM: Chinook Transfer and Storage

I'm Arthur Ashgar, director of data processing at Chinook Transfer and Storage, a regional trucking firm licensed to do business in five Rocky Mountain states. At our Provo, Utah, headquarters we have an NCR 8370 medium-scale computer with one disk drive and six magnetic tape units. The disk drive houses our software library and the rate tables we use to compute shipping charges. All of our data files are on magnetic tape, updated on a batch basis. Each night we update the customer master file, a process that takes about two and a half hours. Billing is done during the day and takes a little over an hour, including updating the accounts receivable file. The rest of the day is spent debugging programs and printing special reports. Most of the reports are for the Interstate Commerce Commission and the various state regulatory commissions. We do very little reporting for our own managers, aside from general accounting documents requested by our controller.

I like my job. We've developed a routine that's easy to follow. The system hasn't changed for about three years, so things run pretty smoothly. You might think that I'm content, that I just rock along without making any waves. Well, maybe I should be, but I'm still young and have my career ahead of me. I feel like I'm really wasting my time. If I can't get some new activity started here, I'm moving on to a larger, more progressive operation.

I've been giving some thought to implementing an MIS. We could put our data base on disk and install a few terminals for online queries. I've even talked with a few of our managers about it. They seem pretty interested. The idea of being able to get current information during the day really appeals to them. As it is now, they make a request one day and get a printout the next—that's for standard reports prepared from the customer master file. Anything special takes up to four weeks.

Oh, pardon me. There's somebody at the door. It's Del Delaney, our magnetic tape sales representative.

"Hey, Del, how are you? Come on in."

Del sits down, but he looks worried. He tells me he heard I was going to install an MIS. He says that would be a big mistake—it would create a lot of new problems. I'm curious why Del cares whether we install an MIS or not. Then it hits me. "Del," I tell him, "you're afraid that if we go to an MIS, we're going to put our data files on disk and you're going to lose our tape business. We're the biggest customer you have. Now, isn't that right?"

I can see that Del doesn't like to admit it. He begins by telling me why it would be a mistake to go from tapes to disks. We wouldn't have any backup files with disks. Disk packs cost about ten times as much as a reel of tape. Sequential storage is much more efficient than direct storage. If we put in disks, we would have to put in terminals too. Our managers don't need immediate inquiry anyway because they don't make decisions that fast. Disks would be too expensive for historical storage. And so on.

I just sit and listen. Finally I tell Del that it isn't definite yet. I've been thinking about it, but that's all. Del is obviously relieved. I can see him relax, and we begin to talk about other things—the chili cook-off this weekend, for instance.

Questions

1. Does Chinook need an MIS?
2. Comment on each of Delaney's criticisms of disks compared to tapes. Are they true? If not, explain.
3. Assuming that Chinook goes ahead with the MIS, what files would be best suited for disk storage? Tape storage?
4. Will Chinook have to install keyboard terminals if it starts to use disks?

Chapter 8

The Data Base

Learning Objectives

After studying this chapter, you should:

- Understand what is meant by the term *data base*
- Understand the role played by the data base management system (DBMS)
- Know the difference between physical and logical data organization
- Know how the pre–data base approach differs from the data base approach
- Appreciate how the DBMS facilitates response to ad hoc (special) requests for information
- Understand how linked lists are used to integrate data in a data base
- Understand how an inverted file is used to extract data from a file in a different sequence
- Gain a working knowledge of DBMS terminology—schema and subschema, data dictionary, data description language, and data manipulation language
- Know the four parts of a DBMS and their functions
- Have an introductory understanding of the ADABAS commercial DBMS
- Know the advantages and disadvantages of a data base and a DBMS
- Be familiar with the role of the data base administrator (DBA)

In the last chapter we studied the devices used for secondary storage. We recognized that the devices house the software library and the data base. The programs of the software library can be stored in secondary storage using a partitioned file organization. They can also be in the form of segments and pages to take advantage of a virtual storage capability. The librarian portion of the operating system retrieves the programs and program segments when they are needed. The data base is also housed in secondary storage, and the contents are made available to applications programs by means of either subroutines in those programs or by systems software.

It is easy to see the importance of the data base. It provides the raw material from which the information product is created. Without the data base there could be no MIS. In this chapter we provide more detail on how data is arranged in secondary storage and how that data is made available to the information processor.

The Data Base in the General Systems Model

We can see the data base in relation to the general systems model in Figure 8-1. Data and information from both the firm and the environment are entered into the data base by means of the input devices described in Chapter 6. Information from the data base is made available to the manager by means of the output devices.

Our interest in studying the data base is to understand how it is used in an MIS. In later chapters we will see how the manager uses this valuable resource. In this chapter we will gain an understanding of how the data is arranged in the data base and how the data base management software manages the data in the data base.

Some Basic Data Concepts

We have seen that data exists in a hierarchy. On the lowest level is the *data item*. The items relative to a particular topic are assembled into a *record*. The space in a record where a data item is stored is called a *field*. All of the records together constitute a *file*. The *data base* consists of one or more files.

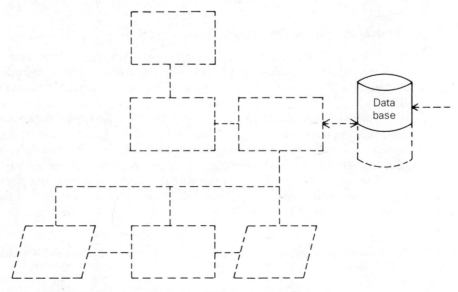

Figure 8-1 The data base in the general systems model.

What is a data base?

The term *data base* can be defined broadly or narrowly. In a broad sense, a data base can include all of the data and information within an organization. Narrowly speaking, we could limit a data base to include only that data and information stored in the computer and available for processing. In this book we use the narrow definition. In doing so, we recognize the potentially large amounts of data and information within an organization that are not stored in the computer.

What is a data base management system?

During the past fifteen years, there has been much interest in a software system to manage the data base. This system is called a *data base management system* (*DBMS*). DBMSes are available from a number of sources (computer manufacturers and software firms) at costs ranging from $100 to over $100,000. We will use the term *commercial data base management system* to describe these preprogrammed systems. Although the systems offer various levels of performance, as a group they represent the most effective way to store, control, and retrieve the contents of a data base.

We should make one point clear at the outset: a firm need not have a commercial DBMS to have a good computer-based MIS. In large organizations the DBMS is almost a necessity, but when the data resource is relatively small and there is little sharing of common data within the organization, the DBMS is not needed. The firm's programmers can prepare programs to manage the data effectively. As computer use becomes more sophisticated and as the DBMS capabilities of minis and micros improve, the number of firms using a commercial DBMS will increase dramatically. Estimates of the annual increase of this market during the 1980s range from 20% to 45%. By 1990 firms are expected to be spending at least $1.8 billion annually for these software systems.[1]

Physical and logical data organization

In our study of secondary storage devices in the last chapter, we were concerned with the *physical organization* of data—the way data is stored in cylinders, tracks, and blocks. This is the computer's view of the data. The user's view can be quite different.

The *logical organization* is the way the user views the data resource. For instance, the user may view a personnel record as shown in Figure 8-2. In fact, however, the physical record could look quite different. For example, it could be blocked, as in Figure 8-3. One physical record represents three logical records.

The important point is that the way the record is stored—its physical organization—need not influence its use. Use can be quite independent of the physical storage arrangement.

---

[1] Peter Krass and Hesh Wiener, "The DBM Market Is Booming," *Datamation* 27 (September 1981): 153.

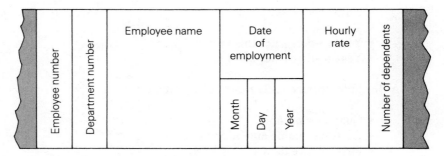

Figure 8-2 A logical record.

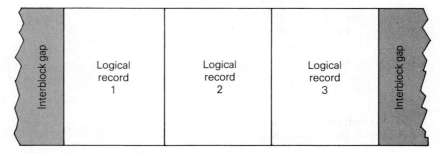

Figure 8-3 A physical record.

The Pre–Data Base Approach

The idea of a data base didn't originate until the late sixties, along with third-generation technology and interest in the MIS. Prior to that time, users recognized the necessity of data files, but the files were regarded as separate entities belonging to particular programs.

As an example, a firm might have a *customer credit file* containing data such as:

- Customer number
- Customer name and address
- Credit code
- Credit limit
- Amount of current accounts receivable

Another file, called a *customer master file,* contains:

- Customer number
- Customer name and address
- Sales region number
- Salesperson number

- Customer class
- Shipping code
- Year-to-date sales this year
- Year-to-date sales last year

A third file, for *accounts receivable,* contains:

- Customer number
- Customer name and address
- First invoice data
    Invoice number
    Invoice date
    Invoice amount
- Second invoice data
    Invoice number
    Invoice date
    Invoice amount

        .
        .
        .

- *n*th invoice data
    Invoice number
    Invoice date
    Invoice amount

Each of these files has one or more purposes. The customer credit file is used for approving customer orders, the cutomer master file is used for invoicing customers, and the accounts receivable file represents the monies owed the firm by its customers. All are *master files.*

You will note the redundancy. All three files include customer number and customer name and address. The customer number is the *key* for all three files—it is used to identify the records and to arrange them sequentially. The customer name and address in the credit file are used when sending letters notifying customers of accepted or rejected orders. The same *field* in the customer master record is used for invoices and for statements when receivables are due.

Figure 8-4 illustrates how these files are used in a pre–data base approach. Although we identified this approach as a late-sixties technique, there are still firms processing data this way today. In the figure, the three master files are shaded. Two other files (accepted orders and billing) are *intermediate files* that simply pass data from one system to another.

The three master files are maintained separately. If a customer moves, the name and address field in all three files must be updated. While some redundancy cannot be avoided, too much is undesirable. Duplicated data wastes storage space, adds processing time, and increases the opportunity for error.

Let's continue our scenario with the pre–data base firm and assume that the sales manager wants a report showing the amount of receivables by salesperson.

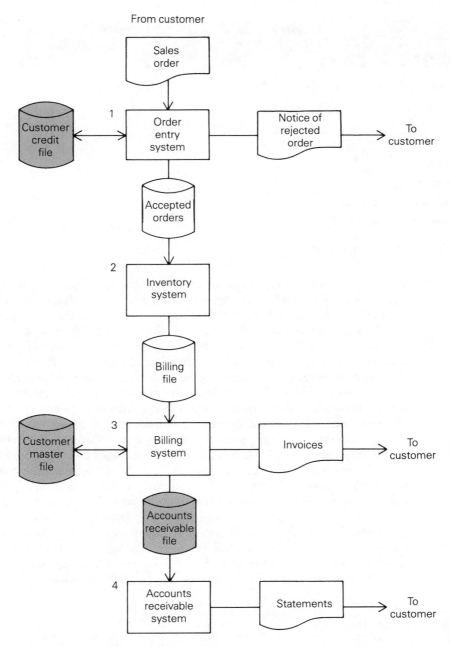

Figure 8-4   The pre–data base approach.

Table 8-1 Integration of Report Data from Multiple Files

Report Data	Customer Credit File	Customer Master File	Accounts Receivable File	Salesperson Master File
Salesperson Number		X		
Salesperson Name				X
Customer Data				
Customer number		X		
Customer name		X		
Credit code	X			
Year-to-date sales this year		X		
Total accounts receivable			X	

The firm's customers haven't been paying their bills promptly, and the sales manager wants to know which salespersons have neglected to follow up on past-due receivables. The sales manager wants the report to include the data listed in Table 8-1. You can see that the special report will require data from four files.

The report will list each customer by salesperson, following the process illustrated in Figure 8-5. In step 1 a program selects data from the three customer files that are maintained in customer number sequence. An intermediate file is created with the selected data (all of the data items listed in Table 8-1 except salesperson name). This intermediate file is sorted into salesperson sequence in step 2. A second intermediate file is created and used with the salesperson master file to prepare the report in step 3. The programs for step 1 and step 3 would have to be specially written to satisfy this ad hoc request. An *ad hoc request* is a special request.

This procedure is inefficient from the standpoints of both the user and the information services department. You can imagine how much time is involved in this type of information request—it could take several weeks to program, debug, test, and run the programs. Considerable programmer time goes into creating programs that may be used only once. This inefficiency was a constraint on MIS performance during the pre–data base era. Managers wanted information but could not get it because the data resource was not in a readily usable form. The lack of software to produce the reports was another limitation.

The Data Base Approach

Essentially the *data base approach* involves the use of logically integrated files to meet the information needs of an organization. The idea is *not* to build one giant file containing everything—that would be impossible. Rather, the contents of files are interrelated in order both to reduce redundancy and to facilitate the retrieval of data from the various files to meet information requirements.

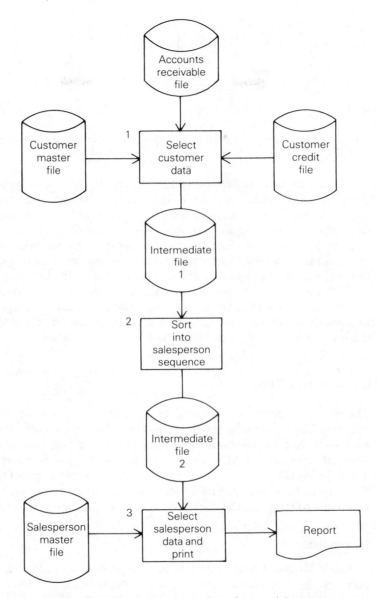

Figure 8-5 Pre–data base preparation of a special report.

Let's go back to our pre–data base firm and see how the sales manager's request is handled with the firm's brand-new DBMS. The manager wants to query the data base and obtain the needed information. He or she can key the query into a terminal or complete a form that is then keypunched or entered into a terminal. The terminal permits an *online query*, with the report displayed within a few seconds or a few minutes, depending on how busy the CPU is. Entering the query offline (by keypunch, for example) will produce the same report, only considerably later—perhaps the next day.

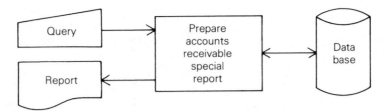

Figure 8-6 Preparation of a special report using a data base.

In Figure 8-6, we see the system flowchart. This approach is clearly much more straightforward, and the design is much cleaner, than the pre–data base approach. The manager keys the query on a terminal keyboard, the data is retrieved from the various files and assembled in the proper format, and the report is printed. The system is responsive, and *no* special programming is required. What makes all this possible? Three primary ingredients: an adequate computer configuration, the necessary data in the data base, and a DBMS.

DBMSes greatly improve a computer's response to ad hoc requests. Similar improvements are realized in other aspects of data base management—creation, updating, control, security, and so on. It is easy to see why the DBMS has captured the interest of managers and information specialists alike.

Logical Integration of Files

The data base approach allows data integration without the redundancy of the pre–data base approach. The integration is achieved logically, not physically. We have seen that the logical arrangement of data can be quite different from the physical arrangement. Although several techniques have been devised for expressing these logical relationships, we will only discuss two: linked lists and inverted files.[2] Data base software uses these logical relationships between data records and items to integrate the data needed to meet managers' information needs.

Linked lists

A *linked list* is a group of data items arranged in an order based on embedded pointers. An *embedded pointer* is a code that links one record to another by referring, for example, to the key of the other record. The code is embedded in the first record—that is, it is a data field within the record.

Linked lists often have a *head,* which is a pointer to the first item, and a *tail,*

[2] For more information on how to integrate data logically, see a data base textbook such as Gordon Everest, *Database Management* (New York: McGraw-Hill, 1982); Jefrey D. Ullman, *Principles of Database Systems* (Potomac, Md.: Computer Science Press, 1980); C. J. Date, *An Introduction to Database Systems,* 3d ed. (Reading, Mass.: Addison-Wesley, 1981); or David Kroenke, *Database Processing: Fundamentals, Modeling, Applications* (Chicago: Science Research Associates, 1977). The Kroenke text is reputedly the most readable; see pp. 57–127 for a discussion of logical structures and how they can be achieved physically.

Customer number				Salesperson number	Salesperson link
22504					
23694				23	25410
24782					
25409					
25410				23	30102
26713					
28914					
30004					
30102				23	30111
30111				23	*
30417					
31715					

Figure 8-7 A linked list.

which points to the last item. You can start at the head and follow the list to the tail, or you can start in the middle and follow the list to the tail. You cannot, however, start in the middle and go back to the head. The linked list is a one-way street. Figure 8-7 is a linked list of customer records. Each row is a record, and only the fields pertinent to our discussion are shown. The records are arranged sequentially. These could be customer credit records, customer master records, or accounts receivable records from our example earlier in the chapter.

Each customer record includes a data item identifying the assigned salesperson. In addition, in the rightmost field is a pointer (a *link*) that chains together all customer records for a particular salesperson—in this case salesperson 23. We can assume that customer 23694 is at the head of the list. The pointer links that record to the record for customer 25410 and so on until we reach the tail, at customer 30111. The asterisk in the link field identifies the tail.

This chaining ability is very powerful. Assume that a sales manager wants to know the total year-to-date sales to all of salesperson 23's customers. The customer file is arranged in customer number sequence. The applications program can initiate a search at the head of the list, looking for the first customer assigned to salesperson 23. When that record is found, the salesperson links enable the program to follow the chain and only process salesperson 23's records. This is much better than searching sequentially through the entire file.

Two-way linked lists

The limitations of a one-way list can be overcome by including a second pointer field that points to the previous record in the chain. This *two-way list* is illustrated

Customer number			Salesperson number	Forward salesperson link	Backward salesperson link
22504					
23694			23	25410	30111
24782					
25409					
25410			23	30102	23694
26713					
28914					
30004					
30102			23	30111	25410
30111			23	23694	30102
30417					
31715					

Forward link   Backward link

Figure 8-8 A two-way linked list.

in Figure 8-8. In the two-way list there is no end-of-chain (tail) marker. Because the list forms a loop, it is sometimes referred to as a *circular* or *ring structure*. The ring structure permits the program to enter the list at any point and process all of the records.

The pointers establish the connections between records and are part of the data file itself. Often it is desirable to establish the logical connections apart from the data base—in the form of indices or directories.

Inverted files

An *inverted file* is one in which records are arranged in a sequence different from the primary one. For example, the customer file is usually arranged in customer number sequence. There are times, however, when we would like to process the data in another sequence, such as by salesperson number or sales region number. One approach is simply to duplicate the customer file and arrange it in the different sequences. This would do the job, but it would require a great deal of storage.

A better approach would be to create an *index* in a sequence other than that of the file. The index can be used to extract file contents based on the index rather than the file sequence. A good example is our earlier example of the sales manager who wanted a special report of receivables by salesperson. All of the receivables data was carried in three files (customer credit, customer master, and accounts receivable) maintained in customer number sequence. By inverting the customer

Salesperson number	Salesperson name	Customer 1	Customer 2	Customer 3	Customer n
16		17042	21096		
20		41854			
23		23694	25410	30102	30111
31		31002			
56		34107	13109		
92		20842			
98		61634			
104		10974			
110		16342	64210	51263	41782

Figure 8-9 An inverted file.

file and creating an inverted file in sequence by salesperson number, we can use the inverted file to retrieve data from the customer sequence files. The inverted file is used as a salesperson index. Figure 8-9 tells the story.

An example of logical integration

The applications program causes the inverted file (index) to be read from secondary storage into primary storage. Once in primary storage, the program can identify the customers assigned to each salesperson. These customer numbers can be used with other indices to locate the credit, master, and receivable files. The data from these files is read into primary storage, where the needed items are selected and the report data assembled. A line is printed on the report including the data for one customer. Then the next customer's records are retrieved. We are able to prepare the report without sorting any records (as we did in the pre–data base approach diagrammed in Figure 8-5). The sequence of the salesperson index helps retrieve customer data in salesperson sequence. Figure 8-10 shows the links and processes.

1. Using salesperson number as the key, the salesperson index is searched to identify the first (or next) customer number.
2. The customer number serves as the key to search the customer index to find the DASD address for the customer credit record. We are illustrating an indexed sequential DASD organization.

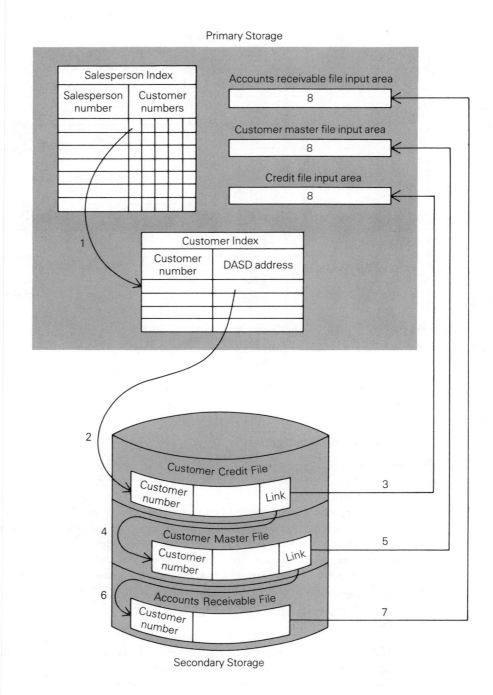

Figure 8-10 Multiple files are linked by pointers.

3. The customer credit record is read into primary storage.
4. The customer master file link in the customer credit record directs the access mechanism to the DASD location of the customer master record.
5. The customer master record is read.
6. The accounts receivable link in the master record directs the access mechanism to the accounts receivable record.
7. The accounts receivable record is read.
8. The report data is assembled.

In this example, indices are used to identify the selected record and its location. Then pointers are used to locate additional records.

Both the linked list and inverted file techniques integrate the data logically using pointers and indices. The data itself remains separated physically, as in pre–data base days.

DBMS Fundamentals

The DBMS makes it possible for a firm to achieve a usable data base. In order to appreciate the role played by the DBMS, you must understand some DBMS fundamentals. These fundamentals apply to each of the commercial DBMSes. In the following sections, we will become familiar with DBMS functions, schema and subschema, the data dictionary, the data description language, the data manipulation language, the way the DBMS is used, and a DBMS model.

DBMS functions

The DBMS is a software system designed to help the user control, retrieve, and store the data resource—the major data management functions.

Control is achieved by authorizing data use and then supervising that use. The data dictionary defines the data base contents in terms of data names and attributes. These definitions are communicated to the DBMS by means of a *data description language (DDL)*. Directories identify users who are permitted to use the system, the system resources they can use, and the specific operations they can perform on each data item. When the user requests data from the data base, the DBMS screens the request using the directories to prevent the misuse of data resources and the loss of data integrity.

Retrieval is achieved by issuing *data manipulation language (DML)* commands to the operating system. When the operating system places the data in primary storage buffer areas, the DBMS arranges and orders the data to meet the specifications of the applications program.

Storage is achieved by identifying the logical relationships among data items and then employing techniques that establish those relationships, such as linked lists and inverted files.

Schema and subschema

Two terms that are often used in relation to the data base are schema and sub-schema. The *schema* is a description of the logical structure of the entire data base. It can be thought of as a list of all of the data item *names* and *attributes* in the data base. Each data item has a name, such as EMPLOYEE-NUMBER, and attributes, such as width (ten positions) and data type (numeric).

If you have experience with programming languages, you know that each data item has a name and its attributes are specified. In COBOL, for example, all of the data items for a record are listed in the data division specification, shown in Figure 8-11. The 01 identifies the record name, and the 02s identify data items. Each item has a name and a "picture." The picture specifies the attributes. For example, HOURLY-RATE has the picture 999V99. The 9s represent numeric positions, and the V is the decimal position. This field can contain any value from 000.00 through 999.99. The picture X(20) for EMPLOYEE-NAME specifies twenty alphanumeric (X) positions.

The example in Figure 8-11 does not represent the firm's total data base. The figure contains only a selected portion of the data base—a *subschema*. If we listed all of the item names and attributes (hundreds or thousands of them), we would have the schema. Each program is concerned with only a portion of the whole, however. Any selected portion is a subschema.

Many different subschemas can be created from a single schema. Users can have their own schemas. This means that data can be presented in many forms, although it only exists physically in one form.

```
01   PAYROLL-RECORD.
     02   EMPLOYEE-NUMBER PICTURE 99999.
     02   EMPLOYEE-NAME PICTURE X(20).
     02   DEPT-NO PICTURE 999.
     02   SOC-SEC-NO PICTURE 9(9).
     02   HOURLY-RATE PICTURE 999V99.
     02   YEAR-TO-DATE-PAY PICTURE 9(6)V99.
     02   YEAR-TO-DATE-TAX PICTURE 9(6)V99.
     02   YEAR-TO-DATE-FICA PICTURE 9(5)V99.
     02   YEAR-TO-DATE-NET PICTURE 9(6)V99.
```

Figure 8-11   A COBOL data specification.

The data dictionary

One of the first steps in developing an MIS is to identify the schema. This is difficult for user and systems analyst alike, because it is impossible to anticipate each item that will be needed. The beauty of the data base approach is that items can be more easily added than if the physical structure provided the integration. An effort is made to identify all data needs initially, but all parties know they will have to expand and improve the data base as time goes on.

Once the items composing the initial data base have been identified, each item is described in detail in a *data dictionary*. A data dictionary, sometimes called a *data element dictionary* (DED), defines all of the data items in the data base.

GENERAL DOCUMENTATION FORM	PROJECT	
	DATE	820506
	PAGE	94

SYSTEM	PART
PHASE	SECTION

DATA ITEM: CUSTNUM

OTHER RELATED ITEMS: ASGNRCNR

                            ASUAANR

                            MEMBER

DEFINITION: A NINE-DIGIT CUSTOMER IDENTIFICATION NUMBER. A NUMBER
IS ASSIGNED TO AN INDIVIDUAL WHO INDICATES AN INTEREST IN
SERVICES AND IS THOUGHT TO BE ELIGIBLE; TO THE SPOUSE OF
A DECEASED MEMBER; TO A NONMEMBER FOR THE
REMAINDER OF A TERM OF AN ASSIGNED POLICY; TO
INDIVIDUALS UNDER AN ASSIGNED RISK PLAN.

        P   S   T

  12345 67   89   DISPLAY ORDER

     89   67 12345 TERMINAL DIGIT ORDER

A PREFIX TO THE POLICY NUMBER WILL BE PRINTED ON OUTPUT
DOCUMENTS TO INDICATE THE COMPANY ISSUING OR POLICY
IDENTIFICATION OR SYSTEM POLICY DATA. THIS DESIGNATION
WILL BE USED FOR MAIL/TELEPHONE CALL ROUTING TO
INDICATE USE OF CICS SYSTEM DISPLAYS FOR ONLINE POLICY
DATA AND/OR INTERNAL WORKFLOW PROCEDURES.
THESE PREFIXES ARE AS FOLLOWS:

  U123   45   67   ASUA COMPANY POLICY
  C123   45   67   CIC COMPANY POLICY
  G123   45   67   GIC COMPANY POLICY
  Z123   45   67   SAIP POLICY (TYPE OF RISK 07)
  N123   45   67   SAIP POLICY (TYPE OF RISK 09)

FORMAT: NNNNNNNNN

ORIGIN: COMPUTER-GENERATED FROM CUSTOMER DISPLAY INPUT
THROUGH CODES/ENTREX BY REG. OP. TO ASSURE TRANSACTION
PROCESSING UNDER CORRECT ASUA NUMBER.

RESPONSIBILITY: (1) UPDATE—CISS

Figure 8-12 A page from a printed data dictionary.

Figure 8-12 is a page from a *printed* data dictionary. The pages can be kept in a
binder, in some sequence (such as alphabetically, by data item name), and they
provide the details about each item. The data dictionary provides a common
definition of the firm's data resource. Both users and information specialists can
then speak the same language when referring to data items. This standard description is especially valuable when the firm follows the *programmer team* concept,
where several programmers work on a system at the same time, subdividing its
processes. The programmer does not have to worry about naming items, determining their attributes, or identifying their sources. All of these details and more
are specified in the data dictionary.

    You will soon learn one thing about computer people—they like to comput-
erize everything. A manual system openly invites computerization. The printed

data dictionary was quickly seen as something that could be maintained in computer storage. Large organizations (or organizations with large data bases) can purchase or lease a *data dictionary system (DDS)*. Some of the DDSes are subsystems of commercial DBMSes, and others are standalone packages. The computerized dictionaries provide various statistics on data use in addition to describing its specifications. For example, you can get a "where-used" list to identify the programs using each data item. Also, you can find out which users receive a particular report.[3]

Data description language

After identifying the data items to be stored in the data base, you must communicate their specifications to the DBMS by means of a *data description language (DDL)*, which is part of the DBMS. For example, if you were using the 80 TOTAL DBMS offered by Cincom Systems, you would define the data items, the records, the data relationships, and the physical characteristics of each file using TOTAL's DDL. These DDL statements are processed by the data base generation program (DBGEN) working in conjunction with the operating system, as shown in Figure 8-13, to produce the data base descriptor. As the data base descriptor is created,

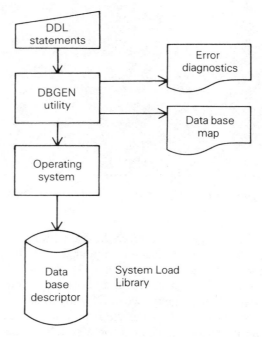

Figure 8-13 A flowchart of TOTAL's data definition process.

---

[3] A survey of nine computerized data dictionaries appears in Robert M. Curtice and E. Martin Dieckmann, "A Survey of Data Dictionaries," *Datamation* 27 (March 1981): 135 ff.

```
BEGIN-DATA-BASE-GENERATION:
DATA-BASE-NAME = ORDERB
BEGIN-MASTER-DATA-SET:
DATA-SET-NAME-CUST
MASTER-DATA:
CUSTROOT = 8
CUSTLKCO = 8
CUSTCTRL = 6
CUSTLKAR = 8
·1·CUSTNAME = 30
·1·CUSTADDR = 30
·1·CUSTCITY = 18
·1·CUSTSTAT = 2
·1·CUSTREVN = 6
END-DATA:
ACCESS-METHOD = ESDS
DEVICE = FBA

VSAM-CONTROL-INTERVAL-SIZE = 4096
TOTAL-LOGICAL-RECORDS = 108000
END-MASTER-DATA-SET:
```

ROOT—REQUIRED BY TOTAL

CUSTOMER NUMBER—LOGICAL KEY
FOR RECORD

LINK TO CUSTOMER ORDER
HEADER RECORDS

LINK TO INVOICES AND PAYMENTS

NAME

ADDRESS

CITY

STATE

TOTAL REVENUE YTD

USE VSAM-ESDS FOR THIS FILE

DESIGNATES EITHER 3310 OR 3370
DISK

Figure 8-14   TOTAL's data description
language (DDL).

DBGEN prints out any error diagnostics and also a data base map. The map relates the physical blocks of records in the DASD to particular files and records. Figure 8-14 illustrates the TOTAL DDL. The name of the data base is ORDERB, and the name of the file or data set is CUST. The customer records in the file contain the typical data items such as name, address, city, state, and total year-to-date revenue. The names for each of these items are listed. In addition, there

Table 8-2 User Directory

User Identification Number	Name	Accounting Reference Code	Systems Resources Allowed
01734	Smith, P. K.	21753-01	70KB primary 10MB secondary 3 tape units
36912	Leong, X. N.	14810-30	120KB primary 5 MB secondary 2 tape units
40654	Zinsmeister, D.	22364-10	50KB primary 10MB secondary
82199	Herrera, M. A.	30412-00	110KB primary 50MB secondary 4 tape units
94076	Winfield, T. R.	60973-01	100KB primary 20MB secondary 2 tape units

are two pointer fields that link the customer record with the order header records and the invoices and payments records. The data base descriptor is a directory of data items that is used by the DBMS to manage the data base.

Other directories in addition to the data definition can be supplied to the DBMS by means of the DDL. A *user directory* can authorize certain persons within the firm to use the data base. Table 8-2 is an example. Another directory is the *field directory,* which lists each data item and identifies the authorized users. This example appears as Table 8-3. These are only two examples. Others can restrict a user's access to certain time periods or give a user exclusive control over the creation, change, or deletion of certain data items. These directories provide different levels of control over the data base contents.

Data manipulation language

Each DBMS includes a *data manipulation language* (DML) that causes operations to be carried out on data base contents. These operations include the retrieval, modification, storage, and removal of data from the data base. The format of a typical Series 80 TOTAL DML appears in Figure 8-15. This is not the command itself, but the format of the command. The user provides specific names such as READM in the area identified as FUNCT, and CUST in the area identified as FILE. The DML format shown here is used in a COBOL program. This particular command enables the user to read selected data items from a file into an area of primary storage, where the items can then be processed. After the command is executed, the user can examine the STATUS field, through programming, to determine whether the operation was completed successfully.

Table 8-3 Field Directory

Data Item	File(s)	Authorized Users	
		I. D. Number	R/W/U*
Employee Number	Personnel	01734	R/U
	Payroll	40654	R
		94076	R
Employee Name	Personnel	01734	R/U
	Payroll	40654	R
		94076	R
Date of Hire	Personnel	01734	R/U
Date of Last Salary Increase	Personnel	01734	R/U
Amount of Last Salary Increase	Personnel	01734	R/U
Current Annual Salary	Personnel	01734	R/U
	Payroll	40654	R

* R—the user may read this data item.
  W—the user may add this data item to the file.
  U—the user may update this data item.

CALL DATBAS USING FUNCT, STATUS, FILE, KEY, ELEM-LIST, USER-AREA, ENDP.

Where:

DATBAS	A Series 80 TOTAL module that acts as an interface between the applications program and Series 80 TOTAL
FUNCT	A field in the user program containing the function to be performed (e.g., "READM")
STATUS	A field into which a status code will be returned. STATUS indicates the success or cause of failure of the operation
FILE	A field in the user program containing the name of the file to be accessed (e.g., "CUST")
KEY	(CONTROL-KEY)—The key field of the record
ELEM-LIST	(ELEMENT-LIST)—An area in the user program containing a list of specific data items requested
USER-AREA	The area in the user program where data contained in the requested data item will be placed
ENDP	The end of the parameter list

When Series 80 TOTAL returns control to the applications program, a status code is given indicating the result of the operation. On successful completion, a status code of "****" is provided. If the operation was unsuccessful, the data base is automatically restored to its condition before the operation, and an appropriate status indicates the cause of the failure.

Figure 8-15 A data manipulation language (DML) command.

DML can be included in programs written in high-level languages such as COBOL, FORTRAN, and PL/I. In this situation, the high-level languages are called *host languages,* and the DML is a *guest.* There are some special data base languages, such as MARK-IV, that include all of the commands necessary to process data in the data base. Languages such as MARK-IV are *self-contained* languages.

Both host and self-contained languages operate in the batch mode. If a manager wants to query the data base from a terminal and to receive an immediate response, he or she must use a special *query language.* These query languages work in conjunction with a data communications monitor, which will be described in the next chapter.

Using the DBMS

Our main concern up to this point has been the manner in which the data items in the data base (the schema) can be logically interrelated so that selected portions (the subschema) can be retrieved for processing. By creating a data dictionary, we identify the items composing the data base. These specifications are communicated to the DBMS by means of a data description language. The DBMS is equipped with the data manipulation language necessary to perform the required processing. Now if we assume that the data has been stored in the data base, we are ready to use the DBMS to provide management information. Figure 8-16 portrays the events. The numbered steps below correspond to the numbered arrows in the figure.

1. An applications program such as a payroll program is being executed. The program requires some data from the data base and contains a command that will cause the needed data items to be retrieved. The control unit of the CPU causes each instruction of the applications program to be executed in sequence. When the DML command is reached, the control passes from the applications program to the DBMS.
2. The DBMS verifies that the data requested has been previously defined in the schema and subschema. In addition, the DBMS uses various indices to determine the DASD address of the first item to be retrieved and to validate the user's authority to use the subschema items.
3. The DBMS requests the operating system to execute an input operation.
4. The operating system signals the channel to initiate the input operation, as described in Chapter 6. The channel causes the data to be accessed, read, and transmitted to a buffer storage area in primary storage. This is a special buffer storage used by the DBMS; it is not the same as the buffer storage in the channel. Control passes from the operating system back to the DBMS.
5. The DBMS transfers the data from the buffer storage to the input area used by the applications program.
6. The applications program processes the data.

Primary Storage

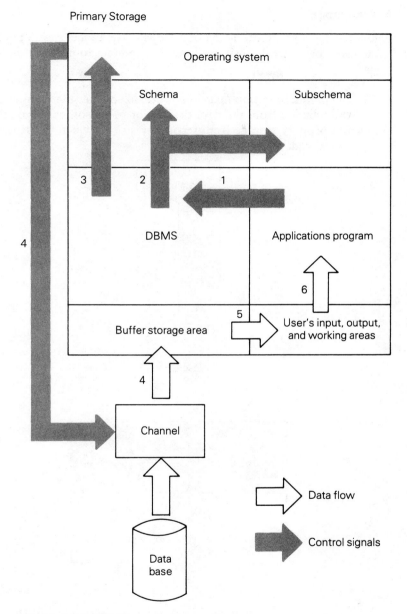

Figure 8-16 DBMS events.

This example recognizes the role of the DBMS in an input operation. A similar chain of events would occur for a write operation. The DBMS provides a software interface between the applications program and the operating system. The operating system in turn provides an interface between the software and the hardware. All of these software and hardware elements work together as an information processor.

A DBMS model

Figure 8-17 is a graphical model of a DBMS. The model shows the four components listed below and illustrates how they interact to perform the DBMS functions.

- The *data description language processor* creates the data base description (the schema) from the data description. This software module is brought into primary storage from secondary storage when the schema is created or updated.

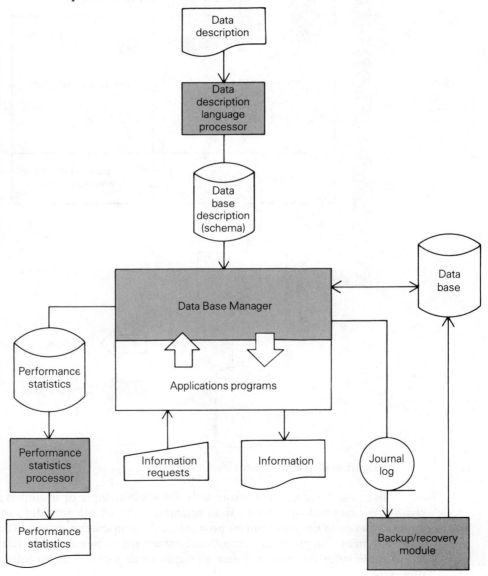

Figure 8-17   A DBMS model.

- The *data base manager* (also called the *data base supervisor*) resides in primary storage to handle requests from applications programs. This element also produces performance statistics and a journal log of data base activity.
- The *performance statistics processor* produces reports from the performance statistics identifying which data is being used and who is using it. The processor is brought into primary storage when the reports are to be prepared. The reports are used by managers in the information services department to manage the data base—identifying areas needing improvement and so on.
- The *backup/recovery module* reconstructs the data base in the event of a catastrophe. As the data base is updated, entries describing the changes are made in a journal log (on magnetic tape). These entries are used to reprocess a backup copy of the data base (created previously) to bring the copy up to date.

There is considerable variation among DBMS offerings on the market today, but most incorporate the basic elements in the model. The systems differ primarily in how the functions are performed.

Commercial Data Base Management Systems

General Electric is credited with developing the first DBMS, *Integrated Data Store* (*IDS*), in the early sixties. Next, IBM joined with North American Aviation to create *Data Language I*, or *DL/I*, the forerunner of one of IBM's current DBMS models—*IMS* (*Information Management System*). During the late sixties and the seventies, IBM was joined by several other firms in providing commercial DBMSes. Presently, IBM offers three DBMSes—DL/I, IMS, and the newer *SQL/DS* (pronounced "sequel"). Cincom Systems markets its *TOTAL* system for use on IBM, Honeywell, UNIVAC, CDC, DEC, Harris, Varian, and Interdata systems. Cullinane Database Systems, Inc., has a package called *IDMS* designed for use on IBM systems. Intel Corp.'s *SYSTEM 2000/80* is available for use on IBM, UNIVAC, and CDC equipment. Software AG of North America, Inc., has developed its *ADABAS* system for use on IBM and DEC computers. A 1979 survey revealed that these five firms (IBM, Cincom, Cullinane, Intel, and Software AG) had provided slightly over 4000 of the 11,000 installed DBMSes and had accounted for over 82% of the derived revenue.[4] The efforts by these firms have accounted for the initial DBMS offerings—packages designed for use on large- and medium-scale systems, as well as some of the more popular minis. In late 1981, there were fifty-four DBMSes offered by fifty companies to this upper end of the computer market.

There is considerable range in the performance capabilities of these DBMSes, as well as in their costs and hardware requirements. The primary storage requirement can be as low as 24KB or as high as 400KB. And the monthly license fee can range from $300 to $950.

---

[4]Krass and Wiener, p. 153.

During recent years, another area of DBMS activity has emerged. Some DBMS vendors have developed special packages for mini and micro systems. At the end of 1981, there were at least forty-one systems available for minis and at least forty-eight systems for micros.[5] Most mini systems are designed for use on the more popular brands—DEC, Data General, Prime, Hewlett-Packard, and so on. Most of the purchase prices are in the $10,000 to $35,000 range. Likewise, the micro systems are intended for popular brands such as Apple, Commodore PET, and TRS-80. Purchase prices for the micro packages are much lower—mostly in the $100 to $1000 range.

In Chapter 10, where we focus on mini/micros, we will study the DBMSes for those systems in more detail. At this point, we can better understand the DBMSes for the larger systems by taking a close look at one popular product: ADABAS.

The ADABAS system

ADABAS (pronounced "aid-a-base") stands for Adaptable Data Base System. It was first installed in July 1972 and has been continually updated and refined ever since. With ADABAS you can have as many as 255 files, each file can have up to

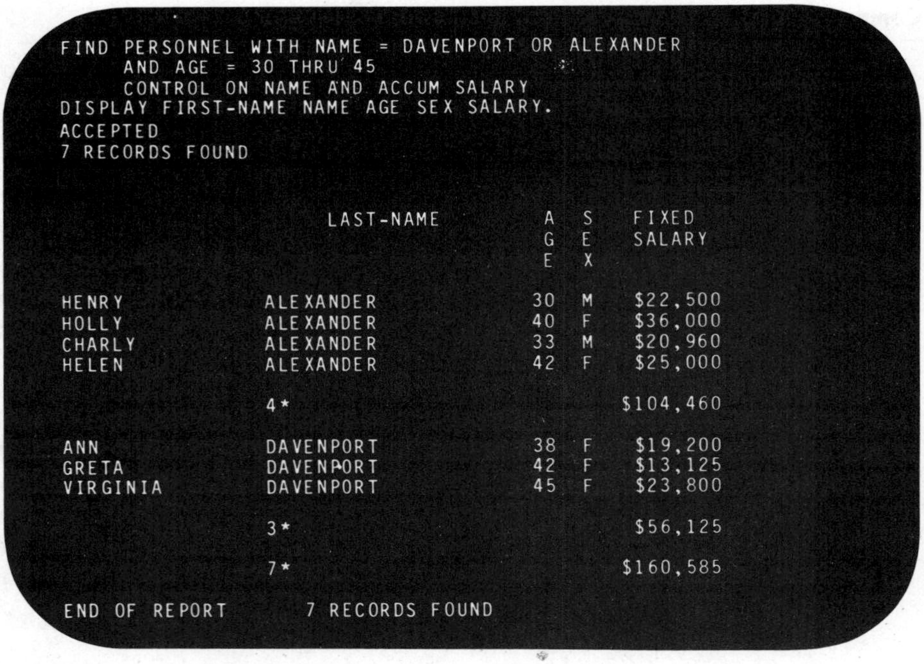

```
FIND PERSONNEL WITH NAME = DAVENPORT OR ALEXANDER
     AND AGE = 30 THRU 45
     CONTROL ON NAME AND ACCUM SALARY
DISPLAY FIRST-NAME NAME AGE SEX SALARY.
ACCEPTED
7 RECORDS FOUND


                         LAST-NAME        A   S    FIXED
                                          G   E    SALARY
                                          E   X

   HENRY         ALEXANDER                30  M    $22,500
   HOLLY         ALEXANDER                40  F    $36,000
   CHARLY        ALEXANDER                33  M    $20,960
   HELEN         ALEXANDER                42  F    $25,000

                 4 *                                $104,460

   ANN           DAVENPORT                38  F    $19,200
   GRETA         DAVENPORT                42  F    $13,125
   VIRGINIA      DAVENPORT                45  F    $23,800

                 3 *                                $56,125

                 7 *                                $160,585

END OF REPORT        7 RECORDS FOUND
```

Figure 8-18 A data base query.

[5] Harvey M. Weiss, "Which DBMS is Right for You?" *Mini-Micro Systems* 14 (October 1981): 157–160; Kathryn S. Barley and James R. Driscoll, "A Survey of Data-Base Management Systems for Microcomputers," *Byte* (November 1981): 208 ff.

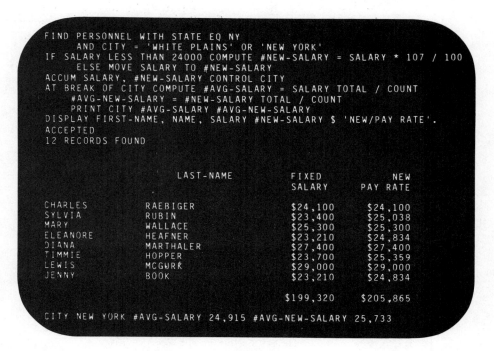

```
FIND PERSONNEL WITH STATE EQ NY
      AND CITY = 'WHITE PLAINS' OR 'NEW YORK'
  IF SALARY LESS THAN 24000 COMPUTE #NEW-SALARY = SALARY * 107 / 100
      ELSE MOVE SALARY TO #NEW-SALARY
  ACCUM SALARY, #NEW-SALARY CONTROL CITY
  AT BREAK OF CITY COMPUTE #AVG-SALARY = SALARY TOTAL / COUNT
      #AVG-NEW-SALARY = #NEW-SALARY TOTAL / COUNT
      PRINT CITY #AVG-SALARY #AVG-NEW-SALARY
  DISPLAY FIRST-NAME, NAME, SALARY #NEW-SALARY $ 'NEW/PAY RATE'.
  ACCEPTED
  12 RECORDS FOUND


                              LAST-NAME          FIXED            NEW
                                                SALARY        PAY RATE

  CHARLES          RAEBIGER                     $24,100        $24,100
  SYLVIA           RUBIN                        $23,400        $25,038
  MARY             WALLACE                      $25,300        $25,300
  ELEANORE         HEAFNER                      $23,210        $24,834
  DIANA            MARTHALER                    $27,400        $27,400
  TIMMIE           HOPPER                       $23,700        $25,359
  LEWIS            MCGURK                       $29,000        $29,000
  JENNY            BOOK                         $23,210        $24,834

                                               $199,320       $205,865

  CITY NEW YORK #AVG-SALARY 24,915 #AVG-NEW-SALARY 25,733
```

Figure 8-19 A data base query with computations.

16.7 million records, and each record can contain as many as 500 data fields. In short, ADABAS can handle a very large data base.

Both online and batch processing are permitted. A language called ADA-SCRIPT+ is used for querying the data base or preparing reports online. A sample of an ADASCRIPT+ dialog between a user and the system appears in Figure 8-18. The user keys in two commands, FIND and DISPLAY (the first four lines), the data is retrieved, and the report is prepared. This is a good example of how a manager can query the data base using a DBMS and receive a response in seconds.

The example in Figure 8-18 contains little computation—only accumulation of salary. In Figure 8-19 ADASCRIPT + causes division, multiplication, and addition to be performed. The user keys in several commands—FIND, IF, ACCUM, COMPUTE, and DISPLAY. This approach is much easier than coding a program, but it is limited to simple jobs.

Another software subsystem, called ADACOM, is used for the batch preparation of reports. ADACOM permits the use of some standard functions such as SUM, MAX, MIN, and AVER. The example in Figure 8-20 is a report prepared from data for several selected states (alphabetically from New York through Utah, excluding Oklahoma). ADACOM counts the number of company employees in each state, accumulates their salaries, and displays the state maximum.

In addition to ADASCRIPT+ and ADACOM, reports on data base schema can be prepared from a computerized data dictionary. In Figure 8-21 a report shows the details of three data items—PERSONNEL-NUMBER, PERSON, and

```
0010 FIND PERSONNEL WITH STATE = 'NY' THRU 'UT' BUT NOT 'OK'
0020 SORTED BY STATE DESCENDING
0030 AT BREAK OF STATE
0040    DO
0050       MOVE OLD (STATE) TO #STATE(A2)
0060       CALL 'STATET' #STATE #LONGNAME(A14)
0070       DISPLAY 'STATE' #LONGNAME
0080       'COUNT' COUNT (SALARY(N8)) (EM=Z,ZZ9)
0090       'TOTAL SALARIES' SUM (SALARY) (EM=ZZ,ZZZ,ZZ9)
0100       'MAXIMUM/SALARY' MAX (SALARY) (EM=ZZ,ZZZ,ZZ9)
0110    DOEND
0120 END


              STATE      COUNT TOTAL SALARIES  MAXIMUM
                                               SALARY
              ---------------  -----  ---------------  ----------

              UTAH           13     150,960          36,000
              TEXAS          22     320,050          50,000
              TENNESSEE      30     276,650          36,000
              RHODE ISLAND    8      74,000          24,000
              PENNSYLVANIA   27     343,950          48,000
              OREGON         20     223,300          48,000
              OHIO           26     250,900          48,000
              NEW YORK       52   1,313,640          29,500
```

Figure 8-20 A report prepared with a report writer.

NAME. These are the first three fields in the personnel file. The report identifies the field width, type of character, date of last maintenance activity, and so forth. Twenty different reports can be produced from the data dictionary.

Data base security is important. ADABAS provides for three levels of password security. Files, fields within files, and fields with certain values can be restricted to only those users who have the right passwords. In addition, data base contents can be encrypted—stored in coded form. Anyone obtaining unauthorized entry will be unable to interpret the scrambled contents.

Each commercial DBMS includes unique features. Selecting a DBMS can be just as involved as selecting a computer. You must first identify your needs and then select the DBMS that best satisfies them.

Data Base Advantages and Disadvantages

The terms *data base* and *DBMS* are not synonymous. The data base is the conceptual resource of the firm, and the DBMS is the software method of managing that resource.

The *advantages* to a firm of having a data base are:

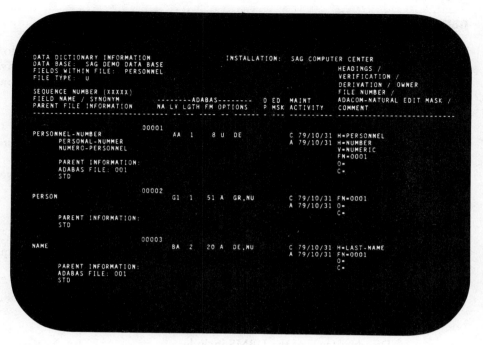

Figure 8-21 A report from the data dictionary.

1. An organized and comprehensive means of recording the results of the firm's activities
2. A reservoir of data to be used in meeting the information requirements of managers and other employees within the firm, and of elements in the firm's environment

The *disadvantages* stem from poor management of the data resource and include:

1. An increased opportunity for persons or groups outside the organization to gain access to information about the firm's operations
2. An increased opportunity for persons to make unauthorized changes in the physical system of the firm through manipulations of the conceptual system; for example, by embezzling funds through computer theft
3. An increased opportunity for poorly trained persons within the organization to misuse the data resource unintentionally; for example, by misinterpreting information output from the data base

As with any resource, the firm attempts to increase the value of the data base by improving both the quality and the quantity of its contents. The firm attempts to minimize the disadvantages by managing the resource better, which involves using a DBMS and improving security measures.

DBMS Advantages and Disadvantages

Although all firms have a data base in one form or another, all firms do not use a DBMS. In fact, only a small portion of firms have one. In general, the advantages of a DBMS relate to improvements in the management of the data base. The disadvantages relate primarily to the cost of the DBMS.

Specifically, the *advantages* of using a DBMS are:

1. A reduction in, but not elimination of, the amount of duplication and redundancy in files
2. Integrated file contents, allowing data to be combined for improved information reporting
3. The ability to handle complex data structures
4. The rapid retrieval of data base contents
5. Better security and integrity of the data base
6. Relatively easy recovery from unexpected catastrophe, such as equipment failure
7. Relatively easy creation and maintenance of the data base
8. "User-friendly" query languages and report generators, enabling nontechnical people to use the MIS

Disadvantages of the DBMS include:

1. Expensive software
2. Greater hardware demands, requiring computers with larger primary and secondary storage capacities than would otherwise be necessary
3. The need for a technically trained staff to oversee the use of the data base and the DBMS

Most computer users apparently feel that the advantages outweigh the disadvantages. They recognize the value of having a data base and of using it efficiently. The DBMS helps achieve both goals.

The Data Base Administrator

Interest in data bases has opened up an entirely new position in computing facilities—the *data base administrator,* or *DBA.* This person manages the data base. In large organizations, more than one person is needed. The duties of the DBA fall into four major categories: planning, consultation, operation, and control.

Planning involves working with users to define the subschemas and the schema. In addition, the appropriate DBMS must be selected. The DBA evaluates the systems on the market and recommends a particular DBMS to top management.

Consultation includes teaching users how to work with the DBMS and providing assistance when needed. The DBA becomes the specialist in data base matters, relieving the systems analyst of much of this responsibility.

Operation consists of creating the data base to conform to the specifications of the selected DBMS and establishing and enforcing policies and procedures for data base use.

Control includes the monitoring of data base activity using statistics provided by the DBMS. In addition, the DBA remains alert to security threats and takes action to correct any weaknesses that appear.[6]

Putting the Data Base and the DBMS in Perspective

The DBMS has made it possible for firms to achieve the type of data base necessary for decision support. Very few firms have a programming staff that could achieve a software system to handle the data management tasks as well as a commercial DBMS. During the late sixties and the seventies, only users of large- and medium-scale systems had the opportunity to obtain commercial DBMSes. More recently, however, many such packages have been developed for mini and micro systems. During this decade, the DBMS picture should get even better, with more packages achieving better performance at lower prices.

A DBMS is a necessary requirement for a firm to achieve a data base that meets the needs of the managers. The combination of the DBMS software, other systems and applications software, and the necessary hardware provide the firm with a valuable information processing capability.

Summary

In this chapter we defined the data base as that data stored in computer storage and available for processing. The DBMS manages the data base by storing, controlling, and retrieving data. You do not need a commercial DBMS to have a data base, but for firms that need to integrate their files, the commercial DBMS is the only practical alternative.

There is a difference between the physical and the logical arrangement of data. The physical structure represents the computer's perspective; the logical structure is how the user sees it. During the pre-data base period, the physical structure was dominant and influenced the way data was processed. Because of physical constraints, many requests for information could not be handled.

Several techniques can be used to make data available in a form that differs from its physical arrangement. The two techniques receiving our attention are linked lists and inverted files. A group of records, each containing one or more links, is called a linked list. A single link in each record permits chaining from one record to another in only one direction. The addition of a second link produces a two-way linked list. An inverted file makes it possible to retrieve records from

---

[6]For additional insight into the duties of the DBA, see the results of a recent survey in Ian B. McCirick and Robert C. Goldstein, "What Do Data Administrators Really Do?" *Datamation* 26 (August 1980): 131–134.

a file in a sequence other than that of the file. For example, a customer master file can be in customer number sequence, and an inverted file can be created that lists those customer numbers in salesperson number sequence. We can use the inverted file to obtain customer master records in salesperson sequence. A combination of inverted files and pointers makes it possible to assemble all of the data required to process a single transaction, even though that data might not be integrated physically.

The terms *file* and *record* are still important data base concepts, but two new words have been added. The schema describes the logical structure of the entire data base, and the subschema describes some particular subset. A single schema can have many subschemas.

When a firm decides to implement a data base, one of the first steps is to identify and define the data items to be included. The data dictionary is the accumulation of these definitions. Some data dictionaries are computerized, permitting the preparation of reports describing the data and detailing how it is used.

The data definition is communicated to the DBMS by means of a data description language (DDL). The DDL is used to build a directory of data items. Other directories restrict data base use in certain ways in order to maintain security and control.

Each DBMS has a data manipulation language (DML) that is used to read and write records, change logical linkages in records, find records that satisfy particular search criteria, and so on. These DML commands are inserted in applications programs at the appropriate points to cause the operations to occur.

Using a DBMS to retrieve or store data in the data base requires coordinating the applications program, the DBMS, the operating system, the channel, and the DASD. The applications program identifies the data base file, record, or item involved. The DBMS checks the schema and subschema and turns control over to the operating system. The operating system issues a command to the channel. And the channel causes the read or write operation in the DASD.

Although each commercial DBMS is unique, most consist of four basic modules. A data description language processor creates the schema. A data base manager controls the functions that occur while the data base is in use. The backup/recovery module helps reconstruct the data base in the event of a disaster. Finally, the performance statistics processor provides reports of data base use.

At the end of the 1970s, five commercial DBMSes accounted for over 82% of the revenue derived from all DBMSes designed for large computers. The situation has changed somewhat since then, with a number of DBMSes available for users of mini and micro systems.

We discussed the ADABAS system to show the kinds of features a DBMS can offer. The ADASCRIPT+ query language and the ADACOM report generator provide the means for generating information output. ADABAS keeps the data contents secure by imposing three levels of password security and by encrypting data records.

The DBMS permits an organization to achieve the advantages of an integrated data base. The main advantages are reduced duplication and the ability to integrate data from several files to produce information output. The main disadvantage of the DBMS is its total cost—including the DBMS package, increased hardware, and a professional staff to implement and maintain it.

If you wanted to have responsibility for a firm's data base, you would apply for the job of data base administrator (DBA). The DBA and his or her department plan how the data base and DBMS will be implemented, consult with users to identify their data and information needs, make the data base available to authorized users, and control the use.

In this chapter we have covered fundamentals of the data base and DBMS that apply to computers of all sizes. In Chapter 10 we will return to this topic and relate the DBMS specifically to mini and micro systems. In Chapters 11 through 15, we will provide examples of how the data base is used in decision support.

Key Terms

data base

data base management system (DBMS)

physical data organization

logical data organization

pre–data base approach

ad hoc request

data base approach

linked list

embedded pointer

list head, tail

two-way list, circular structure, ring structure

inverted file

schema

subschema

data dictionary, data element dictionary (DED)

data dictionary system (DDS)

data description language (DDL)

user directory

field directory

data manipulation language (DML)

host language, guest language

self-contained language

query language

data description language processor

data base manager, data base supervisor

performance statistics processor

backup/recovery module

data base administrator (DBA)

Key Concepts

The difference between a data base and a data base management system

The difference between physical and logical data organization

The pre–data base approach

The data base approach

The manner in which linked lists and inverted files can express logical relationships

How the applications program, DBMS, operating system, and channel hardware work together during an I/O operation

A DBMS model

Questions

1. What is a data base? What is a data base management system (DBMS)?
2. Must a firm have a data base to have an MIS? Must it have a DBMS?
3. What is the pre–data base approach? What is the data base approach? How do they differ?
4. How is an ad hoc request handled with a pre–data base approach? With a data base approach?
5. What are two techniques for expressing logical relationships between data? Provide a one-sentence definition of each.
6. What are the three data management functions?
7. Is the schema the same as the data base? Explain.
8. In what form does the data dictionary exist?
9. What role does the data dictionary play in the programming process?
10. How can the DDL be used to improve the security of the data base?
11. Explain the role of host and self-contained languages in relation to the DML.
12. What are the four components of the DBMS model?
13. Who would use the output of the performance statistics processor?
14. Name the five firms accounting for over 80% of the DBMS revenue in 1979.
15. Which manufacturer's computers are supported by all five of these DBMS firms? Can you explain why?
16. Which ADABAS subsystem provides an online query ability? Which produces reports in a batch fashion?
17. How does ADABAS contribute to data base security?
18. How could there be disadvantages to something as valuable as a data base?
19. If you were to summarize all of the DBMS disadvantages into a single one, what would it be?
20. Which would a firm acquire first—a DBMS or a DBA? Explain.

Problems

1. Assuming that the following records constitute the customer master file, enter the forward and backward links.

Customer Number	Year-to-Date Sales	Salesperson Number	Forward Sales-person Link	Backward Salesperson Link
104	25000.00	12		
109	17500.00	24		
111	12500.00	12		
118	6000.00	12		
124	12000.00	36		
127	300.00	48		
132	18000.00	36		
138	24000.00	12		
142	26500.00	48		
149	120.00	24		
151	8000.00	48		

2. Construct an inverted file in salesperson number sequence for the above customer file.
3. Draw the DBMS model.

CASE PROBLEM: Maple Leaf Industries, Ltd.

You have one of the most successful computer consulting firms in Canada. After completing the MIS program at a large Canadian university, you worked for four years as an analyst programmer for an energy company. Your first consulting jobs dealt with planning computer projects for energy companies, but you have since branched out into other industries. In addition to yourself, you have two systems analysts and a systems programmer.

Last week you presented a data base seminar in Toronto that was attended by over one hundred top executives of some of the largest computer-using firms in the country. The $250 tuition paid by each attending executive made the seminar a huge financial success, but you expect an even greater return in the form of follow-up consulting activity.

While enjoying your morning cup of coffee, you go through the stack of mail that has just been delivered. You notice an envelope from Maple Leaf Industries, and you recall that they had a representative at the seminar. You open the envelope and read

I greatly enjoyed the data base seminar. Although I believed, and still believe, that we have a good MIS, I was surprised to learn of the increased potential that a data base management system offers. It was a shock to my ego to realize that we are what you call a "pre–data base" company, but I want to change that.

We are very interested in implementing a data base management system and would like to consider retaining you as a consultant on the project. At present, we have no in-house data base management expertise. Could you please prepare a short list of the basic steps that we should take in implementing a commercial DBMS. Also, for each step, indicate the person, or persons, responsible. The list will give us a good idea of what we must do and an indication of the support we can expect from you in project planning. I am making the same request of two other computer consultants that I know.

I look forward to receiving your response.

Sincerely,

Anthony Scarmodo, President
Maple Leaf Industries, Ltd.

Questions

1. Provide Mr. Scarmodo with the list of steps he has requested.
2. Identify the person (by title) who should be responsible for each step. Should you, as a consultant, have a role? Are there people within Maple Leaf Industries who should be responsible? Will Maple Leaf have to bring in new personnel to assume any of the responsibilities?

Chapter 9

Data Communications

Learning Objectives

After studying this chapter, you should:

- Understand what is meant by the term *data communications*
- Know the objectives of data communications and how it is used in the MIS
- Be familiar with some of the alternatives in computing and communications equipment that can be integrated into a data communications network
- Understand a number of the more frequently used data communications terms
- Be familiar with some of the common carrier product offerings that can be incorporated into an MIS
- Understand how a manager operates and uses a terminal
- Have a better knowledge of the different kinds of terminals
- Understand the basic principles underlying the movement toward a standard network architecture, and understand the characteristics of that architecture

The Need for a Communications Ability

In our discussion of the computer thus far, we have described the CPU, the I/O units, and secondary storage. In the preceding chapter, we presented the software used with the secondary-storage hardware. We have discussed all of the units that comprise an onsite computer configuration. In this chapter, we expand the scope of our study to include the communication of data from one location to another.

Data communications is the movement of encoded information from one point to another by means of electrical, optical, or electro-optical transmission systems.[1]

We have already encountered data communications in our discussion of information processor hardware. In Chapter 5 we identified several basic approaches to computer processing—online, timesharing, realtime, and distributed—that make use of data communications. In our discussion of input/output devices in Chapter 6, we described hardcopy and CRT terminals. In this chapter we will put these and other topics in perspective by describing the fundamentals of data communications. As we have noted, many firms are distributing their information processors throughout the organization. A data communications ability is an integral part of many modern MIS designs.

Data Communications in the General Systems Model

Data communications can provide the link between the information processor on the one hand and the physical system of the firm and its environment on the other, as shown in Figure 9-1. The circled T symbols in the figure represent terminals. The terminals can be hardcopy or CRT, or they can be other types that we will

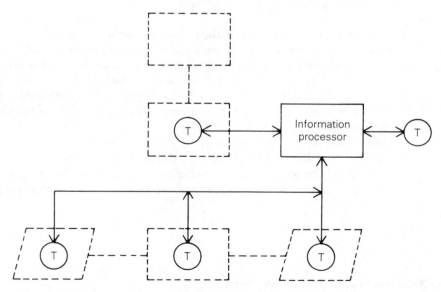

Figure 9-1 Data communications in the general systems model.

[1] Jerry FitzGerald and Tom S. Eason, *Fundamentals of Data Communications* (New York: John Wiley, 1978), p. 4. This excellent text, describing a complex topic in plain English, serves as the basis for much of the material found in this chapter. Another, more recent book on data communications is Vijay Ahuja, *Design and Analysis of Computer Communication Networks* (New York: McGraw-Hill, 1982).

discuss later. In addition, the terminals can be computers, large or small, that communicate with the host information processor.

All of the solid arrows represent two-way flows of data and information. Data can be gathered throughout the firm and from the environment and entered in the information processor. Data and information can also be provided by management. In each situation, data communications facilitates input. Data communications can also be used to transmit information from the information processor to management. For example, a graph can be prepared on a serial printer located in a manager's office. A terminal in a factory can instruct a worker performing a production task. And a terminal in a supplier's office can print out a purchase order for needed materials. In all of these examples, data communications facilitates output. Data communications is needed when any of the inputs and outputs take place some distance from the information processor, such as across town, across the nation, or around the world.

What Is Data Communications?

The most common communications technology until now has been electrical, specifically telephone lines. Recent innovations such as laser and infrared light beams and fiberoptics are opening up new possibilities. The equipment configurations that perform the transmission are often called *data communications networks*.

Data communications networks comprise three basic parts: a sending unit, a transmission channel, and a receiving unit. The sending unit, called the *source*, can be a computer or a terminal. The transmission channel is called the *medium* and can be telephone lines, microwave signals, laser beams, or other means. The receiving unit is called the *sink* and can consist of a computer or a terminal.

Data communications is often referred to as *datacom,* and we will use that contraction in this book in order to save a little ink. You will also hear the term *teleprocessing,* coined during the second computer generation by IBM and still quite popular. The software system within the CPU that interfaces applications programs with datacom networks is often called a *teleprocessing monitor*. We will use the term *data communications monitor*.

Objectives of Datacom

Firms integrate datacom hardware and software into their MIS configurations to accomplish one or more of the following objectives.

- *Capture data at its source.* Datacom enables the data to enter the information processor sooner and eliminates the unnecessary steps of recording and transporting data prior to entry.
- *Facilitate the rapid dissemination of information.* Datacom makes it possible to provide information to users when it is needed.

- *Facilitate organizational policies of either centralized or decentralized control.* Datacom makes it possible for a firm to achieve either objective. How the equipment is used depends entirely on the user's desires.
- *Reduce time and effort needed to perform a task.* With datacom, a person can completely handle a task by interacting with the information processor. For example, a manager can query the data base and receive a rapid reply, regardless of the distance separating the manager from the data base. Without datacom, the manager would have to wait hours or perhaps days to receive the report and complete the activity. The manager's desk would be piled high with semiprocessed work.
- *Reduce data transmission costs.* Datacom can be less expensive than using the mail or physically transporting data from one location to another. For most firms, datacom is the only feasible alternative. With datacom, a firm can transmit data by satellite from Miami to Seattle in seconds. Other methods would be too slow and costly.
- *Facilitate disbursed operations.* A firm can conduct its operations over a much wider geographical area with datacom. Datacom provides the electronic nervous system that enables far-flung operations to work in unison.
- *Facilitate company growth.* As a firm increases in size, it quickly outgrows its communications systems. Datacom enables the communication of large volumes of data and information among many participants at rapid speeds.
- *Contribute to improved management control.* Datacom makes it possible to get the right information to the right person at the right time. Managers can learn of activities as they occur or shortly thereafter. They can take remedial action before it is too late.

Uses of Datacom in the MIS

Much datacom activity is directed at data rather than information processing. In online processing, order entry clerks can enter sales order data using keyboard terminals. Claims adjustors can verify policy coverage by querying the home office data base from claims office terminals. Factory workers can record attendance and job completion from shop floor terminals. In each of these examples, a nonmanager is online to the information processor.

Timesharing, realtime, and distributed processing systems are also frequently data-oriented. For example, a utility company can let its outlying business offices timeshare the central computer to enter accounting data such as meter readings. Most of the current realtime systems (airline reservations and retail point-of-sale recording) are intended to handle data and to provide information to nonmanagement employees. Distributed systems also process data, such as inventory transactions.

The datacom resources are economically justified based on the data processing applications. The resources are therefore available for use in the MIS. In addition, the data processing activity produces an up-to-date data base that serves as a reservoir of data and information for the MIS. Were it not for datacom, such a data base would be impossible in large, geographically disbursed firms.

Datacom provides the link between the manager and the information processor, regardless of the distance between them. *Reports* can be transmitted electronically directly to the recipients, eliminating wasteful handling by intermediaries and improving security. Management *queries* can be handled from any location in the firm, giving outlying managers the same level of information support as those at headquarters. Managers can key in the input data required by mathematical *models* and receive the results of the computations, even though the software and hardware are located elsewhere. In all of these examples physical distance puts no constraint on management's use of the MIS.

Datacom Evolution

Throughout the relatively short history of computers, the use of datacom has swung back and forth between centralized and distributed systems. Figure 9-2 shows the centralized use of the first computers during the early and mid-fifties. Computers were so rare and expensive that large corporations installed them only at their headquarters. During the late fifties and early sixties hardware costs decreased, and large firms installed systems in their area and regional offices. The systems were not interconnected, however, since datacom hardware was extremely primitive.

The third computer generation brought newer and better datacom hardware and the first software. The larger, more powerful CPUs offered "more bang per buck" than smaller models. Firms could process their data more economically on a large, centralized computer than at many outlying sites. Firms began to return the processor power to the central office and to make that power available to the outlying sites by means of telephone communications facilities and terminals.

	1950s	1960s	1970s	1980s
	Centralized	Distributed	Centralized	Distributed
Headquarters	Large systems	Large systems	Large systems	Large systems
Subsidiary Offices and Locations	No computing equipment	Small systems not connected to headquarters	Terminals connected to system at headquarters	Minicomputers, often interconnected with system at headquarters to form an intrafirm computing network
	1950s	1960s	1970s	1980s

Figure 9-2 Periods of centralized and distributed computer use.

Interest in datacom increased, and telephone company officials were predicting that data traffic would outstrip voice traffic by 1980.[2]

Then an unexpected series of events occurred. The minicomputer became popular and began to be applied to business data processing. The minis were so inexpensive that large, widespread firms benefited from distributing the processor power once again. The microcomputer boom only added to the trend. Today a common pattern is for a firm to have a large information processor—a host—at headquarters linked to distributed processors—usually minis—at outlying locations.

As Figure 9-2 indicates, headquarters have always used large systems. Even though considerable computing equipment has been distributed throughout the organization, central control is maintained at headquarters. We can draw two conclusions from this situation. First, firms are not following a program of distributed processing, but rather of "semidistributed" processing. Second, distributed processing does not necessarily mean decentralized control.

Datacom Networks and Equipment

There are two categories of datacom equipment—channels (the media), and the devices attached to channels (the sending and receiving units). Most units attached to a channel can both send and receive data.

Figure 9-3 illustrates a basic datacom network. Here a CPU and a terminal communicate with each other. Communication is achieved by transmitting a message. We will use the term *message* to describe the data or information transmitted through the network. A message can include one or more data items, or it can include many records. A large file would most likely be represented by several messages.

Both the CPU and the terminal are attached to the data transmission channel (such as a telephone line, for example) with modems. *Modem* stands for *modu*lator-*dem*odulator. This unit converts a digital computer signal into an analog telephone signal (it *modulates* the signal) and converts an analog telephone signal into a digital computer signal (it *demodulates* the signal). The modem is required since the computer and the telephone equipment represent data differently. As we have seen, the computer represents data using a code of binary bits—zeros and ones. The telephone equipment represents data with different sound frequencies—cycles per second. The term *hertz* (abbreviated *Hz*) is often used to mean cycles

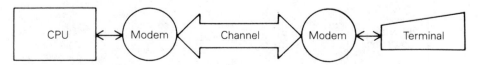

Figure 9-3 A basic datacom network.

[2] "Problems and Predictions for Communications Processing," *Datamation* 22 (June 1976): 117–120.

per second. The different tones that you hear when you use a push-button telephone to dial a number are the different frequencies for the digits.

A modem is not required when the data transmission channel is digital, rather than analog. Although digital equipment is increasingly used, it is not nearly as popular as analog equipment.

The channel pictured in Figure 9-3 is not the same channel described in Chapter 5. The channel we studied earlier connects the CPU to the I/O control units. The CPU channel is obtained from the manufacturer of the CPU. By contrast, the datacom channel is obtained from a communications company such as American Telephone & Telegraph (AT&T).

The network pictured in Figure 9-3 can be used to transmit data in both directions. The CPU can send data to the terminal, and the terminal can send data to the CPU. The modem attached to each end of the channel either modulates or demodulates signals, depending on the direction of the data flow.

One CPU can transmit data to another CPU. This is the case in distributed processing. It is also possible for a terminal to transmit to another terminal without a CPU being involved. This is an example of *offline communication*. We are primarily concerned here with *online communication*—a CPU serving as the source, the sink, or both.

A front-end communication processor

It is becoming increasingly popular to relieve a CPU of much of the work of attending to a data communications network. Mini and micro computers are used for this purpose, and they are called *front-end communication processors*. They are on the "front end"—interfacing with users of the network.

Figure 9-4 shows the network with a front-end processor included. One CPU can have several front-end processors attached, and each front-end processor can control hundreds of datacom channels. The front-end processor performs the following functions:

- It *polls* the terminals on the line, inquiring if they have a message to send.
- It *edits* data received from the terminals and either corrects the errors or orders the sending terminal to retransmit.
- It maintains a *message log* of all messages sent from the CPU or received from the terminals. In conjunction with this logging, it assigns a serial number, date, and time of day to each message for control purposes.
- It *converts character bits* received from the CPU in parallel to the serial form required for channel transmission, and it performs the reverse conversion on data flowing to the CPU.

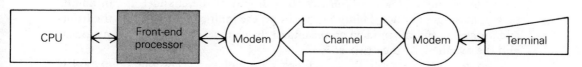

Figure 9-4 A datacom network with a front-end processor.

- It performs a *store-and-forward* service by holding data intended for a terminal that is either busy or out of service. The data is sent later when the terminal is available.
- It *adds codes* to messages so that they can pass along the channel to the correct terminal, and it removes similar codes from messages directed to the CPU.
- It *determines the path* a message will follow when several channel alternatives exist.

As the front-end processor performs these tasks, it communicates with a systems software package maintained in primary storage—the *data communications monitor*. The data communications monitor provides the same type of software interface with the datacom network that the DBMS provides with the data base. When a front-end processor is not installed, the data communications monitor performs all of the above functions and more. The front-end processor relieves the data communications monitor of much of its workload by *offloading* many of the network functions.

Multidrop lines

The two networks illustrated in Figures 9-3 and 9-4 are examples of point-to-point lines. A *point-to-point* line is one that has a single CPU or terminal on one end and only a single CPU or terminal on the other end.

It is possible (and common) to attach multiple CPUs or terminals to a channel, as illustrated in Figure 9-5. This configuration is called a *multidrop line*—multiple terminals or CPUs are dropped along the line. All of these units share the same channel under the control of the front-end processor.

Loop lines

When the terminals are near the CPU (in the same building, for instance) they can be attached by means of a coaxial cable called a *loop line*. The cable is owned by the computer user rather than the communications company. This type of channel is an example of a *private line,* often called a *dedicated line*. Since all data transmission is in digital code, no modems are needed. Figure 9-6 shows an example. When a privately owned cable is used in this manner, the terminals are said to be *hard-wired* to the CPU.

Multiplexers

The communication channel can ordinarily carry only one message at a time. By attaching a unit called a *multiplexer* to each end of the channel, it can handle several messages at once. Figure 9-7 positions the multiplexers between the front-end processor and the modem at one end of the channel, and between the modem and the terminals at the other end.

There are two methods for achieving multiplexing. The oldest method is *frequency division multiplexing (FDM)*. In FDM, the channel is subdivided into

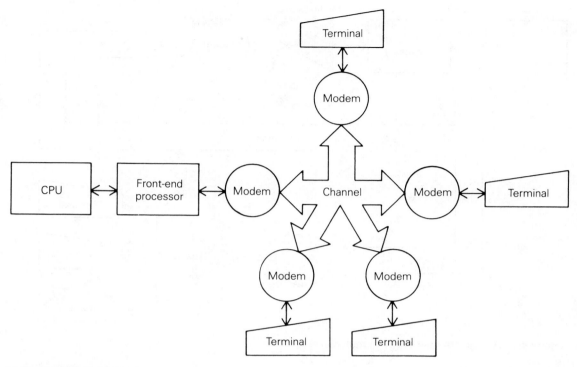

Figure 9-5 A multidrop line.

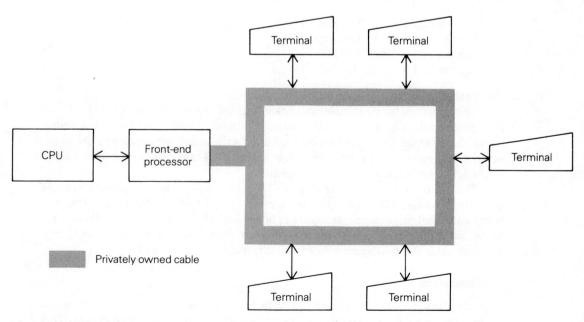

Figure 9-6 A loop line.

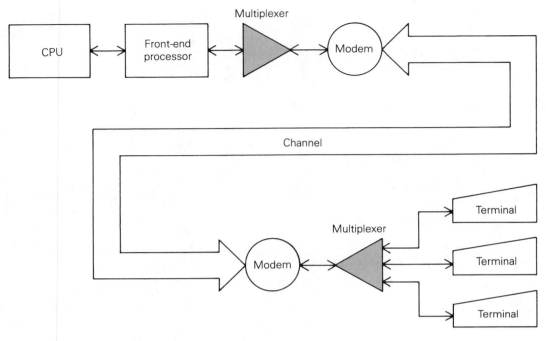

Figure 9-7 A datacom network with multiplexers.

several frequency subchannels. For example, if a channel can handle up to 3000 Hz, it can be subdivided into four subchannels:

Subchannel 1	300–800 Hz
Subchannel 2	900–1400 Hz
Subchannel 3	1500–2000 Hz
Subchannel 4	2100–2600 Hz

The unused frequencies separate the subchannels.

The other multiplexing method is *time division multiplexing* (TDM). TDM merges characters sent to several terminals into a "frame" and sends the frame down the channel. At the receiving end another multiplexer separates the characters and directs them to the appropriate terminals. Transmissions from terminals to the CPU are treated in the same manner.

The main advantage of TDM over FDM is the higher number of subchannels that are possible. TDM can handle as many as thirty-two. But with TDM the subchannels all originate or terminate at one point. Multidrop lines usually require FDM, which permits origins and terminations at any point along the line. Figure 9-8 illustrates the two approaches to multiplexing.

Concentrators

A device similar to a multiplexer can be installed at the same point on the line to "pool" messages from several sending units and transmit them as a group. This

Frequency Division Multiplexing (FDM)

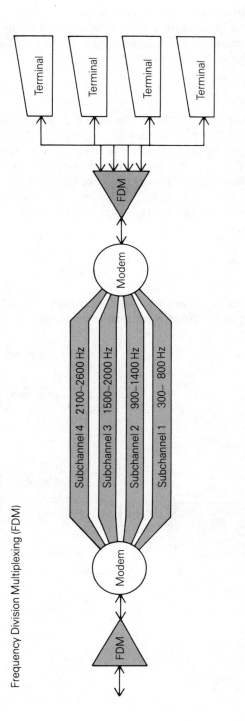

Time Division Multiplexing (TDM)

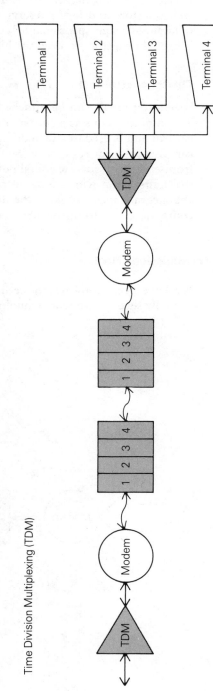

Figure 9-8 Two multiplexing methods.

device, called a *concentrator,* is usually a mini or micro that performs editing as well as a store-and-forward service. Concentrators are normally found at the ends of high-cost, high-speed channels where traffic from several slower-speed channels is brought together to keep the high-speed channel busy.

Cluster control units

Several terminals can be attached to the channel by means of a minicomputer. The mini functions as a *cluster control unit.* As pictured in Figure 9-9, the cluster control unit is used to attach different types of terminals to the line. The terminals can also be of the same type. The cluster control unit offloads activities from the front-end processor—terminal polling, data editing, and so on. Using cluster control units along with front-end processors permits a more even distribution of channel management along the network. The management moves from the host computer closer to the terminal user.

Data Transmissions Media

We have been using telephone lines as an example of a transmission medium. Actually several different technologies provide the transmission medium that con-

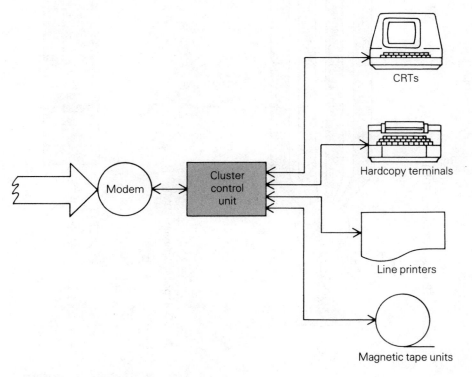

Figure 9-9   A cluster control unit.

nects the source to the sink. These technologies may be provided by communications firms known as *common carriers*. Common carriers include AT&T, General Telephone & Electronics (GTE), Western Union, ITT World Communications, United Communications, and so on.[3]

The vast majority of the media in use today were built to handle voice traffic. These same media can handle data, although not always at the rate and quality level desired. Some of the more important media technologies follow.

- *Telephone wire pairs.* This is the oldest type of medium. Work on our network of telephone lines began over a hundred years ago, and today there are almost one billion miles of circuits blanketing our nation. The lines are constructed of many pairs of wires, twisted and enclosed in a cable covering. Each pair form one voice-grade channel. The telephone lines are designed to carry voice communication, and that level of quality is called *voice-grade*. In certain areas where older telephone equipment is still in use, the quality of voice-grade lines is inadequate for data communications—they create too many errors. In these situations, the lines can be specially conditioned to *above voice-grade* for data transmission.

- *Coaxial cables.* A coaxial cable consists of some type of cylinder containing a single wire conductor. The conductor is separated from the cylinder by insulation. Twenty such cables can be packaged into a large cable, often buried underground, that can carry up to 18,740 telephone calls at a time.[4] These cables are of much higher quality than the wire pairs.

- *Microwave towers.* You have probably noticed towers like the one pictured in Figure 9-10 as you drive around the countryside. These are microwave towers that transmit traffic by means of radio signals. About a hundred such towers are needed to send a message from coast to coast. The signals transmitted by the towers follow the line of sight—they cannot bend with the curvature of the earth.

- *Satellites.* Even though microwave signals cannot bend, they can travel great distances in a straight line. A signal can originate on earth, bounce off a satellite, and return to another location on earth thousands of miles from the sending point. Satellites provide the datacom link for international organizations. A branch office in Sydney, Australia, has the same access to the firm's headquarters in Memphis as an office in Tallahassee. The first commercial satellite was Westar I (still in orbit), launched by Western Union in 1974. Other common carriers in the satellite business are AT&T, GTE, Continental Telephone Corp., Communications Satellite Corp. (COMSAT), RCA, and American Satellite Corporation.[5] A new entry is Satellite Business Systems (SBS), formed in 1979 by IBM, Aetna Life and Casualty Co., and COMSAT. The satellites are usually placed in orbit over the equa-

---

[3] Louise C. Shaw, Marva Levine, and Roseanna Guilsano, "Data Communication Carriers," *Datamation* 26 (August 1980): 107 ff.

[4] FitzGerald and Eason, p. 37.

[5] Shaw, Levine, and Guilsano, p. 107 ff.

Figure 9-10 A microwave tower.

tor at a height of 23,300 miles so that their speed is synchronized with the earth's rotation. Thus the satellites seem to hang in space over a certain point. RCA lost its Satcom III satellite on December 10, 1979, while attempting to put it into orbit over the equator. It hasn't been heard from since. Figure 9-11 shows how a satellite can be used when things go as planned.

- *Lasers.* A laser is a very high frequency, concentrated beam of light that can transmit 100,000 times as much data as a microwave signal. A single laser beam can handle all of the telephone calls for a city the size of Denver. At present lasers have been used only for short-distance transmissions, but they are regarded as the medium of the future. Research is combining laser beams with tiny optical fibers (fiberoptics) to transmit signals at higher speeds and densities than wires or coaxial cables allow.

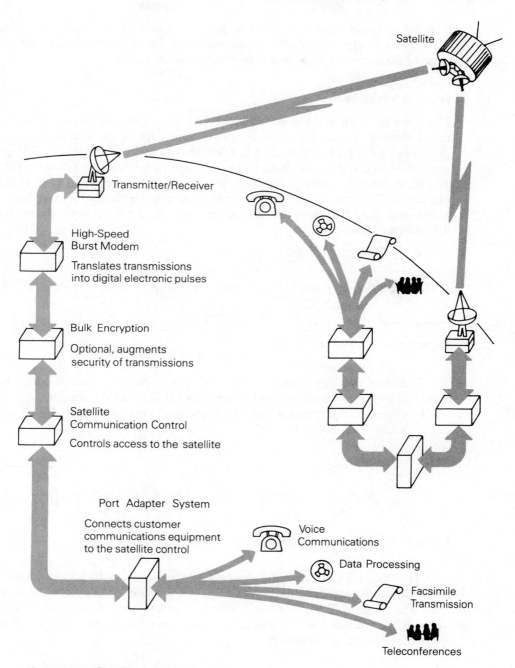

Figure 9-11 Satellite transmission.

Some Data Transmission Fundamentals

In order to understand how datacom equipment is used in an MIS, we should cover some fundamentals of data transmission. These fundamentals deal with types of transmission, data codes, and transmission modes.

Types of transmission

There are three basic types of channels. The most basic and least expensive is called *simplex*. A simplex channel can transmit data in one direction only, as shown in Figure 9-12. An example is a simplex channel connecting the CPU with a terminal in a warehouse that can only receive (a *receive-only printer—ROP*). The ROP can print out a picking list, for example, that the warehouse workers can use in filling the order. But the workers cannot use the terminal to communicate with the CPU. Both the simplex channel and the ROP are intended only for one-way use.

Figure 9-12   Simplex transmission.

A channel that can transmit in either direction, but only one way at a time, is the *half-duplex* channel pictured in Figure 9-13. The half-duplex channel is the best link between the manager and the information processor, since the manager can both send and receive messages.

Figure 9-13   Half-duplex transmission.

The third type of channel is the *full-duplex* channel, which can transmit in both directions simultaneously. Naturally this is the most expensive. It is only used when high-volume, two-way traffic is essential. Since data exists in higher volumes than information, a full-duplex channel is typically used for data, rather than information, transmission.

Data codes

Two coding systems account for practically all datacom traffic today. A 1981 survey of some 1600 users of datacom revealed that over half transmit data using the ASCII and EBCDIC codes.[6] No other codes achieved a use rate higher than 10%.

You recall that we studied both the EBCDIC and ASCII codes in Chapter 5. The *EBCDIC* code used in datacom is the same as that used in computer storage; however, there are two ASCII codes. ASCII-8 (an 8-bit code) is used in storage, and *ASCII-7* (a 7-bit code) is used in datacom. ASCII-7 was adopted as a U.S. standard in 1968. You can represent 128 (2^7) unique character codes with the seven data bits.

The oldest code is *Baudot,* developed in the nineteenth century for telegraph use. Baudot is not used for data transmission because it does not contain a check bit. Baudot can neither detect nor correct errors, and this feature makes it unacceptable as a datacom code.

Transmission modes

Characters are usually transmitted serially—one bit at a time. The bits, represented by frequencies, are generated by the source and received by the sink. How can the sink separate the bits of one character from those of another? Three techniques can accomplish this decoding, and they are referred to as *transmission modes.*

First is the *synchronous* mode, used for the high-speed transmission of a block of characters. Both the sending and the receiving devices are synchronized so that they work as a unit. Just prior to data transmission, a group of "sync" characters is transmitted to establish the coordination. Once coordination is established, the sending device transmits thousands of bits in a block, and the receiving unit, knowing which code is used, counts off the appropriate number of bits for each character. Synchronous transmission is fast because only data bits are sent. Speeds in excess of 9600 bits per second are possible. The main disadvantage is the effect of an error. If a single bit is dropped or an extra one picked up during the transmission, the synchronization between the source and the sink is lost. In this case the entire data block must be retransmitted.

The effect of this type of error is reduced when each character is sent separately. If a single-bit error is made, only that character need be retransmitted. This mode is called *asynchronous* because the sending and receiving units are not synchronized. When the sending unit is ready to transmit a character, the character is sent. There are no preliminary synchronizing characters. Each data character is bounded (preceded and followed) by start and stop bits. An EBCDIC character is preceded by a single start bit and followed by a single stop bit. This approach requires the transmission of the nondata start/stop bits, which effectively slows down the transmission speed. Asynchronous transmission is often referred to as *start/stop* transmission. Of the modes described here, it is the slowest—normally limited to about 1800 bits per second.

The third mode, *isochronous,* combines features of the other two. Each character code includes start and stop bits so that characters can be transmitted at irregular intervals, but the sending and receiving units are synchronized. A clocking mechanism built into both units permits faster transmission than the synchron-

[6] "Computers in Communications: A Ratings Survey," *Datamation,* 27 (July 1981): 106.

ous mode. Isochronous transmission occurs at speeds of up to 9600 bits per second.

The 1981 datacom survey found that synchronous transmission is used more often than asynchronous for all classes of users.[7] The most popular transmission speeds range from 600 to 2400 bits per second (bps), followed by 4800 bps, and then 9600 bps. Although it is possible to transmit at speeds higher than 9600 bps, it is rarely done. Only 8% of the large-scale users transmit at 56,000 bps, which is possible with a digital (not analog) technology available from AT&T called *Dataphone Digital Service,* or DDS.[8]

Common Carrier Product Offerings

The most popular product offering is the *leased voice line* that permits transmissions of up to 2400 bps. These leased lines are dedicated to transmitting a firm's data and are not shared with other users. Next in popularity come *leased high-speed lines* and *direct distance dialing* (DDD). The high-speed lines are specially conditioned so that they can handle up to 9600 bps. With DDD, you can transmit data the same way you make a phone call. The line is shared by many users, and each either pays a monthly charge (for local service) or pays for the amount of time that the line is used (for long-distance service). The least popular product offerings are *DDS* and *privately built lines.* Firms seldom build their own communication lines.

WATS lines

Common carriers have long offered a special bulk arrangement for large volumes of long-distance voice traffic. A firm can lease a WATS (Wide Area Telecommunications Service) line and make any number of calls up to a certain limit, without incurring any charge in addition to the bulk rate. A firm can purchase a block of as little as fifteen hours a month, or it can purchase service around the clock. The common carrier meters the time used.

WATS lines can be either *incoming* or *outgoing,* but not both. If a firm wants its customers to be able to place orders by long-distance telephone, it leases an incoming WATS. If a firm wants to be able to transmit messages to its branch offices, it leases an outgoing WATS.

WATS lines can also be *in-state* or *out-of-state.* With an in-state WATS, all traffic is confined to the home state. With an out-of-state WATS, the firm can transmit messages between its location and any location outside of the home state. A firm can obtain complete coverage and flexibility by leasing four WATS lines—incoming/in-state, incoming/out-of-state, outgoing/in-state, and outgoing/out-of-state. An incoming/out-of-state WATS with full business day use (240 hours per month) costs a firm in Dallas $3873.20 per month, figured in the following manner:

---

[7] Ibid.

[8] Ibid.

Base cost	$ 73.60
First 15 hours @ $20.21/hour	303.15
Next 25 hours @ $18.45/hour	461.25
Next 40 hours @ $16.72/hour	668.80
Next 160 hours @ $14.79/hour	2366.40
	$3873.20

Terminal Equipment

The most popular datacom terminals—CRTs and hardcopy—were discussed in Chapter 6. These units are used in many clerical operations for data entry and data base query. Our interest, however, is confined to the manager's use of terminals.

The managers' use of terminals

When a manager wishes to establish a connection between a terminal and the CPU he or she dials the telephone number of the computer center. When the manager hears a high-pitched tone, indicating that the connection has been made, he or she places the telephone handset in an *acoustic coupler*. The acoustic coupler is a low-cost modem that permits an ordinary push-button telephone to establish the terminal connection. In some of the newer models, the phone itself sits on top of the acoustic coupler as shown in Figure 9-14.

Figure 9-14 An acoustic coupler.

When a manager wishes to use a terminal that is hard-wired into the CPU, there is no need to establish the connection. The manager simply turns on the terminal and presses a key (such as RETURN) to alert the CPU. The CPU responds (actually the operating system does) by displaying a request for identification. The manager keys in the identification, such as an *account number* (used by the operating system to charge computer use to the manager) and a *password* (used to prevent unauthorized access to software and data). When the operating system accepts the codes, it asks the manager to identify the nature of the job. The command structure that the manager uses is the *JCL—job control language*. The JCL varies from one computer to another. If the manager wants to compile a program in BASIC, he or she keys in the word *BASIC*. If a particular program is to be executed that already exists in the software library, that program name is keyed in. The operating system retrieves the program from secondary storage and brings it into primary storage. The operating system may prompt the user by displaying a special character (such as a >) at the left margin.

Using the computer through terminal interaction is referred to as the *conversational mode*—the user and the computer converse with each other. There are three basic methods for achieving this interaction. First, the program can display a *menu* of items available for selection—such as models to execute. This is the *menu-display* technique shown in Figure 9-15. The prompt character, called a *cursor,* is positioned on the first selection. If the manager wishes to execute that

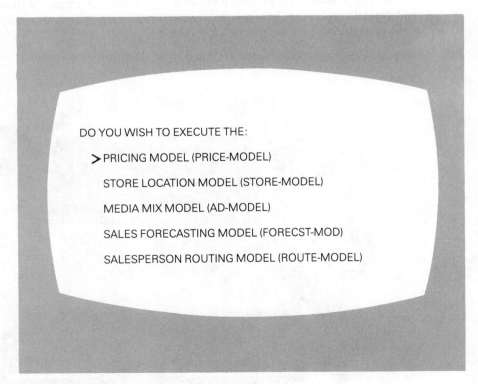

Figure 9-15 Menu-display technique.

model, he or she presses a certain key (such as the letter *Y* for yes). To select another entry, the manager presses the RETURN key. Each time the RETURN key is pressed, the cursor drops to the next item.

Once an entry from the menu has been selected, a second menu can be displayed, then a third, and so on. In this manner, the manager can communicate to the CPU which routine is to be executed as well as the input data for that routine. Menu display is designed for use with a CRT.

A second popular method for inputting data is the *form-filling technique*. An outline of a data form can be displayed on the screen (this technique also is best suited for a CRT), and the manager types the needed data in the appropriate blanks. The cursor is moved from one blank to another by the user or by the program. Figure 9-16 illustrates this approach. This example displays data items needed by the pricing model selected from the previous menu. When the data has been entered, another form can be displayed, asking for additional items.

The third method for entering instructions and data is the *questions-and-answers technique*. You can see in Figure 9-17 that the manager can respond by answering yes or no or by providing data items. The terminal prints or displays the question followed by a question mark. The question mark is the cue for the manager to respond. The response immediately follows the question mark. This technique works equally well with hardcopy and CRT terminals. On either terminal, the questions are asked one at a time. As soon as the manager responds,

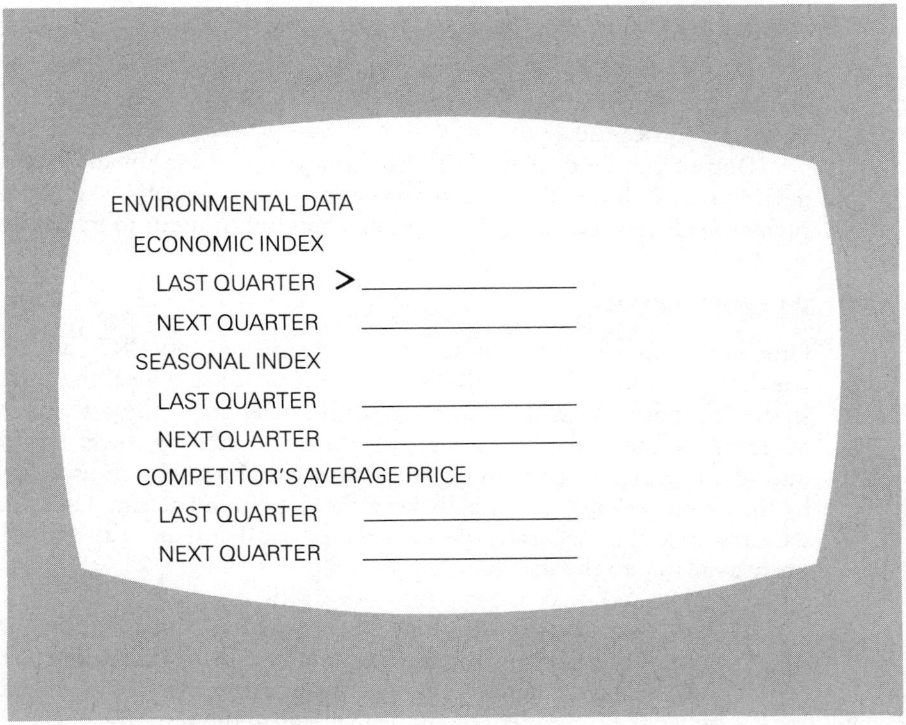

Figure 9-16 Form-filling technique.

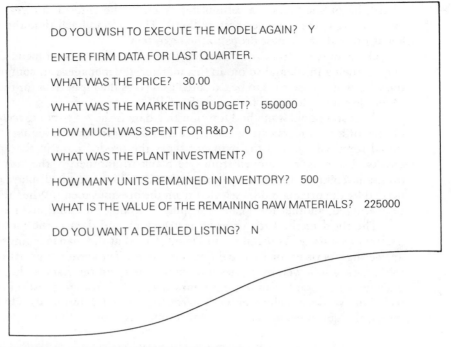

Figure 9-17   Questions-and-answers technique.

another question is asked. When all of the data and instructions have been entered, the data is processed.

Output can be displayed on the manager's terminal or directed to another device such as a line printer or plotter. The manager signs off by keying a command such as OFF and returning the telephone handset (if used) to its base.

Types of terminals

Other types of terminals, in addition to hardcopy and CRT, are push-button telephone, remote job entry (RJE), point of sale, data collection, intelligent, and special purpose. With the exception of the telephone, these terminals are not operated by the manager. Rather, they are operated by lower-level employees during the course of performing their daily activities. The transactions initiated by the employees using terminals keep the data base current. Thus a conceptual data resource that accurately reflects the physical system of the firm is continuously available to the manager.

1. *Push-button telephone.* In Chapter 6 we explained that the manager can use an ordinary push-button telephone to enter data into the computer by pressing the buttons, and that the manager can receive audible responses when the computer is equipped with an audio response device. When used in this manner, the telephone becomes the least expensive type of terminal.

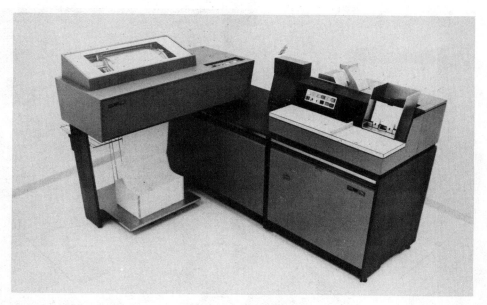

Figure 9-18 A remote job entry (RJE) terminal.

2. *Remote job entry.* An RJE terminal is used when a large volume of input and/or output occurs at a given location, such as in a timesharing network. A good example is an input/output center on a college campus. An RJE terminal, shown in Figure 9-18, includes a punched card reader and a line printer. If users submit their jobs in punched card form, the cards are read and the output printed on the line printer. If users submit their jobs on a CRT, the output is directed to the RJE terminal for printing. The jobs can be weekly payroll calculations, personnel file changes, purchase orders, or other types of transactions that can be handled in batches. The IBM 3780 terminal pictured in Figure 9-18 reads at a speed of 400 cards per minute and prints at a speed of up to 300 lines per minute. Cards can also be punched at a speed of up to 355 cards per minute.

3. *Point of sale.* Two basic types of POS terminals in popular use today are the retail terminals, used primarily in department stores, and the universal product code (UPC) bar code readers, used in supermarkets. The *retail terminal* (described in Chapter 6 and pictured in Figure 6-19) permits data entry from a keyboard or an OCR wand. The units can be online or offline. Offline units typically record transaction data on a cassette tape or floppy disk for processing later. The UPC terminal (discussed in Chapter 6 and pictured in Figure 6-20) is online to either a store mini or a larger system located some distance away.

4. *Data collection.* Data collection terminals are designed for use in factories but can be found elsewhere, as in libraries. The terminal permits data entry on a keyboard or from punched cards or plastic badges. Factory

Figure 9-19   A data collection terminal.

workers use terminals like that in Figure 9-19 for *attendance reporting,* clocking on and off their shift. The terminals are also used for *job reporting,* clocking on and off each job performed. The workers identify themselves for both attendance and job reporting by inserting their badges in the badge reader. Jobs are identified using punched cards that accompany the materials. Variable data, such as the number of pieces rejected, is entered on a keyboard. Libraries use the same equipment to check out books. The units feature a rugged design that stands up well to rough treatment.

5. *Intelligent.* The terminals discussed up to now can perform only input/output operations. They are called *dumb terminals.* When a terminal includes a microprocessor, or when it actually is a microcomputer, it can perform certain operations independent of the CPU. This type is known as an *intelligent terminal.* Intelligent terminals frequently include floppy disk drives for storing the user's data base. They can edit input data and retrieve data from the data base. Certain transactions can be handled locally, or data can be exchanged with the host CPU. Some intelligent terminals rely on routines prerecorded in their chip storage units. The term *firmware* refers to this hardware that performs software functions. An example of an intelligent terminal application is order entry, where the terminal is able to edit input data for possible errors and to conduct a credit check without interacting with the host.

Figure 9-20 A special-purpose banking terminal.

6. *Special purpose*. Computing equipment manufacturers will frequently construct a terminal to meet the special needs of an industry or a firm. A good example is the terminal used at some McDonald's restaurants with keys representing the different products. You want a Big Mac. The clerk presses the appropriate key. The terminal automatically computes the bill and even updates the inventory of ingredients.

   Figure 9-20 pictures three pieces of terminal equipment designed by Burroughs for banking applications. The unit in the center is a printer and the units on either side handle customer deposits, withdrawals, and account balance queries. Another special terminal is designed for use at nurses' stations in a hospital. These special-purpose terminals are usually a type of intelligent terminal.

Datacom Network Architecture

The increasing popularity of datacom over the past decade has created problems for systems designers. The problem stems from the large number of firms manufacturing datacom equipment, and the lack of standards that permit easy integration of the units. In 1980 there were fifty firms with datacom sales over $1.5 million each.[9] Users can encounter problems when they try to integrate hardware and software from several different vendors.

Several manufacturers of computing equipment have recognized the need for standardization. In 1974 IBM announced a plan called *Systems Network Architecture (SNA)*. Two years later Sperry Univac announced its *Distributed Communications Architecture (DCA)*. In 1977 NCR unveiled its *Distributed Network Architecture (DNA)*. The following year Burroughs announced its *Burroughs Network Architecture (BNA)*, aimed initially at host-to-host applications rather than the terminal-to-host orientation of the other three plans. Other firms such as Control Data, Honeywell, Digital Equipment, and Hewlett-Packard have likewise done work in this area.[10]

Network levels and layers

The IBM, Univac, and NCR architectures are characterized both by *levels* of *physical* network connections and by *layers* of *logical* network connections. By separating the logical connections from the physical connections, the management of the datacom network is less dependent on technology.

Figure 9-21 shows the three levels of physical connections—link, path, and end user to end user. The *link level* connects two or more elements (called *nodes*) in the network. Each symbol in the figure represents a node. The *path level* is composed of one or more links connecting the origination and destination nodes. Either the host computer or a terminal can serve as the point of origin or destination of a message. The highest level includes the end users at the points of origin and destination. This is the *end-user-to-end-user level*. End users can be (1) people operating terminals, or (2) applications programs located in the host, a front-end processor, a cluster control unit, or an intelligent terminal.

Each node in the physical network can represent up to three layers of logic. The host and terminal nodes have three layers, as illustrated in Figure 9-22. Intermediate nodes and cluster nodes have one layer and possibly more, depending on the equipment.

The *application layer* includes those routines that cause a user's data to be processed. In the host, the application layer is represented by applications programs. In the terminal node, the application layer is represented by operator actions or by hardware or software (if it is an intelligent terminal).

The application layer interfaces with the *function management layer,* which formats the message for transmission through the network. Formatting can be accomplished by the DBMS in the host node and by hardware and/or software in the terminal node.

---

[9] Ronald A. Frank, "Alive and Well," *Datamation* 26 (June 1980): 112 ff.

[10] For a comparison of the IBM, Sperry UNIVAC, and NCR architectures, see Ralph G. Berglund, "Comparing Network Architectures," *Datamation* 24 (February 1978): 79–85. For information on Burroughs network architecture, see Ronald A. Frank, "Readying BNA for User Nets," *Datamation* 26 (July 1980): 57 ff.

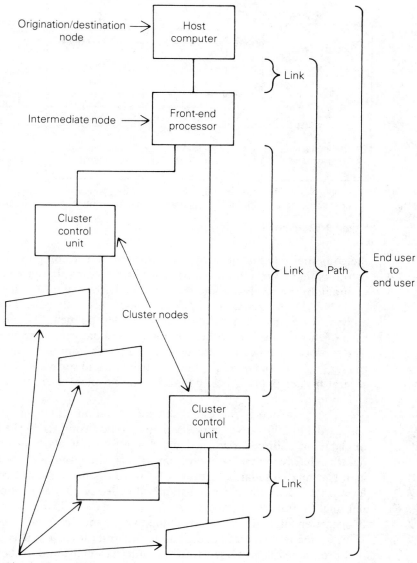

Figure 9-21 Levels of network connections.

The function management layer interfaces with the *transmission management layer,* which schedules, routes, and transmits messages through the network. The transmission management layer is the only one to span the entire end-user-to-end-user level. The other layers are only present in those nodes that interface with end users.

Software for the application layer is provided by the user. Software for the function and transmission management layers is provided by the manufacturer of

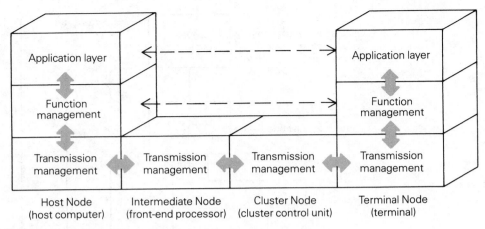

Host Node   Intermediate Node   Cluster Node   Terminal Node
(host computer)   (front-end processor)   (cluster control unit)   (terminal)

Figure 9-22 Three logical layers in the network.

the computer equipment or by a software firm. The computer equipment manufacturers that have announced network architecture plans are committed to providing both the hardware and the software necessary for implementation.

SNA, DCA, DNA, and BNA are master plans that the datacom equipment
and software firms can follow in product development. The main limitation of
each of these plans is that they do not give the datacom user complete flexibility.
The *protocols,* or routines for transmitting data from one node to another, tend
to favor a particular vendor's line of hardware and software. But having to follow
several master plans is better than having no plan at all, which used to be the
situation.

The next step is the establishment of national and international datacom
standards. In 1981 a Network Users Association comprising the largest U.S. users
of datacom equipment formed for the purpose of working toward a national
datacom hardware and software standard.[11] The group is encouraging the American National Standards Institute (ANSI) to establish a standard on the national
level. In 1976 an international standard called X.25 was proposed by the International Standards Organization (ISO). To date X.25 has not received the full
cooperation of either datacom equipment manufacturers or common carriers.
With so many corporate and national interests involved, it is unlikely that any
real progress will be made toward an international standard before 1984, at the
earliest.[12]

Putting Datacom in Perspective

An MIS includes a datacom network when input/output units are not confined to
the computing facility. These I/O units may be within the same building that

---

[11] Edward K. Yasaki, "Network Users Unite," *Datamation* 27 (October 1981): 83 ff.
[12] John L. Kirkley, "Seventh Heaven," *Datamation* 27 (July 1981): 25.

houses the computer room, or they may be located across town, across the nation, or around the world.

The type of I/O equipment used does not depend on the distance to the CPU, but rather on the needs of the users. But the distance to the CPU does influence the type of transmission medium or channel. Short distances can be spanned with coaxial cables or telephone lines. Longer distances require microwave transmission, sometimes via satellite.

Batch processing does not require datacom unless the input origin or the output destination is separated by some distance from the CPU. If such a separation exists, an RJE terminal can transmit batched transactions to the host.

Online processing may or may not require datacom, depending on the size of the system. It is possible to use online processing with a mini or micro by using a CRT terminal attached to the CPU by a cable a few feet in length. But when a user is located elsewhere, online processing demands datacom. Timesharing, real-time, and distributed processing all need datacom as well.

Datacom benefits geographically disbursed organizations in two ways. First, it improves the quality of the firm's operations by providing the necessary communications between units. For example, customer orders can be entered from area sales offices, and if one warehouse is out of stock the order can be filled by another warehouse. The second benefit is an improved MIS. With datacom the data base is updated as each transaction occurs, regardless of location. Management can use this up-to-date data base for decision making. And most importantly, with datacom all managers in the organization have access to the MIS.

If it were not for datacom, the MIS concept would probably never have gotten off the ground. During the early years of MIS, datacom enabled firms to pursue the giant, centralized systems that were then in vogue. More recently, datacom has enabled firms to achieve distributed systems.

Summary

Data communications is also known as telecommunications, teleprocessing, and datacom. The equipment configurations that perform data communications are called networks, and they consist of three basic parts—a source, a medium, and a sink.

Datacom captures data at its source to reduce the time and effort needed to perform a task and to facilitate the rapid transmission of information. Transmission costs can be lower than if other means were used, and a firm's communication network can keep up with organizational growth. Datacom supports either centralized or decentralized control of the information resource and contributes to overall management control.

A firm's datacom equipment is likely to be justified based on data processing tasks, but the equipment also contributes to the development of a sophisticated MIS. Datacom facilitates query responses, model simulations, and the preparation of management reports without system degradation resulting from distance between the user and the information processor.

The simplest datacom network is a point-to-point configuration with source and sink attached to the medium by modems. Networks with many channels use a front-end processor to offload channel management functions from the CPU. The front-end processor may be a mini or micro system (including secondary storage) that is used to log message activity and perform a store-and-forward service.

A multidrop line is more complex, with terminals competing for the use of channels. Multiplexers enable several transmissions simultaneously on the same channel by either subdividing the channel into frequency bands (frequency division multiplexing) or merging data from several terminals into a single transmitted frame (time division multiplexing). Concentrators perform a similar function by merging traffic from several terminals at a single point to make the best use of high-speed channels.

Cluster control units provide an opportunity to offload a host network's processing activity to a point closer to the user. Cluster control units, which may be minis or micros with secondary storage ability, permit some processing separate from the host.

Although a wide selection of transmission media is available, most data traffic uses facilities designed for voice messages. Telephone wire pairs and coaxial cables are being replaced by microwave and satellite transmission. Lasers and other light beams are being refined for future use, possibly using fiberoptics for faster and higher-density movement than wires or cables.

Channels can be simplex, half duplex, or full duplex. The simultaneous, two-way capability of the full-duplex channel makes it ideal for high-volume data processing applications. The half-duplex channel is adequate for MIS designs, since it permits the manager to input queries or model data and then receive the results of the retrieval or simulation at a lower cost than a full-duplex channel.

The highest data speeds can be realized with synchronous transmission, since only data bits move along the channel. Isochronous transmission includes start and stop codes, but a clocking mechanism permits faster speeds than asynchronous transmission.

The most popular transmission codes are EBCDIC and ASCII-7. Both codes permit the addition of an extra bit—the check bit—that is used to detect and sometimes to correct errors.

The common carriers offer both voice-grade and above voice-grade lines. Together with direct distance dialing, these lines account for the majority of datacom traffic. Newer digital technologies are slow to gain widespread use. WATS lines provide a means for firms with much long-distance activity to purchase channels on a time rather than a per-call basis. Different WATS arrangements are available for incoming, outgoing, in-state, and out-of-state service.

Managers use terminals by employing a menu display, form-filling, or questions-and-answers technique. In addition to the telephone, hardcopy, and CRT terminals used by both managers and nonmanagement personnel, other terminal types include remote job entry, point of sale, data collection, intelligent, and special purpose. These latter types are used mainly by nonmanagers.

Network architectures are intended to provide master plans to guide hardware and software development. The IBM, Univac, and NCR architectures all feature levels of physical connections and layers of logical connections. These architectures protect datacom applications programs from changing technology and permit the offloading of host tasks. But the lack of a national or international standard hampers those firms wishing to mix products from several suppliers.

Datacom plays a vital role in the modern MIS. The managers of most organizations are not all located near the computer facility. With datacom, the MIS resource can spread efficiently over great distances.

Key Terms

data communications (datacom)

data communications network

source, medium, sink

teleprocessing

teleprocessing monitor

message

modem

hertz

offline communication

online communication

front-end communication processor

polling

message log

store-and-forward

data communications monitor

offloading

point-to-point line

multidrop line

loop line

private line, dedicated line

hard-wired line

multiplexer

frequency division multiplexing (FDM)

time division multiplexing (TDM)

concentrator

cluster control unit

common carrier

voice-grade line

above voice-grade line

coaxial cable

simplex, half-duplex, full-duplex transmission

receive-only printer (ROP)

Baudot

synchronous, asynchronous, isochronous transmission

start-stop transmission

Dataphone Digital Service (DDS)

direct distance dialing (DDD)

WATS (Wide Area Telecommunications Service)

incoming, outgoing, in-state, out-of-state WATS line

acoustic coupler

password

job control languge (JCL)

conversational mode

menu display technique

cursor

form-filling technique

questions-and-answers technique

remote job entry (RJE) terminal

data collection terminal

attendance, job reporting

dumb terminal

intelligent terminal

firmware

Systems Network Architecture
(SNA)

Distributed Communications
Architecture (DCA)

Distributed Network Architecture
(DNA)

Burroughs Network Architecture
(BNA)

link level

network node

path level

end-user-to-end-user level

application layer

function management layer

transmission management layer

Key Concepts

The basic parts of a datacom network

Contributions of datacom to an MIS

Evolutionary nature of datacom use

Alternate datacom network configurations

Transmission modes

Conversational use of the computer

Network levels and layers

Questions

1. What are the three basic technologies used in datacom systems? Which has been the most commonly used?

2. What are the three basic parts of a datacom network?

3. Does datacom facilitate centralized or decentralized control? Explain.

4. How can datacom reduce the amount of time required for a manager to perform a task?

5. What is the current trend in datacom use?

6. When is a modem required in a datacom network?

7. How have certain datacom functions been offloaded from the CPU?

8. How many terminals can be attached to a point-to-point line? How many CPUs?

9. What are the two basic ways of achieving multiplexing? Name an advantage of each.

10. What roles can minis and/or micros play in a datacom network?

11. What is the similarity between a microwave tower and a satellite?

12. Why would a manager be unlikely to use a simplex channel?

13. Rank the three transmission modes according to their speeds.

14. How many and what types of WATS lines would a firm in Baltimore need to establish a two-way communications link with its sales representatives in all fifty states?

15. In your opinion, which type of terminal best suits a manager? Explain your reasoning.

16. Which of the three basic interactive methods can be used with a hardcopy terminal?

17. Name eight terminal types.

18. What I/O units are a part of a remote job entry terminal?

19. What are the different ways data can be entered into a data collection terminal?

20. What are the three levels that have been defined in a datacom network architecture? What are the three layers?

Problems

1. Draw a diagram of a datacom network consisting of a CPU, a front-end processor, a leased above voice-grade line, and eight CRT terminals attached to the line by means of a multiplexer.

2. Assume that the firm with the datacom network in problem 1 wants to add a loop line with four CRTs. Show the addition.

3. How much would an incoming, out-of-state WATS line cost a company in Dallas for 50 hours of use per month? 100 hours? 200 hours? Use the prices included in the chapter. Assuming that the $14.79 hourly rate applies to everything over 80 hours, what would be the cost of coverage for 24 hours a day, 30 days a month?

CASE PROBLEM: Northwest Paper

Bill O'Brien has just been hired as the new vice-president of marketing for Northwest Paper, a large Oregon-based producer of both consumer and industrial paper products. O'Brien held a similar post with a smaller competitor and had built a top-flight marketing organization in only four years. During his job interview with the Northwest executive committee, Bill revealed that he believed the secret of good business operations was good communication. He emphasized that, if hired, he would need the resources to establish an effective communications system at Northwest.

During his first month on the job, Bill oriented himself to his new company, its resources, its limitations, and its opportunities. During the first four weekly executive committee meetings, Bill maintained a low profile and mostly listened to what Al DuPre, the president, Mal Volding, the vice-president of finance, and Peter Henson, the vice-president of manufacturing, had to say. The purpose of the weekly meetings was to maintain open lines of communication at the top executive level—a practice that received Bill's complete approval.

At the fifth meeting, Al asked Bill how things were going, and Bill replied by saying that he was about ready to start work on his marketing communications system. He asked Mal to invite Don Bender, the director of information services, to the next meeting so that they could all discuss the needed changes. Since Don reported to Mal, Mal was the logical person to extend the invitation.

When the next meeting rolled around, Mal asked Don to briefly describe the Northwest MIS. Don explained that they were using a large-scale CPU with eight disk drives, four magnetic tape units, a card reader and punch, two line printers, and a plotter. Accounting transactions were entered by means of CRT terminals, and similar terminals were located throughout headquarters for handling data base queries. A front-end communication processor polled all of the terminals on the loop line. Systems software included an operating system, a data communications monitor, and a DBMS.

After this explanation, Bill proceeded to tell the group what he felt he needed. He wanted each of the company's thirty-one branch managers to be able to communicate with the computer on a daily basis from their offices located in twenty-six states, including Oregon. Daily sales report data would be transmitted to the computer, and responses to queries for sales statistics would be handled with very little delay. In addition, he wanted each of the firm's 250 sales representatives to be able to query the data base from a customer's office or a pay phone to check on the status of inventory items and unfilled orders. For himself, Bill wanted to be able to obtain summaries of the daily sales report data from a terminal in his office. The reports could be reproduced and distributed to the other members of the executive committee for the weekly meeting. Bill concluded his description by explaining that such a network would enable him, his branch managers, and his sales reps to keep up with their respective areas of responsibility. Information would flow freely, and the result would be an improved efficiency and sales level that would more than offset the cost of the equipment.

Bill clearly had the support of the other members of the executive committee. Mal turned to Don and said, "I want you to give us an idea of exactly what would be required in terms of added hardware, software, and communications facilities in order to meet Bill's request. Why don't you work that up and give us your answer at next week's meeting. I know you can't work up the costs on such short notice—just list the items. Do you need any more information from us?"

"I can't think of any," Don replied. "If I do, I'll make a note of it, and we can discuss it at the next meeting."

"That sounds good," said Mal. "See you next week."

Question

Provide Mal Volding with a list of the hardware, software, and datacom facilities Bill O'Brien needs for his marketing communications system.

Chapter 10

Mini and Micro Systems

Learning Objectives

After studying this chapter, you should:

- Understand the main features of the types of systems composing the small computer market—minicomputers, microcomputers, small business computers, and personal computers
- Appreciate the wide range of small-computer hardware options related to the CPU, I/O units, and secondary storage
- Be familiar with examples of operating systems, programming languages, DBMSes, and applications programs that are tailored to meet the needs of mini/micro users
- Understand some of the basic features of two packaged applications software systems, MAPICS and VisiCalc, and how they can be used to produce management information
- Know how word processing can fit into an MIS design

The Small-Computer Boom

We have already encountered mini and micro systems. In Chapter 5 we recognized the small-computer boom that began in the early sixties with the first *minicomputer*—the DEC PDP-5. The origin of the *microcomputer* can be traced to the Intel 4004 *microprocessor,* announced in 1971. An outgrowth of microcomputer development has been the *personal computer.* The first personal computer was the Altair 880, offered in kit form in 1975. The rest is history. Hardly a day passes without some mention of small-scale, inexpensive computers—systems that you can use for household computations, business purposes, word processing, or entertainment. The small computer is a visible part of our lives. When my two-year-old daughter points to a cover of *Time* magazine and says "Apple," I don't know whether she is pointing at the round red fruit on founder Steven Job's head, or the Apple II micro in the background.

Mini and Micro Systems in the General Systems Model

It is easy to get the idea that minis and micros are used only in small firms. But small computers can also serve as distributed processing systems in distributed networks and as intelligent terminals in timesharing systems. And they can perform the chores of the front-end processor and cluster control unit in datacom networks.

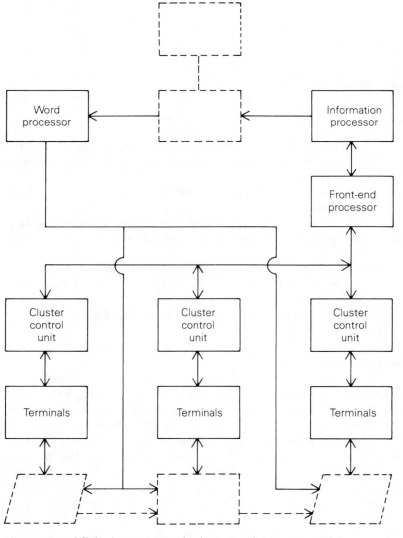

Figure 10-1   Mini/micro systems in the general systems model.

Figure 10-1 reflects the multiple roles of mini/micro systems. The manager can be surrounded by these smaller systems—gathering data from the physical system, processing the data, and enabling the manager to communicate decisions back to the physical system. The figure illustrates the potential of small systems to bridge the gap between the manager and the physical system of the firm.

Confusing Terminology

The name *minicomputer* undoubtedly had its origin in an effort to distinguish the new breed of small computers from their conventional counterparts. Minicomputers can weigh as little as 30 pounds, have primary storage as small as 4KB, represent data and instructions in words of only 8 bits, employ as few as 20 basic instructions, have very limited I/O ability, and cost as little as $2500. These are truly *mini*ature characteristics. Yet this same computer classification can include systems weighing 2000 pounds or more that have several megabytes of primary storage, use 32-bit words, have instruction sets with 200 instructions, include a complete set of I/O and secondary storage devices, and sell for as much as $1 million.[1] Systems such as these were not in mind when the term *minicomputer* was coined.

Today's large minis outperform the small versions of the medium-scale conventional group. The more powerful superminis represent data with 32-bit words, the same size as medium- and large-scale systems. The large words enable the system to process more data during a cycle. At the other end, many small minis perform poorly compared to some of the more powerful microcomputers. These micros have 16-bit words rather than the 8-bit ones characteristic of both early micros and early minis. In the near future, 32-bit micros will be readily available.

The *microcomputer* is characterized by a CPU reduced to *micro*scopic size. The arithmetic and logic unit and the control unit exist in the form of a single semiconductor chip. The first single-chip *microprocessor* was invented by Texas Instruments (TI) in 1970. A chip including primary storage, I/O circuitry, and a clocking mechanism is called a *single-chip microcomputer*. When these goodies occupy a large printed circuit board, they form a *microcomputer module*. A *microcomputer system* results from adding the required support chips, power supply, software, and I/O devices to the chip or circuit board.[2]

The physical size of the CPU circuitry is one way to distinguish between a mini and a micro. Generally the CPU of a micro resides on a single chip, and that of a mini on one or more boards. But—you guessed it—some minis have chips and some micros have boards.

In addition to the mini/micro confusion, you also hear about personal computers and small business computers. We can define a *small business computer* as a small-scale computer, either a mini or a micro, that is oriented toward solving business problems. Small business computer systems such as the IBM System/38

---

[1] Based in part on specification characteristics in Udo W. Pooch and Rahul Chattergy, *Minicomputers: Hardware, Software, and Selection* (St. Paul: West Publishing Co., 1980), pp. 2–4.

[2] A good description of the origin of the microcomputer can be found in André G. Vacroux, "Microcomputers," *Scientific American* 232 (May 1975): 32–40.

Figure 10-2   A small business computer.

(pictured in Figure 10-2), the Burroughs B3900, the CDC Cyber 18, the Radio Shack TRS-80 Model 16, and the TI DS990 offer the hardware and software needed for business data processing. Software, such as graphics packages and "what-if" mathematical simulators, are now being added to the accounting-oriented software that was developed initially. But the emphasis is still on data processing software.

As the name implies, a *personal computer* is one that you own yourself. Invariably these are micros, and their distinguishing characteristic is personal, rather than business, ownership. But this is not to say that the Apple IIs, Commodore PETs, and IBM Personal Computers are not used for business applications. Dataquest, a California marketing research firm, estimates that more than half of the personal computers bought are for business use rather than home and hobby, educational, or technical purposes.[3] These statistics may be misleading. Quite possibly, systems economically justified for business use get much home and hobby use as well.

All of these system types—mini, micro, small business, and personal—are of interest to us in their roles as information processors in an MIS. We will not attempt to pigeonhole certain hardware or software in these categories. Instead we will describe certain popular systems on the market and illustrate some of their business uses.

---

[3] "Computer Stores: Tantalizing Opportunity Selling Computers to Consumers," *Business Week,* 28 September 1981, p. 78.

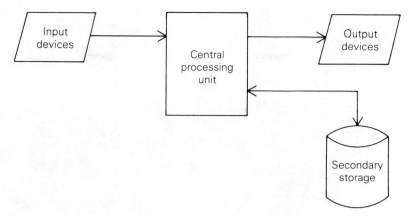

Figure 10-3 The computer schematic.

Mini/Micro Hardware

Minis and micros fit the computer schematic presented in Chapter 5. The schematic is redrawn in Figure 10-3 to provide a guide for our examination of hardware components. All computers consist of the components in the figure, but the packaging varies widely depending on system size.

In the popular Apple II microcomputer system shown in Figure 10-4, the CPU and the input keyboard are housed in the base unit on the left. Above the

Figure 10-4 The Apple II computer system.

Figure 10-5 The TI DS990 Model 36 system.

base unit is a CRT output device and two secondary storage floppy disk drives. On the right is a second output device, a nonimpact printer. All of these units are interconnected by cables. Devices are easily attachable to the CPU—you simply plug them in. You can start with a basic system and upgrade it as your needs expand.

The TI DS990 Model 36, shown in Figure 10-5, comes in a completely different package. This large minicomputer system includes the CPU in the center, two disk drives on the right, and a serial impact printer on the left. At the far left are two CRT terminals. It is also possible to add a magnetic tape unit to back up the data base and the software library. The DS990 can function as a stand-alone information processor or as an intelligent processor in a distributed network.

CPU characteristics

Primary storage is in the form of semiconductor chips with a capacity of from 4 to perhaps 512KB. This storage is of two types—ROM and RAM. *ROM* stands for *read-only memory.* You can read instructions prerecorded by the manufacturer on this part of primary storage, but you cannot use the area for writing. This constraint prevents you from "clobbering" the instructions by writing on top of them. In the TRS-80 Model III, ROM comes in 4KB or 14KB sizes. *RAM* stands for *random-access memory.* Actually a better name would be RWM, read-and-write memory. You can read data or instructions from RAM, and you can write into the same area. RAM is primary storage. In the TRS-80 Model III, RAM starts at 4KB and is expandable to 48KB.

Primary storage is divided into addressable words. Word sizes include 8, 12, 16, 24, and 32 bits. All bits in a word are transferred in parallel within the CPU in one cycle. The *cycle time,* which varies from 400 nanoseconds to 5 microseconds, is the time elapsed between the initiations of two successive, independent primary storage operations. Small word sizes mean slower processing speeds, since

Figure 10-6 The TI DS990 Model 9 with a hardcopy printer.

fewer bits are handled at a time, and also less efficient instruction storage, since two words may be necessary to represent a single instruction.

A CPU is designed to execute a certain number of instructions. This is the *instruction set*. A small micro may only be able to execute 20 instructions, such as read, compare, branch, and so on. A larger system will have a much more complete set. The Wang VS System features 180 instructions, for example. The larger instruction set permits a greater variety of internal logical and arithmetic operations as well as many different I/O operations.

Input/output options

The most common input/output device is the *CRT terminal*. It can be less expensive than its hardcopy counterpart, and the CRT displays output much faster. CRT screens come in different sizes. The Apple II displays 24 lines of 40 characters each, the IBM Personal Computer displays 25 lines of 80 characters each, and the TRS-80 Color Computer displays 16 lines of 32 characters each. The TRS-80 offers eight colors, whereas IBM, Apple, Atari, Mattel, and TI offer sixteen. The graphics capabilities of the CRTs vary as well. Some units, such as Hewlett-Packard's, offer high resolution (many points on the screen that can be blended together to form an image, such as a newspaper photograph), whereas others, such as the PET and the TRS Models II and III, offer low resolution.

If hardcopy output is needed, it can be prepared on a *hardcopy terminal* or a *hardcopy printer*. The most economical approach is to use a hardcopy terminal for both input and output. If you want the rapid display of a CRT, but also need the hardcopy, your system needs a printer. The T1 DS990 Model 9 in Figure 10-6 uses a CRT for both input and output plus a hardcopy printer.

Printers for micros are usually dot matrix, daisywheel, or thermal. The Qume Sprint 5 daisywheel printer, available with the Apple II, operates at an average speed of 45 characters per second. The thermal printer available with the same system operates at 40 characters per second. The TRS-80 line of printers includes dot matrix models capable of from 40 to 160 characters per second. These are typical hardcopy options for small-scale systems. Large systems, such as the Data General ECLIPSE, boast impact line printers achieving 300, 600, or 900 lines per minute.

Small business systems permit the use of additional I/O devices. A manufacturing organization might use *data collection terminals* for attendance and job reporting. A bank might use *teller terminals,* and a retail store might use *point-of-sale terminals. Audio response* is another output option on many systems. No mini/micro systems, business or otherwise, are being offered with punched card input or output.

Secondary storage

The most popular form of secondary storage is the *floppy disk* or *diskette.* Small systems often include disk drives that can hold one or two disks. The Apple II in Figure 10-4 can use one drive to hold a disk containing software and the other drive to hold a disk containing data files. Radio Shack drives handle a single disk containing up to 175KB. These are low-capacity floppies, as are those used with the Apple II (140KB). Floppy disk capacities vary widely, but can go as high as 1MB.

A *magnetic tape cassette* is a much less expensive option. Cassettes are not very popular, however, because they offer sequential, not direct access, storage. The cassettes can be used for program storage, but retrieval time is slow.

It is possible to achieve larger direct access storage capacities and faster data transfer rates than a floppy can offer by using *hard disks.* The disks can be removable or they can be permanently housed in a disk drive or built into the CPU cabinet. One type of permanently mounted DASD is the Winchester disk. A *Winchester disk* is a self-contained unit in which the disk, the access mechanism, and the read/write heads are sealed to protect them from impurities in the air. Since Winchester disks stay cleaner than removable disks, the Winchester read/write heads can be positioned closer to the disk surface, permitting higher-density recording and greater capacity. The first Winchester disks were 14 inches in diameter, but 8-inch and 5¼-inch versions have been developed. The 5¼-inch versions (the same size as mini floppies) typically have capacities in the 6MB range. The 8-inch unit that has become the industry favorite, the Shugart Associates Model SA 1000, has a 10MB capacity. In 1981 3M brought out a three-disk Winchester stack (8-inch disks) with a 60MB capacity. 3M believes that the capacity of the 8-inch unit will ultimately reach 700MB.[4]

---

[4] For information on Winchester technology, see Finis F. Conner, "Introducing the Micro-Winchester," *Mini-Micro Systems* 13 (April 1980): 79–81; and "3M Unveils Winchesters; Casts Lot with ANSI," *Mini-Micro Systems* 14 (June 1981): 16–18.

Figure 10-7 The Data General ECLIPSE MV/8000 system.

Large-capacity, high-performance secondary storage is also possible with conventional *magnetic tape units*. Like cassettes, these units are less appealing than disks because they are serial. They can be used to prepare backup copies of the data base or to log system performance. The Data General ECLIPSE MV/ 8000 system in Figure 10-7 includes two magnetic tape units to the immediate right of the CPU and two DASD disk units at the far right. The removable disk packs are sitting on top of the disk units.

Neither the mini nor the micro was originally designed to solve business problems. In fact, business firms were slow to recognize small systems as information processors. As a result, the variety of I/O and secondary storage units has always been more limited than for larger systems. The limited variety is not as serious a problem now as it was only a few years ago, for two reasons. First, the performance of mini/micro DASD units and serial printers has improved substantially. And second, many of the traditional devices of the larger systems, such as magnetic tape units and punched card I/O, are rapidly becoming obsolete. Users still need a broader selection of peripherals for mini/micro systems, however, to include devices such as plotters, COM units, and OCR units.

Mini/Micro Software

The software available for most minis and micros is more limited than that for larger systems. The systems software—such as operating systems, DBMS, and data communications monitors—handles a narrower range of operations than similar software for medium- and large-scale systems. The past few years have seen considerably more activity in the preparation of applications packages, but most of these perform traditional accounting tasks. There is a much greater need for packaged applications programs than in the larger computer market because many users of mini/micro systems do not know how to program.

Operating systems

The manufacturers of the large 32-bit-word minis, such as Wang, Prime, Data General, and Digital Equipment, all provide powerful operating systems with their hardware. For example, the PRIMOS operating system for the Prime 850 permits the simultaneous support of 128 terminals, provides 512MB of virtual storage, and compiles programs written in COBOL, FORTRAN, BASIC, RPG-II, PL/I, Pascal, and Assembler.

At the 16-bit-word level, an operating system named *UNIX* (developed by Bell Labs and marketed by Western Electric) is the most popular package.[5] UNIX has a license cost of $250 and is used at approximately 2000 sites. UNIX was not designed for any particular computer. It was first applied to a PDP-11, and that effort was so successful that the software was packaged for use on any of a number of systems. Most of the applications, however, have involved the PDP-11, and the VAX. UNIX includes general (not special-purpose) routines that the user can string together to create a powerful operating system. At least one computer manufacturer, Plexus Computers, has designed a computer specifically for the UNIX system.

UNIX has a strong foothold with the 16-bit minis and micros, but its success hardly compares with the operating system that has captured the 8-bit micro market. This operating system, *CP/M (Control Program for Microcomputers)*, is offered by Digital Research, Inc., for $150. It requires 16KB of primary storage but permits only one user at a time—no multiprogramming. It supports a wide variety of languages—COBOL, Assembler, Pascal, BASIC, and FORTRAN. In addition, several service programs (such as sort/merge) are available.[6]

The success CP/M has enjoyed is significant, considering the competition. At least seventy micro operating systems are on the market.[7] Only about forty of these, however, are aimed at the general-purpose demands of a business installation. And only seventeen include a COBOL compiler, which business users consider so important.

Programming languages

A survey of seventy-seven small business systems revealed that BASIC and COBOL are the most frequently supported languages, as illustrated in Figure 10-8.[8] What

---

[5] For more information on UNIX, see Edith Myers, "UNIX: A Standard Now?" *Datamation* 28 (January 1982): 77–80; and Donald A. Norman, "The Trouble With UNIX," *Datamation* 27 (November 1981): 139 ff.

[6] For more details on CP/M, see Jerry Cashin, "CPM—The De Facto Operating System for 8-Bit Micros," *Small Systems World* 10 (January 1982): 11.

[7] The main features of the systems are reported in Jack Hemenway, "Microcomputer Operating System Comes of Age," *Mini-Micro Systems* 13 (October 1980): 97 ff.

[8] Malcolm L. Stiefel, "Choosing a Small Multi-User Business Computer," *Mini-Micro Systems* 14 (June 1981): 87 ff.

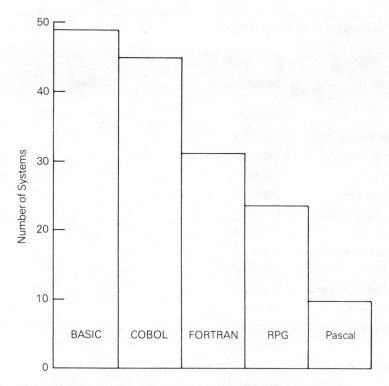

Figure 10-8 Programming languages for small business systems.

the figure does not reveal is an apparent split in the market between those system manufacturers that have long been established in the business computing market and the newcomers. The oldtimers, such as Burroughs, Data General, DEC, IBM, NCR, UNIVAC, and WANG, *all* offer the COBOL language. BASIC, FORTRAN, and RPG are also well supported by this group. The newcomers tend to concentrate on BASIC, making it the most popular language overall. Pascal is not frequently offered, perhaps because it is relatively new.

Data base management systems

Cincom and Software A.G., two of the firms that market DBMSes to medium- and large-scale computers, also have versions for minis. Cincom's TOTAL is available in versions tailored to the IBM System/3, DEC PDP-11, Harris V70, and Interdata 7/32 and 8/32. The Software A.G. ADABAS-M is available for the DEC PDP-11 and DEC VAX line.

In addition, several minicomputer manufacturers have their own systems. DEC offers its DBMS-10/20 and DBMS-11 systems, Hewlett-Packard has its IMAGE, Prime has its DBMS, and TI has its DBMS-990.

Most minicomputer DBMS packages are written specifically for the DEC line—PDP-11, VAX-11, DEC-10, and DEC-20. Table 10-1 lists the DEC-oriented

Table 10-1   DEC-Oriented DBMS Offerings

DBMS Vendor	DBMS Name	PDP-11	VAX-11	DEC-10	DEC-20	Price, Purchase (P) License (L)
Admins, Inc.	ADMINS	*	*			$50,000 P
Advanced Data Management	DRS	*	*			—
Amcor Computer Corp.	AMBASE	*				$17,500 P
Cincom Systems	TOTAL	*				—
Digital Equipment Corp.	DBMS-10/20, 11	*	*	*	*	$16,500–30,000 L
ELS Systems Engineering	Product 3	*				$1900 L
General Electric	MADMAN	*				$20,000 L
International Data Base Systems	SEED	*		*	*	$14,000–35,000 L
Logica, Inc.	RAPPORT	*	*			—
National Information Systems	DPL			*	*	$38,000 P
Relational Software, Inc.	ORACLE	*				$96,000 P
Relational Technology	INGRES		*			$30,000 L
RLG Corp.	UNIBASE	*				$25,000 P
Shipping Research Services, Inc.	SIBAS			*		$40,000 P
Software A.G.	ADABAS-M	*	*			$40,000 P
Software House	System 1022			*	*	$17,000–54,000 P

DBMSes.[9] A few other packages are available for Data General Nova and ECLIPSE, Perkin Elmer, BTI, and Pertec hardware.

Micros represent another market for DBMSes. Many of these packages are written for the popular personal computers—TRS-80, Apple, and PET. Another group is written for any hardware using the CP/M operating system.

Of the forty or more micro DBMS packages, the leader is the MDBS package from Micro Data Base Systems, Inc.[10] Like many other packages, MDBS is compatible with any micros that use the CP/M operating system. Purchase price ranges from $900 to $2000, and over 1000 systems were sold during the firm's first two

[9] Based on data presented in Peter Krass and Hesh Wiener, "The DBMS Market is Booming," *Datamation* 27 (September 1981): 153 ff. See also Harvey M. Weiss, "Which DBMS Is Right for You," *Mini-Micro Systems* 14 (October 1981): 157–160.

[10] For details on twenty micro DBMSes, see Kathryn S. Barley and James R. Driscoll, "A Survey of Data-Base Management Systems for Microcomputers," *Byte* 6 (November 1981): 208 ff. Also see Andrew B. Whinston and C. W. Holsapple, "DBMS for Micros," *Datamation* 27 (April 1981): 165 ff.

years of operation. MDBS offers an error recovery ability along with multiple levels of data security. Most of the DBMSes in this category restrict the number of fields that a record may have. With MDBS, the limit is 255—not very limiting. Some packages have as few as 10 or 20 fields. Like most systems, MDBS contains a report writer, which permits considerable flexibility in formatting various types of reports printed from data.

MDBS is one of the most expensive micro DBMSes. Other systems cost as little as $25. Nobody claims that any of these systems, including MDBS, performs as well as the systems for large computers. But of the lot, MDBS is the most highly respected.

Applications software

Many of the users of mini and especially micro systems are short on programming talent. In some firms, no one can program a computer. These firms rely on either the equipment manufacturers or software firms for their programming. The volume of such software is rapidly increasing, and the quality varies from excellent to poor.

Some applications software is developed to solve the unique problems of specific industries. IBM has an excellent software system for small manufacturers called *MAPICS* (Manufacturing Accounting and Production Information Control System). The system handles many of the routine operational tasks that characterize a production organization—raw material inventory management, material requirements planning, job and attendance reporting, and resource planning. In addition, it maintains a manufacturing data base, prints reports, and responds to queries.

MAPICS does not handle all of the important data processing tasks of a small manufacturer. Two such tasks are sales forecasting and production scheduling. These must be accomplished by some method other than MAPICS—perhaps by other software.

MAPICS consists of the eleven integrated applications charted in Figure 10-9. Data flow is triggered by the receipt of a customer order. The order entry and invoicing subsystem (upper left in the figure) performs the initial processing. Then all of the other subsystems perform their tasks when called for by the chain of events.

Figure 10-10 is an inventory analysis report that can be prepared in several different sequences to provide inventory and financial information. The sample report is printed in vendor sequence, showing sales activity for each vendor. Other sequences can present slow-moving items, high-profit items, high-profit-margin items, and high-investment items first. These are all exception-type reports. The report provides management with the answers to two important inventory questions—how much to order, and when to order.

Another example of a management report available from the MAPICS data base is the cash flow analysis in Figure 10-11. This report projects sales income (inflow) along with expenditures for material, labor, and overhead (outflow) for the next twelve-month period. This information facilitates financial planning.

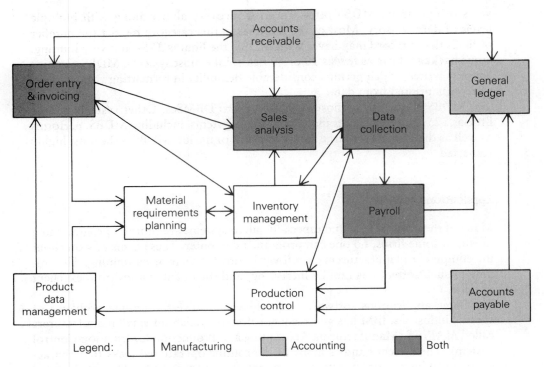

Figure 10-9 MAPICS applications subsystems.

MAPICS is well documented, and it is also supported by an audiovisual training package for users to train employees in MAPICS procedures. It is among the best of the industry-oriented applications packages. At a monthly lease price of $1200, MAPICS is a bargain for a small manufacturer just breaking into the computer game. It provides a system that most manufacturers, large or small, cannot create themselves. Over 150 person-years of effort went into its development.[11]

Other industry packages have been prepared by computing equipment manufacturers and software firms for a number of industries that have heavy data processing workloads. Industries receiving much attention are hospitals, retailing, banking, municipal government, trucking, real estate, and insurance. For example, there are over fifty separate *insurance packages* offered by some thirty software firms.[12] These packages process new business applications, maintain budgets, compute taxes, maintain the securities portfolio, handle claims, and so on. The packages are not cheap—the REASON (REinsurance Accounting System On-Line) system marketed by Nelson & Bauman, Inc., sells for $125,000 to $175,000. The system is written for the Hewlett-Packard HP3000 as well as for larger IBM systems.

---

[11] For more information on MAPICS, see IBM Application General Information Manuals—Order Processing and Accounting Applications, GH30-0220; Financial Applications, GH30-0219; and Manufacturing Applications, GH30-0221.

[12] *ICP INTERFACE Insurance Industry* 7 (Spring 1982).

How much
to order

When to order

```
GATEWAY IND.        INVENTORY ANALYSIS REPORT - STOCK MOVEMENT   DATE 10/12/83  TIME 09.31.20  PAGE 1  AM12J


                              SEQ
           ITEM     WHSE    VENDOR    DATE OF   ESTIMATED  AVERAGE          ORDER    MTD        MTD      MTD       MTD
           NUMBER   NO.     NUMBER  UM LAST SALE ANNUAL USE  USE   E.O.Q.   POINT   ISSUES   RECEIPTS  ADJUSTS   USED

           ITEM                       DATE OF             AVERAGE                     YTD                           YTD
           DESCRIPTION                LAST USE TURNOVERS   LEVEL                     ISSUES                         USED
        VALVE
 1    03021       1     012891    EA  8/20/83    40,000    2,864   5,913*  4,000   2,800       0        0        2,800
                                     10/09/83      207      166                   17,185                         17,185

      COMPRESSOR
 2    27000-02    1     018834    EA  7/18/83    20,000    1,729   1,087   2,400   1,670      300       0        1,670
                                     10/01/83       19    1,121                   10,375                         10,375

      ADAPTER GASKET
 3    27001-01    1     036657    EA  9/29/83    35,000    2,814   2,275   5,833**     0     4,000               2,700
                                     10/11/83       47      725                       0                         16,886

      ADAPTER PLATE
 4    27002-01    1     036657        10/08/83    35,000    2,882   2,273   5,000**     0     1,995      95       2,928
                                     10/09/83       65      532                       0                         17,291

      CONTROL BOX
 5    33480-A     1     042598        10/05/83    45,000    3,627   6,272   4,500   2,650      0        0        2,650
                                     10/10/83      337      129                   21,760                         21,760

      TANK COTER ASSM.
 6    34250-A     1     042598        10/06/83    48,000    3,698  30,151   4,800   2,800      450       0       2,800
                                     10/07/83      334      133                   22,185                         22,185


      NOTE:   *=MANUALLY ENTERED EOQ
             **=MANUALLY ENTERED ORDER POINT
```

Figure 10-10   An inventory analysis report.

The industry-oriented packages for small systems, such as the TRS-80 and the Apple, are much less expensive. Radio Shack markets a medical office system and a manufacturing inventory system priced at $750 each. It also offers a series of five real estate packages on magnetic cassette tape for $29.95 each.

Much of the applications software on the market today is designed to do *basic accounting tasks* for any industry. The Controller system, available for the Apple II Plus, contains accounts receivable, accounts payable, and general-ledger

```
GATEWAY INDUSTRIES          MANUFACTURING CASH FLOW ANALYSIS       DATE 03/06/83  TIME 08.42.44   PAGE   1   AMM3D1
COST - STANDARD ORDERS - BOTH
                    1 03/82  2 04/82  3 05/82  4 06/82  5 07/82  6 08/82  7 09/82  8 10/82  9 11/82  10 12/82 11 01/83 12 02/83  TOTAL
SALES INCOME        568491   503524   670082   584780   553875   585340   452900   497210   646807   375270   556010   424200   6413489
EXPENDITURES
  MATERIAL          302372   177870   347900   245000   252700   332850   203000   206500   399000   137200   280000   165830  3050222
  LABOR              45500    44800    49000    46200    45500    45500    45500    44800    46200    44800    45500    45500   548800
  OVERHEAD          136500   134400   147000   138600   136850   136850   136500   134400   138600   138600   136500   136500  1651390
  TOTAL             484372   357070   543900   429500   435050   515200   385000   385700   583800   320600   462000   347830  5250322
NET MOVEMENT
  MONTH              84119   146454   126182   154980   118825    70140    67900   111510    63007    54670    94010    76370  1168167
  CUMULATIVE         84119   230573   356755   511735   630560   700700   768600   880110   943117   997787  1091797  1168167
```

Figure 10-11   A cash flow analysis.

modules. The system prepares a trial balance, customer mailing list, mailing labels, sales journal, payment journal, invoice register, and cash requirements report. It sells for $625.

Radio Shack offers business applications systems for payroll, general ledger, inventory, accounts payable, accounts receivable, and mailing lists. One payroll package is available in cassette form; other packages require disks. The disk payroll package costs $199.95 and handles up to one hundred employees. You can define up to fourteen earnings and deduction categories. Payroll checks and W-2 forms are printed by a 32KB, two-disk system.

As you can guess from the prices, applications software varies widely. You don't get the same product for $29.95 that you get for $299.95 or for $29,995. Most of the software has a common characteristic, however. It is intended primarily for data, rather than information, processing. The most widely publicized exception is the VisiCalc software package.

VisiCalc

The VisiCalc package is the most popular software of any type. By early 1982 some 200,000 copies had been sold for about $295 each. It is marketed by VisiCorp (founded in 1978 under the name Personal Software), along with six other lesser-known "Visi" packages.

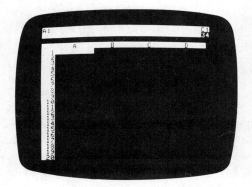

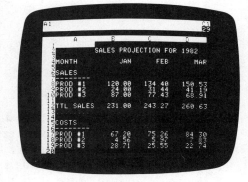

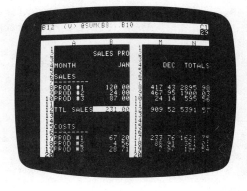

Step 1: Loading VisiCalc.
Your blank VisiCalc worksheet is ready for virtually any number problem you have. The program is simply loaded into the computer from its diskette.

Step 2: Type in your problem.
VisiCalc's row and column format is simple to use. Simple and advanced math, plus business formulas are built in. An on-screen editor allows you to rearrange numbers, words, and formulas to fit your required printout.

Step 3: Play "What if . . . ?
Once your problem is on the worksheet, use VisiCalc's powerful recalculation feature to analyze it. Change one number anywhere on your worksheet and instantly see the results. Sensitivity analysis, projections, estimates, and hundreds of other descisions become clearer, more easily understood—because you can analyze them with VisiCalc.

Figure 10-12   Step-by-step VisiCalc.

The *VisiCalc* package is an electronic worksheet, 63 columns wide and 254 lines deep, that can be created from the CRT keyboard. The user either keys in the data or obtains it from the data base using another product, the *VisiFile* package. Figure 10-12 shows a sequence of building a worksheet from a blank screen (a). In (b) the data has been entered into the rows and columns. This need not be all of the data, since you can display selected portions of the worksheet. In (c) the user is changing a figure—the 231.00 in the "cursor box." The user moves the cursor box to the desired location and types in the data. After building a worksheet, the user can play the "what-if" game. For example, the worksheet may contain a cash flow statement similar to the one in Figure 10-11. The manager can simulate the effect on the cash flow if, say, a 10% increase in worker salaries goes into effect.

A manager can display a standard report, such as a sales analysis by customer or a balance sheet, and make computations using the data. If the manager wants a graph of the output, he or she can use the *VisiPlot* package—available at extra cost, of course. Other members of the Visi family include a financial planning and budgeting package (Desktop/PLAN II and III), a regression-type forecasting package (VisiTrend), a personal appointments calendar (VisiDex), and a software interface to connect your personal computer to a datacom network (VisiTerm). Figure 10-13 illustrates the sequence for using the VisiTrend and VisiPlot packages. The data is entered in (a), transformed in (b), and plotted in (c).

Step 1: Enter your data.
Enter time series into the powerful VisiTrend editor. You can also enter information from a VisiCalc electronic worksheet.

Step 2: Create new time series.
New time series can be developed from mathematical combinations of two or more existing time series.

Step 3: Display graph or printout.
Your time series—either original or new—may be printed out or displayed in a highly flexible graphic format. Graphs may be stored on diskette for later printout or display.

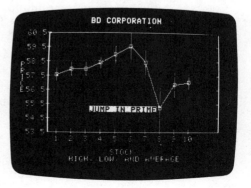

Figure 10-13 Step-by-step VisiTrend and VisiPlot.

If anything explains the VisiCalc package's success, it is its simplicity. No programming is required. It is appealing to managers for this and several additional reasons. First, it presents the data in a tabular format—typical of traditional accounting forms. It is not expensive—the software and the hardware are quite affordable. The VisiCalc package is available on the most popular personal computers—the Apple II and II Plus, TRS-80 Model II, Commodore PET, and IBM Personal Computer. To run the VisiCalc package on your Apple, your system needs 48KB of RAM, a diskette, and a single disk drive.

The success of the VisiCalc package underscores the need for MIS software at the small-systems level. By age 30 the VisiCalc promoter, Daniel Fylstra, had built a $125 million company in four years. Perhaps you should start thinking about a name for your package.[13]

Word Processing

Word processing can be performed by stand-alone, microprocessor-controlled units or by terminals linked to a host. The hardware operates under the control of the operator and of software contained within the stand-alone unit or the host.

Some computer manufacturers have developed a separate line of equipment to handle word processing. The Wang Wangwriter is a good example. A keyboard, CRT, printer, and floppy disk drive under the control of a microprocessor permit the storage of up to seventy-five pages of text, an easy rearrangement of format, and typing at a rate of 200 words per minute. The IBM Displaywriter (see Figure 1-8) is another example of a system designed for word processing. It includes basically the same configuration as the Wang, but it also has an arithmetic calculation function.

The other approach manufacturers have taken is to develop a single system that can be used for both data and word processing. For example, both the TRS-80 Model II and the Apple II Plus offer word processing software. For small organizations, having one system that can perform both tasks is usually less expensive than having two specialized systems. In addition to economy, the combined system permits the use of data base contents in word processing applications. For example, a firm could obtain names and addresses from its data base and use them to prepare promotional mailings.

A photograph of the IBM System/23 Datamaster appears in Figure 10-14. Announced in 1981, the base price is $9830, making it the lowest-priced small business system in the IBM product line. Data processing programs are available for $1025 each, and for $1100 to $2200 the user can attach word processing hardware and software. The system can be equipped with two CRT terminals (IBM calls them *work stations*), enabling two people to use the system at the same time.

---

[13] For more information on the VisiCalc package, see Harry Anbarlian, *Introduction to VisiCalc Matrixing* (New York: McGraw-Hill, 1982). For more details on VisiCalc, Apple, and other success stories, see "Striking It Rich," *Time,* 15 February 1982, pp. 36 ff.

Figure 10-14 The IBM System/23 Datamaster is designed to handle both data and word processing tasks.

Word processing is important to the MIS, whether implemented with word processing or data processing hardware. Figure 10-1 shows a word processor providing the link from the manager back to the physical system. This is the portion of the feedback loop that has been least developed in the MIS. Most of the attention in MIS design has been directed at formal information flows, largely ignoring the informal flows. You recall from Chapter 2 that management theorist Henry Mintzberg distinguished between the hard and soft information flows that affect managerial work. The potential role for word processing in the MIS appears to be in the area of soft information flows—informal flows that have proven difficult for conventional computing equipment. To date, few have attempted to integrate word processing and data processing, and practically no one gives word processing a role in the MIS. There is considerable potential in harnessing the power of word processing to expedite the flow of management information, and no doubt considerable progress will be made in this area during the next several years.

Some Small Business System Applications

Minis and micros can serve as the sole information processor in small firms and as elements in a distributed network in large firms. Although the minis and micros are much more sophisticated in design and use than their earlier counterparts from the first three computer generations, many of them are being applied in basically the same way. The initial applications targeted for computerization by mini and micro users are the traditional data processing applications—inventory, payroll, and so on. These applications are well defined and increased profits from computerization are often possible in the form of reduced expenses and increased revenues. It is common for firms installing mini and micro systems to devote from one to three years to developing these data processing applications.

As soon as the data processing applications are running smoothly and the firm has developed an accurate, up-to-date data base of daily activity, the focus of the mini or micro can be expanded to include management information. The time required for this shift to take place depends on the firm's management. If management possesses a high degree of computer literacy, recognizing the value of the computer as an information processor, the shift will occur quickly. In fact, in firms where management knows the value of computer-generated information, the mini or micro can be installed initially with an information orientation. More often than not, however, the firm elects to gain confidence in its new computing ability through successful implementation of the data processing applications.

Some sample applications are described below to provide an idea of how these small systems are being used to solve business problems.

Manufacturing

Bently Nevada Corporation manufactures products that monitor the performance of equipment such as compressors and pumps. It employs 900 people at its Minden, Nevada, plant, and 1981 sales were $50 million. This is no mini-size company, but its computer is an IBM System/38. The system includes fifty-five terminals—thirty in the manufacturing area. Offices in Houston, Chicago, Buffalo, and Los Angeles also have terminals tied into a datacom network.

The System/38 is used for the typical manufacturing jobs—material requirements planning, production and inventory control, order tracking, and accounting. The computer system is able to keep up with about 2000 production orders a week. In explaining the value of the system, Ron Nino, the vice president of information services, says, "If you can tell the shop foreman daily what he's supposed to do that day, in order of priority, he's going to make money for your company."[14]

The application of small business system hardware and software has improved efficiency in the production process, and it is also valuable for its management information. Data that used to be destroyed can be stored electronically for ninety

---

[14]"With Room to Grow," *Viewpoint,* March–April 1981, pp. 4–5.

days or six months for analysis. Mr. Nino appreciates the value of the small computer–based MIS: "Manufacturers today try especially hard to walk the fine line between customer satisfaction and the high cost of inventory. . . . With the facts from the manufacturing data base, we're convinced that computer-based forecasting can keep us on the narrow path."[15]

Another example in manufacturing involves a very large organization—Owens Corning Fiberglas, with 25,000 employees and sales of $2 billion. In its industrial operating division, a TI DS990 Model 8 is used for attendance and job reporting. Workers clock on and clock off using data collection terminals scattered throughout the plant. The data is transmitted to the TI computer, where it becomes part of the data base. The data is available immediately for response to a manager's query, for use in preparing management reports, and for computing payroll and cost data. As an example of its use, a supervisor can query the data base and learn who is and who is not on the job only moments after a shift begins.

Before implementation of the computerized time and attendance system, supervisors had to gather data daily, sign each time card, and forward them to a payroll clerk. The payroll clerk would determine absenteeism, vacation time, and total hours worked. Now this is all done by computer, relieving the supervisors of this data processing responsibility and freeing them for more important duties.

The DS990 system includes a 256KB primary storage, two disk units providing 100MB of secondary storage, two printers, and several CRT terminals. This system is part of a corporate distributed processing network. The computerization of attendance and job reporting supports lower-level managers and improves their ability to manage the physical system.[16]

Football

Several National Football League teams subscribe to a computerized "scouting service" that analyzes game film data and provides printed reports. All of this is done within strict time constraints.

On the Monday morning after a Sunday game, coaches analyze the game film and record entries on a data sheet. The data is keyed into a Datapoint 1500 system, shown in Figure 10-15; and transmitted to a central computer center in Detroit operated by Quanex Management Sciences. Figure 10-16 shows the data-com network points linking the central computer with fifteen NFL teams. The data is processed in Detroit on Monday evening and the report data is immediately transmitted back to the NFL cities. The Datapoint 1500 prints out a number of reports. Coaches can select from over 300 formats that analyze their own team's and their competitors' strategies. Most coaches use about thirty-five reports a week.

Bart Starr, coach of the Green Bay Packers, says, "We think it is an excellent system. We use it as a method for scouting the opponent and for self-scouting our

---

[15] Ibid., p. 5.

[16] "Owens Corning Fiberglas Application Summary," Texas Instruments, 1981.

Figure 10-15   The Datapoint 1500 dispersed processor.

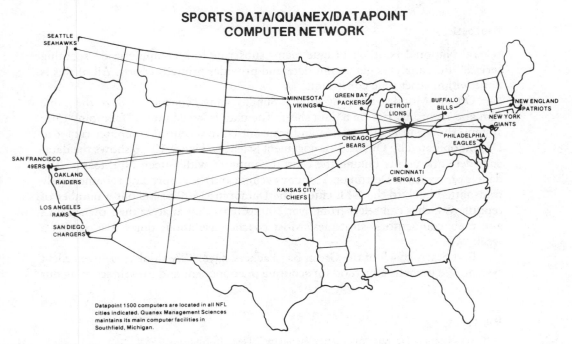

Figure 10-16   The NFL computer scouting network.

own team. Our plans are to continually upgrade and use it to an even greater degree."[17] The Packers liked the results so well that they ordered a larger Datapoint 6600 for accounting work, college draft analysis, concession contracts, season ticket sales, and other applications.

Retailing

Livingston's is the last family-owned women's wear chain in the San Francisco Bay Area. Twelve stores do approximately $20 million worth of sales annually. In 1980 Livingston's made a big switch. It replaced the pencil and paper sales-recording system it had used since 1872 with two IBM System/34s and off-line point-of-sale terminals.

Livingston's uses the retail industry package RMAS (Retail Merchandise and Audit System) along with some specially written programs. Each day the floppy disks from each of the IBM 5260 point-of-sale terminals are taken to the O'Farrell Street offices. Monday's sales information is available by Wednesday afternoon at the latest. The old manual system had a one-week delay.

Livingston's management uses the conceptual information system to monitor the physical system. Executive Chip Livingston says, "At our corporate headquarters we now get a much better idea of what's happening in each store, what's selling and what's not, and what should be reordered immediately."[18]

If a customer wants to buy an item and the store is out of stock, the computer can locate a store that does have the item—in 30 seconds. The buyers use the system to keep track of inventory levels, purchase orders, buying budget, and fast-selling and slow-selling products. One report enables management to analyze sales within certain categories. For example, a report can show how many handbags of a certain type between $50 and $100 have been sold in each store. This is management by exception.

Livingston sums up the firm's computer efforts by saying, "We saw data processing as a necessity for the 1980s. But until we learned what this new system could do for us, we really didn't know how old-fashioned we'd been."[19]

Choosing a Small Computer

Choosing a small computer is no different from choosing a large one. First, you identify, understand, and define your problem, and then you select a hardware and software combination that best meets your needs. This is the systems approach, and it applies just as effectively to small systems as to large ones. In fact, it is particularly important today to use the systems approach to select a small com-

[17] "NFL and College Coaches Increase 'Game Plan' Practice Time Using Datapoint Minicomputers," in *Applied Out-Think,* document 60687 (San Antonio: Datapoint Corp., n.d.), p. 3.

[18] "Retailers in a Dynamic Selling Environment," *Viewpoint,* July–August 1981, p. 8.

[19] Ibid., p. 9.

puter. The low prices encourage many people to make a purchase without seriously considering their needs and what is available on the market.

Before making a purchase, a person or a firm should try to learn as much
about computers as possible. Much information is available from popular magazines such as *Time* and *Newsweek*. And a new group of magazines deals specifically with small systems—magazines like *Byte, Popular Computing, Mini-Micro
Systems,* and *Small Systems World*. Articles frequently offer advice on system
selection.[20] This can supplement information obtained from computer manufacturers' literature and from visits to computer stores. Gathering information yourself is a particularly valuable complement to formal computer courses.

We will not elaborate here on the process that a firm should follow to select
a small computer. That process is described in detail in Part Five of this book.
Just because a computer is small doesn't mean that a small effort should go into
the selection process. The firm should follow the same general selection process
that has been refined over the years by users of large systems. Essentially, that
process is based on the systems approach.

Summary

Small systems are not limited to small organizations. Minis and micros can be
found in large firms as well, functioning as stand-alone systems, serving as information processors in distributed networks, and managing datacom traffic. A manager can be surrounded by these small systems, which form an information link
to the organizational unit.

The terminology can be confusing, but we can consider all small systems to
be either micros or minis. Personal computers are micros that individuals buy for
their own use. Small business systems are micros or minis used to handle small-
and medium-scale business data and information processing.

A microprocessor is a semiconductor chip containing the control and the
arithmetic and logic portions of a CPU. Add primary storage and a few support
chips, and you have a microcomputer. Increase the performance characteristics
beyond a microprocessor, and you have a minicomputer. Primary storage comes
in two types—ROM and RAM. ROM is for program storage; you can read the
manufacturer-supplied instructions but cannot use the area for data manipulation.
RAM permits reading and writing, and this is where applications programs are
stored and data items can be changed and updated.

The first small systems represented data in 8-bit words. Word size has increased,
and now minis often use 16- and 32-bit words for internal data transfer and

---

[20] See, for example, Stan Miastkowski, "Choosing Your Popular Computer," *Popular Computing* 1
(November 1981): 16 ff; idem, "A Computer for Your Small Business," ibid. 1 (November
1981): 35 ff; Malcolm L. Stiefel, "Choosing a Small, Multi-User Business Computer," *Mini-
Micro Systems* 14 (June 1981): 87 ff; "Update: Small Business Computers," *Small Systems World*
10 (January 1982): 14–20; John Seaman, "Mini or Micro: Which Way to Go?" *Computer
Decisions* 13 (October 1981): 90 ff; and Jean-Pierre Frankenhuis, "How to Get a Good Mini,"
Harvard Business Review 60 (May–June 1982): 139–149.

processing. Most micros use 8 bits, but these are being increased to 16 and 32. The expansion of word size is one major reason for the increasing performance of small computers.

Historically the micro and the mini have been characterized by limited I/O hardware and limited software. This is changing. Input is usually accomplished by CRT, but a hardcopy terminal can be used. Hardcopy printed output can also be achieved by using a hardcopy printer—usually a daisywheel or dot matrix unit. Faster line printers are used for high-volume output. Secondary storage takes the form of floppy disk or diskette units in small systems, and hard disks in large configurations. A popular hard disk is the Winchester, a packaged unit offering high capacity and fast data transfer rates. It is also possible to use magnetic tape cassettes and conventional magnetic tape units—primarily for the sequential storage of the software library and for backup data base files.

The systems software for small systems is typically scaled down from that of large systems. Users of small systems generally cannot pay high software prices, and small systems do not usually demand such sophisticated software support. The operating systems for the largest minis are comparable to the systems software of medium- and large-scale computers. But the more modest the equipment, the more modest the operating system. The UNIX operating system is most popular in the middle range, and the CP/M at the micro level. Nonbusiness users like the BASIC programming language, whereas business users like BASIC, COBOL, FORTRAN, and RPG.

Data base management systems follow the same pattern as the operating systems. Popular large computers like the DEC PDP and VAX have DBMSes specially tailored to them. At the lower levels, the MDBS package is widely used. Since so many mini/micro systems are used for nonbusiness applications, as we pointed out in Chapter 5, data base software has not received the same attention as operating systems and language compilers. Much improvement is needed in small system DBMSes to bring them closer in performance capability to the packages available on large systems.

Applications software varies from industry-oriented to task-oriented packages. These packages are available from computer manufacturers and an increasing number of software firms. The quality of the packages varies considerably, from well-documented and -supported products like MAPICS and VisiCalc software to inefficient, error-ridden packages with no documentation and no support from the manufacturer. This is the area where small-system users have suffered from the biggest misconceptions. You need the software, and it must be good. You can't just unpack the hardware and plug it in. Look at the most successful mini and micro systems and you find top-quality software support. Apple is a classic example.

Most of the applications software, however, is intended to facilitate data processing, not management decision making. The wide acceptance of an information-producing tool such as the VisiCalc package highlights the need for more and better MIS software. If you are looking for an area within the computer field that offers wide-open opportunities, the development of small-system MIS software is it.

Similar opportunities exist in word processing. This application area has usually been treated separately from data processing. Today firms are integrating the processes and the data, if not the equipment. The next step will be to incorporate word processing into the MIS. The logical point is in the feedback loop, providing another electronic link between the manager and the firm.

The small business system area is currently receiving the most attention. Small firms are discovering the power of the computer, and large firms are discovering the flexibility of mini/micro systems. We are probably only scratching the surface of possible applications of mini/micro systems in information processing.

A small computer requires as thorough a preselection analysis as a large one does. The systems approach provides a framework that can be followed in defining problems to be solved with the support of small systems, selecting the appropriate hardware and software combination, and implementing the selected configuration. That approach is detailed in Part Five of the text.

This brings us to the end of our discussion of the computer. The final chapter in this part of the book deals with using a computer in an MIS. The focus will not be on technology, but rather on applying technology to produce information for management. We have now laid a foundation of technology on top of the foundation of theory. From this point on, our concern will be with how the MIS is used and how it is achieved.

Key Terms

minicomputer

microcomputer

microprocessor

small business computer

personal computer

ROM (read-only memory)

RAM (random-access memory)

cycle time

instruction set

Winchester disk

work station

Key Concepts

How mini/micro systems can be used to gather data from the physical system of the firm, to transform data into information, and to communicate management decisions back to the physical system

Categories of small-scale systems—minicomputers, microcomputers, microprocessors, small business computers, personal computers

Variability in mini/micro CPU characteristics—word size, cycle time, instruction set

Online nature of mini/micro I/O options

Emphasis on direct access storage devices rather than sequential, and the influence that such an emphasis has on system design

Distinct grouping of systems software into mini and micro categories

Use of programming language availability as an indicator of system orientation—business or nonbusiness

Data processing orientation of packaged applications software

Potential of word processing to help close the feedback control loop for the physical system of the firm

Two basic approaches to word processing—special-purpose word processing hardware and software, or word processing software used on data processing hardware

Evolution of mini/micro applications—first a data orientation, then an information orientation

Questions

1. Is there a clear distinction between minis and micros? Explain.
2. What distinguishes a microcomputer from a microprocessor?
3. Is a small business computer a mini or a micro? Explain.
4. Is a personal computer a mini or a micro? Explain.
5. Name four brands of personal computers.
6. What is ROM? What is RAM? How do they differ?
7. What are two effects of small word size?
8. What is the most popular input device for a mini/micro system? Does this present any problems?
9. What is the most popular secondary storage medium? What option exists when storage requirements increase?
10. What is a Winchester disk?
11. Are mini/micro I/O options becoming more similar or less similar to those of larger systems? Explain.
12. What is the most popular operating system for minis? For micros?
13. What programming languages do users of small business computers prefer? What about nonbusiness users?
14. Name two software firms that offer DBMSes to minicomputer users as well as to medium- and large-scale system users.
15. What minicomputer manufacturer's products are best supported by DBMS packages?
16. What is the most popular DBMS for micros? With what operating system does it interface?
17. What applications does MAPICS perform? Is it a data- or an information-oriented package?
18. How can you explain the wide acceptance of the VisiCalc package?
19. Where does word processing fit into the MIS picture?

20. Which of the sample mini/micro applications (Bently Nevada, Owens Corning, NFL, and Livingston's) enables management to monitor the physical system of the firm? Which is used as a decision support system?

CASE PROBLEM: Tri-Cities Furniture

As part of your MIS course, you are expected to go out into the community and study a data processing system. You are to document the present system and design a new, information-oriented one.

You remember that you once saw a small computer in a furniture store. You drive downtown to the white stucco building with a sign reading "Tri-Cities Furniture: Serving the Endicott, Binghampton, and Johnson City Area." You walk inside and ask to see the owner. There aren't many people in the store. You don't see anyone else who looks like a customer. The man you talked to looks like a sales clerk. An elderly woman sits behind a desk writing in a huge ledger. Three men are unloading a truck and bringing furniture into the store from the alley.

A man wearing a white shirt and tie comes out of an office and says, "Can I help you?" After you explain your situation and introduce yourself, he says, "I'm Albert Mendoza. I'm the owner, sales manager, part-time sales person, and bill collector. Ha ha."

Right away, you know Albert has a sense of humor. Before you stop smiling, he says, "Sure, you can study our operation. Come over here and let me introduce you to Alice and Ray."

You walk over to the woman with the ledger—Alice Cook, the bookkeeper. Alice has been with the firm for 23 years and has been the only person to keep the books. You turn to Albert and say, "I thought I saw a computer in here a couple of months ago."

"That's right," Albert replies. "We have a computer. It's over in this room next to my office. Come over here and I'll show it to you."

You walk into the computer room, and Albert turns on the light. There it is, smaller than you remembered it. But you recognize the parts—a CRT work station, the CPU, a disk drive that can handle two floppies, and a serial printer. The label on the CPU says "IBM System 5110." You don't remember studying that model, and Albert tells you it is one of IBM's earliest small systems.

About that time, the man you first talked to walks in. He is Ray Silva, and he divides his time between operating the computer and selling furniture. The computer work can be done in three or four hours a day. The computer is used to print tags that are placed on furniture arriving from the factory. It keeps inventory records on all items located in this store and in the Binghampton and Endicott stores. The computer also maintains records of installment payments. Tri-Cities caters to lower-middle-class trade, and much of the business is on credit. Albert handles the financing himself.

Albert begins to tell you the story of his computer. On the advice of his accountant, he purchased the computer from a friend who operates a furniture store in Syracuse, some seventy miles away. The friend had purchased the unit from IBM and prepared all of the software himself. When the friend's business prospered, he installed a larger system. The friend made Albert an offer he couldn't refuse, so Albert plunged into the computer game.

As it turned out, it has been a sobering experience. The software doesn't really do the job. It is written to handle the accounts of a single operation, and the three locations of Tri-Cities present problems. Further, the software doesn't balance the accounts. That is why Alice still keeps the books by hand. Albert doesn't trust the computer. Ray processes the inventory and receivables transactions on the computer, and Alice also does them by hand. They have been hoping to cut over to the computer, but problems always come up. Albert hopes that eventually everything will work out so that he can start getting some return on his computer investment.

You ask if there is any documentation for the software (flowcharts, record descriptions, operating procedures, and so on), and find out that there is none. You also learn that anytime anything goes wrong, a systems analyst must come from Syracuse to solve the problem. He is the only person who understands the software. His daily rate is $350 plus mileage. To make matters worse, nobody at Tri-Cities knows anything about programming. Ray knows how to operate the system, but if anything goes wrong, he calls the analyst. Sometimes the trouble turns out to be hardware, and there is a local computer engineer who can fix the trouble.

Albert has problems. Alice is retiring at the end of the year, and Ray has given notice that he plans to leave at the end of the month. He is going into the aluminum siding business. Albert would like to hire a student part-time who knows enough about computers to debug the programs and to add a general-ledger package that came with the system but has never been used. You tell him you'll think about it.

You ask Albert if he is getting any management information out of the computer. "No, I'm not," he says, "though I'd like to. You might think we don't have much business here, but we do. This is just a slack period. Weekends are our busiest time. I have trouble keeping up with everything. I'd like to know what's selling and what isn't, how much profit we're making on our different lines, and so forth. But we just don't know how to get that information out of our computer. And I'm not sure that it's in there. But I bought it with that objective in mind."

You tell Albert you'll get back to him about the term project. You are at a loss for words. You had expected a success story like the ones you heard in class. This seems to be a real can of worms. You say good-bye to everyone, and as you start to walk out the door, Albert calls out, "Hey, I couldn't sell you a good water bed, could I?"

Questions

1. Does Albert need a computer?
2. Would you say that Albert is computer literate?
3. Do you think that Albert should throw out the existing computer and start over?
4. If Albert chooses to stick with the existing system, what would you suggest he do to solve his problems?
5. If Albert chooses to start over, what would you suggest he do differently the next time?

Chapter 11

Computer-Based Decision Support Systems

Learning Objectives

After studying this chapter, you should:

- Know the three basic methods managers use to obtain information
- Know how the methods evolved and how they help the manager identify and solve problems
- Know the basic characteristics of reports, how reports are used by managers, and how to incorporate management by exception into reports
- Appreciate the appeal of data base queries and recognize the resources required
- Have an introductory knowledge of how the INQUIRE User Language and MARK-IV provide a querying ability
- Understand how managers use queries to identify and understand problems
- Know the different attributes of mathematical models
- Understand how linear programming and the Monte Carlo method can provide decision support
- Know the main advantages and disadvantages of modeling

Overview

We have laid the theoretical groundwork, and we have reviewed the hardware and systems software that can be incorporated into an MIS. In this chapter we will build a bridge connecting the theory and technology on the one hand and the business applications on the other. Our approach in this chapter will be to describe how any manager, on any level, and in any functional area can employ the computer as a decision support system. Then in the next four chapters we will see how managers in the main functional areas—marketing, manufacturing, and finance—can harness the power of the computer to help solve their special types of problems.

The Decision Support System (DSS) Concept

We have covered quite a bit of ground since we introduced the DSS concept in Chapter 1. You recall that a DSS is intended to *support* the manager in decision making, not to relieve the manager of this important responsibility. The manager and the DSS work together as an effective problem-solving team. This interaction produces a *synergism* that improves the utility of both resources—the effectiveness of the manager's involvement is improved because of the computer's contribution, and the computer's contribution is improved because of the manager's involvement.

The DSS is aimed at the area of *semistructured problems,* which contain some elements that are well defined and can be quantified and some that are not so well understood and must be considered subjectively. For example, deciding where to locate a new plant is a semistructured problem. Real estate costs, taxes, utilities, and transportation costs can be identified and tabulated. But community, customer, and employee attitudes are difficult to measure. A firm might consider constructing a plant in an area where costs are low. But the same area might suffer from a high crime rate. Should the firm build the plant even though it might have difficulty relocating employees into the area? This is a semistructured problem.

You also recall from our discussion earlier that managers solve *problems* and make *decisions* during the problem-solving process. The systems approach provides a framework for problem solving. As Figure 11-1 illustrates, the six steps of the systems approach produce an operational solution to the problem, and information from the MIS provides support at each step along the way. The task of the manager is to build a strong MIS to provide this type of decision support.

The MIS cannot be expected to provide the same level of support at each problem-solving step. Neither can it provide the same support for all types of problems. We must remember that the idea of a computerized MIS is still relatively recent—less than 20 years old. We are still in the learning stage—learning how to apply this amazing electronic tool to a special and very difficult class of problems. A modern manager attempts to apply the computer to those problems that are recurring and important. Over time, the support provided by the MIS will increase as new problems are identified and applied to computer processing.

Basic Methods of Obtaining Information

There are three basic methods that the manager can use to obtain information from the MIS: reports, data base queries, and mathematical model simulations. Figure 11-2 shows how these methods provide the means of interaction between the manager and the MIS.

The symbols in the figure are the flowchart symbols for input and output media. Starting from the top, the symbol labeled "printed reports" is used to

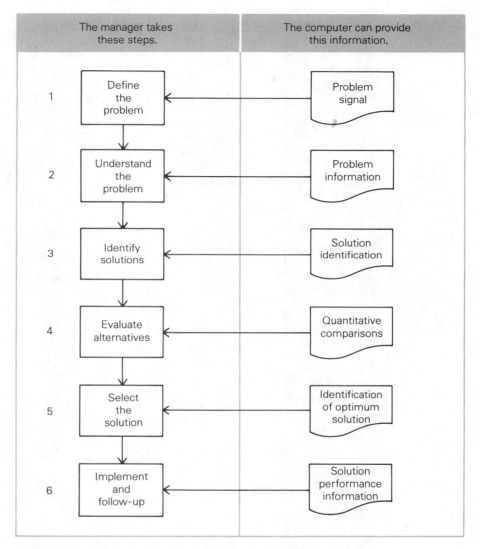

The manager takes these steps.	The computer can provide this information.
1 — Define the problem	Problem signal
2 — Understand the problem	Problem information
3 — Identify solutions	Solution identification
4 — Evaluate alternatives	Quantitative comparisons
5 — Select the solution	Identification of optimum solution
6 — Implement and follow-up	Solution performance information

Figure 11-1 Computer support using the systems approach.

represent any paper document, including a form. The symbol labeled "displayed reports" is used to represent output that is not in hardcopy form, such as information on a CRT. The symbol labeled "query" represents an online keying operation—using a terminal, for example. The punched card symbol in the center represents data punched into cards for entry by a card reader.

Reports come to the manager automatically; they do not have to be requested. They can be *repetitive*—prepared daily, monthly, quarterly, and so on. Some people use the term *periodic* to describe a repetitive report. Alternatively, reports can be *special,* prepared in the event of an extraordinary occurrence such as an accident. Some procedure is established that triggers the reporting process. In some

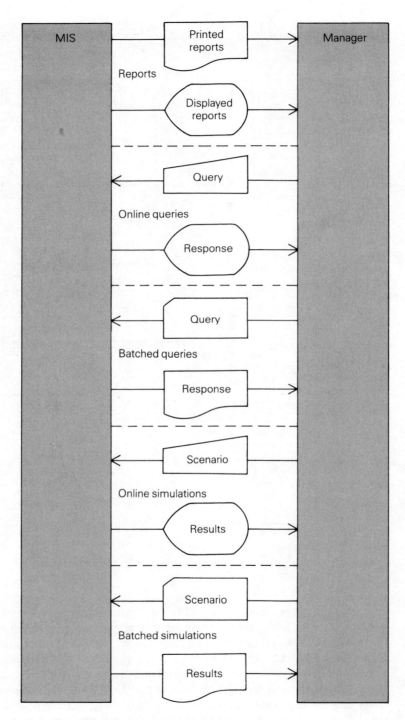

Figure 11-2 Managers obtain information by report, query, and simulation

cases, managers request special reports when they feel that something is going wrong and they want to know more about it.

As Figure 11-2 indicates, some reports are printed, and some are displayed on a CRT. While it is tempting to envision a terminal sitting on each manager's desk, that day has not yet arrived. The majority of reports are produced by line or serial printers and delivered to the manager through the firm's mail service. In some cases a hardcopy or RJE terminal is located in a department for use by all managers in the area.

Queries can be made from a terminal or recorded in punched card form. When the query originates from a terminal, the response usually comes back to that same terminal. It is possible, however, to make a query from a terminal and receive the response in a report printed by a line or serial printer. This would be the case when the manager wants a hardcopy and the terminal is a CRT, or when the report is too big to be accommodated easily on a slow-speed terminal. Although a number of queries are still made on punched cards, that approach is giving way to online methods.

Simulations involve the use of mathematical models to represent the behavior of a real phenomenon. Our specific interest is the simulation of business activity. The objectives of the simulation are to provide the manager with a greater understanding of the system being modeled and to predict how that system might behave, given certain influences. Like queries, simulations can be triggered either online or offline. A manager can enter a scenario from a terminal or in the form of a punched card deck. A *scenario* is the situational data that provides the setting of a simulation. The scenario can describe the firm, its customers, its suppliers, the economy, and so on. Simulation results can come back to the terminal or be printed on the computer printer.

All three methods can generate graphical as well as alphanumeric information. Reports can include graphics, as can query responses and simulations. We will not specifically discuss graphical output during the remainder of the chapter (since it was covered in Chapter 6), but you should keep in mind that graphics are becoming a more important MIS output.

Evolution of the three methods

The oldest method of obtaining information is the report. Business reports have been popular since the first days of commerce. Most likely one of Bob Cratchet's duties was the hand preparation of financial reports for his boss, Scrooge. In your accounting courses, you prepare these same reports by hand—the manual system. Keydriven, punched card, and now computer systems have all used the report as the primary means of output. Although more attention is currently being directed toward the other two methods—queries and simulations—the report is the most widely used method of transmitting information to the manager.

The dominance of the report method can be seen in the conceptual representation in Figure 11-3. The increasing use of the computer in the mid-fifties spawned a corresponding increase in the use of reports. At the same time, simulation became a much-discussed though infrequently used method. Managers still have not embraced simulation to a great degree, mainly because of the demand it places

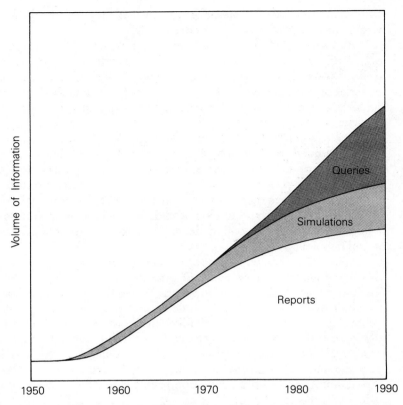

Figure 11-3 Evolution of information-producing methods.

on mathematical skills. Over time, as more computer-literate managers enter business, this hostile attitude will erode, and simulations should enjoy increasing acceptance—although at a modest rate.

At the present time, the query method is stimulating a great deal of interest. Of the three methods of obtaining information, querying is the newest—getting its start in the early seventies with the advent of commercial DBMSes. From all indications, this is the method of the future. Query languages are increasingly *user-friendly*. A person doesn't have to be a programmer to obtain a few data items or to produce a complete report. The query method will probably ride the popularity wave of online processing and will ultimately become the primary method of providing management information.

Two Basic Uses of Information

Managers make two basic uses of information. First, they use information for *problem identification*. Problems are identified, defined, and understood. This use corresponds to the first two steps of the systems approach in Figure 11-1—define the problem and understand the problem. The second use of information is for

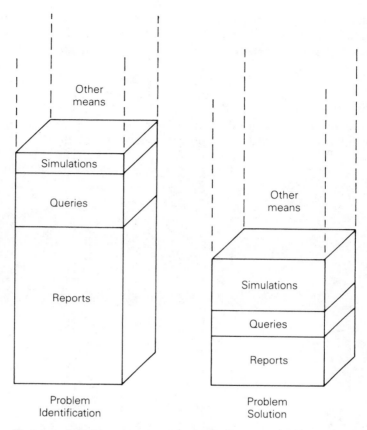

Figure 11-4 MIS support for problem identification and solution.

problem solution, and this use is characterized by the last four steps of the systems approach.

As a general rule, reports and queries are used primarily to identify problems, and simulations are used to solve problems. This means that the MIS provides more support to problem identification than to problem solution, since simulations are not widely used. Figure 11-4 illustrates this condition. Primarily through reports and secondarily through queries and simulations, the MIS handles much of the problem identification workload. Managers also use other means (such as informal information contacts) to identify problems. In fact, more problems may be identified from informal cues than from those provided by the MIS.

Reports can be designed to identify problems or potential problems. Managers can also query the data base to find problems or to learn more about problems that have already been identified. Simulations frequently uncover hidden problems, because weaknesses tend to stand out when part of the firm's operation is manipulated mathematically.

Reports and queries can also help the manager solve problems by identifying alternatives, evaluating and selecting alternatives, and providing follow-up information. But this is the area where simulation really shines. Mathematical models enable the manager to play the "what-if" game—trying out strategies mathematically to predict their consequences.

Reports

In addition to being either repetitive or special, reports can also be detailed or summary. A *detailed report* provides specifics, usually a line of data, about each

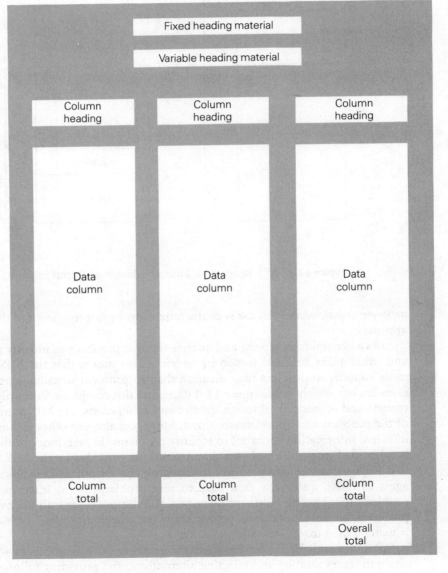

Figure 11-5 Basic report parts.

transaction. For example, a payroll register lists each employee and shows earnings information. This type of report is a list, also called a *detailed listing*.

When a report contains entries that are distillations of multiple transactions, the report is a *summary report*. A departmental earnings report, showing one line of data for each department, is a summary report. Generally, detailed reports are used at lower management levels, and summarized reports are used at upper levels.

Report organization

A general pattern provides a format for all reports. This pattern is pictured in Figure 11-5. A report consists of three main areas—*heading, body,* and *footing.*

In the heading area, centered at the top of the page, is *fixed heading material* such as the name of the report. Immediately below is *variable heading material* such as date and page number.

In the body area are *column headings* that identify the vertical *columns of data* immediately below. The generally accepted convention is to place coded data (such as employee number) on the left, descriptive data (such as employee name) in the center, and quantitative data (such as earnings amounts) on the right.

In the footing area are column total amounts accumulated for each column and also an overall total or group of totals. The sample report in Figure 11-6 contains the basic elements. This is an example of a detailed listing.

Not all reports have all three areas. Some are printed without headings, and some do not have totals. Alternatively, a summary report might contain only a heading and totals.

It is also possible to print subtotals throughout a report at the end of certain sections. For example, all of the employees of a firm can be listed by department, with departmental totals printed immediately following a departmental group. This technique is illustrated in Figure 11-7. Reports are typically printed in some sequence. In this example, employees are listed in each department in *descending order* based on their salary. Departments are listed in *ascending order* based on department number. The point at which the computer recognizes the end of one department and the beginning of another is the *break point*. The departmental totals are printed at the break point.

EMPLOYEES WORKING OVERTIME

MAY 19, 1984

DEPARTMENT NUMBER	EMPLOYEE NUMBER	EMPLOYEE NAME	OVERTIME HOURS
20	10783	STUART, WILLIAM	1.1
20	62943	MCCANN, RALPH	.3
21	10428	WILLIAMS, MAURICE	1.0
23	51640	POTUZAK, ROGER	.8
23	21289	KAHLER, JANE	.5
23	64387	FORKNER, IRV	.1
25	41011	MARTINEZ, ALICE	1.3
		TOTAL	5.1

Figure 11-6 Detailed listing with overall total.

```
                    EMPLOYEES GROUPED BY DEPARTMENT              PAGE    1
                                                                06/08/82
                        AND ORDERED BY SALARY

        EMPLOYEE NAME                JOB              SALARY   CURRENT
                                    TITLE                      DEPT
    ------------------------------------------------------------------------

    **EMPLOYEES IN DEPARTMENT 201

    RONALD GORDON           SR STATISTICIAN          $24,500.76  201

    SAM JACKSON             GRP LDR SYS DEVELOPMENT  $24,000.00  201

    RICHARD HOPKINS         SR SYSTEMS PROGRAMMER    $23,584.75  201

    JAMES PARKS             SR PROGRAMMER            $22,055.79  201

    PAT FLEMING             PROGRAMMER-ANALYST       $19,759.31  201

    TOTAL SALARY FOR DEPT     201                   $113,900.61

    **EMPLOYEES IN DEPARTMENT 316

    JOHN H. WHITE           MGR-CUSTOMER SUPPORT     $27,895.34  316

    BILL APPLE              PERSONNEL MANAGER        $25,485.50  316

    JANET WILLIAMS          SR SYSTEMS ANALYST       $23,500.00  316

    NANCY N MOORE           SR SYSTEMS PROGRAMMER    $22,565.77  316

    GEORGE MILLER           COST ANALYST·            $21,800.00  316

    JAMES GLEASON           ASST MGR-CUST. SUPP.     $21,475.85  316

    SALLY SCHUSTER          SYSTEMS ANALYST          $19,480.00  316

    JAMES R. HILL           APPLICATIONS GRP LDR     $19,259.99  316

    ROBERT P. KELLY         PROGRAMMER               $13,600.00  316

    ANNE SMITH              RECEPTIONIST              $9,000.00  316

    TOTAL SALARY FOR DEPT     316                   $204,062.45

    **EMPLOYEES IN DEPARTMENT 384

    JOE DECKER              CHEMIST                  $16,445.00  384

    TOTAL SALARY FOR DEPT     384                    $16,445.00

    **EMPLOYEES IN DEPARTMENT 401

    WAYNE ROGERS            MGR PERSONNEL TRAINING   $27,845.50  401

    TOTAL SALARY FOR DEPT     401                    $27,845.50

    **EMPLOYEES IN DEPARTMENT 402
```

Figure 11-7 Detailed listing with control breaks.

How managers use reports

Most accounting systems have been designed to produce a set of repetitive reports. Balance sheets and income statements are examples. Both have companywide interest. Other reports have a narrower focus. An aged accounts receivable report is of interest to the credit manager. A sales-by-salesperson report is prepared for the sales manager. And a report of overtime earnings is used by the plant superintendent.

Most of these reports perform a valuable service. Balance sheets and income statements are greatly distilled summaries of hundreds or thousands of separate transactions that show at a glance the financial position of the firm. Reports such as this are read by strategic- and tactical-level managers and are even included in annual reports to stockholders, as in Figure 11-8.

Consolidated Balance Sheet

Aluminum Company of America and consolidated subsidiaries

	(In millions, except share amounts)	
December 31	1980	1979
Assets		(F)
Current assets:		
Cash and time deposits	$ 63.4	$ 135.6
Short-term investments, at cost approximating market	59.5	127.1
Receivables from customers, less allowances: 1980, $2.8; 1979, $3.9	717.5	681.7
Other receivables	55.3	43.2
Inventories (B)	695.6	689.0
Prepaid expenses and other assets	42.7	30.0
Total current assets	1,634.0	1,706.6
Investments (C and P)	764.6	587.2
Other assets and deferred charges	102.2	98.6
Properties, plants and equipment (D)	2,687.3	2,318.9
Total assets	**$5,188.1**	**$4,711.3**
Liabilities		
Current liabilities:		
Accounts payable, trade	$ 331.9	$ 312.6
Accrued payroll and other compensation	134.4	130.3
Taxes, including taxes on income	160.0	277.7
Other current liabilities	156.6	110.5
Long-term debt due within one year	31.1	16.5
Total current liabilities	814.0	847.6
Long-term debt, less amount due within one year (R)	1,017.5	1,020.6
Noncurrent liabilities and deferred credits	118.8	124.4
Future taxes on income (K)	304.0	213.1
	2,254.3	2,205.7
Commitments and contingent liabilities (H)		
Shareholders' equity		
Capital stock:		
Serial preferred stock, par value $100, authorized 1,000,000 shares: $3.75 cumulative preferred stock, authorized 660,000 shares; issued and outstanding, 659,909	66.0	66.0
Common stock, par value $1.00, authorized 150,000,000 shares; issued and outstanding: 1980—73,065,370; 1979—70,340,082 (E and I)	73.1	35.2
Additional capital (G)	190.0	152.8
Retained earnings (C and J)	2,604.7	2,251.6
Total shareholders' equity	2,933.8	2,505.6
Total liabilities and shareholders' equity	**$5,188.1**	**$4,711.3**

Figure 11-8 A balance sheet.

```
                      AGED ACCOUNTS RECEIVABLE REPORT
                              JULY 31, 1983

 CUSTOMER      CUSTOMER              INVOICE   =========AMOUNT DUE=========
   NO.           NAME                 NO.      OVER 30      OVER 60      OVER 90

   2309     AARDVARK REALTY          30422     120.50
   2412     BARNETT'S HOME SALES     23546                   25.25
   3808     BRUCE'S REPAIR           10089                                10.10
   4104     ELKHORN HOME SALES       31209     119.65
   4110     MIDTOWN REAL ESTATE      36363     212.00
   6290     ROYALTY TITLE COMPANY    12362                               359.00
   7363     SHOFFNER FOUNDATION CO.  28290                   50.90
   7508     SUPERIOR DEVELOPMENT     38904      16.35
   8200     WEST GYPSUM COMPANY      21916                  289.50
   8339     ZANZABAR SAVINGS ASSN.   31242     100.10
   9316     ZEBRA LUMBER COMPANY     31619     219.30

           TOTALS                              787.90      365.65       369.10
```

Figure 11-9   An aged accounts receivable report.

Other reports are used by operational-level managers to monitor the performance of their areas. The credit manager uses the aged accounts receivable report (Figure 11-9) to identify poor-paying customers and to direct the firm's collection efforts.

The sales manager uses the sales-by-salesperson report (Figure 11-10) to identify those representatives performing in an extraordinary manner—either very well or very badly. This is done by examining the variance-from-quota columns.

The plant superintendent uses the overtime earnings report (Figure 11-11) to identify those departments adding the most to production costs by paying extra

```
                       SALES BY SALESPERSON REPORT
                              MARCH 31, 1983

 ===SALESPERSON======   ===CURRENT=MONTH======   ===YEAR=TO=DATE======
   NO.      NAME        QUOTA  ACTUAL VARIANCE   QUOTA  ACTUAL VARIANCE

   0120  JOHN NELSON    1200    1083    =117     3600    3505     =95
  10469  LYNN SHERRY    1000    1162    +162     3000    3320    +320
  19261  DARVIN UPSHAW   800    1090    +290     2400    2510    +110
  20234  JANIE EVANS    1500    1305    =195     4500    4110    =390
  61604  TRAVIS BURKE   2000    2333    +333     6000    6712    +712
  62083  CATHY HAGER    1000     990     =10     3000    2319    =681
  63049  STEVE JENNER   1100    1250    +150     3300    2416    =884
  64040  SAM MOSELEY    1050     985     =65     3150    3020    =130

         TOTALS         9650   10198     548    28950   27912   =1038
```

Figure 11-10   A sales-by-salesperson report.

```
                      OVERTIME EARNINGS REPORT
                         AUGUST 31, 1983

                                         OVERTIME HOURS
        DEPARTMENT NO.   DEPARTMENT NAME   CURRENT MONTH   YEAR-TO-DATE

           16-10         RECEIVING            2305.00         5319.20
           16-11         INSPECTION           1025.60         4386.12
           16-12         MATL'S HANDLING      3392.50        12629.00
           16-13         TOOLING                78.00         1049.00
           16-14         ASSEMBLY                .00           792.80
           16-15         PLATING              3504.90        12635.20
           16-16         SHIPPING             5219.16        18294.16

                         TOTALS              15525.16        55105.48
```

Figure 11-11   An overtime earnings report.

premiums for labor. This analysis can relate to the current period or to the cumulative status for the fiscal year.

All of these reports are prepared quite easily by computer. Accounting data stored in the data base describes the period's transactions—sales, payments, hours worked, and so on. At the end of the period, the appropriate computer programs extract data from the data base, sort it into appropriate groupings, summarize the transactions, compute measures of variation, and print the reports. It is also possible to store the report data in the data base for display on a manager's terminal when desired.

The operational-level reports in Figures 11-9, 11-10, and 11-11 reflect *management by exception*. The aged accounts receivable report provides the greatest decision support by reporting only the exceptions (the past-due receivables) and by classifying them in terms of their severity. The overtime earnings report provides less support by reporting the exceptions but not classifying them in any way. The sales-by-salesperson report provides the least amount of support by reporting everything and leaving it up to the manager to analyze the variance and determine whether it falls outside the acceptable range. Clearly the manner in which a report is designed determines the degree of decision support it can provide the manager.

One problem with many repetitive reports is that they were not designed by a manager. The manager receiving the report tosses it into the wastebasket. Perhaps the manager doesn't know how to interpret it or how to use its contents. Or the report may deal with an unimportant aspect of the manager's job.

Queries

You can imagine how appealing the idea of a query ability is to a manager. With a query ability, if you want to know something, you just ask for it. Nothing could be simpler. You can ask a question and have an answer almost immediately. It's a more convenient and responsive information service than you get with a repetitive report. With the report, you have to anticipate the information you will need, and then you might have to wait months before the information services group can do the programming, debugging, and testing. With a query ability, all you need to do is snap your fingers and you have your information—at least that's how it seems.

Actually, the query ability requires a great deal of preplanning also, perhaps more than reports do. To have a query ability, you need two ingredients—a data base and a way to get at the data. Data must be converted to a computer storage medium, such as DASD or magnetic tape, and then organized logically to conform to a particular DBMS. Once the data is under the control of the DBMS, retrieval is possible by using a retrieval, or query, language. The language can be part of the DBMS, like the ADASCRIPT+ query language in the ADABAS DBMS. Or the retrieval language can be a separate software package that functions in conjunction with a DBMS. We will discuss both approaches below.

INQUIRE

INQUIRE is a DBMS for large-scale IBM systems that is marketed by Infodata Systems, Inc. It requires a minimum of 150KB. The purchase price is $120,000, with subsets available for as little as $70,000. At the end of 1981, there were approximately 175 users.

One of the main features of INQUIRE is its *user language,* which permits:

- Selective retrieval of data
- Design of report formats
- Computation of report data

Queries can be either online or batch. The user forms a query by using one or more *commands*. These are listed in Table 11-1. Each *command statement* begins with a command verb. For example, the statement below causes the retrieval of all personnel records with an occupation title of PROGRAMMER and a current salary (CURSAL) greater than (GT) $10,000.

FIND PROGRAMMER AND CURSAL GT 10000

Once this data has been retrieved, it can be printed with the statement

TAB NAME CURSAL ($D) SKIP

The $D causes the salary data to be printed as a decimal, preceded by a dollar sign. SKIP inserts a blank line between the detail lines. The report appears in Figure 11-12.

There are two *retrieval commands*—FIND and SCAN. FIND is used with direct access (indexed sequential and direct organization), and SCAN is used when the data base is organized sequentially. There are three *printing commands*—LIST, TAB, and COUNT. If you instruct

FIND CURDEPT = 316, LIST

Table 11-1 INQUIRE Retrieval and Report Generation Commands

Commands	Function
Retrieval tasks	
FIND	Directly accesses data in the data base
SCAN	Sequentially reads each record in the data base, searching for items
Report generation tasks	
TAB	Enables the user to specify positioning and formatting of data on a report
LIST	Permits vertical listing of all data fields in a record, without formatting
TITLE	Allows the user to print headings over each column of data
FOOTER	Allows the user to print a footer at the bottom of data columns
HEADER	Allows the user to print a title at the top of a report
ONPAGE	Enables the user to print variable information, such as page number, at the top of the report, just below the heading and above the titles
COUNT	Counts the number of records meeting the search criteria
SAVE	Saves selected records for later use
COMPUTE	Permits the user to compute values from retrieved data
TOTAL	Enables the user to print totals at the end of the report or to compute values such as averages, maximums, or minimums
SORT	Permits data sorting for report preparation
BREAK	Allows the users to specify computing, totaling, and printing actions at control breaks

you will receive the listing in Figure 11-13. In this example, there are two employees in department 316, and the data is listed without any special formatting. If you want to format the data in a special way, you can instruct

FIND SKILLS = ENGINEER,
TAB NAME 1 EDTYPE 35 DEGREE 45 SKILLS 54.

and receive the report in Figure 11-14. The numbers identify print positions.

Now that we've learned some basics, we might want to dress up the report with headings and to sort the records. The following statement produces the report in Figure 11-15.

SCAN, TAB NAME CURTITL CURSAL CURDEPT, HEADER 'EMPLOYEES GROUPED BY DEPARTMENT' ' ' 'AND ORDERED BY SALARY', TITLE 'EMPLOYEE NAME' NAME (JOB TITLE) CURTITL SALARY CURSAL (CURRENT DEPT) CURDEPT, SORT CURDEPT (A) CURSAL (D).

NAME	CURSAL
FRED JAMES	$23,500.00
WALLACE COLLINS	$17,285.00
DONALD LEHNERT	$19,378.00
ALTON FUCHS	$25,000.00
TERRY BARANSY	$21,627.70

Figure 11-12 A query response in a simple report format.

```
FIND CURDEPT=316,LIST.

ITEM              31
NAME              JOHN H. WHITE
SSNO              579654901
SEX               M
BIRTH             401011
ADDRESS           6150 ARLINGTON BLVD
CITY              ARLINGTON
STATCODE          VA
ZIP               22044
DEPENDNT          2
TELEPHON          7035788765
CURDIVSN          1
CURDEPT           316
CURSAL            $27,895.34
CURTITL           MGR-CUSTOMER SUPPORT
CLEARANC          TOP SECRET
VACAUTH           15
VACUSED            5
CURJOB            115
CURGRAD           13
CURLOC            2
COMMENTS          EXCELLENT LEADERSHIP AND MANAGEMENT QUALITIES, VERY GOOD FEED BACK
                     FROM CUSTOMERS AND EMPLOYEES REGARDING HIS RESPONSES TO PRO
JOBHIST (   1) 610701630901PROGRAMMER/ANALYST        704 15000001030802
        (   2) 650901670605SYSTEMS ANALYST           892 18500001061002
        (   3) 670606710101SR SYSTEMS ANALYST        316 22350001071102
        (   4) 710101      MGR-CUSTOMER SUPPORT       316 27895341151302
EDUCATN (   1) MIT                 BEE EE       61COLL
        (   2) HARVARD             MBA MANAGEMENT65GRAD
SKILLS  (   1) PROGRAMMER           , SYSTEMS ANALYST
        (   3) PROPOSAL WRITING     , PRESENTATIONS
        (   5) SYSTEMS DEVELOPMENT  , SUPERVISORY
        (   7) CUSTOMER CONTACT
KEYS           CURDEPT=316

ITEM              29
NAME              JANET WILLIAMS
SSNO              149217760
SEX               F
BIRTH             411020
ADDRESS           1429 EVELYN DR
CITY              ROCKVILLE
STATCODE          MD
ZIP               20852
DEPENDNT           3
TELEPHON          3015831497
CURDIVSN          1
CURDEPT           316
CURSAL             $23,500.00
CURTITL           SR SYSTEMS ANALYST
CLEARANC          CONFIDENTIAL
VACAUTH           12
VACUSED            6
CURJOB            107
```

Figure 11-13 Listed data records.

```
                                                              PAGE    1
                                                              06/03/82

NAME                          EDTYPE    DEGREE   SKILLS
---------------------------------------------------------------------

PAUL F SMITH                  COLL      BEE      ENGINEER
                              GRAD               INSTRUMENTATION
                                                 PRODUCTION CONTROL
                                                 ELECTRICAL
                                                 TELEPROCESSING
                                                 SUPERVISORY

ROBERT R JONES                COLL      BEE      ENGINEER

JAMES GLEASON                 COLL      BEE      ENGINEER
                              GRAD      MBA      SYSTEMS DEVELOPMENT
                                                 PROPOSAL WRITING
                                                 SUPERVISORY
                                                 SYSTEMS ANALYST
```

Figure 11-14 Formatted data records.

```
                  EMPLOYEES GROUPED BY DEPARTMENT            PAGE    1
                                                            06/08/82
                        AND ORDERED BY SALARY
     EMPLOYEE NAME             JOB             SALARY   CURRENT
                               TITLE                    DEPT
---------------------------------------------------------------------

RONALD GORDON           SR STATISTICIAN       $24,500.76   201

SAM JACKSON             GRP LDR SYS DEVELOPMENT $24,000.00  201

RICHARD HOPKINS         SR SYSTEMS PROGRAMMER  $23,584.75   201

JAMES PARKS             SR PROGRAMMER          $22,055.79   201

PAT FLEMING             PROGRAMMER-ANALYST     $19,759.31   201

JOHN H. WHITE           MGR-CUSTOMER SUPPORT   $27,895.34   316

BILL APPLE              PERSONNEL MANAGER      $25,485.50   316

JANET WILLIAMS          SR SYSTEMS ANALYST     $23,500.00   316

NANCY N MOORE           SR SYSTEMS PROGRAMMER  $22,565.77   316

GEORGE MILLER           COST ANALYST           $21,800.00   316

JAMES GLEASON           ASST MGR-CUST. SUPP.   $21,475.85   316

SALLY SCHUSTER          SYSTEMS ANALYST        $19,480.00   316

JAMES R. HILL           APPLICATIONS GRP LDR   $19,259.99   316

ROBERT P. KELLY         PROGRAMMER             $13,600.00   316

ANNE SMITH              RECEPTIONIST            $9,000.00   316

JOE DECKER              CHEMIST                $16,445.00   384

WAYNE ROGERS            MGR PERSONNEL TRAINING $27,845.50   401
```

Figure 11-15 A report with headings and sorted data.

The sequential file is scanned. Data items to be printed in columns are NAME, CURTITL, CURSAL, and CURDEPT. The title of the report is EMPLOYEES GROUPED BY DEPARTMENT, followed by a blank line '' and then the words AND ORDERED BY SALARY. The column headings are printed by indicating what is to be printed (EMPLOYEE NAME) followed by the data base identifier (NAME). Enclosing words in single quotes—'EMPLOYEE NAME'—causes the words to be printed on the same line. Enclosing words in parentheses—(JOB TITLE)—causes the words to be printed on separate lines. Before the report is printed, the data is sorted into descending (D) sequence by salary within ascending (A) sequence by department.

There are additional INQUIRE features that we will not cover, such as the ability to compute amounts for printing. But from the material presented you can see the power and flexibility of a query language. Certainly some of the statements are wordy, but they don't approach the wordiness of a programming language. A manager with a programming background can learn to use INQUIRE in one day. One with no computer experience can be productive within a week. Once learned, a query language is easier to use than a programming language. A query can be drafted in only a few minutes.

MARK-IV

Another approach to handling queries is the MARK-IV system by Informatics, Inc. MARK-IV is a batch-oriented approach involving the completion of an information request form.

Assume that a district sales manager believes sales are slipping for the company's new cordless telephone. It has been almost three weeks since the last month's sales analysis report, and she has heard that a rival company has been active in her district. She fills out the information request form in Figure 11-16. The following explanations correspond to the circled numbers in the figure.

1. The sales manager identifies the origin of the query by entering SALES.

2. Entering TODAY in the report date field means that the report will include today's date.

3. The entry SALEYEAR EQ D 84 identifies 1984 as the period for which sales data is to be retrieved. EQ means "equal" and D means "decimal." The year is recorded in a decimal form in the data records.

4. Each data field to be printed on the report is included. BRANCH, YTDSALES, and so on are all fields in the sales records. The data base contains a single record for each branch office.

5. The G indicates that a total is to be accumulated for those fields.

6. The name of the report will appear as entered here.

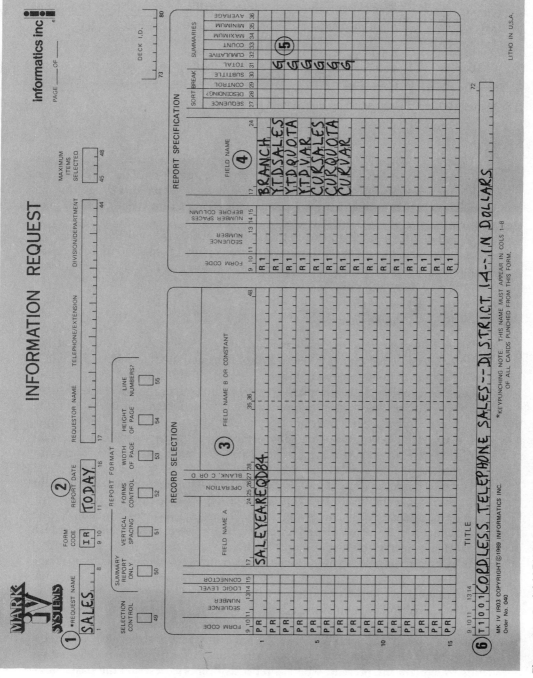

Figure 11-16 A MARK-IV information request form.

10/19/83		CORDLESS TELEPHONE SALES—DISTRICT 14—IN DOLLARS				PAGE 1
BRANCH	YTD SALES	YTD QUOTA	VARIANCE	CURRENT SALES	CURRENT QUOTA	VARIANCE
ALLENTOWN	23715	25000	1285−	1856	2275	419−
ALTOONA	18556	20000	1444−	1432	1800	368−
HARRISBURG	46517	30000	16517	3348	2725	623
LANCASTER	32104	40000	7896−	3104	3625	521−
	120892	115000	5892	9740	10425	685−

Figure 11-17 A sales report produced with MARK-IV.

The data from the information request form is keypunched and the cards read into the computer. The computer retrieves the appropriate data records and prints the report pictured in Figure 11-17. The sales manager can see that all branches except Harrisburg are below quota for the current month and the year to date.

MARK-IV is a batch approach to data base query, whereas INQUIRE is an online approach. Online is much more responsive, but a firm may not really need the fast response or be able to afford the cost. Various factors must be considered when selecting a query language.

How managers use queries

In Chapter 4 we recognized that managers differ in their problem-solving styles. The *problem avoider* tries to block out problems and assume that everything is fine. This type of manager makes little use of the MIS for problem identification. The *problem solver* does not look for problems but solves them when they arise. This person most likely relies on reports to identify problems or potential problems. The *problem seeker* makes full use of the MIS as a problem identification tool. Data base queries provide a convenient vehicle for searching out problems to solve. Reports signal areas for attention, and then queries can probe for specific problems.

Once a manager's attention is called to a problem area, the MIS permits the manager to focus on the source. This can be a step-by-step process, starting with a large area and gradually narrowing down. For example, our sales manager with the poor sales of cordless telephones can start out by reviewing sales by branch office, then sales by salesperson, and finally sales by customer. This method of logically identifying problems is known as *heuristic searching*. Heuristic searching is a tool of the modern manager made possible by computer-based data bases and query languages.

The query ability enables the manager to take an aggressive problem-solving stance—searching out problems to solve. The manager can ask for single data items or a complete report. With queries, the firm's data base becomes a window through which the manager sees what is happening in the firm. Query information tends to explain the present, whereas repetitive reports describe the past. Simulation predicts the future.

Simulation

Simulation can help the manager identify alternatives, evaluate them, and select the best. Simulation is accomplished with a model, and the degree to which a model supports these three steps of the systems approach depends on the type of model used. Some models provide only minimal support, whereas others actually recommend the best alternative.

Basic types of models

In Chapter 3 we recognized four basic types of models: physical, narrative, graphical, and mathematical. Here we are concerned with mathematical models, for that type gives the manager a predictive power.

Attributes of mathematical models

Mathematical models can be static or dynamic. A *static* model represents the entity being modeled at a specific point in time. A firm's balance sheet is an example; it shows the financial condition at a particular time, such as at the close of business on December 31. A firm's income statement, however, is a *dynamic* model since it represents the behavior of the entity (the firm) over a period of time. An income statement might reflect the firm's activity over a quarter or a year.

Mathematical models can also be optimizing or nonoptimizing. An *optimizing* model identifies the single best solution to a problem. An example is a mathematical model that identifies the best selection of merchandise in a warehouse. A *nonoptimizing* model is one that simply projects an outcome of a particular activity—not necessarily the best outcome. A mathematical model can predict sales for a product if the price is set at $79.95. The model doesn't necessarily identify that as the best price. The manager must simulate other pricing strategies and select the one that best achieves the desired result, such as maximum profit.

A final classification deals with the degree of certainty with which the elements or parts of the model can be specified. A *deterministic* model is one where all the elements are known to act in a specific way. The EOQ (Economic Order Quantity) model is a good example.

$$EOQ = \sqrt{\frac{2AS}{R}}$$

The model has only three elements, or variables. A represents the acquisition cost, or the cost to prepare a purchase order, such as $20. S is the annual sales amount for the inventory item. Assume this is 1000 units. R is the retention cost of maintaining the item in inventory, say $0.16 per unit per year.

These numbers are "plugged into" the model to compute an economic order quantity of 500 units.

$$EOQ = \sqrt{\frac{2 \times 20 \times 1000}{0.16}} = \sqrt{250{,}000} = 500$$

There is no other answer. The variables always interact in the same way.

The other form of model is one where the behavior of the variables cannot be predicted accurately. It is known as a *probabilistic* model. This form uses the probability of things happening. Weather forecasters use this approach, for example, when they say there is a 30% chance of rain.

Probabilities are expressed in percentages. If you are 100% certain something will happen, the probability is 1.00. If you are certain it will not happen, the probability is .00. Probabilities usually lie somewhere in between. If you are 60% certain you will get an A in a particular course, the probability is .60.

As we recognized in Chapter 3, models can be general or specific. A *general model* can be used to solve a particular problem facing many organizations. A *specific model* is developed to solve a unique problem facing a single firm. General models are used by firms of all sizes. In many cases the models can be obtained at reasonable prices, well within the budget of many small firms. Specific models, on the other hand, demand an information services or operations research staff skilled in quantitative techniques. Such staffs are generally found only in large firms. This is one reason why modeling is not more widespread. Not all firms can afford to acquire or build their own staff of specialists.

The scope of simulation activity

The term *simulation* can be used in a narrow sense, limiting it to only those mathematical models that describe behavior over time. Hugh J. Watson's text-

Table 11-2 Frequency of Use of Various Management Science Methods

Rank	Method
1	Economic analysis (such as break-even analysis)
2	Statistical analysis (such as decision theory, inference statistics, etc.)
3	Simulation
4	Linear programming
5	Inventory models
6	PERT/CPM
7	Other mathematical programming (such as integer, goal, dynamic, etc.)
8	Search techniques
9	Queuing models
10	Game theory

book on computer simulation adopts this view.[1] According to Watson, simulation is only one of ten analytical tools used to solve business problems. Watson's tools, ranked in order of frequency of use according to a survey, appear in Table 11-2.[2] You will note that simulation is in the third spot, behind economic analysis and statistical analysis. In this text the term *simulation* has a broader sense. We use it to mean "model use," including all kinds of mathematical models.

Since it is impossible to discuss all the types of models in this chapter or in this book, we have singled out those that enjoy frequent use and provide good illustrations of decision support. This chapter introduces two very different types of models—linear programming and Monte Carlo. In later chapters we will discuss economic analysis, statistical analysis, inventory models, and PERT/CPM models.

Linear Programming

Linear programming, or *LP,* is an optimizing technique that identifies the best solution to a static situation.[3] The word *programming* has no special computer-related significance in this case. It means only that a solution can be identified with a certain amount of precision. The word *linear* means that there is a constant ratio between the variables. For example, if $20,000 in advertising produces $100,000 in sales, then $40,000 in advertising should produce $200,000 in sales.

LP has been a popular computer application since the first generation. One reason for this popularity is that the model focuses on a common management problem—achieving a particular goal with limited resources. In LP, the limited resources are called *constraints,* and the goal is the *objective function.* The objective can be to maximize something, such as profits, or to minimize something, such as costs.

Another reason for the popularity of LP is that the objective and the constraints can be stated quantitatively. Once the numeric values have been stated, the computer can make the numerous calculations very rapidly. LP problems can be solved without a computer, but it is a slow process.

Highly versatile, LP solves two basic types of problems: routing and mix. A *routing problem* is one where resources are moved through an area and the task is to find the most efficient route. The most efficient route either minimizes the costs or maximizes the revenues of the routing. Firms can use LP to design the layout of plants, to locate warehouses in certain parts of the country, or to determine the sequences that sale representatives should follow in calling on their customers. A *mix problem* is one where a number of ingredients are used to

---

[1] Hugh J. Watson, *Computer Simulation in Business* (New York: John Wiley & Sons, 1981), p. 2.

[2] Ibid., p. 11.

[3] For an exceptionally readable explanation of linear programming, see Robert Dorfman, "Mathematical, or 'Linear,' Programming: A Nonmathematical Exposition," *American Economic Review* 43 (December 1953): 797–825. This article was reprinted in William Breit and Harold M. Hochman, eds., *Readings in Microeconomics* (New York: Holt, Rinehart and Winston, 1968), pp. 173–94.

produce a product and the task is to find the best combination. The best combination either maximizes customer demand for the product or minimizes costs. The early uses of LP in the late fifties included petrochemical applications—determining mixes of ingredients going into petroleum products. LP has also been used in blending cement, determining the most profitable combination of meats in sausage, and a large number of similar applications.

Example of a linear programming solution

A more detailed description of solving a real business problem with LP can provide a better appreciation of its value to the manager.

Assume that the manager of a retail furniture store in Lexington, Kentucky, has a problem. The problem is how to allocate space in a warehouse to the most profitable items. The warehouse has 6500 square feet, of which 3672 are used for minimum quantities of the seven furniture items carried. The items, the floor space required for each, the minimum quantities, and the total floor space for the minimum quantities are shown in Table 11-3. The question is how best to use the remaining 2828 square feet to maximize profit.

The manager prepares a mathematical expression representing the objective function. To do this, profit figures are assembled for each of the seven furniture items (Table 11-4). A variable name (X_1 through X_7) is assigned to each item to represent the *quantity* of each to be located in the available warehouse area. The LP model will compute the value of each of these variable names.

The manager knows that the total profit from the sale of a certain mixture

Table 11-3 Floor Space for Minimum Quantities

| Item (1) | Floor space (sq. ft.) | | |
	Each (2)	Minimum quantity (3)	Total (4)
Mattress	9.7	4	38.8
Chair	10.7	50	535.0
Sofa	26	40	1040.0
Dining room suite	32.4	25	810.0
Coffee table	12.2	50	610.0
Bedroom suite	32.9	15	493.5
Bookcase	5.8	25	145.0
Total			3672.3

Table 11-4 Item Profit Figures

Item	Variable name	Profit (each)
Mattress	X_1	$ 20
Chair	X_2	40
Sofa	X_3	75
Dining room suite	X_4	170
Coffee table	X_5	60
Bedroom suite	X_6	150
Bookcase	X_7	65

of items will be the sum of the quantity of each times its profit figure. This is the objective function.

$$\text{Maximum profit} = 20X_1 + 40X_2 + 75X_3 + 170X_4 + 60X_5 + 150X_6 + 65X_7$$

For example, the $20X_1$ means that profit from mattresses will be the product of the unit profit ($20) times the number of mattresses (X_1). The LP model can assign any value to X_1, including zero. Zero means that none of that item is to be included in the solution.

The remaining task for the manager is to identify any constraints that may exist. One constraint is floor space. Only 2828 square feet are available for the seven items. This constraint can be stated mathematically, using the floor space figures for each of the items from Table 11-3.

$$9.7X_1 + 10.7X_2 + 26X_3 + 32.4X_4 + 12.2X_5 + 32.9X_6 + 5.8X_7 \leq 2828$$

The floor space area for each item multiplied by the quantity of each, added together, cannot be greater than 2828.

In a similar fashion, the constraints listed below are expressed mathematically.

1. Minimum quantities of each item
2. One mattress for every three bedroom suites
3. Twice as many chairs as sofas
4. Maximum investment of $60,000
5. No more than 60 dining room suites
6. No more dining room suites than coffee tables
7. No more than 55 bookcases

When the manager has reduced the objective function and constraints to mathematical expressions, the linear programming model can be executed.

Using the linear programming model

The mathematical expressions can be entered through an online terminal or punched into cards for input through a card reader. If a terminal is used, the manager must first log on by entering the appropriate account number and password. The manager then specifies which model is to be used by typing in the model name, such as LINPR. The model will be called from the software library by the operating system and entered in primary storage. Execution of the model will begin and the model will cause the instruction MAXIMIZE to be displayed on the manager's terminal. The manager responds by typing in the objective function. The model responds with the instruction SUBJECT TO. The manager then types in each of the constraints. The model can detect certain errors (such as missing arithmetic signs) and prompt the manager with a message ERROR IN LAST LINE. RETYPE. When the manager has entered all of the constraints, he or she types the word END. The model performs the mathematical processes. The model then displays the optimal value of the objective function and the quantities of each furniture item that produce the optimal value. In our example, the model determines that only two items should be located in the available area: chairs and sofas. If 113 chairs ($X_2 = 113$) and 57 sofas ($X_3 = 57$) are stocked, the profit from the use of the available area will be $8783.

LP in perspective as a DSS tool

Now let us review LP in terms of the various forms a model can take. LP is a *static* model. The optimum layout of the furniture warehouse does not change over time. Only one solution is produced, and it is expected to be used until at least one of the factors changes and a new solution is computed. LP is an *optimizing* model. The furniture arrangement provided by LP is the best in terms of accomplishing the maximum profit objective. No other arrangement will produce a higher profit. LP is a *deterministic* model in that it includes no probabilities. The variables are expected to interact in the prescribed manner with 100% certainty. And LP is a *general* model. It solves a class of problems that plague many firms, and it can be widely applied.

LP is designed to handle highly structured problems. It could conceivably be applied to a recurring problem to make the decision each time the problem arises. The manager would have no role in problem solving once the LP model proves effective. In most cases, however, the manager will want to evaluate the LP decision before it is implemented. Even though LP is an optimizing model, it is generally used in a decision-*support*, not a decision-*making*, environment.

A Probabilistic Model: Monte Carlo

We will conclude our discussion of problem solving by computer with a model that simulates an activity over time (it is dynamic), that doesn't identify the single best answer (it is nonoptimizing), that deals in probabilities, and that is special in purpose. This model illustrates the Monte Carlo method of simulating randomly occurring events.

Assume in this case that the manager of a department store in Chicago doesn't know how many sales clerks to assign to a department because the volume of customer activity varies. Different numbers of customers enter the department at different times throughout the day. The customers make purchases of different values. Data describing these variations in customer activity can be gathered. A model can simulate the effect of assigning different numbers of sales clerks to the department.

The store hours can be divided into ten-minute intervals (9:00–9:10, 9:10–9:20, and so on) and a record kept of the number of customers arriving during each interval. The distribution of customers might look like this:

Number of intervals with zero customers	6
Number of intervals with one customer	12
Number of intervals with two customers	20
Number of intervals with three customers	6
Number of intervals with four customers	4
	48

Of the 48 ten-minute intervals during the eight-hour day, six intervals had no customers, twelve had one customer, and so on.

This distribution of arrivals can be converted into a *probability distribution* by calculating percentages (or probabilities) for each customer group. All of the probabilities must add to 1.00 since they account for 100% of the customer activity.

Zero customers	=	$6/48$ =	.12
One customer	=	$12/48$ =	.25
Two customers	=	$20/48$ =	.43
Three customers	=	$6/48$ =	.12
Four customers	=	$4/48$ =	.08
			1.00

The same technique can be used for the dollar values of the customers' purchases. The purchases of the 86 customers are:

No purchase	18
$5 purchase	20
$10 purchase	22
$15 purchase	16
$20 purchase	10
	86

These values are converted into a second probability distribution.

No purchase	=	$18/86$ =	.20
$5 purchase	=	$20/86$ =	.23
$10 purchase	=	$22/86$ =	.26
$15 purchase	=	$16/86$ =	.19
$20 purchase	=	$10/86$ =	.12
			1.00

Now the problem is how many sales clerks to assign to the department to maximize profit. If one sales clerk is required to serve one customer during a ten-minute interval, the number of clerks can range from one to four (since a maximum of four customers is in the department at one time). If only one clerk is assigned, there will frequently be customers who cannot be served and sales will be lost. On the other hand, if four clerks are assigned, no sales will be lost, but there will be some idle clerk time and expenses will be higher.

An important assumption of the model is that there is no pattern to either customer arrivals or purchases. They are both strictly random.

The Monte Carlo Method

A technique to simulate random activity was developed during World War II. *Monte Carlo,* the code name assigned to the technique, is based on the selection of random numbers. The numbers range from 00 through 99. The chance of selecting one of these 100 numbers at random is 1%. It is like putting 100 numbered tags in a hat and selecting one while blindfolded. The chance, or probability, of selecting any particular number is .01.

Series of the hundred numbers can be assigned to each entry in the two probability distributions. For example, the distribution of arrival times looks like this:

Number of Customers	Probability (P)	Number Series
0	.12	00–11
1	.25	12–36
2	.43	37–79
3	.12	80–91
4	.08	92–99

If the computer can randomly generate a number from 00 through 99 (and it can), the chance of generating a number from 00 through 11 is 12%, corresponding to the first probability of .12. Similarly, the chance of generating a number from 12 through 36 is 25% (since this series represents 25 of the 100 numbers), corresponding to the second probability of .25.

In this manner, the computer can simulate the random arrival pattern of the customers. Any number generated will fall within one of the five number series. The series within which the random number falls determines the number of customers arriving during a given ten-minute interval.

Other numbers can be assigned to the customer purchases, and that activity too can be simulated randomly.

Value of Purchases	Probability (P)	Number Series
$ 0	.20	00–19
5	.23	20–42
10	.26	43–68
15	.19	69–87
20	.12	88–99

At the beginning of a ten-minute interval, it is not known how many customers will arrive. A random number is generated, say 45, and it is matched with the number series of the arrivals. The number 45 falls within the range of 37–79, so it is assumed that two customers arrive. The process works the same way for the customer purchases. A random number is generated for each customer; the number determines the value of the purchase for each. If the computer generates a 12 and a 63, the purchase values are zero (the customer is only "looking") and $10, respectively.

The simulation process

A mathematical model is created to simulate the activity of the department, using different numbers of sales clerks. The number of clerks is entered into the model, and output describes the results. In the example in Figure 11-18, only one clerk is assigned, and the activity of only a single hour is simulated. In actual practice, a much larger number of hours would be simulated.

The computer randomly selects the number 23 to represent the number of customer arrivals in period 1. When matched to the number series of customer arrivals, 23 falls within the range of 12–36. This means that one customer arrives in period 1. The computer then selects the number 45 to determine the value of that customer's purchase. The number falls within the range of 43–68; therefore the customer makes a $10 purchase.

INTERVAL	RANDOM NUMBER-- ARRIVALS	NUMBER OF ARRIVALS	RANDOM NUMBER-- PURCHASES	VALUE OF PURCHASE	CLERK NO. 1 SALES	IDLE TIME	LOST SALES
1	23	1	45	$10	$10	0	
2	64	2	14	$ 0		0	
			59	$10			$10
3	79	2	11	$ 0		0	
			28	$ 5			$ 5
4	49	2	46	$10	$10	0	
			47	$10			$10
5	99	4	60	$10	$10	0	
			25	$ 5			$ 5
			97	$20			$20
			41	$ 5			$ 5
6	50	2	81	$15	$15	0	
			31	$ 5			$ 5
			TOTALS	$105	$45	0	$60

Figure 11-18 Computer printout with one sales clerk.

One random number is selected for each time period to represent the number of arrivals. Then a single random number is selected for each customer arriving in that period to represent the value of each purchase.

Since only one clerk is available, he or she can serve only the first customer arriving in a ten-minute interval. Other customers could have made purchases in the amounts shown, but they leave the store and those sales are lost.

In a similar manner, the other numbers of clerks can be simulated. In the example in Figure 11-19, three clerks are assigned to the department. Here the pattern of arrivals and purchases differs from the first example. This difference is characteristic of random process simulation.

In this example, sales totaled $65. There were no lost sales, but idle time totaled 100 minutes (out of 180).

The manager has now used the model to evaluate two alternatives. Most likely, simulations would also be conducted for two and four sales clerks. The nonoptimizing model doesn't identify which alternative is the best. The model only supplies the results that can be expected from each.

The manager can select the best alternative by comparing costs and benefits, as shown in Table 11-5. Costs are calculated by considering the daily or hourly cost of the clerks. The benefits are the sales produced by the clerks.

According to the example, three clerks produce the most profit. While other factors (idle time, value of lost sales, and so on) might influence the final decision, the model has provided the profit and loss figures. This information will provide a basis for the decision.

The model supports the manager by processing data representing the structured portion of the problem. But there are other factors—the unstructured portion—for the manager to consider. These unstructured factors include the store's image, the competitive situation, the sense of community responsibility, marketing strategies, and so on. Together the model and the manager solve a semistructured problem.

INTERVAL	RANDOM NUMBER-- ARRIVALS	NUMBER OF ARRIVALS	RANDOM NUMBER-- PURCHASES	VALUE OF PURCHASE	CLERK NO. 1 SALES	CLERK NO. 2 SALES	CLERK NO. 3 SALES	IDLE TIME	LOST SALES
1	05	0						30	
2	24	1	00	$ 0				20	
3	81	3	30	$ 5	$ 5			0	
			44	$10		$10			
			62	$10			$10		
4	55	2	48	$10	$10			10	
			02	$ 0					
5	10	0						30	
6	63	2	46	$10	$10			10	
			97	$20		$20			
	TOTALS			$65	$25	$30	$10	100	$ 0

Figure 11-19 Computer printout with three sales clerks.

Table 11-5 Cost Benefit Analysis

Number of clerks	Sales	Costs	Profit (loss)
1	$395	$405	$(10)
2	460	435	25
3	515	470	45
4	520	505	15

Monte Carlo in perspective as a DSS model

The Monte Carlo retail salesclerk model is a *dynamic* model in that it simulates activity over time—each ten-minute interval during a day, week, month, or even year. The Monte Carlo model is a *nonoptimizing* model; it does not point out the best solution. The model simply says, "If you decide to use three clerks, this is a likely outcome." The manager must try out different decisions and select the one that looks best. Since the Monte Carlo model uses probabilities, it is a *probabilistic* model. Probabilities are used to describe how certain elements will behave—elements over which the user has little or no control. In this example, customer arrivals and purchase amounts vary randomly. We do not know when an event will occur, but we know the likelihood based on past history. The probabilities represent this likelihood in a mathematical form. Finally, Monte Carlo is a *specific* model. Since the probabilities vary from one firm to another, each user must create a special Monte Carlo model. Because of its special nature, Monte Carlo has been applied on a much smaller scale than LP.

Like the linear programming model, the Monte Carlo model can be initiated from a terminal or from punched card input. The model is located in the software library and is called into primary storage using a program name. When the model is executed online, the manager is asked to input the necessary data, such as the number of time periods to simulate, the number of clerks, the probability distributions, and the costs of the clerks, lost sales, and idle time. When all of the data has been entered, the model is executed and the results displayed or printed. The manager examines the output and then decides whether to run another simulation. The manager can enter new data, such as a different number of clerks, and execute the model again. The manager continues to simulate alternate strategies until he or she feels that all of the feasible ones have been explored. Then the manager makes the decision.

You can see the basic difference between the Monte Carlo model and the linear programming model. The linear programming model provides a greater amount of decision support by identifying the optimal solution. But LP is best suited to highly structured problems, whereas Monte Carlo does best with semi-structured problems. The nature of the problem dictates the choice of the model and, to a great extent, the amount of decision support the model can provide.

How Managers Use Simulation

Models are used to solve specific problems. For a company that has to build a plant on the West Coast, linear programming identifies the best location. For a company that wishes to raise the price of a product, a specific pricing model anticipates the effects on profitability. The pricing decision is made more often than the plant location decision. In today's period of ever-increasing prices, a firm's pricing model gets a real workout.

The systems analyst helps the manager define the problem and identify the type of model to use. The basic decision is, "Do we use a general or a specific model?" If a general model is needed, the next step is to identify the source. If a specific model is needed, the information services staff develops it.

The manager uses the model by providing the scenario and evaluating the results. A model should be tested before it is used for an important decision. For example, a sales-forecasting model can be used to forecast *last* year's sales using prior data. The forecasted sales can be compared with actual sales to measure the model's accuracy. Once developed, the model is called from the software library and used each time its particular type of problem arises.

Modeling advantages and disadvantages

Models offer some real advantages to the manager. They provide a *predictive power*—a look into the future—that no other information-producing method offers. Also, models serve as a *learning tool*. The modeling process can be a learning experience for the participating manager. Models are *less expensive* than the trial-and-error method of making decisions. Once implemented in a firm, a bad decision can cost thousands or millions of dollars. The modeling process is costly too, but not nearly as costly as a bad decision. Finally, the *speed* of the simulation enables decisions to be evaluated in a short period of time. In less than an hour, a manager can simulate the effects of several strategies on several simulated years of operation.

But there are also some disadvantages to models. Most important is the *difficulty of modeling a business system*. Many aspects of a business operation are influenced by the environment, and the firm (1) doesn't control its environment and (2) doesn't completely understand environmental impacts. Additionally, a business organization is a social system composed of one or more people—each with his or her own unique motives, goals, problems, and so on. The resulting system is extremely difficult to quantify. Therefore models only approximate the real world, and some models do this better than others. A second disadvantage is the *high degree of mathematical skill* required. This is a good work area for graduates of business schools. A blend of business and mathematical knowledge, along with computer literacy, is a valuable resource to a firm engaged in modeling activities. At present, people with these mathematical and computer skills are a scarce commodity.

Summary

The MIS provides information for each step of the systems approach. The MIS does not make decisions; it only provides support. This is the DSS concept.

There are three basic methods of obtaining information—report, query, and simulation. These methods are used for two purposes—to identify problems and to solve them. Reports and queries contribute most to identification; simulation contributes most to solution.

Reports are prepared according to a schedule or in response to a special event. Reports can be detailed or summary and contain three basic parts—heading, body, and footing. Managers use reports primarily to review past performance. Management by exception can be built into the report formats to increase their utility.

Queries require a data base and a query language. Some languages, such as the INQUIRE User Language, are online. Others, such as MARK-IV, are batch-oriented. With INQUIRE, statements are formed using commands. The commands permit data retrieval and report generation. Managers use queries to obtain current information. Successive querying—narrowing the scope of a potential problem area—is called heuristic searching. A manager can use queries to seek out problems and to understand them better.

Simulation permits the manager to look into the future, although with less than 100% accuracy. Mathematical models provide this predictive power and can be classified based on the inclusion of a time element, the degree of optimization, the use of probabilities, and the range of applicability. Linear programming is a static, optimizing, deterministic, general model. The Monte Carlo sales clerk model is the opposite—dynamic, nonoptimizing, probabilistic, and specific. Models enable the manager to predict and to learn with economy and speed. But modeling is difficult, and it requires skill in both development and use.

In this chapter we identified the basic ways the manager interacts with the MIS. We will expand on this material in the next four chapters by studying MIS use by marketing, manufacturing, and finance managers.

Key Terms

repetitive report, periodic report	variable heading material
special report	column headings
scenario	break point
user-friendly	command, command statement
detailed report, detailed listing	heuristic searching
summary report	static model
heading, body, footing	dynamic model
fixed heading material	optimizing model

nonoptimizing model
deterministic model
probabilistic model
general model
specific model
linear programming (LP)

constraint
objective function
routing problem, mix problem
probability distribution
Monte Carlo

Key Concepts

The synergistic relationship between the manager and the computer as a problem-solving team

How the MIS provides decision support at each step of the problem-solving process

The basic methods for obtaining computer-generated information—reports, queries, simulations

The basic uses of information—problem identification and solution

How reports can be designed to facilitate management by exception

The software and data resources required for querying

Differences in online and offline querying approaches

Heuristic searching

Model types and attributes

The relatively structured nature of problems solved with linear programming

The semistructured nature of problems solved with Monte Carlo

How Monte Carlo simulates randomly occurring activity

The resources of quantative skills required for simulation

Questions

1. How can management involvement improve the utility of the computer as a decision support tool?

2. Explain how the MIS can help the manager understand a problem. Evaluate alternate solutions? Follow up on solutions?

3. What are the three basic methods for obtaining information?

4. How can you distinguish between a report and a query response?

5. Distinguish between repetitive, periodic, and special reports.

6. What is a scenario?

7. Of the three basic methods of obtaining information, which is the oldest? The newest?

8. What are the two basic uses of information? How do they relate to the three methods of obtaining information?

9. Which of the three basic report parts must be present in a detailed listing?

10. Does a balance sheet (such as Figure 11-8) facilitate management by exception? Explain.

11. Name three commercial software packages that are used to query the data base.

12. Does INQUIRE handle online or batch queries? Does it handle files organized for direct or sequential access?

13. Which of the three basic types of managers is most likely to use data base queries?

14. Can a manager conduct a heuristic search using information from repetitive reports? From special reports? Explain.

15. Which of the three basic methods of obtaining information offers a predictive ability?

16. By what four pairs of attributes can models be classified?

17. What are the two basic types of problems that LP solves? Give an example of each.

18. An LP model can accomplish one of two objectives. What are they?

19. What is the name of the mathematical statement that expresses what the LP model is to accomplish? What is the name of the group of statements that provides the boundaries or limitations of the solution?

20. Considering the potentially high costs of the computer-related resources needed for modeling, how can the technique be economical?

Problems

1. Use the INQUIRE User Language to obtain all of the records for department (DEPT) number 25 from a file organized indexed sequential, and print them with no formatting. Code the necessary instruction(s).

2. Recode the above instruction(s) so that the same operations are performed with a file organized sequentially.

3. Recode the instruction(s) for the first problem to print the employee number (EMPNO) in print position 10, employee name (EMPNME) in position 18, hourly rate (HRATE) in position 30, and hours worked (HOURS) in position 40.

4. Recode the instructions in problem 3 so that the same operations are performed with a file organized sequentially.

5. Fill in the number series for the following probability distribution:

Number of Sales	P	Number Series
0	.05	
1	.10	
2	.30	
3	.30	
4	.10	
5	.15	

6. Using the number series above and the following random numbers, what will be the number of sales for each day?

Day	Random Number	Number of Sales
1	19	
2	78	
3	04	
4	22	
5	76	
6	83	
7	19	
8	27	

CASE PROBLEM: McCullin Wholesale Foods Co.

McCullin is a Los Angeles area food wholesaler selling directly to institutional customers—restaurants, schools, and hospitals. Items are sold in bulk quantities and delivered by a fleet of fifty trucks from a warehouse in Torrance.

Mr. Rao:
Mr. McCullin? I'm Jagdish Rao of Decision Systems Software. My boss, Judith Jordan, told me that you're interested in letting us do some of your programming.

Mr. McCullin:
That's right. Our programming staff has their hands full with the conversion to our new UNIVAC. Besides, our people mainly specialize in accounting systems, and I wanted someone who understands MIS. I thought we might as well start at

the top. I have some information needs that aren't being met, and I would like to explore the possibility of your firm giving us some help. Would you please sit down?

Rao:
Thank you. Just what kind of information do you need?

McCullin:
Well, for one thing, I'm not sure that we're making our deliveries in the most efficient manner. Our drivers leave about six in the morning and return about three in the afternoon. We ask them to report their mileage, but we have no way of knowing if it could be reduced by a more efficient coverage of the routes.

Rao:
Each driver has a separate territory?

McCullin:
That's correct. And we call on the same accounts practically every day—or every two or three days at least. I suppose we could have someone ride along and check on the driver, but that would be too expensive.

Rao:
So you would like to achieve the most efficient routing?

McCullin:
Yes. I'd like to know how many miles the drivers should cover each day when they leave in the morning. It would be sort of like a budget. We could measure how well they keep within the budget.

Rao:
What would the drivers think?

McCullin:
They'd go for it. I'd be willing to give them some kind of bonus for meeting the budget. *That* they would like!

Rao:
Do you have any other information needs?

McCullin:
I really need more information on who my best customers are, what they're buying, and when they're buying. All I get now is a detailed listing of all our sales, sorted by customer, with monthly totals. I don't even look at it—it's too detailed.

Rao:
How many customers do you have?

McCullin:
Over 3000, but all of them aren't active. I imagine that perhaps 500 customers account for 80% of our sales. Another thousand or so account for the remaining 20%.

Rao:
Are you sure about that?

McCullin:
You know, I'm really not. That's what I mean. I'm not getting the information I need.

Rao:
You're doing inventory, billing, and receivables on the UNIVAC, aren't you?

McCullin:
We certainly are.

Rao:
Well, it seems to me that you have the data you need. You just aren't retrieving it in a properly summarized form.

McCullin:
I'm sure that's true. And we have one of those data base management systems. I've never been checked out on it, though. Do you think that would solve my problem?

Rao:
Partially. Let's pursue this a little further. You would like to be able to identify those customers accounting for the most sales, and then do an analysis of their purchases—what they are buying and when? How often would you want to do this?

McCullin:
If I could get a good monthly analysis, that would be great. Say on the third of the month, if I could get a printout of key customer activity, I'd be satisfied.

Rao:
Do you ever need any one-time information? In other words, do you ever need information that you never needed before, and that you'll probably never need again?

McCullin:
No, that's not my style. I like to get a system established and then follow it.

Rao:
Which would you say is your main interest: what's happening now, what might happen in the future, or what happened in the past?

McCullin:
Without a doubt, I want to look to the future. I want to see trends developing, like good customers who start to buy elsewhere, so I can pass the information along to my other managers.

Rao:
You say you *want* to. Aren't you able to do that now?

McCullin:
Not with the information I'm getting.

Rao:
Your sales transactions are processed on the UNIVAC each day, aren't they?

McCullin:

Yes. It's batch processing all the way. We make our computer runs in the evening so we can load the trucks next morning. Does all this make sense to you, Mr. Rao?

Rao:

Yes, its beginning to. I think I have enough to get started. Let me think this over and get back to you in a couple of days.

Questions

1. How could McCullin solve the problem of inefficient delivery routing? Explain how your solution would work.

2. Which of the three basic information-producing methods would be used to inform McCullin of key customer sales?

3. Does McCullin need data base query?

4. How can the MIS advise McCullin of emerging trends?

5. Would you characterize McCullin as a problem seeker, solver, or avoider? Explain your answer.

Part Four

FUNCTIONAL INFORMATION SYSTEMS

One of the characteristics of the systems approach described earlier is the subdivision of a system into subsystems. In Part Four this technique is used to develop a better understanding of the MIS. The MIS is described in terms of its users—the managers. Since managers are most commonly organized by functional area, that is the way the MIS is subdivided. This part describes functional information systems used by managers of marketing, manufacturing, and finance.

An introductory chapter relates why the functional subdivision is appropriate and introduces each functional information system. Each system is described as containing two basic types of subsystems: input and output. Input subsystems gather data from within the firm and from its environment. This data is stored in the data base and converted into information by the output subsystems. Each of the three functional information systems is represented by a graphical model and is described in a separate chapter. The intent is to illustrate some of the ways a manager can use an information system.

You should understand one key point at the outset. Although we describe the MIS as a collection of subsystems, you must not get the idea that these subsystems are separate and isolated. On the contrary, they are integrated into an overall MIS, serving the interests of the entire firm.

Chapter 12

Introduction to Functional Information Systems

Learning Objectives

After studying this chapter, you should:

- Understand how functional organization structure can influence the design of an MIS
- Appreciate the high level of interest in marketing that has provided structural models to be used in designing functional information systems
- Recognize how the marketing concept can provide a unity of direction useful to the manager implementing an MIS
- Visualize a functional information system as a group of input and output subsystems
- Understand how the input subsystems gather data and information internally and from specified environmental elements
- Recognize that the output subsystems are tailored to meet the information needs of the functional managers
- Know the basic manner in which the managers in marketing, manufacturing, and finance use their information system

Functional Organization Structure

Business firms have traditionally been organized along functional lines. These are not the same management functions that Henri Fayol identified (plan, organize, staff, direct, and control). Rather, they are the major jobs that the firm performs, such as marketing, finance, and manufacturing. Some other functional areas are not uncommon—such as engineering, and research and development. They are not as common, however, as the three that we will describe: marketing, finance, and manufacturing.

For years management analysts have criticized the functional structure and pointed to its many shortcomings. For systems theorists the functional structure makes it extremely difficult to mold the various parts together so that they perform as a single system. Each part tends to operate as a separate system, independent of the others.

There have been partial movements toward other, more modern, structures. The giant consumer products companies such as Procter & Gamble, General Foods, General Mills, and Pillsbury have used a *brand management* organizational structure for years. Resources of both a production and distribution nature are grouped under a brand manager. A popular product, like the Nestlé Company's Taster's Choice coffee, has its own designated resources, functioning as a separate organization within the overall company structure.

Another approach that crosses functional boundaries is the establishment of a *physical distribution,* or *logistics,* division within a firm. This division is responsible for *all* material flow—from vendors, through the firm's production facilities, to customers. The physical distribution division combines the material flow from both the manufacturing and marketing areas. This approach is the most dramatic evidence of the flow network concept that characterizes a systems theory of organization. Unfortunately, the physical distribution approach has been limited mainly to industrial organizations. Both the physical distribution and the brand management structures usually exist within an overall functional organization. Firms have been hesitant to give up completely on the functional structure.

A functional organization chart of a manufacturing firm can be seen in Figure 12-1. In this chart, information services is shown as a fourth major area, on the same level as marketing, manufacturing, and finance. More will be said of the information services operation in the final part of the book; it is not included as a major functional area in this or the next three chapters.

Two major functions that many firms perform are manufacturing and marketing. The firms make things and then distribute them to their customers. The things made can include either products or services. The manufacturing function has the production responsibility; the marketing function distributes the product or service once it has been created.

This interpretation of production, which encompasses both products and services, is very broad. It means that firms other than manufacturers have a production function. Banks produce financial services, hospitals produce medical care, legal firms produce legal services, and symphonies produce music. Such a broad interpretation was made in Chapter 3 when the general model of the firm was presented. The model described how input resources are transformed into output resources. This transformation is the production function.

It is easier to see the universality of the marketing function. Every organization that provides products or services must sell them to its customers. Most organizations have marketing departments, including nonmanufacturing types such as banks, insurance companies, colleges, military branches, and churches.

According to our definition, then, practically all types of organizations include manufacturing and marketing. The functional approach therefore provides a good general model of organization that can be applied to many situations. And it works.

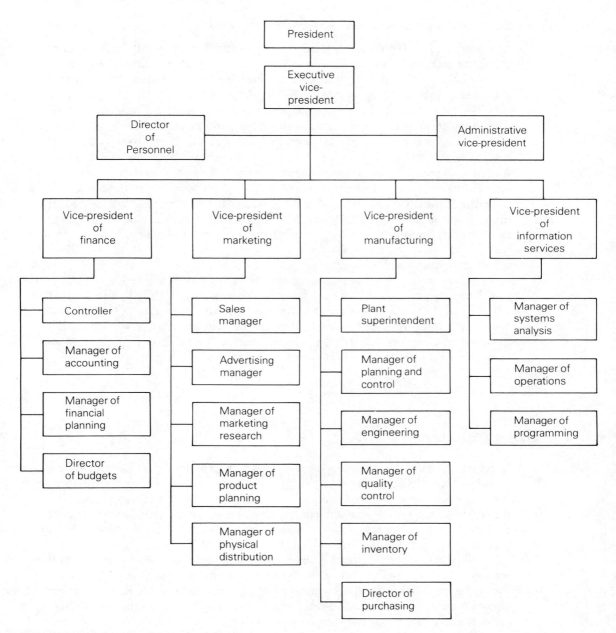

Figure 12-1 A functional organization.

A third functional area has not yet been mentioned. That function is finance—an important part of any organization. Finance lends support to the other two functions by assuring that sufficient operating funds are available and by controlling the use of those funds. It takes money to run any type of operation; therefore the financial function exists in all organizations.

Functional organization and the flow network concept

In Chapter 2, the systems approach to organization recognized flows of basic resources (personnel, materials, and so on). Although the flow network approach has not been embraced by the real world of business as an organizational method, it can be used to explain the roles of the three functions.

The two concepts are not totally dissimilar. The financial function is concerned with the money flow. The manufacturing and marketing functions represent the material flow. In this context, material includes both products and services. The marketing function determines what material should flow from the firm to its customers, and the manufacturing function creates that material flow.

Only the machine and personnel flows lack representation in the functional structure. This is because both of these resources are used in all three functional areas. They are not employed separately. Very often a firm has a personnel function, but it is responsible only for certain parts of the personnel flow. And no firm has a separate organizational unit with sole responsibility for all the machines used throughout the company.

So a close parallel exists between the two approaches, but not an identical one. Both the money and material flows can be seen quite readily in a functional structure. But the personnel and machine flows diffuse throughout all functional areas. This diffusion creates problems when the firm attempts to work together as a system. The key resource in achieving efficient operation is the personnel resource, which unfortunately is organized functionally.

Functional Information Systems

Every business organization encompasses a multitude of activities. These activities constitute the physical system of the firm and are usually grouped according to the major functions shown in Figure 12-1. When trying to implement a conceptual information system that will reflect the physical system, the manager finds it difficult to ignore the functional influence. It is only logical for the information system to be organized functionally as well (Figure 12-2).

This is what has happened. The conceptual information system representing the physical marketing system has been named the *marketing information system*. The same logic has created a *financial information system* and a *manufacturing information system*. A review of business literature will yield a number of references to these functional information systems—especially in the marketing area.

When information systems are organized functionally, a question arises concerning the information needs of the chief executive officers—the board chairperson, the president, the executive vice-president, the administrative vice-president, and so on. These positions do not fit within any function, but rather tie them together at the top level. This problem could be solved by organizing the information systems by management level. There could be a strategic-management information system as well as ones for the tactical and operational levels. This approach makes a great deal of sense. The information needs of the various man-

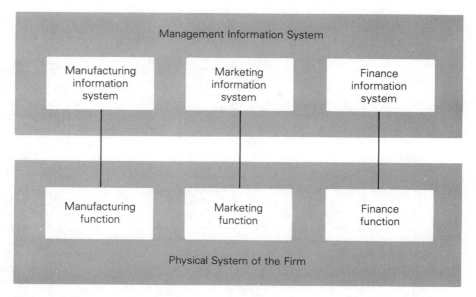

Figure 12-2 Functional information systems represent functional physical systems.

agement levels are different, and separate information systems could be created for each.

A major problem with this approach is that business firms are not organized by levels. The strain of functionalism would exist within each level, fragmenting the system. The strain would not be too strong on the strategic level, where the welfare of the entire firm is of prime importance. But on the lower levels functional interests tend to supersede those of the firm.

Although other structures are possible for an information system, the one most readily accepted by business firms is the functional structure (Figure 12-3). For this reason it will be the structure presented here. A concept of information management is presented based on functional subsystems representing functional physical systems. We will not describe a separate information system for the chief executive officers. It is assumed that their information is a distillation and synthesis of that produced by each functional information system.

As we proceed with our discussion of the functional approach, it is important to remember that functional information subsystems do not diminish the importance of an integrated overall system for the firm—the MIS. The functional subsystems must work together. They must share a common data base, and decisions made in one area must be compatible with those made in others and with the overall objectives of the firm.

The remainder of this chapter will introduce each of the three functional subsystems, identifying the information needs of the managers in each area as well as the primary sources of information. These information inputs and uses will be used to construct a graphical model of each subsystem. The purpose of these models is to provide a structure showing what each subsystem can include. Then, in the following three chapters, each subsystem will be described in greater detail.

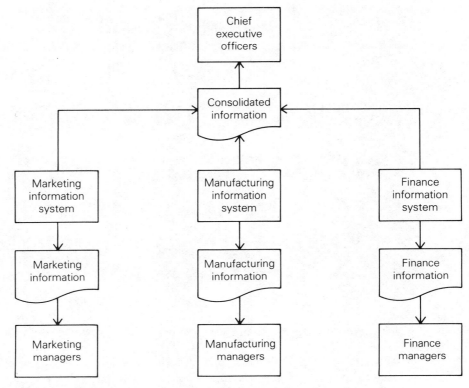

Figure 12-3 Users of functional information output.

Marketing Information Systems

We will start with the marketing information system, not because it is more important, but because its composition is better defined than the others. Marketers have spent considerable time studying the subject of the marketing information system and have developed some excellent models showing how it should be constructed.[1]

Marketing and the marketing concept

Many people think of marketing in very narrow terms—selling and advertising only. Marketers, however, define it very broadly. William J. Stanton, author of a leading marketing text, defines marketing as

[1] For information on different approaches to modeling a marketing information system, see Richard H. Brien and James E. Stafford, "Marketing Information Systems: A New Dimension for Marketing Research," *Journal of Marketing* 32 (July 1968): 19–23; Donald F. Cox and Robert E. Good, "How to Build a Marketing Information System," *Harvard Business Review* 45 (May–June 1967): 145–54; W. J. E. Crissy and Frank H. Mossman, "Matrix Models for Marketing Planning: An Update and Expansion," *MSU Business Topics* 25 (Autumn 1977): 17–26; William R. King and David I. Cleland, "Environmental Information Systems for Strategic Marketing Planning," *Journal of Marketing* 38 (October 1974): 35–40; and David B. Montgomery and Glen L. Urban, "Marketing Decision-Information Systems: An Emerging View," *Journal of Marketing Research* 7 (May 1970): 226–34.

a system: of business activities designed to: plan, price, promote, and distribute something of value: want-satisfying goods and services to the benefit of: the market—present and potential household consumers or industrial users.[2]

Recently a large number of firms have moved toward a *marketing orientation*. This means that the entire organization is dedicated to the objective of marketing—the satisfaction of customer wants and needs at a profit. This is called the *marketing concept.* The marketing concept is important in terms of the opportunity it offers the firm to contribute to the improving standard of living and also to meet its social obligations. More importantly here, the marketing concept has a special significance to the subject of information systems.

Much has been said in previous chapters about the importance of the firm's acting as an integrated system. In reality, this integration is very difficult to achieve. One of the most demanding tasks of the chief executive officer is to integrate the functional elements of the firm into a smoothly operating unit. The marketing concept implies that integration is best achieved through marketing goals. This does not mean that the marketing function should dominate the company. But it does mean that everyone in the organization should work toward the basic goal of the marketing function—satisfying customer needs.

The marketing concept could provide the rallying point for the integration of information systems within the firm. In order for all parts of a firm to work together and to share information resources, there has to be some all-encompassing sense of purpose. The marketing concept could provide this unity of direction. All other things being equal, achieving an MIS is easier in a firm that has implemented the marketing concept than in a firm that has not.

Sources and uses of marketing information

One of the first people to recognize the importance of a marketing information system was Philip Kotler, distinguished marketing professor at Northwestern University. Kotler created a model that divides the marketing information system into four subsystems based on the sources and uses of information—internal accounting, marketing intelligence, marketing research, and marketing management science (see Figure 12-4).[3] These subsystems take data from the environment and transform the data into information for the marketing executive.

By including the *internal accounting system,* Kotler recognizes the symbiotic, or dependent, relationship among the functions of the firm. In fact, it is the internal accounting system that provides a common bond throughout the firm, gathering data describing actual operations and using that data to prepare basic accounting documents and management reports.

---

[2] William J. Stanton, *Fundamentals of Marketing,* 6th ed. (New York: McGraw-Hill, 1981), p. 4.

[3] For a description of his landmark work, see Philip Kotler, "A Design for the Firm's Marketing Nerve Center," *Business Horizons 9* (Fall 1968): 63–74. Kotler's model of the marketing information system first appeared in his text *Marketing Management: Analysis, Planning, and Control,* 2d ed. (Englewood Cliffs, N.J.: Prentice-Hall, 1972), p. 295. It has also appeared in subsequent editions.

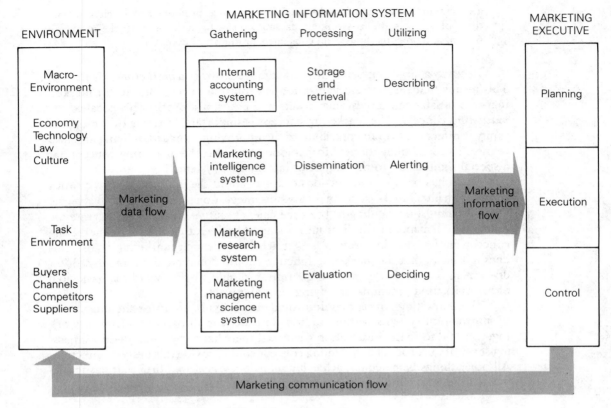

Figure 12-4 Kotler's model of the marketing information system.

The *marketing intelligence system* is concerned primarily with disseminating information to alert the manager to new developments in the marketplace. The marketing intelligence system differs from the accounting system in that the output information is oriented toward the future, rather than the present or the past. Information of this nature, such as an announcement that a competitor is developing a new product, is used mainly in planning.

The systems that evaluate alternative strategies and either decide which alternative is best or provide information to the manager so that he or she can make this decision are the marketing research system and the marketing management science system.

Marketing research is a twofold activity carried on in many firms. It involves (1) gathering current data describing all parts of the marketing operations, and (2) presenting the findings to management in a form that facilitates decision making. The emphasis is on the timeliness of the information; it is usually necessary to design and conduct projects that will gather data describing what is currently happening. The techniques used for analyzing the data are most frequently quantitative in nature, although some analysis is qualitative. The quantitative techniques can be either basic or complex.

In *marketing management science,* the emphasis is on the use of only sophisticated quantitative techniques, such as simulation. The data sources can be either the marketing research system or the internal accounting system.

The marketing research and marketing management science systems therefore represent the most modern methods of analyzing data to assist the manager in problem solving. The marketing manager uses the information output for the basic process of planning, executing, and controlling.

Kotler has produced a good structure for identifying the primary methods of generating marketing information. His model assigns most of the sophisticated problem-solving techniques to the marketing research and marketing management science subsystems. For our purposes, we need a finer breakdown so that we can see the different types of decision support provided by a marketing information system. We will achieve that finer breakdown by subdividing the marketing information system into information-producing subsystems based on the marketing mix.

The marketing mix

Like managers in other areas, marketing managers recognize that they have a variety of resources with which to work. The objective of the marketing manager is to develop strategies that enable these resources to be used in marketing the firm's products and services. The marketing strategies consist of a mixture of ingredients that has been termed the marketing mix.

The *marketing mix* is the package of products and/or services presented to the prospect (or customer) as a means of satisfying the prospect's needs and wants. The marketing mix consists of "the four Ps"—product, promotion, place, and price. *Product* is what the customer buys to satisfy the perceived need or want. Product in this sense can also be some type of service. *Promotion* is concerned with all the means of encouraging the sale of the product, including advertising and personal selling. *Place* deals with the means of physically distributing the product to the customer. This ingredient includes transportation, storage, and distribution on both the wholesale and retail levels. *Price* consists of all the elements relating to what the customer must pay for the product or service, including discounts and bonuses.

Marketing mix subsystems

The manager is concerned primarily with achieving an optimal mixture of the marketing ingredients to meet the needs of a particular target market. Therefore it seems logical to approach the study of marketing information systems by addressing the ingredients of the marketing mix.[4] The overall information system can be divided into subsystems for each of the mix ingredients.

---

[4]The first model of a marketing information system to employ the mix approach was the Brien and Stafford model. The Crissy and Mossman model also took the same approach. See footnote 1.

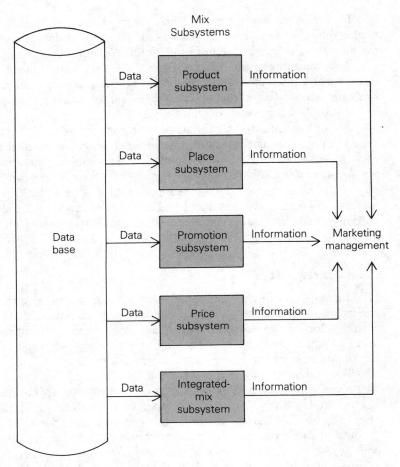

Figure 12-5 Marketing mix subsystems provide information output.

The mix subsystems in Figure 12-5 provide the interface between the manager and the data base. Each subsystem provides information about its part of the mix. The *product subsystem* provides information about the firm's products. The *place subsystem* provides information about the firm's distribution network. The *promotion subsystem* provides information about the firm's advertising and personal selling activities. And the *price subsystem* helps the manager make pricing decisions.

In addition there is a fifth subsystem labeled the *integrated-mix subsystem*. This subsystem enables the manager to develop mix strategies by considering the effect that each ingredient has on the others. For example, a manager might want to know the effect of lowering the advertising budget while also raising the price of the product. The integrated-mix subsystem helps the manager see how the mix ingredients interact.

Each of the five *output subsystems* consists of programs in the software library. Programs can include applications programs, such as report writers and mathematical models. The programs can also include systems programs, such as query language processors and data base management systems.

The marketing information system model

A model of the marketing information system should also recognize the *sources* of the data used to provide the needed information. Kotler's model identifies the three main sources: the internal accounting system, the marketing intelligence system, and the marketing research system. The marketing management science system emphasizes data processing over data gathering. When the three data sources are added to the basic mix subsystems, the result is a model that views the marketing information system in terms of both its output information and its input data sources. The model can be seen in Figure 12-6.

This model provides a finer breakdown of how information systems help solve marketing problems. For this reason it will serve as the basis for the discus-

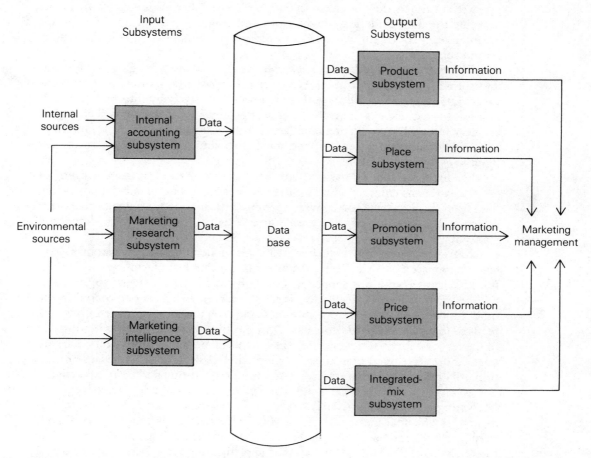

Figure 12-6 Model of a marketing information system.

sion of the marketing information system in the next chapter. Its basic structure of input and output subsystems will also be used to describe the manufacturing and financial information systems.

The model of the marketing information system shows the three *input subsystems* gathering data from internal and environmental sources. The *internal accounting subsystem* appears in the other two functional systems as well because it is a corporate resource whose activities cut across functional boundaries. The accounting subsystem includes data entry devices such as terminals and optical character readers. It also includes the procedures and personnel needed to enter the data into the data base and the computer programs needed to process the data for output reporting.

The *marketing research subsystem* consists of personnel conducting the research and entering the data into the data base. It also includes any equipment used for data gathering and input. In addition, some computer programs might be used to process the data before it is stored. The data comes from the environment and describes the firm's customers and prospects. As presented here, the marketing research subsystem does not have an output responsibility. Although we are incorporating the data-gathering activities of marketing research into our model, we are integrating the traditional marketing research reporting activities in the various output subsystems.

The *marketing intelligence subsystem* comprises the personnel, equipment, and software concerned with gathering environmental data describing competitors. Marketing intelligence is gathered almost exclusively by informal means. It is soft information, and there are no indications that this situation will change in the near future. But marketing intelligence is an important source of information concerning competitive activity, and for this reason it is included as one of the input subsystems.

We have developed a basic structure for an information system consisting of input subsystems entering data into the data base, and output subsystems taking data from the data base and converting it into information for management. This structure is a product of the considerable activity in marketing to describe a marketing information system—its composition and its uses.

Marketers have shown much more interest in defining an information system tailored to meet their own needs than have managers in manufacturing and finance. It is not clear why this has happened. Certainly marketing managers' appreciation for the importance of information is no greater than their counterparts' in the other functional areas. One possible explanation is that the literature of business tends to focus on unsolved problems. Once a problem is solved, it has less interest to the readers. Perhaps the information systems in manufacturing and finance are much more developed than those in marketing. This is possible because of the primarily internal and quantitative focus of manufacturing and financial activity.

Marketing, on the other hand, has an environmental and subjective focus. Marketing activity is completely keyed to the customer—an environmental element over which the marketer exercises little or no control. Because it is so difficult to quantify the relationship with the customer, implementing a marketing MIS is a real challenge. This is not to say that implementing an MIS in manufacturing and finance is easy. But it is relatively easier to computerize those areas than to computerize marketing. The generally higher level of computer use in manufacturing and finance tends to bear this out.

How marketing managers use the information system

Marketing managers use the information system to learn about needs and wants in the marketplace that can possibly be filled with new or improved products and services. Their planning horizon is usually quite long. It takes several years from the time a need or want is recognized until the product or service appears on the market. The marketing information system makes it possible for firms to react more quickly to consumer needs.

Once the product or service has been provided, marketing managers use the information system to follow up on how well the consumers' needs are being satisfied. The marketing information system provides feedback information from the marketplace, and this information is used to modify, improve, or delete products and services.

Manufacturing Information Systems

The manufacturing manager is concerned mainly with material flow from vendors, through the transformation process, and to marketing for distribution. Both personnel and machines are used to expedite and facilitate this flow and transformation. In a manufacturing firm, most of the employees work in the manufacturing function. Also, much use is made of machines that move material by conveyors, cranes, and trucks, and that transform raw materials into finished goods. Many of these machines are controlled by computers.

The manufacturing manager must create the physical system that transforms input materials into finished goods. He or she must also obtain information describing the performance of the physical system so that decisions can be made when necessary. A model of a system that can supply the manufacturing manager with such information is illustrated in Figure 12-7.

Input subsystems

In Chapter 9 we described how data collection terminals can be scattered throughout the production area and used for attendance and job reporting. Although these terminals can be used to input more than accounting data, they are regarded here as part of the *internal accounting subsystem* in Figure 12-7. Most of the data collected by these terminals relates to accounting and is used for payroll and cost-accounting applications. Manufacturing management uses information produced from this accounting data for planning and controlling its operations.

The *manufacturing intelligence subsystem* gathers data from the environment. The two elements in the environment of particular interest to the manufacturing manager are vendors and labor. The vendors provide both material and

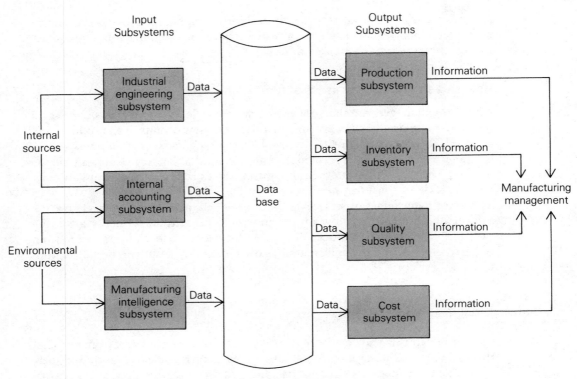

Figure 12-7 Model of a manufacturing information system.

machine resources; they also provide information in the form of catalogs and sales literature. In addition, the firm can generate much information as a result of past vendor performance in terms of quality, price, and service.

Data describing the labor element in the environment is much less formal and specific. This data can be gathered by reading newspapers and union publications, through personal contact with employment agencies and placement centers, and from government statistics. Such data rarely finds its way into the computerized portion of the MIS but instead is communicated by word of mouth and in the form of typed documents.

The *industrial engineering subsystem* is like the marketing research subsystem in that it relates to special data-gathering projects. The subsystems are dissimilar in that the industrial engineering subsystem gathers data from inside the firm rather than from the environment. Industrial engineers (or IEs) study the manufacturing operation and make recommendations for improvement. The industrial engineering subsystem is the direct descendant of Frederick W. Taylor's scientific management group.

Output subsystems

The manufacturing manager must both design and use production systems. An information system must explain how the physical system functions. The *produc-*

tion subsystem describes each phase of the transformation process, from the ordering of raw materials from a vendor to the release of the finished goods to marketing. A great many activities are tracked by this subsystem—purchasing, receiving, material handling, and the production process itself. This subsystem reports on everything that is done to the material flow through the firm.

As the material flows, the manager wants to know how well the objectives of quantity, quality, and cost are being met. The *inventory subsystem* reports on quantity by keeping a record of how much material flows from one step to the next—from raw materials to work in process and finally to finished goods. A special *quality subsystem* is used to assure that the quality level of raw materials received from vendors meets the required standards. Then this subsystem reports on the quality level at each critical step of the transformation process. Statistics play an important role in the quality control process. Many problems addressed in college statistics classes deal with the measurement of production quality.

The *cost subsystem* tells the manufacturing manager exactly what the transformation process is costing. While all managers are, or should be, concerned with costs, such costs can be reported more easily to the manufacturing manager than to many others. This is because the costs of labor, materials, and machines can be reported very specifically in production units or even in seconds. The data collection input devices record the exact time a worker or a machine starts a job and the exact time the job is finished. The same devices can also report exactly how much material is used. The data can be reported to the manufacturing manager and compared with predetermined standards. Excessive costs call for decisions that make the material flow and transformation process more efficient.

The four output subsystems consist of programs in the software library—applications and systems programs. In a small organization, packaged programs such as the MAPICS system (see Chapter 10) can provide most of the software needed by these four subsystems. Linear programming is used extensively in the design of production systems. Query languages can enable manufacturing management to track the flow of jobs through a plant.

How manufacturing managers use the information system

Manufacturing managers have a shorter planning horizon than marketing managers. Manufacturing managers are concerned with maintaining the steady flow of materials through the plant. They focus primarily on the current year's operations, with special attention to the current month, week, and even day.

The manufacturing information system enables manufacturing managers to plan and prepare for the production process and then to monitor that process to assure that the schedule is met. It provides a means by which they can view the production operation—practically in realtime.

Financial Information Systems

Business people have tried to develop mechanized financial information systems for fifty or more years. Punched card machines were used primarily by the financial function. Actually, their use was generally restricted to the processing of account-

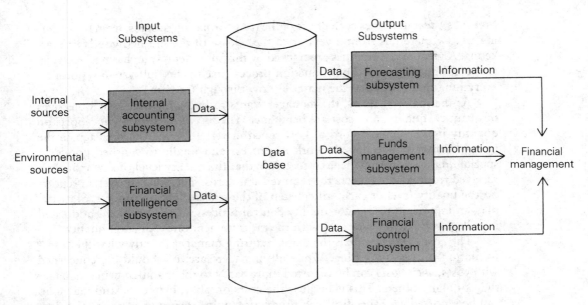

Figure 12-8   Model of a financial information system.

ing data, and little attention was paid to the information needs of management—even of financial managers. When computers were developed, they too were applied to the same accounting problems. It wasn't until the mid-sixties that financial information systems were developed beyond the basic accounting tasks.

The financial function is concerned with the money flow through the firm. First it is necessary to acquire enough money to support the manufacturing and marketing activities. Then it is necessary to control those funds to assure that they are used in the most effective way.

Information describing the money flow—both anticipated and actual—permits managers in all functional areas to meet their financial responsibilities. This information is provided by the financial information system. The function of this system is to identify future money needs, to assist in the acquisition of those funds, and to control their use. These three tasks are represented as output subsystems in the financial information system. The model of this system is illustrated in Figure 12-8.

Input subsystems

The model of the financial information system includes two input subsystems: the internal accounting system and the financial intelligence system. The *internal accounting subsystem* gathers both internal and environmental data. We have seen how data collection terminals in the manufacturing area provide much of this data. Other data is captured from source documents and entered in the data base from keyboard terminals located throughout the firm. Much of this accounting data is originated by employees other than those in the accounting department. For example, a clerk in the receiving department enters data into a terminal to describe a shipment that just arrived. This data triggers the preparation of a check by the accounts payable system to pay the vendor.

The accounting subsystem also gathers environmental data as a result of business transactions with other firms. The environmental data describes the transactions and provides a basis for analyzing vendors' performance and customers' purchasing habits. Both manufacturing and marketing managers use the information produced from this accounting data.

The *financial intelligence subsystem* gathers data from the financial community—banks, governmental agencies, securities markets, and so forth. This subsystem monitors the pulse of the nation's economy and informs the firm's executives of trends that can affect the financial condition of the company. Within the past few years, the environment that this subsystem monitors has broadened from national to international in scope. The interdependence of U.S. and foreign economies requires that attention be given to international conditions.

Output subsystems

The *forecasting subsystem* projects the activity of the firm for any period of up to ten years or more. The activity of the coming year is influenced primarily by market demand and internal constraints, such as the size of the sales force, production capacity, and available finances. As the forecast period lengthens, the importance of the environment increases. The changing needs of consumers must be anticipated, as should the climate of the national and international economies. Forecasting models have been developed that include both internal and environmental data to provide a basis for immediate and long-term planning. These models constitute the bulk of the forecasting subsystem.

The *funds management subsystem* uses projections of company activity to determine the flow of money into and out of the firm. The manager can simulate several strategies designed to achieve the best balance in the inflow and outflow during a future period, such as the coming year. Balanced flows reduce the need to borrow operating capital and increase the return on invested surplus funds.

The use of available funds is controlled by the *financial control subsystem*. This subsystem primarily uses data gathered by the internal accounting subsystem to produce reports showing how monies are being spent. The reports compare actual financial performance to a budget and provide ratios between financial figures as a measure of good performance. As business becomes more competitive and the costs of operations increase, good budget performance becomes increasingly important. The control subsystem enables managers to track their cost control activity.

More packaged software has been developed for the financial area than for any other. These are mostly accounting packages such as payroll, inventory, accounts receivable, and so on. The VisiCalc package (see Chapter 10) can be used in this part of the MIS. It can be used in the funds management subsystem for manipulations such as cash flow analyses and in the financial control subsystem for developing operating budgets.

These packaged programs enable small firms to achieve good financial control without investing in large information services staffs. In large firms, much analyst and programmer time is devoted to accounting systems in the financial area.

How financial managers use the information system

Financial managers use the information system to manage the money flow. The manager must look into the future and identify the monetary needs of the firm. Sources of these funds must be identified and relationships established so that the funds flow into the firm when needed. These activities are long-range and environmental in focus. The financial manager uses the information system to keep current on the financial environment and to cultivate that environment so that it represents an asset of the firm rather than a constraint.

As the funds flow through the firm, they are managed so that they are used as effectively as possible. This management is guided by the annual operating budget. The information system gathers data describing the financial transactions of the firm and reports, in a summarized form, the results of those transactions to managers throughout the firm. This feedback information enables managers to adjust their systems and procedures in order to meet the financial objectives.

The financial manager also uses the information system to identify the best places to invest surplus funds. Like the acquisition of funds, investment activity involves the financial community and demands anticipating future financial environments.

The Conceptual Nature of Models

The models of the three functional information systems in Figures 12-6, 12-7, and 12-8 all provide nice, neat pictures of how an MIS can be organized. But you must understand that these conceptual representations do not exactly match what exists physically. The models help you understand functional information systems by showing the data-gathering tasks they can perform and the types of information they can provide.

The models can convey the mistaken impression that each box contains its own unique contents, independent of the rest of the system. Such is not the case. Much data is shared among the three functional areas. The firm has a common data base, not separate data bases for each functional area. And many software packages have multiple uses. Linear programming, for example, can determine the optimal mix of products rolling off a production assembly line, the optimal blend of advertising media in a promotional campaign, and the optimal combination of securities in a firm's investment portfolio.

The models can also convey the mistaken impression that data and information flow easily from one function to another, and from one information subsystem to another. The ease with which these flows are achieved varies widely from one firm to the next. Even in firms with good information flows, often there are a number of intermediate steps as the information passes from one area to the next. These intermediate steps do not appear in the models.

Some of the subsystems identified in the models are difficult to locate in most firms. You probably will never see a door with a sign reading "Industrial Engineering Subsystem," even when there are IEs on the payroll. And you will probably never find a person in charge of "Manufacturing Intelligence"—even in the largest corporations. These are all jobs relating to the flow of management information. Somebody performs these jobs in all firms, but in many cases it is not a full-time responsibility, and the person may never know that he or she is doing it. When a controller playing golf hears a new stock offering touted as a good investment opportunity, he or she doesn't say, "My, what an interesting bit of financial intelligence." Nevertheless, the controller does realize that the information is valuable, even without assigning it to a particular information subsystem of the firm.

With all of these disclaimers, you might wonder why we bother with the models in the first place. This is not the first discussion of models in the text, as you know. The general systems model of the firm in Chapter 3, the model of the systems approach in Figure 4-11, and the computer schematic in Figure 5-6 are all graphical models that present structural relationships. As you surely must appreciate by now, the subject of the MIS encompasses many topics. Models help organize information. They provide a structure that might not be immediately apparent and thus serve as a blueprint for study and application. The real beauty of the models is that they rarely change. In a field like the computer industry, where change is the name of the game, anything that lends stability is invaluable.

In this chapter we have built a conceptual framework for our study of functional information systems. During the next three chapters we will describe actual information processing applications that relate to each of the conceptual subsystems. Our models will enable us to see how all of the activities fit into an overall system designed to facilitate the flow of information to managers.

Summary

The objective of this chapter has been to provide a structure for studying the MIS. The MIS has been discussed previously in general terms, and it is necessary to be more specific about how management uses it. Since organizations and managers are grouped according to the functional areas of finance, manufacturing, and marketing, the uses of the MIS can also be grouped this way.

A functional approach to the MIS is probably the most realistic because functional organization is prevalent in the business world. Constructing the MIS as a composite of these functional subsystems, however, should not imply that a total, integrated MIS is unnecessary. The end objective of every firm's information program should be the attainment of an integrated MIS in which all parts work in harmony. If parts of the information system do not work together, the MIS will not be effective. And it is doubtful that the physical system of the firm can be any more efficient. The two systems must work together. An efficient physical system demands an efficient information system, and vice versa.

The main functional areas identified in this chapter are marketing, manufacturing, and finance. It is assumed that all managers except chief executives fit within one of these three areas. Functional information systems are developed for each area, and all of the managers—including the chief executive officers—derive their information from them. It is logical to subdivide the MIS into functional information systems. The managers in these areas have unique information needs and the functional information systems meet these needs.

Our model of the marketing information system is based on the pioneering work of Philip Kotler. Input subsystems gather internal and environmental data and enter it into the data base. Output subsystems convert data into information for management. We use the same model format for the manufacturing and financial information systems.

Key Terms

brand management

physical distribution, logistics

marketing information system

financial information system

manufacturing information system

marketing orientation, marketing concept

internal accounting subsystem

marketing intelligence subsystem

marketing research subsystem

marketing management science subsystem

marketing mix

product subsystem

place subsystem

promotion subsystem

price subsystem

integrated-mix subsystem

output subsystem

input subsystem

manufacturing intelligence subsystem

industrial engineering subsystem

production subsystem

inventory subsystem

quality subsystem

cost subsystem

financial intelligence subsystem

forecasting subsystem

funds management subsystem

financial control subsystem

Key Concepts

The fact that functional subsystems do not detract from the objective of an integrated MIS

The development of functional information systems corresponding to the functionally organized physical resources of the firm

The manner in which the marketing concept can unify the various functional areas so that they work together as a single system

The pervasive nature of a firm's internal accounting system as it cuts across functional boundaries

The manner in which each of the three intelligence subsystems is responsible for gathering information from certain environmental elements

How the marketing mix provides an effective means of subdividing information outputs

The need for an integrated-mix subsystem

The informal nature of intelligence describing competitive activity and the labor element of the environment

The environmental focus of the financial information system in acquiring and investing funds, and the internal focus in accounting for use of resources within the firm

Questions

1. If the MIS is an integrated system that meets the information needs of the entire firm, how do you explain the use of functional information systems?
2. Describe two methods that firms have used to achieve a flow network effect in a functional organization.
3. Can you think of an organization that cannot be considered in manufacturing terms? If so, explain why it doesn't fit a manufacturing description of transforming a raw material into a finished product.
4. Does a military branch, such as the army, have a marketing function? Explain your answer. What about a church?
5. Would a nonprofit organization like the United Way have a financial function? Explain.
6. What functional area of the firm is responsible for the personnel flow?
7. Name a method that can be used to subdivide a firm's MIS other than by functional area. Why would it have difficulty succeeding?
8. In a firm with information systems organized functionally, where do the top executives get their information?
9. How could a firm's manufacturing function adopt the marketing concept?
10. What did Philip Kotler contribute to the concept of functional information systems?
11. Which subsystem exists in all three functional information systems? Which functional area of the firm is responsible for this subsystem?
12. What are the two main activities of marketing research?
13. Which marketing mix ingredient is represented by a firm's TV commercials? By a fleet of delivery trucks? By a two-for-one sale?
14. How does the marketing research subsystem differ from the marketing intelligence subsystem?
15. What is the relationship between data collection terminals and the cost subsystem?
16. Which functional subsystem is represented by the MAPICS package?
17. In what functional area were a firm's punched card machines located? How did this influence early computer applications?

18. Has financial intelligence become more important or less important during the past few years? Explain.

19. Which financial output subsystem is concerned with the budget? With performance ratios?

20. For which functional subsystem has the most packaged software been prepared?

CASE PROBLEM: Great Lakes Boat and Marine

Your career is progressing nicely—six successful years with one of the Big Eight accounting firms in its management services division. Your performance as a computer consultant was so outstanding that you got a job offer from one of your clients. You managed the conversion from a batch to an online data processing system for Great Lakes Boat and Marine so well that the company offered you the position of vice-president of information services. Sue Rankin, the president, told you that the next step was to develop an MIS and she needed someone to implement it. The system you installed earlier does all the essential data processing tasks—order entry, inventory, billing, accounts receivable, purchasing, and receiving. You know that Great Lakes has a sound internal accounting system, which should make it possible to achieve an excellent MIS.

During your first day on the job, you meet with Rankin to learn more about her expectations. She tells you she has formed an MIS committee consisting of Rick Guenther (vice-president of manufacturing), Don Lehnert (vice-president of marketing), Cheryl Mitchell (vice-president of finance), and you. Rankin wants you to call on each member, introduce yourself, and set a date and time for the first planning meeting.

You already know Mitchell, having worked with her on the installation of the data processing system. You know she is extremely computer literate and anxious to expand the scope of the computer applications. You have heard of Guenther and Lehnert but haven't met them. As you leave, you remember to ask Rankin, "Aren't you going to be on the MIS committee?"

"No," Rankin replies, "I'm too busy planning our entry into the New England market area next year. I just don't have time. That's why I hired you."

Your first stop is Guenther's office. You find him extremely likeable—a warm handshake, boundless energy, contagious optimism, and a great sense of humor. You spend two hours in his office, getting to know him and talking about the computer. Guenther wants to get started immediately.

"We've just been waiting for someone like you," he says. "We've known about MIS and how it can help us in manufacturing, but we haven't had anyone to pick up the ball and run with it. I want data collection terminals in every work area. We should be able to implement attendance reporting immediately, and I would like to be reporting all production activities within three months. I need good data to establish some good production standards. I want all manufacturing managers to have terminals in their offices, and I want each to attend a course on how to use the computer. I've seen what a good MIS can do in manufacturing, and I can't wait to get started."

Neither can you. You are so excited after talking with Guenther that you almost run down the hall to Lehnert's office. When his secretary ushers you into his office and his greeting is, "Well, what do *you* want?" you suspect rough sailing. You introduce yourself and explain your purpose. You feel uncomfortable when Lehnert nervously jingles coins in his pocket as you talk. When you pause to catch your breath, he says, "Listen, I don't have time to get involved with Sue's MIS. We're planning to expand our market area and I have to find eight new distributors by the end of the month. I can't do that sitting around talking about computer programs. If I can't get my marketing job done, there won't be any company to put an MIS in.

"Now, I have to go. Why don't you talk with my manager of marketing administration, Willie Campbell. The MIS would really be in Willie's area. He'll get you fixed up. Just a minute, and I'll have my secretary take you to his office.

"I've appreciated meeting you, and I wish you all the luck in the world. I'm sure you'll give us a good MIS."

Questions

1. Is there a problem here? If so, what is it?

2. From the information you have, how would you rate the chances of Great Lakes' achieving a "good MIS."

3. Assuming Lehnert won't cooperate, should you go ahead with work on Guenther's and Mitchell's areas?

4. Assuming Rankin insists that Lehnert must get involved, list two alternate ways that his cooperation might be gained. Which do you recommend, and why?

Chapter 13

Marketing Information Systems

Learning Objectives

After studying this chapter, you should:

- Understand how data and information are gathered by the marketing intelligence and marketing research subsystems
- Be familiar with some of the programs in the software library that provide the marketing manager with information relating to product, place, promotion, price, and the integrated mix
- Know the difference between marketing research and the marketing information system
- See how the computer can be used both to establish and to operate distribution channel systems
- Appreciate the difficulty of modeling promotion and pricing decisions
- Understand how the manager uses a nonoptimizing model

Overview

The concept of functional information systems was presented in the previous chapter. This chapter analyzes the marketing information system in greater detail. The marketing information system precedes the manufacturing and financial systems for two reasons. First, more has been done in marketing to develop a description of a functional information system. Second, the marketing information system concerns that element of the environment that should represent the point of origin for everything the firm does, i.e., the customer.

The second marketing information system model developed in Chapter 12, including input and output subsystems, will provide the basis for this chapter. The model is reproduced here as Figure 13–1. All of the subsystems, except that

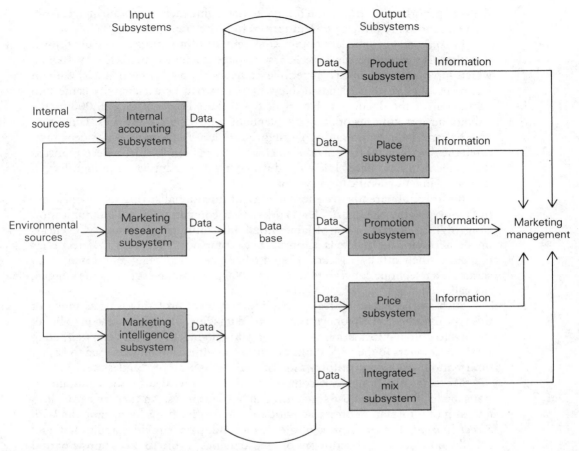

Figure 13-1 Model of a marketing information system.

of internal accounting, will be addressed in this chapter. The accounting subsystem will be discussed in Chapter 15, when the financial information system is studied.

Marketing Intelligence Subsystem

The discussion in Chapter 4 focused on the various elements in the environment of the firm. Certain functional areas within the firm have prime responsibility for each of the elements. The two elements identified with the marketing function are the customers and the competition.

Marketing has no responsibility to establish a communication flow *to* the competition, but it must establish an incoming flow. The activity associated with this gathering of *competitive* information is called *marketing intelligence*. This term may bring to mind visions of spying—an activity called *industrial espionage*. A certain amount of undercover work surely goes on in the competitive world of business, although few instances have been reported. Firms are hesitant to report thefts of proprietary information for fear of damaging their corporate image. Also, such violations are difficult for authorities to prosecute.

In some cases, outsiders obtain confidential information by accident. Such was the case involving the loss of a sixty-page document prepared by Exxon, which apparently contained competitive strategies against Tenneco. A Mr. William Dunn, Jr., was visiting friends in New Orleans when he accidentally came into possession of the document. He tried to sell it to Tenneco for $20,000 at the Atlanta airport after negotiating by telephone with Tenneco officials. Dunn was arrested and later found guilty. During the trial, a Tenneco vice-president indicated the report might have a value of close to $1 million. Until Tenneco reported the incident, Exxon never knew the document was missing, even though Exxon uses a document classification system.[1]

But there apparently are enough cases of intentional spying to make executives wary of the threat. A New York–based company, CCS Communication Control, Inc., markets a line of James Bond–like antibugging devices.[2] CCS deals in counterespionage and sells its products to companies that want to detect bugs planted in their offices, to learn when a telephone call is being monitored, or to scramble a telephone conversation so that it will be meaningless to anyone bugging the call.

Such stories make interesting reading, but there probably isn't as much of this type of industrial espionage as one would imagine. There is no reason to break the law to obtain information that is so easy to obtain legally. The term *marketing intelligence* refers to the wide range of ethical activities that may be used to gather information about competitors, and not to the unethical or clandestine.

Much information about competitive firms is revealed by the communications media, especially those specializing in business news. An executive can glean a wealth of information on the activities of competitive firms by reading the *Wall Street Journal*. The trade press of the various industries provides additional, and usually more detailed, descriptions of such activities. Table 13-1 contains a partial list of publications specializing in industry-oriented information. These publications do not contain all the information a manager would like to have on a subject, but they do provide the initial signal that some type of activity is underway. Additional information-gathering efforts, also conducted in an ethical manner, can provide more facts to fill out the picture. For example, marketing intelligence might trigger a marketing research project. A firm learning that a competitor is test marketing a new product can design its own research project to evaluate the competitor's success.

In addition to exposure to mass-circulation media, information-gathering efforts can take the form of attending stockholder meetings and reading stockholder announcements such as the annual report, attending open-house celebrations to dedicate new facilities or announce new products, purchasing competitive products for engineering and design analysis, and visiting competitive stores to learn what is being sold and what prices are being charged.

[1] Raymond Klempin, "Industrial Spying: The Shady Business of Stealing Secrets," *Houston Business Journal,* 15 December 1980, pp. 1, 12.

[2] Lynn Ashby, "Perilous Times," *The Houston Post,* 5 October 1980, p. 1B.

Table 13-1 Some Industry-Oriented Publications

Air Conditioning, Heating & Refrigeration News	Housing
American Druggist	Industry Week
Automotive Industries	Infosystems
Aviation Week & Space Technology	Iron Age
The Banker	Journal of Purchasing & Materials Management
Best's Review—Life/Health Insurance and Property Casualty Insurance Editions	Journal of Retailing
	Labor Law Journal
Broadcasting	Merchandising
Chain Store Age Executive	Modern Plastics
Chemical Week	National Petroleum News
Computer Decisions	Oil and Gas Journal
Computers and People	Personnel
Credit and Financial Management	Pipeline & Gas Journal
Datamation	Progressive Grocer
Drug & Cosmetic Industry	Public Utilities Fortnightly
Electronic News	Pulp & Paper
Financial World	Quick Frozen Foods
Fleet Owner	Textile World
Food Processing	Transportation Journal
Forest Industries	World Oil
Fueloil & Oil Heat and Solar Systems	

The sales force of the firm is also expected to play an important role in this feedback of competitive information. The salesperson is expected not only to communicate information from the firm to the marketplace, but also to communicate information back to the firm. When the salesperson establishes a good relationship with a customer, it is possible to learn much about competitive activity. The customer can pass along information just obtained from competitive salespersons. When this system works as it should, competitive operations can be monitored practically in realtime.

Unfortunately, in the few reported instances of companies' monitoring feedback from their sales staff, the system didn't work very well. Some firms have planted competitive information so that it would be obtained by their sales reps. Either the information was never reported to headquarters, or it took forever to get there, or it was utterly distorted during the feedback process. If a firm wishes to rely on salesperson feedback, a concerted effort should be made to install a formal system. The formal system should include forms, procedures, and so on for reporting competitive information.

Many of a firm's marketing intelligence activities are informal. Much of the information gathered is not entered into the computer-based MIS. It is soft information. Some of the intelligence does enter the computer, however. This computer data is purchased from firms such as A. C. Nielsen, Market Research Corporation of America, and Brand Rating Index Corporation, which gather data about transactions such as retail food and drug sales. This data can be purchased in either magnetic tape or hardcopy form.

Purchased data answers key questions about who is buying, who isn't, what they are buying, and so on. The data is gathered using marketing research techniques (described in the next section) and sold to clients. JFY, Inc., of Melville, New York, gathers data by telephone survey or mail questionnaire and records the findings on "Data-Tapes."[3] JFY does not make its data available to competitive firms. When a company contracts with JFY for competitive information, it can be assured that the information is not flowing in the other direction as well.

Even though much competitive data can be purchased and the amount is continually increasing, marketing intelligence remains essentially an informal system. Usually there is no set plan for gathering such information and disseminating it throughout the firm. This part of the MIS can be characterized as an informal system handling primarily soft information.

Marketing Research Subsystem

Marketing research is concerned with gathering information about customers or prospects. The scope of analysis could be much broader, addressing the entire marketing system, but that has not been the practice. Marketing researchers are interested in the customer and why the customer buys the firm's products. Marketing research is a common business activity, in practice since about 1911. Large firms have marketing research departments, and an increasing number of marketing research firms perform the service for their clients. The research process is much more formal than gathering marketing intelligence.

The marketing researcher works with two types of data—primary and secondary. *Primary data* is data gathered as a result of a special effort, such as a survey. *Secondary data* is data someone else has already gathered. Secondary data is used when possible because it is much less expensive and can be acquired more quickly than primary data. A great deal of secondary data is available from the federal government in the form of statistics. Some of this government data is purchased; some is free. Secondary data can also be purchased from commercial sources. Mailing lists are probably the most frequently purchased marketing research data. These lists are available on magnetic tape and can be prepared for special consumer groups, such as retired military officers living in the Southwest.

---

[3] Bernie Whalen, "Data-Tapes Let Marketers Selectively Target Coupons, Samples," *Marketing News,* 27 November 1981, sec. 1, p. 4.

Figure 13-2 A personal interview.

Means of gathering data

It is difficult to find a person who is unfamiliar with marketing research. When asked about marketing research, the common response is "Oh yes, you mean surveys." Almost everyone has been approached at one time or another, in person, by mail, or by telephone, for information about shopping habits, product preference, brand loyalty, and so on.

Actually, the survey is only one method of gathering data through marketing research. A *survey* is conducted when the same questions are asked of a number of persons, by whatever method (personal interview, telephone, or mail). The number of persons surveyed may be relatively small, say thirty, or quite large, say several thousand. Figure 13-2 shows a personal interview being conducted in a shopping mall—a convenient place to contact shoppers and ask them questions about their shopping habits.

When different questions are asked of a small number of people, such as three or four, the technique is known as an *in-depth interview*. The time devoted to the interview is much longer than that spent with any single survey participant. Also, the emphasis is on probing for information explaining why customers behave as they do. This approach is based on similar techniques developed in psychology.

Another technique from the behavioral sciences is *observation*. It presumes that the best way to learn of a behavior is either to observe that behavior taking place or to obtain indications that the behavior has occurred. The technique has been used quite effectively in anthropology and sociology and has been adopted by marketers. Marketing researchers note license plate numbers in a shopping center parking lot in order to learn how far people have driven to patronize the center. Or they set up movie or television cameras in supermarkets to record the response of shoppers to displays.

Marketers have even adopted the technique of the *controlled experiment* from the physical and behavioral sciences, and both the real marketplace and the classroom serve as laboratories. Very often college students serve as subjects in experiments designed to measure the effect of a particular treatment (say a certain type of ad) on behavior (the ability to recall the ad).

Relationship of marketing research to the MIS

Although marketing research has been around for a long time, the MIS concept is quite new. As the concept evolved, there was some confusion within marketing as to how MIS related to marketing research. Some authorities believed MIS was simply a new name for marketing research. This was especially the case when the term *marketing information system* was used.

Most authorities now seem to regard marketing research as a subset of the marketing information system, which in turn is a subset of the management information system. The marketing research subsystem is responsible for linking the MIS to that important element in the environment—the customer.

There is one important difference between marketing research and the MIS. The definition of the MIS offered in the first chapter referred to a *continuous* flow of information. Marketing research, on the other hand, is primarily concerned with special information-gathering projects. If a firm needs a certain type of information, a research project will be designed to provide it. Usually, no effort will be made to keep the information up to date once it has been gathered. One marketer compared marketing research to a flashbulb and MIS to a candle: Marketing research lights up a small area vividly for a short period of time, whereas the MIS provides general illumination for a large area over a long period of time.

Computer-assisted interviewing

Today's large marketing research firms use multistation microcomputer systems in the interviewing process. The interviewer reads the question from the CRT and enters the response either by keying it in or by using a *light pen* to "check" the response displayed on the CRT. For example, with a multiple-choice question, the interviewer need only touch the selected answer with the light pen. The light pen provides a means of entering data through the CRT. For a photograph of a light pen in use, see Chapter 1, Figure 1-1.

These micro-based interviewing systems, including the necessary software, can be leased from firms such as Sophisticated Data Research, which offers an eight-station (CRT) micro with both hard and floppy disk for less than $24,000 per year. The light weight and compact size of the micro have also made it an attractive device for personal interviewing, such as in shopping malls. Using a computer increases interviewers' productivity by about 20% and eliminates the intermediate step of entering responses on a printed form.

Product Subsystem

The product is usually the first specified ingredient in the marketing mix. The firm decides to provide a product to satisfy a particular market need. Subsequently, the remaining ingredients (place, promotion, and price) are identified and described.

You should keep in mind that each of these marketing mix decisions assumes the existence of corporate goals. The firm must know where it is and where it wants to go. The goals, along with the available resources, are the primary constraints at each step of the decision-making process. For example, a firm may have an overall goal of providing equipment and supplies to the medical profession. In this case, the firm would not consider any activity outside of that field. The goals of the firm dictate the activity area.

The resources of the firm also play an important role. A firm usually develops both a production and a marketing capability for a particular product or family of products. Attempting to manufacture and market a completely different type of product could prove extremely difficult. For example, what problems would be created if the Head ski company decided to add frozen food products? Product diversification is normally accomplished by acquiring other firms.

The product life cycle

The marketing manager is concerned with developing strategy and tactics for each ingredient in the marketing mix and then integrating these into an overall marketing plan. A framework called the *product life cycle* guides the manager in making these decisions. As its name implies, the product life cycle charts the development of the product from introduction, or birth, through various growth and developmental stages, to deletion, or death. Names have been given to four stages in the life cycle: introduction, growth, maturity, and decline. The cycle and its stages are shown in Figure 13-3.

Although the product life cycle consists of four stages, there are three time periods during which the marketing information system helps the marketing manager make product-oriented decisions. The first period precedes the introduction of the product, when a decision must be made whether to develop and market the product. The second period is during the introduction, growth, and maturity stages, when the product is healthy. The final period is during the decline, when product deletion must be considered. These three decision periods also appear in Figure 13-3.

A number of techniques have been developed to provide the manager with the information needed for making product-oriented decisions. The technique discussed below helps the manager decide which product should be selected for introduction to the market. Techniques such as this, plus others relating to product decisions, constitute the product subsystem of a firm's marketing information system.

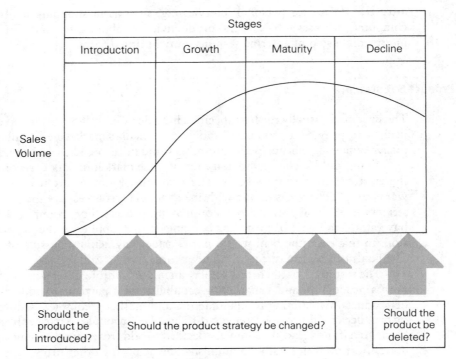

Figure 13-3 Product life cycle and decisions.

Product development

The decision to develop a new product should be carefully considered, have a sound financial basis, and be made by top corporate management. Prior to the decision, information should be available to indicate, with a high degree of certainty, the profit potential of the proposed product. Many firms have developed an orderly and systematic approach to the consideration of new products that considers a variety of factors, such as profitability and utilization of resources. Scores can be computed for products under consideration, and management attention can focus on products with the best scores.

Figure 13-4 illustrates this quantitative approach to new-product evaluation.[4] In this example, new products are evaluated on both their marketing and their production features. A product selected for introduction scores high in both categories. The decision criteria are listed for both production and marketing considerations along with a weighting (criterion weight) that reflects the relative importance of each. The center portion of the tables consists of ratings that each criterion receives, from very good to very poor. The ratings each have values from

---

[4]Based on Stewart H. Rewoldt, James D. Scott, and Martin R. Warshaw, *Introduction to Marketing Management,* 3d ed. (Homewood, Ill.: Richard D. Irwin, 1977), pp. 253–62. The technique is not new—an early description appeared in John T. O'Meara, "Selecting Profitable Products," *Harvard Business Review* 39 (January–February 1961): 83–89.

A--UTILIZATION OF PRODUCTION RESOURCES (PROPOSED NEW PRODUCT JXL5005)

DECISION CRITERIA	CRITERIA WEIGHT	VERY GOOD (10)		GOOD (8)		AVERAGE (6)		POOR (4)		VERY POOR (2)		TOTAL	CRITERION EVALUATION (TOT. EV X WEIGHT)
		P	EV	P	EV	P	EV	P	EV	P	EV		
PLANT CAPACITY	.20	.2	2.0	.6	4.8	.2	1.2	0	0	0	0	8.0	1.60
LABOR SKILLS	.30	.2	2.0	.7	5.6	.1	.6	0	0	0	0	8.2	2.46
ENGINEERING KNOW-HOW	.30	0	0	.2	1.6	.2	1.2	.6	2.4	0	0	5.2	1.56
EQUIPMENT AVAILABILITY	.10	0	0	0	0	.7	4.2	.3	1.2	0	0	5.4	.54
MATERIAL AVAILABILITY	.10	0	0	0	0	.1	.6	.6	2.4	.3	.6	3.6	.36

TOTAL PRODUCTION RESOURCES VALUE 6.52

B--UTILIZATION OF MARKETING RESOURCES

DECISION CRITERIA	CRITERIA WEIGHT	VERY GOOD (10)		GOOD (8)		AVERAGE (6)		POOR (4)		VERY POOR (2)		TOTAL	CRITERION EVALUATION (TOT. EV X WEIGHT)
		P	EV	P	EV	P	EV	P	EV	P	EV		
PRODUCT COMPATABILITY	.20	0	0	.2	1.6	.5	3.0	.2	.8	.1	.2	5.6	1.12
SALES KNOWLEDGE	.20	.1	1.0	.5	4.0	.3	1.8	.1	.4	0	0	7.2	1.44
DISTRIBUTION FACILITIES	.30	.3	3.0	.5	4.0	.2	1.2	0	0	0	0	8.2	2.46
LONG-TERM DEMAND	.30	0	0	.2	1.6	.6	3.6	.2	.8	0	0	6.0	1.80

TOTAL MARKETING RESOURCES VALUE 6.82

C--UTILIZATION OF FIRM RESOURCES

RESOURCE	VALUE	WEIGHT	WEIGHTED VALUE
PRODUCTION	6.52	.40	2.61
MARKETING	6.82	.60	4.09
TOTAL			6.70

Figure 13-4 Quantitative evaluation of a new product: (a) utilization of production resources (proposed new product JXL5005); (b) utilization of marketing resources; (c) utilization of firm resources.

a high of 10 for very good to a low of 2 for very poor. In the column beneath each rating is listed the probability (P) of the new product's scoring the indicated rating on each specific criterion. For example, the probability of the new product's receiving a rating of very good on the criterion of plant capacity (in Figure 13-4a) is .2. This probability is multiplied by the rating value of 10 to obtain an "expected value" (EV) of 2.0. The second column from the right contains a summation of the expected values for each criterion, and these are multiplied by the appropriate criterion weight to obtain the figures in the rightmost column. The total of these figures represents a "total production resources value" of 6.52 for the new product. The table reflecting the marketing consideration (Figure 13-4b) is constructed in the same manner. Both the production and marketing resource utilization scores are multiplied by respective weights (to reflect the relative importance of production and marketing considerations for the new product), and the weighted values are added. The final score of 6.70 represents the company production and marketing resource utilization for the new product (Figure 13-4c). Similar scores are developed for the other products under consideration to aid management in selecting the new product to be produced and marketed. The products with the highest scores receive the highest consideration.

In order to use such an approach, it is necessary to quantify a number of essentially subjective measures. Numbers must be assigned to criterion weights, probabilities of performance, and relative weights of production and marketing. It is extremely difficult to quantify these estimates. Even so, such an approach has an inherent value. It forces the manager to identify the factors influencing the decision and to consider the relative significance of each.

This new-product evaluation model is a static, probabilistic, nonoptimizing, specific model. Using a model like this is justified only in firms that develop a large number of new product possibilities. Managers evaluate the products and enter the evaluations in a terminal. Output can be printed on a terminal or a printer. Hardcopy output provides a record of the evaluation.

The new-product decision is semistructured. The product subsystem supports the manager by providing a quantitative analysis of possibilities. When using a model such as the new-product evaluation model, the manager must understand that much of the input data is subjective.

Place Subsystem

Firms must make their products and services available to their customers. This distribution is accomplished by channel systems. For some firms the channels are short—the Fuller Brush Company, for example, sells door-to-door. For others, the channels are quite long—farmers' products reach the supermarket through a number of intermediaries, including wholesalers, brokers, and distributors.

The method by which the firm makes its products available to the customer is identified as the "place" ingredient in the marketing mix. Place decisions fall into two categories: (1) the establishment of channel systems, and (2) the performance of the distribution functions.

Establishing channel systems

In most cases, the manufacturer must establish the channel. The manufacturer has created a product and must deliver it to the market. In creating a channel system, the manufacturer needs information about the activity of the product at each step. It is not sufficient, though, for the feedback to the manufacturer to stop when the product has been delivered to the wholesaler. Just because the wholesaler bought the product does not assure that it will appeal equally well to the retailer. The same can be said of sales at the retail level—there is no assurance that the consumer will buy. If the manufacturer is to know what is happening in the channel, feedback must be obtained from each channel link—and in many cases, from the consumer as well.

If the manufacturer expects feedback from the channel members farther down the line, something must be offered in return. Quite possibly this need only be information—a type of *feedforward* to the wholesaler and the retailer. Just as the manufacturer needs information *after* the physical product flow occurs, the wholesaler and the retailer need information *before* the flow begins. Feedforward information from the manufacturer to the channel members can include announcements of new products, sales and promotion aids, forecasts of demand, and so on. If the participants in the channel system realize the value of the information flow and the improved performance it offers, then an efficient interfirm information system is possible.

It is important to understand that information is one of the resources flowing through the channel. It flows in both directions, as shown in Figure 13-5. These

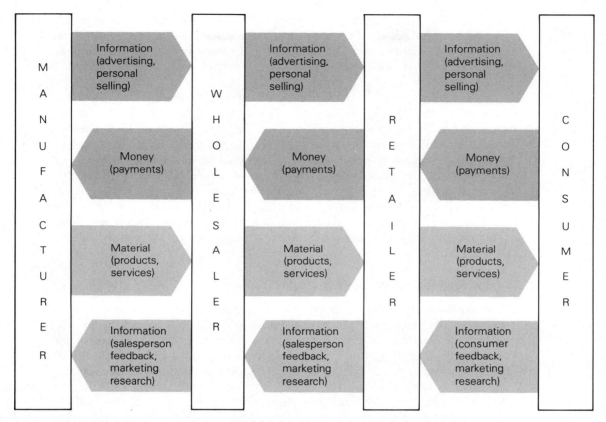

Figure 13-5 Resource flow through the channel.

flows are accomplished in various ways. Sales representatives of the channel members are responsible for preparing written reports and for communicating information by word of mouth. Very often information or data is transmitted by punched card, magnetic tape, or data communications network. A channel system that permits information to flow freely among the firms provides an edge over competitive systems without that capability.

Computer mapping for dealer location

Companies that sell their products through dealers, such as Yamaha Motor Corp. U.S.A., are faced with the problem of where to locate the dealerships. Dealerships must be in areas where the level of business is high, yet existing dealership areas must be protected.

Demographic Research Company helped Yamaha make these decisions by blending computer graphics with behavioral demographics.[5] *Behavioral demo-*

---

[5] Daniel H. Straub, "Targeting Markets with Computer Mapping and Graphics," *Marketing Communications* 7 (February 1982): 21–23.

graphics links psychological, life-style, and household-expenditure data to geographic location, often by zip code. Two mathematical models have been developed—one to identify areas of high potential sales and the other to compare Yamaha sales goals with actual sales in high-potential areas. The first model was tested several times in the Houston market.

The models produce a series of maps drawn on a plotter. The first map shows the configuration of the trading area. The second adds an overlay to the first showing actual sales by dot density. An example appears in Figure 13-6. The third map shows that dealer boundaries could shrink if potential sales are not lost, since dealers could achieve a higher level of sales in the immediate vicinity. The fourth map identifies the volume of business for each dealership in the reduced areas.

Yamaha has used the model and mapping techniques to locate new dealerships in Chicago, Kansas City, Missouri, and Orange County, California. The models enable Yamaha to obtain answers to important "where" questions—Where is the potential need? Where are the unexpected pockets of consumers?

Performance of distribution functions

Once the distribution systems have been established, the firm needs to set machinery in motion to facilitate the flow of resources along the channel. In no other area of the firm's marketing operations has the computer been applied so successfully. Physical distribution, or logistics (the names given to the physical flow), has greatly improved during the past decade through the application of computers and quantitative problem-solving techniques. The main reason for this success is that physical distribution problems are largely deterministic, not probabilistic. The variables are physical rather than behavioral, and their interrelationships can be specified very clearly. In this respect, the physical distribution part of marketing is very similar to the manufacturing function.

Computer-controlled warehouse operation

The Levi Strauss & Co. garment distribution center in Waco, Texas, provides a good example of how computers can be used in both the physical and the conceptual system.[6]

In 1981 Levi opened a 1-million-square-foot automated warehouse controlled by a warehouse control system (WCS) consisting of two IBM Series 1 small computers. The warehouse has a capacity of 11 million items of clothing, which if placed on hangers, would stretch 270 miles. Now that's a walk-in closet!

As cartons of garments arrive from plant sites, laser scanners read data from bar codes to identify the type, style, size, and color of the contents. The model in

---

[6]Information concerning the Levi operation was obtained from a Levi Strauss & Co. press release and from "Twenty-Three Acres of Automation," *CWIPS*, July–August 1980. (*CWIPS* is the magazine of the Cutler-Williams consulting firm, which was retained to assist Levi in the implementation.)

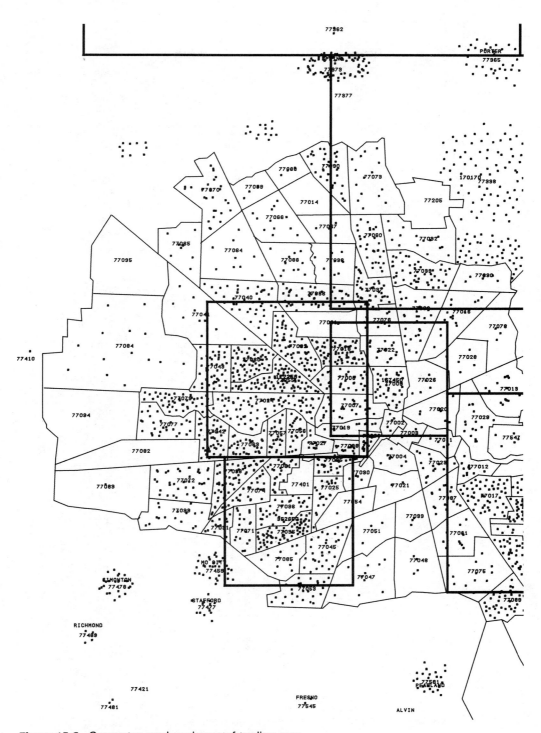

Figure 13-6 Computer-produced map of trading area.

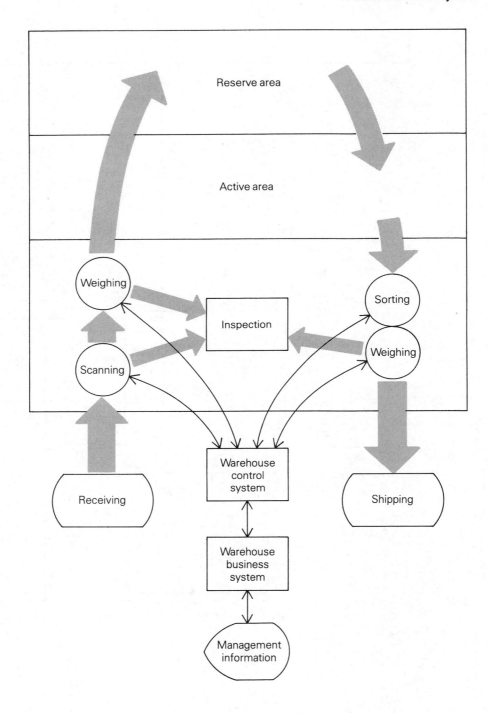

Figure 13-7   Graphical model of Levi distribution center.

Figure 13-7 is a conceptual representation of the warehouse processes. After the scanning process, a scale built into the conveyor system weighs each carton. Under the control of the WCS computer, actual weight is checked against the expected weight of the particular contents. If the variance is greater than half a pound, the carton is selected for inspection. Cartons are stored in a reserve area, which accounts for about nine-tenths of the floor space. Here cartons are held until they are needed in a smaller active area. Orders are filled from garments in the active area.

The conceptual system is called the warehouse business system (WBS), and it consists of an IBM 4341 computer linked by a datacom network to an IBM System/370 at a distribution center in Amarillo, Texas. At the end of each day, the WBS can tell Waco, Amarillo, and San Francisco management exactly what happened that day.

Warehouse workers communicate actual warehouse location to the WBS by radio. Each worker carries a portable bar code scanner attached to an FM radio transmitter. Once merchandise has been stored, its location is relayed to the WCS. and the data base is updated. When an order is to be shipped, the WBS instructs warehouse workers to select the appropriate merchandise. The selected cartons are placed on a conveyor belt where the WCS scans the bar code and directs the carton to the proper shipping area. Again, each carton is weighed, and any discrepancies are checked. Managers of the distribution center can query the data base at any time to review the stock level of any product and any warehouse location.

The primary purpose of the automated distribution center is to improve service to retail customers. Retailers can obtain merchandise much more quickly, improving the quality of their service to their customers. Levi management expects the computer to have almost as great an influence on sales success as the copper rivet—not quite, but almost.

Promotion Subsystem

Comprising both personal selling and advertising, promotion is an important ingredient in the marketing mix. But it has been extremely difficult to harness the power of computerized information systems in this area. Companies have had salesperson-reporting systems for years, but these systems provide only a record of past performance. Even less has been accomplished in advertising.

Advertising decisions

Advertising is more an art than a science. Creativity plays a big role in advertising, and marketers know little about why some ads encourage purchases whereas others do not. An ad may have a high entertainment value but be ineffective in stimulating sales. For years, marketers have tried to create *media planning models* to support generally unstructured advertising decisions. These models are typically developed by academicians and see only limited use by advertising agencies. The models select combinations of media for campaigns and develop a time schedule for their use. More success has been enjoyed with computer analyses that relate advertising and other variables (such as price) to sales. Programs in canned statistical packages ordinarily analyze this data. In some cases, relatively sophisticated econometric models are used. An *econometric model* is one combining statistical techniques with economic data.

Of all the areas of marketing—and perhaps of all the areas of business—advertising has enjoyed the least DSS success. This is another area of business that presents an opportunity to make your first million. If you have any idea how to harness the power of the computer to improve the quality of advertising decisions, you won't have any trouble finding listeners.

Personal selling decisions

Decisions relating to personal selling are more structured because they depend less on the whims of the buying public. Sales managers perform all of Henri Fayol's functions—they plan, organize, staff, direct, and control. The MIS provides the greatest support in planning and controlling.

Many firms use computer-based *planning* techniques to plan activities for the coming year. These plans, based on a sales forecast, provide a basis for determining recruiting and training needs. Personnel plans can schedule new hires and training programs throughout the year in order to meet annual sales objectives.

Controlling the sales force is made possible by a sales information feedback system. Sales representatives make daily or weekly reports of activity in their territories, and the data is transmitted to headquarters by mail, telephone, or datacom. This type of reporting is typical of the food industry, where sales reps cover territories comprising a large number of retail outlets. Procter & Gamble sales reps complete a form like the one in Figure 13-8 to record the results of each sales call. The form describes not only sales, but also information about the status of the account, such as ads, displays, and out-of-stocks. Sales call data is entered into the data base and used to prepare reports like the one in Chapter 11, Figure 11-10, which compares actual performance with quotas. Reports like these, combined with the ability to query the data base, enable sales managers to control their sales forces.

Sales support

Hopkins Manufacturing Company of Emporia, Kansas, employs 100 people to manufacture a line of automotive products including windshield ice scrapers, headlight aimers, and beverage container holders. The IBM System/38 computer processes data describing customer orders and prints sales reports that enable regional marketing managers to do a better job than was previously possible.

When the managers call on the company's 200 sales agents or call directly on buyers, they are armed with the sales information. At a glance, they can identify which products in what volumes were purchased by which customers through which agents over the two previous years. The managers use this information to identify opportunities and potential problems, both of which might have been missed without the computer output.

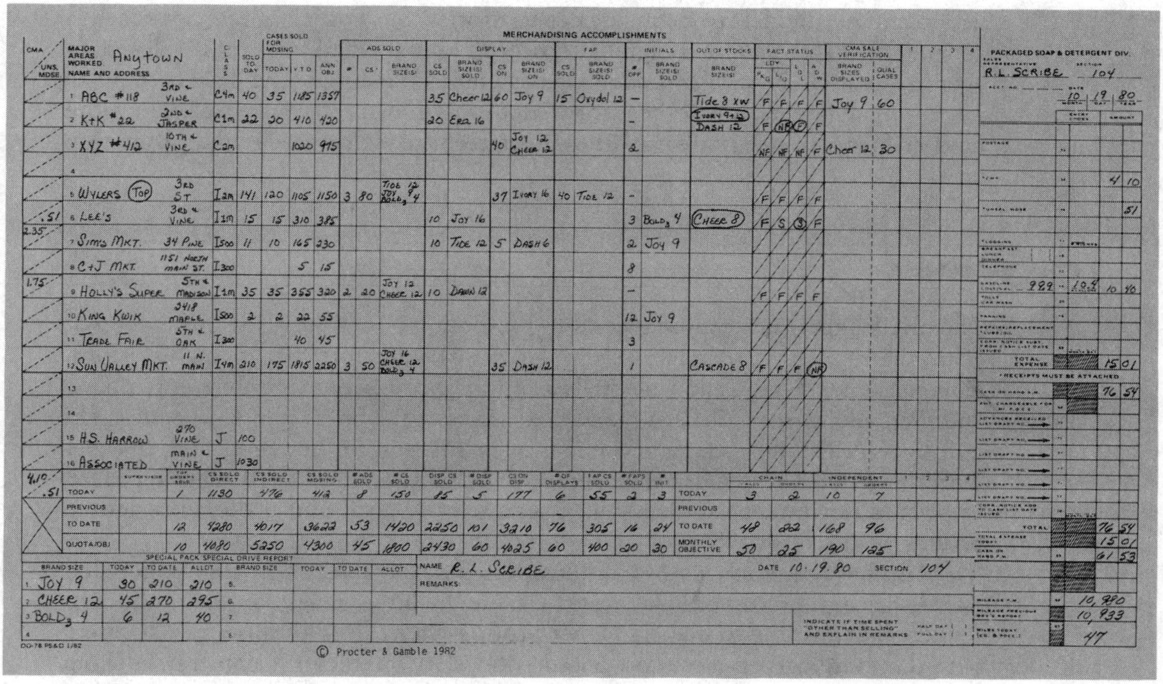

Figure 13-8 A Procter & Gamble sales call form.

An indirect promotional benefit comes when customers call to ask about an order. Previously, someone had to look through stacks of paper files to get the answer and then call back. Now the operator says, "Just a moment," and keys a query into a CRT. The information is available in seconds.

The computer helps Hopkins do a better job of meeting its customers' needs. This, in turn, helps Hopkins meet its objectives of growth and profitability.[7]

Realities of promotion support

The MIS provides a valuable service to marketing managers in the promotional area by supplying current, accurate, and complete information on sales campaigns, group sales performance, and individual accomplishments. These computer applications are easily justified by the amount of time saved for the manager and the sales representatives, who are relieved of monotonous, time-consuming record-keeping duties. Salespersons are not bookkeepers, and their time should be spent selling, not processing data.

This is not to say, however, that the MIS is used for making every promotional decision. Some decisions can be made very well with little direct support from the MIS. Sales territory assignment is a good example. We saw earlier how Yamaha

[7] "Finding the Right System," *Viewpoint,* September–October 1981, pp. 2–4.

uses computer models to define dealer territories. Such an elaborate approach is generally not justified for assigning territories to individual sales reps. Sales managers generally rely on their knowledge and understanding of the market to make territorial assignments. In other words, not everything is computerized. The more modest forms of decision support systems seem to work best in the promotion area.

Price Subsystem

The pricing area runs a close second to promotion in terms of DSS difficulty. For years the marketing manager received very little support for pricing decisions. Companies tended to follow a *cost-based pricing* policy of determining their costs and then adding some desired markup to arrive at the price. In the ski equipment industry, for example, the markup is usually 100 percent based on cost. In other words, a retailer buys a down jacket for $55 and sells it for $110. This approach to pricing is a rather cautious one; if you sell the item, you make your desired profit.

Another approach is less cautious. It is a *demand-based pricing* policy that establishes a price compatible with the value the buyer places on the product or service. It is possible to make a higher profit from a sale with this approach than with the more conservative cost-based policy. The marketer is constrained from setting the price too high, however, even though the product may be valued at that level by the customers. When the price gets too high and profits are large, competitors are attracted to the market. This leads to lower prices and profits.

The MIS can support the manager in both pricing policies. With the cost-based approach, the MIS can provide accurate cost-accounting data upon which to base a decision. With the demand-oriented approach, the MIS enables the manager to engage in "what-if" modeling to locate the price level that maximizes profit yet retards competitive activity.

Model of an Interactive Pricing Strategy

A mathematical model can simulate the effect of a firm's pricing strategy on profits. The model is dynamic—it simulates the effect of the price over a period of time, such as a year. It is nonoptimizing, telling the manager what the results of a strategy might be rather than selecting the best price. It can be deterministic or probabilistic, depending on the approach. And it is specific, incorporating characteristics unique to the user firm.

The model can be designed to consider both environmental and internal influences.

Environmental influences
- National economy
- Seasonal demand
- Competitors' pricing strategy
- Competitors' marketing budget

Internal influences
- Plant capacity
- Raw materials inventory
- Finished goods inventory
- Marketing budget

Data representing each of these influences is entered into the model. The data represents the scenario that, along with a particular price, will produce a likely output. The pricing model is designed for interactive use—it prompts the manager to input the scenario items and the price. The simulation is performed and the results are printed or displayed on the terminal in the form of an income statement.

Figure 13-9 shows the dialog between the model and the manager. The manager can obtain figures for the economic index and seasonal index from the financial information system, and for the plant capacity, raw-materials inventory, and finished-goods inventory from the manufacturing information system. The competitors' price and marketing budget figures can be provided by the marketing intelligence subsystem.

Figure 13-10 illustrates how these data items can be retrieved by data base query before using the model. Queries are represented by the arrows coming from the data base on the left. In addition, the manager enters an estimated market demand, a marketing budget, and a price to be simulated. This is a loosely coupled pricing model. A *loosely coupled* model is not interconnected to other models or other systems by computer-controlled data flows. In this approach the pricing model is a stand-alone DSS, and the manager provides the scenario and decision data.

Another approach is a *tightly coupled* model, pictured in Figure 13-11. Here the model does not ask the manager for data that can be obtained from other systems. The data is retrieved automatically. The pricing model can even interface both with a forecasting model that estimates demand and with a marketing budget model that provides next quarter's budget. The manager need only input one data item—the price.

```
ENTER THE FOLLOWING ENVIRONMENTAL DATA
   ECONOMIC INDEX--LAST QUARTER ? 1.10
   NEXT QUARTER ? 0.95
   SEASONAL INDEX--LAST QUARTER ? 0.75
   NEXT QUARTER ? 1.10
   AVERAGE COMPETITOR PRICE--LAST QUARTER ? 120
   NEXT QUARTER ? 115
   AVERAGE COMPETITOR MARKETING BUDGET--LAST QUARTER ? 500000
   NEXT QUARTER ? 750000

ENTER THE FOLLOWING FIRM DATA
   PLANT CAPACITY (IN FINISHED GOOD UNITS) ? 325000
   RAW MATERIALS AVAILABLE (IN F.G. UNITS) ? 1375000
   FINISHED GOODS INVENTORY (UNITS) ? 15000
   MARKETING BUDGET FOR NEXT QUARTER ? 375000

ENTER YOUR ESTIMATE OF NEXT QUARTER'S DEMAND (UNITS) ? 425000

ENTER NEXT QUARTER'S PRICE ? 125
```

Figure 13-9 Pricing-model dialog.

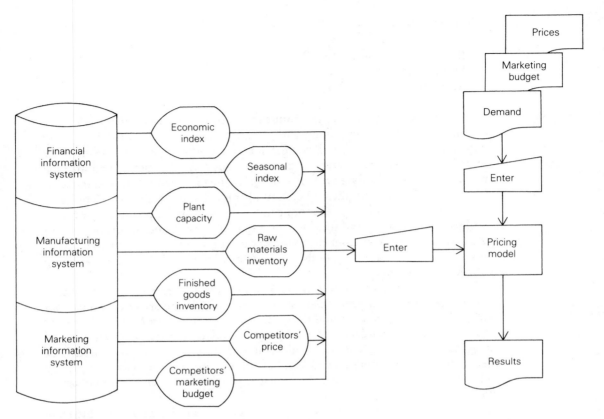

Figure 13-10   A loosely coupled pricing model.

The tightly coupled model certainly requires less work from the manager. But developing the model is more complex because it must interface with the other models. The loosely coupled approach is characteristic of initial DSS efforts in the 1970s. As firms get farther along with their DSS programs, models can be interconnected to permit the automatic exchange of data.

The model consists of a number of mathematical equations. For example, one equation multiplies price times sales volume to get sales revenue. Another equation multiplies plant value times a depreciation percentage to get depreciation expense. After all the calculations have been made, the results of the simulation are printed as an income statement, shown in Figure 13-12.

Since the model is nonoptimizing, the manager must try several pricing strategies. During this iterative process, the manager has only to enter the new price, and another income statement is printed. If desired, the manager can also manipulate the marketing budget to see what effect it, in conjunction with the price, will have on profit.

Figure 13-13 illustrates graphically how the iterative modeling process can lead to an optimal price. The manager starts with a price of $125 and gradually

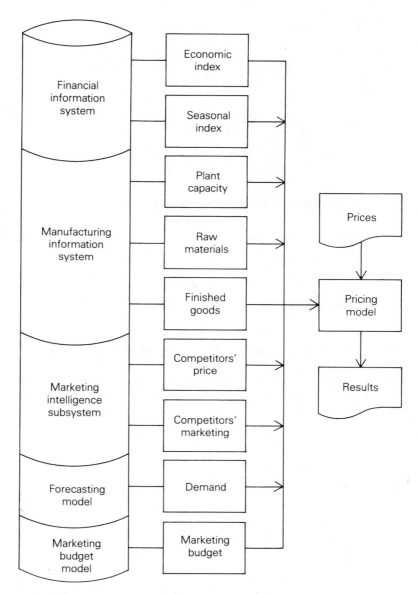

Figure 13-11 A tightly coupled pricing model.

raises it on the second, third, and fourth iteration. Each time, profit also increases. During iteration 5, the price of $145, when compared with the competitors' price, causes sales to be lost and profit to drop. The manager sees that a price of $145 is too high, so the price is gradually decreased during repetitions 6 through 9 until profits increase to the earlier level. A price somewhere between $141 and $142 is optimal. In iterations 10, 11, and 12, the model identifies $141.75 as the price yielding the most profit.

SALES REVENUE	$15,542,580
EXPENSES	
MARKETING	500,000
RESEARCH & DEVELOPMENT	500,000
ADMINISTRATION	275,000
MAINTENANCE	82,005
LABOR	675,725
MATERIALS	683,379
REDUCTION, FINISHED GOODS	180,000
DEPRECIATION	614,687
FINISHED GOODS CARRYING COSTS	0
RAW MATERIALS CARRYING COSTS	68,750
ORDERING COSTS	52,000
PLANT INVESTMENT EXPENSES	490
FINANCE CHARGES	0
SUNDRIES	260,900
PROFIT BEFORE INCOME TAX	11,649,643
INCOME TAX	5,588,453
PROFIT AFTER INCOME TAX	6,061,189

Figure 13-12 Pricing model output.

A word of caution should accompany the illustration in Figure 13-13. A model is only as good as the mathematics and the data. In this example, the manager has to estimate some values such as the competitors' expected price and marketing budget, along with the national economy. As the manager uses the

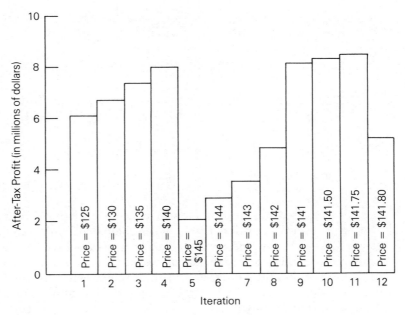

Figure 13-13 Iterative simulation of different prices.

model output, he or she must keep these estimates in mind. The model most likely isn't accurate enough to pinpoint a price of exactly $141.75. The manager can use the output, however, to establish a price *range* (say, from $138.00 to $145.00). The model gives a certain structure to the problem, but the manager must respond to the unstructured portion.

Integrated-Mix Subsystem

A good example of an integrated-mix model is BRANDAID, an online model consisting of submodels for advertising, promotion, price, personal selling, and retail distribution. BRANDAID simulates the activities of a manufacturing firm selling to customers through retailers in a competitive environment.[8] This environment, including the main elements and the influences that interconnect them, is shown in Figure 13-14.

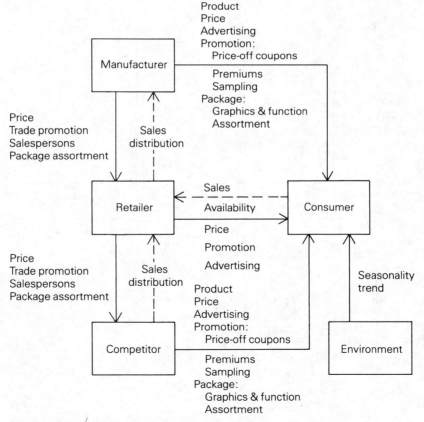

Figure 13-14 The market system modeled by BRANDAID.

[8] John D. C. Little, "Decision Support Systems for Marketing Managers," *Journal of Marketing* 43, (Summer 1979): 9–26. For a detailed description of BRANDAID, see John D. C. Little, "BRANDAID: A Marketing-Mix Model, Parts I and II," *Operations Research* 23 (July–August 1975): 628–73.

The basic approach of the model is to estimate the effect of various influences on the firm's sales. Four categories of influences are considered—those of the manufacturer, the retailer, the competition, and the general environment. Manufacturer-controlled variables include product characteristics, wholesale price, advertising, personal selling, packaging, and production capacity. Retailer-controlled variables include retail price, promotions (such as coupons and stamps), and advertising. Competitor-controlled variables are the same as for the retailer. Environmental variables include seasonality, trends, and other influences.

Each influence is modeled with one or more mathematical expressions. The results of the influences do not simply add together, but interact multiplicatively. For example, if packaging is expected to increase sales by 20% (from 1.00 to 1.20) and retailer promotion is expected to increase sales by 20% (from 1.00 to 1.20), the combined influence will be 44% (1.20 × 1.20 = 1.44) rather than 40% (.20 + .20 = .40). This feature recognizes the synergism among ingredients in the marketing mix.

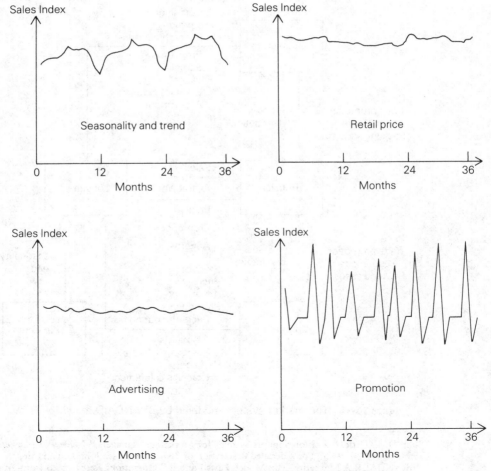

Figure 13-15 Influences of four variables considered separately.

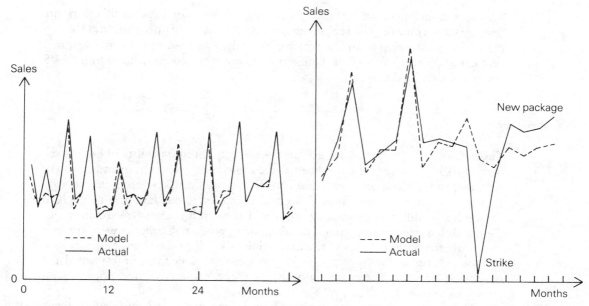

Figure 13-16 Influences of four variables, taken together.

Figure 13-17 A model cannot cope with unexpected events.

Figures 13-15 and 13-16 illustrate this interaction. Figure 13-15 shows the behavior over time of four of the influencing variables. If only one of these variables were present, sales would fluctuate as shown. The combined influences can be seen in Figure 13-16. The graph shows sales projected by the model along with actual sales.

As you can see, BRANDAID does a good job of projecting sales based on mix strategy. The model is only able to consider built-in factors, however. If some unexpected event occurs, the model cannot handle it. This is what happened when a company using BRANDAID was hit by a strike, followed by an unexpectedly good sales response from a change in packaging. The effect of these influences is pictured in Figure 13-17.

BRANDAID was initially intended for use in annual planning, to be put on the shelf during the interim. What happened, however, was that the firm's managers began to use the model during the year for strategy decisions. In one case, a brand manager heard a rumor that his advertising budget was going to be cut in half. By 5 o'clock he had a complete analysis of what the effect on sales and profits would be if the cut went into effect. In other cases, managers have used the model to simulate the effect of certain anticipated competitive actions.

An integrated-mix model such as BRANDAID can be a powerful tool, not only for marketing managers but for others as well. But such a tool is not created overnight. Work on BRANDAID started in 1969 and efforts to improve it have continued. A firm implementing BRANDAID can anticipate a start-up period of two or more years.

This modeling effort demands the managers' time. For a successful effort, the firm needs to commit (1) a senior executive to oversee the entire project, (2) a top marketing manager, (3) an information specialist, and (4) general management support at the top level. All of these resources are required in addition to the MIS resources identified earlier.

Summary

The marketing information system has the important responsibility of linking the firm to its key environmental element—the customers—whom it intends to serve with its products and services. Input subsystems provide data describing the customers and also the competition. This data is entered in the data base of the firm for use by the different processing routines that constitute the software library of the marketing information system. In this chapter, processing routines were grouped according to the ingredients of the marketing mix. All of the routines, programs, or models helping the manager make product-related decisions are part of the product subsystem. The composition of the place, promotion, and price subsystems is determined in the same way.

There are no set rules concerning which managers will use which subsystems. The policy is determined by the unique interests and capabilities of the personalities involved. But some general pairings can be made between subsystems and likely users. This is done in Table 13-2. Note that the chief executive is included,

Table 13-2 Users of the Marketing Information System

User	Subsystem				
	Product	Place	Promotion	Price	Integrated mix
Chief executive officer	X	X	X	X	X
Vice-president of marketing	X	X	X	X	X
Brand manager	X	X	X	X	X
Sales manager			X	X	
Advertising manager			X	X	
Manager of marketing research	X	X	X	X	X
Manager of product planning	X				
Manager of physical distribution		X			
Other managers	X	X	X	X	X

and that he or she uses all subsystems. As stated earlier, the subsystem output used at this level is of a highly summarized form. The chief executive officer, the vice-president of marketing, and the brand manager have the greatest interest in the integrated-mix subsystem.

Of course, other functional managers could use output from the marketing information system as well. For example, an engineering manager could use the new-product evaluation model, and a financial officer could use the pricing model.

The marketing information system will play an increasingly important role in the information system of the firm. Since problems relating to customers are essentially probabilistic, they take much time to solve. As the firm becomes better attuned to the task of meeting the needs of the customer, more resources will be directed to understanding this critical element in the environment. This focus will demand greater active participation by marketing management, both line and staff, in the design and implementation of marketing information systems. In addition to understanding the operation of their firm as a system, managers must also understand the environmental influences on this system. They also must understand the task of management and know how modern-day techniques and devices can be applied.

Much has been accomplished in marketing information systems during the past decade. Many marketing managers have shown great interest in using the computer as a decision support system. The challenge of the 1980s will be to make such systems available on a broader scale, especially to marketing managers in small firms using mini and micro systems.

Key Terms

industrial espionage	feedforward information
primary data, secondary data	behavioral demographics
survey	media planning model
in-depth interview	econometric model
observation	cost-based pricing
controlled experiment	demand-based pricing
light pen	loosely coupled model
product life cycle	tightly coupled model

Key Concepts

The informality of marketing intelligence	How computers can be a part of both the physical and the conceptual warehouse systems
The nonrepetitive nature of marketing research	The subjective nature of promotional decision making
How information support can span the product life cycle	

The iterative use of a nonoptimizing
model

The coupling of models to facilitate
data exchange

The high degree of accuracy with
which a model can handle the
variables incorporated into it

Questions

1. Which environmental element is the responsibility of the marketing intelligence subsystem? The marketing research subsystem?

2. Is there a difference between industrial espionage and marketing intelligence? If so, explain.

3. List five things a firm can do to keep informed of competitive activities.

4. Distinguish between primary and secondary data.

5. What are the four basic means of gathering data? Which has been computerized? In what way?

6. Is a marketing research system the same as a marketing information system? Explain your answer.

7. What are the three time periods in the product life cycle where information support is provided?

8. What type of firm would use the quantitative new-product evaluation model? What should a manager keep in mind when using the model?

9. What is feedforward information?

10. Which marketing area resembles manufacturing in that it involves easily quantifiable variables?

11. Does Levi Strauss use the computer as part of its physical warehouse system or its conceptual system? Explain.

12. How is data entered into the Levi Warehouse Control System (WCS)?

13. As the sales manager carries out Fayol's management functions, which receive the most support from the MIS?

14. Who uses the sales support system at Hopkins Manufacturing Company?

15. Are salesperson call report forms (such as the one used by Procter & Gamble) an example of marketing intelligence, marketing research, or neither?

16. What are the two basic approaches to pricing? Which receives support from the MIS? How?

17. How is data exchanged between loosely coupled models? Between tightly coupled models?

18. Why did profit fall when the manager raised the price from $140 to $145 in Figure 13-13?

19. Why does profit increase when price decreases from $145 to $141?

20. What are the four categories of influences on consumer behavior in the BRANDAID model?

CASE PROBLEM: National Foods, Inc.

National Foods is one of the leading manufacturers and distributors of food products, competing directly with firms like General Mills, General Foods, and Nestlé. A large-scale computer is installed at headquarters in Minneapolis, with distributed processing systems at plant and distribution centers across the country. Each of the firm's 625 sales representatives is equipped with a portable keyboard terminal that can be attached to an ordinary push-button telephone. At the end of each day, the sales reps transmit sales call data to headquarters using the incoming WATS. The data includes sales figures (products and units) plus reports ‚pecial promotions such as cooperative ads, coupons, contests, and the like. The computer operation at National is managed by Dan Kennerly, vice-president of information systems.

It's the Friday afternoon before Memorial Day weekend, and Dan is just about to leave the office when the phone rings. Fred Ennen, vice-president of marketing, is on the line. Dan cradles the telephone between his shoulder and ear while tossing some papers into his briefcase.

Fred congratulates Dan on the new sales tracking system that has just been installed. "It's absolutely fantastic," Fred says. "We're able to track the sales volume of any of our products on a daily basis throughout the life cycle. The reps are following the procedure and reporting their data daily. We can even see the effect of our advertising and promotional campaigns—something we've never been able to do before."

This is all sweet music to Dan's ears, but he is anxious to get on the road. He interrupts, saying, "Listen Fred, I'm on my way out the door the pick up Alice so that we can head for the lake. If this can wait until Tuesday, I'd rather discuss it then."

Dan thinks Fred will take the hint and is surprised to hear, "I understand, Dan, but just let me tell you what's on my mind. It'll only take a minute, and I'd like you to think about it over the weekend. Then we can talk more on Tuesday.

"I have a great idea. Why don't we install a sales tracking system that will track competitive sales? We could limit it to only selected items at first. Maybe we could start off with a single line, like dog food, where the number of competing brands is small. I'd like to know about the competition's plans to put a new brand on the market before it actually hits. Then I'd like to track the sales during the life cycle. When we see the volume dropping off, we can anticipate a new product to take its place and increase our intelligence activity. Doesn't that sound like a good idea? Now, I'd like you to give me your suggestions about the data inputs we'll need and where they can come from. Why don't you think it over, and we can get together first thing Tuesday morning."

Dan's feelings are a mixture of surprise, flattery, and dejection. He manages to say, "Sure, Fred. That sounds like a good idea. I'll think it over." With that, he hangs up the phone, shuts his briefcase, puts it in the closet, and leaves the office.

Questions

1. Is Fred's idea of a competitive tracking system feasible?
2. How could National learn of competitive products before they are introduced?
3. How could they track competitive product sales?
4. Could a system be designed using secondary data only?
5. Would the National sales reps be involved in any way?
6. Which subsystems of the marketing information system would be involved in the new system?

Chapter 14

Manufacturing Information Systems

Learning Objectives

After studying this chapter, you should:

- Understand how the MIS can be used to make plant location and layout decisions
- Appreciate the essentially informal nature of the flow of labor information within the firm
- Know how a formal procedure for gathering vendor information contributes to meeting manufacturing schedules and achieving desired levels of quality
- Recognize that the industrial engineer (IE) is concerned with both physical and conceptual manufacturing systems
- Appreciate the contribution that a data collection network can make to gathering attendance and job data on a realtime basis
- Understand the basic mechanics of inventory management
- Be familiar with the process of vendor rating
- Understand the concept of material requirements planning (MRP)
- Appreciate the potential for providing the manufacturing manager with specific and up-to-date information on production costs

Overview

In the introduction to the previous chapter, we commented that marketing was the logical function to study first, since its focus on the customer is the starting point for everything a firm does. Now that we have taken the first step, it is time for the second. The most logical area is manufacturing. After strategic-level management decides to produce the products forecasted for sale by marketing, it is the responsibility of manufacturing to accomplish that production. The production process is our topic in this chapter. We will look at the physical manufacturing system and identify the basic responsibilities of manufacturing management. We will then describe the subsystems that compose the manufacturing information system—the conceptual information system that enables manufacturing management to manage the physical manufacturing system.

The Physical System

The general systems model of the firm (see Chapter 3) describes a manufacturing organization in a general way. At the bottom of the model is the physical system. The physical system is composed of system inputs received from the environment, transformation processes, and systems outputs directed to the environment. Manufacturing management is responsible for (1) constructing this physical system and (2) using the system to produce the firm's products. Our discussion here will focus on products, not services. We have recognized earlier, however, that a broad definition of manufacturing encompasses services as well.

Constructing the physical system

The decision to construct a physical manufacturing system such as a plant is made at the strategic level because the decision has long-term effects and represents a giant investment. Once the first decision is made, the firm must decide where to locate the plant, and this involves tactical-level management as well. First, management must select a particular region of the United States or another country. Some of the factors influencing the selection of a *region* include the concentration of customers, availability of a labor supply, land costs, availability of raw materials, climate, and strength of unionization.

Once the region has been selected, management must decide on a particular *city*. This decision considers customer concentration, labor supply, land, taxes, transportation, community services (police, fire, and so on), community attitudes, cultural resources, and management preferences.

Finally, management must choose a particular *area* of the selected city. Factors influencing this decision include customer concentration, land costs, transportation, utilities, and zoning restrictions.

These are semistructured decisions. Some factors, such as land costs, taxes, and transportation facilities, can be measured quantitatively. Other factors, such as community attitudes, and cultural resources, are difficult to measure.

The MIS can help the manufacturing manager make any of the location decisions. A model can consider both quantitative and subjective factors, or quantitative factors only. Linear programming (LP) is frequently used to consider quantitative factors to identify the best location.

A plant location model

Assume that a firm has three plants, one in Denver, one in St. Louis, and one in Pittsburgh. These plants manufacture ice chests that are shipped to distribution

Unit Shipping Charges

Plant	Distribution Center			
	Atlanta	Seattle	Los Angeles	New York
Pittsburgh	1.10	1.35	1.50	0.75
St. Louis	1.35	2.05	1.60	1.10
Denver	1.50	1.75	1.55	1.80

Figure 14-1   A production and distribution network.

centers in Los Angeles, Seattle, Atlanta, and New York. Figure 14-1 shows the site locations and indicates the unit shipping charges from each plant to each distribution center.

The firm attempts to minimize shipping costs by shipping from the plant closest to each distribution center. This is not always possible because the plants have different capacities and the distribution centers serve market areas with different demand levels.

Plant capacities are:

$$
\begin{array}{ll}
\text{Pittsburgh} & \text{10,000 units} \\
\text{St. Louis} & \text{15,000 units} \\
\text{Denver} & \text{23,000 units}
\end{array}
$$

Distribution center demand levels are:

$$
\begin{array}{ll}
\text{Atlanta} & \text{12,500 units} \\
\text{Seattle} & \text{10,000 units} \\
\text{Los Angeles} & \text{8,000 units} \\
\text{New York} & \text{17,500 units}
\end{array}
$$

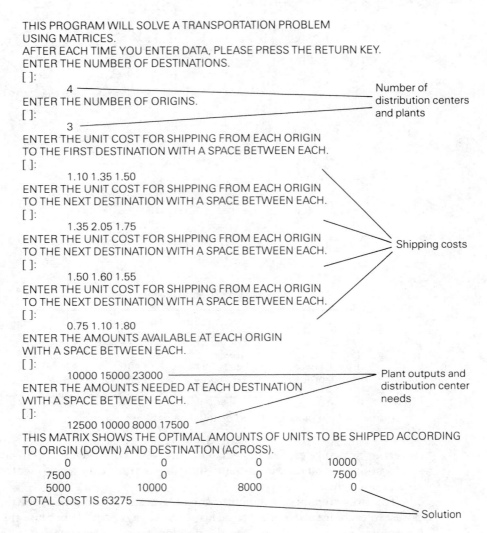

THIS PROGRAM WILL SOLVE A TRANSPORTATION PROBLEM
USING MATRICES.
AFTER EACH TIME YOU ENTER DATA, PLEASE PRESS THE RETURN KEY.
ENTER THE NUMBER OF DESTINATIONS.
[ ]:
    4 ——————————————————————————————— Number of
ENTER THE NUMBER OF ORIGINS.   distribution centers
[ ]:   and plants
    3 ———
ENTER THE UNIT COST FOR SHIPPING FROM EACH ORIGIN
TO THE FIRST DESTINATION WITH A SPACE BETWEEN EACH.
[ ]:
    1.10 1.35 1.50
ENTER THE UNIT COST FOR SHIPPING FROM EACH ORIGIN
TO THE NEXT DESTINATION WITH A SPACE BETWEEN EACH.
[ ]:
    1.35 2.05 1.75
ENTER THE UNIT COST FOR SHIPPING FROM EACH ORIGIN
TO THE NEXT DESTINATION WITH A SPACE BETWEEN EACH.   Shipping costs
[ ]:
    1.50 1.60 1.55
ENTER THE UNIT COST FOR SHIPPING FROM EACH ORIGIN
TO THE NEXT DESTINATION WITH A SPACE BETWEEN EACH.
[ ]:
    0.75 1.10 1.80
ENTER THE AMOUNTS AVAILABLE AT EACH ORIGIN
WITH A SPACE BETWEEN EACH.
[ ]:
    10000 15000 23000 ——————————————————————— Plant outputs and
ENTER THE AMOUNTS NEEDED AT EACH DESTINATION   distribution center
WITH A SPACE BETWEEN EACH.   needs
[ ]:
    12500 10000 8000 17500
THIS MATRIX SHOWS THE OPTIMAL AMOUNTS OF UNITS TO BE SHIPPED ACCORDING
TO ORIGIN (DOWN) AND DESTINATION (ACROSS).

0	0	0	10000
7500	0	0	7500
5000	10000	8000	0

TOTAL COST IS 63275 ————————————————————————————

                                                   Solution

Figure 14-2 Model dialog—three plants.

The company uses an LP model to allocate plant output according to distribution center demand. Using an interactive model, the shipping costs, capacities, and demands are entered from the terminal. The model dialog and entered data appear in Figure 14-2. The model asks for data by typing ENTER. . . . The data entered appears on the line below and to the right of the []: symbol. This symbol is the *cursor* that tells the user to enter the requested data. The model uses the term *origin* for the plants and the term *destination* for the distribution centers.

At the bottom of the printout is a matrix showing the number of units to be shipped from each plant to each distribution center to produce the minimum cost. Just below the matrix is the total cost amount—$63,275.

Table 14-1 Optimal Shipping Allocations—Three Plants

	Distribution Centers			
Plant	Atlanta	Seattle	Los Angeles	New York
Pittsburgh	0	0	0	10,000
St. Louis	7500	0	0	7,500
Denver	5000	10,000	8000	0

The solution matrix is reproduced in Table 14-1 showing the plant and distribution center names. Pittsburgh ships all of its output to New York. St. Louis ships 7500 units to Atlanta and 7500 units to New York. Denver ships 5000 units to Atlanta, 10,000 units to Seattle, and 8000 units to Los Angeles.

The model printout in Figure 14-2 does not show how the cost figures are computed; that detail appears in Table 14-2.

The firm is considering the construction of a new plant in the southeast United States as part of a long-range plan to expand that market area. Top management first decides on Florida and then picks Orlando as a possible city. The LP model is executed a second time, entering new shipping costs from the Orlando site, and the capacity of the Orlando plant (4000 units are to be transferred from Pitts-

Table 14-2 Shipping-Cost Computations—Three Plants

	Distribution Centers			
Plant	Atlanta	Seattle	Los Angeles	New York
Pittsburgh				.075 × $10,000 = $7500
St. Louis	1.35 × $7500 = $10,125			1.10 × $7500 = $8250
Denver	1.50 × $5000 = $7500	1.75 × $10,000 = $17,500	1.55 × $8000 = $12,400	

THIS PROGRAM WILL SOLVE A TRANSPORTATION PROBLEM
USING MATRICES.
AFTER EACH TIME YOU ENTER DATA, PLEASE PRESS THE RETURN KEY.
ENTER THE NUMBER OF DESTINATIONS.
[ ]:
     4
ENTER THE NUMBER OF ORIGINS.
[ ]:
     4
ENTER THE UNIT COST FOR SHIPPING FROM EACH ORIGIN
TO THE FIRST DESTINATION WITH A SPACE BETWEEN EACH.
[ ]:
     1.10 1.35 1.50 0.75
ENTER THE UNIT COST FOR SHIPPING FROM EACH ORIGIN
TO THE NEXT DESTINATION WITH A SPACE BETWEEN EACH.
[ ]:
     1.35 2.05 1.75 2.00
ENTER THE UNIT COST FOR SHIPPING FROM EACH ORIGIN
TO THE NEXT DESTINATION WITH A SPACE BETWEEN EACH.
[ ]:
     1.50 1.60 1.55 1.40
ENTER THE UNIT COST FOR SHIPPING FROM EACH ORIGIN
TO THE NEXT DESTINATION WITH A SPACE BETWEEN EACH.
[ ]:
     0.75 1.10 1.80 1.15
ENTER THE AMOUNTS AVAILABLE AT EACH ORIGIN
WITH A SPACE BETWEEN EACH.
[ ]:
     6000 15000 23000 4000
ENTER THE AMOUNTS NEEDED AT EACH DESTINATION
WITH A SPACE BETWEEN EACH.
[ ]:
     12500 10000 8000 17500
THIS MATRIX SHOWS THE OPTIMAL AMOUNTS OF UNITS TO BE SHIPPED ACCORDING
TO ORIGIN (DOWN) AND DESTINATION (ACROSS).

0	0	0	6000
3500	0	0	11500
5000	10000	8000	0
4000	0	0	0

TOTAL COST IS 62275

Figure 14-3 Model dialog—four plants.

burgh). The number of destinations and their demand levels remain the same. Figure 14-3 illustrates the model dialog; Table 14-3 details the computations.

The addition of the Orlando plant will not reduce shipping costs very much— only by $1000 (to $62,275). That savings alone would not sufficiently justify the plant; but perhaps other, subjective, factors would. The better customer service, long-range market expansion, and so forth must also be considered.

The managers can consider other options. They can simulate other Florida locations instead of Orlando, or they can consider another area, such as the midwest. They can even consider adding a new distribution center—perhaps in Florida. These are all possibilities, and the LP model can quickly provide cost information. In this fashion, the MIS helps management make the long-range decision of plant location.

Table 14-3 Shipping-Cost Computations—Four Plants

	Distribution Centers			
Plant	Atlanta	Seattle	Los Angeles	New York
Pittsburgh				0.75 × $6000 = $4500
St. Louis	1.35 × $3500 = $4725			1.10 × $11,500 = $12,650
Denver	1.50 × $5000 = $7500	1.75 × $10,000 = $17,500	1.55 × $8000 = $12,400	
Orlando	0.75 × $4000 = $3000			

General layout of the plant

After the plant site has been selected by top- and middle-level management, the next step is to determine the details of the plant layout. Primary attention is given to efficiency of operations—moving the materials the shortest possible distance to keep costs down and eliminate bottlenecks and delays. Lower-level management becomes involved in the plant layout decision, since they will be using the arrangement on a day-to-day basis.

A plant typically includes the areas shown in Figure 14-4. The portion corresponding to the input element in the general systems model consists of a *receiving* area, a *receiving inspection* area, and a *raw-materials storeroom*. The *shop floor* area corresponds to the transformation element in the general model. The shop floor consists of several work stations—areas where different types of processes are performed. The area corresponding to the output element in the general model includes a *final inspection* area, a *finished-goods storeroom*, and a *shipping* area.

The key to a profitable production operation is timing. Vendors' raw materials should arrive at the plant precisely when they are needed. Too early means unnecessary inventory-carrying costs. Too late means missed production schedules. Materials also should arrive at the work stations precisely when they are needed, and the finished goods should be shipped to the customer immediately after passing final inspection. The MIS can play a vital role in achieving this precise timing.

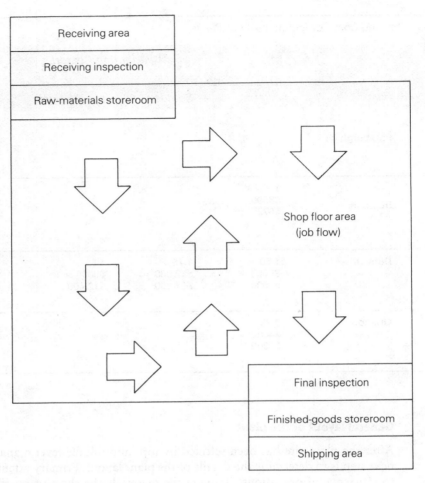

Figure 14-4 General plant layout.

A plant layout model

Figure 14-5 illustrates how several different layouts can be considered. All three consist of the same work stations; only the arrangements differ.

There are about 30 or 40 mathematical models available to help manufacturing management decide on a plant layout.[1] The models fall into two categories—construction heuristics and improvement heuristics. A *construction heuristics* model starts with an open floor space and constructs a single floor layout

---

[1] For more information on plant layout models, see James M. Moore, "Computer Methods in Facilities Layout," *IE* 12 (September 1980): 82 ff; Jarrold M. Seehof and Wayne O. Evans, "Automated Layout Design Programs," *Journal of Industrial Engineering* 18 (December 1967): 690–95; Robert S. Lee and James M. Moore, "CORELAP—Computerized Relationship Layout Planning," *Journal of Industrial Engineering* 18 (March 1967): 195–200; and Elwood S. Buffa and Thomas E. Vollmann, "Allocating Facilities with CRAFT," *Harvard Business Review* 42 (March–April 1964): 136–50.

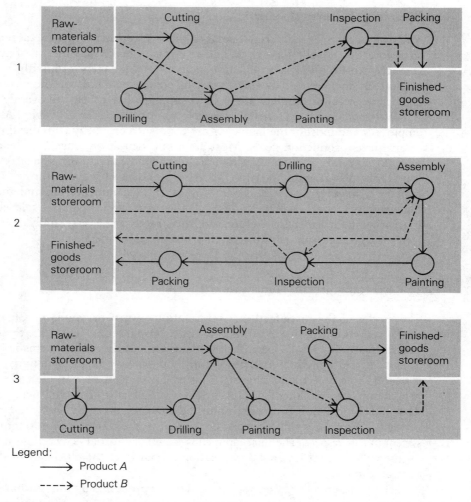

Legend:

⟶ Product A

----➔ Product B

Figure 14-5 Evaluation of alternate plant layouts.

logically, using input data, a relationship chart, and space allocations. The first model of this type was CORELAP (COmputerized RElationship LAyout Planning), which is still in use.

An *improvement heuristics* model requires inputting a feasible layout which it then improves by swapping areas and scoring the revised layouts until no further improvements can be made. The first of these models was CRAFT (Computerized Relative Allocation of Facilities Technique), and it is still one of the most popular.

The output from these models must be checked and reviewed before a decision is made to implement a layout. The logic of the layout must be verified, and some manual fine tuning can almost always achieve additional efficiencies. Although the plant layout problem is one of the most structured in business, it is extremely difficult to solve with a mathematical model.

Operating the physical system

The task of the manufacturing manager (plant superintendent, general manager, shop foreperson, shift supervisor, and so on) is to make the best use of available resources to accomplish production objectives. Managers ordinarily are constrained by their resources—personnel, machines, material, and money. At any given time, certain resources are in short supply, while others are overabundant.

The manufacturing function is largely an operational-level activity. All of the employees and most of the managers are concerned primarily with meeting operational-level production goals. Most attention focuses on what is to be accomplished today, this week, and this month. Very few manufacturing managers address long-range planning and control. The vice-president of manufacturing is a strategic-level manager, and the general manager of manufacturing and the plant manager are tactical-level managers. All others are on the operational level. Manufacturing management, therefore, can be characterized as essentially operational level, with the most highly structured problems in business.

The Model of the Manufacturing Information System

The model of the manufacturing information system presented in Chapter 12 contains the same basic structure as the one for marketing. There are three input subsystems used mainly for gathering data. One of these subsystems is internal accounting. Although internal accounting is typically a financial activity, part of it relates directly to manufacturing. This part is concerned with the collection of production data. Another input subsystem is manufacturing intelligence; it obtains data and information from environmental elements involved with the manufacturing function. This subsystem is very similar to the marketing information subsystem in this respect. The final input subsystem is industrial engineering; it focuses on the collection of internal data relating primarily to the efficiency of the production process.

Data gathered by these input subsystems is processed by four output subsystems to prepare information for management use. Most of the information is used by manufacturing managers, but the chief executive officer and other functional managers can use the output when appropriate. The four output subsystems relate to four basic dimensions, or characteristics, of the production process: quality, cost, inventory control, and the process itself. Figure 14-6 shows the manufacturing information system model.

The remainder of this chapter will describe each of the manufacturing-oriented information subsystems.

Manufacturing Intelligence Subsystem

The two environmental elements of particular importance to the manufacturing function are labor and vendors. All production organizations make some use of personnel. Even in highly automated processes, people are needed to initialize,

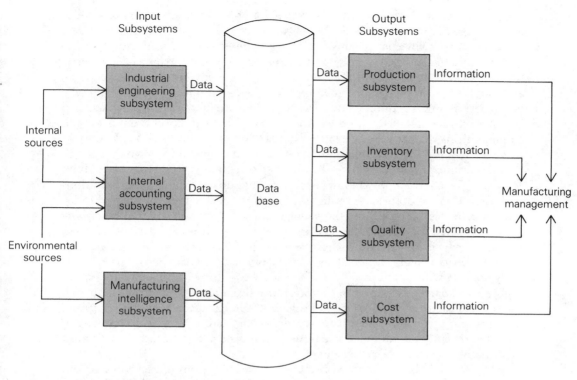

Figure 14-6 Model of a manufacturing information system.

maintain, and monitor the automated machinery. And all organizations use input material resources acquired from vendors or suppliers. The manufacturing manager should remain aware of the status of these personnel and material sources so that they flow through the firm as needed.

Labor information

The labor element in the environment can be regarded as the pool of potential employees available to the firm. The size of this pool fluctuates with the economy, the geographic region, and the category of employee. At the present time, for example, the pool available to a computer software firm in the Santa Clara Valley south of San Francisco is quite small. Conversely, the pool available to General Motors in Detroit is quite large.

Since the personnel resource is the most important to the manufacturing function, the manufacturing manager should keep abreast of the environmental supply of labor. The situation is analogous to that of a purchasing agent establishing multiple sources of supply for production materials. Just as the materials must keep flowing and be available when needed, so a good supply of employees should be available for employment when personnel openings exist.

Identifying the labor pool and cultivating it to be available when needed is usually not the responsibility of the manufacturing manager. Rather, it falls on the firm's personnel department to advertise for applicants, screen and test them, and arrange for interviews with the managers of the areas where the openings exist. The personnel department is therefore a buffer between manufacturing management and the labor element in the environment. It is the personnel department that must cultivate sources of the labor resource—employment agencies, colleges and universities, trade schools, government agencies, and the local community.

There is one condition, however, that causes manufacturing managers to become actively involved with the labor element. That condition is unionization. In many firms the personnel resource is organized into labor unions. A contract or agreement is established between the firm and those employees who belong to the union. Some firms must deal with more than one union, with a separate contract for each. The contract provides the basic information describing the expectations and obligations of both the firm and the union members. This contractual information provides the guidelines the manager must follow. Information describing the actual performance of both the firm and the union members must be gathered so that management can ensure that the terms of the contract are being met. This information is usually obtained by supervisory-level managers as part of their daily contact with union members. The supervisors forward this information to higher-level managers by personal contact or written report. The firm's industrial relations department can play a vital role in this information flow, initiating and expediting it throughout the manufacturing organizaton. Very seldom does this information enter the computerized information system, but the information must be available for effective management.

Figure 14-7 shows the flow of labor information from the several environmental elements to the personnel department. The two-way formal flow between the manufacturing management and the personnel department consists of written requests for personnel and data sheets on applicants. A formal flow can also exist from manufacturing management to upper-level corporate management. This flow consists of reports detailing the degree to which the contractual terms are being followed.

Vendor information

Substantially more data and information are gathered about the firm's material sources than about its personnel. For one reason, firms have many material suppliers, or vendors. And transactions involving those vendors occur each day. Another reason for the greater volume of input is that several of the firm's employees gather and use vendor data and information. These employees are called *buyers,* and they work in the purchasing department. Most purchasing departments have several buyers, and they usually specialize in contacts with certain classes of vendors. For example, one buyer will specialize in procuring electronic components, and he or she will be well informed about the electronics suppliers. Another buyer will specialize in adhesives, another in maintenance supplies, and so on.

The selection of reliable vendors is an important step toward production quality and efficiency. Ordered raw materials must arrive on schedule, at the expected quality level. One approach to building reliable vendor relationships is to screen possible vendors before making a purchase commitment. This screening can be a two-step process. First, a firm asks a prospective vendor to complete a

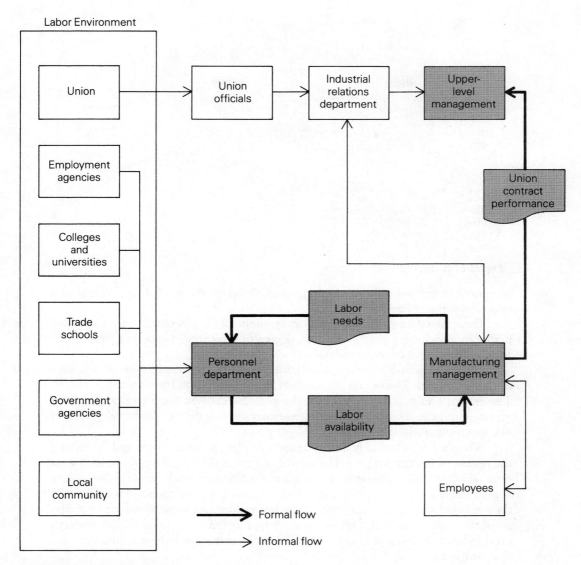

Figure 14-7 Flow of labor information.

questionnaire inquiring about production resources, the importance placed on quality control, and so on. Data from these forms is stored in the data base and reviewed and updated periodically.[2]

The second step involves an in-depth financial analysis of the vendor. For large vendors, data can be obtained from annual reports or from Securities and Exchange Commission reports. For small vendors, managers must request information directly from the organizations. An analysis of balance sheet and income

---

[2]For a good description of vendor data forms, see "Qualify Your Sources to Be Assured of Quality," *Purchasing,* 18 December 1980, pp. 45 ff.

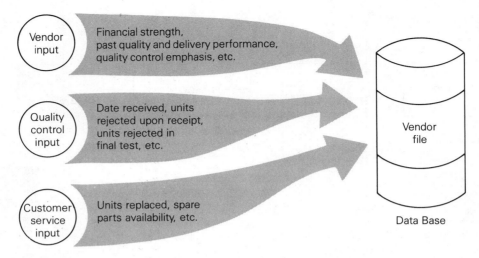

Figure 14-8 Input to vendor records.

statement items will indicate the long-term ability of the vendor to perform as a reliable source of supply.[3]

These two data-gathering steps can be augmented by personal visits to vendor plants by purchasing personnel. This degree of screening is especially important for the vendors of critical materials.

Once a vendor has been selected, buyers should remain current on the vendor's capabilities. The buyers get much of their information from the vendor itself. The vendor's sales representatives make personal calls on the buyers and furnish manuals and catalogs. Also, buyers frequently contact the vendor by telephone to ask specific questions.

When a firm obtains materials from a vendor, a record is created describing the results of the transaction. The record is kept in the data base along with data obtained from the vendor survey forms and the financial analyses. Additional data is provided by quality control inspections during the production process and by the customer service department. A complete vendor record will provide an analysis of the organization and the performance of its materials from receipt through production to end-product use. Figure 14-8 illustrates these three sources of vendor information.

Industrial Engineering Subsystem

Modern industrial engineering is a combination of basic engineering knowledge and quantified management techniques integrated with applied mathematics and statistics. Industrial engineers (IEs) are prepared by college programs to plan, control, design, and manage complex industrial organizations. In performing their work, IEs use the computer as a tool for analyzing and designing industrial systems. They also are concerned with the human element in industrial systems—the

---

[3] For more details on the financial analysis of vendors, see Rebecca Lipman, "Know Your Suppliers' Financial Profile," *Purchasing*, 28 May 1981, pp. 69 ff.

behavior of people working together in organizations and interacting with mechanized and computerized processes.

Industrial engineering can be traced back to Frederick W. Taylor and his scientific management. But industrial engineering has come a long way since those early days. The modern IE is not just an "efficiency expert" with stopwatch and clipboard, shaving seconds off production processes. The IE is a systems analyst—a specialist in the design and operation of physical systems who is knowledgeable in conceptual systems as well. Much of the work of the IE concerns conceptual systems, such as quantitatively determined order quantities and reorder points in inventory systems. It is difficult to distinguish between the work of the IE in the manufacturing area and the work of the systems analyst. Both work with conceptual systems, but the IE also works with physical systems.

IEs provide support to manufacturing managers in making the plant location and layout decisions described earlier. The IEs are skilled in the use of modeling techniques such as linear programming. IEs also spend a great deal of time assisting manufacturing management in the establishment of production standards. These *standards of performance* (traceable to Taylor) enable management to control the production process. Actual performance is compared with the standards. As we have seen, the computer can play an important role in this comparison by gathering the data describing actual performance, making the comparison with the standards, and reporting discrepancies to management—*management by exception*. The data describing actual performance comes from the third input subsystem—internal accounting.

Internal Accounting Subsystem

Internal accounting is usually identified with the financial function. But part of internal accounting relates directly to the manufacturing function. This part is the data collection network—the main source of input data describing production activities.

Data collection terminals were described in Chapter 9. These terminals accept input from punched cards, plastic badges, or keyboard entry and transmit the data to a computer. This flexible data-gathering ability enables the terminals to serve as "sensors" throughout the manufacturing area (Figure 14-9). Each time an action is initiated or completed, an entry can be made in a nearby terminal. The central computer uses this input to update the data base so that it reflects the current nature of the physical system. This is *job reporting*.

Figure 14-9 shows twelve data collection terminals located throughout a factory. Terminal 1 is in the receiving area. When raw materials are received from vendors, receipt data is entered in the terminal. All material receipts then undergo a quality control inspection, and the results are recorded on terminal 2. As the accepted receipts enter the raw-materials inventory, that action is logged on terminal 3. The same terminal is also used to record the release of materials to the production process. Terminals 4 through 10 are used by production employees to signal the start and completion of each step of the production process. When the final product is finished, terminal 11 is used to show that the goods are now in the finished-goods inventory. Terminal 11 also signals the release of finished

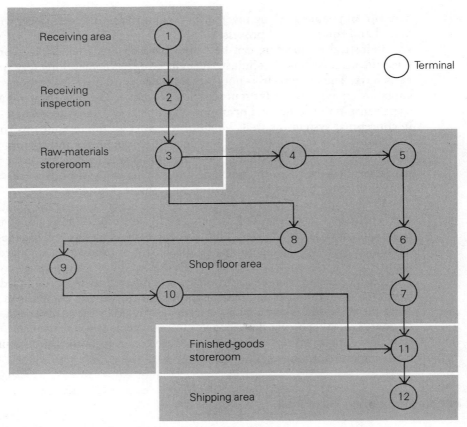

Figure 14-9 Location of data collection terminals.

goods to the shipping department. When the goods are shipped to customers, that action is recorded on terminal 12.

The data collection terminals track the flow of materials through the plant every step of the way. In addition to reporting material flow, the terminals also record the use of personnel and machine resources. The same terminals can be used for *attendance reporting,* with workers using their plastic badges to "punch in" in the morning and "punch out" in the afternoon. Also, as production steps employing machines are started and completed, the computer can determine how long the machines are in use.

Since the data collection system records the use of the three main manufacturing resources (material, personnel, and machines), it effectively records every important production action. Manufacturing management can use this information to monitor—in realtime—the activities of the entire production system.

A data collection example

National Cash Register (NCR) offers a hardware/software data collection package called the *Data Pathing System.* The system is in use at Rexnord, Inc., a manufacturer of industrial equipment that employs some 1200 workers. For years data was collected by telephone from the shop floor. Forty-five phones were used to

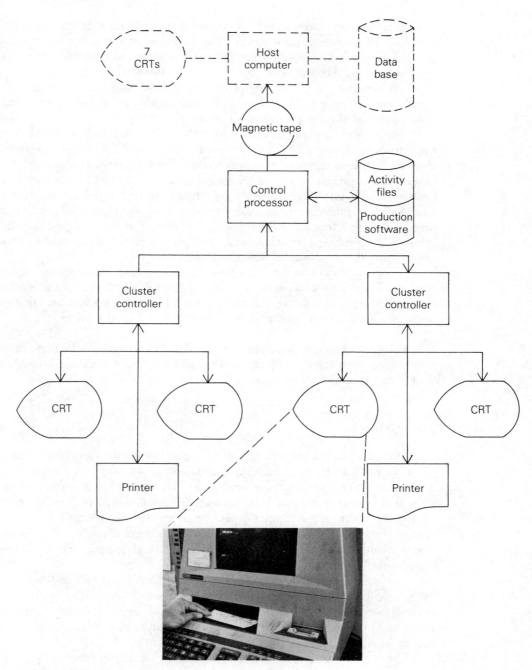

Figure 14-10 An NCR Data Pathing System.

relay attendance and job data to four keypunch operators. During peak periods, it was impossible for the keypunchers to keep up with the workload.

A Data Pathing System was installed, consisting of the configuration diagrammed in Figure 14-10. The data collection network interfaces with the host computer through a control processor—a microcomputer that maintains its own data base of shop floor information. The data base retains labor and production data for three days, enabling shop floor management to base decisions on more than just the current status.

Workers use the CRT terminals for attendance and job reporting. The terminals accept badge and punched card input, as well as keyboard entry. Instructions to the employees are displayed on the screen.

Two cluster controllers, each with 64KB of storage and software, interface the control processor with the shop floor terminals—25 CRTs and 6 printers. The cluster controllers can send messages to shop floor supervisors and employees so that corrective measures can be taken. For example, if an employee tries to clock on a job that is not in the schedule, a message can be printed for the supervisor. Each half-hour, the control processor prints reports for supervisors of any exceptions requiring attention. Each report is a snapshot of the status of the physical system. The combined reports represent a dynamic model of the production operation, using the principles of management by exception.

Supervisors can use the Data Pathing System to communicate decisions to workers. For example, supervisors can establish job sequences for the workers to follow. This is one of the very few instances where management uses the MIS to communicate decisions to the physical system in a formal manner.[4]

This concludes our discussion of how data is entered into the manufacturing information system by the three input subsystems. The remaining discussion will deal with the output subsystems.

Inventory Subsystem

Manufacturing management has always been responsible for inventory. Records show the on-hand balance, and physical counts assure that the conceptual system accurately reflects the physical one. This maintenance of inventory records is known as *inventory control*. With the current focus on operating costs, managers have given attention to another aspect of inventory—the reduction of inventory cost to the lowest possible level consistent with desired service. This is an area where quantitative techniques have proven successful, and their application is called *inventory management*.

The annual cost of maintaining or carrying an inventory can be as much as 30% of its value. This maintenance cost includes factors such as spoilage, pilferage, obsolescence, taxes, insurance, and so on. If the raw-materials storeroom contains $1 million in inventory, the inventory can run up an annual maintenance cost as high as $300,000.

These maintenance, or carrying, costs vary directly by inventory level—the higher the level, the higher the costs. And the inventory level of an item is influenced primarily by the number of units ordered from a vendor at one time. In

[4]"NCR's Source Data Management System," *Production & Inventory Management Review and APICS News* 1 (September 1981): 63–65.

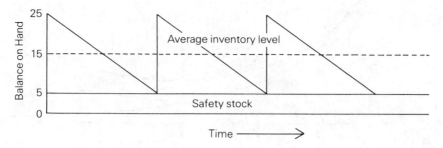

(a) Order quantity of 20; average level is 15.

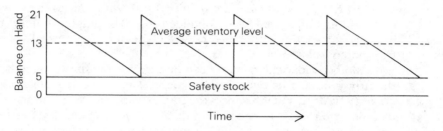

(b) Order quantity of 16; average level is 13.

Figure 14-11 Order quantity affects inventory level: (a) order quantity of 20, average level is 15; (b) order quantity of 16, average level is 13.

simplified terms, the average inventory level is usually half of the order quantity plus any safety stock. *Safety stock* is an extra quantity that is maintained to prevent or minimize stockouts and backorders. A *stockout* is a condition when no items remain in inventory—the cupboard is bare. A *backorder* is an order from a customer that cannot be filled because of a stockout. Backorders can lose customers, and therefore management attempts to hold them to a minimum.

The model in Figure 14-11 shows the effect of order quantity on average inventory level. A reduction in order quantity from 20 to 16 lowers the average level by 2. If the item happens to be an expensive electric motor costing $5000, the reduction in annual maintenance costs could be $3000 (2 × $5000 × .30).

In the upper example, a quantity of 20 is ordered from the vendor. Sometimes (just after receipt) there are 25 units in inventory. Sometimes (just before receipt) there are only 5. On the average, there are 15 units in inventory.

In the lower example, a smaller quantity is ordered and the average level drops accordingly. This effect would seem to identify lower order quantities as the best goal for the manager. That conclusion would be true were it not for another cost that *increases* as the order quantity decreases. This is the purchasing cost. It costs a fixed amount to prepare a purchase order, perhaps $45, regardless of the number of units ordered. Therefore, the fewer the units, the higher the *per-unit* purchasing cost. If the firm orders one unit at a time, the per-unit purchasing

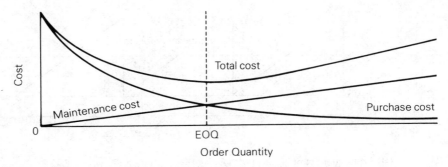

Figure 14-12 The EOQ represents the lowest total cost.

cost is $45. This cost can be reduced to $22.50 per unit when two are ordered, to $15 when three are ordered, and so on.

The *EOQ* (*economic order quantity*) *formula* balances these two inventory costs and identifies the lowest combined cost. The graphical model of this technique is included in Figure 14-12. An EOQ can be established for each item in raw-materials inventory.

Another economic quantity can be used for the finished-goods inventory if the firm produces its own finished goods. This is the *economic manufacturing quantity* (*EMQ*), and it balances the costs of carrying the inventory with the costs of production inefficiencies. These quantities—EOQ and EMQ—are optimum. They cannot be improved upon without changing the values of the variables. The manager therefore need not decide how much to order.

In a similar fashion, the MIS can decide when to order replenishment items. An order point can be calculated for each item to trigger a purchase order to the vendor (in the amount of the EOQ) or a production order to the factory (in the amount of the EMQ).

The formula for the reorder point is:

$$R = LU + S$$

where: L = vendor lead time (in days)
          U = usage rate (number of units used or sold per day)
          S = safety stock level (in units)

For example, if it takes the vendor 14 days to provide the ordered materials, and you use ten units per day, you will use 140 units while waiting for the vendor to fill the order. Add to this a safety stock of 16, and the reorder point is 156.

These two decisions—*when* to order and *how much* to order—represent the two key decisions in inventory management. They can both be made by the inventory subsystem with little or no management intervention. Once these quantities have been established, the manager need not get involved until they need to be updated.

An inventory success story

Inventory has long been recognized as an application area offering excellent opportunities for improvement in several areas of operations. Such has been the case at the Qyx Division of Exxon Office Systems Company, a fast-growing manufacturer of electronic typewriters.

Qyx selected Cincom's Manufacturing Resource Planning System (MRPS) for use in inventory management, purchasing, and other areas. MRPS was implemented to do three important tasks—minimize inventory investment, maximize customer service, and optimize plant efficiency.

Three months after selecting the Cincom package, the Qyx information services staff delivered it to manufacturing management for implementation. Four months later, the inventory management system was fully implemented. Such quick development time is possible with packaged software, supported by cooperation between the users and the information specialists.

The MRPS results are impressive. Inventory accuracy has increased 60%—from 35% to 95%. This increased accuracy enabled inventory levels to be reduced 30%. Purchasing has also been improved by increasingly accurate purchase orders. Outstanding (unfilled) purchase orders have been reduced by 55% due to better control. In addition, in-bound freight charges have dropped 30% and overtime expense in the inventory and production department is down 55%.

Describing the need for inventory management such as that provided by MRPS, Gus Modica, project leader, said: "Maintaining inordinately high levels of inventory can tie up needed cash. And in a high-technology field such as ours, where product obsolescence is a high risk, stagnant inventories can have a dramatic effect on our bottom lines."[5]

Quality Subsystem

Quality standards are normally established for all the products a firm manufactures. But it is not sufficient to establish quality controls on only the finished-goods output. If the end product is unacceptable, where does the manager look for a solution? The manager must establish quality control (QC) checks at each key point in the system. One vital checkpoint is the input function, where raw materials are received from vendors. If the output products of the firm are to meet an expected quality level, the input materials must be of equal or higher quality. We have seen how the manufacturing intelligence subsystem can provide information on vendor quality performance.

Most manufacturing firms have several potential sources of supply for each item purchased. This practice prevents a catastrophe if one supplier shuts down. This is one way the firm can protect against environmental impacts.

Buyers in the purchasing department have the job of selecting the best vendor for a particular order. This decision has always been largely unstructured because of the frequent changes in the variables. Vendors go out of business, new ones come on the scene, prices change, and so on.

Each time a buyer selects a vendor, the quality subsystem can provide information to support the decision. The past performance of each potential vendor

---

[5] "Controlling Growing Manufacturing Ops with Cincom's MRPS," *Production & Inventory Management Review and APICS News* 1 (July 1981): 20–22.

can be reported in a format that facilitates comparison and evaluation. Numeric scores can be computed for each vendor, and the ones with the highest scores are given prime consideration for the order.

There are three approaches to developing numeric ratings.[6] First is *raw scoring,* where you simply count late deliveries and rejects or compute percentages of on-time and accepted units. Next is *weighted raw scoring,* where criteria are weighted based on importance. Third is *point scoring,* where points are awarded for doing certain things right (such as 100 points for being on time with no rejects) and points are deducted for doing things wrong (such as minus 10 points when a shipment is one week late).

As for an example of weighted raw scoring, assume that a manufacturer of radios and TVs has identified two important measures of vendor performance: product quality and speed of delivery. These measures are weighted as follows:

$$\text{Material quality} = 60$$
$$\text{Speed of delivery} = 40$$

The formulas for the measures are:

$$\text{Material quality} = 60 \times \frac{\text{number of orders accepted}}{\text{total number of orders}}$$

$$\text{Delivery speed} = 40 \times \frac{\text{number of delivery promises met}}{\text{total number of delivery promises}}$$

One of the vendors has the following performance record:

$$36 \text{ of } 40 \text{ orders accepted}$$
$$5 \text{ of } 15 \text{ promised delivery dates met}$$

The vendor's performance score would be calculated as:

$$\text{Material quality} = 60 \times \frac{36}{40} = 54$$

$$\text{Delivery speed} = 40 \times \frac{5}{15} = 10$$

$$\text{Total performance score} = 64$$

Vendor rating is not a perfect solution to the problem of vendor selection. The scores only provide a starting point. The buyers can supplement the ratings with special analyses of vendor data. The data can be obtained using a query

---

[6] Somerby Dowst, "The Many Faces of Vendor Evaluation," *Purchasing,* 26 February 1981, pp. 44 ff.

COMMODITY CODE	VENDOR	NUMBER OF EMPLOYEES	PRIMARY LINE OF BUSINESS	SALES ($000)	PURCHASES ($000)	PURCHASES AS PERCENT OF SALES
40312	AMERICAN MACHINE WORKS	87	ELECTRONIC CONNECT.	1281	304	0.24
	DUDLEY CONTROLS, INC.	112	SEMICONDUCTORS	5286	567	0.11
	HAMILTON VALLEY MFG.	193	SEMICONDUCTORS	3083	1876	0.61
	ONTARIO INDUSTRIES	84	ELECTRONIC PARTS	2835	160	0.06
	WHITLEY-BOWLES, INC.	216	ELECTRONIC PARTS	1087	307	0.28

Figure 14-13 Example of vendor analysis data.

language. An example of the type of data available appears in Figure 14-13.[7] The report lists all vendors supplying a particular material (commodity code 40312), showing the number of vendor employees, the vendors' annual sales, and the amount of purchases from each vendor last year. Buyers can evaluate the sale and purchase amounts to gauge each vendor's dependency on the buying firm's business. The report shows Hamilton Valley to be extremely dependent on the buying firm. Some buying firms try to cultivate this type of relationship because it gives them considerable power over the vendor. Other firms, sensitive to the ethical issues, set a limit on the firm's percentage of a vendor's total business. Regardless of policy, a report like the one in Figure 14-13 can help buyers maintain the relationships they want.

In this example of the quality subsystem, we have addressed vendor selection. This is only the first place where quality is considered. Quality control can be evident in each phase of the firm's operations.

Production Subsystem

The production subsystem is the most complex of the output subsystems. It is concerned with all of the actions performed on the material flow. These actions are performed by two other basic resources: personnel and machines. The production subsystem is therefore a conceptual representation of how these three resources (material, personnel, and machines) are used together to create finished products.

Managers on all levels make production decisions. The decisions of where to locate plants and how to arrange them are made on the upper levels. These are production decisions, and the production subsystem provides support, as described earlier. Managers on the lower levels are given the authority to make decisions relating to the day-to-day operation of the plant.

Determining material requirements

A good example of system operation decisions is *material requirements planning* (*MRP*). MRP is a technique of managing production inventories that takes into

---

[7]Based on an example in Robert Ditmars and Richard Paige, "Information Systems Development," *Purchasing World* 24 (May 1980): 70 ff.

account the specific timing of material requirements.[8] MRP is a schedule of material required in each time period covered by the firm's production schedule. The production schedule is determined by the sales forecast provided by the marketing information system.

MRP is a positive approach to materials management—anticipating material needs and planning their acquisition. This is in contrast to the old technique (still used by some firms) of waiting for customer orders to arrive and then reacting to those orders with material requisitions.

MRP interacts with two other systems—production scheduling and capacity requirements planning—as pictured in Figure 14-14.

1. The firm's sales forecast for the coming period is used by the production scheduling system to prepare a *master production schedule* (MPS).

2. The material requirements planning system performs the following steps:
   a. It uses the master production schedule to determine the number of finished goods needed during each time period.
   b. It uses the bill of materials file to determine the raw materials and their quantities, by time period, to produce the needed finished goods. The total quantities of raw materials are called the gross requirements.
   c. The gross requirements are reduced by the quantities of raw materials on hand to determine the net requirements.
   d. The net requirements are allocated to different time periods to reflect vendor lead times and specific steps during the production process when the materials will be needed.

3. A check is made by the capacity requirements planning system to ensure that the firm has sufficient production facilities (equipment, fixtures, and the like) to meet the schedule.

The outputs from the MRP system include those that are required to carry out the production schedule along with some optional management reports. The required outputs include (1) a *planned order schedule,* which lists needed quantities of each material by time period and is used by buyers to negotiate with vendors; (2) *order releases,* which are authorizations to produce the products on the planned order schedule; and (3) *changes to planned orders,* which reflect canceled orders, modified order quantities, and so on.

Optional outputs include (1) *exception reports,* which flag items requiring management attention; (2) *performance reports,* which indicate how well the system is operating in terms of stockouts, backorders, and so forth; and (3) *planning reports,* which are used by manufacturing management for future inventory planning.

---

[8] For an excellent primer on MRP incorporating computer methodology, see William S. Donelson II, "MRP—Who Needs It?" *Datamation* 25 (May 1979): 185 ff. Our discussion draws from Donelson and from Norman Gaither, *Production and Operations Management* (Hinsdale, Ill.: Dryden, 1980), pp. 531–38.

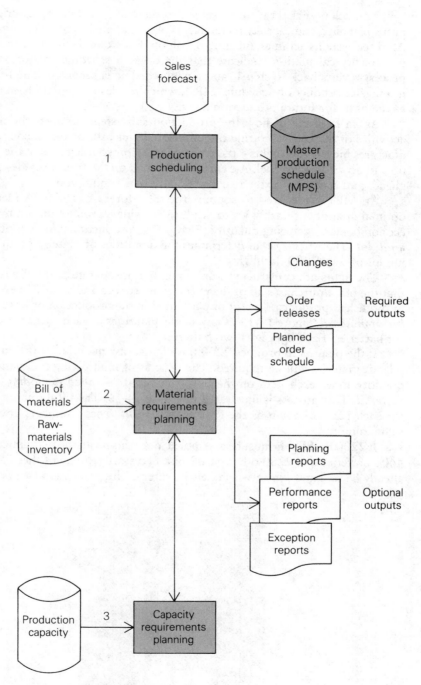

Figure 14-14 Production planning.

You will note that the three systems (production scheduling, material requirements planning, and capacity requirements planning) are linked by two-way arrows. All three systems act in an integrated fashion. For example, if either the materials or capacity calculations indicate that the original schedule cannot be met, the process reverts back to step 1, and a new schedule is prepared. The final output is a master production schedule (MPS), which resides in the data base and serves as the basis for future production activity.

As an example of how the production subsystem supports the day-to-day activities of the manufacturing organization, let us assume that a company manufactures bicycle flashlights—the type you strap on your leg so that the light bobs up and down as you pedal. A clear lens mounted on the front provides some light ahead, and a red lens at the rear warns motorists behind you.

An MPS is prepared to support the sales forecast. The MPS identifies the optimal quantity of flashlights to produce in a single production run by using the economic manufacturing quantity (EMQ). The production run quantity is called a *job lot*. The MRP system determines the quantities of materials required for a job lot of, say, 2200 flashlights.

The lights are constructed from a number of separate parts. We can assume that the plant purchases all of the parts from vendors and simply assembles them into finished products. The list of parts used in the production process is called a *bill of material* (Figure 14-15). Only single quantities of each part are used, except for batteries. Each light uses two batteries.

If the plant is to produce 2200 flashlights, raw materials sufficient for 2200 bills of material will be required. The process of multiplying the manufacturing quantity times each item on the bill of materials is called *exploding the bill of material*. This process is illustrated in Figure 14-16. The total quantity required for each part is known as the *gross requirement*. These numbers appear in the right column.

If 2200 flashlights must be assembled, does this mean the plant must purchase 4400 batteries and 2200 other parts? Not necessarily. Some of these parts might already be on hand—in raw-materials inventory. The production subsystem checks

Part	Quantity
Plastic cylinder	1
Plastic top	1
Strap	1
Switch	1
Spring	1
Reflector	1
Bulb	1
Lens, red	1
Lens, clear	1
Battery	2

Figure 14-15   Bill of material for bicycle flashlight.

Part	Qty. per Final Product		Number of Final Products		Gross Requirement
Plastic cylinder	1	x	2200	=	2200
Plastic top	1	x	2200	=	2200
Strap	1	x	2200	=	2200
Switch	1	x	2200	=	2200
Spring	1	x	2200	=	2200
Reflector	1	x	2200	=	2200
Bulb	1	x	2200	=	2200
Lens, red	1	x	2200	=	2200
Lens, clear	1	x	2200	=	2200
Battery	2	x	2200	=	4400

Figure 14-16 An exploded bill of material.

the inventory status of each part to determine the *net requirement* (gross requirement minus parts on hand). This process is shown in Figure 14-17.

You can see that all of the parts are available in the needed quantities except two: switches and bulbs. The firm has only 800 switches on hand, and it needs 2200. The firm also needs to order bulbs, since there are no bulbs in raw-materials inventory. Again, the EOQ is used.

It is possible that additional purchase orders will be triggered by the net requirements computation. These orders are for items still in stock, but with a balance below the reorder point. The reflector is one of these items. There are enough reflectors on hand, but only four will be left after the flashlights are produced. The requirement for the flashlights will drop the balance on hand below the reorder point.

The production subsystem uses the raw-materials file in the data base to determine the net requirements. The inventory subsystem then uses the EOQ and

Part	Gross Requirements	Inventory on Hand	Net Requirements
Plastic cylinder	2200	3000	0
Plastic top	2200	2250	0
Strap	2200	6000	0
Switch	2200	800	1400
Spring	2200	2999	0
Reflector	2200	2204	0
Bulb	2200	0	2200
Lens, red	2200	3625	0
Lens, clear	2200	5500	0
Battery	4400	5005	0

Figure 14-17 Net raw-material inventory requirements for flashlight parts.

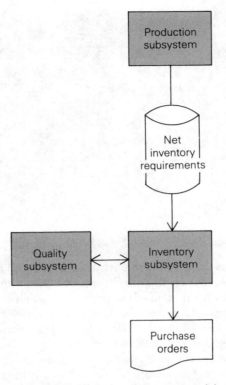

Figure 14-18 Ordering the raw materials.

the net requirements to determine the quantity to order. The specific vendor is selected with information provided by the quality subsystem. In this manner, all three subsystems work together to requisition needed materials, as illustrated in Figure 14-18.

Production cannot start until all the parts are available. When the switches and bulbs arrive, the production subsystem notifies manufacturing management, by transmitting data to the central computer from terminals located in the receiving and the receiving inspection areas. The computer then notifies the appropriate managers, such as the schedulers and dispatchers, by transmitting messages to terminals in their offices.

Scheduling production

The flashlights are assembled one step at a time from the required parts. The items move from one work station in the plant to another as the assembly process proceeds. Figure 14-19 shows this flow through the plant.

The production flow starts by releasing the raw materials from inventory. In this example there are two main flows: one for assembling the cylinder and one for the top. Work can be done simultaneously on the cylinder and the top to reduce the length of time required for the job. The steps in the cylinder flow are

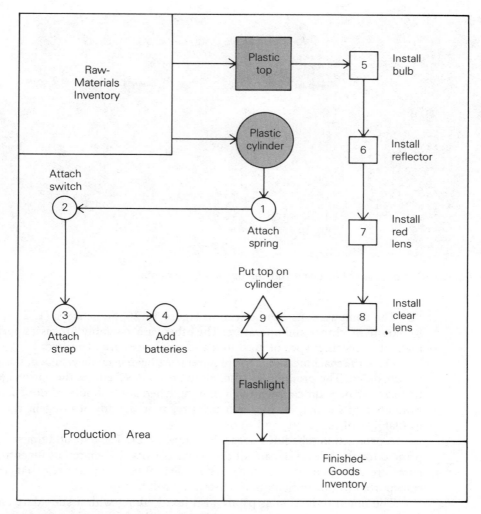

Figure 14-19 Job flow through the plant.

numbered 1 through 4 and are circled. The steps for the top are numbered 5 through 8 and are enclosed in squares. In step 9 the top assembly is attached to the cylinder assembly, and the result is a finished flashlight that enters the finished-goods inventory.

The production schedule determines when the flashlights will be produced. To determine the schedule, the job lot quantity must be multiplied by the performance standards for each step. For example, if the first step is the attachment of a battery spring to the plastic flashlight cylinder (step 1 in Figure 14-19), a special spring insertion machine can be used. The machine must have an operator. The standard insertion time of 0.16 minute means that 352 minutes of both machine and operator time will be required to attach 2200 springs. Similar computations can be made for each remaining step of the process to identify the total machine and personnel requirements.

```
                    MACHINE AND MANPOWER REQUIREMENTS

PRODUCT--BICYCLE FLASHLIGHT
PRODUCTION QUANTITY--2200

                       -------MACHINE------        ------EMPLOYEE------
         STEP          TYPE  STD.  TOT. TIME        TYPE   STD.  TOT. TIME

    1--ATTCH SPRG       129   .16    352           0-129   .16    352
    2--ATTCH SW         402   .30    660           0-402   .30    660
    3--ATTCH STRP       ---   ---    ---           ASSY    .10    220
    4--ADD BATTS        ---   ---    ---           ASSY    .08    176
    5--INST BULB        202   .16    352           0-202   .16    352
    6--INST REF         ---   ---    ---           ASSY    .30    660
    7--INST LNSR        602   .20    440           0-602   .20    440
    8--INST LNSC        604   .20    440           0-604   .20    440
    9--ATTCH TOP        ---   ---    ---           ASSY    .16    352
```

Figure 14-20   Computation of machine and personnel requirements.

The computations can be seen in Figure 14-20. Some steps (1, 2, 5, 7, and 8) require machines and operators. The others are assembly processes performed manually. Specific types of machines and employees are identified.

Once the machine and labor requirements have been determined, the job can be scheduled. The production scheduling program schedules the various jobs for the best use of plant capacity. Determining when a job should be done hinges on a number of factors, such as job priority, time already waiting in the queue, availability of resources, and so on.

A production schedule appears in Figure 14-21. The date and time of day are printed for the release of each of the 10 parts from raw-materials inventory. The parts are not released until they are needed. When they are released, they are transported to the work station where they will be used.

The nine production steps are also listed, along with a start date and time for each. A production step is scheduled to begin no later than 30 minutes after the raw materials have been delivered to the work station. Steps 5 through 8 require a total of 1892 minutes of production time, compared with 1408 minutes for steps 1 through 4. The start time for the cylinder assembly (steps 1–4) is therefore delayed so that the tops can be attached (step 9) as soon as the cylinders are assembled.

The production process

The production subsystem triggers the production process. Information is prepared for employees in the inventory and production areas, telling them what to do, when to do it, and (if necessary) how to do it. One approach is for the computer to transmit signals to the appropriate terminals as the actions are scheduled to begin. Another approach calls for the computer to print all of the information on forms that are put in a folder called a *shop packet*. The shop packet accompanies

```
                              PRODUCTION SCHEDULE

  JOB NAME=BICYCLE FLASHLIGHT
  JOB NO. 79-133

  RAW              RELEASE        PRODUCTION        START          COMPLETION
  MATLS          DATE   TIME      STEP          DATE   TIME        DATE   TIME

  CYLINDER       10-24  0800
  SPRING         10-24  0800    1-ATTCH SPRG  10-24  0838        10-24  1430
  SWITCH         10-24  1430    2-ATTCH SW    10-24  1500        10-26  0900
  STRAP          10-26  0930    3-ATTCH STRP  10-26  0950        10-26  1330
  BATTERY        10-26  1345    4-ADD BATTS   10-26  1404        10-26  1700
  TOP            10-23  0900
  BULB           10-23  0900    5-INST BULB   10-23  0930        10-23  1522
  REFLECTOR      10-23  1530    6-INST REF    10-23  1600        10-25  1000
  LENS RED       10-25  1030    7-INST LNSR   10-25  1100        10-26  0920
  LENS CLEAR     10-26  0930    8-INST LNSC   10-26  1000        10-26  1620
                               9-ATTCH TOP   10-27  0800        10-27  1352
```

Figure 14-21 Example of a production schedule.

the job as it moves through the plant. The timing of the actions is specified on a separate printed production schedule.

As work begins on a step in the production process, the worker uses the terminal at his or her work station to advise the computer of:

- Job identification
- Step number
- Work station
- Employee identification
- Start time

The first three items are entered from a punched card or on a keyboard. The employee can be identified by inserting his or her plastic badge. Start time is recorded by the computer as the message is received.

When the job step is completed, the worker advises the computer by using the terminal. Again the computer enters the time of day. In this way the computer can calculate the time required to complete the step (stop time minus start time).

The production subsystem can keep the manager informed of job progress by means of exception reporting. If a step took too long to complete, subsequent steps may be delayed. Perhaps management can take action to prevent the delay. If a step is completed earlier than scheduled, it might be possible to speed up the completion of the job in order to make an earlier shipping date.

The computer has relieved operational-level management of many decisions. Formerly, people in the production planning and control office made all of the decisions based on little more than wall charts and keyboard calculators. Now these people are able to concentrate on solving unstructured problems as they arise. The manufacturing information system, with its data base of up-to-date production data, can provide decision support for the most difficult decisions a manager can face.

Cost Subsystem

Inventory costs can be minimized through the use of economic order and manufacturing quantities. Production costs can be controlled through the use of accurate cost standards. On a periodic basis the manufacturing manager can receive a report showing how the actual production costs compare with the standards. An example is shown in Figure 14-22.

The manager can key a query into a terminal, and cost data for each department can be displayed. The computer program compares total standard hours with total actual hours and calculates the variance. When the actual hours exceed the standard, the job numbers contributing to that excess are printed. In the figure, the painting department exceeded the standard by 35 hours on jobs 79-283 and 79-291.

If the manager wants more information on the excess, another query can be made and the data can be reported by employees. Figure 14-23 is an example. Analysis of this data indicates that employee 8514 accounted for a six-hour overage on job 79-283. Now the manager has the information needed to determine the cause. The foreperson of the painting department can meet with the employee to discuss what happened on job 79-283. Once the causes are identified, action can be taken to eliminate or minimize them in the future.

The two required ingredients for an effective cost control program are standards of comparison and accurate reporting of actual costs. The data collection network of the production subsystem helps meet both requirements. Data describing actual job performance is collected, and over a period of time this data is used to set standards. When start and stop times are recorded for each step of the

```
                PRODUCTION COST REPORT
                     BY DEPARTMENT

             WEEK ENDING 10-22-83

   DEPARTMENT      STD.    ACT.    VAR.    SEE JOB     JOB
                   HRS.    HRS.            NUMBERS     VAR.

   WELDING         1090    1085    -5

   PAINTING         330     365    35      79-283      10
                                           79-291      25

   PLATING          523     522    -1

   INSPECTION        78      85     7      79-303       7

   ASSEMBLY        2027    2423   396      79-292      23
                                           79-295     107
                                           79-298      47
                                           79-313     219

   CLEANING         293     278   -15
```

Figure 14-22   Production cost report.

```
              PRODUCTION COST REPORT
            BY DEPARTMENT AND BY JOB

          WEEK ENDING 10-22-83

DEPARTMENT        JOB      EMP.     STD.     ACT.     VAR.
                  NO.      NO.      HRS.     HRS.

PAINTING       79-283     3124       11       13        2
                          3309       18       18        0
                          4119       62       65        3
                          7218       42       40       -2
                          7301       10       11        1
                          8514       73       79        6

               TOTALS . . . . . .   216      226       10
```

Figure 14-23   A second production cost report.

production process, accurate actual times can be computed. When the conceptual system is able to track the flow of resources through the physical system in the manner described, the manager is able to control all dimensions of acceptable performance: quality, time, quantity, and cost.

Summary

The manufacturing function of the firm primarily involves the flow of material resources. Managers in this area must design and operate a system to handle this flow.

Computers have been applied in the manufacturing area in two basic ways: to control production processes and machines and to serve as information systems. The manufacturing information system can be used in both the design and the operation of the production system. Design decisions are made infrequently, but they are important in that they commit large sums of money for long periods of time. These unstructured decisions are made on upper management levels. Although the information system probably cannot supply all the information the manager would like when making these decisions, it does provide a good deal of information and can help structure some parts of the decision.

Operational decisions are of a different type. They are made on a daily basis and can be structured to a great extent. This is because most of the important variables can be identified and measured in quantitative terms.

The model of the manufacturing information system includes three input and four output subsystems. The output subsystems can be used in both the design and the operation of the production system. The information from the output subsystems is used by different managers in the manufacturing area, and by others as well. This usage is shown in Table 14-4.

As with the marketing information system, the chief executive officer receives information from all output subsystems in summary form. Both the vice-president

Table 14-4 Users of the Manufacturing Information System

| | Subsystem | | | |
User	Inventory	Quality	Production	Cost
Chief executive officer	X	X	X	X
Vice-president of manufacturing	X	X	X	X
Plant superintendent	X	X	X	X
Manager of planning and control	X		X	
Manager of engineering		X	X	X
Manager of quality control		X		
Director of purchasing	X	X		X
Manager of inventory control	X			
Other managers	X	X	X	X

of manufacturing and the plant superintendent also use highly summarized output describing the entire operation.

Managers in marketing and finance will probably also make use of the output. Marketers will be interested in all aspects of production (cost, quality, and availability) since these factors influence the product that is to be sold. Financial managers will have a special interest in output from the cost subsystem.

Information systems have become a vital part of modern manufacturing techniques. Today they account to a large extent for the stream of quality products available to consumers and users around the world.

Key Terms

origin, destination
receiving area, receiving inspection
   area
raw-materials storeroom

shop floor area
final inspection area
finished-goods storeroom
shipping area

construction heuristics model

improvement heuristics model

inventory control

inventory management

safety stock

stockout

backorder

economic order quantity (EOQ)

economic manufacturing quantity (EMQ)

raw scoring

weighted raw scoring

point scoring

material requirements planning (MRP)

master production schedule (MPS)

planned order schedule

order release

job lot

bill of material

gross requirement

net requirement

Key Concepts

The operational-level nature of most manufacturing managerial work

The design of physical manufacturing systems along flow network lines

The informal nature of labor information

The potential for developing a formal vendor data-gathering system

The role of the industrial engineer (IE) in analyzing and designing both physical and conceptual manufacturing systems

Data collection as a means of gathering accounting data in the manufacturing area

The structured nature of inventory management

The quantitative evaluation of vendors

The integrative nature of production scheduling, material requirements planning, and capacity requirements planning

The step-by-step manner in which a production schedule evolves—considering inventory, machine, and personnel constraints

The realtime ability that data collection terminals provide a manufacturing information system

Questions

1. What types of decisions do strategic- and tactical-level manufacturing managers make? What about operational-level managers?

2. What is structured about a plant location decision? What is unstructured?

3. What type of model can be used to support the plant location decision? How could this same model be used to locate a network of distribution centers and retail stores?

4. What areas of a plant layout correspond to the input element of the general systems model? the transformation element? the output element?

5. How do construction heuristics and improvement heuristics models differ? Do these models solve perfectly structured problems? Explain.

6. What two environmental elements are the focus of the manufacturing intelligence subsystem?

7. What document establishes the basis for the flow of information concerning unionized workers. What department is responsible for facilitating this flow?

8. What are the two steps of gathering vendor data?

9. How does the work of the IE contribute to management by exception?

10. How are data collection terminals used for attendance reporting? for job reporting?

11. Does the NCR Data Pathing System provide the manufacturing manager with a snapshot or a motion picture of the manufacturing operation? Explain.

12. What distinguishes inventory management from inventory control?

13. How do firms minimize stockouts?

14. What two costs are incorporated in the EOQ formula?

15. When would an EMQ be used instead of an EOQ?

16. What is the relationship between the manufacturing intelligence subsystem and the quality subsystem?

17. What is MRP?

18. How are gross requirements computed? How are net requirements computed?

19. How are production performance standards used to prepare the production schedule.

20. What is the relationship between the internal accounting subsystem and the cost subsystem?

Problems

1. Using the formula in the chapter, compute the reorder point for the following items.

Item	Vendor lead time	Usage rate	Safety stock	Reorder point
1	8	4	6	
2	12	3	7	
3	24	8	20	
4	5	1	2	
5	38	19	40	

2. Using the formula in Chapter 11, compute the economic order quantity for the following items.

Item	Acquisition (purchase) cost (dollars)	Annual sales (units)	Retention (maintenance) cost (dollars)	EOQ
1	40	12,000	2.50	
2	40	500	5.00	
3	40	2,500	12.50	
4	40	100,000	.25	
5	40	150	10.00	

3. Assuming an 80% weighting for quality and a 20% weighting for delivery speed, rate the following vendors.

Vendor	Total no. of orders	No. of orders accepted	Total no. of delivery promises	No. of delivery promises met	Vendor rating
1	30	28	12	9	
2	4	4	4	2	
3	12	8	5	3	
4	2	0	2	2	
5	8	5	8	7	

CASE PROBLEM: Interstate Hydraulic Manufacturing Co.

Interstate Hydraulic Manufacturing Co. is an established, family-owned manufacturer of hydraulic devices used in automobile suspensions and forklift trucks. From the factory in Muncie, Indiana, products are shipped to customers throughout the United States and several foreign countries. All data processing is performed by a service bureau, which uses a computer to handle payroll, billing, accounts receivable, inventory, and cost accounting. Workers clock on and off the job using time clocks, and they report job progress by filling out a forms packet that accompanies each job lot. Data from the time cards and forms packets is keypunched by the service bureau.

Ben Lambert is in charge of customer service, handling complaints, conducting plant tours, and providing information to the plant manager on product performance. One day Lambert is sitting at his desk, handling the backlog of correspondence he has accumulated. He picks up his office recorder and dictates:

Ms. Ellie Nostrom
Purchasing Director
McCullin Enterprises

Dear Ms. Nostrom,

Thank you very much for being so understanding last week when you called to inquire about your order. As I explained, we have a large number of jobs in process at any one time, and many more waiting in line. It is simply impossible to locate where one is without spending considerable time looking through our records.

I later learned that your order was held up due to a lack of materials. We have been having difficulty obtaining the nylon bushing that attaches the actuating arm to the housing. We have had only one supplier that could meet our high quality standards, and we have recently learned that their factory has been on strike for almost half a year.

We finally located another supplier in California and placed an order with them. But when the bushings arrived, the receiving report was misfiled, and we didn't know that they were here. The receiving report, which is normally sent to our accounting department, was sent to purchasing by mistake.

After your call, I talked with the supervisor of receiving, and he said he remembered seeing the shipment. We finally located it in raw-materials inventory and have issued a production order. The job is presently in process and should be completed either by the end of next week or early the following week.

Again, thank you for calling attention to your order. Our customers are our most valuable asset, and we appreciate your business. You have our pledge that we will continue to be responsive to your needs and supply you with the same high level of service that has been our trademark. Please do not hesitate to call on me at any time.

Sincerely,

Ben Lambert, Manager
Customer Service Department

Questions

1. Which manufacturing information subsystems were involved with Ms. Nostrom's problem?
2. What computing equipment would be necessary to help prevent this problem from recurring?
3. What is the fundamental problem at Interstate, as reflected by the mishandling of Ms. Nostrom's order?
4. Will the problem be solved with the equipment specified in your answer to question 2? Explain your answer.

Chapter 15

Financial Information Systems

Learning Objectives

After studying this chapter, you should:

- Know how the financial function manages the firm's money flow
- Understand that the internal accounting system is an integrated set of subsystems
- Know the basic features of the internal accounting subsystems used to process an order—the processing and the input/output documents and files
- Understand how a corporation gathers information from its stockholders
- Appreciate the importance to a firm of information describing the financial community
- Recognize how the format of the *Wall Street Journal* enables the manager to stay current on the business environment
- Understand the two basic types of forecasts—short-term sales and long-term environmental
- Have an introductory understanding of how forecasting can be accomplished with a packaged software system
- Understand how a nonoptimizing model can be used for cash flow decision making
- Appreciate the value of the budget and performance ratios to the financial control of a firm
- Have an introductory understanding of how a natural language can be used in "what-if" modeling

Importance of Accounting Data

Had this book been written twenty years ago, it would have dealt primarily with the internal accounting system of the firm. That system was the conceptual information system until a more complete treatment of management information was developed.

The accounting system is still important, even though it is only one part of the MIS. Accounting is important because it provides a detailed record of the activity of the firm. Accounting tells what the firm has done in the past and, in certain instances, what is happening now. It is important for the manager to understand this, but it is also necessary to project what is likely to happen in the future. More sophisticated techniques than accounting must be used to provide the manager with information about what lies ahead.

The internal accounting system provides a common data base linking all three functional information systems. Each system shares in gathering and using this data. A good accounting system is a prerequisite of an MIS. Without one, an MIS cannot exist.[1]

Model of the Financial Information System

Figure 15-1 shows a model of the financial information system. There are only two input subsystems and three output subsystems. There is no input subsystem analogous to marketing research or industrial engineering, which conduct formal studies of system efficiency and performance. Studies of the firm's financial operation are usually conducted by independent auditing firms. The three output sub-

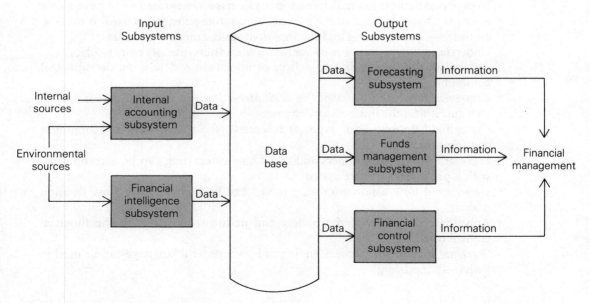

Figure 15-1 Model of a financial information system.

---

[1]Aside from the fact that accounting data is important to the MIS, a firm that cannot implement a good accounting system probably cannot implement the more comprehensive MIS.

systems are concerned with forecasting the future financial condition of the firm, managing the flow of funds into and out of the firm, and controlling expenditures by the organizational units.

The financial information system is concerned with the money flow. Information is gathered to track the flow through the firm. Output information in the form of management reports and traditional accounting statements keeps management and members of the firm's environment informed of the firm's financial condition.

The firm's stockholders, members of the financial community, the government, and vendors require different kinds of information that describe the firm's financial condition. But the responsibility for providing information to the environment is not unique to the financial information system. Marketing is responsible for keeping its customers informed, and manufacturing is responsible to its vendors. But in the case of the financial information system, much of the financial information is directed to groups and organizations that never have been and never will be directly associated with the firm—securities analysts, educators, potential investors, and so forth.

Internal Accounting Subsystem

Accounting data provides a record of everything of monetary importance that happens in the firm. A record is made of each transaction, describing the important facts—what happened, when it happened, who was involved, and how much money was represented. This data is useful in that it can be analyzed in various ways to meet management's information needs. If a wholesaler wants to learn more about customers who have bought more than $25,000 worth of merchandise in the past month, those accounting records can be selected for analysis. If a retailer wants to know how sales fluctuate by day of the week, that information, too, can be obtained. Virtually any type of information can be produced from this accounting data.

There are three key features of accounting data. First, it deals only with the firm and the activities of environmental elements dealing with the firm. The firm must be directly involved. If information is needed about environmental elements never involved in the firm's business transactions, the accounting system cannot provide it.

Second, the data represents thousands of facts, which, presented separately, would only confuse management. This data must be processed to convert it into information. This is the task of the MIS.

Third, the data is largely historical. In no way does it describe everything happening now. This situation is not due to the slowness of the data processing, but to the delay in entering the data into the system. Modern data-gathering techniques are doing much to make accounting data more current. Data collection terminals in the manufacturing area are an example of how accounting data can be gathered without delay.

Each day, hundreds or thousands of transactions occur within a firm. Even though there are a lot of these transactions, many result from chain reactions, with one or more triggered by a single activity. A large number are triggered by a customer order. This is not surprising, since all of the firm's subsystems are intended to respond, in one way or another, to customers' requests for products and services.

   A number of accounting systems handle the transactions initiated by a customer order. These are subsystems within the overall internal accounting system. One internal accounting subsystem is the *order entry system,* which enters the orders into the accounting system. Another is the *billing system,* which sends bills or invoices to customers. A third is the *accounts receivable system,* which collects the money. Figure 15-2 shows how these systems interface with the customer and how they are linked with the inventory subsystem of the manufacturing information system. If the firm is not a manufacturing organization, the product subsystem of the marketing information system replaces the inventory subsystem. The numbers in the figure are keyed to the numbers in the explanation below.

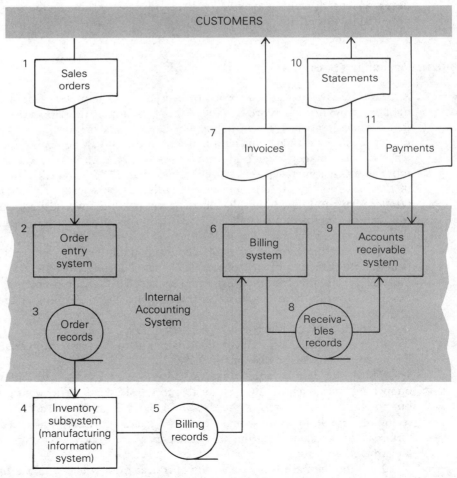

Figure 15-2 Subsystems in the internal accounting system.

1. Sales orders. When a customer such as a wholesaler or retailer decides to purchase something from the manufacturer, some type of *order form* is prepared. In many cases, a salesperson for the manufacturer will complete the form. The order form identifies the customer, the salesperson, the items ordered, the quantity of each, and the price to be paid. Other data completes the description of the sales order.

2. Order entry system. When the sales order is received by the firm, several processes occur. Since most sales are on credit rather than for cash, a credit check can confirm the customer's ability to pay. The decision whether to grant customer credit is a structured one and can be programmed. Usually a credit limit in dollars is established for each customer, and the amount of money owed the firm must remain within this limit. As long as the customer pays its bills to the firm, the firm will continue to accept the customer's orders for amounts within the credit limit.

Another process performed by the order entry system establishes a control over orders received. A record is made of the important data for each order. Data, such as customer number, order number, and order date, is keyed into a terminal. An order suspense record is created from this data and entered into the data base. A program checks each suspense record daily to assure that the order is filled within a reasonable time. If an order is not filled within a specific period, the system generates a signal. An employee in the order department can then investigate the cause of the delay. This is an example of how the conceptual information system can make structured decisions to improve the performance of the physical system.

Other order data must be entered in the system in addition to that used for control, including identification and quantity of each item ordered. This data too can be entered from a terminal, or it can be keypunched or read optically.

The output from the order entry system is a file of order records. In Figure 15-2 these records are on magnetic tape, but they could just as easily be on a disk. The figure also illustrates another important condition. The systems and subsystems are connected by data files. One system creates a file and passes it on to another for additional processing.[2]

3. Order records. The order records include the data from the sales order that will be needed to complete the processing. All that is required is the customer identification, a specification of what was ordered, and how much. At this point, the firm doesn't know whether these orders can be filled or not. Perhaps some of the items are not in stock. These records simply reflect what the customers have ordered.

---

[2] The system flowchart in Figure 15-2 represents a batch processing system. Many firms process accounting data in batches because of the economy. The main reason for using a batch processing example, however, is that it illustrates the subsystems involved and shows their linkages. This detail is not included in a system flowchart of an online system. In an online approach, intersystem communication is accomplished in primary storage rather than with intermediate files.

4. Inventory subsystem of the manufacturing information system. In the previous chapter, we explained that the finished-goods inventory subsystem of the manufacturing information system determines whether the order can be filled. That process occurs here. The inventory record for each ordered item is obtained from the finished-goods inventory file, and a check is made to determine whether sufficient stock is on hand. If so, the order will be filled and shipped. If not, the manufacturer will have to produce additional stock, as described in the previous chapter.

The finished-goods inventory file can be on either magnetic tape or DASD. If on tape, the order records must be sorted into the file sequence before processing. If online processing is being used, the order records can be in random order.

When the finished-goods inventory record is obtained from the data base, the needed data is extracted. This includes item description and price, and the location in the warehouse where the item can be found. Any computations, such as checking the reorder point or determining backorder quantity, are also done at this point.

5. Billing records. The inventory subsystem of the manufacturing information system communicates with the billing system by means of a file of billing records. These records represent the items on the order that can be filled. If a customer orders four items and three can be filled, those three will be included in this file. The record for the single item that cannot be shipped is retained by the inventory system as a backorder.

The billing records include only the important data relating to the transactions: customer identification, item identification, and quantity and price of items to be shipped. They need not include descriptive data relating to the customer (customer name and address, shipping instructions, etc.). That data can be extracted from the data base by the billing system when it is needed.

6. Billing system. At this point, the firm knows which items will be shipped to the customers. But no activity has yet occurred within the physical system. All has been accomplished within the conceptual information system. Conceptual data files confirmed the customer's credit ratings and the availability of items in inventory. The actual filling of the orders in the storeroom remains to be done. This activity is triggered by the billing system.

7. Invoices. The outputs of the billing system are used in three vital tasks. First, the invoices advise the customers of the amounts owed for the merchandise received. Second, copies of the invoice are used by clerks in the warehouse to fill the order. And third, the billing system advises the accounts receivable system of the amounts due.

Figure 15-3 illustrates an *invoice* that also serves as a *picking ticket* and a *packing list*. The invoice is printed in triplicate. The original is mailed to the customer, and the other two copies are sent to the warehouse. Multiple inventory items on the invoice are printed in a sequence that facilitates efficient picking. After the warehouse clerk fills the order using the picking ticket copy, the packing list copy is enclosed in the carton with the merchandise.

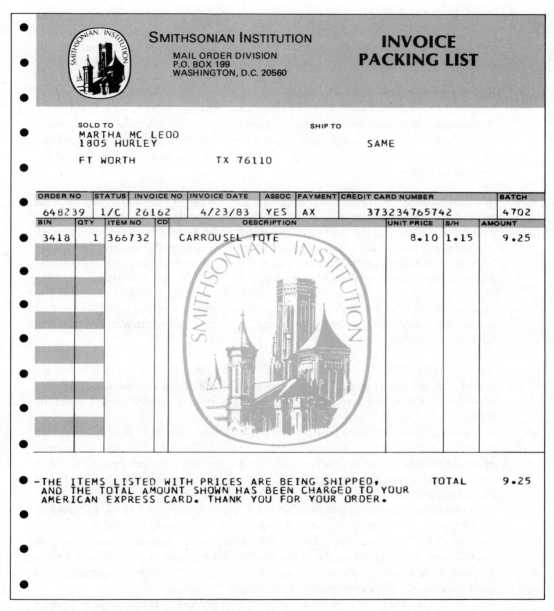

Figure 15-3 A multipurpose invoice form.

The physical system responds to signals generated by the conceptual information system. The conceptual information system determines what should be done, and the physical system does it. For a firm to rely on its conceptual system, that system must be accurate. It is the conceptual system that determines whether the physical system can fill the order. For the procedure to work smoothly, the conceptual system must be an accurate reflection of the physical system.

8. Receivables records.   The third important output of the billing system is the communication to the accounts receivable system. This communication can be in the form of a magnetic tape or disk. It is a file of *receivables records,* or records of money owed the firm by its customers—an *accounts receivable file.* A single record is included for each invoice, giving the vital data—invoice number and date, customer identification, and amount due.

9. Accounts receivable system.   This system is responsible for collecting all money owed the firm. In many cases, the customers will send their payments upon receipt of the invoice, or within thirty days. Very often a discount will be allowed for prompt payment.

10. Statements.   Some customers do not pay when they should. They must be reminded. The document that serves as the reminder is the *statement.* A line is printed in the body of the statement for each invoice on which an amount is owed. The amounts can be printed in separate columns based on the length of time they have been due. Amounts due over ninety days represent critical receivables situations demanding management attention.

Credit managers can receive notice of these past-due amounts for follow-up action. An overdue receivables report can be prepared weekly, listing those customers with amounts due over ninety days. This type of report was illustrated in Chapter 11, Figure 11-9.

11. Payments.   When payments are received, the corresponding amounts due are removed from the receivables file. The receivables file therefore contains only records of outstanding customer debts; the file is an inventory of money owed the firm.

It is common for some type of *turnaround document,* such as a punched card or optical reading slip, to accompany the payment. This computer-readable input relieves the firm of the necessity of keying the payment into a terminal or other keydriven machine.The turnaround document was described in Chapter 6 and illustrated in Figure 6-10.

The three systems described above are just a sampling of those included in the internal accounting system. Another group of systems interfaces with the firm's vendors. These systems are involved with purchasing, receiving, and accounts payable and are triggered by the manufacturing information system when it detects a need for replenishing raw materials. Still other systems handle transactions with stockholders, the firm's personnel, and the government.

As defined here, the internal accounting system performs two important roles in the MIS. First, it relieves operational-level managers of many routine decisions that can be programmed into the computer's logic. The manager specifies how the decisions are to be made, and the MIS carries out those instructions without further manager involvement. Second, the accounting system provides the data base of the firm's financial activity. This data base makes it possible to see where the firm has been in the past. In some cases, the data base describes what is happening currently. And accounting data is required by many of the mathematical models to enable managers to look into the future.

Faster billing with timesharing

The Composite Can Products group of Owens-Illinois Forest Products Division makes paper and metal combination containers for frozen orange juice and motor oil at eight plant locations. The old billing system required each plant to mail invoice data to the headquarters in Toledo, where the invoices were prepared on an IBM System/34 and mailed to the customer. The billing delay caused by mailing the data to Toledo was in turn delaying the receipt of customers' payments.

By installing terminals at each plant site, the firm has reduced the payment delay by a minimum of seven days. This means that the firm can use the money seven days sooner than before. At today's interest rates, the extra time will pay for the system in the first year.

With the new system, invoice data is transmitted to Toledo for processing. Output data is transmitted back to the plants, where invoices are printed on the terminal. The plants mail the invoices to their customers. The billing system, along with two production reporting systems, required fifty-five programs and was implemented in about five weeks by one analyst/programmer and one programmer.

According to Charles Eberlin, manager of planning and administration: "From a management standpoint, we emphasize to our plant staff that return on investment is the name of the game. They can see very quickly that gains in information processing speed will allow them to make decisions faster and improve our return on investment."[3]

Financial Intelligence Subsystem

The financial intelligence subsystem is responsible for gathering data and information from stockholders, the financial community, and the government. Since the financial function controls the money flow through the firm, information is needed to expedite this flow. The day-to-day flow of money from customers and to vendors is controlled by the internal accounting subsystem. The financial intelligence subsystem is concerned with flows other than those involved in daily operations. This system seeks to identify the best sources of additional capital and the best investments of surplus funds.

Stockholder information

All but the smallest corporations have a stockholder relations department within the financial function. This department is concerned with the flow of information between the firm and its stockholders. Most of the information flows from the firm to the stockholders in the form of annual and quarterly reports. Figure 15-4, a page from the Alcoa annual report, shows how several key financial indicators have fluctuated over a five-year period. Both current and potential stockholders use this information to appraise the investment opportunity offered

---

[3] Moving Invoice Data," *Viewpoint*, March–April 1981, p. 18.

Five-Year Summary

Years ended December 31	1980	1979	1978	1977	1976
Earnings (millions of dollars)					
Total revenues	$5,195.9	$4,847.0	$4,072.5	$3,433.1	$2,943.6
Cost of goods sold and operating expenses	3,801.0	3,452.9	2,976.3	2,593.5	2,216.7
Selling, general administrative and other expenses	351.1	305.9	276.1	239.5	207.7
Provision for depreciation and depletion	261.3	247.0	227.5	203.9	191.3
Interest expense	71.8	86.1	87.8	89.8	90.9
U.S. and foreign taxes on income	251.1	270.2	189.0	97.4	75.0
Other taxes	73.9	73.4	60.3	52.4	43.8
Equity earnings (losses) from entities not consolidated	84.2	93.1	57.2	38.6	25.6
Net income	469.9	504.6	312.7	195.2	143.8
Preferred stock dividends declared	2.5	2.5	2.5	1.9	2.5
Common stock dividends declared	114.3	91.3	66.3	46.6	47.3
Percent return on:					
Sales and operating revenues	9.1	10.5	7.7	5.7	4.9
Average shareholders' equity*	17.3	22.0	16.0	11.2	8.9
Average invested capital*	13.6	16.3	11.5	8.3	6.8
Financial position (millions of dollars)					
Working capital	820.0	859.0	735.6	667.1	581.6
Properties, plants and equipment, net	2,687.3	2,318.9	2,164.6	2,029.6	1,953.4
Investments	764.6	587.2	490.6	446.7	446.5
Other assets, net*	(16.6)	(25.8)	7.4	5.5	1.2
Long-term debt (noncurrent)	1,017.5	1,020.6	1,130.0	1,166.0	1,158.1
Future income taxes*	304.0	213.1	178.7	153.3	159.0
Shareholders' equity*	2,933.8	2,505.6	2,089.5	1,829.6	1,665.6
Share data					
Per common share (dollars)					
Net income	6.54	7.15	4.45	2.79	2.07
Dividends declared	1.60	1.30	.95	.675	.6925
Equity (based on year-end outstanding shares)*	39.25	34.68	28.86	25.42	23.30
Price range					
High	38.1875	30.25	26.50	29.75	30.625
Low	26.125	23.25	19.25	20.4375	19.25
Number of shareholders					
Preferred	2,169	2,264	2,386	2,496	2,592
Common	28,170	28,587	29,405	28,751	28,451
Average number of common shares outstanding (thousands)	71,475	70,251	69,755	69,020	68,188
Property, plant and equipment expenditures (millions of dollars)	637.8	420.0	349.8	281.7	243.7
Cost of materials, services, etc. (millions of dollars)	2,736.2	2,475.4	2,124.9	1,852.3	1,592.5
Wages, salaries and employee benefits (millions of dollars)	1,487.7	1,369.5	1,215.3	1,070.5	922.8
Average number of employees	45,600	46,800	46,000	45,200	43,300
Capacity, production and shipments (thousands of short tons)					
Primary aluminum production—United States	1,535	1,543	1,470	1,376	1,280
Primary aluminum capacity—United States	1,725	1,700	1,700	1,675	1,675
Primary aluminum production—consolidated	1,596	1,603	1,531	1,431	1,409
Primary aluminum shipments—consolidated	376	301	206	171	231
Total shipments of aluminum products—consolidated	1,833	1,886	1,779	1,688	1,638
Primary aluminum production, worldwide, including affiliates	2,054	2,038	1,938	1,836	1,690
Primary aluminum capacity, worldwide, including affiliates	2,324	2,227	2,185	2,160	2,160

*Restated for years 1976 through 1979 (Note F)

Figure 15-4 The annual report synthesizes the financial condition of the firm.

Figure 15-5 An annual stockholders meeting.

by the firm. Stockholder reports are prepared by the stockholder relations department working closely with top management. They contain information in a highly summarized form.

Stockholders have an opportunity to communicate information (complaints, suggestions, ideas, etc.) to the firm through the stockholder relations department. Also, once a year an annual stockholders meeting (Figure 15-5) is held where stockholders can learn firsthand what the firm is doing. Very often, stockholders use these meetings as an opportunity to communicate directly with top management.

Information gathered informally from stockholders is seldom entered into the computerized system, but it is disseminated by verbal communication and written memo to key executives in the firm.

Financial community information

The relationship between the firm and the financial community also receives attention from financial management. There should be a balanced flow of money through the firm, but this equilibrium is not always achieved. At times additional funds are needed or investments of surplus funds are desired. It is the responsibility of the financial intelligence subsystem to compile information on sources of funds and investment opportunities.

An important indirect environmental effect influences this money flow through the firm. The federal government controls the money market of the country through the Federal Reserve System. There are various means of releasing the controls to expedite the money flow and of tightening the controls to reduce the flow.[4]

The firm therefore must gather information from both financial institutions and the Federal Reserve System. This information permits the firm to remain current on national monetary policies and trends and possibly to anticipate future changes. A variety of publications can be used for this purpose. They are prepared by both the financial institutions and the government. Two examples are the *Monthly Economic Letter* prepared by the First National City Bank of New York and the *Federal Reserve Bulletin* prepared by the Federal Reserve System.

In addition to the need to acquire funds, the firm frequently must invest surplus funds on either a short- or long-term basis. These funds can be invested in a number of different ways—in United States Treasury securities, commercial paper, or certificates of deposit (CDs). Since the terms and rates of return for some of these vary over time, it is necessary to monitor these investment opportunities continually so that the optimum ones can be used when needed.

Gathering information from the financial environment is the responsibility of the financial intelligence subsystem. As with the other two functional intelligence subsystems, the information is usually handled outside the computer system. This subsystem is one area where computer use could improve.

The *Wall Street Journal* as an information source

Possibly the most widely read business periodical, the *Wall Street Journal* (WSJ), contains news of happenings throughout the business community. It provides especially informative descriptions of the economic environment in which businesses operate. Simply by reading a periodical such as the *WSJ*, you can keep up with many of the important environmental influences that shape a manager's decision strategy.

The *WSJ* is published Monday through Friday, following the format illustrated in Figure 15-6 to cover a wide variety of topics.[5] Each day the front page contains a "What's News" section in columns 2 and 3. The "Business and Finance" column offers a distillation of the day's major corporate, industrial, and economic news. The "World-Wide" column captures the day's domestic and international news developments.

"Special Reports" appears in column 5 each day. On Monday, "The Outlook" provides an economic overview, analyzing the economy from every conceivable angle. On Tuesday, the "Labor Letter" addresses work news of all kinds—government policy, management, unions, labor relations, and personnel. Wednesday brings the "Tax Report," which alerts readers to new tax trends. The "Business Bulletin" appears each Thursday and tries to spot emerging trends. The idea is to make information available while managers can still act on it. Finally, every Friday

---

[4] For a description of how Federal Reserve policies can affect the economy, see George J. Church, "Paying More for Money," *Time,* 8 March 1982, pp. 74 ff.

[5] Material for the discussion of the *Wall Street Journal* was taken from *A Future Manager's Guide to the* Wall Street Journal, published by the *Wall Street Journal*, Educational Service Bureau, Princeton, N.J.

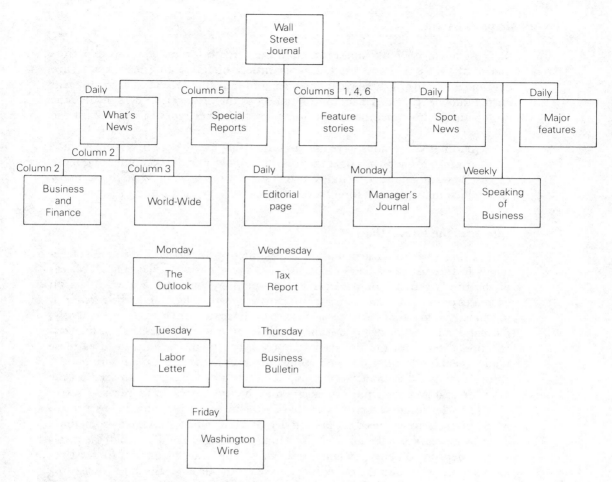

Figure 15-6 Organization of the *Wall Street Journal*.

brings the "Washington Wire," providing an interpretation of government policy and its possible impacts on business.

Other sections of the *WSJ* include a daily editorial page, feature stories in columns 1, 4, and 6 on the front page (and every day except Monday on the back page), the "Manager's Journal," "Spot News" (which provides insight into what competitors are doing), "Speaking of Business," and major features.

We have seen that upper-level managers need environmental and future-oriented information. Business periodicals such as the *WSJ* can provide much of this soft information flow.

The internal accounting and financial intelligence subsystems furnish input data and information to the financial information system. The remainder of the chapter is devoted to the output subsystems that provide information to managers throughout the firm—not only in the financial function.

Forecasting Subsystem

Business managers have long recognized the need to forecast the future performance of the firm. As a result, a large variety of forecasting techniques have developed.[6] Many of these techniques are informal and depend to a great extent on the knowledge, experience, and intuition of the manager. Others involve the use of quantitative methods to project sales and other types of activity for the firm.

Quantitative methods were used in forecasting long before they were applied to other areas of the firm's operations. But the power of the computer and more sophisticated quantitative methods such as simulation have improved the accuracy with which managers can forecast the future.

Who does the forecasting?

Forecasting is very often accomplished by marketing. In these instances, the objective is to forecast sales. Sales forecasts serve as the basis for planning all phases of the firm's activity for the near future—perhaps the coming year. Based on estimates of the firm's sales, the manufacturing function determines the personnel, machine, and material resources needed to produce the firm's products. Similarly, the marketing function determines the required marketing resources, and the financial function determines the financial resources. The financial function uses these requirements to identify the total money needs of the firm for the future period. In this manner, the financial planning for each functional unit is based on the sales forecast and is intended to ensure that the firm meets that forecast.

The sales forecast serves as the basis for short-term planning in most firms. Many firms, however, need to plan activity for a longer period of time—sometimes eight to ten years into the future. With a long planning horizon, much of the firm's success depends on environmental influences. The firm must try to forecast the national economy and the effect it can have on the firm. Long-range forecasting of this type normally belongs to the financial function.[7]

Forecasting methods

Forecasting techniques can be divided into two categories—quantitative and nonquantitative. All techniques, however, are based on projections of what has happened in the past.

A nonquantitative approach does not involve computations of data. The manager says something like, "We sold 2000 units last year, and we should be able to improve on that. So I think we will sell 2500 next year." Forecasts such as this can have little or no basis, or they can result from an informed firsthand

---

[6] For an analysis of eighteen different forecasting techniques, see John C. Chambers, Satinder K. Mullick, and Donald D. Smith, "How to Choose the Right Forecasting Technique," *Harvard Business Review* 49 (July–August 1971): 45–74.

[7] The use of forecasting in long-term planning is discussed in Terry W. Rothermel, "Forecasting Resurrected," *Harvard Business Review* 60 (March–April 1982): 139–147.

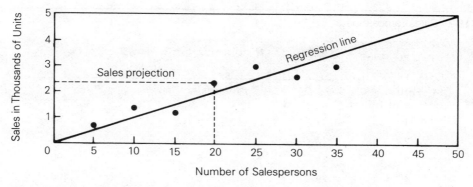

Figure 15-7   Relationship of sales to number of salespersons.

knowledge of the situation. Many managers are extremely adept at the nonquantitative approach.

Not all managers are so gifted, however, and many businesses are too complex for this simple method. In these situations the manager can use a variety of quantitative techniques to assure the most accurate forecast possible using the available data. One such technique is *regression analysis*. It involves the relationship of the activity to be forecast, such as sales, to some other activity, such as the number of salespersons. This relationship is shown in Figure 15-7.

Seven points are plotted on the graph. They represent the relationship between the two variables during previous periods, say the past seven years. For example, in one year twenty salespersons were employed and sales were approximately 2300 units (dotted lines). It is apparent from the plot of points on the graph that a positive relationship exists between the two variables—the more salespersons the firm employs, the higher the sales.

Regression analysis permits the use of a mathematical model to specify the relationship very exactly. When the model is executed, a regression line can be drawn through the points so that the total distance from each of the points to the line is at a minimum. This line is the "best fit" to the points. The management can then use the regression line to forecast sales based on a particular number of salespersons. For example, if the firm employed fifty salespersons, it could assume that sales would approximate 5000 units.

This example involves only two variables: an *independent variable* (salespersons) and a *dependent variable* (sales). Sales depend on the number of salespersons. This type of regression is known as *bivariate regression*—only two variables are involved.

Many business activities, such as sales, are sufficiently complex to defy predictions based on a single *independent* variable. In those cases more than one can be used; this technique is called *multivariate regression*. For example, it might be necessary to relate sales to (1) the number of salespersons, (2) the advertising budget, (3) the number of retail outlets, and (4) the number of customers.

The calculations required for bivariate regression (sometimes called *simple regression*) can be easily made on an electronic calculator. You have probably

Table 15-1   Sales forecast data

	Historical Data		
Year	Sales (Y)	Advertising (X_2)	Price ratio (X_3)
1	24	4	80
2	27	4	80
3	31	5	90
4	29	5	100
5	33	6	100
6	38	7	110
7	37	8	120
8	40	8	100
9	45	9	90
10	49	10	100

made such calculations in a statistics or operations research course. The calculations for multivariate regression (often called *multiple regression*) are much more involved and require the use of a computer.

Prewritten programs are used to perform regression analysis on the computer. Usually these programs are part of a set that performs different types of statistical analyses. Some of the more popular sets, or stat packages, are BMDP 77, OMNITAB, SAS®, and SPSS.

SAS—Statistical Analysis System

The SAS (pronounced "sass") package is a product of the SAS Institute Inc.[8] We will use it as an example of forecasting with a stat package. Assume that you own a creamery that sells ice cream to supermarkets. You have been in operation for ten years and have accumulated some statistics on your operation. The statistics presented in Table 15-1 represent your annual sales (Y) in thousands of dollars, your advertising budget (X_2), also in thousands of dollars, and a ratio (X_3) of your price compared with your competitors' average price. To compute the ratio, your price is divided by the competitors' average price.

Both the data and the SAS instructions can be entered through a terminal or keypunched. It is possible to use data already stored in the data base, in which case you only have to enter the SAS instructions. We will assume that the historical data in Table 15-1 is *not* in your data base, so you must enter it from a terminal.

---

[8] SAS is the registered trademark of SAS Institute, Inc., Cary, N.C. For an introductory description of SAS, see the *SAS Introductory Guide,* (Cary, N.C.: SAS Institute, 1978).

You would like to use SAS to develop a regression equation that expresses the slope of the regression line. The equation will be based on the historical data. All you need to do is enter the data and the SAS instructions as follows:

```
DATA;
  INPUT SALES 1-2 ADVER 4-5 PRICE 7-9;
  CARDS;
  24   4   080
  27   4   080
  31   5   090
  29   5   100
  33   6   100
  38   7   110
  37   8   120
  40   8   100
  45   9   090
  49  10   100
PROC GLM;
  MODEL SALES = ADVER PRICE;
```

The word DATA tells SAS to create a file. The word INPUT is used to define the format of the input record. The first field is SALES, which appears in the first two positions. The next field is ADVER, which is in positions 4 and 5. PRICE appears in positions 7 through 9. The word CARDS is used when the data is entered in card form or through a terminal. The ten data records follow.

The instruction PROC (pronounced "prock") is a request for SAS to process your data. GLM stands for general linear model, the part of SAS that performs the regression. The MODEL expression first identifies the dependent variable (SALES) and then the independent variables (ADVER and PRICE). The dependent variable appears first with the independent variables(s) to the right of the equals sign. In this model, sales *depend* on advertising and price.

The SAS output appears in Figure 15-8.

Funds Management Subsystem

The general systems model of the firm shows how resources flow from the environment, through the firm, and back to the environment. One of these flows is money. Money flow is important in that it makes possible the other resources; and, in the form of profits, it reflects the ability of the firm to meet its responsibilities to the owners.

The money flow can be managed to achieve two goals: (1) to assure that the inflow in the form of sales revenue is greater than the outflow in the form of expenses, and (2) to assure that this condition remains as stable as possible throughout the year.[9] A firm could show a good profit on the year's activities,

---

[9] For an explanation of how the cash flow can be managed, see Bradley T. Gale and Ben Branch, "Cash Flow Analysis: More Important than Ever," *Harvard Business Review* 59 (July–August 1981): 131–136.

S T A T I S T I C A L   A N A L Y S I S   S Y S T E M   14:07 WEDNESDAY, MAY 12, 1982   2

GENERAL LINEAR MODELS PROCEDURE

DEPENDENT VARIABLE: SALES

SOURCE	DF	SUM OF SQUARES	MEAN SQUARE	F VALUE	PR > F	R-SQUARE	C.V.
MODEL	2	556.41542632	278.20771316	110.12	0.0001	0.969196	4.5027
ERROR	7	17.68457368	2.52636767			STD DEV	SALES MEAN
CORRECTED TOTAL	9	574.10000000				1.58945515	35.30000000

SOURCE	DF	TYPE I SS	F VALUE	PR > F	TYPE IV SS	F VALUE	PR > F
ADVER	1	551.00594059	218.10	0.0001	443.50691568	175.55	0.0001
PRICE	1	5.40948572	2.14	0.1868	5.40948572	2.14	0.1868

PARAMETER	ESTIMATE	T FOR H0: PARAMETER=0	PR > |T|	STD ERROR OF ESTIMATE
INTERCEPT	16.50961065	3.94	0.0056	4.18787189
ADVER	3.92557910	13.25	0.0001	0.29627964
PRICE	-0.07338590	-1.46	0.1868	0.05015139

Figure 15-8 SAS forecast output.

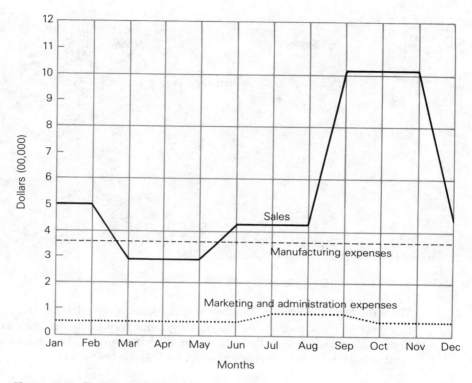

Figure 15-9 Fluctuating sales influence monthly profit.

yet have periods during the year when expenses exceeded revenues. This situation can be seen in Figure 15-9, where a manufacturer of garden equipment enjoys high sales in the fall and low sales in the spring. From March through May, the monthly sales of $300,000 are not high enough to cover the monthly manufacturing expenses of $360,000. Money outflow during March through May exceeds inflow by $262,000, even though profit for the year is $1,908,000.

The funds management subsystem can prepare a report such as that in Figure 15-10, showing money flow for the next twelve-month period. The report can be printed by a mathematical model that uses the sales forecast plus expense projections as the basis for the calculations.

Although the annual results are good, the money flow throughout the year is anything but stable. Since the sales to wholesalers are made mostly in the winter months, there is a big inflow of money from September through February. But the plant operates at a fixed output throughout the year, and this puts a drain on money from March through August. This feast-or-famine condition presents problems for financial management. What can be done with the surplus during the winter months? And what about the deficit during the summer?

The model the manager uses to solve the money flow problem is called the *cash flow model*. The term cash flow is common in finance and refers to a period-by-period simulation of cash inflow and outflow. The model produces a printed report, such as the one in Figure 15-10, in a format familiar to financial managers.

PROJECTED MONEY FLOW

	JAN•	FEB•	MAR•	APR•	MAY	JUN•	JUL•	AUG•	SEP•	OCT•	NOV•	DEC•	TOTAL
MONEY INPUT SALES	$500	$500	$300	$300	$300	$400	$400	$400	$1000	$1000	$1000	$500	$6600
MONEY OUTPUT MANUFACTURING EXPENSES													
WAGES	82	82	82	82	82	82	82	82	82	82	82	82	984
MATERIALS	220	220	220	220	220	220	220	220	220	220	220	220	2640
OTHER MFG• EXPENSES	58	58	58	58	58	58	58	58	58	58	58	58	696
TOTAL MANU- FACTURING EXPENSES	360	360	360	360	360	360	360	360	360	360	360	360	4320
MARKETING AND ADMIN• EXP•	26	26	26	28	28	28	40	40	40	30	30	30	372
NET CHANGE IN MONEY	+114	+114	-86	-88	-88	+12	0	0	+600	+610	+610	+110	1908

Figure 15-10   An unbalanced money flow.

The cash flow model in this example is dynamic, deterministic, nonoptimizing, and specific. The manager can also obtain general-purpose models such as VisiCalc to perform a *cash flow analysis*. Since the models are nonoptimizing, the manager must simulate several scenarios in order to find the best strategy.

First simulation—variable production schedule

One alternative is to develop a new product that would increase revenues during the first part of the year. But because such a development program normally spans a period of several years, it is not a feasible solution to the immediate problem.

Another way to achieve a better balance between sales and expenses is to match production to sales rather than spend constant amounts for wages, materials, and manufacturing expenses, as in Figure 15-10. The financial manager schedules production output in one month to equal the sales forecast for the next. Of course this change would have to be approved by the manufacturing manager. This new strategy is illustrated in Figure 15-11.

The figure shows a peak manufacturing period during the summer, creating the products for fall sales. The effect of this strategy is illustrated by the money flow model in the form of the report shown in Figure 15-12.

Second simulation—delayed materials payments

It is clear that the above change helped the situation during the first four months, but the money drain during May through August increased. The main reason for these negative balances is the high materials expenses for May–July of $400,000 per month. If the manager can shift these expenses to months with high sales revenues, the negative balances can be eliminated or reduced. It probably would

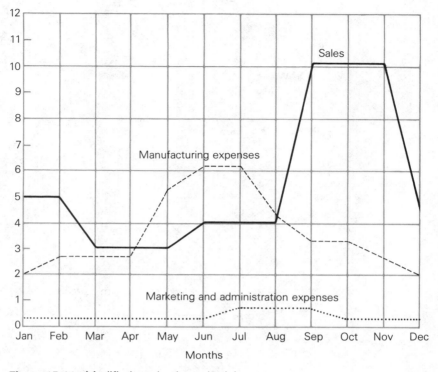

Figure 15-11 Modified production schedule.

	JAN	FEB•	MAR•	APR•	MAY	JUN•	JUL•	AUG•	SEP•	OCT•	NOV•	DEC•	TOTAL
PROJECTED MONEY FLOW													
MONEY INPUT													
SALES	●500	●500	●300	●300	●300	●400	●400	●400	●1000	●1000	●1000	●500	●6600
MONEY OUTPUT													
MANUFACTURING													
EXPENSES													
WAGES	44	44	60	60	60	150	150	150	74	74	74	44	984
MATERIALS	120	160	160	160	400	400	400	200	200	200	120	120	2640
OTHER MFG•													
EXPENSES	46	46	50	50	50	80	80	80	56	56	56	46	696
TOTAL MANU-													
FACTURING													
EXPENSES	210	250	270	270	510	630	630	430	330	330	250	210	4320
MARKETING AND													
ADMIN• EXP•	26	26	26	28	28	28	40	40	40	30	30	30	372
NET CHANGE IN													
MONEY	+264	+224	+4	+2	-238	-258	-270	-70	+630	+640	+720	+260	1908

Figure 15-12 Effect of production changes on money flow.

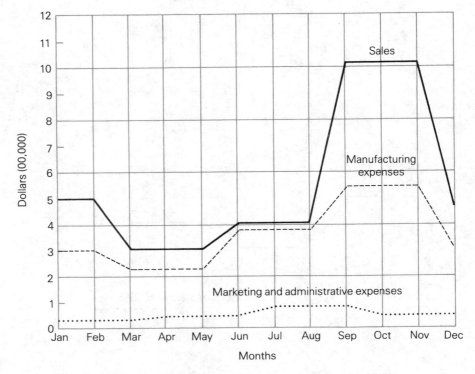

Figure 15-13 Modified payment schedule.

not be practical to shift the acquisition of the materials to an earlier or later period, but the payment might be delayed. Materials could be acquired for the May–July production peak, and payment delayed until September–November. Vendors would have to approve a 120-day delay in payment without an interest charge.[10] Assuming that vendors would be receptive to such an arrangement, the finance manager can simulate this solution. The results are illustrated in Figures 15-13 and 15-14. You can see that there is a positive cash flow each month except for very small negative flows from June through August. If this flow is satisfactory to the financial manager, no further simulations are performed.

The cash flow analysis usually takes the form of a printed report. But it can also appear graphically in a format similar to the graphs used here. A software package such as Trend-Spotter '82 or DISSPLA can convert the data into a form suitable for output on a plotter or CRT.

The cash flow model enables the manager to simulate the effect of various strategies to achieve the best use of available money. The finance manager can use the model to evaluate strategies and then work cooperatively with other functional managers to select and implement the optimal strategy.

---

[10]The likelihood of a vendor agreeing to a 120-day delay in payment depends on several factors. One is the economy. During periods of tight money and high interest rates, the vendor will probably insist on payment within 30 days. Another factor is the manufacturer's power relative to the vendor's. If the manufacturer purchases most of the vendor's output, the vendor may have no alternative but to go along with the delayed payment.

	JAN	FEB•	MAR•	APR•	MAY	JUN•	JUL•	AUG•	SEP•	OCT•	NOV•	DEC•	TOTAL
PROJECTED MONEY FLOW													
MONEY INPUT													
SALES	•500	•500	•300	•300	•300	•400	•400	•400	•1000	•1000	•1000	•500	•6600
MONEY OUTPUT													
MANUFACTURING													
EXPENSES													
WAGES	44	44	60	60	60	150	150	150	74	74	74	44	984
MATERIALS	200	200	120	120	120	160	160	160	400	400	400	200	2640
OTHER MFG.													
EXPENSES	46	46	50	50	50	80	80	80	56	56	56	46	696
TOTAL MANU-													
FACTURING													
EXPENSES	290	290	230	230	230	390	390	390	530	530	530	290	4320
MARKETING AND													
ADMIN. EXP.	26	26	26	28	28	28	40	40	40	30	30	30	372
NET CHANGE IN													
MONEY	+184	+184	+44	+42	+42	-18	-30	-30	+430	+440	+440	+180	1908

Figure 15-14 Effect of delayed materials payments on cash flow.

Control Subsystem

One of the basic management functions is control. Managers compare actual performance with predefined standards to assure that overall objectives are being met. This occurs on all management levels.

Managers have operational objectives to achieve, such as producing or selling a certain value of items. Managers are given an amount of money to use in meeting these objectives; this money is called the *operating budget* (often simply called the "budget"). The budget provides the operating funds for a fiscal (financial) year.

Establishing a budget is an unstructured decision. Managers must enter into the process and prepare a budget that will be realistic and yet will stimulate efficient operations.

Each organizational unit has its own budget. Together these budgets constitute the budget of the entire firm. Managers on all levels are evaluated not only on how well they meet their operational objectives, but also on how well they stay within their budgets.

The budgeting process

Because firms have paid so much attention to the budgeting process over the past twenty years, it is now very refined. Firms have learned that the best budget is developed jointly by all participants. A purely *top-down* budgeting approach is likely to fail when it is imposed on lower-level managers by those above. The lower-level managers feel that it is not their budget, but their superiors'. A purely *bottom-up* approach would most likely offer little improvement. Lower-level managers would tend to play the "Army game" of asking for much more funding than they think they need, knowing that their requests will be cut.

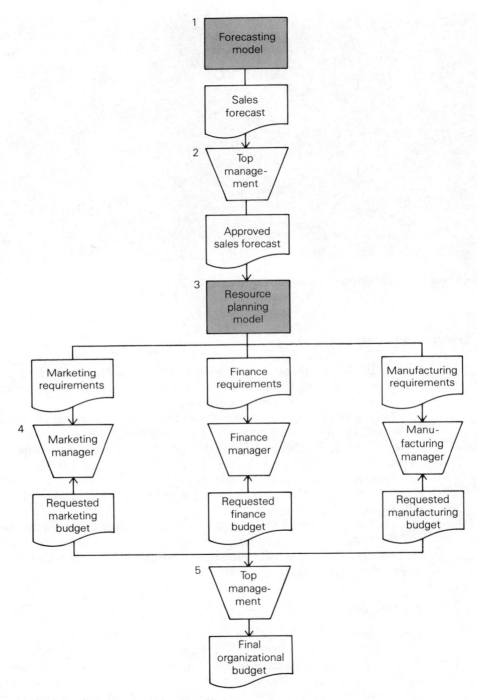

Figure 15-15 The budgeting process.

The most effective budgeting approach combines the participation of lower-level managers with overall direction (but not manipulation) by upper-level managers. Such an approach is termed an *integrative* approach. Figure 15-15 illustrates this budgeting process. The numbered paragraphs below correspond to the numbers in the figure.

1. The starting point is the sales forecast. This forecast can be prepared by a forecasting model, perhaps using multiple regression.

2. Top management examines the forecast and makes adjustments to it based on their subjective evaluations plus other inputs.

3. The approved forecast data is then entered into a resource-planning model that converts the quantitatively stated sales objectives into resource requirements for each functional area. For example, if the firm is to sell 230,000 units next year, eight new salespersons must be hired, a new drill press must be purchased, two new accounting clerks must be added, and so on.

4. The model's programmed projections are then evaluated by each of the managers of the units to which they apply. These managers use their knowledge of the business to increase or (very infrequently) to decrease the budgeted amounts. Each manager works in conjunction with his or her superior to arrive at an acceptable budget. The two-way arrows connecting this and the next step illustrate the give and take between top management and functional management before the budget is finalized.

5. The combined approved functional budgets represent the organizational budget. Once budgets are established, they are seldom changed. They represent the standards of acceptable financial performance.

Budget reports

The operating budget for a unit, such as a department or division, usually consists of amounts for each of the basic expense items (salaries, telephone, rent, supplies, and so on). These expense items are usually allocated monthly throughout the budget period.

Each month, each manager with budget responsibility receives a report showing actual expenditures compared with the budget. An example of such a report appears in Figure 15-16. Managers pay considerable attention to these reports. In some firms, management compensation plans are geared, in part, to budget performance. Perhaps bonuses are paid when performance is within budget. The important goal is to meet the total budgeted amount for the year. The manager works toward this objective by monitoring the monthly reports and responding to unusual variances.

The manager can use the report to identify areas for follow-up and then can query the data base to obtain more detailed information. For example, if the office has exceeded its telephone budget, the manager may be able to determine who is

```
                                      BUDGET REPORT
                                 AS OF JANUARY 31, 1982
                                    MIDWESTERN REGION

                        CURRENT MONTH                        YEAR-TO-DATE
         ITEM       BUDGET    ACTUAL      DOLLARS       BUDGET    ACTUAL      DOLLARS

   SALARIES        $23,500   $22,000    -$1,500       $59,000   $54,250    -$4,750
   TRAVEL            8,250     9,000    +   750        23,500    28,100    + 4,600
   ENTERTAINMENT     1,400     1,635    +   235         4,200     5,100    +   900
   TELEPHONE           200        85    -   115           600       225    -   375
   RENT                535       535          0         1,605     1,605          0
   FURNITURE             0         0          0           420       505    +    85
   SUPPLIES            625       410    -   215         1,875     1,320    -   555
   MISC.               400       620    +   220         1,200     1,965    +   765

   TOTAL           $34,910   $34,285    -   625       $92,400   $93,070    +   670
```

Figure 15-16 Sample budget report for a regional sales office.

responsible. Of course, the detailed information must first be in the data base in order to answer this query.

All managers on all levels throughout the firm use budget reports. The reports are provided by the financial information system.

Performance ratios

In addition to the budget, the control subsystem produces a number of *performance ratios* that enable managers on all levels to compare their performance with internal standards and also with those accepted as desirable by financial analysts. Many industries also have standards that member firms seek to attain in order to remain competitive. These ratios are computed using summary totals of accounting transactions.

There are quite a few ratios. Among the most popular is the *current ratio*, which measures the extent to which a firm can cover its short-term debts with assets easily converted into cash.

$$\text{Current ratio} = \frac{\text{current assets}}{\text{current liabilities}}$$

A ratio of 1.0 or greater is desirable, since it means the firm can cover its debts without having to sell its fixed assets (such as inventory).

Another popular ratio is *inventory turnover*.

$$\text{Inventory turnover ratio} = \frac{\text{cost of goods sold}}{\text{average inventory value}}$$

Generally, the higher the ratio, the better. The ratio is an indication of the managers' abilities to "keep that stock moving." If the ratio is too high, however, inventory ordering costs can become excessive.

Ratios such as these are used by managers and by outsiders (such as financial analysts, potential investors, and stockholders) to monitor the performance of the firm. The ratios represent highly distilled representations of a mass of accounting data. They provide a handy way to come to grips with the data to make meaningful observations.

The MIS cannot take credit for making these ratios possible. Most of the ratios were around long before the computer—laboriously cranked out by manual, keydriven, and punched card systems. Computers have made it easier to calculate the ratios. The ratios can be computed and stored in the data base, waiting for a manager to ask for them. Or the ratios can be computed at the time a query is made.

Putting the control subsystem into perspective

The MIS has done a better job in the control area than in any other. It provides the manager with accurate, complete information showing how the firm's performance compares with its objectives. A major shortcoming of this support is the historical nature of the information. In some firms, the information is out of date before it is available and so cannot help prevent problems. Managers are aware of this limitation, however, and recognize the value of computer systems that can speed the information flow. Today's online systems—featuring DASD, datacom, and DBMS—make it possible to report control information quickly enough to minimize the impact of emerging problems.

IFPS—Interactive Financial Planning System

We have encountered several software systems designed to make it easier for the manager to obtain information. The VisiCalc package, a computerized worksheet, permits "what-if" modeling on small systems. For large systems DBMS query languages such as INQUIRE and ADASCRIPT+, standalone query languages such as MARK-IV, and report writers such as ADACOM enable the manager to obtain information without programming.

Another popular software system of this nature is especially useful for decision making in the financial area. This package is IFPS—*Interactive Financial Planning System*.[11] IFPS, a product of Execucom, is a natural language system that permits a manager to build a model to test alternate strategies.

IFPS is similar to the VisiCalc package in that it views data as a table of numbers. But IFPS is much more powerful. It runs on medium- and large-scale

---

[11] Most of the information presented here on IFPS came from the *IFPS Tutorial* (Austin: Execucom, 1980).

systems as well as on superminis. With IFPS you can also incorporate probabilities into the model, and you can use the Monte Carlo method.

IFPS is one of a new breed of *natural-language* software—software designed to encourage greater manager participation and use through easier dialog. We will use IFPS as an illustration of how easily a manager can obtain information—especially information that must be generated through simulation.

An IFPS example

Assume that you want to project the performance of a new product over five years. You key in values as shown in Figure 15-17. The lines with asterisks serve as comments or separators. Most of the other lines consist of mathematical expressions. For example, line 9 instructs that variable cost will be computed by multiplying volume times unit cost. If you are familiar with a programming language such as BASIC or FORTRAN, you will note that these statements resemble those languages. But IFPS performs many functions automatically that must be coded when a programming language is used.

```
? MODEL INCOME
READY FOR EDIT. LAST LINE IS 30
? LIST

MODEL INCOME   VERSION OF  06/08/82  13:58
1 COLUMNS 1-5
2 *
3 *          INCOME STATEMENT
4 *
5 VOLUME = VOLUME ESTIMATE,PREVIOUS VOLUME * 1.045
6 SELLING PRICE = DATA FOR 2, PRICE ESTIMATE,PREVIOUS SELLING PRICE * 1.06
7       SALES = VOLUME * SELLING PRICE
8 UNIT COST = .85
9 VARIABLE COST = VOLUME * UNIT COST
10 DIVISION OVERHEAD = .15 * VARIABLE COST
11 STLINE DEPR(INVESTMENT,SALVAGE,LIFE,DEPRECIATION)
12       COST OF GOODS SOLD = VARIABLE COST + DIVISION OVERHEAD + DEPRECIATION
13 GROSS MARGIN = SALES - COST OF GOODS SOLD
14 OPERATING EXPENSE = .02 * SALES
15 INTEREST EXPENSE = 15742,21522,21147,24905,21311
16 *
17 NET BEFORE TAX = GROSS MARGIN - OPERATING EXPENSE - INTEREST EXPENSE
18 TAXES = TAX RATE * NET BEFORE TAX
19      NET AFTER TAX = NET BEFORE TAX - TAXES
20 *
21 INVESTMENT = 100000.125000,0,100000,0
22 *
23 RATE OF RETURN = IRR(NET AFTER TAX + DEPRECIATION,INVESTMENT)
24 *
25 *  DATA ESTIMATES
26 TAX RATE = .46
27 VOLUME ESTIMATE = 100000
28 PRICE ESTIMATE = 2.25
29 SALVAGE = 0
30 LIFE = 10
END OF MODEL
```

Figure 15-17 The manager enters the IFPS statements using a keyboard terminal.

After the instructions have been entered into a terminal, the model is executed and the output appears on the terminal or a printer. Figure 15-18 is an example of the type of output that could be received, using the input from Figure 15-17. The output is in the form of an income statement comparing product performance for each of the five years.

IFPS permits you to engage in "what-if" modeling. For example if you feel that the income statements in Figure 15-18 can be improved, you can input changed values and perform the simulation again. You might want to see what the results would be if unit cost (line 8) were $0.80 instead of $0.85. To do so, you would not have to rekey the entire model—only the line(s) changed.

Use of natural language software in the MIS

IFPS is generally regarded as the type of software managers need. There will undoubtedly be much more activity in natural languages in the future. The availability of such languages has real significance to the manager.

```
? SOLVE
MODEL INCOME  VERSION OF  06/08/82  13:58 -- 5 COLUMNS 21 VARIABLES
ENTER SOLVE OPTIONS
? ALL
```

	1	2	3	4	5
INCOME STATEMENT					
VOLUME	100000	104500	109203	114117	119252
SELLING PRICE	0	0	2.250	2.385	2.528
SALES	0	0	245706	272168	301481
UNIT COST	.8500	.8500	.8500	.8500	.8500
VARIABLE COST	85000	88825	92822	96999	101364
DIVISION OVERHEAD	12750	13324	13923	14550	15205
DEPRECIATION	10000	22500	22500	32500	32500
COST OF GOODS SOLD	107750	124649	129245	144049	149069
GROSS MARGIN	-107750	-124649	116460	128119	152412
OPERATING EXPENSE	0	0	4914	5443	6030
INTEREST EXPENSE	15742	21522	21147	24905	21311
NET BEFORE TAX	-123492	-146171	90399	97771	125071
TAXES	-56806	-67239	41584	44975	57533
NET AFTER TAX	-66686	-78932	48815	52796	67539
INVESTMENT	100000	125000	0	100000	0
RATE OF RETURN					-.1795
DATA ESTIMATES					
TAX RATE	.4600	.4600	.4600	.4600	.4600
VOLUME ESTIMATE	100000	100000	100000	100000	100000
PRICE ESTIMATE	2.250	2.250	2.250	2.250	2.250
SALVAGE	0	0	0	0	0
LIFE	10	10	10	10	10

Figure 15-18 Output from the IFPS model.

First, the manager need not invest so much time in the development of the MIS. Instead of communicating needs to the systems analyst, who will in turn communicate them to the programmer, the manager creates a model in a very short time.

Second, the need to communicate with the systems analyst is eliminated or greatly reduced. This solves the communication problem that has haunted users and technicians since the early days of the computer.

Third, by being able to do their work themselves, managers help relieve the backlog of unfilled requests for computer applications. Information specialists no longer work with users on those projects where users have become self-sufficient. The specialists can then concentrate on applications where their input is required.

Summary

The financial information system helps the manager achieve an efficient flow of money through the firm. The heart of the system is the internal accounting subsystem, providing details of transactions to all three functional information systems. Many of the internal accounting systems are closely related. Three of these systems (order entry, billing, and accounts receivable) are concerned with handling customer orders. These systems communicate with each other using files of data.

The other input subsystem, financial intelligence, gathers information and data from the environment. Stockholders, the financial community, and the national economy are the primary sources of financial intelligence.

The data and information gathered by the input subsystems are used by the forecasting subsystem to project the status of the firm's environment for long-term planning.

The forecasting subsystem projects future activity in the light of possible environmental influences. Statistical packages such as SAS include regression models that can forecast activity using one or more independent variables. These models, combined with environmental data gathered by the three intelligence subsystems, represent a powerful forecasting tool.

The funds management subsystem provides an estimate of the money flow into and out of the firm for the near future. Expected excesses or shortages of funds are flagged before they occur. Alternate strategies can then be considered to realize the best use of available funds.

Finally, the control subsystem enables the manager to measure the degree to which financial objectives are being met. The operating budget and financial ratios represent powerful tools that compare actual performance with acceptable standards.

The financial output subsystems are used by managers throughout the firm because the subsystems deal with an important resource—money. Money not only is necessary to obtain other resources but provides the basic measure of success.

The chief executive officer makes use of selected information from each of the output subsystems and from the internal accounting subsystem. Top managers in the financial area, such as the vice-president of finance and the controller, also use all of the subsystems. Lower-level financial managers tend to favor those

Table 15-2 Users of the financial information system

User	Subsystem			
	Forecasting	Funds management	Financial control	Accounting
Chief executive officer	X	X	X	X
Vice-president of finance	X	X	X	X
Controller	X	X	X	X
Manager of accounting			X	X
Manager of financial planning	X			X
Director of budgets			X	X
Other functional managers	X	X	X	X

subsystems relating directly to their area of responsibility. It is important to note that managers in other functional areas use the financial system's output. Every day, managers throughout the firm use financial information. Table 15-2 identifies the users of the financial information system.

Key Terms

order entry system

billing system

accounts receivable system

order form

invoice

picking ticket

packing list

accounts receivable file

statement

turnaround document

regression analysis

dependent variable

independent variable

bivariate regression, simple regression

multivariate regression, multiple regression

cash flow model

cash flow analysis   performance ratio
budget, operating budget   current ratio
top-down budgeting approach   inventory turnover
bottom-up budgeting approach   natural language
integrative budgeting approach

Key Concepts

The integrated nature of internal   The management of the firm's
  accounting subsystems   money flow by regulating inflows
The importance of internal   and outflows
  accounting to the MIS   The budget and performance ratios
The importance of environmental   as standards of acceptable
  information to managing the   financial performance
  money flow of the firm   Different approaches to budgeting
The responsibility of the financial   Natural-language software as a con-
  function for long-term forecasting   tributor to increased managerial
                                            use of the MIS

Questions

1. Does the firm provide accounting data only to those individuals and organizations directly involved with the firm's activities? Explain.
2. Name three key features of accounting data.
3. What is the input to the order entry system? What is the output?
4. Which subsystem prepares invoices? statements? picking tickets?
5. What are the three tasks performed by output from the billing system?
6. How can the keying of customer payment data into the computer be reduced or eliminated?
7. Describe the two important roles played by the internal accounting subsystem in the MIS.
8. Name two ways the corporation communicates information to its stockholders.
9. Name two publications of environmental financial information, and identify their sources.
10. Which organizational function usually prepares the sales forecast? the long-range economic or environmental forecast?
11. What are the two categories of forecasting techniques?
12. What is regression analysis? What is the regression line?
13. What distinguishes multivariate regression from bivariate regression?

14. Where does the data come from when using SAS as a forecasting model?

15. What are the two goals of money flow management? Does a cash flow model help achieve these goals? Explain.

16. Is a budget the same as an operating budget? What time period is usually covered by a budget?

17. What are the three basic approaches to budgeting? Which works best? Why?

18. What is the relationship between sales forecasting and the budgeting process?

19. In what way is IFPS similar to the VisiCalc package? What differentiates the two software systems?

20. What special significance do natural languages have for the MIS?

Problems

1. Calculate the current ratio for Alcoa for the years 1980 and 1979, using data in Figure 11-8.

2. Using data in Figures 11-8 and 15-4 calculate the inventory turnover ratio for Alcoa for the years 1980 and 1979. Use *total cost of goods sold and operating expenses* and *inventories*.

CASE PROBLEM: Aurora Outdoor Kits, Inc. (A-OK)

A-OK was founded in 1973 in Aurora, Colorado, by Faye and Bill Stuart. The firm manufactures kits for making various outdoor and camping items such as tents, parkas, sleeping bags, and down mittens. The kits are described in a catalog mailed to approximately 250,000 households a year. All business is by mail order, and the customer can return the kit if not completely satisfied. Returns are rare because the kit is well designed and the instructions are easy to follow.

Bill is vice-president of production and supervises sixty to seventy production employees. An office staff of twelve is supervised by Faye, who is president and chief administrative officer. The remaining employees are in marketing—a small staff of half a dozen supervised by the sales manager, Oley Tumwater.

Although the accounting system uses keydriven machines, A-OK has decided to order a computer. The company has retained a local consulting firm to help select equipment, design a system, program, and recruit a full-time analyst-programmer and an operator.

The consultant assigned to the account, Itzak Amitag, has been interviewing the various managers, learning what information they will need from the new system. Today Itzak is scheduled to interview Oley Tumwater.

Itzak taps on Oley's door as he walks in, and Oley motions for him to sit down. After a few minutes of chatting, Itzak gets down to business by asking,

"Oley, what kinds of information do you think you will need from the new system?"

Oley thinks for a few minutes and says, "Oh, the usual sales analysis figures. You know, sales by product, sales by geographic area, sales by season. I think the geographic analysis would be especially helpful. We could record sales by zip code, for example, to pinpoint exactly where our customers are. That information would really be helpful in planning new catalog mailings."

Itzak takes notes as Oley talks. Then he asks, "How would you like this information presented?"

"Oh, just summaries," Oley replies. "The product report could contain a line for each of our seventy products. We could show the item code, description, and monthly sales. If I could get that report monthly, I'd be happy. We could store all the monthly summaries and then print a seasonal analysis at the end of the year. For the geographic analysis, if we could show sales totals by zip code, that would be fine."

Itzak scribbles some more and then asks, "Any more information needs?"

"Nope, not for now," Oley replies.

Itzak studies his notes and mumbles to himself as he sketches a diagram on his pad. "We'll have to capture all of the needed data from the order form and update a sales statistics file right after the billing run. Then we just pull what we need out of the statistics file when we're ready to print the reports."

"What's that?" Oley interrupts.

"Oh nothing," Itzak replies. "Just talking to myself. I'll run along now and put this together and get back to you." With that, Itzak and Oley shake hands—each satisfied that he has taken an important step toward the new computer.

Questions

1. What data will have to be entered into the system so that Oley can have his reports?
2. At what point in the internal accounting system will the data be entered? (Refer to Figure 15-2)
3. At what point in the internal accounting system will the sales statistics file be updated?
4. What file will be used to update the sales statistics file?
5. Draw a rough sketch of the reports Oley has requested. Use sample reports in Chapter 11, starting with Figure 11-5, for reference.

Part Five

DEVELOPMENT AND CONTROL

At this point, three major topics have been discussed: the theoretical basis of systems, computing equipment, and functional uses of the computer. A major topic remains: how a firm can develop an MIS. This remaining topic is the subject of Part Five.

The following four chapters describe the process of MIS development. As this development unfolds you must understand two key points. First, the process is accomplished in steps. Second, the users of the information and the information specialists work together.

The organization of the chapters is intended to convey this step-by-step process. Each chapter deals with a major step. Planning the MIS project is described in Chapter 16. The analysis and design work leading to the specifications of the MIS is the subject of Chapter 17. The implementation of the MIS in the firm is treated in Chapter 18. The control of the operating MIS concludes the discussion, in Chapter 19.

Therefore, the MIS has a life cycle consisting of four major phases. But unlike other life cycles, MIS development is a never-ending affair. Attaining an MIS does not signal the end of management involvement. Over time the present MIS will become deficient and the process will have to be repeated.

Chapter 16

Information Systems Development: The Planning Phase

Learning Objectives

After studying this chapter, you should:

- Know which top-level executives in a firm can assume overall responsibility for the MIS project
- Understand the role played by an MIS committee in MIS planning and control
- Know the benefits of planning the MIS project
- Understand two basic approaches to the MIS project
- Be familiar with what the planning steps accomplish and who performs them
- Recognize the importance of a formal report as a basis for receiving management approval to proceed to the next phase
- Appreciate that planning is a necessary prerequisite to the achievement of control
- Understand how control evolves as project specifications are defined in greater detail
- Have an introductory understanding of network analysis as a control mechanism

Overview

One of the characteristics of the systems approach is to start with the big picture, which is what we will do as we begin our study of the MIS life cycle. This chapter and the next three will introduce you to a number of actiities that lead to an MIS. You will need a view from the top before you get involved with the details. Figure 16-1 provides an overview of the basic relationship between the manager (or user) and the information specialists. You will note that the manager either plans or controls. A plan is established during the first phase that provides the

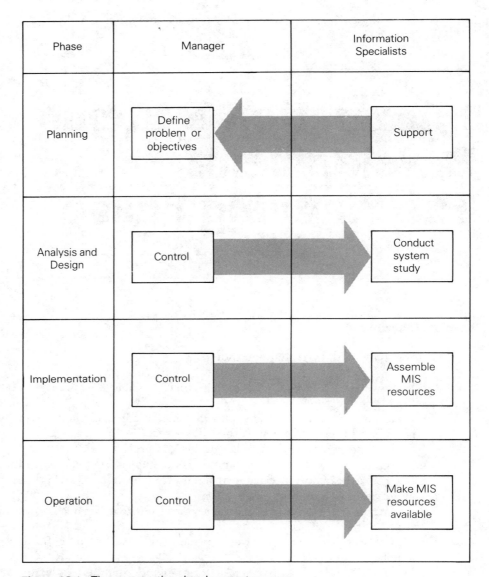

Figure 16-1 The cooperative development process.

control mechanism for the following phases. The information specialists support the manager during the planning phase and then are responsible for performing the tasks in the remaining three phases.

Figure 16-1 is the big picture. Each chapter in Part Five also contains a model of the activities for the phase under discussion, showing the steps in greater detail.

Importance of Planning

Chapter 2 described the management functions identified by Henri Fayol. The first, planning, is the key to the satisfactory performance of the others. For this reason, managers have learned that time spent in planning pays dividends when the other functions are performed.

The efforts of a firm to implement an MIS represent a large-scale activity involving many people and facilities, much money and equipment, and considerable time. The MIS project can require as many resources as the development of a new product, the construction of a new plant, or entry into a new market. Therefore, the MIS project should receive the same management attention as any expensive, time-consuming project.

Difficulty of the Task

This chapter deals with the planning that must be done *after* a decision is made to consider implementing an MIS and *before* work begins to design and implement the system. It is important that this planning be accomplished before work on the project actually starts. If not, it is likely that much of the work will be misdirected and have to be redone. Poor planning only delays the benefits of the MIS and adds to the cost of the project.

The difficulty of the development will depend on several factors. Three appear especially critical. These are (1) the attitude of the employees toward the MIS, (2) the availability of objectives for the firm, and (3) the adequacy of the existing information system. These three influences are illustrated in Figure 16-2.

When the firm's employees have a positive attitude toward the MIS, when the existing system is fairly adequate, and when the firm has good objectives, the

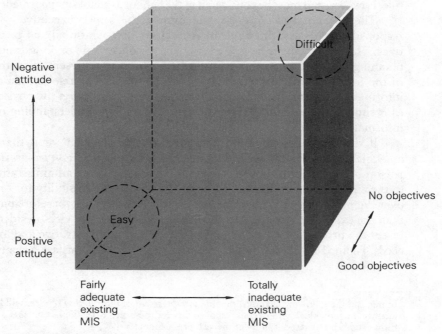

Figure 16-2 Difficulty of the MIS development.

development can be relatively easy. A healthy environment does not reduce the importance of planning but should reduce the time management spends on it. When the three conditions do not exist, development will be difficult and much time must be devoted to planning.

Responsibility for the MIS Project

Someone within the organization must have overall responsibility for the MIS *project*. This should *not* be the manager, such as the vice-president of information services,[1] who is responsible for the computer. Rather, it should be a high-level manager representing the users of the information system output.

There is nothing wrong with the president of the firm having this responsibility. In fact, that would be an ideal situation. The MIS will provide information needed by all types of managers on all levels. The system is so important to the success of the firm that the president's involvement is justified. But the president might not be able to devote as much time to the MIS project as it deserves. In this case, the president delegates primary authority for achieving the MIS to a key top-level executive.

Positions within a firm lending themselves to the type of direction needed are the executive vice-president and administrative vice-president. Generally, a functionally oriented executive, such as the vice-president of finance, should not be selected, because this could impede the achievement of a total MIS serving all areas of the firm. The vice-president might be tempted to devote primary attention to his or her own area, to the disadvantage of the others. This is only a general rule, however, and must be considered in the light of available management resources.

The *executive vice-president* is usually the senior executive with overall responsibility for assuring that the firm meets its operational and tactical objectives. This arrangement frees the president to concentrate on long-range strategic planning. The executive vice-president therefore can represent *all* of the interests of the firm in terms of the needs of both its physical system and its conceptual information system. And if the information system supports the physical system, as it should, the executive vice-president has the best understanding of the total information needs.

If the firm does not have an executive vice-president or if that person is unavailable, the logical second choice is the *administrative vice-president*. This person occupies a staff position responsible for providing administrative support to the entire firm. Unfortunately, he or she has no responsibility for or authority over the physical system. This person's scope of activity is therefore more limited than the executive vice-president's. But the administrative vice-president can represent the firm as a whole, in terms of meeting its administrative and information needs. Figure 16-3 shows how the various executive positions are generally ordered

---

[1] In this and the following chapters, the title *vice-president of information services* will be used to identify the individual with overall responsibility for the firm's MIS. We recognize that not all firms establish this responsibility at the vice-presidential level.

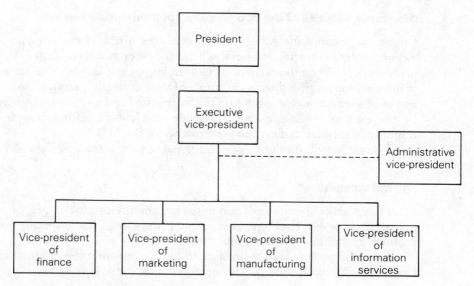

Figure 16-3 Executive positions within a firm.

within a firm. Solid lines indicate superior/subordinate relationships. The dotted line indicates the staff relationship of the administrative vice-president to the other executives.

In this discussion we will assume that the executive vice-president has primary responsibility for the MIS project. This title is used to simplify the discussion; in no way is it implied that this individual has responsibility in all cases. Designation of the responsibility depends entirely on the conditions within a particular firm.

MIS responsibilities of the executive vice-president

The executive vice-president is responsible for determining what the MIS will do and then for assuring that it is done. This task involves communicating with other executives and managers in the firm to determine their *general* information needs. The executive vice-president, assisted by the vice-president of information services, meets with the president and the functional vice-presidents to determine the major subsystems of the MIS. This information is then augmented with more specific details provided by lower-level managers.

MIS responsibilities of the functional executives

The vice-presidents of finance, marketing, and manufacturing all play active roles in the MIS project. First they communicate with the president, executive vice-president, and vice-president of information services to develop the overall description of the MIS. Then the functional vice-presidents work with the vice-president of information services to develop the overall description of their functional information systems.

MIS responsibilities of the vice-president of information services

During the preimplementation period, when the firm is considering an MIS, the vice-president of information services helps the other managers identify their information needs. When the decision is made to implement an MIS, the vice-president of information services directs the efforts of the information services staff in design and implementation. Once the MIS is implemented and its performance approved by the executive vice-president, the vice-president of information services is responsible for maintaining the performance of the MIS.

The responsibilities of these executives are summarized in Table 16-1.

The MIS committee

Most firms make liberal use of committees. Committees exist on practically every management level. They are used to pool knowledge for a specific project or problem and to improve communication.

The MIS project clearly justifies an executive committee. Many companies have followed this approach. The membership of the *MIS committee* includes the

Table 16-1 Executive responsibility for the MIS

Executive	Preimplementation period	Implementation period	Postimplementation period
President		Overall responsibility for the MIS	
Executive vice-president	Take primary responsibility for the design and implementation of the MIS		Approve the performance of the MIS
Vice-president of finance	Design the overall MIS Design the financial information system	Implement the financial information system	Make suggestions for improvement
Vice-president of marketing	Design the overall MIS Design the marketing information system	Implement the marketing information system	Make suggestions for improvement
Vice-president of manufacturing	Design the overall MIS Design the manufacturing information system	Implement the manufacturing information system	Make suggestions for improvement
Vice-president of information services	Design the overall MIS Design the functional information systems	Implement the overall MIS and its functional information systems	Oversee the operation and maintenance of the MIS

executive vice-president, the functional vice-presidents, and the vice-president of information services. The executive vice-president is chairperson and keeps the president informed of the committee activities. The other members serve as advisors.

The initial responsibility of the committee is to agree on what the MIS should do, in general terms, and to approve the expenditure of funds for the planning phase of the project. During the project, the committee monitors progress and approves funds for the next phase. Once the MIS is implemented, the committee formally approves the system's performance in terms of its objectives. When such a committee is not formed, these responsibilities belong to the key executive assigned to the project, such as the executive vice-president.

Summary of MIS responsibility

Responsibility for the design and implementation of the MIS lies in two general areas: (1) managers, who will use the MIS output, and (2) the information services staff, who will create the MIS. In addition, responsibility for the overall MIS, the functional subsystems, and parts of the functional subsystems is distributed among managers on several levels.

A top executive (the president or executive vice-president) is responsible for the overall effort and is assisted by the other managers who will use the MIS output. The vice-president of information services lends support when and where needed. The implementation of an MIS is decidedly a team effort.

There has never been any doubt about the necessity of management involvement in a computer project. The scenario presented here, describing active, informed participation at the top level, is a normative model—it describes how the MIS *should* develop. Not all projects are managed in this fashion. But the closer the project management conforms to the description presented here, the greater the chances for success.

Benefits of Planning the MIS

Managers engage in planning to facilitate the achievement of certain goals, such as the development of an MIS. Managers expect the time invested in planning to pay off in benefits not realized when planning is bypassed or done poorly. In terms of the MIS project, good planning is expected to have the following benefits:

1. Identify tasks necessary for goal achievement. The scope of the project is defined. Which activities or subsystems are involved? Which are not? *In general terms,* what types and amounts of work will be necessary? This information provides management with an initial idea of the scale of resources required.

2. Recognize potential problem areas. Good planning will point out things that might go wrong. It is better to know of potential problems than to wait for them to appear. In most cases, the problems can be eliminated before they become serious, or the project can be planned so that its success is not impaired by the preexisting constraints.

3. Arrange a sequence of tasks.   Most likely, hundreds of separate tasks will be necessary to implement the MIS. These tasks are arranged in a logical sequence based on information priorities and the need for efficiency. For example, a sales-forecasting model is of such importance to the firm that it should be implemented before a less important model, such as a warehouse location model. Also, the sequence of tasks has an impact on efficiency. One task usually follows another. The computer should not be scheduled for delivery until the room has been prepared, for example.

4. Provide a basis for control.   The means to achieve and maintain control must be determined in advance. Certain project goals and methods of performance measurement must be specified. When the time comes to direct company resources toward the MIS effort, the executive vice-president, assisted by the other managers, knows what needs to be done, who will do it, and when it will be accomplished.

These planning benefits enable the manager to understand what is to be done. The project can then be executed in the most efficient manner and the manager can maintain continuous control.

Alternate Planning Approaches

There are two basic ways to approach an MIS project. One is an *objective orientation,* where the firm uses its objectives as the starting point. The other is a *problem orientation,* where the firm designs an MIS to address specific problems. A new firm must begin with objectives, for there has been no opportunity to encounter problems. The firm establishes objectives and designs an MIS to help meet those objectives. An existing firm, however, can take either approach. Table 16-2 presents both approaches.

The existing firm does not merely select between the two approaches; it follows the route dictated by the situation, according to Figure 16-4. If a firm does not have objectives, they must be defined before proceeding with MIS planning. Then the firm must determine whether it is meeting its objectives. There is no need to develop a new MIS if the existing one is doing its job.

Table 16-2   Alternate approaches to planning

Type of firm	Objective orientation	Problem orientation
New	Establish objectives and design an MIS to help achieve them	
Existing	Evaluate existing objectives and improve when needed; use as a basis for MIS design	Identify problems and design an MIS to help solve them

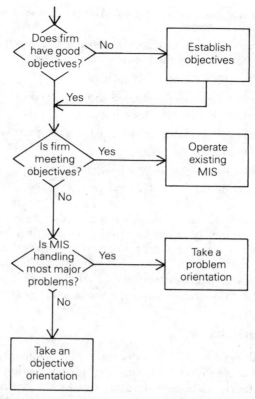

Figure 16-4 Determining the MIS approach.

If the firm is not meeting its objectives, it must choose between the two planning approaches. The choice depends on how well the MIS is handling most of the major problems encountered. If the MIS is doing a good job, a comprehensive redesign is unnecessary—the existing system need only be modified to correct its minor flaws. If, on the other hand, the MIS has serious faults, the firm needs a fresh approach and should follow an objective orientation.

Objective orientation

Basing MIS design on organizational objectives is called *strategy set transformation*.[2] According to this concept, overall company strategy is an *information set* consisting of goals, strategies, environmental constraints, sophistication of the management resource, and so on. Strategic MIS planning converts the information set into an *MIS strategy set* consisting of MIS objectives, constraints, and strategies.

---

[2] W. R. King, "Strategic Planning for Management Information Systems," *MIS Quarterly* 2 (March 1978): 27–37.

The process of developing an MIS strategy set consists of six steps:

1. Defining the internal and environmental groups influencing the long-term performance of the firm
2. Identifying the goals of each group
3. Identifying and developing the organizational strategy for achieving the desired interface with each group
4. Identifying alternate MIS strategies that support the organizational strategy
5. Evaluating the alternate MIS strategies
6. Selecting the best MIS strategy

It is strategic management's responsibility to accomplish steps 1 and 2. Tactical management becomes involved in step 3. Systems analysts perform steps 4 and 5. Step 6 is the primary responsibility of the vice-president of information services.

Strategy set transformation is a good example of the systems approach. It assures that MIS strategy supports the long-range strategies of the firm.

Problem orientation

If a firm designs an MIS to solve particular problems, it must have a good set of objectives and a physical system capable of achieving those objectives. The problem orientation requires a situation in which specific problems prevent the firm from achieving its objectives. It assumes that the problems can be solved with the right kind of information.

A problem orientation can focus on existing problems and on the development of *decision support systems* to help solve those problems. An overall MIS framework already exists, and the decision support systems can fit into that framework. It would be unwise to pursue a DSS approach without first establishing an overall MIS structure.

MIS Performance Criteria

Although the point of origin for the objective and problem approaches differs, the end product should not. An MIS should support the firm's objectives. This is accomplished by providing the firm's managers with the information they need to achieve their objectives. The standards of performance for the MIS are based on how well the information needs of the managers are supported.

The firm's objectives determine the objectives that each functional area—and the managers in those functional areas—should attain. The manager's objectives, in turn, determine their information needs. And the manager's information needs determine the *performance criteria* of the MIS—what it is expected to achieve. This hierarchy is illustrated in Figure 16-5.

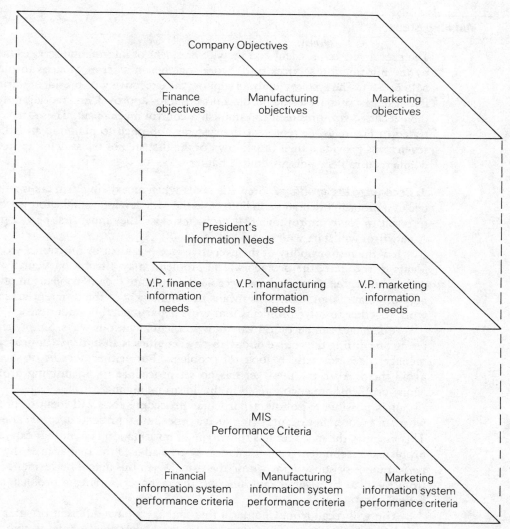

Figure 16-5 Relationship between objectives, information needs, and MIS performance criteria.

For example, a firm might have an objective of realizing a 12% return on investment during the coming year. To help achieve this objective, the marketing function might have an objective of $25 million in sales revenue with operating expenses under $1.2 million. In order to meet these marketing objectives, the vice-president of marketing might require periodic sales and expense reports. Later in the MIS life cycle, the report requirements will be stated very specifically. At this point in the planning phase, however, the criteria are stated only in general terms, such as "Provide a monthly expense report that compares actual expenses with budgeted expenses for each operating unit." Similar statements establish the general performance criteria for each subsystem of the MIS.

Planning Steps

The executive vice-president and the vice-president of information services (assisted by the information services staff) work together in a series of steps to plan the MIS project. The systems analysts support the executive vice-president during the initial stages, prepare a study project proposal for approval, and work jointly with the executive vice-president to establish a control mechanism. These steps, illustrated in Figure 16-6, represent the systems approach to planning an MIS. The seven steps provide a finer breakdown of the first step of the systems approach—define the problem—discussed in Chapter 4.

1. Recognize the problem. Step 1 is taken when an existing firm takes an objective or a problem orientation. In both cases the MIS developmental effort is expected to result in some improvement. If problems exist, they must first be recognized. A new firm will start with step 3.

It is the responsibility of the executive vice-president or functional vice-presidents to recognize the problems. The problems may affect a particular organizational unit, but they need not necessarily originate there. Problems in one area may originate in another. This means that managers of the different areas must work together to solve problems that cross departmental boundaries.

A manager can become aware of a problem in various ways. Simply encountering one during the course of day-to-day activities is an *informal* approach. The manager does not actively look for problems, but neither does he or she try to avoid them. Also, the manager has no set procedure for identifying problems. Many problems are encountered in this informal manner.

It is possible to follow a particular procedure that will identify problems when, or before, they occur. Using such a procedure represents a *formal* approach. This assumes the manager has some type of information system that can identify problems. Essentially, the information system advises the manager of the actual performance of subsystems within the firm. When this actual performance varies from the plan by a significant amount, the manager initiates a problem-solving action.

You will recall from Chapter 4 that managers have different orientations to problem identification. The informal approach described above is that of the *problem solver*. The *problem seeker* follows the formal approach. The *problem avoider* follows neither.

2. Define the problem. Once the manager (the executive vice-president or functional vice-president) realizes that a problem exists, he or she must understand it well enough to pursue a solution. At this point the manager doesn't attempt to gather all of the information describing the problem. That would require a full-scale systems analysis. The manager is interested only in understanding the problem well enough to direct an effort aimed at solving it. At a minimum, the manager should know where the problem exists. Which management level is involved? Perhaps there is more than one level. Which functional area is involved? Again, the problem may exist in more than one area. In addition, the manager should know which system or subsystem is deficient and what the general difficulty is.

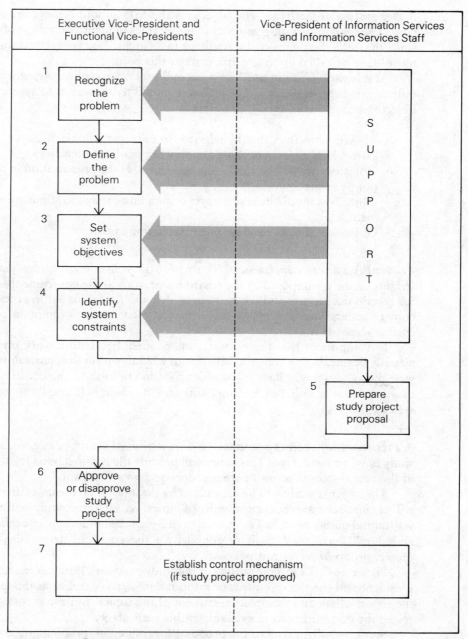

Figure 16-6 Steps in the planning process.

Most likely the manager will be assisted by the analyst in defining the problem in these terms. Once there is agreement on the problem, its location, and its general nature, the findings should be put in writing. This written description can serve as a useful guide for the work that follows.

3. Set system objectives. The objectives the MIS should achieve are specified next. The functional vice-presidents play key roles in identifying these objectives, since the MIS should meet the needs of their areas. Lower-level managers will most likely be called upon to participate at this point.

At this early point in the developmental process, the objectives can be stated only in rather general terms. The manager should try, however, to assure that the objectives have the following characteristics:

- All MIS objectives should help the firm achieve its objectives.
- Lower-level objectives should support upper-level objectives.
- Objectives should be valid—they should steer the organization in the direction it wants to go.
- Objectives should be realistic, yet demanding enough to stimulate improvement.
- Objectives should produce measurable standards.

4. Identify system constraints. The new MIS will operate under many constraints. Some are imposed by the environment, such as the government's demand for certain tax reports and the customers' demand for billing information. Other constraints are imposed by the firm's management, such as limits on computer cost or response times.

It is important that these constraints be identified before work on the MIS actually begins. In this way, the MIS design will fall within the constraints. Otherwise the system might have to be redesigned to conform to the constraints once they are known. Other constraints will arise as more is learned about the new system.

5. Prepare study project proposal. Before a new MIS can be designed, a systems study must be conducted. This study will provide the *detailed* basis for the design of the new system in terms of what it does and how it does it.

The systems study will be conducted by the analyst or a team of analysts and will require several weeks or months of effort. As such, the study will require a substantial outlay of cash. The executive vice-president must approve this expense and should have some basis or support for the go-ahead decision. The *study project proposal* serves this purpose.

Figure 16-7 is a sample outline of the study proposal. Both the executive vice-president and the vice-president of information services realize at this point that the report offers an incomplete treatment of the topics. But the report does represent the best information available at this early stage.

Sections 1 through 3 of the proposal (introduction, problem, objectives and constraints) are developed jointly by the systems analysts and the executive vice-president during the first four steps of the planning phase.

Sections 4 through 7 are developed by the systems analysts. The analysts gather information, primarily by personal interview with the managers, to identify the subsystems of the functional information systems and the major programs to be included in each subsystem. Section 4 identifies the possible system solutions,

1. Introduction—reason for the proposal

2. Problem definition

3. System objectives and constraints

4. Possible alternatives

5. Recommended course of action
    a. Tasks to be accomplished
    b. Resource requirements
    c. Time schedule
    d. Cost recap

6. Anticipated results
    a. Organizational impact
    b. Operational impact
    c. Financial impact

7. General implementation plan

8. Study project objectives
    a. Tasks
    b. Budget

9. Summary

Figure 16-7 The study project proposal.

and each is briefly described. The analysts determine which alternative appears to be best suited for the particular situation, and that alternative is described in section 5, along with a brief explanation of the resources needed for implementation. Section 6 describes the effects, both positive and negative, on the firm and its operations. Section 7 presents a general implementation plan.

The first seven sections of the proposal relate to the MIS. Section 8 relates to the study project leading to the MIS. In this section, the analysts identify the tasks involved in conducting the study project and the funds needed. The summary section simply concludes the report.

The study project proposal is strictly a preliminary report. Although the problem is defined in as much detail as possible, more will be learned about it as the study progresses. All possible alternatives are stated generally—including the one recommended by the analysts. The purpose of the report is to identify an objective that will guide the participants during the coming months.

One point should be made about the selection of the best alternative. The final selection must be made by the manager. It is not the systems analyst's responsibility to make this decision. Rather, the analyst provides the manager with enough information to make a sound decision. The two parties must work together closely at this point.

6. Approve or disapprove study project. In preparing the proposal, the analyst must be careful not to advocate an unjustified study. The facts should be reported honestly, with equal attention given to the reasons why the study should not be conducted and to weaknesses in the proposed general design. The executive vice-president will decide whether to continue the project, and this decision must be based on the best information available.

The executive vice-president weighs the pros and cons of the proposed project and the system design and takes one of three actions. The first question the executive vice-president asks is, "Do I have enough information?" If the answer is "no," he or she tells the analyst what additional information is needed. When this information is obtained, the review process is repeated. The executive vice-president will not reach a final decision on the project until all of the necessary information is at hand.

Once the executive vice-president feels that sufficient information is available, the *go/no go decision* is made (Figure 16-8). If the decision is "go," the project proceeds to the study phase. If the decision is "no go," both the executive vice-president and the systems analysts turn their attention to other matters.

As the executive vice-president considers approving the project, two key questions need answers:

1. *Will the proposed system solve identified problems or enable the firm to meet its objectives?* These are the performance criteria. This will be the

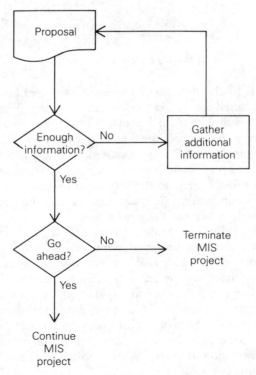

Figure 16-8 The "go/no go" decision.

basis for evaluating the performance of the MIS once it is implemented; it also should be the basis for evaluating the proposed MIS.

2. *Is the proposed study project the best way to determine the specific design of the proposed MIS?* There is no pat answer to this question. The executive vice-president must be assured that the analysts have considered all of the feasible approaches to the study. If the executive vice-president is to have this assurance, he or she must have a good understanding of the MIS concept and computer implementation. One reason why managers must learn about computer processing is that they must approve the expenditure of large sums of money for computer projects.

7. Establish a control mechanism.   Before the study begins, the executive vice-president must take steps to establish control over the project. This executive has overall responsibility for the final system and the efforts leading to it—a responsibility that should not be delegated to the information specialists.

Project control must be developed in phases. Complete control depends on a detailed specification of the work to be done, and no such specification exists at this point. Still, the general specification is adequate for establishing initial control. As the implementation project unfolds, the information specialists will develop the detailed specification. This specification provides the basis for control throughout the project.

General Project Control

The executive vice-president and the vice-president of information services must work together closely to establish the control mechanism. They need a thorough understanding of the task ahead, which the vice-president of information services can provide.

Throughout the project, both executives must receive progress reports showing how actual performance compares with the plan. This requires two things: performance standards and a progress-reporting system.

1. Performance standards.   Standards of acceptable performance are established for three dimensions of the activity: time, cost, and quality. At this stage, the standards can be established only in general terms. This is especially true for the standard of quality.

2. Progress reporting.   The executive vice-president must remain up to date concerning the progress of the MIS project. The vice-president of information services is responsible for keeping the executive vice-president current, which is done through scheduled meetings. The meetings usually are held weekly but can be supplemented by special sessions as the need arises. The meetings take the form of progress reports by the vice-president of information services. Quite often, visual aids are used to illustrate what has been accomplished, what has not been accomplished and why, upcoming activities, and possible trouble spots. At a minimum, the meetings include the executive vice-president and the vice-president of information services. If an MIS committee is formed, that group also attends. At times managers from functional areas and members of the information services staff are invited to participate. The meetings employ management by exception in that the managers devote their attention to critical areas and do not dwell on things going as planned.

Detailed Project Control

Once the executive vice-president and the systems analysts have specified the basic components of the MIS, the analysts must specify the details—what needs to be done, who will do it, and when will it be done.

1. What needs to be done?   The preliminary planning meetings between the top managers and the members of the information services staff should produce a list of jobs for the MIS to perform. For example, in the marketing information system the jobs could include:

> *Product Subsystem*
> > New-product evaluation model
> > Product deletion model
>
> *Place Subsystem*
> > Warehouse location model
> > Warehouse layout model
>
> *Promotion Subsystem*
> > Territory assignment model
> > Advertising media scheduling model
>
> *Pricing Subsystem*
> > Pricing model

2. Who will do it?   The vice-president of information services next decides who will be responsible for designing each of the subsystem models. For example, in the marketing information system, analyst A might be assigned to the two product models, analyst B to the place models and the advertising media scheduling model, and analyst C to the sales territory assignment model and the pricing model.

There may not be enough analysts to do all the specified work. In this case, new employees must be recruited and hired. If so, the general design specifications identify the type of employees needed. For example, the two warehouse models will probably use linear programming. If a linear programming specialist is not presently on the staff, one will have to be added. The firm must acquire personnel who have the skills necessary to achieve the MIS.

3. When will it be done?   The vice-president of information services must establish a time schedule for the MIS project. Certain things will have to be done at specific times. For example, new computing equipment might have to be scheduled for delivery. The firm will want the equipment delivered when it can be used—not before and not after. For example, if a new disk file is required for the customer master file, delivery should coincide with the completion of the programs that will load data into the file and use the contents.

Assignment of responsibility

The project schedule is based on the time required to do the different tasks. Once the tasks have been identified and assigned to persons or teams, an estimate can be made of the time required to do each subtask. For example, the following subtasks might be required to develop the product deletion model:

1. Identify the processes that the appropriate marketing managers will use to make product deletion decisions.
2. Identify the information requirements of the managers making the deletion decision.
3. Identify the input data necessary to produce the required information.
4. Prepare a program flowchart or pseudocode description of the computer processing to convert input data to information output.
5. Code the program.
6. Test the program.
7. Obtain confirmation from the managers who will be using the model that the model satisfies their information needs.
8. Implement the model.

The vice-president of information services then determines who will perform each of the subtasks, and how long each should take. Table 16-3 illustrates how

Table 16-3 Detailed subtask planning

	Functional System: Marketing Subsystem: Product Model: Product Deletion	
Subtask	Responsibility	Time Estimate (person days)
1. Identify deletion criteria	Systems analyst and product manager	7
2. Identify output information requirements	Systems analyst and product manager	5
3. Identify input data requirements	Systems analyst	4
4. Prepare program flowchart or pseudocode	Programmer	5
5. Code program	Programmer	15
6. Test program	Programmer and operations staff	10
7. Approve program performance	Product manager and vice-president of marketing	7
8. Implement model	Operations staff	7

responsibility is distributed for the product deletion model, and how time estimates are made for each subtask.

The assignment of responsibility is usually not too difficult. The type of system to be designed and the type of design work involved specify personnel or types of personnel who should have the responsibility. The estimation of time duration is more difficult. At this stage of the project, these estimates can be only broad approximations. They are based on the experience of the people involved. The vice-president of information services and the information services staff are expected to have this experience. For example, they might estimate that the product deletion model will require approximately 1000 lines of program code. If work standards indicate that a programmer can prepare fifty lines of code per day, the total time duration for coding should be twenty working days.

Monitoring project progress

Once the MIS project has been defined in terms of (1) the models or programs to be prepared, (2) who is responsible for them, and (3) when the work should be done, the executive vice-president has a basis for control. The next step is to document the project plan in a manner that will maintain control as work progresses.

There are a number of documentation techniques. The executive vice-president and the vice-president of information services select the one with which they feel most comfortable. One technique is the *Gantt chart,* showing when work on each subtask should be performed. You recall from Chapter 2 that the Gantt chart is a product of the classical management school.

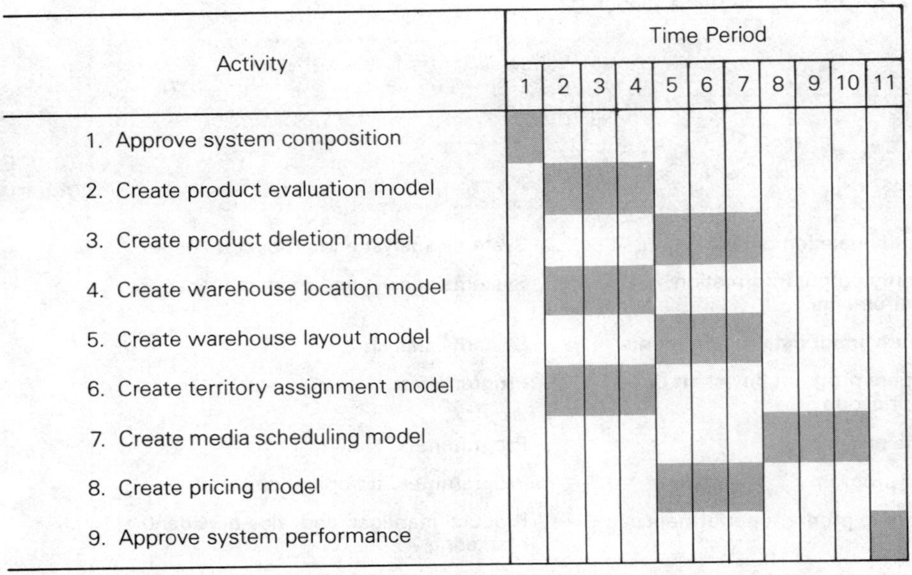

Figure 16-9 Gantt chart of marketing information system activity.

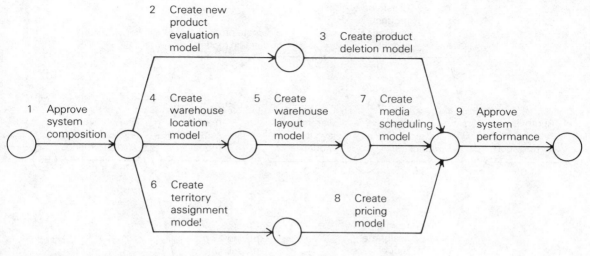

Figure 16-10 Network diagram of marketing information system activity.

The Gantt chart in Figure 16-9 illustrates how the work on the seven marketing models is phased over time. During the progress report meetings, the managers can use charts such as this to compare actual performance with planned performance.

The main shortcoming of the Gantt chart is that it doesn't show how the activities interrelate. It doesn't show that work on the seven models (steps 2–8) cannot begin until the system composition is approved (step 1). Also, it doesn't show that the same information specialist is going to create both of the product models (steps 2 and 3).

These interrelationships can be represented by another documentation technique—*network analysis*. In network analysis, *activities* are represented by interconnected arrows to show how one relates to another. In Figure 16-10 the bars in the Gantt chart have been redrawn as interconnecting arrows. The network diagram shows that activity 9 cannot start until activities 3, 7, and 8 are completed. Activity 3 cannot start until activity 2 is completed, and so on.

The circles are called *nodes,* and they do more than simply connect the arrows. The nodes can be numbered, as in Figure 16-11, to provide a better identification of the activities. Each activity has a unique pair of node numbers, and is identified by those numbers. For example, when referring to the activity to create a new pricing model, you would speak of "activity 40-70."

Figure 16-11 also shows estimated times just below the arrows. These numbers can represent any time increment—days, weeks, months, and so on. In this example they represent months. By adding up the times for each path through the network, we can identify the critical path. The *critical path* determines overall project time. In the example, the critical path connects nodes 10, 20, 50, 60, 70, and 80. This path requires eleven months. The upper path (nodes 10, 20, 30, 70, and 80) requires eight months, as does the lower path (nodes 10, 20, 40, 70, 80). The upper and lower paths thus allow for extra time, called *slack time*. Both the

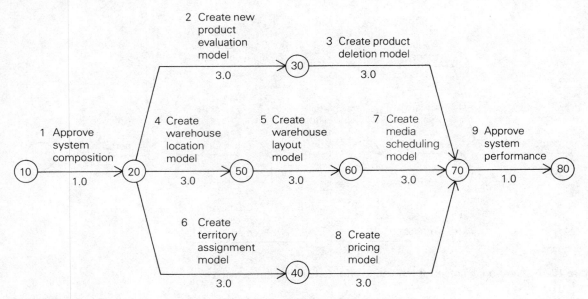

Figure 16-11   Network diagram with node numbers and activity times.

upper and lower paths contain three months of slack. Work in activities 20-30 and 30-70 could be delayed up to three months without affecting project time. The same holds true for activities 20-40 and 40-70. There is no slack along the critical path.

Figure 16-11 is an example of a *Critical-Path Method (CPM)* network. CPM uses a single time estimate for each activity. The other popular type of network is the *Program Evaluation and Review Technique (PERT)* chart. PERT differs from CPM in using three time estimates—pessimistic (T_p), most likely (T_m), and optimistic (T_o). A formula is used to weigh the most likely estimate more heavily than the pessimistic and optimistic.

$$\text{Activity time} = \frac{T_p + 4T_m + T_o}{6}$$

For example, if $T_p = 1.2$, $T_m = 4.0$, and $T_o = 5.0$, the activity time would be

$$\frac{1.2 + 16.0 + 5.0}{6} = \frac{22.2}{6} = 3.7$$

There are a number of prewritten computer-based CPM and PERT packages.[3] Most are offered by manufacturers of computing equipment—Honeywell, UNIVAC, IBM, DEC, Control Data, Burroughs, and NCR. Some are offered by

---

[3] A survey of computer-based CPM and PERT systems is included in Perry Petersen, "Project Control Systems," *Datamation* 25 (June 1979): 147 ff.

NODE NUMBERS	ACTIVITY	TIME	EARLY START	LATE START	EARLY COMPLETION	LATE COMPLETION	SLACK
10-20	APPROVE COMPOSITION	1.0	1/10	1/10	2/10	2/10	0
20–30	NEW PRODUCT MODEL	3.0	2/10	5/10	5/10	8/10	3
20–40	TERRITORY ASSIGNMENT MODEL	3.0	2/10	5/10	5/10	8/10	3
20–50	WAREHOUSE LOCATION MODEL	3.0	2/10	2/10	5/10	5/10	0
30–70	PRODUCT DELETION MODEL	3.0	5/10	8/10	8/10	11/10	3
40–70	PRICING MODEL	3.0	5/10	8/10	8/10	11/10	3
50–60	WAREHOUSE LAYOUT MODEL	3.0	5/10	5/10	8/10	8/10	0
60–70	MEDIA SCHEDULING MODEL	3.0	8/10	8/10	11/10	11/10	0
70–80	APPROVE SYSTEM	1.0	11/10	11/10	12/10	12/10	0

Figure 16-12   Project calendar printed by a network software package.

software firms—Atlantic Software, CINCOM, and Structural Programming. Also, some service bureaus and timesharing services—Service Bureau Corporation, University Computing, and Dataline—have packages of their own.

The real value of the network method is the discipline it imposes by requiring that a project be planned in detail before work begins. For small MIS projects the networks can be drawn by hand and the critical-path calculations made with an electronic calculator. For large projects a computer-based network package is very helpful. The computer package makes it easy to update the network, which is a real advantage. Also, the computer can compute the *start date* and the *completion date* for each activity. You specify when the project will begin, and the software computes the dates. For example, if you specify that the product deletion model project will begin on January 10, the network package will compute the dates shown in Figure 16-12. You can see that there are both early and late start dates and early and late completion dates. When the early and late dates are the same, as for activity 10-20, that activity is on the critical path. As the righthand column indicates, there is no slack. Each of the four activities not on the critical path has three months of slack. The slack is the amount of time between the early and late dates, either start or completion.

Computerized network analysis is an excellent control mechanism for complex projects. In addition to printed listings like the one in Figure 16–12, network analysis can provide various graphs. Figure 16-13 shows a plotted network diagram and Figure 16-14 shows a graph—both drawn with the EZPERT package from Systonetics.

Summary

This chapter has dealt with planning. Responsibility for planning the MIS project must be placed in the hands of a top executive. This executive must understand what needs to be done so that resources can be allocated and the effort controlled.

It is important to understand why planning and controlling the MIS project are a top executive's responsibility. The project is large enough to require high-level attention. The responsible person should not be the manager of the computer facility, but should be someone who can represent the users of the MIS output.

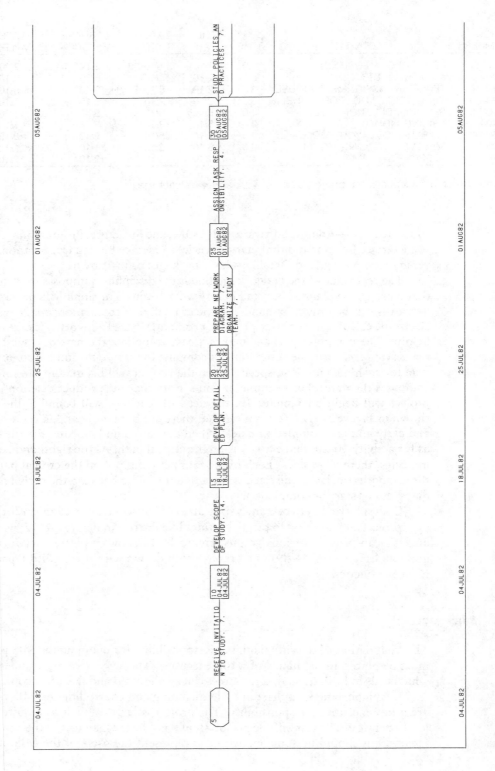

Figure 16-13 A plotted network diagram.

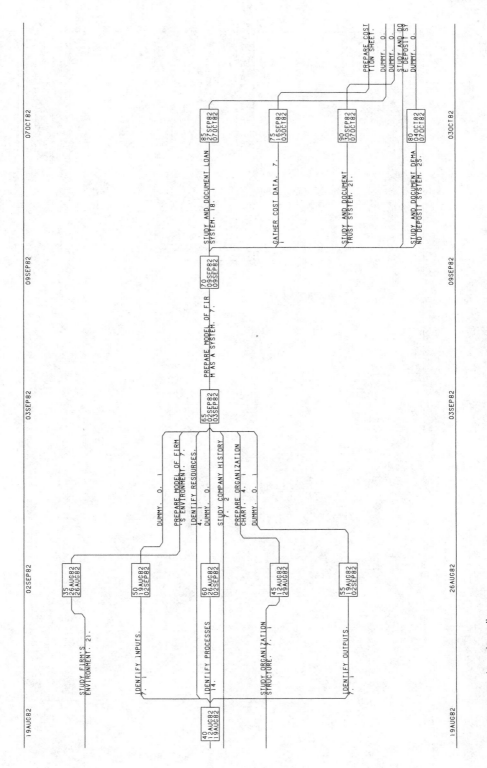

Figure 16-13 (continued)

536

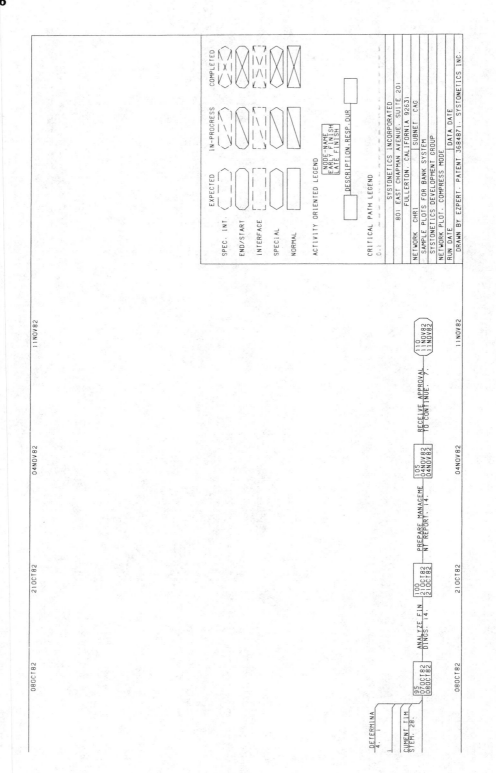

Figure 16-13 (continued)

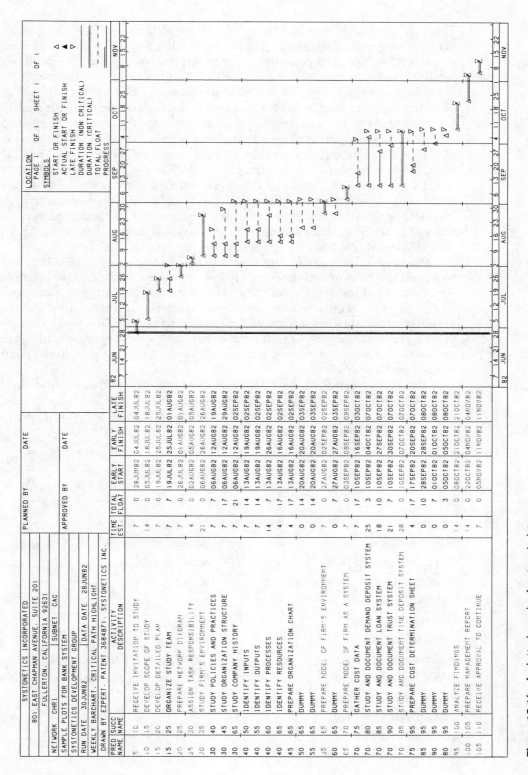

Figure 16-14 A plotted graph of network data.

The only purpose of the MIS is to help managers manage. For this reason, a manager or group of managers should decide what the MIS will do and assure that it is done. The ideal person to have this responsibility is a top executive with total-firm interests and involvement, such as the executive vice-president.

Planning an MIS project requires some knowledge of what the MIS will do. Some assumptions must be made about system design, and these provide the basis for planning. As more information is gained about design, the plans can be updated.

At a minimum, the managers must know whether the MIS will be designed to solve specific problems or to help the firm meet certain objectives. Then they must decide whether to redesign the existing MIS or to create a completely new one. Discussions with functional vice-presidents then identify the subsystems of each functional information system. With this basic knowledge, the executive vice-president or the MIS committee can set the specifications and authorize a systems study. The study, described in the next chapter, will shed new light on the MIS and will provide the basis for continuing the project.

Planning an MIS project requires that the executive vice-president and the vice-president of information services follow seven steps. The first four determine the objectives of the MIS and identify its constraints. These steps are the responsibility of the executive vice-president, but assistance is provided by the vice-president of information services and the systems analysts. This group then prepares a study project proposal to serve as the basis for the systems study. If the proposal is approved, a control mechanism for the project is established jointly by the two vice-presidents.

The vice-president of information services and the systems analysts divide each task into subtasks, assign responsibility, and estimate the time requirements. These details provide the basis for project control. Graphical techniques, such as Gantt charts and network diagrams, provide a useful means of tracking the progress of MIS development.

Key Terms

MIS committee	detailed project control
objective orientation	network analysis
strategy set transformation	activity
information set	node
MIS strategy set	critical path
problem orientation	slack time
performance criteria	CPM (critical path method)
informal problem recognition	PERT (project evaluation and review technique)
formal problem recognition	
study project proposal	start date
go/no go decision	completion date
general project control	

Key Concepts

Factors influencing the MIS project that determine the degree of difficulty

The necessity for top-level management control of the MIS project

The benefits of planning

Two basic approaches to MIS design—objectives and problems

The sequential nature of MIS project planning

The formal written report as the basis for the go/no go decision

How the control mechanism evolves from planning

Questions

1. What are the phases of the MIS life cycle? What happens after the last one is completed?

2. Is there any relationship between the sequence of the planning phase and the sequence of Henri Fayol's management functions—plan, organize, staff, direct, control? If so, explain.

3. What three factors influence the difficulty of the MIS task?

4. Which top-level executives are candidates for MIS project director? Which one would be best? Why?

5. What distinguishes the responsibilities of the executive vice-president from those of the administrative vice-president?

6. What role do the functional vice-presidents play in MIS planning?

7. Does a firm always establish an MIS committee? Who serves on it?

8. List four benefits of planning the MIS.

9. What are the two basic approaches to the MIS project?

10. What is strategy set transformation? List the six steps and identify who is responsible for each.

11. Is strategy set transformation an example of the systems approach? Explain.

12. What determines the performance criteria for the MIS?

13. Would you rather develop an MIS for a new firm or an existing one? Explain your answer.

14. Where do MIS constraints originate?

15. Does the systems analyst determine which system design will be studied during the next phase? Discuss.

16. Is it a good idea to devise a project plan before you know all the details of the project? Explain your reasoning.

17. What decision is made immediately before the go/no go decision?

18. What two basic questions influence the go/no go decision?

19. What three questions must be answered to establish detailed project control?

20. What distinguishes network analysis from a Gantt chart?

Problems

1. Using the activity times in the diagram, (1) determine total project time, and (2) identify the critical path.

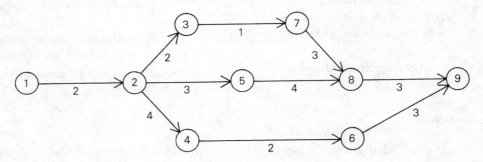

2. Using the following pessimistic (T_p), most likely (T_m), and optimistic (T_o) times, compute total project time for the diagram in problem 1. What is the critical path?

Activity	T_p	T_m	T_o
1-2	3	2	1
2-3	3	2	2
2-4	5	3	2
2-5	4	3	2
3-7	2	1	1
4-6	4	2	1
5-8	7	3	1
6-9	5	3	2
7-8	4	3	3
8-9	4	3	2

3. Draw a critical path diagram of an Indianapolis 500 pit stop. After the car stops, one crew member gives the driver a drink and then cleans the windshield. After the car is raised off the ground, one crew member fills the gas tank, and four each remove a wheel and replace the removed wheel with a new one. When the wheels have been replaced and the gas tank filled, the car is lowered to the ground. The car then resumes the race.

CASE PROBLEM: Saito Electric Corp.

Saito Electric is one of Japan's largest manufacturers of electric and electronic consumer products, including sound recorders, kitchen appliances, and power tools. You are the manager of systems analysis, reporting to Mr. Kiyoshi Hoshina, vice-president of computer services. In your weekly planning meeting with Mr. Hoshina and the other computer managers, you learn that top management wishes to establish some performance criteria for the computer division. Mr. Hoshina has given you the task of establishing the standards for the firm's manufacturing information system.

When you get back to your office, you look at your copy of the Saito long-range plan and review the firm's objectives. You find them to be stated in very general terms—"to offer a balanced package of consumer products . . . to maintain a position of leadership . . . to identify new consumer needs . . . to strengthen and maintain community and employee relationships. . . ."

You know that the company objectives are the place to start, but you feel they are too broad to be of specific help on your assignment. You decide that the next source of information is Mr. Mitsu Saito, vice-president of manufacturing. You make an appointment and, after a brief discussion of the weather, ask Mr. Saito about the objectives of the manufacturing division. He opens a desk drawer, retrieves a small notebook, and begins to read: "To make efficient use of manufacturing resources. To maintain production quality at the established level. To manufacture the right quantity at the right time for the firm to meet its sales forecast. To provide safe working conditions for all employees."

As Mr. Saito puts down the notebook, you are still not convinced that you have gotten the specifics you need. You ask Mr. Saito, "Could you describe how the computer group might help you meet your objectives?"

Mr. Saito replies, "For us to meet our objective of efficient resource use, we must first know what resources we will need. We get this from our material requirements and capacity requirements planning models. Our production scheduling model permits us to have the right quantity at the right time. We achieve our quality objective primarily by selecting vendors who provide high-quality raw materials. We pursue our objective of worker safety by receiving statistics on accidents so that they might be anticipated and prevented."

Now you're getting somewhere. But you still need more specifics before you can begin to put together performance criteria. You ask Mr. Saito exactly what he expects from his MRP, capacity requirements, and scheduling systems: "Is it enough that we simply have those models available?"

"Of course not," Mr. Saito replies. "The models must be accurate. They must be able to handle our volume and variety of production. They must be designed in such a manner that we can use them as frequently as we like, from terminals in our offices, without running up unreasonable computer charges."

"Fine," you say as you jot down some notes. "But what about vendor selection? How should the MIS support you in that area?"

"First," Mr. Saito explains, "we must have in our data base up-to-date financial information on each vendor. Second, we must have an up-to-date price list for each of our vendors. And third, we must be able to query the data base and retrieve summary reports showing the quality records of each vendor's shipment."

"Excellent," you respond, confident you are on the right track. "One more point—what about the safety statistics?"

Mr. Saito adjusts his tie as he talks. "Right now we're getting monthly reports on accidents—where they happen, when, the cause, and the resulting cost in lost production hours. I would like to develop some type of point scoring system involving lost production hours, so each department can be ranked by its safety record. We could implement a reward system as a means of making our supervisors more sensitive to the safety issue. I would like to be able to get a weekly status report comparing the safety records of each department."

Before you can thank Mr. Saito for his time, he gets up from his chair and leads you out of his office, explaining, "You must excuse me. I must meet a group of Americans who want to tour our plant. They are very interested in learning as much as possible about our methods and most likely will want to take some pictures. Please come back again when you have developed your performance criteria. I will tell you if you are on the right track. *Sayonara*."

Questions

1. Was it a waste of your time to start by reading the company's objectives?

2. Is Mr. Saito using the MIS to meet manufacturing objectives? Explain your answer.

3. State the general performance criteria for the MRP, capacity requirements, and scheduling systems.

4. State the criteria for the vendor information portion of the manufacturing intelligence subsystem.

5. State the criteria for the safety-reporting system.

6. Do you still need more information to help you state the above performance criteria completely? If so, specify.

Chapter 17

Information Systems Development: The Analysis and Design Phase

After studying this chapter, you should:

- Know the major career paths for information specialists, and know how specialists are organized to develop and maintain information systems
- Understand the importance of communication in the design of an MIS and the roles played by information specialists and managers
- Know the three basic approaches to MIS design
- Understand what systems analysis and systems design mean
- Understand how the systems study evolves in steps, taken jointly by managers and information specialists
- Understand how the systems analyst identifies the manager's information needs
- See how specific MIS performance criteria are developed from the general statements developed during the planning phase
- Understand how a computer configuration is determined
- Recognize some of the types of analysis and design documentation that can be used
- Be able to prepare documentation of basic information systems using flowcharting and HIPO

A Shift in Emphasis

The previous chapter described the role of the firm's management in planning and controlling the MIS project. In this chapter, the emphasis shifts to the work performed by the information services staff. This is the work that creates an MIS to meet the objectives identified by the firm's management. It is the responsibility of the vice-president of information services to see that this work is carried out in the prescribed manner and that the schedule is followed. As the work is performed over a period of months, the vice-president of information services reports the progress to the executive vice-president or the MIS committee. As problems arise, actions are taken to get the project back on course.

Although this chapter focuses on the information services staff, it is important to understand that their work is aimed at creating an MIS that meets the managers' needs. And those managers, through the executive vice-president or MIS committee, exercise control over the work.

In addition to playing a role in the planning and control of the MIS project, managers play an active part in the analysis and design of the MIS. Managers must communicate to the information services staff their exact information needs. If this communication is to be effective and efficient, the manager must understand the tasks of the information services staff as well.

The purpose of this chapter is to help you understand the needs and tasks of the information services staff. Subsequent chapters will again take up the manager's perspective.

The Information Services Staff

Most of the computer-related jobs in organizations using computers fall within four broad categories: operations, programming, systems analysis, and data base administration.

The operator

Like any machine or device, the computer must be operated. A small computer requires only a single *operator,* while a large one can require three or four. The operators communicate instructions to the computer through the console, place appropriate card files in the card reader, mount and dismount tape reels and disk packs, and put the correct paper forms in the printer.

The operators are part of the computer operations department. This department, under the supervision of an *operations manager,* is responsible primarily for running jobs on the computer.

In addition to those working directly with the computer, other members of the operations department operate keydriven data input machines, maintain controls over computer input and output, schedule jobs on the computer, and maintain library files of tapes and disk packs.

The programmer

The people preparing the programs are the *programmers*. Programmers can use a variety of special computer languages to write programs. The choice of a language is determined by the type of problem and the manner in which it is to be solved. A mathematical problem is usually solved with FORTRAN (FORmula TRANslation). A similar problem can be solved by using a data terminal with BASIC (Beginner's All-purpose Symbolic Instruction Code). A business problem can be solved with COBOL (COmmon Business Oriented Language). There are several other languages to choose from.

The programmer has the important responsibility of communicating with the computer. If the computer is to do what is expected, the program must be accurate. Before a program is put into operational use, the programmer subjects it to many tests to assure that it contains no errors, or "bugs."

Firms usually have more than one programmer. In some cases, each programmer specializes in writing certain types of programs. For instance, a programmer might specialize in writing programs for marketing or for accounting.

The programmers are supervised by a *programming manager*.

The systems analyst

It is the responsibility of the *systems analyst* to define the computer solution to a problem. The systems analyst must gain an understanding of the problem from the manager. In some cases, the manager knows precisely what is needed. In other cases, the analyst serves as a catalyst by informing the manager of the kinds of information available. Obviously the analyst must have a good understanding of the manager's responsibilities and duties in order to identify information needs.

Typically the manager and the analyst engage in long discussions. These discussions provide the analyst with a sufficient understanding of the manager's needs to develop a computer approach to the solution. Once the approach is defined, it is communicated to the programmer. This communication is accomplished both verbally and in writing. Much of the written communication incorporates diagrams and tables.

The systems analysts in a firm are directed by a *systems analysis manager*.

The analyst programmer

The jobs of systems analyst and programmer are not separated in all firms. One person often performs both jobs, particularly in small firms where the information systems staff is not large enough for specialization. Perhaps the firm has only one person available to do the analysis and design work. That person becomes the *analyst/programmer*.[1]

In many large organizations one person does both jobs. These are organizations where the computer applications are not too complex for one person to handle the analysis, design, and programming duties. In other industries the applications are so complex that they require one person to do the analysis and design work and someone else to do the programming.

---

[1] The term *programmer/analyst* is also used. We use *analyst/programmer* because it reflects the sequence of activities: analysis first, then programming.

When the analyst and programmer duties are combined in one position, the problems of communication and coordination are eliminated. But as a result, the analysis and design work might suffer since each is handled only on a part-time basis.

The data base administrator

The *data base administrator* (DBA) is responsible for implementing, maintaining, controlling, and making available the firm's data base. In small firms, only one person performs these duties. In large firms, the DBA may comprise a group of people organized so that each can specialize in certain areas.

By interacting with both the user and the analysts to define data needs, the DBA relieves the systems analyst of much of the responsibility for data input. This frees the analyst to concentrate on the information output and the processes creating that output. The DBA's work also affects the programmer, who no longer needs to worry about how the data is represented physically.

Organization of the information services staff

The information services staff consists of systems analysts, programmers, operators, and data base administrators. All of these people play important roles in the MIS project. The manner in which they participate depends on the size of the staff. Figure 17-1 illustrates one way to organize a large staff.

Grouping analysts and programmers by functional subsystems enables the

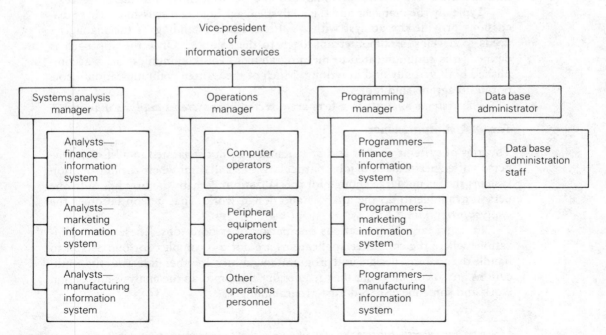

Figure 17-1 The information services staff.

specialists to develop a better understanding of the information needs of the managers. This approach can do much to overcome the communication barrier between managers and the information services staff.

Within each functional information system group, several *analysis and design teams* can be formed to specialize in certain subsystems. For example, a team of analysts and programmers might be responsible for developing a pricing subsystem or a manufacturing intelligence subsystem.

Another popular way to organize the staff is to divide the analysts and programmers into two groups. One group is responsible for *systems development,* or the creation of new systems. Both analysts and programmers are included. The other group is responsible for *systems maintenance,* or the updating of systems already in use. This group too includes both analysts and programmers. Within each development or maintenance group, the analysts and programmers can be organized into subsystem teams.

Whatever the organizational arrangement, the information services staff must interact with managers on different levels and in different functional areas. Figure 17-2 illustrates the interactions between functionally organized teams of information specialists and managers.

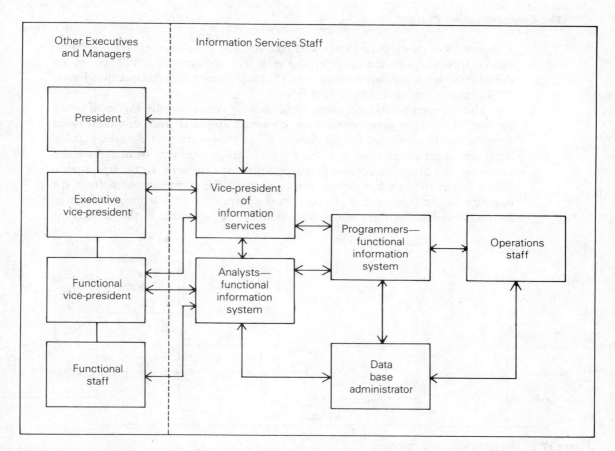

Figure 17-2 Relationships between information services staff and other executives and managers.

As shown in the figure, the vice-president of information services works with the president, the executive vice-president, and the functional vice-presidents to develop the specifications for the MIS. The appropriate analysis team works with the vice-president of the functional area, such as marketing, and with the staff managers in that area, such as the sales manager, advertising manager, and the like.

Once the analysts have developed detailed specifications for a functional information system, the specifications are communicated to the appropriate functional programming group, which will develop the needed computer programs. It is then the task of the operations staff to run these programs on the computer to generate the output information.

The broad scope of data base administration duties is illustrated at the bottom of the figure. The DBA works with the analysts to define the users' data needs, with programmers to make the logical structure of the data available, and with the operations staff to create and maintain the physical structure.

All of the arrows in the diagram are bidirectional, indicating the two-way communication that must take place.

The Communication Process

The process of developing a computer solution to a problem involves communication. It begins with the manager and ends with the computer. In between are the information specialists—the analyst, the programmer, and the operator. Figure 17-3 illustrates this communication flow.

The manager needs information and verbally communicates this need to the analyst. The analyst prepares the basic computer approach and communicates it verbally and in writing to the programmer. The programmer creates the detailed computer approach and communicates it to the computer in the form of a written program. The programmer also prepares written instructions for the operator to follow when running the job on the computer. The communication from the operator to the computer is physical, in the form of switch settings and keyed instructions. Finally, the communication from the computer to the manager is

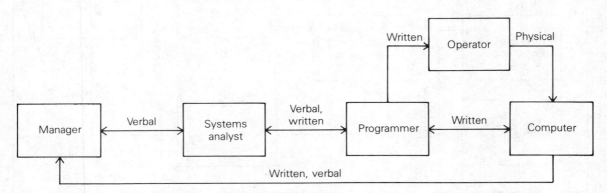

Figure 17-3 The communication process.

usually in written form, either as a printed report or as information displayed on a terminal. When the computer configuration includes an audio response unit, output can be in the form of a verbal message.

The communication problem

The design of an MIS requires two broad types of knowledge: management and information systems. The manager furnishes the management knowledge, and the systems analyst furnishes the information systems knowledge. Representatives from these two areas must communicate, and this is not always easy. Both areas have their separate jargon, educational and career development paths, and professional interests. At some point, however, these two bodies of knowledge and experience must come together. That point is the verbal communication between the manager and the systems analyst in Figure 17-3. This is potentially the weakest link in the chain. If it breaks down, no further communication is possible.

Solving the communication problem

Both the analyst and the manager can take steps to assure that the communication link between them does not break. They can both learn as much about each other's job as possible. This provides a shared knowledge that can form the basis for a strong communication tie. Much of this shared knowledge can be gained in college and university programs in management and computer science. The remainder is gained through experience by jointly solving business problems.

Another approach to solving the communication problem is to eliminate the need for information specialists. If the manager can communicate directly with the computer, there is no need to use information specialists as intermediaries. This approach, illustrated in Figure 17-4, is becoming increasingly popular, especially among users of mini and micro systems. The manager prepares the programs (the written communication) and then executes them on the computer by performing the necessary operating tasks (the physical communication). The computer responds with the information in written or displayed form.

What about eliminating th manager?

Analysis and Design of the MIS

In the previous chapter, we explained that the MIS can be designed to help the firm meet certain objectives or to solve particular problems. A decision made during the planning phase defined the general approach. Knowing the approach,

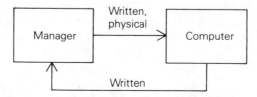

Figure 17-4 The emerging communication process.

the vice-presidents were able to make some assumptions about what the MIS could achieve and what could be required for implementation. It is now time to perform the detailed analysis and design work leading to the MIS.

Approaches to MIS design

There are three basic approaches to the design of an MIS. One is the *top-down approach,* in which the specifications for the MIS are defined on the strategic level and then filtered down through the management layers. This approach works best with the objective orientation. The top managers know the objectives and design an MIS that will support their attainment. But this imposes an MIS on lower-level managers that might not satisfy their needs.

The problem is solved by taking another approach—the *bottom-up approach.* When this is followed, operational-level managers design an MIS to help them meet their objectives or solve their problems. It is likely that the problem orientation will predominate, since the firm's objectives are often obscured by day-to-day problems. Whatever the orientation, the manner in which these lower-level systems operate may have a restricting influence on upper-level systems.

A third approach can overcome the limitations of the other two when performed correctly. This is a *modified top-down approach,* which permits managers on all levels to influence the design. Activity starts on the top level, which identifies an MIS structure that will enable the firm to meet its objectives. This design is presented to lower-level managers for approval or modification. The managers on the lower level make changes, additions, or deletions and return the design to the top level for approval. The revised design is evaluated at the top level and perhaps sent down again in a modified form for further consideration. This evaluation, modification, and approval process continues until it produces a design that is satisfactory to all levels.

The modified top-down approach is identical to the way many firms establish their operating budget, as discussed in Chapter 15. The vertical interaction produces a plan that supports top-level objectives, yet assures lower-level acceptance.

During the early years of computer use, the bottom-up approach flourished. Today, however, the top-down approach is more popular. Those who recommend the top-down approach do not intend to force a system on the lower levels. Rather, they assume that vertical interaction is part of the top-down approach. From this point on, we will use the term *top-down* to mean the modified top-down approach described above.[2]

What is systems analysis?

Analysis is another word for study. In an MIS project the firm is studied as a system. In an existing firm, the study aims at the physical system and its conceptual information system. Some information system exists; the question is whether it

---

[2] For a similar description of a modified approach, see Gideon Samid, "Modified Top Down Design," *Datamation* 27 (November 1981): 175–176.

meets the needs of the managers of the physical system. The analysis job requires the systems analyst to gain some understanding of the physical system. The analyst spends time in the production area, in the warehouse, and in the sales office in order to understand what is happening. He or she talks with the various managers to become familiar with what they do and what information they need. Sometimes this familiarization process takes weeks or even months.

The systems analyst rarely gets involved in making improvements to the physical system. That is the work of the industrial engineer. The analyst only tries to become familiar with the physical system, not to change it. As the analyst studies the existing physical system, he or she focuses on its conceptual information system. Is the information system adequate? If not, what does it need?

In a new firm, there is no information system to study. One must be created. the study emphasis is on understanding the operation of the planned physical system in order to anticipate information needs. Perhaps there is no factory, warehouse, or sales office yet. In that case, the analyst meets with the people who will be managing those operations in order to learn about the planned work and its demand for information.

The discussion that follows involves a systems study in an existing (not a new) firm.

What is systems design?

After interviewing the managers during the study process, the analyst has secured enough information to design the MIS. The planning phase identified the subsystems of the functional information systems. Now the analyst knows what the managers will need from each subsystem in terms of information output.

As the analyst starts to work on these systems and subsystems, he or she considers different designs and selects the one that best enables the firm to meet its objectives. This design is documented in detail, using graphic as well as narrative descriptions.

When the documentation has been prepared, it is given to the programmer for coding. The work of the programmer can be considered part of either design or implementation. In this discussion, programming and the role of the operations staff in testing the programs and building the data files are included in the implementation phase.

An example of the systems approach

The way the systems analyst learns about information needs and then designs an MIS is an example of the systems approach. The analyst first defines the problem by discussing it with the managers. Then the analyst considers various solutions or system designs.

The analyst doesn't have to follow the systems approach. There have surely been many instances when a system was designed before the problem was defined or understood, or when an inferior alternative was selected. Some of these efforts might have met with success, but the odds are heavily against it. The systems approach doesn't guarantee success; it just offers the best chance.

The Analysis and Design

The preceding chapter described the planning by the executive vice-president and the vice-president of information services. A study project proposal was prepared and approved, and a control mechanism was established. As the analysis and design work proceeds, the executive vice-president retains overall control, but the work of the information services staff is the responsibility of the vice-president of information services. Figure 17-5 illustrates how these two executives continue to work together.

The bulk of the work in this phase is performed by the systems analysts. A systems study is conducted in steps 3 and 4 to define the needs, and then a system is designed in steps 5 through 8 to meet those needs. When the design work is completed, the analysts, under the close direction of the vice-president of information services, prepare a second proposal. This proposal recommends the continuation of the project through implementation.

Although it is unlikely that a firm would get this far and then decide to drop the project completely, it is possible. In the beginning, very little is known about the MIS and what it will do for the firm. As more is learned, management might decide that the results do not justify the cost. The process of implementing an MIS is a series of two key go/no go decisions. One decision determines whether the firm will go through the expensive and time-consuming analysis and design phase. The other decision determines whether the firm's resources will be harnessed in an implementation effort. The information services staff must provide the justification for proceeding from one phase to another.

The following paragraphs correspond to the numbered steps in Figure 17-5.

1. Announce the study project.   Perhaps no project affects as many employees in a company as an MIS effort does. All managers should be involved, and many workers will participate in the analysis and design effort and will perform important roles in the MIS.

It is important to recognize the positive effects of the MIS in order to obtain the cooperation and participation of the employees. Nothing is more fearful than the unknown, and it is easy to generate rumors about the effect of the MIS on jobs. For this reason, *top* management must inform the employees of what is planned.[3]

In the case of large firms, a computer has probably been in use for several years, most likely as a data (rather than an information) processing system. If this is the situation, the employees have come to accept the computer as a positive resource and not as a device aimed at replacing people. Management then only has to explain the new use of the computer as an information system and to ask for the employees' support.

If a firm has no computer history, the situation is different. Here management must explain what the computer is intended to do in order to overcome the

---

[3] For a description of the importance of good communication to employee morale, see Randall S. Schuler, "Effective Use of Communication to Minimize Employee Stress," *The Personnel Administrator* 24 (June 1979): 40–44.

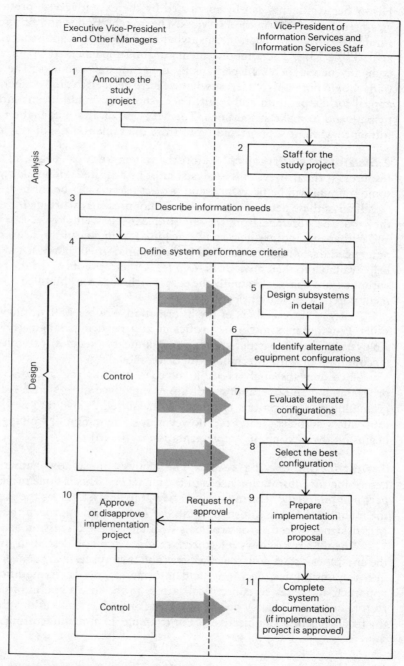

Figure 17-5 The system study project.

employees' fears. A company meeting can be called, with the president presiding. His or her comments can be supported by the executive vice-president and the vice-president of information services. The presentation is not technical; it simply summarizes, in very general terms, what the MIS can do and what it will take to achieve the 'MIS. The announcement can be supplemented by an article in the company newspaper, and perhaps by departmental meetings. The communications should not imply, "Here is what we have decided to do." Rather, they should appeal for cooperation and input. Each employee should be encouraged to participate and to make suggestions. The MIS cannot attain its highest level of performance without support and input from the rank and file of employees.

2. Staff for the study project.   Before the system study can begin, all of the needed resources (primarily systems analysts) must be acquired and made ready. Perhaps some training will be necessary, and project teams must be formed.

If all of these personnel resources are not presently working for the company, they must be obtained from the environment. New employees can be recruited, and perhaps temporary help can be acquired from consulting firms or even computer vendors. Some vendors—IBM, for example—make analyst and programmer help available to their customers for a fee. Other vendors make the help available without extra charge. (Actually the cost is included—or "bundled"—in the equipment purchase or lease price.)

Many of the members of the information services staff will have specialized skills. Programmers might be proficient in a particular language, say COBOL. Analysts might have experience with an industry (airlines) or with a subsystem (accounting) or with a technique (decision modeling).

Since only the analysts are involved in the analysis and design phase, the programming and operations staff are not involved at this time. Additional programming and operations resources are acquired as they are needed. The firm must allow sufficient lead time, however, for orientation or training before work begins on the next phase: implementation of the MIS.

3. Describe information needs.   The analysts must now gather information describing the information needs of the managers. This is done primarily through *personal interviews*. During an interview, the analyst guides the discussion with the intent of defining information needs. The general approach the firm takes in MIS design—objectives or problems—influences the discussion as well.

When a firm follows an *objectives orientation* as described in Chapter 16, the analyst can start with the objectives and then successively convert the findings into responsibilities, decisions, and information needs. A modification of this approach addresses certain critical factors in the firm's operations. The *critical-factors approach* focuses on the few areas of business operations that are key to the firm's meeting its objectives.[4] For example, in a manufacturing organization,

---

[4] Management consultant Peter Drucker is credited with initially recognizing the critical-factors approach in *The Practice of Management* (New York: Harper & Row, 1954). For a more recent application of the technique, see John F. Rockart, "Chief Executives Define their Own Data Needs," *Harvard Business Review* 57 (March–April 1979): 81–93.

the critical factors might be labor relations, vendor relations, inventory management, and production scheduling. In this situation, manufacturing management and the analysts concentrate on defining the information needed to perform these four critical activities. The objective is an MIS designed to support the management of critical activities.

When a firm follows a *problem orientation,* the analyst focuses initially on problems, then on the decisions necessary to solve the problems, and finally on the information needed for decision making.

Regardless of whether an objectives or problem orientation is pursued, the discussion path always leads to the manager's decisions. As the analyst focuses on the decisions, he or she might pursue the following line of questioning.[5]

1. What decisions do you regularly make?
2. What information do you need to make these decisions?
3. What information do you get?
4. What information would you like?
5. What specialized studies do you request?
6. What magazines and trade reports would you like to have routed to you on a regular basis?
7. What specific topics would you like to be informed of?
8. What do you think would be the four most helpful improvements that could be made in the present information system?

Personal interviews represent the most effective way for the analyst to gather information describing the manager's information needs. During the interview, the analyst can react to the manager's answers and direct the line of questioning along the desired path.

In addition to personal interviews, *observation* may yield insight into information needs by revealing how managers and employees go about their duties. Another source of information is *data search,* where the analyst reviews historical records in order to understand the details of the firm's operations. Finally, the analyst can conduct a *survey* using a questionnaire to gather information from a large number of managers by mail and telephone as well as by personal interview. The survey is increasingly important as firms implement distributed systems, making it more difficult for the analyst to personally interview all of the participants. Analysis ends when the analyst understands the specific information needs of all managers concerned.

4. Define system performance criteria. For the first time in the project, the specific needs of the managers are known. Up to this point, the needs have only been defined in general terms, and some have been assumed. It is now possible to specify

---

[5] Adapted from Philip Kotler, *Marketing Management: Analysis, Planning and Control,* 3d ed. (Englewood Cliffs, N.J.: Prentice-Hall, 1976), p. 423.

in exact terms what the MIS should accomplish. These are the performance criteria that were stated in general terms during the planning phase.

For example, a marketing manager might want a certain level of performance from a pricing model. The manager can insist that it consider a five-year projection of the national economy, probable reactions by competitors based on the past five years' performance, and production and marketing costs. Further, the manager might specify that the model be interactive and that the resultant accuracy (projected results compared with actual) be within 5%.

Of course, what the manager wants and what he or she gets can be two different things. Perhaps the firm cannot afford a computer configuration that could provide the needed information. Or perhaps the information is not available because of environmental constraints. Finally and most importantly, a manager's requests must be evaluated in terms of how they support the firm's attempts to meet its objectives.

If acceptable, the specifications become the performance criteria for the MIS subsystems, such as the pricing model. How well the pricing model does its job will be determined by comparing the model with these criteria. Efforts are made to establish similar criteria for each part of the MIS and for each computer program. These criteria should be quantitative, rather than subjective, so that performance can be measured exactly.

5. Design subsystems in detail. When the analyst understands what the new system must accomplish, he or she must next describe the processes that the computer can follow. Attention is paid to basic computer capabilities rather than to particular pieces of equipment. For example, the analyst recognizes that an online master file is necessary but does not specify that the file be DASD, magnetic tape, or whatever.

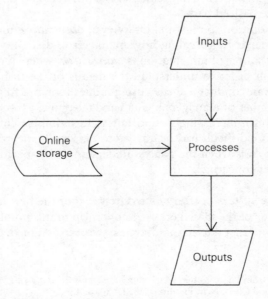

Figure 17-6 General system design.

Each subsystem of the system is described in terms of its inputs, processes, secondary storage, and outputs, using *general* flowcharting symbols as in Figure 17-6. These general symbols are *hardware-independent* (that is, they do not specify any particular type of hardware).

As an example, assume that one of the subsystems in the MIS will process customer orders. This is the *order entry system*. Using information gathered up to this point, the analyst prepares the general system flowchart shown in Figure 17-7.

Input will include *order data* specifying customer number, customer order number, item numbers, item quantities, and item prices. This data can be entered in a variety of ways, but the analyst is not concerned with those details here.

Immediately upon receipt, an entry is made in an online *order log* to serve as a control to assure that no orders are lost. The log entry includes customer number, customer order number, the firm's own sequential control number, and date.

Next, input data fields are edited to detect errors such as missing data, alphabetic characters in a customer number or item number field, item numbers outside an acceptable range, item prices that appear unreasonable, and so on. When errors are detected, a record is written on an *error listing*.

Orders passing the data edit are subject to a credit check. In order to make the check, it is necessary to compute the amount of the order and obtain an accounts receivable amount and a customer credit code from an online *customer credit file*. If the order amount causes the accounts receivable amount to exceed the credit limit, the order data is recorded on an online *rejected-orders file*. The records will stay in that file until the credit manager decides what to do—accept them or return them to the customers. This decision is semistructured. The MIS

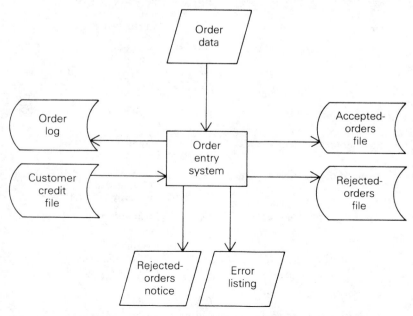

Figure 17-7 General system flowchart of the order entry system.

helps the credit manager make the decision by writing a *rejected-orders notice,* which provides information to support the decision. Orders passing the credit check are written onto the *accepted-orders file,* which serves as input to the inventory subsystem.

In this manner, the analyst "thinks through" the subsystem design. It is a *detailed* design in that the analyst identifies the input data, secondary storage data, basic processing and logic, and output data. The design will become more detailed once a particular hardware configuration is selected. But at this point, the design is detailed enough to serve as a basis for the hardware decision.

6. Identify alternate equipment configurations.   It is now time to think about the computer configuration. All of the systems have been documented in the above manner. A configuration must be selected that allows the programs to function efficiently. The needs of the systems will determine the configuration.

The selection of a configuration is a sequential process, starting with the identification of various configurations that can execute each program. For example, the order entry system can accept order data from punched cards, CRT or hardcopy terminal input, or OCR documents. The order log, customer credit file, rejected-orders file, and accepted-orders file can be on magnetic tape or DASD. The error listing and the rejected-orders notice can be produced by a printer, a CRT terminal, or a hardcopy terminal. In addition, data can be processed in

Table 17-1   System alternatives

System Elements	Alternatives
Input	Punched card CRT terminal Hardcopy terminal OCR
Order log	Magnetic tape DASD
Customer credit file	Magnetic tape DASD
Rejected-orders file	Magnetic tape DASD
Rejected-orders notice	Printer CRT terminal Hardcopy terminal
Accepted-orders file	Magnetic tape DASD
Error listing	Printer CRT terminal Hardcopy terminal
Processing	Batch Online

batches or online. These alternatives are summarized in Table 17-1. In all there are 1152 different configurations ($4 \times 2 \times 2 \times 2 \times 3 \times 2 \times 3 \times 2$).

Now, this doesn't mean that the analyst carefully considers all 1152 possible combinations. Some alternatives need not even be considered. For example, punched card input can be dismissed as an option if the firm has no card punch equipment. And OCR input can be dismissed if this is the only place in the overall system design where OCR could be used and the volume of activity does not provide adequate justification. By eliminating obviously unacceptable options, the analyst can reduce the feasible system alternatives to a reasonable number, say from three to six, for detailed study. Table 17-2 identifies three alternatives for evaluation.

7. Evaluate alternate configurations. The analyst, working closely with the manager, evaluates the three order entry alternatives. They select the one that best enables the subsystem to meet its objectives, given the constraints.

Each subsystem is evaluated in the same manner, with the analysts and the manager identifying the best configuration. Then they must consider all of the subsystems together to identify the configuration that offers the best support to the subsystems as a group. Table 17-3 compares the subsystems of the internal accounting system. You must understand that the evaluation considers all of the subsystems in the MIS—not just those of internal accounting or any other system.

8. Select the best configuration. We can use the internal accounting subsystems in Table 17-3 as an example of how a configuration is selected.

The analysts evaluate all of the subsystem configurations and adjust the device mix so that all subsystems conform to a single configuration. For example, OCR input might be replaced with CRT terminal input for the inventory and accounts receivable subsystems. In the same manner, plotter and COM output might be replaced as output options with printer and magnetic tape respectively. After the analysts have adjusted the configurations, they present their recommendation to the executive vice-president or MIS committee for final approval.

Table 17-2 Alternatives selected for detailed study

Alternative	Input	Order Log	Customer Credit File	Accepted- and Rejected- Orders File	Rejected- Orders Notice	Error Listing
1	CRT	Magnetic tape	DASD	Magnetic tape	Printer	Printer
2	Hardcopy terminal	DASD	DASD	Magnetic tape	Printer	Printer
3	Hardcopy terminal	DASD	DASD	DASD	Hardcopy terminal	Printer

Table 17-3 Comparison of subsystem configurations

Subsystem	Input Devices			Secondary Storage		Output Devices				
	Hardcopy terminal	CRT terminal	OCR	Magnetic tape	DASD	Printer	Hardcopy terminal	CRT terminal	Plotter	COM
Order entry	X				X	X	X			
Inventory	X		X		X	X	X			X
Billing					X	X				
Accounts receivable			X		X	X		X		
Purchasing	X				X		X			
Receiving		X			X			X		
Accounts payable	X			X		X				
General accounting	X	X		X	X	X	X	X	X	

In the event that the selected configuration does not provide the support the manager identified initially, the performance criteria should be modified accordingly. The system will be evaluated by the performance criteria, so the performance criteria should be achievable with the selected configuration. In this manner, the executive vice-president selects an equipment configuration, such as the one in Figure 17-8, that best fits the needs of the entire organization.

As the firm defines its MIS resource needs, it follows a logical progression of events. First, the firm develops a basic system design to support the information needs of the managers. This basic design identifies the procedures and data requirements. Next, it identifies a basic hardware configuration to execute the procedures (software). At this point, the analysis and design phase ends. During the next phase, the firm will select the hardware vendor or vendors, determine whether to develop software or purchase it from vendors, and select the software vendors if that option is pursued. All of these decisions are interrelated.

9. Prepare implementation project proposal. Although much has been accomplished toward achieving an MIS, considerable work remains. None of the computer programs has been coded or purchased at this point, for example. But before additional funds are allocated to the implementation phase, management requires as much information as possible to justify proceeding. Now that the system has been designed, it is possible to provide this information.

The information services staff prepares an *implementation project proposal*

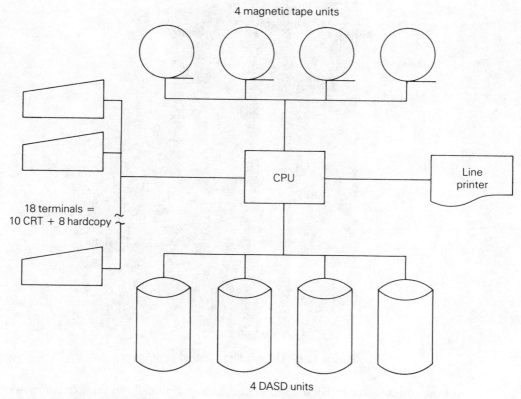

Figure 17-8 The selected equipment configuration.

outlining the work to be done, the expected benefits, and the costs. The format of this proposal is similar to the one prepared for the study project. Figure 17-9 presents a sample outline for a proposal.

Sections 2, 3, and 5 of the figure represent updated versions of corresponding sections in the study project proposal. Because we know more about these sections now, the information can be more specific.

Unlike the study project proposal, the implementation project proposal does not describe possible alternatives for the firm to follow. The selected design and computer equipment configuration are presented in section 4 along with the performance criteria. The anticipated results of that design are described in section 5.

The study project proposal contained a general implementation plan, which is now presented in detail. Since the revised plan is such an improvement over the old one, new documentation of the implementation phase should be prepared— new bar charts, network diagrams, and so on.

10. Approve or disapprove the implementation project. The vice-president of information services reports the progress of the information services staff through-

1. Introduction—reason for the proposal

2. Problem definition

3. System objectives and constraints

4. System design
   a. Summary description
   b. Performance criteria
   c. Equipment configuration

5. Anticipated results
   a. Organizational impact
   b. Operational impact
   c. Financial impact

6. Detailed implementation plan
   a. Objectives
   b. Tasks to be accomplished
   c. Resource requirements
   d. Time schedule
   e. Cost recap

7. Summary

Figure 17-9 The implementation project proposal.

out the systems study. These reports are made periodically to the executive vice-president or the MIS committee. The key executives in the firm are therefore able to intervene and take appropriate action as problems arise. At the conclusion of the study, the managers not only understand the work that has been done, but feel a genuine satisfaction from having actively participated. This is a healthy situation when proposal review time rolls around. The executive vice-president (or the MIS committee) reviews his or her own proposal, not one produced entirely by the information services staff.

In some cases, approval might be conditional, requiring changes to the design or the implementation plan. If the executive vice-president (or MIS committee) has been informed of the progress throughout the analysis and design phase, he or she will most likely approve the implementation project.

11. Complete system documentation. The executive vice-president's or MIS committee's approval to proceed with implementation is evidence of a successful analysis and design effort. The analysts have studied the existing system and prepared the design of a new system that is satisfactory to the firm's management. One important step remains, however. The approved system design must be thoroughly documented. It is a mistake to proceed with implementation if documentation is incomplete.

Each system (or subsystem) within the MIS must be documented. Such documentation often includes:

1. System documentation
   a. System description (narrative)
   b. Global design representation (such as a system flowchart or HIPO documentation)

2. Program documentation (for each program or program module within the system)
   a. Program description (narrative)
   b. Logical design representation (such as a program flowchart or pseudocode)
   c. Output record layouts (such as printer spacing charts and display screen formats)
   d. Input layouts (such as DASD or magnetic tape layouts)

A system usually includes more than one program or program module, with the documentation assembled as in Figure 17-10.

All of the materials for a system together constitute the *system documentation package*. All of the materials for a program constitute the *program documentation package*. It is the systems analyst's responsibility to provide the initial contents of these packages during the analysis and design phase. The programmer adds to the contents during the implementation phase. The packages are filed in the information services department.

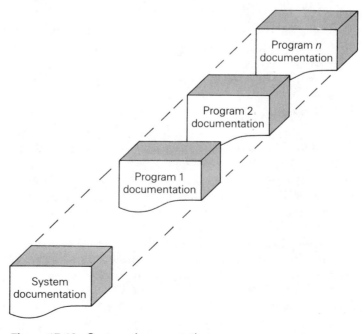

Figure 17-10 System documentation.

System Description
Order Entry System

The Order Entry System processes customer sales orders
and performs the following tasks:
1. Makes an entry in an order log for all orders
   received

2. Edits orders for error data

3. Conducts a credit check

4. Records data for accepted orders in an
   accepted-orders file

5. Records data for rejected orders in a rejected-
   orders file

6. Prints a rejected-orders notice for each
   rejected order

7. Prints an error listing of all orders rejected
   because of error data.

The order log provides a record of all orders received.
Records remain in the rejected-orders file until
the credit department determines their status.
The accepted-orders file serves as input to the inventory
system.

Figure 17-11 A system description.

A flowchart-based documentation example

Let us use the order entry system to illustrate the documentation. This system is described in narrative form in the *system description* shown in Figure 17-11. The system is also described graphically in the system flowchart in Figure 17-12. Both of these overview descriptions deal with inputs and outputs rather than with processing details. The latter are described in program documentation.

The order entry system in the flowchart appears to consist of only a single step. This is characteristic of an online system. If orders were processed in batches, the system would consist of several observable steps.

The analyst uses a plastic template (see Figure 17-13) to draw the flowcharts. Flowcharting is described in detail in the Appendix.

The program flowchart in Figure 17-14 shows the series of steps required to perform the processing. The two diamonds represent the logical decisions of determining whether error data or exceeded credit limits have been encountered. The

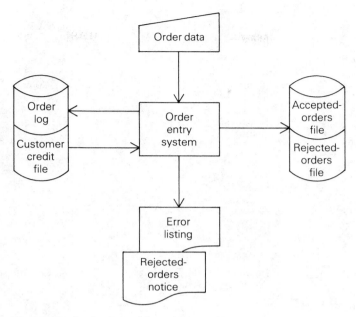

Figure 17-12 A system flowchart.

parallelograms represent input and output steps, and the rectangles represent processing. The small circles containing the letter *A* are connectors—they connect points on the page. There are twelve steps in the program flowchart, but considerably more programming instructions will be required. Some of the flowchart steps represent several programming instructions.

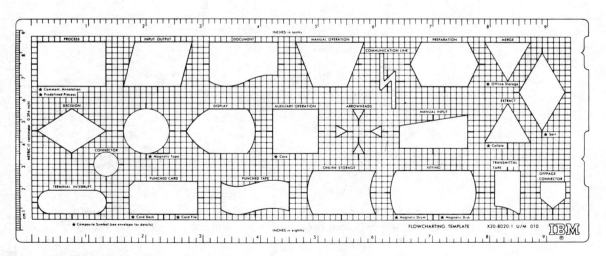

Figure 17-13 A flowchart template.

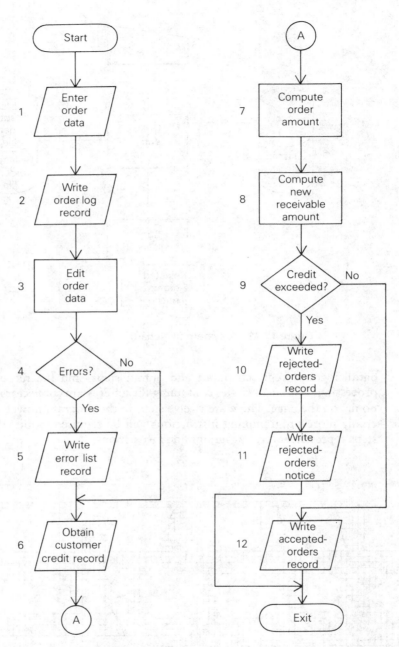

Figure 17-14 A program flowchart.

Each input and output record format is usually documented with one or more layout forms. A sample layout of a customer credit record is shown in Figure 17-15, using a *record layout form*.

The layout of the rejected-orders notice appears in Figure 17-16. This form is called a *printer spacing chart* or a *print layout form*. It permits both horizontal

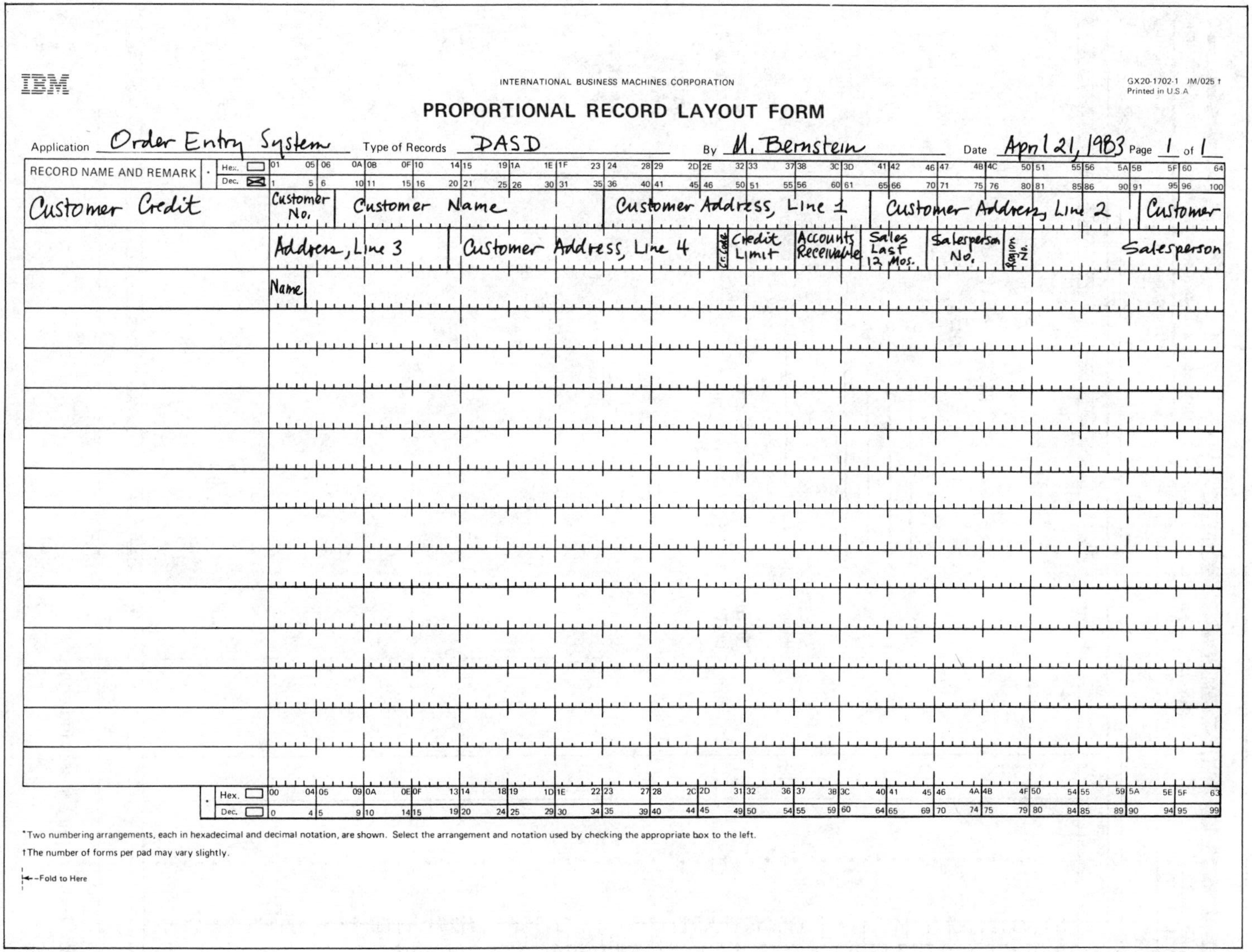

IBM

INTERNATIONAL BUSINESS MACHINES CORPORATION

GX20-1702-1 JM/025 †
Printed in U.S.A.

PROPORTIONAL RECORD LAYOUT FORM

Application: Order Entry System
Type of Records: DASD
By: M. Bernstein
Date: April 21, 1983
Page 1 of 1

RECORD NAME AND REMARK	Fields (positions 1–100)
Customer Credit	Customer No. / Customer Name / Customer Address, Line 1 / Customer Address, Line 2 / Customer
	Address, Line 3 / Customer Address, Line 4 / Cr. Code / Credit Limit / Accounts Receivable / Sales Last 12 Mos. / Salesperson No. / Region No. / Salesperson
	Name

Hex. / Dec. scale: 00–63 (hex), 0–99 (dec); 01–64 (hex), 1–100 (dec).

*Two numbering arrangements, each in hexadecimal and decimal notation, are shown. Select the arrangement and notation used by checking the appropriate box to the left.

†The number of forms per pad may vary slightly.

←Fold to Here

Figure 17-15 A record layout form.

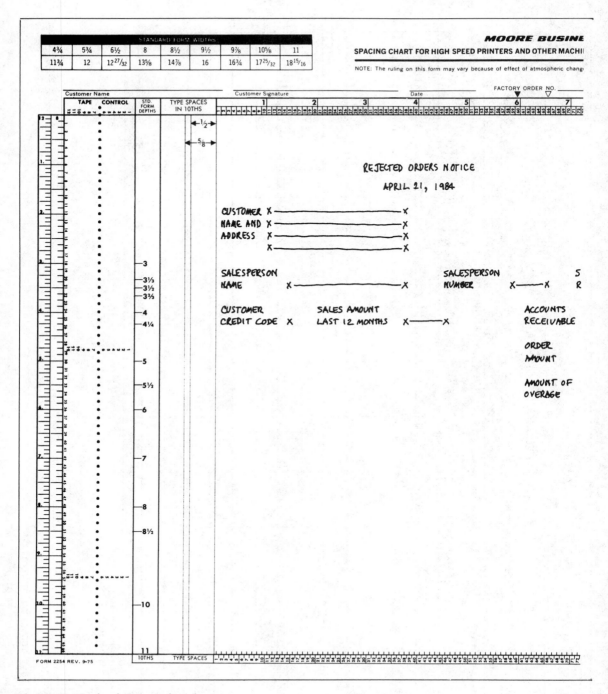

Figure 17-16 A printer spacing chart.

'SS FORMS, INC.

NE-WRITTEN BUSINESS FORMS WITH 1/10" HORIZONTAL SPACING

es on paper. To insure accurate reproduction draw copy according to printed ruling.

NARROW OR STRIP COATED CARBON, CARBON SPOT OPAQUE OR TISSUE

These features are shown by using an overlay to designate the areas of carbon coating. The overlay is placed over the copy for the part on which the carbon impression will be made and the areas to be carbon coated are outlined in red pencil.

_____ COPY FOR FACE OF PART _____ SAME AS PART _____ EXCEPT _____

$\frac{1}{10}$ HORIZONTAL $\frac{1}{8}$ VERTICAL

| 8 | 9 | 10 | 11 | 12 | 13 | 14 | 15 | 16 | STD. FORM DEPTHS |

ILES

EGION XXX

X———X

X———X

X ——— X

3
3½
3½
3¾
4
4¼
5
5½
6
7
8
8½
10
11

and vertical mapping of a report printed on a hardcopy printer. A similar layout form is available for designing a report to be displayed on a CRT.

The examples of documentation illustrated above represent a typical selection describing a system. All of the methods and forms have been in use for a number of years, since they were originally developed to document punched card systems. During recent years, several new documentation methods have been developed. Two are *HIPO (Hierarchy plus Input-Process-Output)* and *pseudocode*. HIPO is best suited to showing a system overview and therefore represents an alternative to a system flowchart. Pseudocode is best suited to showing program detail and therefore represents an alternative to a program flowchart.

Using HIPO for design and documentation

HIPO consists of three types of diagrams. One, the *hierarchy diagram* or *structure chart,* shows the subdivision of a system by levels. A hierarchy diagram for the order entry system appears in Figure 17-17. This example identifies system inputs and outputs (as in the system flowchart in Figure 17-12) and basic processing steps (as in the system description in Figure 17-11). The upper box represents the system (box 1.0). On the next lower level are the basic processes of the system (boxes 2.0 through 5.0), which are described in greater detail on successively lower levels. The narrative in each process box consists of a verb and an object.

A second type of HIPO diagram is the *overview diagram,* which relates inputs and outputs to the processes identified in the hierarchy diagram. In Figure 17-18 the input files and output files are linked to the basic processes by arrows. The files are represented by rectangles in this example. Some analysts prefer to use the flowchart symbols for the various file media.[6] No effort is made to relate specific files to specific processing steps or to show the detail of the processing. That detail is described in successively lower-level detail diagrams.

Each of the four processing boxes in the overview diagram is described by a detail diagram. The *detail diagram* for step 4.0, compute credit check, appears as Figure 17-19. In the first processing step, unit price is multiplied by quantity for each item ordered. These input data items are enclosed in boxes to indicate that they are already in primary storage. The output, order amount, is also placed in storage. The second processing step computes the credit limit overage. The customer credit file is accessed to obtain the credit limit and the accounts receivable amount. The accounts receivable amount is added to the order amount, and the updated receivable amount is compared with the credit limit. If the sum exceeds the credit limit, the amount of the overage is recorded in a storage area. The detail diagram for module 4.0 does not show the detail of the computations in steps 1 and 2. HIPO is not intended to provide detailed documentation or to replace coding.

---

[6]The HIPO technique used here is described in detail in Harry Katzan, Jr., *Systems Design and Documentation: An Introduction to the HIPO Method* (New York: Van Nostrand Reinhold, 1976). For an example of how flowchart symbols can be used in the overview diagram, see Marilyn Bohl, *Tools for Structured Design* (Chicago: Science Research Associates, 1978), pp. 172–173.

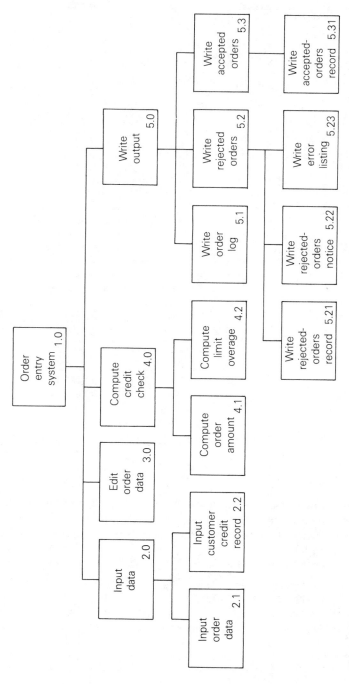

Figure 17-17 A hierarchy diagram.

System/Module No._____ System/Module Name_____

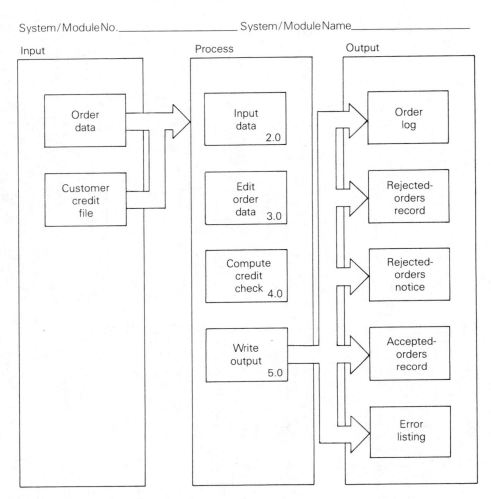

Figure 17-18 An overview diagram.

The dark arrow labeled "From 1.0" links module 4.0 to the module on the higher level, module 1.0. Also, the dark arrow labeled "return" recognizes that control will be returned to the upper-level module as soon as this series of steps is complete.

HIPO was developed by IBM in the mid-seventies.[7] Its main advantages are that it facilitates top-down design and permits the manager to be involved in system design farther into the project than if flowcharting were used. Thus far HIPO hasn't been used very much by computer users. Whether it will become a popular design and documentation technique in years to come remains to be seen.

[7] For more information on HIPO, see *HIPO—A Design Aid and Documentation Technique* (White Plains, N.Y.: IBM Corporation), GC20-1851.

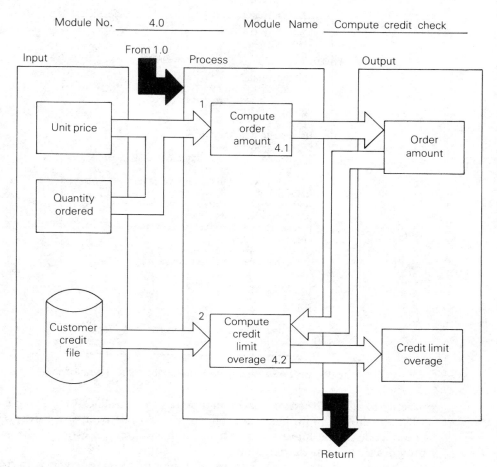

Figure 17-19 A detail diagram.

Using pseudocode for design and documentation

Unlike HIPO, pseudocode has been generally accepted by computer users as an alternative to flowcharting. *Pseudocode* is not a computer language, but it is quite similar to languages such as FORTRAN and PL/I. A programmer can use pseudocode instead of a program flowchart, and it is easy to convert the pseudocode into programming language.

A pseudocode description of the order entry system appears in Figure 17-20. It uses the same logic illustrated in the program flowchart in Figure 17-14. Compared to flowcharting, there are very few rules in pseudocode.[8] Some key words such as IF and DOWHILE are usually written in capital letters. Also, it is common

---

[8] For a thorough explanation of pseudocode, see Bohl, pp. 17–60.

```
Start
Enter order data
Write order log record
Edit order data*
IF order contains errors THEN
      write error list record
(ELSE)
ENDIF
Read customer credit record
DOWHILE this order
      Multiply order quantity times unit price
      giving price extension
      Add price extension to invoice amount
ENDDO
Add invoice amount to accounts receivable
giving new accounts receivable
IF new accounts receivable greater than
credit limit THEN
      Write rejected orders record
      Write rejected orders notice
ELSE
      Write accepted orders record
ENDIF
Exit

*The detail of the editing process is not shown.
```

Figure 17-20   A program description using pseudocode.

practice to indent the statements of an IF statement and a DOWHILE and DOUN-TIL (not shown) loop. One advantage of pseudocode over flowcharting is that pseudocode can be entered as comments in the program. A listing of the program provides the documentation along with the coding.

Pseudocode facilitates a *structured design* of programs, which is currently very popular. The fact that pseudocode facilitates structured design partly explains its popularity. Another reason is that pseudocode *replaces* program flowcharts, and many programmers do not like flowcharting. This attitude is especially prevalent among new programmers, who are initially taught structured programming and prefer the flexibility of pseudocode to the rather inflexible rules of flowcharting.

Putting the documentation techniques in perspective

You should recognize that system and program documentation requirements vary widely from one installation to another. Everyone agrees that documentation is desirable because it performs two basic functions. First, it facilitates *communication* among the participants in the system design (primarily among users, analysts, and programmers). Second, it facilitates system *maintenance* at a later date. But many installations demand only a bare minimum of documentation—perhaps nothing more than a program listing. Proponents of complete documentation believe that the time spent in documenting pays dividends elsewhere during the system life cycle. Computer users should remain open-minded to the different documentation techniques, recognizing that each is best suited to particular situations.

The subject of documentation is very important to users of packaged software. If a user purchases a poorly documented software package, the ultimate cost can exceed that of a higher-priced, documented package. In the first place, the user never really knows what the package will or will not do. Second, when something goes wrong and a programmer must be brought in to fix the problem, the programmer wastes precious (spelled "expensive") time finding the cause of the trouble.

There is no doubt that much of the documentation of business installations over the years has been busy work. But it would be a big mistake to do away with documentation altogether. Computerized business systems are used by many people over a long period of time. For this reason alone, documentation is a must.

In this chapter we have described only a few of the most popular documentation tools. A number of these tools have been devised during recent years to keep pace with the changing nature of computer use.[9] The tools are similar to golf clubs in a golfer's bag—each is designed for a certain situation. The professional systems analyst is skilled in the use of all the tools needed to do a particular job. If managers are to become more self-sufficient in satisfying their own information needs independently of the information services staff, they too must become more proficient in the use of documentation tools.

Summary

The information services staff is composed of systems analysts, programmers, operations personnel, and data base administrators. This staff is responsible for developing an MIS. Development includes an analysis of the existing system and the design and implementation of the new MIS. The work of the staff is directed by the vice-president of information services, but the overall control is exercised by the executive vice-president or the MIS committee.

This chapter describes the analysis and design phase, work performed primarily by systems analysts. Programmers and operations personnel perform their work during the implementation phase.

The general system design can be controlled by top executives (the top-down approach), by the operational-level managers (the bottom-up approach), or by interactions among managers at all levels (the modified top-down approach). Although the latter approach is the most effective in meeting the information needs of all managers, all three approaches require the analyst to understand the

---

[9] For a good documentation of the evolution of systems analysis and design methods, see J. Daniel Couger and Robert W. Knapp, *Systems Analysis Techniques* (New York: John Wiley & Sons, 1974); and J. Daniel Couger, Mel A. Colter, and Robert W. Knapp, *Advanced System Development/Feasibility Techniques* (New York: John Wiley & Sons, 1982). Other sources of information on analysis and design can be found in Jerry FitzGerald, Ardra F. FitzGerald, and Warren D. Stallings, Jr., *Fundamentals of Systems Analysis*, 2d ed. (New York: John Wiley & Sons, 1981); Edward Yourdan and Larry L. Constantine, *Structured Design* (Englewood Cliffs, N.J.: Prentice-Hall, 1979); and Tom DeMarco, *Structured Analysis and System Specification* (Englewood Cliffs, N.J.: Prentice-Hall, 1979).

managers' needs. The analyst gains this understanding by employing a variety of information-gathering techniques, with an emphasis on personal interviews. The process of gaining an understanding of the existing system and the managers' information needs is called *systems analysis*. Once this understanding is gained, the different approaches to the new MIS are defined and evaluated. The selection of the design believed to best enable the firm to meet its objectives concludes the *systems design*.

The analysis and design phase is initiated by an announcement to the employees, followed by staffing any vacant positions. Analysis includes a description of information needs and a definition of system performance criteria, conducted by both the analysts and the managers. Design includes detailing subsystem designs, identifying and evaluating alternatives, and selecting the optimal configuration. The analysts do most of the designing, soliciting management's input as the design unfolds.

The analysts prepare an implementation project proposal to gain approval to proceed to the next phase of the MIS life cycle. Approval is the signal for the analysts to complete all of the system documentation. The purpose of the documentation is to facilitate communication and maintenance. Flowcharting is the traditional documentation technique, but newer approaches (such as HIPO and pseudocode) are gaining support.

Key Terms

operator	order data
operations manager	order log
programmer	error listing
programming manager	customer credit file
systems analyst	rejected-orders file
systems analysis manager	rejected-orders notice
analyst/programmer	accepted-orders file
analysis and design team	implementation project proposal
systems development	system documentation package
systems maintenance	program documentation package
top-down approach	system description
bottom-up approach	record layout form
modified top-down approach	printer spacing chart, print layout form
personal interview	
critical-factors approach	HIPO (Hierarchy plus Input-Process-Output)
observation	
data search	hierarchy diagram, structure chart
survey	overview diagram
hardware-independent	detail diagram
	pseudocode

Key Concepts

The organizational structure of the information services department

The communication process involving managers and information specialists

Basic approaches to information systems design

The difference between systems analysis and systems design

The analysis and design process

The analyst's information-gathering techniques

The logical process of determining a computer configuration

Documentation packages for systems and programs

Levels of documentation detail

Reasons for documentation

Questions

1. What jobs are performed in the operations area?
2. Compare the duties of a systems analyst and an analyst/programmer.
3. What factors influence whether a firm assigns the analysis and programming responsibilities to different individuals?
4. Identify three ways that analysts and programmers can be grouped within the information services department.
5. Explain the difference between systems development and systems maintenance.
6. How is the data base administrator involved in the analysis and design process?
7. What is the MIS communication process? How do participants communicate with each other?
8. What is the communication problem? How can it be solved?
9. What are the three approaches to MIS design? How do they relate to the two approaches to the MIS project described in Chapter 16?
10. What is the difference between systems analysis and systems design?
11. Which information specialists are involved with the analysis and design phase?
12. Name the four basic ways a systems analyst identifies a manager's information needs.
13. What are some strategies a systems analyst can use during a personal interview?
14. Why are general flowcharting symbols used early in the design process? What term is used to describe these general symbols?
15. What two types of transactions are recorded in the rejected-orders file?
16. Assume that a firm is considering the system alternatives in Table 17-1 and decides against punched card and OCR input. How many different configuration possibilities remain?
17. What is the difference between a system flowchart and a program flowchart?

18. What are the three types of documentation included in HIPO?

19. Explain why pseudocode is so popular.

20. What are the two basic functions of documentation?

Problems

1. Draw a system flowchart of the following steps:

   a. A sales clerk fills out a sales receipt form.

   b. The sales receipts are accumulated in batches and sent to the data entry department.

   c. Data from the sales receipts is recorded on floppy disks using a key-to-disk unit.

   d. Data from the floppy disks is read into the computer and added to a monthly sales file on DASD. During the same process, a daily sales report is printed.

   Refer to the description of flowcharting in the Appendix, if necessary.

2. Draw a system flowchart of the following steps:

   a. A raw-material requirement file on DASD is read by the computer. For each raw-material item, possible vendors are identified by directly accessing vendor records in the vendor file, also on DASD. A buyer notification form is printed on a hardcopy terminal in the purchasing department.

   b. A buyer makes a purchase decision, using information on the buyer notification.

   c. The purchase decision is entered into the computer from the terminal.

   d. Using the purchase decision data, the computer prints purchase orders on the line printer and writes records in a pending-receipts file on magnetic tape.

3. Draw a HIPO hierarchy diagram for the process described in problem 1.

4. Draw a HIPO hierarchy diagram for the process described in problem 2.

5. Draw a HIPO overview diagram for step d in problem 1.

6. Draw a HIPO overview diagram for step d in problem 2.

7. Draw a HIPO overview diagram of the following processes:

   Process 2.0   Input data from a payroll transaction file and an employee master file.
   Process 3.0   Compute gross earnings.
   Process 4.0   Compute income tax.
   Process 5.0   Compute social security tax.
   Process 6.0   Compute net pay.
   Process 7.0   Write output on a payroll register form.

8. Draw a separate HIPO detail diagram for each process in problem 7. The payroll transaction file is on magnetic tape, the employee master file is on DASD, and the payroll register form is prepared on a line printer. Gross earn-

ings are computed by multiplying hourly rate (from the employee master file) times hours worked (from the transaction file). Income tax is computed by multiplying gross earnings times an income tax percent (in primary storage). Social security tax is computed by multiplying gross earnings times a social security tax percent (in primary storage). Net pay is computed by subtracting income tax and social security tax from gross earnings. The payroll register form contains employee number and name (read into primary storage in process 2.0), gross earnings, income tax, social security tax, and net earnings.

CASE PROBLEM: Metroscope Realty

Master of ceremonies:
First I'd like to thank the nice folks at the Granada Inn for such a delicious meal. Now it's our pleasure to welcome as our speaker Mr. Arnold Whitmarsh, owner of Metroscope Realty, who will address this monthly meeting of the Fort Wayne Microcomputer Club. Mr. Whitmarsh.

Mr. Whitmarsh:
Thank you, Mr. President. It's my pleasure to be here this evening to tell you about our new MIS—that stands for *management information system*. Last summer when my wife and I were vacationing in Iowa, I noticed that one of those computer stores was having a sale. We checked it out and they made me an offer I couldn't refuse. Got a brand new microcomputer for 35 percent off. Brought it back to the office and learned my first lesson about software—you need it. I called the store in Iowa and they sent me five real estate programs for only $29.95 each. Well, I tried to get those programs to work, but I just couldn't do it. I was talking with my brother-in-law, and he said I needed a programmer. So I ran an ad and hired Ray Fletcher, whom you all know. Ray got the programs to run in nothing flat. We started using them and found we didn't even need our desk calculator any more. We're doing calculations now that we never dreamed of before—rental property income analysis, mortgage analysis, depreciation calculations, and much more. (*Pause*) One day Ray came to me and said, "Mr. Whitmarsh, we ought to think about installing a management information system." I said "What's a management information system?" Ray proceeded to tell me how my agents and I could get a lot of valuable information from the computer. It sounded good, and I gave Ray the green light. "Put as much as you can on the computer," I told Ray. Since then, Ray has been working night and day getting our MIS ready. I thought you might want to ask Ray some questions, since he's the expert, so I brought him along. Take a bow, Ray. (*Applause*) Now, does anybody have any questions?

Club member:
Ray, what programs are you writing?

Fletcher:

Mostly accounting systems—general ledger, billing, receivables, commission accounting, and inventory.

Club member:

Did you consider canned programs?

Fletcher:

Not really. Mr. Whitmarsh hired me as a programmer and I felt obligated to give him his money's worth. Besides, I know what we need, and our programs will be tailored to us, not somebody else.

Club member:

Have you had a good experience working with the people who will use the system?

Fletcher:

I haven't bothered them yet. They're all busy selling, and I don't want to waste their time. I've been in the real estate business off and on for over ten years, and I know what's needed. I plan on getting everything put together in a nice package and then having a training seminar to show everyone how to use it.

Club member:

What language are you using, and what kind of documentation are you preparing?

Fletcher:

BASIC. And the program listings are pretty much it as far as documentation goes. I include a data dictionary at the beginning of each program, defining all the variables. Documentation isn't a real problem. I have a good understanding of what's going on and can make changes to the programs very easily if the need arises.

Master of ceremonies:

Pardon me, folks. I'm going to have to cut this short. The cleanup crew has to come in and get the room ready for the American Legion dance tonight. See you all next month.

Questions

1. What was the major error Mr. Whitmarsh made in hardware selection?
2. Have any errors been made in the software area? Explain.
3. Is Ray Fletcher doing a good job of developing the MIS? Support your answer.
4. Assume you are a Club Member giving Mr. Whitmarsh a ride home after the meeting. He says, "I'd be interested in any suggestions that might help us improve our MIS." Briefly, what would you say?

Chapter 18

Information Systems Development: The Implementation Phase

Learning Objectives

After studying this chapter, you should:

- Appreciate how specific and accurate the implementation plan can be, given a good system design specification
- Understand the purpose of the two major communications to employees: the announcement of the implementation, and the educational program
- See how the sequence of the implementation tasks is influenced by software and computer decisions
- Understand the basic process of soliciting and evaluating vendor proposals
- Understand the process of developing an applications program
- Know the key elements of structured programming, how it fits within the larger sphere of structured development, and how structured development influences MIS design and use
- Be introduced to natural programming languages and their potential influence on the MIS
- Appreciate the difficulty of data base preparation in certain circumstances
- Understand the scope of the educational program and how outside resources can be used
- Know the basic strategies for cutover to the new system

Significance of the Final Approval

The executive vice-president's or MIS committee's approval of the implementation project proposal signals the final go-ahead for the MIS. This approval indicates that the firm's management is sufficiently satisfied with the system design and its anticipated benefits to authorize an additional expenditure of funds.

Much work has been accomplished up to this point—perhaps the most difficult part of the project. The systems analysts have been able to communicate with the managers to identify their information needs. This is never easy, since it requires a positive and cooperative attitude mixed with a good portion of creativity and ingenuity.

Once the MIS is designed, implementation tends to be more automatic. Certain important tasks remain to be done. These tasks can be planned and executed with considerable precision. Reaching this point in the MIS project, indicates that the firm has a highly competent management and information services staff. Recognizing this competence should give the firm's management confidence that the implementation will proceed successfully.

Implementation of an MIS

The implementation phase includes all of the tasks necessary to convert the MIS design into a working system. The analysis and design phase describes the new system and how it will work. The description exists only on paper; it is a model of the planned MIS. What is necessary now is the conversion of that model to the real thing—the MIS. The MIS will be a physical system consisting of machines (the computer and peripheral or auxiliary equipment), personnel (managers, employees, and the information services staff), and materials (tapes, disks, cards, paper forms, and so on). *Implementation* is the acquisition and integration of these resources to form a working MIS. Once this operational status has been achieved, the MIS enters its fourth and final phase—operation.

Implementation tasks

Many separate tasks make up the implementation effort. These tasks involve practically everyone in the firm, whereas the planning and the analysis and design phases involved primarily the managers, systems analysts, and data base administrators. The implementation phase involves these same people as well as operational-level employees throughout the organization and the remainder of the information services staff.

The tasks involved in implementation include:

1. Plan the implementation
2. Announce the implementation project
3. Organize the MIS staff
4. Select the computer
5. Prepare and/or purchase the software library
6. Prepare the data base

7. Educate participants and users
8. Prepare physical facilities
9. Cut over to the new system

The sequence in which these tasks are performed depends on the organization. The selection of the computer equipment and, in some cases, the selection of the software vendor are key tasks and determine the sequence of several other tasks. If a firm has a programming staff and intends to develop its own software, the computer selection is made prior to preparing the software library, the data base, the physical facilities. This sequence is shown in Figure 18-1. If, on the other

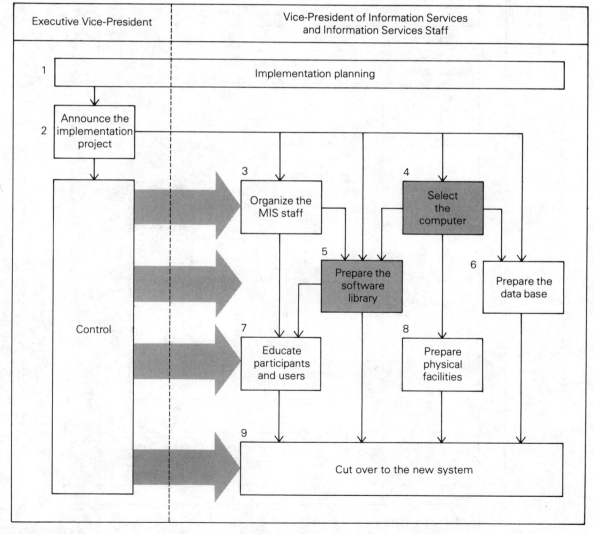

Figure 18-1   The implementation phase—the firm prepares its own software.

hand, a firm intends to obtain its software from a vendor, the software decision most likely precedes and influences the computer selection. Take, for example, a small manufacturing firm that evaluates the different applications software on the market and decides to use IBM's MAPICS package. This decision narrows the computer selection choice to those IBM systems that use MAPICS. This sequence is shown in Figure 18-2.

Two important points should be made about Figures 18-1 and 18-2. First, you will notice that several tasks are going on at the same time. In the earlier life

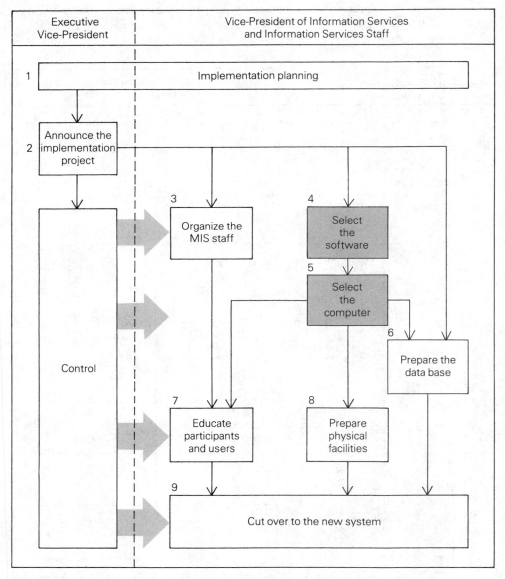

Figure 18-2 The implementation phase—the firm purchases its software.

cycle phases the manager and the analyst took steps sequentially. In this phase other resources (such as programmers and operators) are involved, and several of them can be working at the same time.

The second point concerns the conceptual nature of the diagrams, which are intended to show a general pattern. In an activity as complex as the implementation of a computer, you cannot represent all of the possible combinations of tasks in the form of nice, neat boxes. For example, it is quite possible that a firm will prepare some of its software and purchase the rest. This firm's implementation plan would be a combination of Figures 18-1 and 18-2. Another firm may need only slight modifications in its MIS, which will require few changes in the physical facilities. In this second firm, the facility preparation can be delayed until very late in the project. A third firm may be implementing its first large-scale computer, requiring significant changes in the physical facilities. Work on those changes can begin very early in the implementation phase so that the facilities will be ready at cutover time.

As you study these two diagrams and read the description of the implementation, keep these points in mind. These diagrams, together with those in the preceding life cycle chapters, serve as general guidelines of the work to be done in developing an MIS.

Implementation Planning (1)

You recall that a control mechanism was established at the end of the planning phase in the form of a Gantt chart or network diagram. As more was learned about the project during the analysis and design phase, the control mechanism was updated and made more detailed. Now only one phase remains before cutover, and the managers and information specialists have a very specific knowledge of the MIS design. This knowledge can be used to develop a detailed—and quite accurate—implementation plan.

Software selection

The system design identifies the particular software packages needed. All firms will acquire systems software from vendors of operating systems, data base management systems, data communications monitors, and the like. Many firms, especially those planning the installation of a mini or micro, will acquire applications programs. The software vendors must be identified and time estimates made for vendor responses to requests for bids.

Programming

Each of the programs has been designed and documented. There is now an accurate list of all the programs that will be required. The relative complexity of each program can be estimated quite accurately. The program documentation provides a picture of the work each program is to do. This documentation can also be used to estimate the time required to prepare each program.

In addition to a better knowledge of the required programs, the firm also has a better understanding of the resources that will do the work—the programmers. Quite possibly, the programming staff has already been assembled. Their numbers and capabilities are known. Specific programmers can be assigned to specific programs.

Data base preparation

The system design includes an identification of all the required data files as well as their contents. Some of these files might currently exist in computer-readable form, such as punched card or magnetic tape. Perhaps they will remain as is, or they may be converted to another form, such as magnetic disk. Whatever the file medium, there is a good chance that additional data will be required and must therefore be added. Also, there is a good chance that completely new files will have to be created. This is especially likely for files of environmental data that may not have existed previously. The system design permits a detailed plan of the file building that will provide the data base for the MIS.

If a data base management system (DBMS) will be used, it is the data base administrator's (DBA's) responsibility to teach the personnel how to use the DBMS. This is part of the overall education program. Also, it is the DBA's responsibility to use the DBMS to prepare the data base.

Putting the plan into action

The control mechanism graphics (such as the network diagram) are updated to reflect the details of the implementation plan. Periodic meetings of all participants continue and will increase in frequency as the cutover approaches. From this point on, management attention shifts from planning to control. The final plan has been made; it is time to put it into action.

Announce the Implementation Project (2)

Just as the analysis and design phase was announced to the employees, so top management must communicate the plans for the implementation phase. This communication should be less sensational than the previous one. The rank and file of employees know of management's interest in an MIS and probably expect the project to continue through completion.

Although all employees were not involved in the analysis and design phase, communications were aimed at all levels. This approach was intended to stop rumors about negative impacts of the MIS on employment and duties. Now most employees will be expected to play a role in the implementation. An appeal must be made for their cooperation. Management should explain the roles employees will play and the benefits they will receive.

Since significantly more material must be communicated now, the announcement can be made in phases (Figure 18-3). The president can address the entire employee force (if possible) or can make a statement for the company's publication, explaining the plan in general terms. Then the executive vice-president and

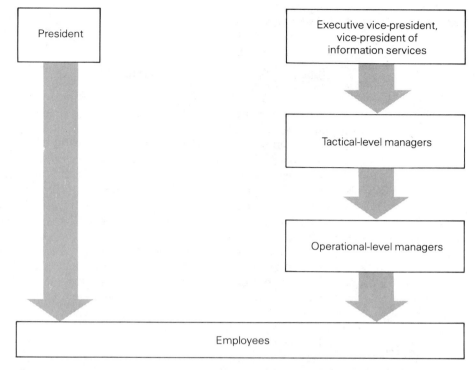

Figure 18-3 Announcement of the implementation flows from top to bottom.

the vice-president of information services can meet with key managers to discuss how each area will be involved. These managers will then meet with their staffs to acquaint them with the upcoming events. The final step includes meetings with each section and department to discuss in specific terms how the implementation will be handled. These meetings are not intended to educate the employees about their role in the operating MIS, although this topic might be covered briefly. The objective is to inform the employees of their role in implementation.

Organize the MIS Staff (3)

Most of the information services staff has already been acquired, and in some cases training has begun to prepare staff members for their upcoming roles. The systems analysis group has been in place for quite some time and has completed the bulk of its work in designing the new MIS. Because the hiring plans for the programmers and operators included sufficient lead time, the staff will be ready to start work when the time comes.

During this period, the final additions will be made to the information services staff, training programs will continue, and the staff will be organized into functional groups or teams. The implementation plan specifies what staff members are needed and when their work will begin.

Select the Software and the Computer (4)

Not too long ago, firms automatically assumed they would do all their own applications programming. Today applications software offered by computer manufacturers and software houses can handle the data and information processing of large and small firms alike.[1] The decision of whether to *make or buy* applications software is further complicated by the increasing variety and improving quality of the packages.

Figure 18-4 lists some of the more important factors influencing the make-or-buy decision. Factors 1–6 concern the firm and its software needs. Factors 7–11 concern the software vendors and their products. A firm can use the eleven factors as a self-administered questionnaire. Responses to each factor will indicate an overall "make" or "buy" orientation, or something in between. Each factor can be weighted, and points are computed by multiplying the weight times the checked rating. The factor points can be added to produce a total score. In Figure 18-4, the firm has a moderate "buy" orientation, which means that it will probably obtain most or all of its applications software from vendors.

The process followed for selecting both software and computer vendors varies widely, depending on the firm. A large firm developing a giant MIS can exercise considerable clout with vendors because of the size of the potential business. A large firm can impose exceptionally stringent requirements on vendors that are to compete for the business. A small firm does not have this clout and must use existing information to evaluate the vendors' offerings. In the discussion that follows, we will assume that the firm is large enough to go through a formal process of requesting vendor bids, evaluating them, and making a selection.

Requests for bids

The system design should be made available to the vendors offering all or any of the types of computing equipment in the configuration selected at the end of the system study. Many vendors supply only certain units, such as plotters, terminals, or OCR readers. Some of these units may be superior to similar devices supplied by vendors like IBM, Honeywell, and Control Data Corporation, who offer complete configurations. The best configuration might integrate hardware from more than one vendor. Since many firms produce computing equipment, some screening process usually precedes the offering of invitations to bid.

Each vendor selected should be provided with a document called a *request for bid* or *request for proposal (RFP)*. This document is a summary of the relevant

---

[1] At the end of 1980 there were some 1400 vendors of large-system software and 2800 vendors of mini/micro software. The origins of the software industry are described in Larry Welke, "The Origins of Software," *Datamation* 26 (December 1980): 127 ff. For the results of a survey of users' ratings of fifty-nine applications software packages, see "Applications Software Survey 1982," *Datamation* 28 (May 1982): 94 ff.

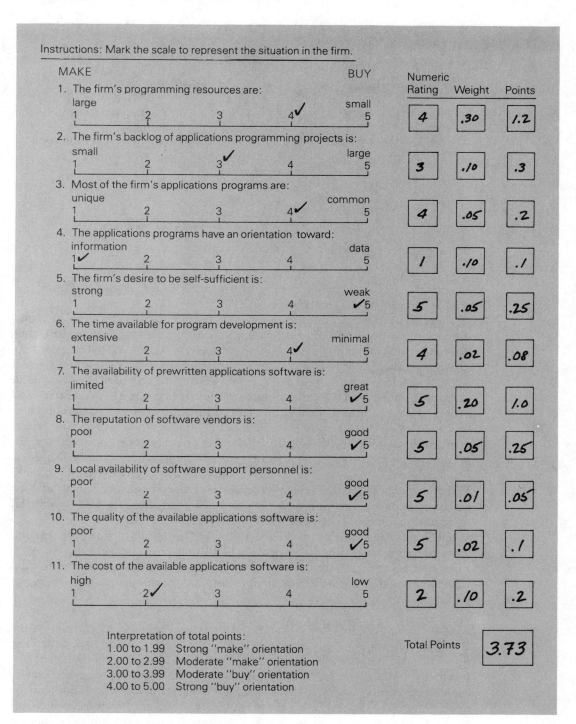

Figure 18-4 Self-administered make-or-buy questionnaire.

1. Letter of transmittal

2. System objectives and constraints

3. System design
   a. Summary description
   b. Performance criteria
   c. Equipment configuration
   d. Program documentation packages
      (selected portions)
   e. Estimated transaction volume
   f. Estimated file sizes

4. Installation schedule

Figure 18-5 The request for bid.

parts of the system study and the implementation project proposals. Figure 18-5 presents an outline of a bid request.

The letter of transmittal explains to the vendor what is expected, including the type of proposal and the deadline for submission. Descriptions of the system objectives and constraints, design, performance criteria, and equipment configuration are taken directly from the implementation project proposal (see Figure 17-9). The selected portions of the program documentation packages will enable vendors to understand what the equipment is intended to do. The estimated transaction volume and the estimated file sizes will permit vendors to determine how much time will be required to process the data. Vendors therefore propose equipment configurations to meet specific processing requirements. By specifying the system design for the vendors, the firm assures that all vendors will be proposing equipment to do the same job. If the vendors are left to propose configurations of their own choosing, the firm has no clear basis for comparison. The installation schedule, included as the final section of the RFP, enables vendors to schedule equipment deliveries to arrive at the appropriate time.

The same approach can be followed to solicit proposals for software. In some cases, the computer equipment vendor will also propose prewritten applications software packages. In other cases, software firms will prepare packages to meet a firm's special needs. The RFP provides a format for vendors' recommendations.

Preparation of vendor proposals

If vendors choose to compete for the order, they prepare a *proposal* describing how their equipment meets the performance criteria. For larger orders, vendors inevitably want to conduct personal interviews with the key people involved in the selection decision. Ostensibly they do this to gather more information, but the main objective is to promote their products. It is difficult not to grant vendors access to the key managers in the firm. A good understanding of the managers and their needs cannot help but contribute to a proposal that more completely meets the needs of the firm.

1. Letter of transmittal

2. Summary of recommendations

3. Advantages

4. Equipment configuration

5. Equipment specifications
   a. Performance data
   b. Prices

6. Satisfaction of performance criteria

7. Delivery schedule

Figure 18-6   The vendor equipment proposal.

Presentation of vendor proposals

In practically all cases, the vendors prepare written proposals. Some proposals may be nothing more than a letter, while others may be lengthy volumes. An outline of a vendor equipment proposal is shown in Figure 18-6.

Section 2 summarizes the vendor's recommendations relating to the type of equipment proposed and the major benefits expected. This section does not elaborate, but condenses the relevant points of the proposal into a succinct management summary. Section 3 lists the advantages of selecting this vendor's equipment over another's. Sections 4 and 5 identify the proposed computer system components along with their performance specifications (speeds, accuracy ratings, and so on) and their price. Section 6 addresses the performance criteria, program by program. When included, this is the lengthiest section of the proposal. Finally, in section 7 the vendor quotes a delivery schedule, which should meet the installation dates in the implementation plan.

Very often the vendor will also make a formal oral presentation to the key executives or the MIS committee. This presentation gives the firm's executives an opportunity to ask questions about specific points in the proposal.

Selection of vendors

When all vendors propose the same types of equipment or software, the selection decision boils down to which one best meets the performance criteria at the lowest cost. How does the firm know that the proposed systems can meet the performance criteria? One approach is to establish *benchmark problems* for the vendors to solve, using the proposed hardware and software. These benchmark problems can be a few of the more important programs or the entire system.

As an example of the benchmark approach, the U.S Public Health Service sent RFPs to over ninety potential vendors for a multimillion-dollar timesharing service bureau contract.[2] Each vendor was expected to write its own software to handle twenty-two different types of transactions involving a data base of over one million records. Only five vendors responded, each spending over $100,000 to compete for the business. The results were enlightening to the Public Health Service officials. The IBM System/370 using the ADABAS DBMS couldn't handle the transaction volume. The winner was a Tandem computer that cost about one-third the price of the UNIVAC and IBM systems. The vendors were not constrained in any way in selecting hardware or software. This approach was intended to assure that no competitive alternative would be overlooked.

An even more demanding selection criterion was imposed by the U.S. Air Force when UNIVAC and Burroughs competed in a "compute-off" for a contract worth $500 million.[3] Seeking to update its computer systems, the Air Force provided space in a Montgomery, Alabama, air base building for two computers to compete side by side. The computers, a UNIVAC 1100/60 and a Burroughs 5930, processed the same data to determine which system would be installed at 105 air bases. As an indication of how serious the vendors were about the compute-off, Burroughs assigned 150 employees to the project. In contrast to the Public Health Service RFP, the Air Force constraints were very rigid. Both systems, for example, had to feature punched card input. Such rigid constraints discouraged many vendors from bidding.

When vendors must respond to benchmark tests, the test results determine who gets the business. The vendor that meets the performance criteria at the lowest cost wins the contract. Most business firms, however, are in no position to engage in such testing. The vendor selection decision in most instances is semistructured, not based strictly on quantitative proposal data. Consideration must be given also to the vendor's record of meeting previous commitments. A survey of some of the vendor's customers can indicate the consistency with which promises are fulfilled.

When all of the vendor data has been received and analyzed, the executive vice-president and the vice-president of information services (or the MIS committee) select the vendor. The president approves the selection, and the firm places an order with the selected vendor.

Prepare the Software Library (5)

Systems programs, such as operating systems, compilers, and utility programs, are usually obtained from the vendor of the CPU. Sometimes, however, they are obtained from software houses. Software from the houses is often more efficient (that is, it requires less storage and is faster) than software from computer vendors.[4] Other software, such as data base management systems, graphics packages, and data communications monitors, are also obtained from outside sources.

---

[2] Malcolm A. Gleser, Judith Bayard, and David D. Lang, "Benchmarking for the Best," *Datamation* 27 (May 1981): 127 ff.

[3] George Anders, "We Have Play-Offs, Runoffs, Bake-Offs; Now, a Compute-Off," *Wall Street Journal,* 21 September 1981, pp. 1, 29.

[4] For a description of the experiences of four firms with packaged software, see "Picking and Perfecting the Packages," *Datamation* 26 (December 1980): 139 ff.

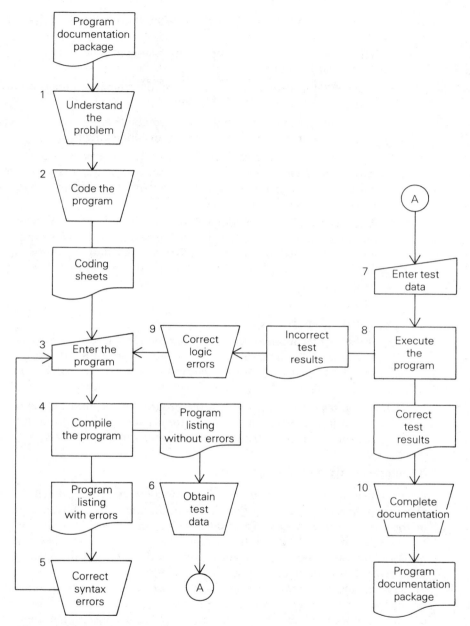

Figure 18-7 The programming process.

The programming process

When a firm decides to create its own applications software, it follows a process like the one pictured in Figure 18-7.

    1. The programmer must first understand the problem. He or she reviews the contents of the program documentation package and then prepares

the logical design representation—that is, the program flowchart or pseudocode.

2. The program is coded in a particular language, such as BASIC, FOR-TRAN, or COBOL.

3. The program is entered from a keyboard terminal or punched into cards that are read by a card-reading unit.

4. The language compiler translates the *source program* (coded by the programmer) into an *object program* (in machine language).

5. The output from the compilation is called the *source program listing*. Any *error messages* identify syntax errors. *Syntax errors* occur when the rules of the programming language are violated. Perhaps a hyphen or a period has been omitted.

6. After achieving a "clean compile"—a compilation with no syntax errors—the programmer uses data to test the program logic. Sometimes test data will be fabricated; other times the firm uses real data to test the programs. The test data should be carefully selected to trace each logical path in the program.

7. The test data is entered.

8. The program is executed.

9. If test results are incorrect, the programmer corrects the *logic errors*. An example of a logic error is an arithmetic expression with parentheses in the wrong place, producing the wrong answer. The corrected program is recompiled, and steps 3, 4, 5, and 8 are repeated.

10. When test results are correct, the programmer completes the documentation in the program documentation package. The programmer adds the source program listing, the test data listing, and the test data results.

Modular and structured programming

Programmers today are encouraged to follow a structured approach. Structured programming is an expansion of modular programming, which gained popularity in the early sixties. In *modular programming,* the program is subdivided into modules. Each module is a self-contained unit that accomplishes a particular process, such as computing overtime earnings. Figure 18-8 illustrates the basic arrangement of a modular program.

The sequence in which the modules are executed is controlled by a master module called the *driver module*. The driver module performs no processing; it causes the other modules to be executed. As the figure shows, the driver module causes module 1 to be executed. When that processing is completed, control returns to the driver module, and then module 2 is executed, and so on. There can be several levels of modules. Module 1 can cause modules 1.1 and 1.2 to be executed, and so on.

If you turn Figure 18-8 on its side, you get a HIPO hierarchy diagram. The HIPO technique encourages a modular program structure.

Modular programming allows several programmers to work on the same program at the same time—the *programmer team approach*. Modules can be

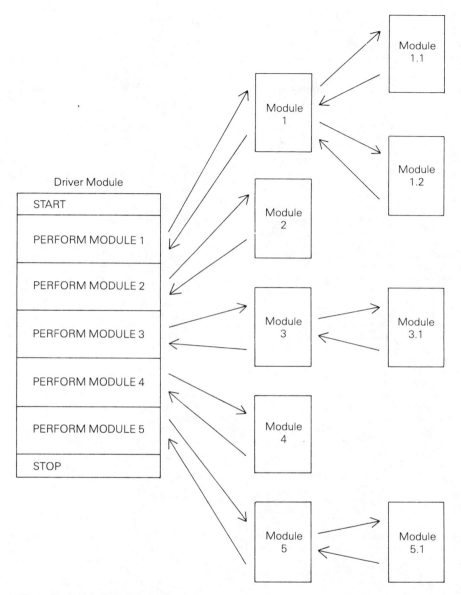

Figure 18-8 Modular program structure.

assigned to different programmers, and then the modules can be integrated into a modular program.

Structured programming is a disciplined modular approach requiring three conventions in program design.

1. Only one basic task is accomplished in each module.
2. Each module has only one entry and one exit point.

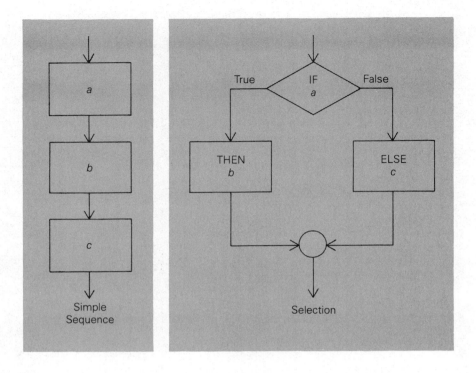

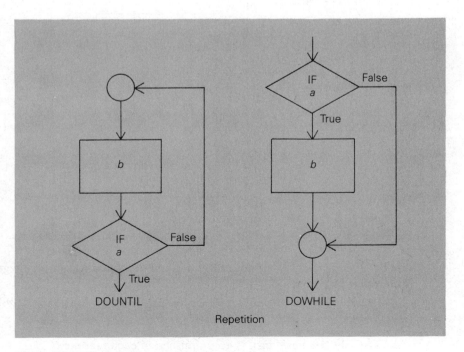

Figure 18-9 Three basic programming structures.

3. Only three basic structures are followed in coding: simple sequence, selection, and repetition. These three structures are diagrammed in Figure 18-9. In a *simple sequence,* processes *a, b,* and *c* follow one after the other. In a *selection sequence,* a test is made to determine IF condition *a* exists; if so, THEN execute process *b,* ELSE execute process *c.* The *repetition sequence* produces a loop. The DOUNTIL form waits until the end to determine if it is time to get out of the loop; the DOWHILE form makes the test at the beginning.

The pseudocode example in the Chapter 17 (see Figure 17-20) contained a DOWHILE sequence. Pseudocode is well suited to developing the three structures of structured programming. The ability of both pseudocode and HIPO to facilitate structured programming accounts for much of the popularity of the two documentation tools.

Structured programming can be used with any programming language, but it is easier to achieve with some languages than with others. PL/I and Pascal are especially well suited.

Structured system development

Structured programming is one part of a large effort—*structured development.* The development of structured information systems begins long before coding time. When the manager and the systems analyst first begin to explore the design of the new system during the analysis and design phase, the design evolves from the top down. In fact, the term *top-down* is used to describe the complete set of system development efforts that reflect a modular, hierarchical structure—top-down analysis, top-down design, top-down coding, top-down testing, and top-down cutover.[5]

The HIPO hierarchy diagram is a good starting point for a structured design. The systems analyst prepares this diagram and possibly specifies more details using a HIPO overview diagram. At some point the documentation responsibility is passed along to the programmer, who prepares a HIPO detail diagram and then a pseudocode description. The point at which design responsibility passes from the analyst to the programmer is influenced by the policies of the firm, the system being designed, and so forth.

You should understand that HIPO and pseudocode are only two of several possible documentation tools that can be used in a structured design. Other tools include decision logic tables, decision trees, and data flow diagrams.[6]

---

[5] Structured development is described in greater detail in J. Daniel Couger, Mel A. Colter, and Robert W. Knapp, *Advanced System Development/Feasibility Techniques* (New York: John Wiley & Sons, 1982), pp. 89–91; and Edward Yourdon and Larry L. Constantine, *Structured Design: Fundamentals of a Discipline of Computer Program and System Design* (Englewood Cliffs, N.J.: Prentice-Hall, 1979).

[6] For information on decision logic tables, see Michael Montalbano, *Decision Tables* (Chicago: Science Research Associates, 1974); and Herman McDaniel, *An Introduction to Decision Logic Tables,* (New York: John Wiley & Sons, 1968). For a description of how decision trees can be used to document decision models, see Barbara Bund Jackson, *Computer Models in Management* (Homewood, Ill.: Richard D. Irwin, 1979), pp. 420–440. Data flow diagrams are explained in Tom DeMarco, *Structured Analysis and System Specification* (Englewood Cliffs, N.J.: Prentice-Hall, 1979), pp. 47–122.

Significance of structured development to management

The structured, top-down approach to system development permits the manager to make a *greater contribution* to system design. Tools such as HIPO enable a manager to remain involved longer, as the design evolves gradually from the top. The term *iterative refinement* has been used to describe how the design is gradually made more detailed. The longer the manager can play an active role, the better the opportunity for the design to meet the manager's needs.

Also of significance to the manager is the ability of the structured techniques to handle *large and complex systems*. The systems approach is followed, continually subdividing large systems into smaller modules until they become manageable. This approach applies equally well to data processing systems and decision support systems.

Systems developed using the structured approach are more *easily maintained* once they are implemented. When a system is designed in a modular, structured fashion it is easier for the systems analyst and programmer to revise, update, and improve it. In today's world, where the costs of analyst and programmer talent are increasing while hardware costs are decreasing, any approach that makes more efficient use of the information specialists' time is a step in the right direction.

Natural programming languages

Along with structured programming, natural languages are making applications programs easier to prepare. *Natural languages* are more "user-friendly" than languages such as FORTRAN, COBOL, and BASIC. The natural languages permit the programmer or manager to prepare a program using language that is closer to conversational language than traditional programming languages are. Programs can be written in less time, using fewer instructions.

Examples of natural languages are Mathematical Products Group's RAMIS II, National CSS's NOMAD, Software A.G.'s NATURAL, and Cincom's MANTIS. The languages permit easy file building and use of the file data by applications programs. Figure 18-10 shows how the MANTIS system enables a user to create a data file using the form-filling technique. Figure 18-11 shows how applications programs can be coded.

Natural languages are just now emerging as a viable means of preparing programs. The languages are especially significant to the MIS in that they make it easier for managers to obtain information. With natural languages, managers don't have to go through the firm's information services department every time they need a new application or a new information output.

Prepare the Data Base (6)

Earlier discussions have explained the data base in terms of what it is, how it is organized, and how it is used. The discussion here centers on how the data base is prepared.

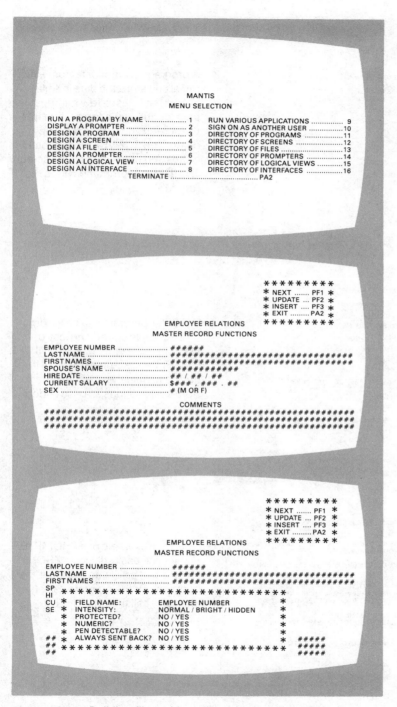

After the user signs on, MANTIS displays a menu. Each user's menu can be specially tailored to a particular application. This tailoring makes the system easy to use and contributes to security. The user selects the function to be executed—such as DESIGN A FILE.

Screen design is usually the first step in implementing an application. The user keys in all headings and data fields. The # sign indicates data fields.

Field attributes can now be assigned. MANTIS automatically highlights the field being defined.

Figure 18-10   Building files with applications development software.

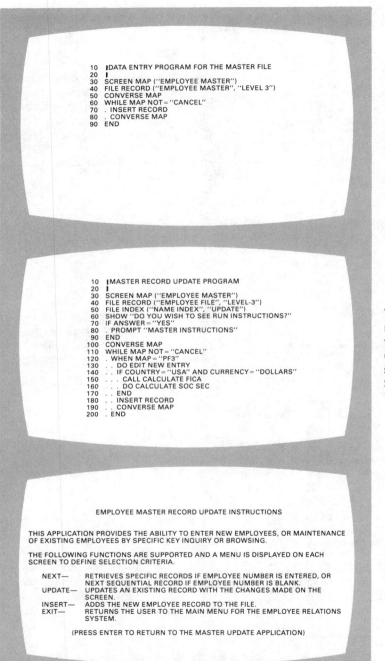

```
10   IDATA ENTRY PROGRAM FOR THE MASTER FILE
20   I
30   SCREEN MAP ("EMPLOYEE MASTER")
40   FILE RECORD ("EMPLOYEE MASTER", "LEVEL 3")
50   CONVERSE MAP
60   WHILE MAP NOT = "CANCEL"
70   . INSERT RECORD
80   . CONVERSE MAP
90   END
```

A program to enter data from a terminal and store the data in a file can be written in just a few minutes. The user identifies the format ("map") of the screen and the file to be updated. The CONVERSE command writes and reads data on the screen. The INSERT command writes the record in the file.

```
10   IMASTER RECORD UPDATE PROGRAM
20   I
30   SCREEN MAP ("EMPLOYEE MASTER")
40   FILE RECORD ("EMPLOYEE FILE", "LEVEL-3")
50   FILE INDEX ("NAME INDEX", "UPDATE")
60   SHOW "DO YOU WISH TO SEE RUN INSTRUCTIONS?"
70   IF ANSWER = "YES"
80   . PROMPT "MASTER INSTRUCTIONS"
90   END
100  CONVERSE MAP
110  WHILE MAP NOT = "CANCEL"
120  . WHEN MAP = "PF3"
130  . . DO EDIT NEW ENTRY
140  . . IF COUNTRY = "USA" AND CURRENCY = "DOLLARS"
150  . . . CALL CALCULATE FICA
160  . . . DO CALCULATE SOC SEC
170  . . END
180  . . INSERT RECORD
190  . . CONVERSE MAP
200  . END
```

The initial program can be made more complex by adding instructions. In this example, a PROMPTER (see screen example below) is inserted to help the user enter data. Some calculations are also added.

EMPLOYEE MASTER RECORD UPDATE INSTRUCTIONS

THIS APPLICATION PROVIDES THE ABILITY TO ENTER NEW EMPLOYEES, OR MAINTENANCE OF EXISTING EMPLOYEES BY SPECIFIC KEY INQUIRY OR BROWSING.

THE FOLLOWING FUNCTIONS ARE SUPPORTED AND A MENU IS DISPLAYED ON EACH SCREEN TO DEFINE SELECTION CRITERIA.

NEXT—   RETRIEVES SPECIFIC RECORDS IF EMPLOYEE NUMBER IS ENTERED, OR
            NEXT SEQUENTIAL RECORD IF EMPLOYEE NUMBER IS BLANK.
UPDATE—   UPDATES AN EXISTING RECORD WITH THE CHANGES MADE ON THE
            SCREEN.
INSERT—   ADDS THE NEW EMPLOYEE RECORD TO THE FILE.
EXIT—   RETURNS THE USER TO THE MAIN MENU FOR THE EMPLOYEE RELATIONS
            SYSTEM.

(PRESS ENTER TO RETURN TO THE MASTER UPDATE APPLICATION)

This is an example of a PROMPTER. A user can easily design a PROMPTER and can call it into use from the terminal. Or the program can automatically call the PROMPTER.

Figure 18-11 Coding programs with applications development software.

Preparation can be easy or difficult, depending on the circumstances. The task becomes difficult when (1) the firm is converting from a system of manual files to computer media, (2) the files are large, (3) the files contain very old data, and (4) some of the data has not been maintained in the past. The degree to which any of these conditions exist determines the difficulty of the task.

During the 1960s most large firms converted their data bases to computerized systems. These firms now have accurate and up-to-date data bases, and preparing the data base no longer presents a problem. But for small firms installing their first computer—a mini or micro system—preparing a data base involves the same problems large firms faced twenty years ago. In fact for these small firms, preparing the data base can be just as difficult as preparing the software library.

Preparation difficulties

Manual files create conversion problems because they usually contain errors, omissions, and inconsistencies. These flaws can go unnoticed in a manual system, but are unacceptable to the computer. For example, if a programmer defines a salesperson number field to consist of eight digits, it must be exactly that. Each record must contain the salesperson number, it can be no larger or smaller than the eight positions, and it can contain neither alphabetic nor special characters. Flaws such as these must be corrected before the data is acceptable to the computer.

Large files simply add to the size of the task. Conversion can take weeks or even months and demand more personnel and equipment than the firm has available.

Old files add yet another dimension to the difficulty. Over the years, forms and coding systems change, creating a hodgepodge of data. Files with these variations must be converted to a standardized format. Any efforts to confirm the accuracy of data elements or to reconstruct missing elements are usually very difficult. The source documents used to prepare the files have probably long since been destroyed.

When data is *not maintained,* special data-gathering activities must be performed. This can be expensive, especially when the data is gathered from the environment. Competitors' plans and customers' attitudes are particularly difficult to obtain.

These difficulties are not minimized when a DBMS is used to build the data base. The data dictionary and the data description language provide a framework for specifying the data base contents, and the data manipulation language is used to record the data in a format compatible with the DBMS. But the data must be in an edited, computer-readable form before the DBMS becomes involved. It is this pre-DBMS effort that makes base preparation so difficult in some firms.

Basic routes to the data base

Figure 18-12 shows the three basic ways to prepare a data base. The most direct path starts with computer-readable media such as punched cards, magnetic tapes,

Existing Files

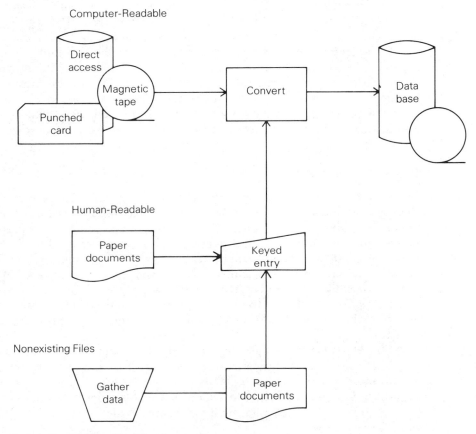

Figure 18-12 Preparing the data base.

and DASD. Data from these media is read into primary storage, edited for accuracy, recoded when necessary, and arranged in the new format. The data is then written on a data base medium, usually DASD or magnetic tape.

Very often data will be maintained, but not in a computer-readable form. It may be in manila file folders, for example. This data must be entered into the computer using a keyed entry device. Once the data is in primary storage, the procedure above can be followed to build the output files. OCR can sometimes be used to read data from paper file documents. Usually, however, the poor condition of the paper and variations in the shape and location of characters prevent OCR use.

The third route to the data base shows the special data-gathering step required for new data. Data is usually recorded on a form specially designed for the purpose.

Responsibility for data base preparation

We have seen that the data base administrator (DBA) is responsible for all phases of data base activity. This includes the preparation of the data base, which is often the most important and difficult of the DBA's responsibilities. Additional people may have to be hired to help prepare the data base.

Another alternative is to contract with a computer service bureau to provide the personnel, hardware, and software necessary to prepare the data base. The DBA is responsible for overseeing the work of the service bureau.

Importance of the data base

When we discussed the manufacturing information system, we recognized that the quality of a finished good cannot exceed the quality of its raw materials. The same reasoning applies to the quality of a firm's management information—it cannot exceed the quality of its data base. If a firm has a data base containing accurate, complete, and current descriptions of its resources and transactions, it is not too difficult to transform that data into information. This is especially true with the current user-friendly software—report writers, query languages, and natural languages. The time and money a firm invests in its data base is repaid many times over as that data is transformed into management information.

Educate Participants and Users (7)

The MIS will affect many people. Some will make the system work and others will use its output. All must be educated concerning (1) their role in the system and (2) how the system will benefit them.

The education program is aimed not only at members of the firm, but at elements in its environment as well. Table 18-1 identifies the different groups that need education and the type of education they need. The education can be provided by the systems analysts, instructors in the personnel department, or outsiders (such as consultants).

The only groups not needing education concerning the expected benefits of the MIS are the members of the information services staff and strategic-level management. We assume that both have already received this information during their previous involvement with the system.

Operational-level employees, such as clerical personnel, factory workers, and salespersons, must learn how to do specific tasks. These tasks include filling out forms, operating terminals, and using output. This education is very detailed and specific. All these people must understand exactly how the system works.

Managers on all levels receive less specific instruction. Departmental managers must understand the role of their departments, including the flow of data and information to and from other departments, and the effect on the system of not performing the work as specified. All managers must also understand how to interpret and use the information output. Quite probably, the managers will need

Table 18-1 Structure of the MIS education program

	Group	Type of education
INTERNAL	Information services staff	How to perform specific tasks
	Other employees (clerical, production, sales, etc.)	How to perform specific tasks; how to interpret output; benefits
	Operational- and tactical-level management	Departmental duties and responsibilities; how to interpret output; benefits
	Strategic-level management	How to interpret output
ENVIRONMENTAL	Vendors	The role of the vendor in the system; benefits
	Customers (industrial)	The role of the customer in the system; benefits
	Customers (individual)	Changes to billing and collection procedures; benefits
	Organized labor	The role of union workers in the system; benefits
	Government, stockholders, local community, financial community	No specific education program required

hands-on training in the use of a terminal. This training can be provided by representatives of the equipment vendors.

Education for internal employees is best handled face to face, giving an opportunity for two-way communication. Education for members of the environment, although important, is not personalized or as thorough.

Vendors and industrial customers generally need more information on the new MIS than other members of the environment. Both vendors and industrial customers must understand that they are participants in an interfirm information network. The benefits accruing to all participating firms in the network should be stressed. This program should be communicated in person, when possible, to key individuals by representatives of the firm's purchasing and sales departments. Direct mail can support these personal contacts.

The new MIS often changes the procedures relating to individual customers, or consumers. These changes usually affect the way the firm bills and collects for

⟨A⟩ Clyde Campbell Menswear

Dear Customer:

This is your new computer statement. We hope you like it.

As you know, we are not a big corporation--we are a small group of men's specialty shops in Fort Worth, Dallas and Austin. And our main specialty, being small, is personal service to you--your salesman knows you by name, knows your tastes, your wardrobe, and probably has a record of your sizes. If we get in something he thinks you will like, you'll usually get a phone call or a note. We pride ourselves in doing things the giants can't do.

Same with this statement. You'll find it's almost identical to the one you've been getting with the charges, credits and balance in the right place. You won't have to keep your original sales ticket to know what you've bought, or find a number in the fine print on the back with a vague description. You'll still get another copy of your signed ticket with your statement. You won't be billed in the middle of the month--we will still close our books on the 25th. You won't have to carry another credit card, or remember your account number--your salesman will personally handle this when you make a purchase. And your salesman's initials follow the ticket number on the face of the statement.

So ... we hope you will like this kind of old-fashioned statement.

There's only one thing we're a little nervous about. In putting all of our accounts on the computer at one time, we may have misspelled your name, or perhaps gotten the wrong address. Will you please check this first statement very carefully and give us a correction on anything you find wrong. Be sure to check your balance, too. We have taken every precaution in making the changeover, but if there is any possibility of a mistake, we want to know and correct it quickly, right now at the start. There's a place below for you to tell us. Send it to us with your payment, or mail it now if you prefer.

Sincerely yours,

Clyde Campbell Menswear

"With you from College to Career to Chairman of the Board"

Correct Name and Address (please print)

_____

_____

_____

Anything else wrong?_____

_____

Figure 18-13 Letter advising customers of the installation of a new computer.

purchases, and consumers should be informed of these changes by a letter inserted in bills or statements. Figures 18-13 and 18-14 present two letters mailed to the customers of a men's clothing store, informing them of the firm's new computer system.

If the firm's workers are members of organized labor unions, local union officials should be included in the education effort. The sessions with labor rep-

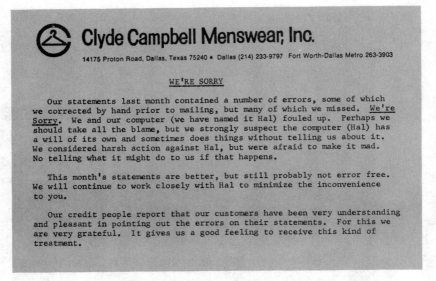

Figure 18-14 Letter reporting computer installation progress to customers.

resentatives are much like those directed at lower- and middle-level managers: they stress general procedures and benefits. The sessions can be conducted by members of the firm's industrial relations department, assisted by the information services staff.

There is no need for specific education programs for other members of the environment. Any information needs can be handled as they arise.

Outside education programs

Many hardware and software vendors conduct education programs for their customers. Some courses are free, others require a fee. These courses are aimed at both managers and information specialists. IBM offers a full range of courses and is noted for its customer executive program. One-week sessions at IBM plants give top-level executives firsthand knowledge of how computers produce management information.

Control Data Corporaton (CDC) is another computer manufacturer with a strong customer education program. CDC is noted for its courses tailored to information specialists. Some of the courses, however, are helpful for managers. Examples are the Pascal Programming Workshop, Successful Application of Minicomputer Systems, Forecasting Techniques for Decision Making, and Fundamentals and Applications of Data Processing.

The Datamation Institute offers similar courses for both information specialists and managers. Courses offered in twenty-one cities in the U.S. and Canada feature tight, fast-paced one- and two-day formats. Some courses of special interest to managers are Management's Use of Computer Graphics, DP Concepts for Management and Users, and Decision Support Systems.

The American Management Association also offers computing courses for managers. In its catalog for the last half of 1982, some twenty-nine courses were included—from Fundamentals of Data Communications to Developing Computer-Based Marketing Information Systems.

Courses such as these offer excellent opportunities for both managers and information specialists to prepare themselves for their roles in the MIS. The people needing education and the types of education needed should be identified early in the MIS life cycle and scheduled at the appropriate time—usually just before the learned material would be applied.

Prepare Physical Facilities (8)

The work required to prepare the physical facilities depends on the amount of computing equipment needed. If only a few additional units are to be installed (disk drives, terminals, etc.), they can be housed in existing areas. If a new computer system is needed, a complete construction project may be necessary.

Such a project begins with the specification of the equipment environment (power, temperature, space, and humidity) by representatives of the equipment vendor. These same representatives also recommend the best arrangement of the equipment units for operating efficiency. Once the layout of the computer area has been developed (Figure 18-15), attention is given to surrounding areas (offices, peripheral equipment rooms, libraries, etc.). The layout and design of these areas is often done by architects and interior designers. Finally, the design is implemented by a general contracting firm.

Constructing computer facilities is similar to constructing facilities to house any piece of expensive equipment. Representatives of architectural and contractor

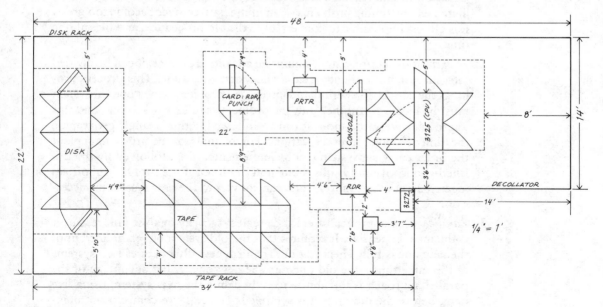

Figure 18-15 Layout of a computer area.

firms, along with those of the computer manufacturer, can supply expert consultation. All of these activities are incorporated into the overall implementation plan and are controlled in the same manner as work performed by the firm's own employees. If is very common for the manager of computer operations to have primary responsibility for representing the firm to the various outside groups.

Cutover to the New System (9)

When the above implementation work has been completed, it is time to cut over to the new system. The larger the firm and the more complex its operations, the more difficult the cutover becomes. As with a human patient undergoing a heart or kidney transplant, the total system must be kept alive while converting to the new vital organ. There is a long history of successful computer conversions, and there is no reason to fear failure when these conversions are performed correctly.

Basic approaches to cutover

Cutting over to the new MIS involves three basic approaches: immediate, phased, and parallel. The one selected will depend on the characteristics of the firm—the type and scope of operations, resources, and so forth. The three approaches are illustrated in Figure 18-16.

1. *Immediate.* The simplest approach is to convert from the old system to the new one on a given day. When possible, this approach should be selected since it is the least expensive and time-consuming. This approach is feasible in small firms, but not in large ones. As the scale of the operation increases, the timing problems of an immediate cutover become too great. It is almost impossible to convert all of the old procedures and files at one time.

2. *Phased.* If the entire system cannot be converted at once, it can be divided into subsystems and converted a subsystem at a time. This process prolongs the conversion period and introduces problems when one subsystem must be linked to another. But the problems can be worked out, and this approach is very common. It can be followed within a single geographic location or among several locations. For example, at the firm's main plant the order entry subsystem can be implemented first, followed by the finished-goods inventory subsystem, and so on. Or if the firm has suboffices located across the country, each can convert to the new system in succession.

3. *Parallel.* This approach offers the greatest security against failure, but it is the most expensive. It requires that the old system be maintained until the new one is fully checked out. The firm actually operates two systems at the same time—the old one and the new one. A big advantage of the parallel approach is the ability to fully debug the new system, using live data, before the old system is scrapped. The expense comes from main-

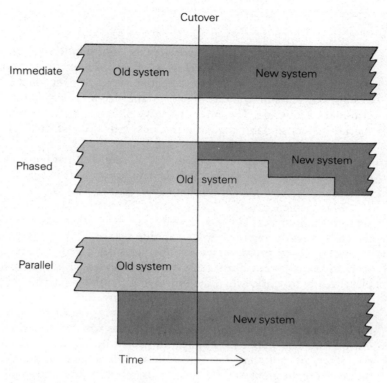

Figure 18-16 The three basic approaches to cutover.

taining two systems at once, including people, equipment, supplies, and so on. It is possible, however, to hire temporary help or contract with computer service bureaus to perform much of the duplicated work during the conversion period.

Maximizing the opportunity for success

Effective planning offers the best opportunity for a successful cutover. In addition, two special techniques can be used to identify trouble spots before full-scale cutover is attempted. *Simulation* is especially effective for checking out online systems, where a mathematical model can simulate the new online system in operation. The model estimates the load on the CPU during peak periods to assure that the equipment configuration is adequate. Such models are often available from computer equipment manufacturers and computer consulting firms.

A *pilot test* can be used first to test the performance of the system on a limited scale. The entire system is put to test, but only in a restricted area. For example, if an airline is installing a realtime reservation system, initial use can be limited to travel agents and airline offices in a single city. The pilot test works equally well for batch systems. Both the pilot test and simulation can be used as a preliminary to any of the three basic approaches.

Summary

The implementation of an MIS requires the coordination of many activities. This coordination is achieved by developing a detailed implementation plan and maintaining continuous control. The executive vice-president (or the MIS committee) exercises this planning and control, and the vice-president of information services also plays a key role. The latter executive directs the activities of the information specialists, coordinates their interactions with the rest of the firm, and reports progress and problems to top management.

The implementation can take several months, involving most of the firm's employees and certain elements in the environment. It is a costly process, and its success depends on good planning and cooperation.

Management gets the process started by announcing the implementation project to the employees. The announcements are intended to gain the cooperation of the employees during the implementation period.

Any needed programmers or operators are hired and trained. Information services management must allow sufficient lead time for the personnel to be in place, ready to work, when the time comes to play an active role.

Selecting a computer and selecting software are interrelated. For small-system users, the availability of software may be a major factor in computer selection. In these situations, the software selection comes first. In situations where there is less dependence on outside applications software, the key decision is selecting the computer, and software decisions follow. This is the point in the implementation phase where the greatest difference exists between large and small computer users.

Firms attempt to minimize the costs of applications software by pursuing a structured programming approach, which exists within a larger structured development framework. A top-down design, incorporating documentation techniques such as HIPO and pseudocode, enables management to play a more significant role during the initial stages. More and more firms are using natural languages and thus spending less time and effort on programming. For some applications, the manager can develop the programs without assistance from the information specialists.

Preparing the data base requires a substantial effort when first converting to computerized systems, when files are large and contain old data, and when data has not been maintained. Most large firms accomplished the majority of their data base preparation during the 1960s, when they converted to computerized systems. Today small firms are following the same process.

Education is a vital part of a successful implementation. An educational program is designed for the firm's management and employees, and for members of the environment, to prepare participants for their roles and to emphasize the benefits of putting forth a full effort. Outside programs offered by computer and software vendors, institutes, and associations provide high-quality, concentrated coverage of key topics.

The effort going into the physical installation varies. Large firms adding only a few pieces of equipment may not have to make any special preparations. Small firms installing small systems may also make only minor alterations to existing facilities. But for firms constructing their first special-purpose computing facility, the project can be expensive and time-consuming.

When all of these preparations have been completed, it is time to cut over to the new system. Cutover can be immediate, phased, or parallel. A successful cutover is most likely when preceded by planning and by the use of techniques such as simulation and a pilot test. Once the cutover has been accomplished, the MIS is operational. This phase is the topic of the next chapter.

Key Terms

implementation

make or buy

request for bid, request for proposal (RFP)

proposal

benchmark problem

source program, object program

source program listing

error message

syntax error

logic error

modular programming

driver module

programmer team approach

structured programming

simple sequence

selection sequence

repetition sequence

structured development, top-down development

iterative refinement

natural language

immediate cutover

phased cutover

parallel cutover

pilot test

Key Concepts

The overlapping of several tasks during the implementation phase

The opportunity for detailed and accurate implementation planning

The need for communication to employees concerning their role in the implementation and the operation of the MIS

The variable influence of software and computer decisions on the implementation process depending on the firm's characteristics

Two-way communication with software and computer vendors

The varying amounts of proposal-related effort a vendor will expend, depending on the size of the potential order

Structured development and structured programming

Factors influencing the difficulty of the data base preparation task

Comprehensive nature of the educational program— encompassing all levels within the firm plus key environmental elements

Different approaches to cutover, influenced by firm size and resources

Questions

1. Under what conditions will a firm make software decisions before it makes computer decisions?
2. How many implementation tasks can be going on at the same time in a firm preparing its own software? What are the tasks? (Use Figure 18-1 as a guide)
3. What is the main purpose of the implementation announcement?
4. Does the make-or-buy decision relate to software? The computer? The data base? Explain each answer.
5. Is the make-or-buy decision a structured decision? Explain.
6. Why include estimated transaction volumes and file sizes in an RFP?
7. Why do vendors often insist on conducting interviews in the firm, even though proposal specifications are very detailed?
8. What is a benchmark problem? When does a vendor participate in a benchmark process?
9. Did the U.S. Public Health Service impose strict proposal requirements on its vendors? Explain.
10. What is a source program? An object program?
11. What is a syntax error? A logic error?
12. Are modular and structured programming the same? Explain.
13. How does HIPO facilitate modular program structure?
14. What are the three conventions of structured programming?
15. What are the three structures of structured programming?
16. What is iterative refinement? How does it affect the manager?
17. Name three advantages of structured development.
18. Describe the situation in which data base preparation would be most difficult.
19. What type of material is included in the educational program for strategic-level managers? For union officials? For the government?
20. Which cutover approach would the U.S. Air Force be likely to follow in implementing its new computer systems at 105 air bases? Explain your answer.

CASE PROBLEM: New Canaan Business Forms

It seems like only yesterday that you, Jill Marquez, graduated from college with a degree in MIS. The past two years have flown by—moving to New Canaan, Connecticut, and starting your own computer consulting firm; getting the big inventory system contract that paid the bills while you made new contacts; and hiring your first employee, a part-time typist.

All of these thoughts cross your mind as you drive to your 9 A.M. appointment with Betty Kornegay, the president of New Canaan Business Forms. You met Betty at the DPMA (Data Processing Management Association) meeting last week. She was the guest speaker, and you chatted with her afterwards about her plans to get a computer. A few days later she called and asked you to come by and talk further. It looks like a good opportunity. New Canaan Business Forms is a growing company, just now reaching the size where it needs to computerize its data processing and begin thinking about an MIS.

Betty:

Hi, Jill. Come on in. I'm glad you have time for us to finish our talk. As I mentioned, we've decided to get a computer and have made quite a bit of progress. We hired two systems analysts about eight months ago, and they have just finished their systems study. I'm pleased with the work they're doing. They've established a good rapport with our managers and put together very professional-looking documentation. I'd like you to take a look at it and let me know what you think.

Jill:

I'd be happy to. Is that the reason you asked me to drop by?

Betty:

No, it isn't. We need to decide immediately whether to do our own programming or buy software packages. I recognize that that decision needs to be made by me and the other members of the computer committee. But frankly, we don't have the expertise. We need your help. I'd like to retain you as a consultant to give us guidance as we consider the make-or-buy decision. What about it?

Jill:

I'm flattered. I've been involved in these decisions before and know how challenging they can be. I'm sure I can help. But to help me understand your situation better, I'd like to ask you some questions. First, you didn't mention hiring any programmers.

Betty:

We haven't gotten that far. We've delayed hiring any until we've made the make-or-buy decision.

Jill:

That's good. Could you give me some idea of the size of your programming task. Do you have a lot of applications programming to do?

Betty:

Not too much initially. We plan to implement only the basic accounting systems at first. Our systems are pretty standard—"plain vanilla," I'd say. The analysts tell me we handle things in a typical fashion.

Jill:

There's nothing wrong with that. Now tell me, what are your plans for management information?

Betty:

At present we're going to hold off. We'd like to get the basic information outputs from the accounting systems and then build on that. We're in no big hurry. I'm a firm believer in taking it slow and easy.

Jill:

Do you mind relying on outsiders for your programming?

Betty:

Not at all. We rely on outsiders for practically everything else—customers, materials, finances. I can't see that computer programs are any different.

Jill:

From what you say, I don't believe you'll have any trouble finding the software you need—not initially, anyway. Later, when you get more involved in management information needs, it might be a different story. I know of several software vendors in the area who have good products and excellent service organizations. I wouldn't hesitate to recommend any of them. And from what I know, their prices are very reasonable—at least compared to what you would have to pay in Boston, for example.

Betty:

It's good to know that. I feel that either way we go, we can end up with a quality computer installation. Do you have any other questions?

Jill:

Only one. What seem to you to be the most important factors influencing your make-or-buy decision?

Betty:

That's a tough one. Let me see. First, I would say our modest computer staff. We don't have any programmers, and from what I hear the market in this area is pretty tight. There aren't many good ones who are looking. Second, I would say the quality of local software service—if it's good, that would be a big encouragement to buy. Cost doesn't really play much of a role. I've learned long ago that you get what you pay for. Any more questions?

Jill:

No, I think you've answered all of them.

Questions

1. Use the eleven-item scale in Figure 18-4 to determine a make-or-buy score for Betty's firm. Your instructor will give you a blank form. Use the case material as a basis for your entries.

2. What decision do you recommend?

3. What assumptions did you have to make to complete the form?

Chapter 19

Operation and Control of the MIS

Learning Objectives

After studying this chapter, you should:

- Know the role played by control in achieving and maintaining computer security
- Know the three basic properties that every MIS should have
- Know the three basic types of MIS controls
- Understand how the manager achieves and maintains control
- Know how the MIS development process can be controlled
- Be able to distinguish between an information audit and an accounting audit, and know why each is necessary
- Know how both hardware and software controls can be incorporated into system design
- See how any system can be divided into basic parts, and design controls incorporated into each part
- Know how system operation can be controlled
- Be familiar with the duties performed by computer operations personnel
- Appreciate the necessity of disaster planning, and understand the types of plans and programs that are possible

Overview

Now that the MIS has been implemented, it can be used on a daily basis to provide the benefits that justified its development. The first three phases of the MIS life cycle (planning, analysis and design, and implementation) probably took several months to a year or more to complete. The firm hopes that this fourth and final phase, operation, lasts several years before it becomes necessary to start the life cycle over again.

We are going to address the operation of the MIS in this chapter. We are also going to recognize the importance of control to the operating MIS. But as we have shown, management does not wait until the operation phase to establish control. Control begins with the planning phase and continues throughout the life cycle.

The Importance of Control

According to Henri Fayol, control is one of management's functions. One of the purposes of the MIS is to support managers as they control their areas of operations. But even though the MIS facilitates control, the MIS itself must be controlled. Managers exercise control over the work of the information services staff during the design and implementation of the MIS. After the MIS is implemented, its operation must be carefully controlled. With stories of computer crime frequently in the news, the subject of control takes on new dimensions.[1] But computer crime is only one dimension of inadequate control. Other forms include the loss of confidential company information to competitors, inadequate accounting systems, and information that does not live up to management expectations. In this chapter we focus on the subject of control—where it should be established and how. This is an appropriate topic to conclude our analysis of current MIS technology and methodology. Only by developing a well-controlled MIS can managers have confidence in its output.

Introduction to System Control[2]

Control is the mechanism used to regulate and guide the operation of a system. Control procedures represent one of three protective measures designed to maintain security. The other two are physical measures and backup and recovery measures. *Physical measures* include precautionary steps, such as building locks, fire extinguishers, and closed-circuit TV. *Backup and recovery measures* include duplicate data files at cross-town locations and an agreement with another computer user for the purchase of computer time in the event of an emergency.

Security is the goal of all these measures. *Security* may be defined as the protection of people, facilities, and data from both natural and human hazards. The subset of data security is our area of interest. Although a breach of data security can take many forms, all fall into the six categories in Table 19-1. The loss can be accidental or intentional, and it can result in the modification, destruction, or unauthorized disclosure of data.

---

[1] See, for example, "The Spreading Danger of Computer Crime," *Business Week,* 20 April 1981, pp. 86 ff; and "Crackdown on Computer Capers," *Time,* 8 February 1982, pp. 60–61.

[2] Based on *Data Security Controls and Procedures—A Philosophy for DP Installations,* G320-5649 (White Plains, N.Y.: IBM Corporation, 1977).

Table 19-1 Six ways to breach data security

	Accidental	Intentional
	1. Modification	4. Modification
	2. Destruction	5. Destruction
	3. Disclosure	6. Disclosure

Actually, accidental breaches of data security are a greater threat than intentional breaches. Accidents happen more frequently, but the average cost is less than the highly publicized intentional acts.

We should make one point clear at the outset. It would be prohibitively expensive to make a computer installation 100% secure. Firms should augment preventative measures with mechanisms to detect violations after they occur and to consistently and publicly punish the violators.

System properties

An information system should have three properties: integrity, auditability, and controllability.

A system has *integrity* if it performs according to its specifications. These specifications should describe system performance when things go wrong as well as when things go right. System designers attempt to develop a system that has *functional integrity,* the ability to continue operating even when one or more components have failed. Such systems are said to have a *fail-soft* capability. A good example is an airline reservation system that includes a backup CPU for use when the primary system goes down. When the computer is inoperative because of a malfunction, it is said to be *down*. The computer is unavailable for use during *downtime.*

Auditability means that it is relatively easy to examine, verify, or demonstrate the performance of a system. People who are independent of the system organization conduct the audit. For a system to be auditable, it must meet the tests of accountability and visibility. *Accountability* means that responsibility for each event occurring within the system must be traceable to a single individual. *Visibility* means that unacceptable performance is called to the attention of the system managers. A computer program, for example, is auditable if the programmer follows standard practices of coding and documenting the program, and if the program documentation package provides a clear view of what the program does. Auditability is a major reason for documentation.

Controllability permits management to exercise a directing or constraining influence over the behavior, use, and content of the system. System controllability is achieved by dividing the system into subsystems that handle separate transactions. A breach of integrity in one subsystem should not compromise the entire system. For example, one subsystem in a bank is for opening and closing accounts. Another subsystem processes deposits and withdrawals. The first subsystem controls the second to prevent unauthorized manipulations of funds, such as someone's opening a fictitious account and transferring funds into it from other accounts.

The MIS Control Task

The process of developing the MIS must be controlled. The system *development controls* assure that objectives are identified and that work toward those objectives proceeds according to plan.

During the development of the MIS, management must assure that the design minimizes the chance of error, detects errors when they are made, and corrects the errors for reentry. These are system *design controls,* and they include both hardware and software controls. The hardware controls are incorporated into the equipment by the vendors. The software controls are incorporated into systems software by vendors and in applications software by the firm's systems analysts and programmers. Once the MIS is implemented, system *operation controls* preserve the integrity of the system.

Methods of achieving and maintaining control

Management can exercise control in three basic ways, as illustrated in Figure 19-1.

First, management can take direct control, evaluating progress and performance and determining what corrective actions are necessary. This approach requires a substantial knowledge of computers and information systems. Such knowledge is gained by reading books, taking courses, learning through informal contacts with knowledgeable people, and gaining experience.

Second, management is represented indirectly in the design effort on a full-time basis by the vice-president of information services. This person is an executive who owes allegiance not only to the technical staff, but to the using managers as well. This person's main responsibility during the design effort is to assure that the system design is acceptable to the users.

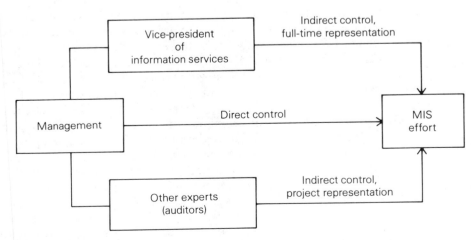

Figure 19-1 Control of the MIS effort.

Third, management makes use of internal or external auditors to evaluate the system and influence its design from a technical standpoint. These specialists represent management on a project basis and provide the computer expertise the managers do not possess.

Control of the Development Process

Management should control the development of the MIS from initiation through completion. This control attempts to assure an acceptable MIS by following a well-planned procedure:

1. Establish overall project control.
2. Identify user requirements.
3. Establish performance criteria for the MIS.
4. Establish standards for the design and operation of the MIS.
5. Specify an acceptance testing program.
6. Specify a postinstallation review program.
7. Establish a procedure for maintaining and modifying the MIS.

Each of these control actions is taken at a specific point in the life cycle of the MIS, as shown in Figure 19-2. And each action is taken before the system goes into operation.

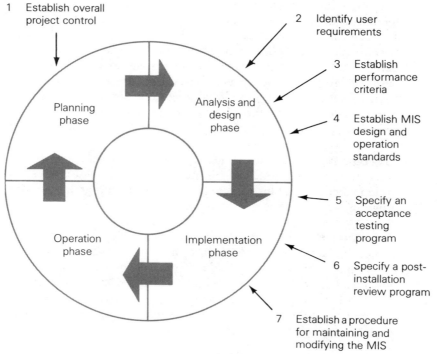

Figure 19-2 Control actions in the MIS life cycle.

1. Overall project control. Top management establishes overall project control during the planning phase. The top executive assigned to the MIS project establishes a working relationship with the top information services executive, forms an MIS committee (if needed), determines the basic specifications of the MIS, and creates some type of project control mechanism (such as network analysis).

2 and 3. User requirements and performance criteria. These two activities are addressed as the systems study proceeds. It is the system analysts' responsibility to identify user requirements. Once defined, the requirements are expressed in terms of what the MIS must do to meet them; that is, the performance criteria. The ultimate success of the MIS rests on how well these criteria are met.

4. Design and operation standards. Standards are the guidelines of acceptable performance by members of the information services staff. There are many sources of standards that a firm can consider. There are *standards organizations,* such as ISO (International Organization for Standardization) and ANSI (American National Standards Institute, Inc.). The flowchart symbols we have used are those accepted by ISO and ANSI. In addition, there are *user groups* of different manufacturers' equipment. Many of the names of these groups convey the spirit of cooperation and unity among the members, such as SHARE and GUIDE (IBM users). But none says it better than the Honeywell Users Group—HUG. Certain standards are also developed by the *computer manufacturers,* such as the format of file labels and job control languages. A firm can evaluate these various standards and decide whether they are applicable. Or the firm can create its own standards.

It is a good idea to have a *standards manual* that spells out the conventions the members of the information services staff are expected to follow. Standards are established for each area of MIS activity (systems analysis, programming, operations, and data base administration. For example, a systems analysis standard would specify the contents of the system documentation package. A data base standard would specify names to be used for data files, records, and elements. Figure 19-3 contains a sample table of contents for a standards manual. The manual is developed by the information specialists under the guidance of the vice-president of information services.

5. Acceptance testing program. The requirements for approval of each computer program are spelled out in detail. This approval is necessary before the programmer satisfies his or her responsibility for program development and the program is entered into the software library.

6. Postinstallation review program. Shortly after the cutover, the information services department should conduct an audit to determine how well the MIS is performing. This is not an audit of the system's compliance with accounting practices, but of the system's ability to meet its decision support commitments.

The best way to conduct an *information audit* is for systems analysts to interview all of the firm's managers personally. These interviews take place thirty to ninety days after cutover. Managers are asked how satisfied they are with the

TABLE OF CONTENTS

	PAGE #
CHAPTER #3 - PROGRAMMING STANDARDS & PROCEDURES	
3.1 Introduction	1.3.1
3.2 Structured Programming	1.3.1
3.2.1 Guidelines	1.3.1
3.2.2 Basic Control Patterns	1.3.2
3.2.3 Control Logic Structures	1.3.3
3.3 Modular Programming	1.3.8
3.3.1 Benefits	1.3.8
3.3.2 General Consideration	1.3.8
3.3.3 Data Allocation/Assignment	1.3.10
3.3.4 Input/Output	1.3.11
3.3.5 Subroutines	1.3.11
3.4 COPYLIB/Data Dictionary	1.3.12
3.4.1 General	1.3.12
3.4.2 Source Program Library Facility	1.3.13
3.4.3 COPY Statement	1.3.13
3.5 Table Searching	1.3.15
3.5.1 General Information	1.3.15
3.5.2 Examples	1.3.16
A. Indexed Loop Search	1.3.16
B. Search Verb Loop	1.3.16
C. Simple Serial Search	1.3.17
D. SEARCH ALL Verb	1.3.17
E. Binary Search	1.3.18
F. Segmented Search	1.3.19
3.5.3 Indexing - Subscripting Difference	1.3.21
3.5.4 Comparisons of Searching Techniques	1.3.22
3.6 Programming	1.3.23
3.6.1 General Language Selection	1.3.23
3.6.2 General Programming Standards	1.3.24
3.6.3 Dates & Control Data	1.3.29
3.6.4 Job Classing Structure	1.3.40

Figure 19-3 Table of contents for a standards manual.

MIS and whether they have any suggestions. The information services department uses the input from these interviews to fine tune the system and to add new applications.

Considering the scarcity of systems analysts and the scope of many MISes, it is unrealistic to assume that all managers can be interviewed personally. This is a good place to use a mail questionnaire. The MIS can prepare a mailing list of all managers receiving information output (reports, simulation results, or query responses). The computer-printed questionnaire can ask specific questions about each form of information produced for the manager. Figure 19-4 shows an example. Managers can comment on each type of information output they receive. A

```
TO:          F.A. AKERS
             MANAGER OF PRODUCT PLANNING

FROM:        F.D. DRY
             VICE PRESIDENT OF INFORMATION SYSTEMS

SUBJECT:     PERIODIC EVALUATION OF MIS PERFORMANCE

DATE:        JUNE 30, 1980

LISTED BELOW IS EACH FORM OF INFORMATION OUTPUT PRESENTLY BEING
SUPPLIED BY THE INFORMATION SYSTEMS DIVISION.  PLEASE INDICATE
YOUR EVALUATION OF EACH OUTPUT BY CHECKING THE APPROPRIATE BLANK.
RETURN THE COMPLETED QUESTIONNAIRE BY JULY 15.

OUTPUT 1--NEW PRODUCT EVALUATION MODEL

1. THE ACCURACY OF THIS OUTPUT IS:
      ACCEPTABLE (NO EXPLANATION NEEDED)
   ---
      MARGINAL: EXPLAIN      -------------------------------------------
   ---
      UNACCEPTABLE: EXPLAIN  -------------------------------------------
   ---

2. THE TIMELINESS IS:
      ACCEPTABLE (NO EXPLANATION NEEDED)
   ---
      MARGINAL: EXPLAIN      -------------------------------------------
   ---
      UNACCEPTABLE: EXPLAIN  -------------------------------------------
   ---

3. THE COMPLETENESS OF THE INFORMATION IS:
      ACCEPTABLE (NO EXPLANATION NEEDED)
   ---
      MARGINAL: EXPLAIN      -------------------------------------------
   ---
      UNACCEPTABLE: EXPLAIN  -------------------------------------------
   ---

4. THE PRESENTATION MODE (PRINTED REPORT, CRT DISPLAY) IS:
      ACCEPTABLE (NO EXPLANATION NEEDED)
   ---
      MARGINAL: EXPLAIN      -------------------------------------------
   ---
      UNACCEPTABLE: EXPLAIN  -------------------------------------------
   ---

OUTPUT 2--PRODUCT DELETION MODEL

DO YOU HAVE ANY INFORMATION NEEDS THAT ARE NOT BEING MET
PRESENTLY?
      YES
   ---

      NO
   ---
```

Figure 19-4 MIS evaluation questionnaire.

"yes" response to the final question triggers a personal call from the systems analyst.

This information audit is intended to assure that the MIS meets the managers' needs. The audit should be conducted annually during the operating life of the MIS.

Another type of audit—the *accounting audit*—should be conducted annually by professionals independent of the information services department. Conducted by an EDP auditor, the accounting audit is intended to verify compliance with generally accepted accounting and business standards.[3] An *EDP auditor* is a person trained in both auditing practices and computer processing. These auditors can be acquired from public accounting firms, such as Arthur Andersen & Co., or from general management consulting firms, such as Booz·Allen & Hamilton. EDP auditors often use packaged programs that track test data through the system to assure that data is being processed correctly.

EDP auditors also frequently use a questionnaire to identify potential weaknesses in MIS management. The vice-president of information services completes a questionnaire like the one in Figure 19-5. Responses to the computer performance evaluation form indicate to the EDP auditors which areas need attention.

7. Maintenance and modification of the MIS. Many cases of computer fraud have been reported in which persons made unauthorized changes to operational programs or to contents of the data base. One bank programmer rounded interest computations down to the lower penny and added the fractional amount to his personal account.

To prevent such unauthorized changes, or to catch them when they are made, controls can be established on program changes. Some computer users have established *program change committees* to evaluate each request for change. The request is described on a special form, and all of the detailed documentation is attached. No change can be made to a program without this committee's approval.

Formal procedures such as this should reduce the number of unauthorized changes but will not eliminate them. Other controls must also be instituted, such as having the computer print out reports of unauthorized data requests or exceptionally high activity for certain financial accounts.

System Design Control

It is possible to design an information system without any built-in controls. The design cost would be less than a system with controls. While that result might seem appealing, management is usually quick to spot the weaknesses. The penalties in operating such a system would outweigh the savings in design. It would

---

[3] For a description of EDP auditing techniques, see Ron Weber, *EDP Auditing: Conceptual Foundations and Practice* (New York: McGraw-Hill, 1982); *Systems Auditability and Control: Audit Practices* (Altamonte Springs, Fla.: The Institute of Internal Auditors, 1977); and *Computer Audit Guidelines* (Toronto: Canadian Institute of Chartered Accountants, 1975).

1. Is some particular resource limiting production at the installation?
   a. What is the limiting resource? (processors, memory channels, peripherals, communication, people, etc.)
   b. How do you know this is the limiting resource?
   c. When was this resource last augmented?
   d. Can this resource be augmented on a step-by-step basis?

2. Is there a regular procedure for tracking and reporting the number of production jobs that are rerun?
   a. What is counted as a rerun? (abnormal terminations, normal terminations but wrong data, human-ordered reruns, etc.)
   b. What percent of production runs are reruns?
   c. What percent of resource usage is caused by these reruns?
   d. Are causes for reruns tracked by job?
   e. Who keeps track of reruns?
   f. What is done to control repeated reruns of the same job?

3. Are there restrictions to keep operators from modifying scheduling, priority, or execution parameters or options at their discretion?
   a. How often do operators modify scheduling parameters?
   b. What parameters do operators modify?
   c. What are their reasons for modification?

4. Is there a continuing effort to improve the performance of applications programs?
   a. How much resource or cost saving has resulted from improvement projects?
   b. Which systems are current candidates for performance improvement projects?
   c. How were these programs chosen?
   d. How much could be saved monthly by improvements to these programs?
   e. Which programs are the major users of the installation's limiting resource?
   f. Who is responsible for reviewing applications programs?
   g. What was the cost for running the largest application for the past twelve months?

5. Is there an established group or individual with overall responsibility for computer performance evaluation?
   a. What CPE tools are available for this group's use?
   b. What projects have been completed in the last year?
   c. How much has this group saved in the past year?
   d. Who is responsible for the CPE group?

6. Are the costs of online systems examined with regard to their value or revenue produced?
   a. What portion of computing resources, or their costs, is used for online support?
   b. What would the effect be if online services were severely restricted or eliminated?
   c. How do online applications save money for users?

7. Is there a formal process to determine the value of new data processing projects before their development is undertaken?
   a. How are the project costs and potential benefits determined?
   b. What controls are used to keep development costs in check?
   c. For the most recently implemented project, how do actual benefits compare with projected benefits?

Figure 19-5 Computer performance evaluation questionnaire.

d. For this project, how do actual costs compare with projected costs?
e. How many people had to be contacted, and how long did it take, to answer the two preceding questions (c and d)?

8. Has top management established system performance goals for the computer center?
a. What are these performance goals?
b. Are these goals being met?
c. How does management know whether or not these goals are being met?

SOURCE: "What to Do about Those Expensive Computers," *Management Focus* (Peat, Marwick, Mitchell & Co.) 28 (January-February 1981), pp. 18–19.

Figure 19-5 (continued)

be like buying a car without a spare tire, a fuel gauge, bumpers, and door locks. The cost would be lower, but the reduced safety and security would present serious problems. The cost savings would not be worth the trouble.

Some subsystems of the MIS demand greater controls than others. Generally, anything involving money needs the tightest controls. A firm cannot afford to make a mistake in calculating an employee's payroll check or a vendor's payment. But a nonmonetary subsystem, such as a report of sales statistics, might still be useful even if it contains some minor errors.

Computer control is based on a key point. Systems controls cost money. And a control should not be implemented if its cost exceeds its value. This is an important decision to make in systems design—what level of control is justified in each subsystem? Management cannot make this decision alone—they need the assistance of the information services staff and EDP auditors.

Areas of system design controls[4]

The MIS includes many subsystems, and most are unique in one way or another. Each one can be subdivided into basic parts, however, and controls should be considered for each part. Figure 19-6 illustrates these basic subsystem parts.

The first part is devoted to *transaction origination*. This procedure usually involves recording several data items on some type of source document. The document might be a sales order form, a payroll time card, or a bank check. This origination is external to the computer equipment and precedes any computer processing.

After the transaction is originated, it is converted into a computer-readable form, a process called *transaction entry*. This part does involve the use of computer

---

[4]The format for this study of design controls, and much of the content, was obtained from *Systems Auditability and Control: Control Practices* (Altamonte Springs, Fla.: The Institute of Internal Auditors, 1977), pp. 45–86. This document reports the results of a study conducted by SRI International and funded by IBM.

or data processing equipment. The transaction data can be keyed into a terminal or a keypunch, key-to-tape, or key-to-disk unit.

In some subsystems, data is communicated from one location to another. This is the *data communication* part. In other subsystems, data is entered by transaction entry directly into the computer for processing.

Once the data is entered into computer storage, it is processed by programs in the software library. In many instances, this *computer processing* results in data added to or taken from the data base.

When the processing has been completed, some *computer output* is created. This output can be information for management or data for use by another subsystem.

The following paragraphs address each part of a subsystem. Some examples of control for each part will be described briefly to provide an idea of the alternatives available.

1. Transaction origination. Each subsystem part in Figure 19-6 can be subdivided further to identify specific control areas. In Figure 19-7 this is done for the transaction origination part of the subsystem.

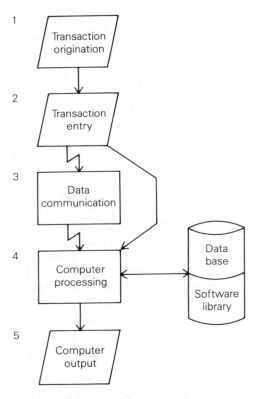

Figure 19-6 Basic subsystem parts.

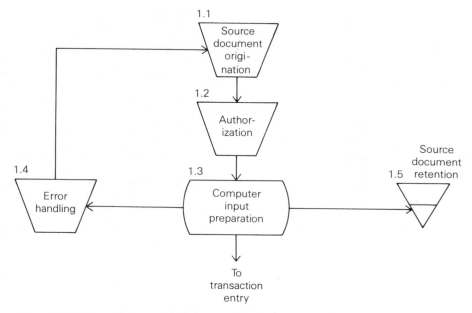

Figure 19-7 Transaction origination control areas.

Controls of transaction origination start with the *source document origination*—the order form, the payroll card, or the check. These controls deal with procedures for (1) designing source documents for use, (2) assuring the security of documents before use, and (3) handling the documents.

Authorization controls describe how data entries are to be made to the documents and by whom. This is accomplished by requiring signatures on source documents, involving several persons in the preparation of each document, devising written procedures, and establishing limits on the approval of certain transactions, such as customer credits.

Computer input preparation controls establish a means of identifying input records found to be in error and assuring that all input data is processed. Examples of controls of this type are maintaining transaction logs, which serve as a record of transactions to be processed, and batching source documents.

Error-handling controls provide a systematic way to correct errors and resubmit records for input. This control area is not concerned with detecting errors, but with correcting them once they have been detected. Each subsystem part has an error-handling area.

Finally, controls of *source document retention* specify how documents will be stored after use and under what conditions they will be made available to potential users.

2. Transaction entry. Transaction entry converts the data from a source document to computer-readable format. The controls attempt to maintain the accuracy

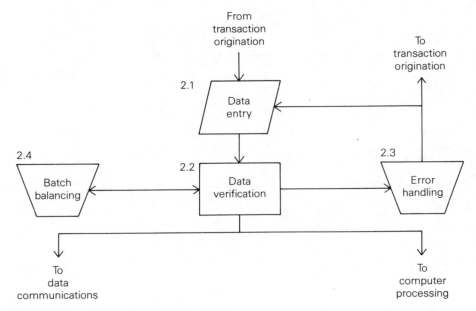

Figure 19-8 Transaction entry control areas.

of data to be transmitted over a communication network or entered directly into a computer. Figure 19-8 shows how this subsystem part is divided into four control areas.

Controls over *data entry* can apply to either offline processes (such as key-punching) or terminal input. The controls exist in the form of written procedures and the input equipment itself. The equipment should be located close to the point of transaction origination to reduce delays in entry. Also, an effort should be made to capture the input on a computer-readable medium such as a cassette tape or floppy disk.

After the data is recorded, it is *verified* for accuracy. The use of a key verifier machine is a good example of *data verification*. The data is keyed a second time and the key depressions are compared with holes in the card. An unequal comparison indicates an error. These errors are corrected by the *error-handling* area.

A *key verification* operation can also be performed with terminal input, requiring a second terminal operation to rekey the data. Software in the host, the cluster control unit, or the terminal can detect differences in the two keying processes. A simpler verification of terminal input can be performed by the operator, who visually checks the data that has just been entered and is now displayed on the screen. This process is called *sight verification*. Additionally, the software can perform *input editing*—checking fields for the wrong types of characters, invalid codes, and so forth.

Control totals such as document count and dollar amounts are accumulated for each batch in a *batch-balancing* process. These totals are later compared with similar totals prepared on the input data by the computer. An equal comparison indicates all transactions have been processed.

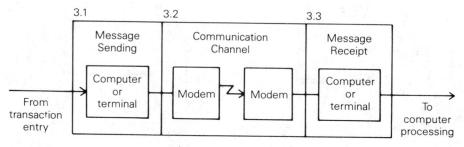

Figure 19-9 Data communication control areas.

3. Data communication. In subsystems where data is transmitted over a communication network, there are three areas where controls are possible: message sending, the communication channel, and message receipt (Figure 19-9). Error handling is not a separate area, but is accomplished by the communication equipment.

Control can be established over *message sending* by securing all phone equipment rooms to prevent wiretapping, by using a code to identify each user or terminal or both, and by restricting terminals or users to entering only certain approved transactions. In addition, a message log can be maintained of all transactions for periodic audit or follow-up.

Most of the controls of the *communication channel* involve hardware rather than software. An example of a hardware control is data *encryption,* which scrambles the characters to make the data meaningless to an unauthorized receiver. Figure 19-10 illustrates encryption by simply rearranging the characters. IBM contributed the encryption algorithm that has become the Federal Data Encryption Standard in the U.S.

Controls of *message receipt* include the automatic detection of errors by the receiving units and requests for resubmission. Errors can be detected when "check bits" or "check characters" are transmitted along with the data, and the bits or characters are inappropriate for the data received. For firms using dial-up lines, telephone numbers for the modems can be changed frequently and kept confidential. All calls can be intercepted by a computer operator, who obtains proper identification before permitting transmission.

4. Computer processing. Up to this point, all of the controls have been placed on entering data into the computer. With that now accomplished, controls can

In the above figure, a pay rate of $0,875.62 would be transmitted as 620758.

Figure 19-10 Encryption can confuse unauthorized data users.

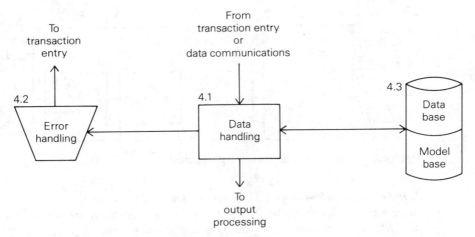

Figure 19-11 Computer processing control areas.

be built into the programs and the data base. These control areas are shown in Figure 19-11.

Data-handling controls properly identify input transactions and assure the accuracy of data manipulation and computation. Assume that three types of input transactions—identified by codes 1, 2, and 3—can be processed. Through programming, the computer can determine if a transaction is a code 1 or 2. If not, it is a mistake to assume the code is a 3. Perhaps an error was made in keying in a 1 code, and an A was entered instead. It is neither a 1 nor a 2, and it most certainly isn't a 3. Figure 19-12 shows examples of good and bad program logic to test the transaction code.

One example of a control of data manipulation and computation might test the result of an arithmetic operation for reasonableness. The monthly commission for a sales representative can be checked for a maximum limit, say $5000. Any exceptions can be flagged for follow-up to verify accuracy.

The *error-handling* control area is concerned with reporting and correcting errors and with reentering correct data. When a transaction is found to contain an error, processing of that transaction is suspended. The transaction record is entered into an error suspense file and held until it is corrected. An error report is printed by the computer, specifically identifying the error. Errors in money data fields are corrected with proper debit and credit entries rather than deletion and replacement. If deletion and replacement were allowed, any figure could be entered as a replacement amount and an error could be difficult to detect. The error suspense file can be used periodically to prepare statistical reports on types of errors, frequency, and source.

Processing controls can also be established on changes to both the *data base* and the *software library*. No changes to data files or programs are permitted without a proper departmental security code and an individual password. Only certain types of changes are permitted for each code and password. A log of all

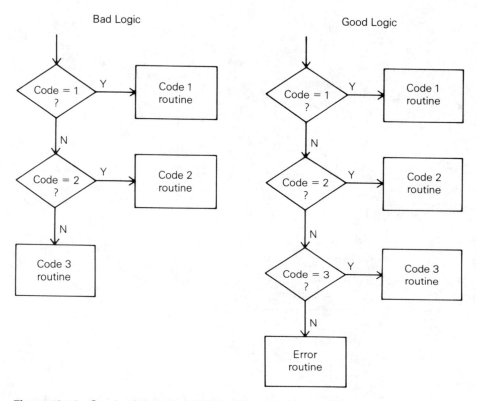

Figure 19-12 Good and bad approaches to code testing.

changes to data and programs is maintained in secondary storage. The log identifies the date and time of the transaction, identification of the terminal (if used), security codes, and password.

A very common method of controlling the use of data files is to incorporate header and trailer labels into the files. Header labels can assure that the proper file is being used and that a file is retained for the required length of time. Trailer records can contain control totals for data in the file.

5. Computer output This subsystem part is responsible for delivering the finished product to the customer. See Figure 19-13.

The *computer operations balancing* area verifies that all batches and transactions received from user departments are processed. This procedure is accomplished by balancing computer output totals to totals established at input. Additional controls can be established on money amounts. Computer reports can also be prepared on changes to programs and on transaction volume by terminal to detect unauthorized use.

Controls on report *distribution* attempt to assure that only the appropriate persons receive the output. A cover sheet identifying the recipient is attached to

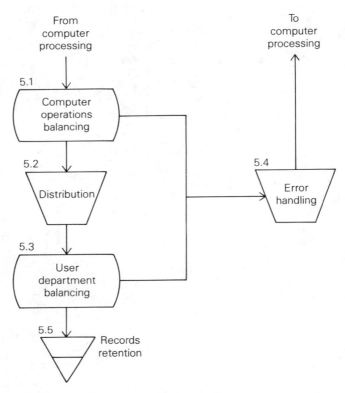

Figure 19-13   Computer output control areas.

each report, and a log is maintained showing when each output is distributed. Only the correct number of copies is prepared. The recipient can be asked to acknowledge receipt by returning a special form. The thoroughness of these controls varies with the type of information distributed.

User department balancing also involves balancing computer output to control totals established when input data was prepared. This type of balancing is usually more thorough than that of computer operations. It is the responsibility of the user department to establish and maintain controls that guarantee system integrity.

Error handling consists of an error log maintained by a special control group. Errors are corrected, following written procedures, and the corrected transactions are reentered. Upon acceptance by the system, the transactions are removed from the error log. The error log is periodically scanned to identify transactions where correction is overdue.

The final area of *record retention* is the responsibility of the user department. The objective is to maintain proper security over computer output and to control waste disposal. Paper shredders of out-of-date reports and aborted computer runs represent a control of this type.

It is the systems analyst's responsibility to assure that the system design includes the proper level of controls. The analyst can take the hardware controls as given and can then build in the software controls where needed. The analyst must be careful not to over- or undercontrol the system.

Control of System Operation

The two control areas discussed above deal with actions taken prior to cutover to the MIS. After cutover a third control phase becomes necessary. This is the control over the actual operation of the MIS.

System operation controls are intended to achieve efficiency and security. Computer operations are a complex system composed of the computer, peripheral equipment, personnel, facilities, and supplies that must work together in a coordinated fashion. In addition, the operations are meant to be safe from disruption or abuse by unauthorized personnel both inside and outside the firm.

Controls that contribute to the desired efficiency and security can be classified into six areas:

1. Organizational structure
2. Input/output scheduling and control
3. Library control
4. Equipment maintenance
5. Environmental control and facilities security
6. Disaster planning

Organizational structure

The information services staff is organized along lines of specialization. Analysts, programmers, and operations personnel are usually kept separate and develop the skills required of their work area only. This structure contributes to the efficiency of the overall operation, and also to security. It is much more difficult to violate the system when the cooperation of several individuals is required. Controls are built into the system by each category of personnel. One type of employee (say a programmer) might be able to bypass his or her controls, but no others.

In addition to the separation of operations from analysis and programming, it is desirable to separate the different areas within operations. The main areas are input/output scheduling and control, data entry, media library, production control, and equipment operations. In a department organized as in Figure 19-14, it is difficult for user departments or operations personnel to violate the system.

The different units within the operations department play special roles in the flow of computer jobs through the department. These roles are illustrated in Figure

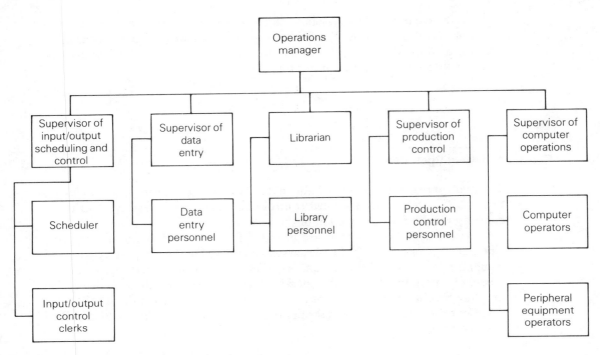

Figure 19-14 Organization of the operations department.

19-15. Data entry personnel convert input data into a computer-readable form. Computer operators perform the necessary computer setups to run the jobs. Operators of peripheral equipment such as decollators and forms bursters (machines that separate the carbons from multiple copy forms and pull apart the separate pages) make the computer output available for distribution. Library personnel make data files available for processing. Input and output control personnel establish controls at points of data entry and exit. Production control personnel assure that jobs are run as scheduled. The scheduler establishes the production schedule for all operations activities.[5]

Computer operations can be viewed as a manufacturing operation. Work flows through the plant. One measure of the efficiency of the production process is the speed with which work flows. *Response time* measures from the time the user releases the source data (point 1 in Figure 19-15) until he or she receives the output (point 6). *Turnaround time* runs from the time the operations department receives the data (point 2) until the output is transmitted to the user (point 5). Turnaround time measures the efficiency of all of the operations units. *Throughput time* is the time from input into the CPU (point 3) until output from the CPU (point 4). Throughput time measures the efficiency of only the computer processing within operations.

[5] For a very thorough description of duties performed by the various types of operations personnel, see Marjorie Leeson, *Computer Operations: Procedures and Management,* 2d ed. (Chicago: Science Research Associates, 1982).

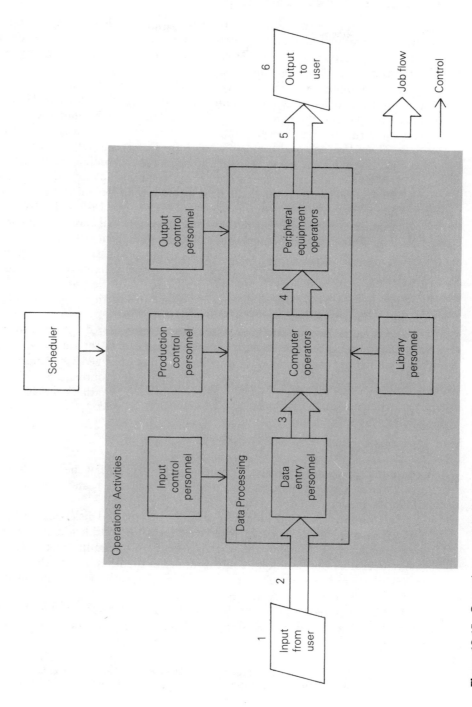

Figure 19-15 Operations organization facilitates job flow.

Input/output scheduling and control

In a factory it is necessary to input raw materials, schedule the flow of materials through the production area, and distribute the finished output to the customers. In the computer operations "factory," these tasks are the responsibility of the input/output scheduling and control section.

Often an important responsibility of this section is to serve as a link between the computer and its users, performing an *input/output control* function. This relationship exists in a pure batch environment, where users submit data in source document form for data entry, batch processing, and the delivery of hardcopy output. The relationship also exists when online users submit jobs to be batch processed. But when input, processing, and output are all online, the input/output control section is effectively bypassed. These relationships are diagrammed in Figure 19-16. The controls applied by the input/output control section are based primarily on the balancing activities illustrated in Figures 19-8 and 19-13.

The supervisor of the input/output control section is also responsible for *job scheduling*. The scheduler prepares the daily schedule from one day to one week in advance, based on historical data describing computer use, the recurring jobs and their characteristics, special jobs to be run, and situations unique to that day—operator absences, jobs to be rerun, changed priorities, and so on. Scheduling computer work is very similar to scheduling production work in a factory, and many of the same techniques are effective.[6]

The schedule is given each day to the *production control* section responsible for coordinating the schedule with computer operations. Separating scheduling from production control makes it difficult to run unauthorized programs or make unauthorized changes to the data base. In an online environment, however, that possibility exists. Security must be achieved by incorporating controls (codes, passwords, and so on) into the programs.

Library control

A computer media library is similar to a book library, in that there is a librarian, a collection of data and information media, a storage area, and a procedure for making the media available to users.

The computer media include reels of magnetic tape and disk packs (see Figure 19-17). These are stored in racks, some with locks for confidential material. The racks are housed in a walled area that is secure from unauthorized access. The same temperature and humidity controls apply to the library as to the computer room. Only library personnel are allowed in the library, and computer media are released only to computer operators.

Two types of records provide the basis for control: a record of each reel and disk pack, and a record of each data file. These records can be kept in the data

---

[6]For a good description of computer scheduling, see *Managing the Data Processing Organization,* GE19-5208 (Lidingö, Sweden: IBM Corporation, 1976), pp. 71–78. This manual is available from your local IBM office.

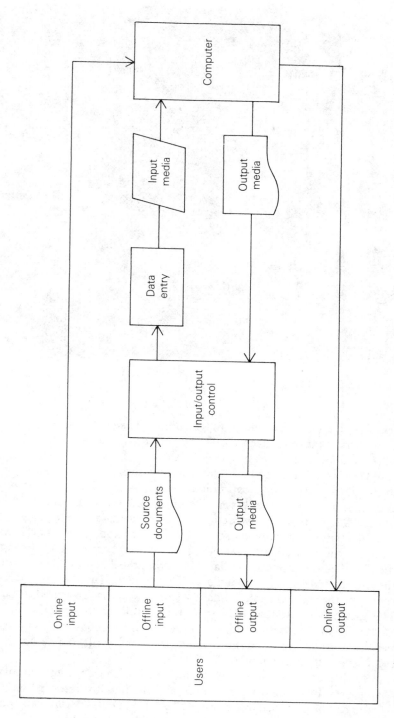

Figure 19-16 Input/output control interfaces with batch users—input or output.

Figure 19-17   A tape library.

base. As reels or disk packs and files are checked out to computer operators, entries are made to the records. The records are updated upon return. The records reflect the location and use history of the items.

Duplicate copies of files and programs should be maintained, although not in the library. Another location is desirable as a hedge against a disaster in the computer area. Additionally, it is common practice to maintain two *generations* of data files so that reconstruction can be performed if necessary.

In a batch environment, sequential files are updated on a cycle basis, such as daily or monthly. The file created on Wednesday contains data from the Tuesday file plus Tuesday transaction data. Likewise, the Tuesday file was prepared from the Monday file plus Monday data. The Monday, Tuesday, and Wednesday files represent three generations of data. (This concept is illustrated in Figure 19-18.) The data on the Monday file is not erased until the Wednesday file is created. If anything happens to the Wednesday file, it can be reconstructed by again processing the Tuesday transactions against the Tuesday file. These batch files can be recorded on magnetic tape or DASD.

A different procedure must be followed in an online environment. Here file changes can be made from terminals, and the files are recorded on a DASD. File backup can be provided by "dumping" the DASD files periodically onto magnetic tape. The transaction data also is saved so that the DASD file can be reconstructed if necessary.

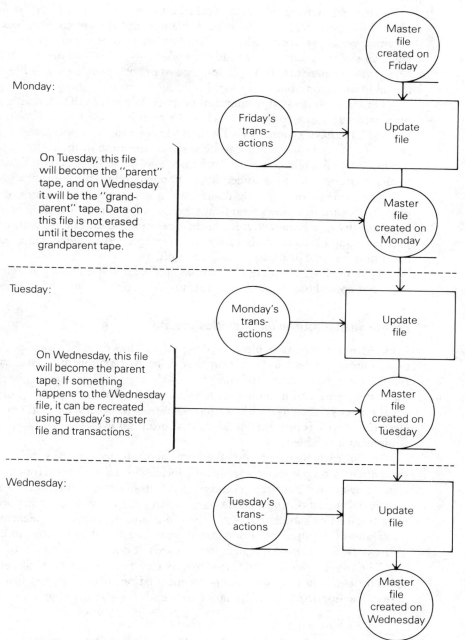

Figure 19-18 Three generations of magnetic tape files.

Equipment maintenance

It is the computer manufacturer's responsibility to keep the equipment in running order. This service is included in the monthly lease charges or is contracted separately.

The computer repair persons, called *customer engineers* (CEs) or *field engineers* (FEs), perform both scheduled and unscheduled maintenance. *Unscheduled maintenance* is performed when the computer develops unexpected problems, as when an electronic component suddenly goes bad. *Scheduled maintenance,* called *preventive maintenance* (PM), is designed to prevent problems. It is like changing the oil in an automobile every 4000 miles.

On larger systems it is common practice to provide the FEs with a specific time each day to perform PM, such as from 8:00–9:00 A.M. It is also common for the FEs to have a room solely for their test equipment, supplies, repair manuals, and so on. One or more FEs can be assigned full-time to the installation. PM is less frequent on a minicomputer, and there may be no PM at all on a micro. With a micro, you just wait for something to happen and then have it fixed.

The manager of computer operations monitors the performance of the computer to ensure that downtime is not excessive. The manager monitors the performance by observing activities in the operations area, talking with operations personnel and FEs, and receiving reports of system performance. The reports show downtime by time of day, by computer unit, and so on.[7]

Time for PM, adequate FE facilities, and a good monitoring system are controls that contribute to good equipment operation.

Environmental control and facilities security

Computers are expensive pieces of equipment. They must be given special care to protect the investment and ensure against damage or malfunction. The large models require special environmental conditions—the computer room must be clean, and the temperature and humidity must remain within tolerance limits. Backup electrical power is often available so that operation will continue even when normal electrical service is interrupted. Some organizations even have backup computing equipment available.

In the early years of computer use, many firms regarded their systems as showpieces. Computers were frequently located in sidewalk-level rooms with large viewing windows. Passersby could note the progressive nature of the firm.

Social unrest during the late sixties changed all that. Some computer centers were bombed or sabotaged. Now, the trend is to maximize the security of computer areas.[8] Equipment rooms are inaccessible to all but authorized persons. Those persons must use magnetic-stripe cards or doorlock combinations to enter.

The trend toward distributed processing has an effect on facilities security. Instead of having only one computer installation to protect, the firm now has many. The opportunity for someone to breach the security is greater, since more

---

[7] Examples of reports the operations manager can use to monitor system performance are included in *Managing the Data Processing Organization,* pp. 112–120. For a complete description of the duties of the operations manager, see Robert J. Thierauf and George W. Reynolds, *Effective Information Systems Management* (Columbus: Charles E. Merrill, 1982).

[8] For additional information on physical security, see *The Considerations of Physical Security in a Computer Environment,* G520-2700 (White Plains, N.Y.: IBM Corporation, 1972); and Ludwig Stern, "Security for Your Computer Facility," *The Office* 88 (August 1978): 18 ff.

installations exist. But when a breach occurs, it is not as serious as in a centralized installation. Generally, only a portion of a firm's data base is available at a distributed site. Also, even with one or a few distributed sites inoperative, the remainder of the network can function.

Disaster planning

The firm that establishes the above controls on system operation can expect a high level of performance. But unforeseen disasters may occur. For example, a fire in another part of the building could destroy remote equipment, such as terminals. A program tape could be erased by mistake, vendor supplies and services could be terminated for a variety of reasons. Management should anticipate and plan for these possible disasters so that the firm can recover from minor as well as major emergencies.

Rather than devise a single, all-encompassing plan, a more manageable approach is to define multiple plans, programs, and procedures. Management can prepare formal, written documents outlining (1) measures to prevent a disaster, (2) means of alerting members of the organization to an impending disaster, (3) emergency precautions intended to minimize the damage, and (4) a procedure for recovery. The plans below are the most common.[9]

An *emergency plan* is designed to assure the safety of the firm's employees and to protect other critical resources in the event of either natural or human threats. The idea is to identify those resources necessary for the organization to function and to map a strategy of alarm, evacuation, and protection.

A *backup plan* details how the firm can continue to function from the time it suffers a loss of capability until it has recovered. Users must identify information processing jobs that will be necessary during the recovery period. These jobs in turn identify the minimum equipment configuration required. Arrangements can be made for the use of a backup system, either with another user or with the computer manufacturer. When very little system degradation can be tolerated, even for a short time, backup equipment can be located on the premises. Airlines, for example, have a backup CPU for their reservation system.

A *recovery plan* is intended to restore the firm's operating capability after a disaster. The recovery plan complements the emergency and backup plans by specifying how the MIS resources can be reassembled. The plan identifies alternate computer sites and sources of replacement equipment, communication facilities, and supplies.

A *vital-records plan* identifies critical data files and specifies where duplicate copies are stored. The storage location should be some distance from the computer installation.

In addition, firms can establish programs dealing with topics such as *data classification*. This program determines the relative importance of data and information items and specifies those employees who can have access. You recall from Chapter 13 that Exxon didn't realize it was missing an important document, even

---

[9]Based on *Data Security Controls and Procedures*, pp. 17–22.

though it had a *document classification* system. Implementing a control system is one thing—using it properly is something else.

Plans and programs such as these have only recently been considered necessary. Few firms have achieved the level of disaster planning described here. The plans are costly and are only implemented when they can be economically justified.[10]

Putting MIS Control in Perspective

Why is the manager concerned about controlling the MIS? For one thing, if the MIS is inoperative for any length of time, there probably will be no physical system of the firm to manage. Employees on all levels depend on the MIS for day-to-day support. Recall the important role the MIS plays in the manufacturing area, for example.

In addition, losing the MIS effectively isolates many managers from the physical system. This is especially critical on the lower levels, since those managers depend heavily on the MIS to signal problems needing their attention. Although upper-level managers also rely on the MIS, their longer planning horizon minimizes the disruption caused by short periods of computer downtime.

More serious than the temporary disruption of MIS output is the effect data base tampering can have on decision-making. Recall that data can be modified, destroyed, or disclosed by unauthorized persons. The worst act would be undetected modification. In this case, the MIS would produce erroneous information that could cause the wrong decisions to be made. And if the modification were detected, management's confidence in the information from the MIS could be seriously damaged.

If data base contents are destroyed, then a recovery procedure would recreate the files from backup copies. The disruption to decision making would only be minimal for this type of data base tampering.

The third possibility, disclosure, could cause the firm to lose its competitive position in the marketplace. A competitor could engage in a form of electronic espionage to tap the firm's data base. Conceivably, the competitor could have available as much information on the firm's operations as the firm's own managers.

These are the reasons that managers are concerned about MIS control. This concern was stimulated first by the social unrest mentioned above and second by the publicized instances of computer crime during recent years. Many firms are

---

[10]The best sources of information concerning MIS controls are the auditors associations. See, for example, *Control Objectives 1980,* (Carol Stream, Ill.: EDP Auditors Foundation, 1980); *Executive Report, Audit Practices,* and *Control Practices* (Altamonte Springs, Fla.: The Institute of Internal Auditors, 1977); and *Computer Control Guidelines* (Toronto; Canadian Institute of Chartered Accountants, 1970). Other good sources are the manufacturers of computing equipment. *Staying in Charge,* G505-0058 (White Plains, N.Y.: IBM Corporation, 1981), is addressed to the CEO and includes an excellent bibliography. See also John G. Burch, Jr., and Joseph L. Sardinas, Jr., *Computer Control and Audit: A Total Systems Approach* (New York: John Wiley & Sons, 1978).

increasing computer security with the intent of minimizing their vulnerability to computer crime. As safeguards are installed to discourage thefts of the firm's financial assets, another valuable resource will also be protected—information. In the long run, protecting information might be more important to the performance of the firm than protecting of the firm's financial assets.

Summary

Security is achieved by physical measures, backup and recovery measures, and controls and procedures. Data security can be breached either intentionally or accidentally, resulting in modification, destruction, or disclosure.

A system should possess three properties: integrity, auditability, and controllability. A system has integrity if it performs according to its specifications. A system has auditability if it exhibits accountability and visibility. Accountability means that responsibility is established for each transaction, and visibility means that exceptions from standard performance are called to the attention of the system's managers.

The MIS control task is focused on three areas: development, design, and operation. The manager can achieve control in these areas directly, through the vice-president of information services, or through other experts such as auditors.

Control of the development process spans the three life cycle phases leading to cutover. Managers initially achieve control by establishing a project plan based on a mechanism such as network analysis. The analysts identify the managers' information needs and establish the performance criteria of the new system. The information services department performs its tasks according to standards, such as flowcharting symbols and system documentation contents. The work of the programmer must adhere to an acceptance test that stipulates exactly how the program must perform. Before cutover, managers specify how a postinstallation review will be conducted, and they establish a procedure for maintaining and modifying the MIS. These developmental controls are applied over time to anticipate problems before they arise and to assure continuous control throughout the MIS life cycle.

System design is controlled by incorporating both hardware and software controls into the five basic parts of a system—transaction origination, transaction entry, data communication, computer processing, and computer output. Hardware controls are provided by the manufacturers of the computing and data communications equipment. Examples are key verifier machines and encryption devices. Software controls are incorporated into the system design by vendors and systems analysts. Examples are passwords, batch control totals, and data editing.

The control of systems operations is based on the organizational structure of the operations department, the activities of units within the department (such as input/output scheduling and the media library), equipment maintenance, environmental control, facilities security, and disaster planning. Most of these controls are the responsibility of the manager of operations.

Managers are interested in MIS control because a breach of security can cripple a firm's operations, cut off the managers from the physical system, produce manipulated information that leads to wrong decisions, and make confidential information available to competitors.

With this chapter we have finished tracing the MIS through its life cycle. In the next and final chapter we take a look at the MIS of the future.

Key Terms

control

physical measure

backup and recovery measure

security

integrity

functional integrity

fail-soft

downtime

auditability

accountability

visibility

controllability

development control

design control

operation control

standards organization

standards manual

information audit

accounting audit

EDP auditor

program change committee

transaction origination controls

transaction entry controls

key verification

sight verification

data communication controls

encryption

computer processing controls

computer output controls

response time

turnaround time

throughput time

input/output control

job scheduling

file generations

customer engineer (CE),
  field engineer (FE)

unscheduled maintenance

scheduled maintenance

preventive maintenance (PM)

emergency plan

backup plan

recovery plan

vital records plan

data classification

document classification

Key Concepts

The relationship of control to security

Auditability of a system

The time dimension of control: system development through operation

The two measures of MIS acceptability: information content and accounting integrity

Areas of system design controls

Balancing computer input with output, performed both by the user and the information services group

The manner in which organizational structure facilitates control

The differences between response, turnaround, and throughput times

Generations of sequential files

Different types of disaster plans

The importance of MIS control to the manager

Questions

1. Does the MIS help the manager control, or does the manager control the MIS? Explain.
2. What are the three protective measures that achieve security?
3. What are the different ways that data security can be breached?
4. How can a distributed data processing network provide functional integrity?
5. What is auditability? How do documentation tools contribute to auditability? How does structured design contribute?
6. What are the three types of controls that can be applied to the MIS?
7. How can a manager control the MIS when he or she is not an information specialist?
8. Who has the initial responsibility for establishing a control over the MIS? When and how is this accomplished?
9. Who establishes design and operation standards?
10. What is an information audit? Who conducts it? What are they looking for?
11. Answer the previous question in terms of an accounting audit.
12. What are the five areas of system design controls? Identify the one(s) not directly involved with computing equipment.
13. What are some ways that the accuracy of input data can be verified?
14. At what point in the system can encryption be used as a design control?
15. What is the effect on system control when one person in a small organization performs all of the operations duties?
16. Which is most important to the manager—turnaround, response, or throughput time? Which is most important to the vice-president of information services? a computer salesperson?
17. Which type of file offers the best backup protection—sequential or direct? Explain.
18. How can the operations manager minimize downtime?
19. What effect does distributed processing have on facilities security?
20. Which management level suffers most when the system goes down? Why?

CASE PROBLEM: Artesia, Tucson, and Grand Canyon Railway

The Artesia, Tucson, and Grand Canyon Railway (AT&GC), headquartered in Artesia, New Mexico, provides freight service to four southwestern states. A progressive firm, AT&GC has a marketing research department staffed by three analysts. Abner McCann, the director, is assisted by Elizabeth Patton and Richard Hall. All took computer courses in college but have had little opportunity to use those skills at AT&GC.

The AT&GC computer is located within the controller division and is understaffed. A high turnover of analysts and programmers has made it impossible to respond to many demands for computer support. The marketing research department has one of the lowest priorities and has been unable to get any computer work done internally. During the past year, the marketing researchers have been going outside to a computer service bureau, but costs have soared. Abner was able to convince top management to allow marketing research to get its own micro. He was also able to obtain some systems analysis assistance to conduct a system study and select a computer. An order has been placed for a Sony SMC-70—a keyboard/CPU unit with 64KB RAM and 32KB ROM, a floppy disk unit that handles two 3½-inch disks, a dot matrix printer, and a CRT.

The system is due to arrive next week, and Abner is telling Elizabeth and Richard about the new system operation.

Abner:
I've found a place down the hall where we can put the Sony. It's the vacant office next to the janitorial closet.

Richard:
You mean the closet where they keep all the cleaning materials? I don't know if I can stand the odor. Every time I walk by, the fumes from those solvents nearly knock me down.

Abner:
You'll get used to it. We can keep the door closed.

Elizabeth:
What about the chance that somebody will come in at night and walk off with it? You remember my radio was stolen last year. There aren't any locks on the doors inside this building.

Abner:
The night security guard keeps everything under control. He makes his rounds every hour or so, and I can instruct him to check on the computer.

Elizabeth:
What else is going to be in the room besides the Sony?

Abner:

I've already got some furniture moved in. Let's walk down there, and I'll show you the layout.

(Abner, Elizabeth, and Richard walk to the new computer room.)

Abner:

We'll put all of the units on this table, and we can keep the disks on the bookshelves. We'll move the shelves right next to the table. They'll be so close, you won't have to get out of your chair to change disks.

Richard:

We'll keep *all* the program disks *and* the data disks on those shelves?

Abner:

Right.

Elizabeth:

Are we going to be the only ones using the computer?

Abner:

That's the way it's intended. Any time we want to use it, we just come on down, turn it on, and start computing. It's really easy to operate.

Richard:

Say, isn't it getting warm in here? I'm burning up.

Elizabeth:

I noticed that myself. The air conditioner doesn't seem to be working.

Abner:

Oh, its working, all right. It's just that there is some kind of boiler on the other side of the back wall.

Elizabeth:

Oh, great.

Richard:

What about performance? Is the Sony pretty reliable?

Abner:

The best. You know their reputation. That was one of the big pluses when we evaluated their proposal.

Richard:

What happens when it goes down?

Abner:

We'll call a repairperson. There are quite a few in Roswell.

Richard:

But that's forty miles away. Does anybody else around here have a Sony?

Elizabeth:

Somebody has one of their radios. That's the kind I had stolen.

Richard:
No, I mean a Sony *computer*.

Abner:
I don't know. What difference does that make?

Richard:
Can we go back to the office? The heat and the fumes are making me sick.

Questions

1. Which of the six operation control areas appear to be critical to the satisfactory use of the Sony?
2. What hazards exist?
3. How could these hazards be eliminated?

Chapter 20

The Future of the MIS

Learning Objectives

After studying this chapter, you should:

- Recognize the necessity for the computer user to develop self-sufficiency in system development
- Understand current hardware trends
- Understand current software trends
- Appreciate the value of flowcharting as a graphical documentation tool
- Recognize the effect of distributed processing on security
- Appreciate current trends in the three basic parts of the MIS: office automation, data processing, and decision support systems

The Challenge of Change

The computer industry is in the midst of change—the most dramatic change in its short history. The computer has spread out from corporate headquarters and into branch offices, small businesses, and even homes. People of all ages are exposed daily to ads on TV and in print touting the powers of the computer. No area of our society has failed to grasp the significance of computers in our daily activities and to our future hopes.

Nobody is certain where computers will lead us. Undoubtedly there will be new problems. But there will also be new opportunities. Many people have ideas about what may evolve, and in this final chapter we will examine some that relate to the MIS.

As you embark on your business career, you will be caught up in the MIS evolution. You don't simply have to go along for the ride, though. With your preparation you can influence the direction the evolution will take. There are many opportunities to improve the way computers are used as decision support systems. The imaginative and resourceful newcomers to the business scene—people like you—will shape the MIS of the future.

The Changing Role of the Information User

The business environment is becoming increasingly computer literate. People are learning about computers at an earlier age and are getting better training than ever before. Computer courses are common in high schools and are becoming more popular at the junior-high and elementary levels.

Take, for example, the Lyons Township High School's two campuses in La Grange and Western Springs, Ill., where 4000 students a year gain hands-on experience with a computer.[1] The school has spent $200,000 to provide 240 computer terminals. The entire faculty can use the computer, and faculty members have written sixty programs that are used in courses. Some of the program names are intended to stimulate student interest, such as "Pounds Away" for a program dealing with nutrition and weight, and "Spelling Demons," designed to improve spelling.

Many high-school graduates will go on to college and take more computer-related courses before pursuing a career. Others will take jobs in industry and government and will become either users or producers of management information. More and more people on all levels will be computer literate and open-minded to new applications. The result will be twofold. First, there will be a greater demand for computer use within firms. Second, users will be able to put their own jobs on the computer, without relying completely on specialists in the information services department.

The communication problem

The most serious problem to plague computer users has been communicating with the information professionals—systems analysts and programmers. This problem is being solved by making the communication less necessary. If the user can do his or her own work, there is little or no need to communicate. The user can identify and define the problem, identify alternate solutions, evaluate the solutions and select the best, implement the system, and use and improve the system. All of this activity can occur within the user's area without involving the information services staff. In many cases, users will have their own mini or micro.

User-friendly software

For this utopian use of the computer to become a reality, the computer must become easier to use. It is one thing to expect clerical employees or first-line supervisors to put their data and information processing jobs on the computer. Expecting the same performance at upper management levels, where problems are less structured and time constraints more pronounced, is something else.

Continued improvements in software will be necessary. Languages must become more user-friendly. The trend toward natural languages must continue. Data base query languages such as the INQUIRE User's Language, MARK-IV, and ADA-SCRIPT+ are steps in the right direction. These languages are easy to learn and use. This capability should be equally available to small systems.

---

[1] Casey Banas, "Illinois High School Trains Entire Faculty to Use the Computer," *Houston Post,* 17 November 1981, p. 1B.

Simulations also need to be easier to use. Managers are acquiring a greater quantitative sophistication in their college courses and are less afraid of statistical packages (such as SAS) and of management science tools (such as linear programming). The popularity of general-purpose models (such as VisiCalc and IFPS) is evidence of how positively management will respond to a package that is easy to use.

The Changing Role of the Information Supplier

What effect will this trend toward user independence have on the traditional roles of systems analyst, programmer, and data base administrator? These people are currently in short supply, and the shortage is expected to increase.

Recently it has been common for some users to wait as long as five years to get an application on the computer. These are jobs that the firm and the information services department regard as low priorities. Even if a job shouldn't go on the computer at all, the user equates the long waiting period with poor service. Lack of support by the central computing facility has encouraged the use of small, distributed systems—often without an overall master plan.

An IBM study found that the backlog of computer applications is equivalent to 68% of the currently installed applications base.[2] In addition, IBM estimates that there is another backlog of yet unidentified jobs equal to 112% of the installed base. This combined backlog of 180% will be practically impossible to eliminate. Assume, for example, that it would take a firm five years to reprogram all of its current applications. (This is a conservative estimate.) It would take nine years to eliminate the backlog. By that time, still more jobs would be waiting.

The seriousness of this problem is augmented by the inability of colleges and universities to meet industry's needs for computer professionals. Dr. John Hamblen, of the University of Missouri at Rolla, has studied the problem of filling computer job openings with college graduates.[3] The situation in 1978/79 is illustrated in Table 20-1. Only at the two-year level is supply greater than demand. The need for graduates of higher-level programs is not being met. And the situation

Table 20-1   Demand for college-prepared computer professionals

College Level	Graduates (annual)	Demand (annual)
Two-year	33,000	26,000
Four-year	13,000	54,000
Masters	3,400	34,000
Doctorate	300	1,300

[2] David C. Mollen and Van Bakshi, "How to Support Company End Users," *Data Processor* 24 (May–June 1981): 6–8.

[3] Bernie Ward, "The Computer Age: Where Will We Find the Talent?" *Sky* 11 (March 1982): 79.

is expected to get worse. Employment in computer occupations is projected to increase from 1.4 million in 1980 to 2.1 million in 1990—a 50% increase.[4]

A Possible Solution

The information services department cannot continue to attempt to meet all of the information needs of its users. The department must first identify that portion of the firm's information-producing activity that it can handle and then gain expertise in performing those services. The remaining jobs are going to have to be performed by the user or by outside service organizations. Emphasis in the information services department must shift from trying to do all the work to helping users do their own work. The information services staff must assume the roles of information consultant and educator—helping users solve especially difficult problems and enabling users to become self-sufficient in solving routine problems.

Industry must recognize that it will not be able to hire analysts and programmers in the numbers needed. And industry must also recognize that colleges and universities cannot continue to prepare graduates for traditional systems analyst and programmer roles when those roles are going to be different tomorrow.

Colleges and universities must prepare their students for an environment of distributed systems analysis, design, and implementation accomplished with only specialized help from the information services department. Students should be prepared to function as either users or information specialists in this environment. Students aiming at a career in management should be exposed to MIS in their disciplines—marketing, finance, accounting, real estate, and so on. Students aiming at a career as information specialists should acquire consulting skills. These skills include the identification and analysis of information alternatives, planning and controlling the MIS life cycle, decision support, data base management, top-down development, and natural languages. In addition to these consulting skills, information specialists should stay familiar with current hardware and software so that users can be kept up to date.

The evolution of the roles and responsibilities of both users and ifnormation specialists will not occur overnight. Realistically, it will never occur completely. Many information services departments will cling to the old practice of encouraging user dependence. But the trend is clear, and the end result will be users who are both willing and able to implement their own decision support and data processing systems.

The Changing Nature of Computer Systems

Practically all areas of computer technology are changing. During the next few years, we anticipate a continued movement of processor power toward the user. Vendors will develop hardware dedicated to managing the data base, and improvements in storage technologies will increase storage capacities. The methods of entering data into the MIS and receiving information from it will also

---

[4] Ibid., p. 77.

change. And the interest in automating the office may well dwarf the interest in computer use in an MIS or DSS.

Distributed processor power

Computing hardware is moving toward the user. Purely centralized computer installations are giving way to processors located in the manager's area. The most extreme evidence of this distribution is the micro installed to serve the processing needs of a single department or person. Other evidence comes from datacom systems in which much communications processing is offloaded to front-end network processors, intelligent terminals, and cluster controllers, as in Figure 20-1.

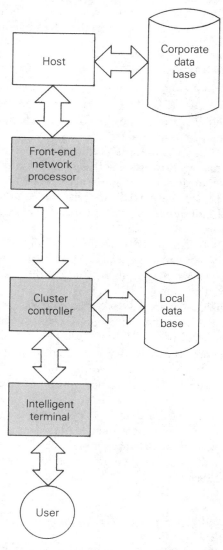

Figure 20-1 Offloading communications processing.

In the figure, the user has an intelligent terminal that can perform specialized processes independently of the other systems. A cluster controller can include a local data base, facilitating certain processing independently of the host computer and its centralized corporate data base.

This distribution of processor power has been underway for almost ten years and will continue as hardware costs continue to fall. Equipment manufacturers are providing users with hardware capable of meeting information needs. The software, however, is more difficult to provide. The systems software, such as operating systems and data communications monitors to support distributed systems, are more complex than those packages that support a centralized batch system. And the data base management systems for small computer systems do not compare with those for large systems. The effective use of distributed systems will hinge on improved software (rather than hardware) capabilities.

Data base processors

In addition to the movement of processor power toward the user, there will be a movement toward the data base. A micro will be dedicated to interfacing the data base with the CPU, freeing up the CPU for information processing. Figure 20-2 illustrates the offloading of data base responsibility to a *back-end data base processor*. Once this offloading is accomplished, computer processing will be performed by three separate processors designed to accomplish three types of processing: data base, information, and datacom network.

Interest in data base hardware (also called *data base processors*) has existed for years. ICL announced a system called CAFS (Content Addressable File Store) in 1977.[5] More recently, Cullinane announced a data base processor selling for about $300,000 (compared with about $150,000 for a DBMS) that included a report writer, query language, and I/O peripherals—a terminal, printer, and backup tape drive. The system was subsequently withdrawn, apparently because its price was considered too high.[6]

Meanwhile, Software A.G. is considering converting about 8000 of the 200,000-odd instructions comprising ADABAS to chip storage. Intel, the chip giant, acquired the firm that developed the System 2000 DBMS and is expected to make liberal use of hardware in future DBMSes. A California firm, Britton Lee, Inc., has developed a data base processor that will be sold not to users, but to computer equipment manufacturers. This machine is supposedly ten times faster than a software DBMS.

The trend toward a data base processor is one approach to improving the DBMS. New firms will most likely follow this path. The old DBMS firms will probably stick with a software emphasis and work to improve efficiency. Computer users will ultimately be able to select between hardware- and software-oriented DBMSes.

---

[5] Olin Bray and Kenneth J. Thurber, "What's Happening with Data Base Processors?" *Datamation* 25 (January 1979): 146 ff.

[6] Jan Johnson, "DBMS: Out of the Closet," *Datamation* 27 (September 1981): 64 ff.

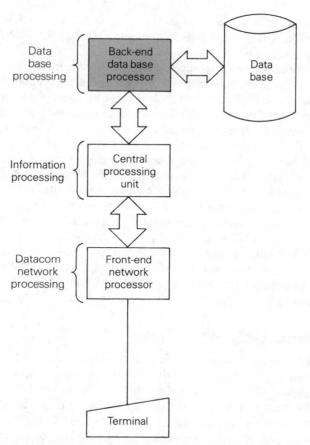

Figure 20-2 Offloading data base processing to a
back-end processor.

Increasing storage capacity

No breakthroughs in storage technology are anticipated during the next few years.
Semiconductor chips will continue to provide primary storage, with chip capacity
increasing from the 64KB in 1982 to 512KB by 1985.

It is possible that innovations in chip technology will produce storage capabilities for the late eighties that are difficult to comprehend by today's standards.
One avenue is the *biochip* now being developed by the combined efforts of phys-
icists, genetic engineers, chemists, and neurologists.[7] These scientists are working
to produce a molecule that passes current in only one direction, just as a transistor
does. Such chips could consist of proteins and could possibly be produced by
bacteria. The chips could be made in a three-dimensional form, which has proven
difficult for makers of two-dimensional semiconductor chips. To illustrate the

---

[7]Sharon Begley, "A Chip Off the Old Block," *Newsweek,* 8 March 1982, p. 92.

potential of biochip storage, one chip could store all of the information ever recorded by human beings in a cube measuring 1/200 of an inch on each side—the width of two human hairs.

Perhaps biochip storage will replace bubble memory as the storage technology of the future. Bubble memory was pegged as the replacement of magnetic disks for secondary storage. But disk storage just won't go away. For years industry experts have predicted the demise of disk storage, but it only gets better—with larger capacities and faster access. Disk storage is very well established and will probably be good for another decade at least.

There has been work toward developing other disk technologies, such as *optical disks,* that might eventually replace magnetic disks or tapes. An optical disk records data in the form of holes one-millionth of a meter in diameter burned into a recording material by a laser. The main shortcoming is that once the data is recorded, it cannot be changed. The main advantage is the large capacity—one 12-inch optical disk can contain the data recorded on twenty-five reels of magnetic tape. The cost per byte stored on an optical disk is about one-tenth that of magnetic tape. The high-density recording and the low cost make the optical disk a good candidate for archival (or historical) storage. In this application, permanent recording is not a problem—it's actually desirable.[8]

Elimination of keyed input media

Offline keyed input, such as keypunch, key-to-tape, and key-to-disk, is giving way to online input using terminals and to direct input media such as OCR documents. This evolution is illustrated in the conceptual model in Figure 20-3. You will notice that MICR is on the decline, being replaced by electronic funds transfer systems such as automated teller machines. OCR will continue to gain ground in high-volume transactions such as credit card invoices, billing turnaround documents, retail sales, and so on. The mini/micro boom will make online keyed entry using terminals the most popular input method of the future. It is still too early to tell whether voice recognition will compete with keyed entry. Most likely, voice recognition will not be popular until the late eighties.

Reduction of printed output

Similar evolutions are underway in output, as shown by the conceptual model in Figure 20-4. Output from computer printers once accounted for practically all the information available to the manager. In those days, stacks of computer printouts represented the manager's data base. Today these printouts not only are costly to produce and take up unnecessary space, but they lack immediacy and convenience. It is much easier to query the data base from a terminal and receive the information right away. Hence, much of the printed matter that is now simply

---

[8] For a detailed description of how optical disks can be used for data base storage, see Dick Moberg and Ira M. Laefsky, "Videodiscs and Optical Data Storage," *Byte* 7 (June 1982): 142 ff.

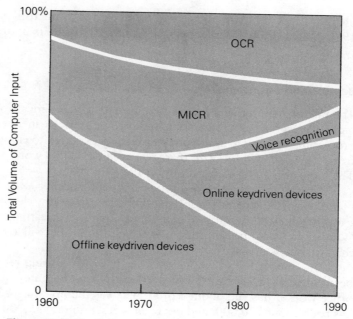

Figure 20-3 Evolution of input devices.

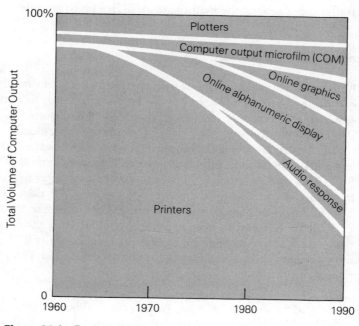

Figure 20-4 Evolution of output devices.

filed away for future reference will be converted to microfilm. By the end of the 1980s, most printed output will be from serial printers attached to mini/micro systems.

Booming office automation

The microcomputer as a means to automate office clerical routines may attract more widespread attention than similar applications in data and information processing. The micro as a word processor is expected to enjoy a tenfold increase from 1974 to 1989. In 1974, there were some 200,000 word processors installed. The number may hit 2 million by 1989.[9]

Riding the surge of word processing will be other examples of office automation—voice-actuated typing, facsimile transmission, electronic work stations featuring microform retrieval and online data base updating, and electronic mail. Within ten years, transmitting a letter electronically will cost substantially less than first-class postage.[10]

Automating the office makes a lot of sense. During recent years, little has been invested in increasing office productivity. The automation investment per office worker has run about $2000, whereas the investment per factory worker has been about $30,000, and per farm worker about $55,000. During the 1960s, factory productivity increased by 83%, whereas office productivity increased by a mere 4%.[11]

As firms start to implement office automation systems, their plans should define how these systems integrate into the MIS. If office automation and MIS are regarded separately, neither area will live up to its potential.

The Changing Nature of Software

Both applications and systems software are moving toward the user in the same manner as hardware. There has always been interest in making the computer easier to use, but only recently have efforts been directed toward the end user. Previously the aim was to ease the programmer's workload.

In Figure 20-5 you can see three clusters of software. The first cluster in the lower left includes the traditional high-level languages, such as FORTRAN, COBOL, PL/I, APL, and Assembler. These *procedural languages* require the programmer to specify the procedure for processing the data. Of these first languages, only FORTRAN ever enjoyed much use outside the information services department. FORTRAN has always been extremely popular with engineers, actuaries, scientists, and so on. Although all of these languages are still in use (COBOL is the most popular business language), they were designed for computing environments typical of the 1960s.

[9] Len Corlin, "Astounding Technology Portends Drastic Office Changes in '80s," *Contract* 22 (January 1980): 129.

[10] "Electronic Mail Can Cut Costs," *Nation's Business* 69 (December 1981): 18.

[11] Elio R. Rotolo, "Entering the '80s with a Challenge," *IE* 12 (July 1980): 32.

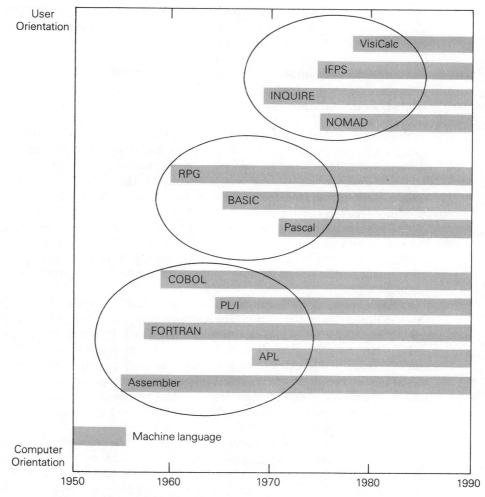

Figure 20-5 Movement of software toward the user.

The trend toward online computer use and micro systems contributed to the acceptance of BASIC, whereas the popularity of structured design provided a ready market for Pascal. These two languages, along with RPG (Report Program Generator), form the second cluster moving closer to the user. You can see that RPG was ahead of its time—it was developed in the second computer generation for the IBM 1401 system.

The software of the 1980s, designed specially for users, represents the third cluster. These are the *nonprocedural languages* or *natural languages* that only require the user to specify what information is desired—not how to produce it. We have discussed IFPS, VisiCalc, and the INQUIRE User's Language. NOMAD is similar to INQUIRE in that it is data base–oriented. Other examples of user languages are Ramis II, and INFO. IBM has announced BETA, a business-oriented language designed for small systems, as well as a language called QBE (Query By Example). At the present time, interest in these languages is high, and more packages of this type are expected.[12]

User-Friendly Documentation Tools

If the user is to gain self-sufficiency in programming by means of the user languages, he or she must also be proficient in the use of documentation tools. Among current tools, HIPO and pseudocode are the most user-friendly. HIPO is best suited to designing the overall system structure and that of lower-level modules. Pseudocode is best suited to designing the detailed program logic within each module. This top-down use of the tools is illustrated in Figure 20-6.

There are two other tools in the figure that were only mentioned in Chapter 18—decision logic tables (DLTs) and decision trees. Both have been around for quite a while, and both are user-friendly. They were never as popular as flowcharts, but perhaps their day has come. Both are effective in designing decision support logic.

The days of flowcharting as *the* system documentation tool are numbered. System flowcharting is best suited to batch systems, and those systems are diminishing in popularity. While program flowcharting is effective for designing terminal-oriented programs, the new breed of system designers seems to support pseudocode. Pseudocode is easier for new analysts to learn than flowcharting because pseudocode has fewer rules. Programmers like pseudocode because it so closely resembles certain popular programming languages, such as PL/I and FORTRAN. And, as we have mentioned, pseudocode is especially adaptable to structured programming.

But flowcharting has its advantages. Once the rules are learned, flowcharting permits a faster and easier communication of a system design or program logic than any other method. The saying "One picture is worth a thousand words" sums up the value of flowcharting as a documentation tool. A person skilled in flowcharting can merely glance at a flowchart and understand the essence of the design or logic. System and program logic can be complex, and flowcharting can describe that logic graphically. This ability will assure flowcharting a role in system and program design for years to come. But the role is much narrower than it was during the early years of the computer.

---

[12] For information on NOMAD, see Daniel D. McCracken, "The NOMAD Approach," *Datamation* 26 (May 1980): 165 ff. For information on RAMIS II, a product of Mathematica Products Group in Princeton, N.J., see *Datapro 70: The EDP Buyers Bible,* vol. 3 (Delran, N.J.: Datapro Research Corporation, 1981), pp. 70E-610-01a through 70E-610-01d. INFO is described in "INFO: A User's Language," *Computing Newsletter* 14 (May 1981): 2. BETA is described in "A New User-Oriented Business Language," *Computing Newsletter* 14 (March 1981): 3. See also M. Hammer et al., "A Very High Level Programming Language for Data Processing Applications," *Communications of the ACM* 20 (1977): 823–840. QBE and two other IBM languages, ADRS II and APL/DI, are described in "End-User Systems Available from IBM," *Computing Newsletter* 15 (December 1981): 2.

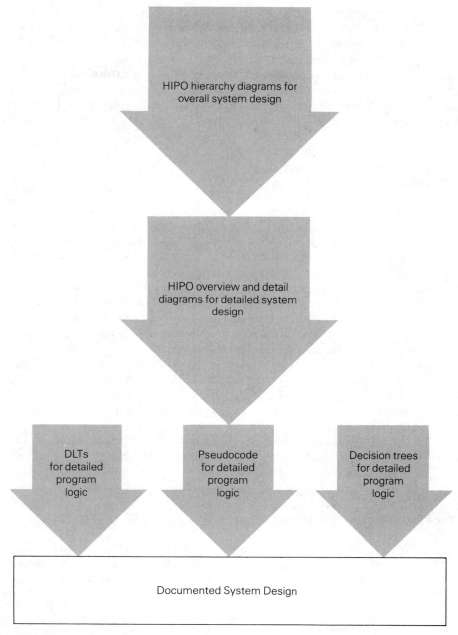

Figure 20-6 Top-down design by users.

Managers and future managers should learn to use these documentation tools so that they can design some of their own systems. Colleges and universities should ensure that all business students—future MIS users as well as future information specialists—learn to use the tools. And colleges and universities must remain alert to newer and better tools. To do this, the schools must stay in close touch with computer users, quickly recognize the value of new tools and techniques, and pass that information on to the students. Perhaps some new tools will be developed through academic research.

Colleges and universities will not shoulder the entire education burden, however. Industry has a giant task during the next few years to help the current group of managers become self-sufficient. Perhaps colleges and universities can help industry with this educational task. That would be a proper arrangement. But industry must do much of its own educating.

MIS Security

The distribution of processor power throughout the organization is going to influence security and control. In one respect, security will be improved by spreading the risk rather than relying on one giant system. If the single system is out of order, the firm may not be able to function. The result would not be nearly so devastating if one or even a few distributed systems shut down.

In another respect, overall security might decline. The firm can go to great lengths to protect its central facility with all types of physical safeguards. But it is far more difficult to take such precautions at numerous distributed sites. The person responsible for the office micro may not give security the same priority as the operations manager of the central system would.

In terms of data base security, the distributed system is most secure because illegal access exposes only a portion of the firm's data resource. In terms of data communications, the distributed system is again most secure because there is more processing on site and less need to transmit data, which exposes it to unauthorized interception.

All things considered, the trend toward distribution should improve security and control. But firms will have to give local managers enough resources to safeguard their distributed systems.[13]

The Final Analysis—MIS Trends

You recall from the first chapter that we identified three subsystems of the MIS: office automation, data processing, and decision support. We will conclude our description of the MIS by commenting on the trends to expect in each of these areas.

Office automation

We know that office automation includes several areas of activity in addition to word processing. All of the areas affect the flow of management information, but

---

[13] Frederick G. Withington addresses the problem of controlling distributed projects in "Coping With Computer Proliferation," *Harvard Business Review* 58 (May–June 1980): 152–64.

the most visible impact during the next few years will involve word processing. Some firms have already begun integrating their word processing and data processing systems. More firms will include word processing in their overall MIS planning. Word processing can electronically capture some of the flows of informal information that have escaped the computer so far. Firms will sponsor word processing training courses for their managers. In cases where word processing software is used on conventional computing equipment, the manager's terminal can provide a convenient means of facilitating the information flow. Stand-alone systems will be less convenient, but not necessarily less effective.

Data processing

It is easy to get caught up in the aura of DSS, content that computers have been processing data for a quarter of a century and thus have solved all possible data processing problems. That conclusion would be a mistake. Many small firms now implementing their first computers are going through the same evolution (although more quickly) that large firms experienced in the first generation. In fact, this *is* the first generation for small-system users. These users are primarily concerned with building a data processing base and are implementing billing systems, payroll systems, and so forth.

The data processing problems of small firms will be solved largely by packaged software and eventually by hardware specially built for certain applications. Much improvement is needed here before people with little or no computer knowledge can use the applications packages effectively.

As difficult as it is to believe, many large firms still struggle with data processing problems. The list even includes Fortune 500 companies. Packaged programs are not the solution here. These firms need to determine why they have been unable to implement data processing systems successfully. Once they understand the reasons, they must solve the problems. The shortage of information specialists will hit hardest here. Large numbers of specialists are needed, and they are not available. Perhaps by using applications development software (such as MANTIS and NATURAL), a few programmers can implement all of the data processing systems that a firm needs.

Decision support systems[14]

Several firms, including American Airlines, Sun Oil, and Del Monte, have already established DSS departments. TYMSHARE, a vendor of the DSS software package EXPRESS, has formed a consulting group to work with client firms. DSS is no longer just a concept—it's a reality in many organizations.

The continued success of DSS efforts depends on contributions from both information specialists and users. The specialists must understand how DSS differs from data processing and early MIS concepts. In addition, the specialists should be proficient in the wide variety of technical skills required, and they should

---

[14] Based on Ralph Sprague, "DSS Trends," *Computing Newsletter* 14 (March 1981): 2.

understand their role as catalysts. Users should be willing to invest their valuable time in the design and use of their systems.

Improvement will be realized in *dialog management*—making it easier for managers to interact with the DSS. English-like languages, light pens to enter data and instructions into the CRT, and greater use of the menu display technique will facilitate manager-DSS dialog. Improvements in *data management* will make it easier for a manager to access a small subset of the data base (say forty to a hundred data items) and to work with that data extensively. As we learn more about how managers use a DSS, the value of making a few key items available becomes clearer. In *model management,* we can expect to see new modeling languages that permit the user to create a special-purpose model independently of the information services staff, or with only minimal assistance. And as time goes on, more efforts will be directed toward an area that has enjoyed only scattered attention until now—*artificial intelligence (AI).*[15] Proponents of AI anticipate that the computer can be programmed to do more problem analysis and to contribute more to decision guidance.

Summary

Computer use is changing rapidly, prodded by the increasing shortage of resources—primarily systems analysts and programmers. The role of the information services department is shifting from doing the work to advising and educating the users so that they can do their own work. This shift in industry roles will be reflected in college and university programs preparing future users and information specialists. The key to the success of this shift of responsibility will be the continued development of user-friendly software and the ability of educators and information specialists to teach users how the software works.

Computer systems are also changing from centralized configurations to distributed networks. In these networks, the orientation of hardware is moving toward the user in the form of terminals, micros, cluster controllers, and front-end processors. Hardware will also orient more toward the data base to perform functions presently handled by DBMS software. Storage capacities will continue to increase, even though the form of that storage (chips and disks) will probably remain the same during the next few years. Input is moving away from source media, such as punched cards, toward medialess input from online terminals. Output is moving away from printed reports to displayed reports and query responses. While many changes will occur in the way data is processed, more changes will occur in office automation, where there is tremendous room for improving productivity.

Software is also moving toward the user. Newer packages such as query languages and DBMS report writers are making it possible for users to specify what they want without having to worry about how it will be done. Firms will

---

[15] For information on artificial intelligence and how it can affect the DSS, see Robert H. Bonczek, Clyde W. Holsapple, and Andrew B. Whinston, "Future Directions for Developing Decision Support Systems," *Decision Sciences* 11 (1980): 616–31.

still need information specialists to use the more traditional languages to prepare data processing programs.

Users must also master the use of design tools such as HIPO, pseudocode, DLTs, and decision trees. These user-friendly tools will restrict flowcharting to use only in documenting batch systems and in diagramming program logic, where graphical capabilities are needed.

Security has been a problem with centralized computing facilities, and new challenges must be met with distributed systems. If the people responsible for small systems have sufficient resources, securing distributed networks will be easier than securing large, central sites.

During the 1980s we can expect to see word processing playing a more vital role in MIS designs and small organizations using micros for data processing. Firms that are further along in computer use will expand their decision support systems by concentrating on improvements in the user-DSS dialog, restructuring data bases for easier use, and providing users with modeling languages. Throughout the decade, managers and information specialists will focus on DSS.

A Final Note

The MIS can be defined in one sentence: It is a system that provides information to management. But understanding the resources needed for an MIS and how they interrelate requires considerable analysis. A broad view of the MIS encompasses ideas and techniques from all the business disciplines—accounting, management, management science, finance, marketing, production, and so on. This is the approach we have taken. Our task has been to show that the MIS is much more than a computer. We recognized that the computer satisfies only a portion of the manager's information needs, and that other information comes from less formal activities such as personal conversation and reading. But most importantly, the MIS involves people. As we presented the various topics, we described them in relation to the information specialists, who create the MIS, and to the managers, who use it. You will play one or both of these roles—perhaps soon. Above all, we aimed to describe how these roles can be played so that you might contribute to the success of your firm and to your own professional development.

Key Terms

natural language	procedural language
data base processor	nonprocedural language
front-end network processor	dialog management
back-end data base processor	data management
biochip	model management
optical disk	artificial intelligence (AI)

Key Concepts

Increasing computer literacy

The emergence of user-friendly software

The shifting role of the MIS user from dependence on the information services staff to self-sufficiency

The inability of colleges and universities to meet the growing demand for information specialists to function in an environment of user dependency

The necessity for changes in academic MIS programs to keep in step with industry's needs

The changing nature of computer use and equipment configurations

The potential for significant improvements in office efficiency through automation

The effect of distributed systems on MIS security

The continued importance of data processing system development— primarily in small firms implementing their first computers

The three thrusts of DSS improvements: manager-system dialog, highly usable data subsets, and modeling languages

Questions

1. What effect will greater computer literacy have on future MIS designs and use?

2. What basic problem has continuously haunted computer users?

3. Give some examples of user-friendly software.

4. What situation is forcing information services departments to change their relationships with MIS users?

5. What type of college is doing the best job of meeting the demand for its MIS graduates?

6. Will the manager of the future do all of his or her MIS development work? Explain.

7. What types of jobs will the information specialist of the future handle?

8. In what directions is processor power moving?

9. What is a data base processor?

10. Distinguish between a front-end and a back-end processor.

11. Are future increases in storage capacity going to involve primary storage or secondary storage? Explain.

12. Why is the optical disk not suited for use as master file storage?

13. In 1990 what will probably be the most common means of entering data into a computer? What about computer output?

14. In recent years, how much has been invested to automate each farm worker? each factory worker? each office worker? During the 1960s, how much did factory productivity increase? What about office productivity?

15. What is a procedural language? Give some examples. What is a nonprocedural language? Give some examples.

16. How can a manager use a HIPO hierarchy diagram, overview diagram, detail diagram, and pseudocode in developing a DSS?

17. What unique feature of flowcharting makes it a valuable documentation tool?

18. What net effect will the trend toward distributed processing have on MIS security?

19. Comment on the statement "Firms solved their data processing problems long ago."

20. Will data management of the future focus on larger or smaller files for manager use?

CASE PROBLEM: Broadmoor College

Broadmoor is a private liberal arts college in Ohio. The school of business offers an undergraduate major in MIS. The spring semester is drawing to a close, and Amy Klatzkin, head of the MIS department, has called a meeting of the MIS faculty to discuss next year's textbook orders. The faculty includes Irv Fetinger, who teaches programming, Gwynne Larson, who teaches systems analysis, and Ike Markowitz, who teaches the introductory computer course.

Amy:
We need to get our textbook orders in for the fall, so I'd like to know if you want to reorder the same texts we used this year. Do you plan to change your courses any?

Ike:
I've been reading a lot lately about some of the newer languages such as RAMIS and NOMAD. Should we be introducing our students to them in addition to COBOL, instead of it, or what? I'm talking about the introductory course.

Amy:
That's a good point. I'd like to know what the rest of the group thinks.

Irv:
I definitely think we should expose our students to them. That's the wave of the future. COBOL is a necessity, but if we limit our students to that, we're short-changing them.

Gwynne:
What do you mean? COBOL is the number one business language. RPG is number two, and nobody ever recommended teaching it. I can't understand all the fuss over RAMIS. I think we should wait and see if it is really going to be used. It costs a lot of money to buy a package, implement it on our system, develop our lab assignments, and everything. We could waste a lot of money and time jumping

at every new software package that comes along. I think we should stick with COBOL for the time being.

Amy:
Ike, what do you think?

Ike:
I really don't know. I guess it depends on what we're trying to accomplish. Are we trying to prepare students to be information specialists or users or what?

Amy:
Well, we're preparing our MIS majors to be information specialists. But Ike, you've got a lot of future MIS users in your introductory classes. About three-fourths of your students are taking your course because it's required of every business major. And it's the only computer course they ever take.

Gwynne:
Do we have the funds to put RAMIS on our computer?

Amy:
I'm sure we do. We've got quite a bit of money left in the budget. But is that the package we want to add?

Irv:
I don't see how we can answer that now. We haven't even identified the possibilities. There are many others. Ike mentioned NOMAD. There's NATURAL, MANTIS, and QBE. And what about graphics software such as DISSPLA? There are a lot of user-friendly packages we could consider.

Ike:
Irv, do you think they should be included in your programming courses for our MIS majors?

Irv:
I'd rather see them in your introductory course. That's where we have the future MIS users. I can't see that the MIS professional needs that kind of knowledge. I would rather emphasize good program design methods and succinct coding featuring traditional languages such as COBOL, Assembler, or PL/I. Our MIS majors will be expected to develop efficient data processing programs. If we don't give them the basics, nobody else will.

Ike:
You're teaching structured design, aren't you?

Irv:
Right. That's what I mean by stressing good programming skills.

Ike:
Gwynne, are you still teaching structured design in your systems course?

Gwynne:
Yes. We've gotten completely away from flowcharting. I'm teaching HIPO hierarchy diagrams and pseudocode. The students love it.

Ike:

I wish the introductory students had a chance to learn some of those tools. We don't have time to do anything beyond flowcharting. And structured programming is out of the question. We just don't have the time.

Amy:

Speaking of time, my next class is in ten minutes. Everybody give me their book orders by Wednesday. Thanks for coming. We need to have more meetings like this.

Questions

1. Discuss Broadmoor's MIS department in terms of the general systems model. Is the department deficient in terms of any of the model elements?

2. Is there a problem? If so, describe it and explain how it can be solved.

3. What should be done, if anything, about the introductory computer course?

4. Should the MIS majors receive exposure to user-friendly software as well as traditional languages? Support your answer.

5. How do you feel about the systems analysis course? Are the proper tools included? Explain.

Appendix

Flowcharting

Basic Types of Flowcharts

Tasks performed by the computer can be complex. This complexity can confuse the person designing the system (the systems analyst) or the person preparing the computer program (the programmer). Also, confusion can arise as these people attempt to explain the system to each other and to other people, such as managers.

It didn't take computer professionals long to realize that flowcharts of the systems could overcome much of the complexity. The *flowcharts* consist of specially shaped symbols that identify the type and sequence of steps that solve a particular problem.

There are two basic types of flowcharts. One is used by the systems analyst to illustrate how programs and/or noncomputerized processes are linked to form a system. This type of flowchart is the "big picture" of the system and is called a *system flowchart*. The system flowchart is a *global design representation*.

The other type of flowchart is used by the analyst or the programmer to show the steps executed in a single program. These flowcharts are called *program flowcharts*. The program flowchart is a *logical design representation*.

Flowchart Symbols

Both types of flowcharts are drawn with the template pictured in Figure 17-13. These symbols are internationally accepted standard shapes and represent a common language among computer professionals around the world.

Some of the shapes are used only with one type of flowchart, some are used only with the other, and some can be used with either. The remainder of the appendix will be devoted to an explanation of these symbol shapes.[1]

---

[1] For more information on flowcharting, see Marilyn Bohl, *Flowcharting Techniques* (Chicago: Science Research Associates, 1971); Michel H. Boillot, Gary M. Gleason, and L. Wayne Horn, *Essentials of Flowcharting* (Dubuque: William C. Brown, 1975); and Nancy Stern, *Flowcharting: A Tool for Understanding Computer Logic* (New York: John Wiley & Sons, 1975). See also Bohl, *Tools for Structured Design* (Chicago: Science Research Associates, 1978).

System flowchart symbols

Data or information processing systems (the procedures, not the equipment) consist of a series of *processes* linked by *files* of data or information.

1. Process symbols. There are three primary ways to process data: manually, with a keydriven device, and with a device such as a punched card machine or computer that can be programmed.

Processes performed *manually* are illustrated with this symbol:

Examples are:

Appropriate lettering is entered in the symbol to provide more information about the exact process involved.

Processes performed by operating an *offline keydriven machine* such as a keypunch, a cash register, or a desk calculator are represented by:

Examples are:

Processes performed by operating an *online keydriven machine* such as a terminal are represented by:

Examples are:

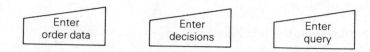

Finally, processes performed by the *computer* are illustrated by:

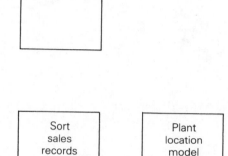

Examples are:

Print payroll checks	Sort sales records	Plant location model

System flowcharts are prepared by arranging the processing symbols in the correct sequence (Figure A-1). For example, a procedure might involve (1) opening the mail, (2) keying the sales order data onto floppy disks, (3) sorting the sales records, and (4) printing a sales report.

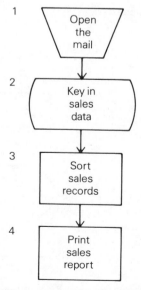

Figure A-1 Process steps.

Symbols are usually arranged in a vertical sequence. Arrows show the direction of the flow, steps are often numbered, and a brief description is enclosed in the symbol.

2. File symbols. It is also common practice to include symbols representing the files of data or information linking the process steps. These symbols can take the following forms, depending on the file media used.

File Medium	Symbol Shape	Example
Punched Card		Sales cards
Desk calculator tape		Batch totals
Magnetic tape (reel or cassette)		Inventory file
Direct access storage device (DASD)		Customer file
Printed document (hardcopy)		Sales report
Displayed output (not hardcopy)		Simulation output
Online storage (magnetic tape or DASD)		Customer master file

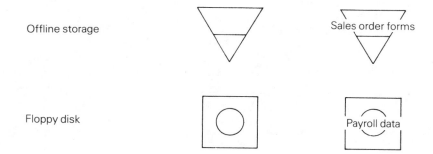

Offline storage

Sales order forms

Floppy disk

Payroll data

The symbol for the floppy disk is not a recognized standard. Neither is there a standard symbol for a magnetic tape cassette (we use the tape reel symbol). The absence of symbols for these popular media presents problems when documenting modern systems. In addition, there is no symbol for computer output microfilm (COM) and no symbol that can be used for both terminal input and output.

When the file symbols are added to the four process symbols linked in Figure A-1, the system flowchart is complete. See Figure A-2.

The brackets to the right of steps 2 and 3 are *annotation symbols*. They explain the processing of the related step in greater detail.

Program flowchart symbols

The analyst or the programmer must prepare a program for each of the computer steps in a system. In Figure A-2, for example, a program is prepared for step 4. A prewritten sort program can be used for step 3.

While a large number of different computer instructions can be used in a program, they fall within one of five categories. These categories are (1) preparation, (2) input and output, (3) data movement and manipulation, (4) logic, and (5) program terminal points.

The *preparation* symbol is:

Examples are:

Total = 0

Set
calendar
to 250

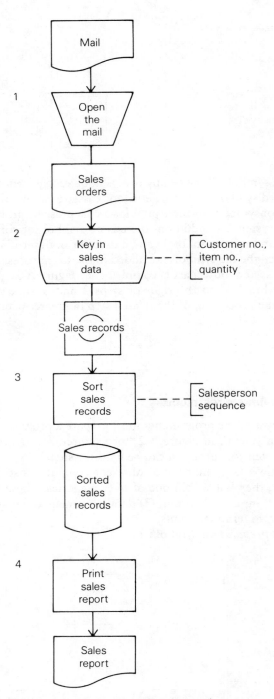

Figure A-2   System flowchart example.

The preparation symbol is usually included at the beginning of the program to *initialize* certain data values, to set switches that can be tested with program logic, or to clear primary storage areas.

An *input* or *output* instruction can be illustrated with:

Examples are:

Read
sales
record

Print
report
line

The above are general-purpose input/output symbols; they apply to any type of media.

Data movement and manipulation instructions include the different types of arithmetic processes and also data elements moving from one location to another. The rectangle represents all of these.

Examples are:

Add sales
to
total

Multiply
rate by
hours

Compute
square
root

Move name
to
output

The *logical decisions* the computer makes usually involve selecting one of two alternatives. A condition either exists or it doesn't. These decisions are illustrated with a diamond.

Examples of yes/no decisions are:

Both of these examples ask a question. The answer is either yes (Y) or no (N). One arrow leads into the diamond, and two exit from it. It makes no difference which points on the diamond are used.

Examples of a true/false decision are:

A statement is made, and the statement either is true or it is false. This technique is especially applicable to IF statements in programming languages.

The diamond is strictly a program flowcharting symbol. It is not used in a system flowchart.

Another symbol limited to use in program flowcharts is the oval.

The oval represents a *terminal point* in a program: the beginning or the end of the program or a major subroutine within it. The beginning and end of the program are illustrated with:

Figure 17-14 provides an example of the use of the oval.

Program flowchart example

A program flowchart for the "Print sales report" program in the preceding system flowchart (Figure A-2) might be drawn as in Figure A-3.

In step 1, a single record is read from the sales file. The program only handles one record at a time and repeats itself for each record in the file. This repetition is indicated by the loop made with steps 1 through 5.

In step 2, the computer makes a logical decision. Have all records in the file been read? The computer can answer this question using the results from step 1. When the computer is unable to read a record in step 1, it becomes apparent in step 2 that all of the records have been read and processed. In that case, step 6 follows step 2. If the end of the input file has not been reached, step 3 follows step 2.

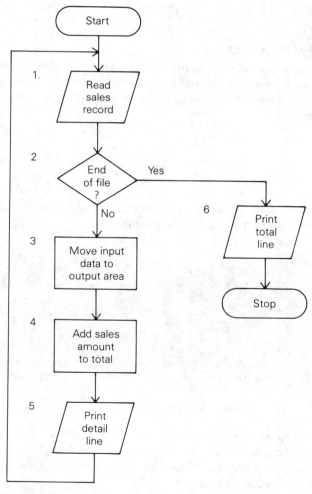

Figure A-3 Program flowchart example.

In step 3, data elements from the record just read are moved to an output area in main storage for printing later. This sample program flowchart does not indicate the specific data elements moved. They can be explained with an annotation symbol.

The arithmetic is performed in step 4 by adding the amount of the sales transaction to the previous total.

In step 5, a detail line is printed, showing the data for the transaction just processed.

After printing the detail line, the program loops back to step 1, where another record is read or an attempt is made to read another record (in the case of an end-of-file condition).

When all of the input records have been read and processed, the program branches from step 2 to step 6. There, a total line is printed with the amount accumulated from all transactions. Then the program ends.

Lengthy flowcharts

Some problems might require a flowchart too lengthy to fit on a single page. In these cases, some technique must be used to connect the lines on one page with those on another. A special symbol, the *off-page connector,* is used for this purpose.

If the flow goes from the bottom of page 1 to the top of page 2, a pair of off-page connectors makes the connection.

Bottom of Page 1   Top of Page 2

A letter or number is entered in both symbols to show the relationship. This permits the use of more than one set of connectors.

Another connector eliminates long connecting lines on a single page, and is called the *on-page connector.*

A pair of on-page connectors could have been used in Figure A-3 to eliminate the line looping back to step 1 from step 5.

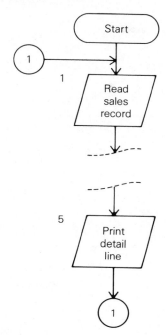

Either letters or numbers are entered in sets of related on-page connector symbols. If letters are used for off-page connectors, numbers can be used for on-page, or vice versa.

Flowcharting suggestions

You will often be required to draw flowcharts for assigned problems. Your instructor will specify particular requirements that must be met for a satisfactory grade. No attempt will be made here to list all of the possible dos and don'ts of flowcharting. We will offer some suggestions, however, that should make the task easier and more productive.

1. Draw the flowchart *before* designing the system or coding the program.
2. Use a template.
3. Draw a preliminary flowchart, using a pencil. Then draw a neat version (using pencil or pen) when the final form is certain.
4. Make the flow go from the top of the page to the bottom, and from the left to the right.
5. Use on-page connectors to eliminate long lines on the page.
6. Don't try to cram too many symbols on a page. Use off-page connectors for flowcharts that need additional pages.

Your instructor will identify which of the above suggestions you should follow, and he or she may add others to the list.

Index